RADIO AND TELEVISION SERVICING

Editor
R. N. WAINWRIGHT
T.Eng.(CEI), F.S.E.R.T.

**Radio and Television Servicing
1980-81 Models**

**MACDONALD
MACDONALD FUTURA PUBLISHERS
LONDON**

ISBN 0 354 04725 6

ISBN 0 354 04725 6

Typesetting by Impact Typesetters, Letchworth, Herts.
Printed in Great Britain by
Hazell, Watson & Viney Ltd., Aylesbury, Bucks.

CONTENTS

PREFACE

Many technical innovations have been introduced by the domestic electronics industry in recent years and the desirability of video tape recorders, electronic games, remote control, Teletext, etc., has been extensively promoted by the manufacturers to good effect despite the difficult financial climate existing at this time.

Surprisingly, the small-screen portable monochrome television receiver, which for some time has been predicted to become virtually extinct, has actually seen an increase in sales. The reason for this is certainly the attraction of the comparitively low price and choice offered by a flood of Far Eastern imports and the infrequent repair requirement reported by service departments. It would, however, seem likely that with a larger range of colour television portables becoming available at cheaper prices, the monochrome tube will eventually become relegated to the visual display section of the home computer.

Although receiving far less publicity than it deserves, a significant development is the much improved reliability which may now be confidently expected of all current production. This is of course a natural outcome of the transition from thermionics to semiconductors and was inevitable as it became possible to largely eliminate the generation of heat associated with valve operation. In general applications, components are no longer subjected to unsuitable ambient conditions and lower operating voltages place less stress on capacitors and insulation. The situation has been further improved by the application of the B.E.A.B. Code of Practice which requires that certain critical components must have 'fail-safe' characteristics and an extension of this approach, implemented by some British manufacturers, calls for strict standards of .long-term reliability for all components used in a piece of apparatus.

The present cost of service has to be considered in relation to the value of the equipment and there is a growing tendency to consider certain low-price items as expendable when repairs are necessary. In this respect, Philips Service has already issued a list of such products (see Supplementary Servicing) for which no service information or spares will be made available. Nevertheless, much equipment continues to be of a complex nature and despite the increasing use of integrated circuits, faults do occur and adequate service information is essential before any attempt can be made by an experienced engineer to return the apparatus to a safe and satisfactory condition. Regular users of the *Radio and Television Servicing* volumes will appreciate the vital assistance offered in these pages in maintaining the goodwill of their customers. It is perhaps interesting to note that, although component reliability has improved, a greater proportion of failures are attributable to 'dry joints' which can give rise to elusive and intermittent symptoms.

PREFACE

In view of the specialised knowledge and equipment required, no attempt is made in these pages to provide any guidance on the servicing of video tape recorders. Most distributors offer short courses to familiarise engineers with the techniques of servicing such apparatus and it is stressed that no attempt should be made to interfere with any part of these machines without prior study of the problems involved.

As in previous years, this volume contains a representative collection of current colour and monochrome receiver circuits and service information in the first section. The second section presents a selection from the wide range of available audio equipment including portable radios, clock radios, tape-recorders and entertainment centres. The usual addendum of supplementary items contains abstracts from technical bulletins issued during the year and should be used in conjunction with information previously published.

In presenting this information, grateful thanks are extended to the manufacturers and their representatives for the generous help and co-operation in providing the technical information used in the preparation of this volume. It is emphasised that whilst every effort is made to ensure that the information given is correct, errors occurring in original service manuals may be reproduced here. The publishers and editor of this volume can therefore accept no responsibility for injury or damage to persons or property as a result of inaccuracies in circuits or text.

R.N.W.

TELEVISION SERVICING
(Colour and Monochrome)

ACKNOWLEDGEMENTS

Alba (Radio and Television) Ltd.
Crown Radio Ltd.
Decca Radio and Television Ltd.
Grundig (Great Britain) Ltd.
Hitachi Sales (U.K.) Ltd.
I.T.T. Consumer Product Services
J.V.C. (U.K.) Ltd.
National Panasonic (U.K.) Ltd.
Philips Service
Photopia Ltd.
Rank Radio International
Roberts Video
Sanyo Marubeni (U.K.) Ltd.
Sharp Electronics (U.K.) Ltd.
Sony (U.K.) Ltd.
Thorn Consumer Electronics
Toshiba (U.K.) Ltd.
Technical and Optical Equipment (London) Ltd.
Waltham Electronics (U.K.) Ltd.

BUSH

Model BC7300
Chassis Group T26A

General Description: The tuner, I.F. and decoder sections of this receiver are basically similar to those used in the Bush T22A chassis which is described in the 1979-80 volume of *Radio and Television Servicing*. The timebases have been designed to accommodate the latest type C.R.T. which requires minimum convergence correction. The revised sections of the circuit are given here, together with waveforms, and should be used in conjunction with information previously given.

Mains Supply: 240 volts, 50Hz.

Scan Coil Removal and Re-assembly

Removal: Remove the connector from the scan coils. The connector latch must be pushed forward whilst withdrawing the connector.
Remove the Tube Base T157A.
Loosen the clamp screw on the tube neck.
Slide off the scan coil assembly.

Replacement: Slide the scan coils onto the tube neck, the potentiometer should be at approximately 10 o'clock (45° to left of top centre).
Gently push them forward and twisting the coils to the right and left locating the coils into the keyway.
Push the coils snug against the tube and tighten the neck clamp.
Replace the connector on the scan coils.
Replace Tube Base T157A.

(T11) CIRCUIT DIAGRAM (C.C.U.)—MODEL BC7300

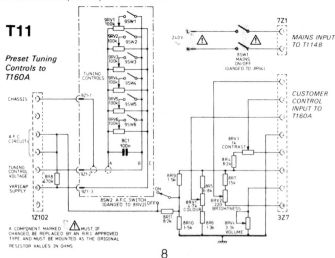

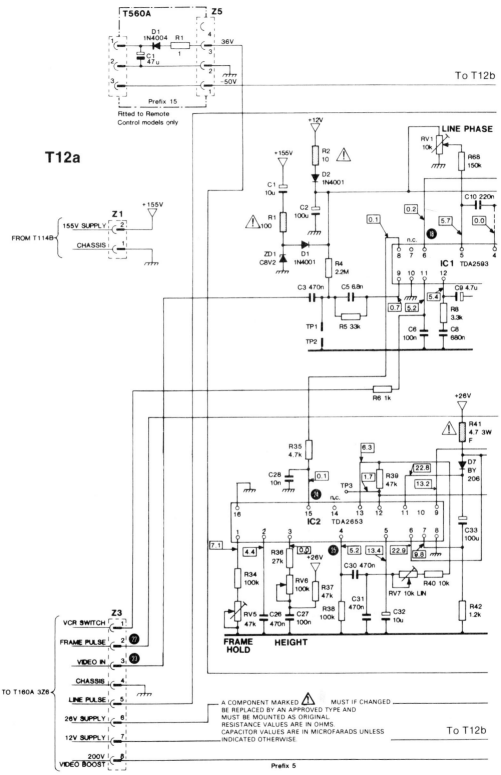

(T12a) CIRCUIT DIAGRAM (T156A TIMEBASE PANEL)—MODEL BC7300 *(PART)*

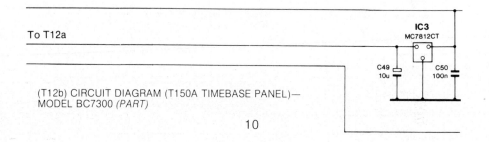

To T12a

T12b

TO POWER
SUPPLY

+26V

To T12a

(T12b) CIRCUIT DIAGRAM (T150A TIMEBASE PANEL)—
MODEL BC7300 (PART)

10

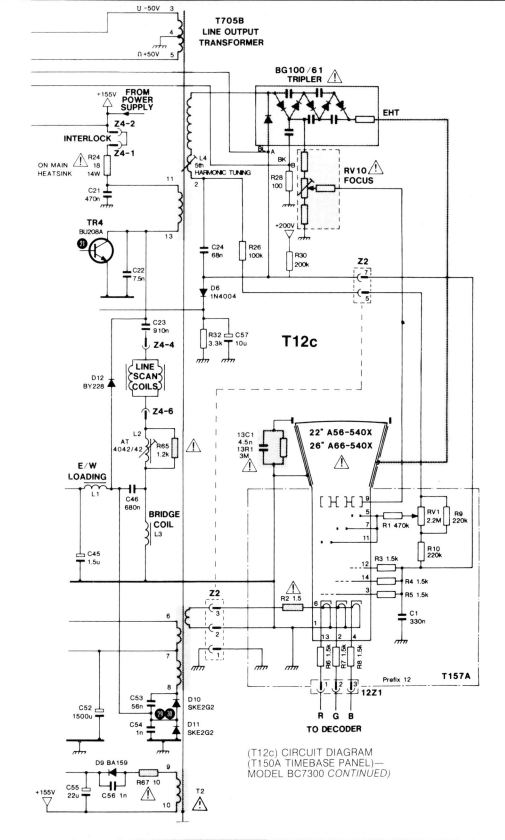

(T12c) CIRCUIT DIAGRAM
(T150A TIMEBASE PANEL)—
MODEL BC7300 *CONTINUED)*

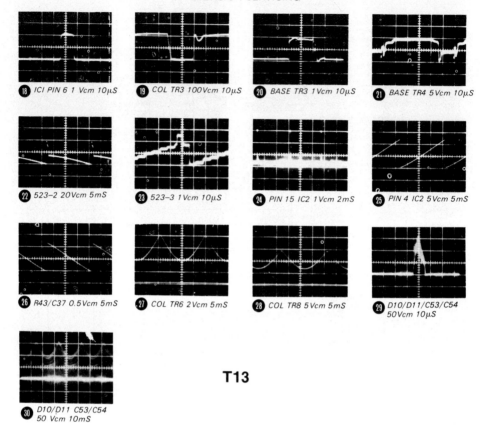

18 ICI PIN 6 1 Vcm 10µS

19 COL TR3 100Vcm 10µS

20 BASE TR3 1Vcm 10µS

21 BASE TR4 5Vcm 10µS

22 523-2 20Vcm 5mS

23 523-3 1Vcm 10µS

24 PIN 15 IC2 1Vcm 2mS

25 PIN 4 IC2 5Vcm 5mS

26 R43/C37 0.5Vcm 5mS

27 COL TR6 2Vcm 5mS

28 COL TR8 5Vcm 5mS

29 D10/D11/C53/C54 50Vcm 10µS

30 D10/D11 C53/C54 50 Vcm 10mS

T13

(T13) CIRCUIT WAVEFORMS (18-30)—MODEL BC7300

12

CROWN Models 5TV-62R, 5TV-63R, 5TV-64R, 5TV-65R, 5TV-67R, 5TV-68R

General Description: A portable 4.5-in. monochrome television receiver with A.M./F.M. radio and designed for world-wide distribution. Model 5TV 65R is aligned for the U.K. standards and the circuit given here relates to this version. The other models follow similar practice with alternative tuner and frequency standards.

Mains Supply: 240 volts, 50Hz.

Radio Wavebands: (5TV 65R): L.W. 150-300kHz; M.W. 525-1605kHz; F.M. 88-108MHz; I.F. 470kHz:10.7MHz.

Dismantling

Place the unit upside down on a soft cloth and remove 6 screws from the base.

Removal of T.V. Circuit Board (Fig. T14a): Remove the 2 screws (1 and 2) holding the T.V. circuit board and remove the selector knob.

Removal of Chassis: Remove the 4 screws (1-4).
Remove the tuning knob, volume knob and radio selector knob. (Fig. T14b).

Removal of Radio Board: Remove the 3 screws (5-7). (Fig. T14b).

Removal of Escutcheon: Remove the 3 screws (3, 8 and 9) holding the escutcheon and pull the escutcheon upward. (Fig. T14b).

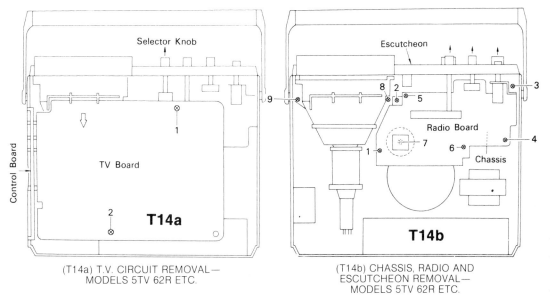

(T14a) T.V. CIRCUIT REMOVAL—
MODELS 5TV 62R ETC.

(T14b) CHASSIS, RADIO AND
ESCUTCHEON REMOVAL—
MODELS 5TV 62R ETC.

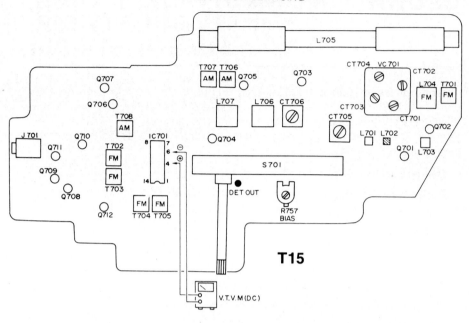

T15

(T15) ADJUSTMENT AND TEST POINTS (RADIO SECTION)—MODELS 5TV 62R ETC.

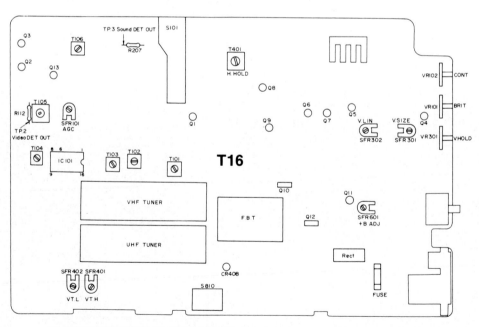

T16

(T16) ADJUSTMENT AND TEST POINTS (T.V. SECTION)—MODELS 5TV 62R ETC.

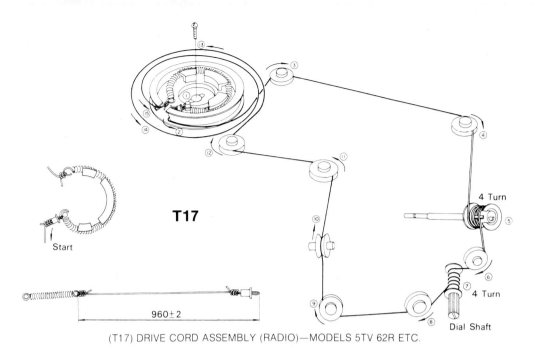

T17

Start

960±2

(T17) DRIVE CORD ASSEMBLY (RADIO)—MODELS 5TV 62R ETC.

Radio (Fig. T17): Cut 0.3mm dial cord to a length of 1070mm.
Using a spring and grommet, arrange the cord as shown in figure T17.
Thread in numerical order and finally strain the spring.
Note: When winding the thread four times at point 5, be careful, at third time
of winding, not to let the thread slip to the underside of drum claw.

T.V. (Fig. T18): Cut 0.3mm dial cord to a length of 750mm.
Using a spring and grommet, arrange the cord as shown in figure T18.
Thread in the order shown and finally strain the spring.
Note: When winding the thread four times at point 7, be careful, at third time
of winding, not to let the thread slip to the underside of drum claw.

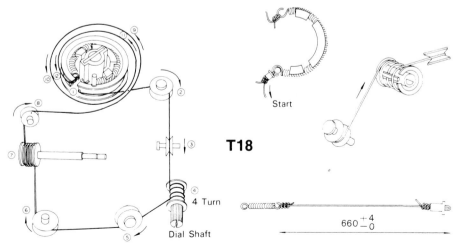

T18

Start

4 Turn

Dial Shaft

660 +4 −0

(T18) DRIVE CORD ASSEMBLY (T.V.)—MODELS 5TV 62R ETC.

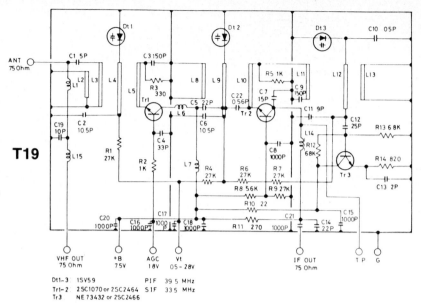

Dt1-3   1SV59   PIF 39.5 MHz
Tr1-2   2SC1070 or 2SC2464 S1F 33.5 MHz
Tr3   NE 73432 or 2SC2466

(T19) CIRCUIT DIAGRAM (U.H.F. TUNER)—MODEL 5TV 62R

Adjustments

Note: E.H.T. is 6.5KV at 35μA beam current.

+B Adjustment: Set the channel selector to an empty channel and turn Contrast VR, Bright VR fully clockwise (Max. position).
Connect V.T.V.M. to +B line on the T.V. board.
Adjust SFR601 on the T.V. circuit board for 7.4 ± 0.1V.

Channel Coverage: Set the dial to CH21 (U.H.F. low) and turn SFR402 for best picture quality.
Set the dial to CH69 (U.H.F. high) and turn SFR401 for best picture quality.
Repeat the above procedures two or three times to make sure that the dial is set correctly to the received channel.

IC701 (LA-1201) Bias Adjustment: Connect V.T.V.M. between No. 4 pin and No. 6 pin of IC701. Adjust the semi-fixed resistor R757 until V.T.V.M. indicates 0.5V of reading, with the tuner placed in a no signal position.

Raster Adjustment:
Centring Adjustment: Receive a test pattern and adjust the centring magnet on the deflection yoke so that the centre of the pattern is centred on the C.R.T. screen.
Focus Adjustment: Focus adjustments (R417, 418) are located near Flyback Transformer.
V. Hold: VR301.
H. Hold: Set the horizontal OSC coil (T401) to give instant 'pull-in'.
V. Line: Adjust resistor SFR302 so that the upper and lower sections of the pattern are equally displayed.

16

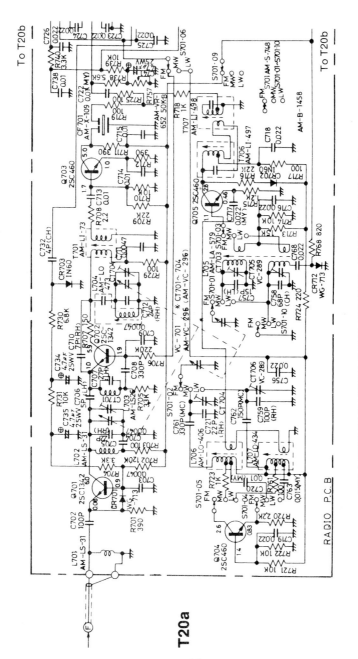

(T20a) CIRCUIT DIAGRAM (RADIO SECTION) — MODEL 5TV 65R (PART)

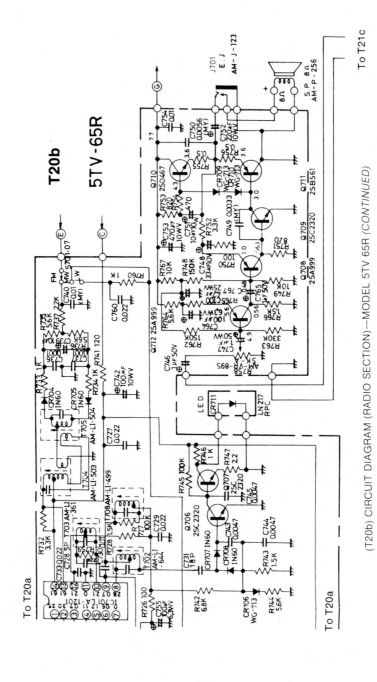

(T20b) CIRCUIT DIAGRAM (RADIO SECTION)—MODEL 5TV 65R (CONTINUED)

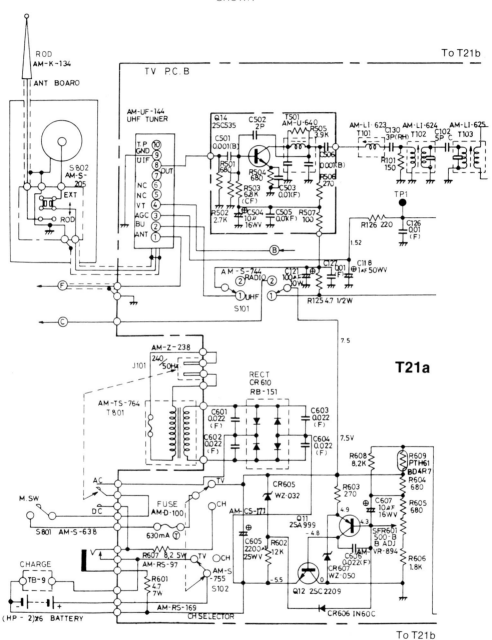

(T21a) CIRCUIT DIAGRAM (T.V. SECTION)—MODEL 5TV 65R *(PART)*

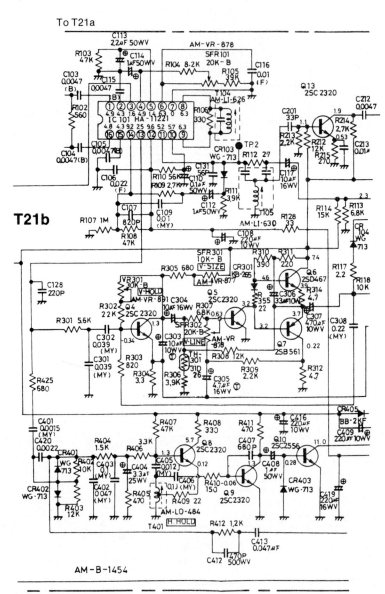

(T21b) CIRCUIT DIAGRAM (T.V. SECTION)—MODEL 5TV 65R *(PART)*

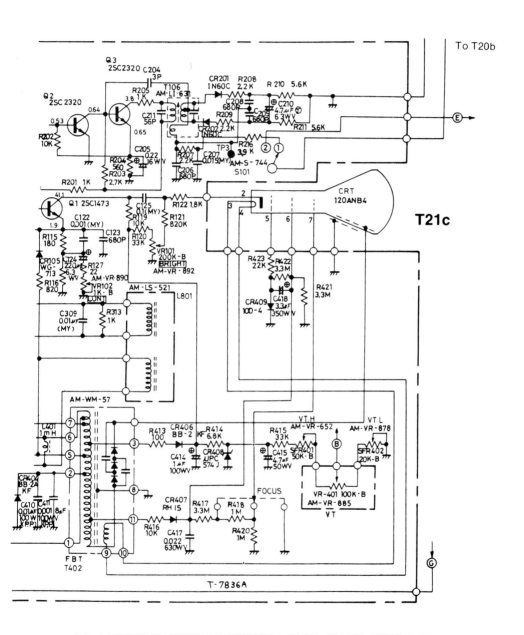

(T21c) CIRCUIT DIAGRAM (T.V. SECTION)—MODEL 5TV 65R *(CONTINUED)*

DECCA Chassis Series 71, 75, 90, 91, 95.
Models CN0704, CN0704-R10, CT0901, CT0901-RC10, CV0950, CV0950;RC10

General Description: This series of receivers incorporates a chassis which is based on the Decca 70 Series design which is fully described in the 1978–79 volume of *Radio and Television Servicing*. Subsequent modifications are listed here together with the circuit for the Control Unit and Channel Selector Assembly.

Modifications

2C3 and 2C14, 4μ7 capacitors. Type changed to electrolytic, LRVB 4.7/25 E.C.C. —10+75% 50V.

2R14 resistor, value changed from 150R to 1k0 5% 0.25W carbon film.

R611 resistor is 220R on chassis type 91, 95 and 150R 5% 0.25W on chassis types 71, 75.

D200, zener diode type BZX79 C6V8, in series with R200 3k9 5% 0.25W resistor, are added and connected between the junction of R202/2SK2 pin 7 and anode of D214. Anodes of D200 and D214 together.

2R9, 180R 5% 0.25W resistor, is added and connected between the junction of 2R14/2L1 and the junction of 2R12/2C6.

D402 diode type BY206GP is changed to type BA157.

On later models, the TDA2571 is replaced by a TDA2571A in the IC301 position. These I.C.s are not interchangeable and the complete modification entails the following component changes:

1. The direct sync. sub-panel (ASS 5-0733-4) is not fitted.
2. C302 (2n2) becomes 2n7 1% 63V polystyrene.
3. R306 (22k) becomes 18k 2% 0.25 metal film.
4. VR305 (4k7) becomes 2k2 20% 0.05W carbon min. pre-set.
5. R311 (100k) becomes 47k 5% 0.25W carbon film. This resistor is connected between IC301 pin 5 and the +12V line.
6. IC301 (TDA2571) becomes TDA2571A.
7. A wire link is added, connecting IC301 pin 1 to TP302 (R322).

A MkII version of the Decoder sub-panel (ASS 5-0714-8) is now being fitted; this is compatible with the MkI version and can be used as a direct service replacement. No special adjustments are necessary when changing panels; the alignment procedure remains the same.

This new decoder has been introduced in order to reduce the very tight specification necessary for the chroma delay line 2DL1 and also some

peripheral components associated with the previous 2IC2 (TDA2522) have
been integrated within the TDA 2524.

These voltage measurements replace those given for 2IC2 (TDA2522).

Integrated Circuit 2IC2 (TDA2524).

Pin	V	Pin	V
1	5.5	9	2.4
2	5.5	10	10.3 (30V range).
3	5.5	11	11.7 (30V range).
4	0	12	6.8
5	2.8	13	1.2
6	2.8	14	4.6
7	9.0	15	1.6
8	9.0	16	4.1

These voltage measurements are added under the heading

'Transistors'.

Ref.	Emitter	Base	Collectors
2Tr1	0	0.9	4.3
2Tr2	4.9	5.5	11.3
2Tr3	4.9	5.5	11.3
2Tr4	4.9	5.5	11.3
2Tr5	9.1	8.4	0

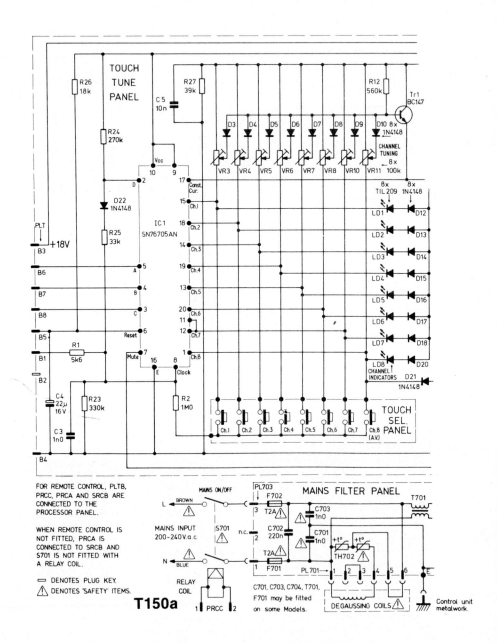

(T150a) CIRCUIT DIAGRAM (CONTROL UNIT)—CHASSIS 71 ETC. *(PART)*

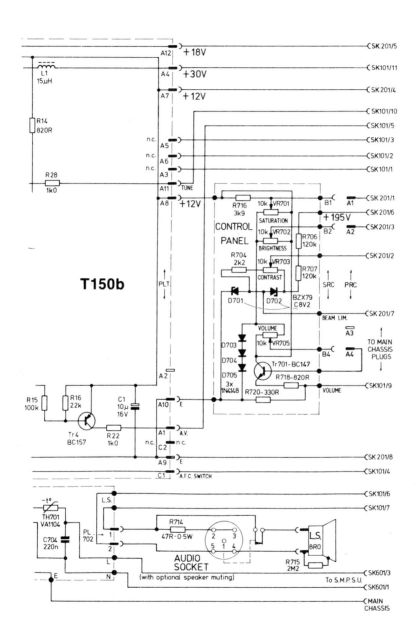

(T150b) CIRCUIT DIAGRAM (CONTROL UNIT)—CHASSIS 71 ETC. *(CONTINUED)*

GRUNDIG   Models P1221GB, 'Triumph 1221', 'Record 1221'

General Description: A portable monochrome television receiver for reception of U.H.F. transmissions and operating on mains or battery supplies. Integrated circuit techniques are widely used with self-contained modules for sound and vision I.F. stages. The chassis is isolated by mains transformer and a socket is provided for the connection of an earphone.

Mains Supply: 240 volts, 50Hz.

Battery: 12 volts, 1.6 amps.

Circuit Diagram Notes: The indicated voltages are measured with a Grundig UV4 with signal applied (values in brackets without signal) at maximum contrast and minimum brightness.

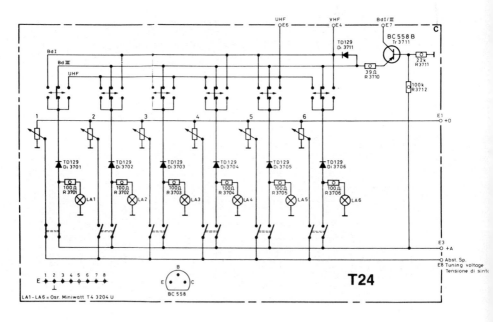

(T24) CIRCUIT DIAGRAM (PROGRAMME SELECTOR)—MODELS P1221 ETC.

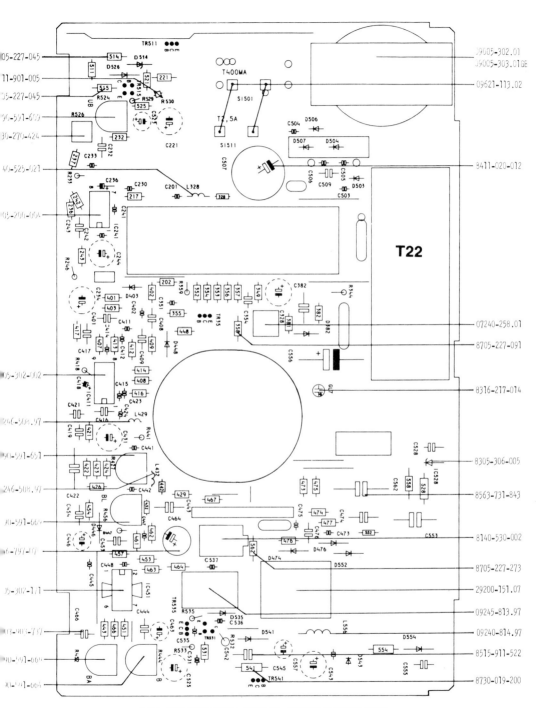

(T22) COMPONENT LAYOUT—MODELS P1221 ETC.

27

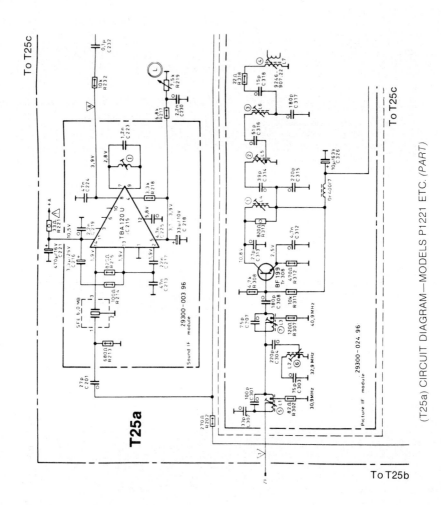

(T25a) CIRCUIT DIAGRAM—MODELS P1221 ETC. *(PART)*

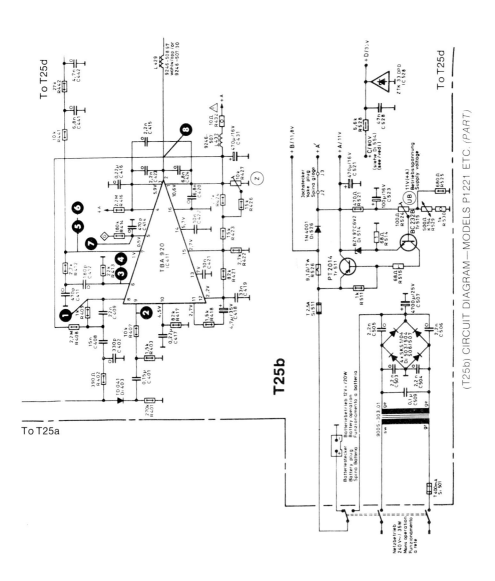

(T25b) CIRCUIT DIAGRAM—MODELS P1221 ETC. (PART)

29

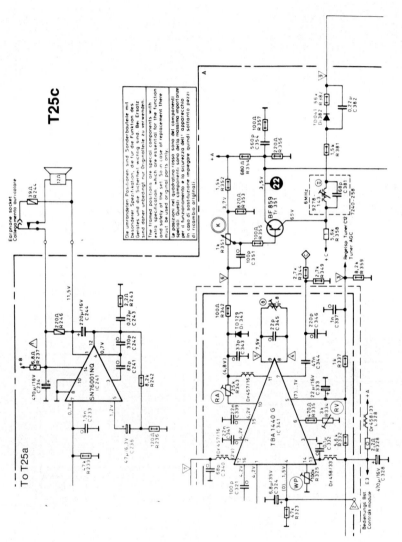

(T25c) CIRCUIT DIAGRAM—MODELS P1221 ETC. (PART)

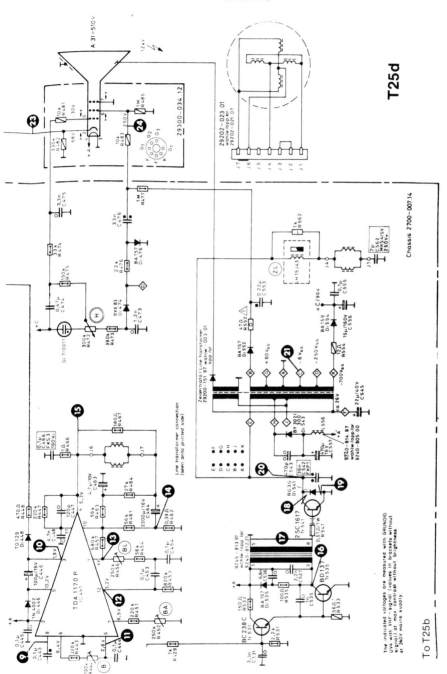

T25d

Chassis 2700-007.14

(T25d) CIRCUIT DIAGRAM—MODELS P1221 ETC. (CONTINUED)

The indicated voltages are measured with GRUNDIG UV4 with VHF-signal (values in brackets without signal) at max contrast without brightness at 240V mains supply

To T25b

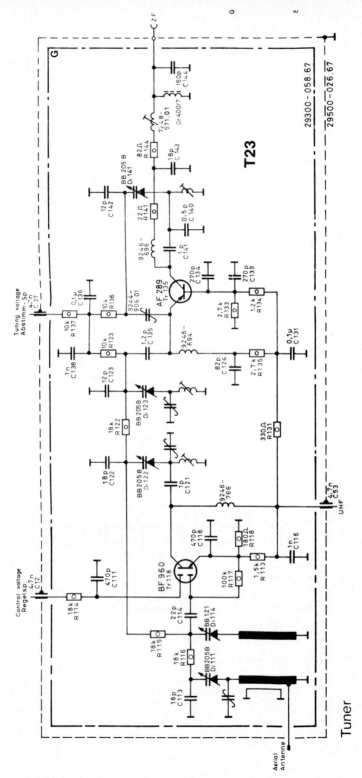

Tuner

(T23) CIRCUIT DIAGRAM (U.H.F.) TUNER—MODELS P1221 ETC.

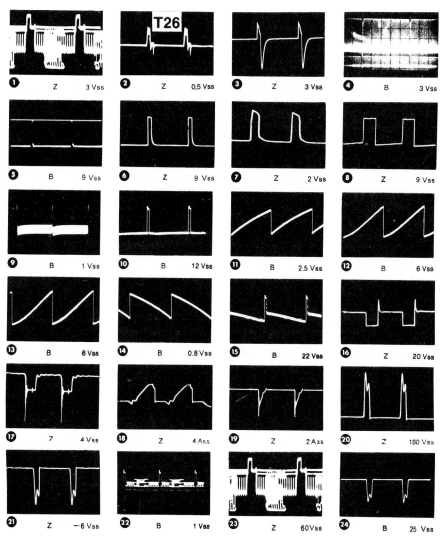

(T26) CIRCUIT WAVEFORMS—MODELS P1221 ETC.

GRUNDIG Models 1510b, 1613, 1632, 4613, 6232, 6612, 6632

General Description: A series of colour television receivers featuring a basic chassis comprising a 'mother' board with a number of plug-in modules. The basic circuit for Model 1510b is given here with additional information on modifications for other versions.

Mains Supplies: 240 volts, 50Hz (1510b, 1613, 4613); 220 volts, 50Hz (1632, 6232, 6632).

Receiver Options: See chart below.

Model	CRT	Screen diagonal	Programme selection on set	Remote control	Power consumption	Sound output power (sine)	Head/ earphone socket
1510b	370 DLB 22-TC 02 (SK)	16″	8 electronic touch buttons	—	100W	1.5W	•
1613	420 BMB 22-TC 02 (PK)	16″	8 electronic touch buttons	—	100W	1.5W	•
1632	420 BMB 22-TC 02 (PK)	16″	1 button for 16 programmes	TP 120	100W	1.5W	•
6612	560 BYB 22-TC 01 (PK)	22″	12 sensors	—	100W	2W	—
6232	560 BYB 22-TC 01 (PK)	22″	1 button for 16 programmes	TP120E	100W	2W	•
6632	560 BYB 22-TC 01 (PK)	22″	1 button for 16 programmes	TP120E	100W	2W	•

Adjustments

Power Supply Unit +F Voltage: Adjust +F voltage at point 29 to 15V with control g.

Adjustment of E.H.T. Voltage: Whenever a repair is undertaken in the E.H.T. section, and especially when the 2903-035.03 control module has been replaced, the E.H.T. must be reset. A calibrated high voltage voltmeter must be used and the circuit adjusted as follows, using the HS control (on the E.H.T. control module).

Adjust contrast, colour contrast and brightness to minimum. Adjust control HS to obtain the required E.H.T. (see the main circuit diagram for the television receiver in question). In exceptional cases the following test method can be used to check the E.H.T. setting.

Set contrast, colour contrast and brightness to minimum. Connect a multirange voltmeter to point c of the line transformer. A voltage reading of 49

34

± 1V must be obtained. Under these conditions the supplies to the C.R.T. are correct. It is also pointed out that the adjustments to the stage must be correctly carried out to avoid contravening safety standards concerning harmful radiation from colour television receivers.

Basic Brightness: Inject any aerial signal/switch oscilloscope to D.C.
Set to maximum brightness.

Connect D.C.-oscilloscope to amplifier output (R 379) or to MP 23 (tube socket board).

Adjust black level to 120V with control HI. It is permissible for the 'white' peaks to be limited at this stage, but the limiting must stop at normal brightness (black level approx. 160V).

White Level Adjustment/Stop Point: Inject monochrome signal or turn colour contrast control to minimum.

Set service switch to 'line' position.

Turn grid controls Sr, Sg, Sb to left hand stop (chassis in vertical position).

Adjust control Sp until a single coloured line just becomes visible. (The controls for contrast and brightness located at the front of the set are inoperative when the switch is in the 'line' position).

Adjust the grid control of both the weaker colours until all three lines have the same intensity, producing a white line.

Set service switch to 'normal'.

Adjust brightness and contrast of the test pattern for normal viewing conditions.

Adjust controls KI and KII until the picture is equivalent to that produced on a black-and-white tube for all grey values between black and white and no colouration can be detected.

Green Intensity of the Adjustment Bar: Feed in test signal.

Connect plus pole of electrolytic capacitor C 1167 on SL-module to voltage point +F/15V C3. The adjustment bar will then become continuously visible.

Turn contrast K to minimum.

Adjust green intensity using control GI. It must not be so bright as to cause reduction in picture contrast.

Contrast Adjustment:
Feed in signal.
Connect oscilloscope to 'blue' cathode of the picture tube.
Set the composite signal to 80V$_{pp}$ with contrast control.

Line Amplitude: Adjust control HS to obtain the correct picture width. Any variation in the picture width can be corrected by adjusting coil KA.

Focus: Adjust the focus control S so that when viewing a normally adjusted standard test pattern the picture is equally in focus over the entire screen surface.

Line Linearity: Adjust the ring magnet of coil ZL so that the horizontal distances to the left of picture zones equal those of the right. Do not reverse polarity of magnet—the linearity must be adjustable only at the left picture edge.

Colour Contrast Basic Value:
Feed in colour test signal.
Adjust to max. contrast, medium brightness, medium colour saturation.
Connect oscilloscope to module contact 9 of the colour module.
Set the —(B-Y) signal to 1.5V$_{pp}$ with control FKI.

East-West Pin Cushion Correction: Correct pin cushion distortion with control O/WA. The vertical lines at the left and right hand picture edges must be as straight and as vertical as possible.

Trapezium Distortion: Correct any distortion in the raster with control Tr. The two outer vertical lines of the convergence grid must be parallel. Repeat adjustment to controls O/WA and Tr.

Picture Centring:
Horizontal: If the picture has moved sideways on the screen it can be centred with control BZ.
Vertical: If the picture has moved too far up or down on the screen, it can be centred with potentiometer BZ.

Volume, Coarse Adjustment: Adjust control LG so that every time the receiver is switched on it will be set for normal loudness (normal-level function).

Fault-finding Procedure (E.H.T. Control Module):

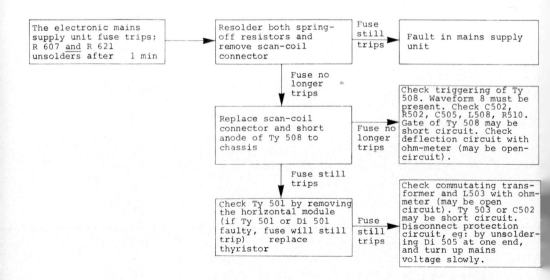

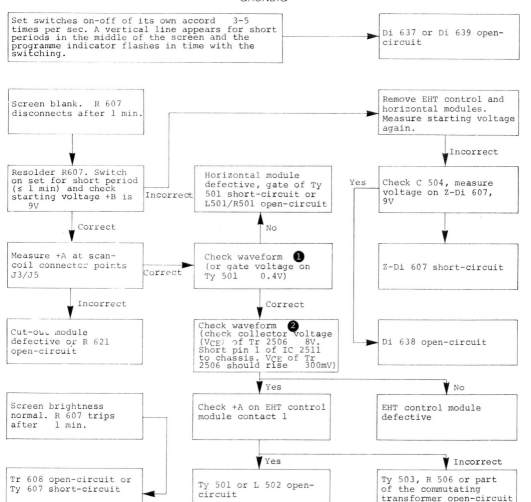

Set switches on-off of its own accord 3-5
times per sec. A vertical line appears for short
periods in the middle of the screen and the
programme indicator flashes in time with the
switching.

→ Di 637 or Di 639 open-
circuit

Screen blank. R 607
disconnects after 1 min.

Remove EHT control and
horizontal modules.
Measure starting voltage
again.

Incorrect

Resolder R607. Switch
on set for short period
(≤ 1 min) and check
starting voltage +B is
9V

Incorrect

Horizontal module
defective, gate of Ty
501 short-circuit or
L501/R501 open-circuit

Yes

Check C 504, measure
voltage on Z-Di 607,
9V

Correct

No

Measure +A at scan-
coil connector points
J3/J5

Correct

Check waveform ❶
(or gate voltage on
Ty 501 0.4V)

Z-Di 607 short-circuit

Incorrect

Correct

Cut-out module
defective or R 621
open-circuit

Check waveform ❷
(check collector voltage
(V$_{CE}$) of Tr 2506 8V.
Short pin 1 of IC 2511
to chassis. V$_{CE}$ of Tr
2506 should rise 300mV)

Di 638 open-circuit

Yes

No

Screen brightness
normal. R 607 trips
after 1 min.

Check +A on EHT control
module contact 1

EHT control module
defective

Yes

Incorrect

Tr 608 open-circuit or
Ty 607 short-circuit

Ty 501 or L 502 open-
circuit

Ty 503, R 506 or part
of the commutating
transformer open-circuit

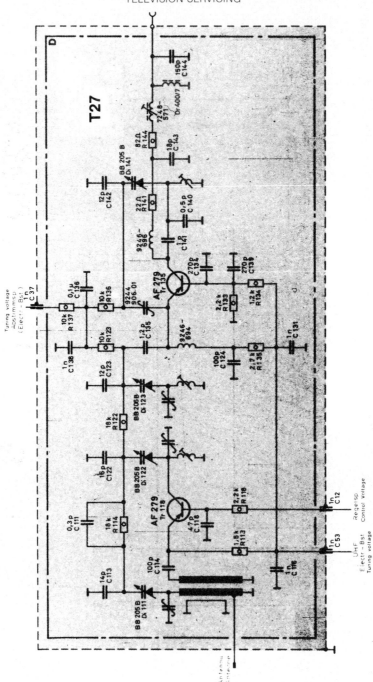

(T27) CIRCUIT DIAGRAM (U.H.F. TUNER)—MODELS 1510b ETC.

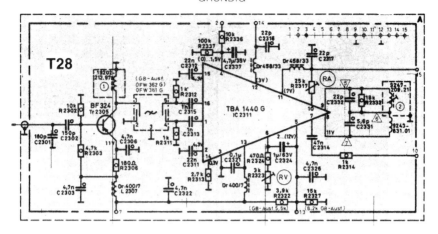

(T28) CIRCUIT DIAGRAM (VISION I.F. MODULE)—MODELS 1510b ETC.

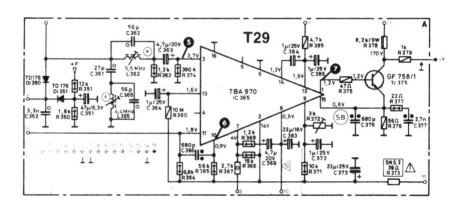

(T29) CIRCUIT DIAGRAM (VIDEO MODULE)—MODELS 1510b ETC.

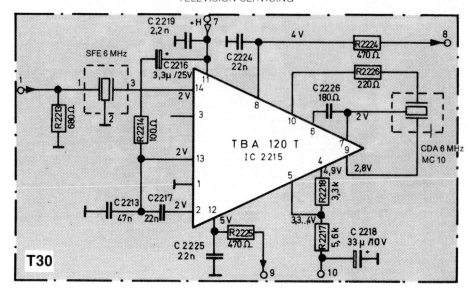

(T30) CIRCUIT DIAGRAM (SOUND I.F.)—MODELS 1510b ETC.

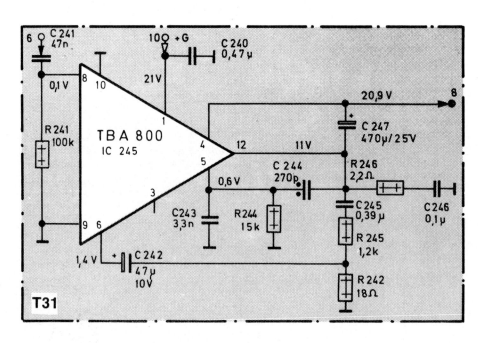

(T31) CIRCUIT DIAGRAM (A.F. STAGE)—MODELS 1510b ETC.

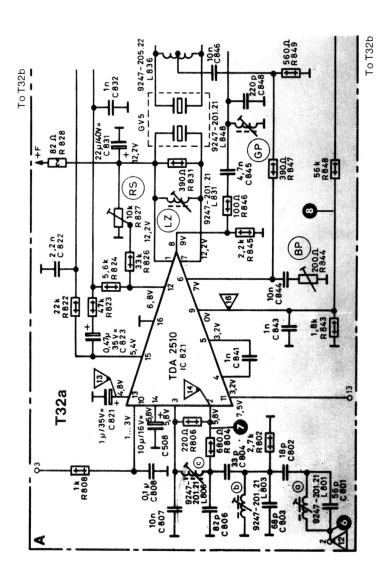

(T32a) CIRCUIT DIAGRAM (DECODER MODULE)—MODELS 1510b ETC. *(PART)*

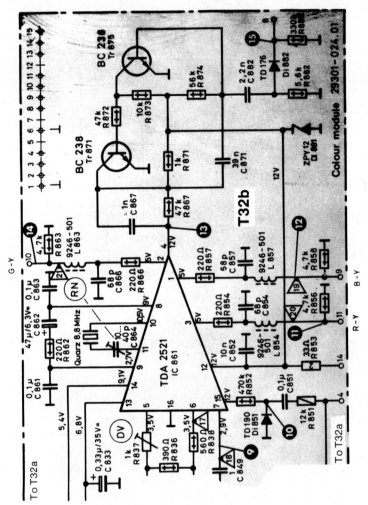

(T32b) CIRCUIT DIAGRAM (DECODER MODULE)—MODELS 1510b ETC. (PART)

Z=L   B=F   Vss=Vpp

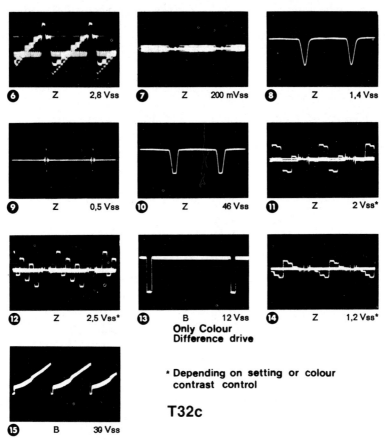

⑥   Z   2,8 Vss   ⑦   Z   200 mVss   ⑧   Z   1,4 Vss

⑨   Z   0,5 Vss   ⑩   Z   46 Vss   ⑪   Z   2 Vss*

⑫   Z   2,5 Vss*   ⑬   B   12 Vss   ⑭   Z   1,2 Vss*
Only Colour
Difference drive

⑮   B   30 Vss

*** Depending on setting or colour
contrast control**

T32c

(T32c) CIRCUIT WAVEFORMS (DECODER)—MODELS 1510b ETC. *(CONTINUED)*

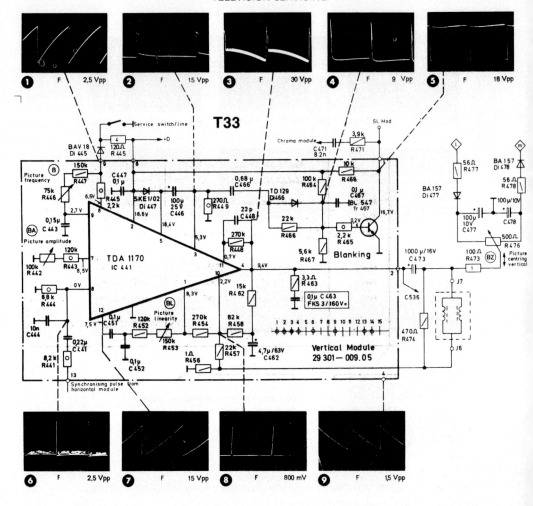

T33

(T33) CIRCUIT DIAGRAM (FIELD MODULE)—MODELS 1510b ETC.

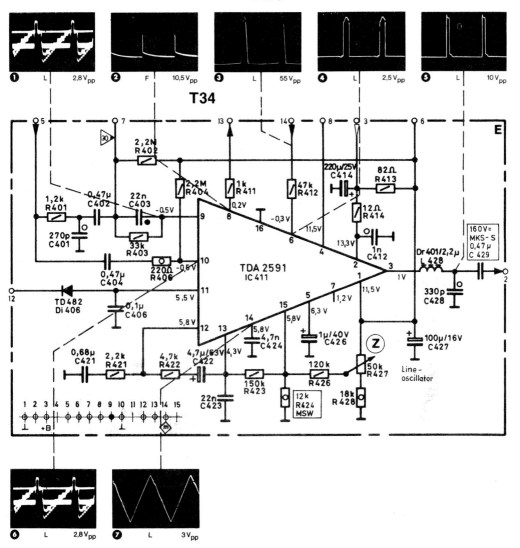

T34

① L   2,8 V_pp
② F   10,5 V_pp
③ L   55 V_pp
④ L   2,5 V_pp
⑤ L   10 V_pp

⑥ L   2,8 V_pp
⑦ L   3 V_pp

(T34) CIRCUIT DIAGRAM (LINE TIMEBASE)—MODELS 1510b ETC.

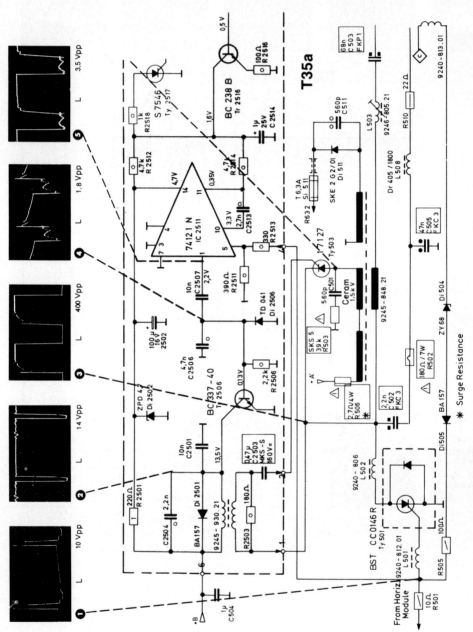

(T35a) CIRCUIT DIAGRAM (LINE OUTPUT)—MODELS 1510b ETC. (PART)

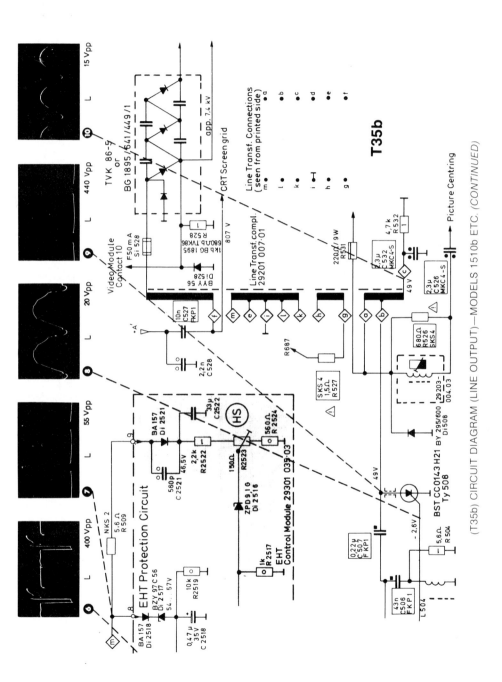

T35b

(T35b) CIRCUIT DIAGRAM (LINE OUTPUT)—MODELS 1510b ETC. (CONTINUED)

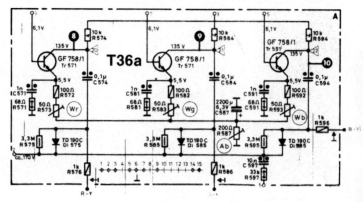

(T36a) CIRCUIT DIAGRAM (R.G.B. DRIVE MODULE)—MODELS 1510b ETC.

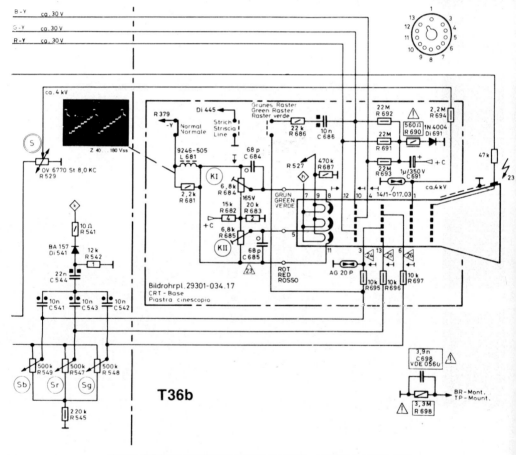

T36b

(T36b) CIRCUIT DIAGRAM (C.R.T. PANEL)—MODELS 1510b ETC.

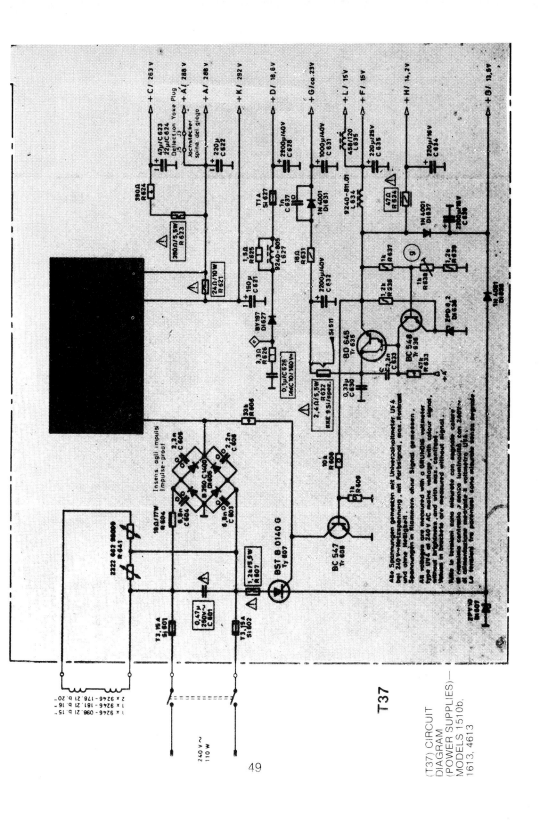

T37

(T37) CIRCUIT
DIAGRAM
(POWER SUPPLIES)—
MODELS 1510b,
1613, 4613

49

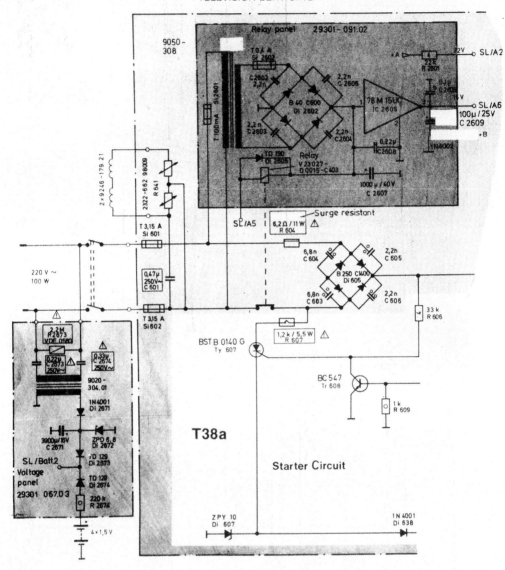

(T38a) CIRCUIT DIAGRAM (POWER SUPPLIES)—MODELS 1632, 6232, 6632 *(PART)*

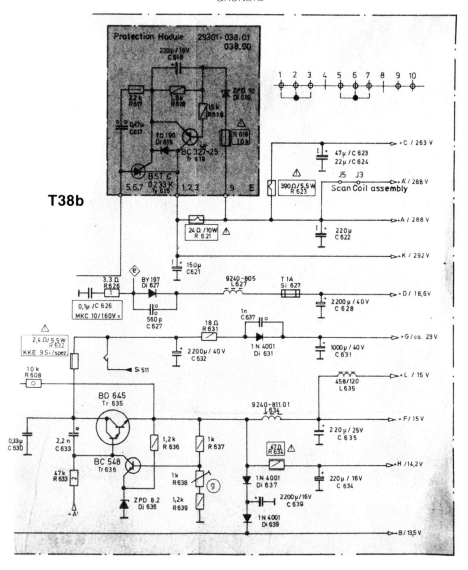

T38b

(T38b) CIRCUIT DIAGRAM (POWER SUPPLIES)—MODELS 1632, 6232, 6632 *(CONTINUED)*

HITACHI

General Description: A basic colour television chassis with the option of manual, touch, or remote control. The circuit of the CAP-162 version is given here as a general guide to all models. 13-in. and 16-in. cathode ray tubes are used making these instruments portable although operating from mains supplies only.

Mains Supply: 240 volts, 50Hz.

Adjustments (Fig. T78)

Horizontal Frequency: Connect TP701 and TP702 by a capacitor 10μF/50V and align R707 so as to obtain the correct line frequency.

Horizontal Centring: Align R720 to obtain the correct horizontal centring.

Horizontal Picture Width: Align the H. Size jumper wire (cut ore resolder) to obtain the correct picture width.

Vertical Frequency: Connect TP601 and TP602 by a resistor 100KΩ. Adjust R605 so as to obtain the correct field frequency.

Picture Height: Adjust R610 so as to obtain the correct picture height.

Vertical Centring: Connect the V. Cent link to either N, D or U to obtain the correct vertical centre.

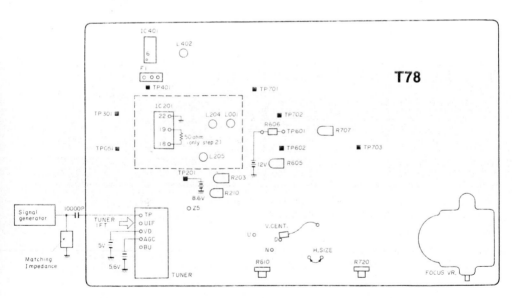

(T78) ADJUSTMENT AND TEST POINTS (MAIN BOARD)—NP8C CHASSIS

HITACHI

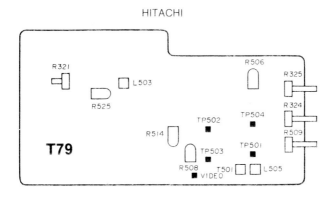

(T79) ADJUSTMENTS AND TEST POINTS (DECODER)—NP8C CHASSIS

A.G.C. Delay: Adjust the input R.F. (U.H.F.) level to —56dBm.
Channel adjustment must be correct or A.F.C. switched ON.
Warm up the set for at least 2 minutes.
Connect a D.C.-Voltmeter to the TP051.
Align R203 so that the meter reads V_1 8.0 +0.1 $^{0.1}_{0.05}$ V with signal.

Grey Scale Tracking. Fig. T80: *The receiver should be soaked (warm up) at least 10 minutes before carrying out the adjustments.*
Receive a white raster test card and set the Drive controls at their middle positions.
Turn the Back Ground Level (B.G.L.) controls (green, red and blue) fully anti-clockwise. (The picture will be darkened.)
Turn the screen control fully anti-clockwise.

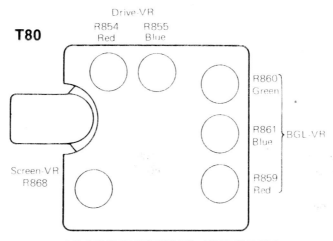

(T80) C.R.T. DRIVE ADJUSTMENTS—NP8C CHASSIS

Disconnect the Y-connector from the video and chroma board and connect TP602 and TP601 with a short link.

Turn up the screen control gradually until one of three coloured lines faintly appears on the screen (e.g. blue).

Turn the screen control fully clockwise, then adjust the blue-, red- and green-B.G.L. controls so that three coloured lines equally appear on the screen.

Keep one of the B.G.L.-controls which corresponds to above colour (e.g. blue-B.G.L.) as it is, and turn up other two controls (e.g. green and red) until their coloured lines also faintly appear on the screen.

Disconnect the short link from TP602 and TP601 (Field oscillator operates), and connect the Y-connector to the video and chroma board.

Turn the Contrast control and the Brightness control fully to minimum.

Set the Sub-brightness control (R321) so that the white raster faintly appears on the screen.

Adjust two B.G.L.-controls (e.g. green and red) so that the correct grey scale tracking at low brightness is obtained.

Turn up the Contrast control and adjust the Drive controls (blue and red) so that the correct grey scale tracking at high brightness is obtained.

Turn down the Contrast control and check the correct grey scale tracking at low brightness.

Otherwise readjust two B.G.L.-controls (e.g. green and red) for the correct grey scale tracking.

Repeat steps several times, until the ideal grey scale tracking is obtained over whole brightness range.

Sub Brightness Alignment: Set the Brightness control at its middle-position and the Contrast control at its minimum.

Release the field locking by V. Hold control (R605) and let the blanking part appear on the screen.

Observe the black level and turn up the Sub-brightness control (R321) gradually until that level can be seen to turn grey.

Purity and Convergence: This chassis television receiver incorporates Hitachi in-line type tube, with saddle-toroidal scan coil. Since the convergence quality is strictly controlled in the factory, reconvergence is not normally required.

When it is needed, in case of the replacement of a picture tube or a scan coil etc., read and follow the adjustment procedure step by step to obtain the best results, because this is rather different from the conventional tube system.

Set the television receiver facing to the south, and soak it at least 10 mins.

Check the horizontal and vertical linearity, the picture width, and the focus as already described on the previous pages.

Receive a cross-hatch test card.

In case of the replacement of the picture tube, wind the adhesive tape (bandage type is preferable) around the neck, for securing of scan coil.

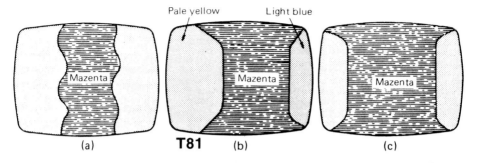

(T81) PURITY ADJUSTMENTS—NP8C CHASSIS

Purity (Figs. T81–T82): Before proceeding please perform preliminary static convergence adjustment.

Push the scan coil fully up to funnel part of the picture tube. Disconnect the (G-Y) plug from the signal board and see the broad magenta belt appears on the screen (Fig. T81a).

Pull out the scan coil gradually towards you and see that two oval parts (coloured pale yellow and light blue) appear on each side of the screen (Fig. T81b).

Rotate the purity magnet (c) (Fig. T82a), and set two coloured parts to become equal in area (Fig. T81c).

Insert preliminary rubber wedge between the funnel and the scan coil at the top position, and tilt the scan coil backward at the top.

Pull out the scan coil gradually towards you again until two coloured parts disappear simultaneously. See that the white purity (connect (G-Y) plug) is all right, if not, pull out the scan coil until ideal white purity is obtained. Fasten the scan coil securely by tightening the screw.

Unless the red purity (disconnect both (G-Y), (B-Y) plugs) is obtained, repeat the adjustments again.

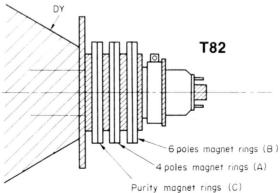

(T82) C.R.T. NECK ADJUSTMENTS— NP8C CHASSIS

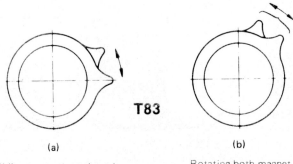

(a)

(b)

Sliding two magnet ring tabs
foward or away from each other

Rotating both magnet
rings together

(T83) STATIC CONVERGENCE ADJUSTMENTS—NP8C CHASSIS

Static Convergence (Figs. T82–T83): This procedure is the convergence alignment for the centre part of the screen.

Step	Convergence lines	Magnet (Fig. T82)	Movement (Fig. T83)
1	Vertical Blue and Red	4 poles (A)	sliding (a)
2	Horizontal Blue and Red	4 poles (A)	rotating (b)
3	Vertical B/R and Green	6 poles (B)	sliding (a)
4	Horizontal B/R and Green	6 poles (B)	rotating (b)
5	Repeat steps 1 to 4		

Dynamic Convergence Alignment (Fig. T84): This procedure is the convergence alignment for the circumference of the screen.

Push in the preliminary rubber wedge between the funnel part and scan coil gradually until both horizontal and vertical lines are converged at the circumference of the screen.

Proceed according to the arrangements on the screen (Fig. T84a & b).

Case (a)

(i) Insert fixing wedge at 9 o'clock position, until three coloured squares are converged.

(ii) Insert two fixing wedges at 1 and 5 o'clock positions and fix three wedges by highly adhesive tape. Then pull up preliminary wedge.

Case (b)

(i) Insert fixing wedge at 3 o'clock position, until three coloured squares are converged.

(ii) Insert two fixing wedges at 7 and 11 o'clock positions and fix three wedges by highly adhesive tape. Then pull up the preliminary wedge.

HITACHI

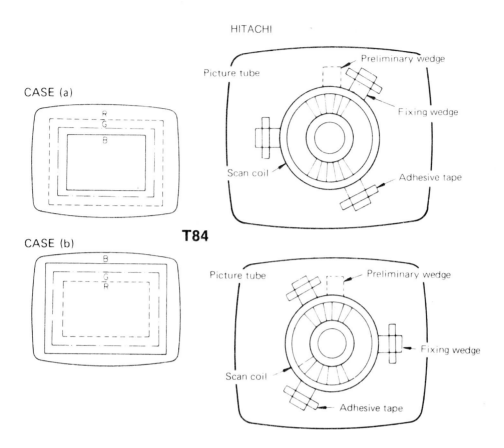

CASE (a)

CASE (b)

T84

(T84) DYNAMIC CONVERGENCE ADJUSTMENTS—NP8C CHASSIS

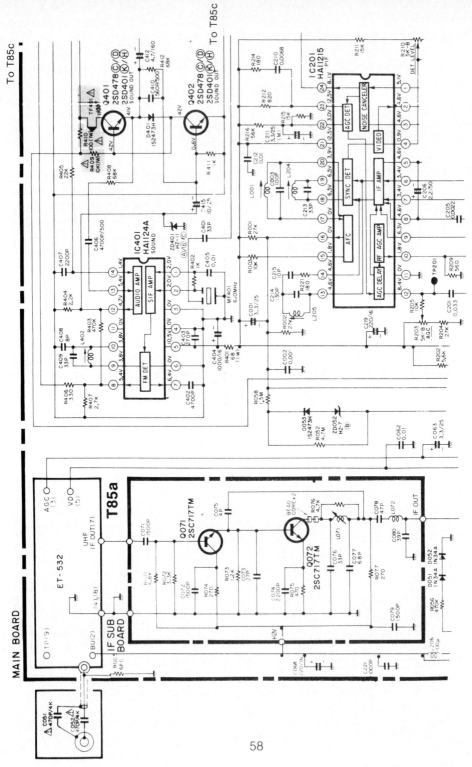

(T85a) CIRCUIT DIAGRAM—NP8C CHASSIS (CAP-162) (PART)

58

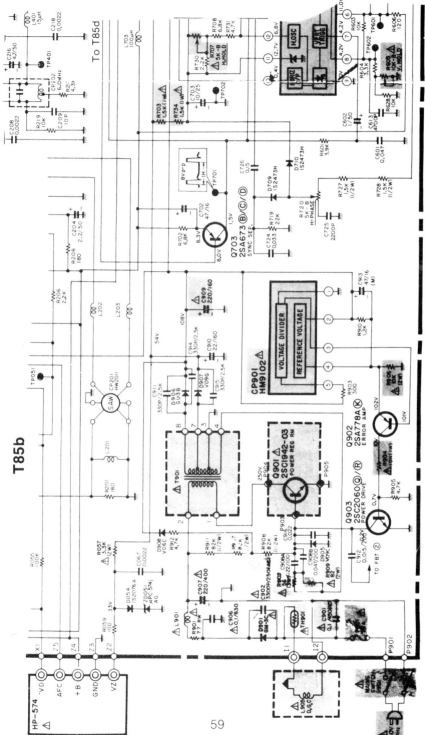

(T85b) CIRCUIT DIAGRAM—NP8C CHASSIS (CAP-162) (PART)

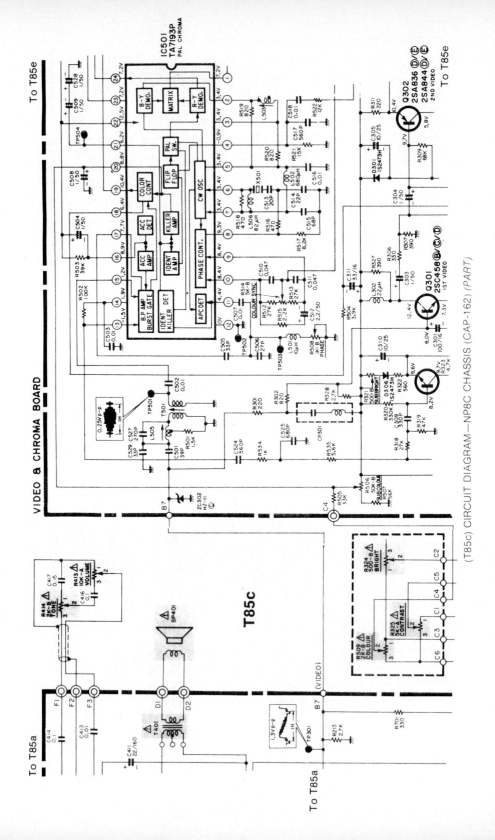

(T85c) CIRCUIT DIAGRAM—NP8C CHASSIS (CAP-162) (PART)

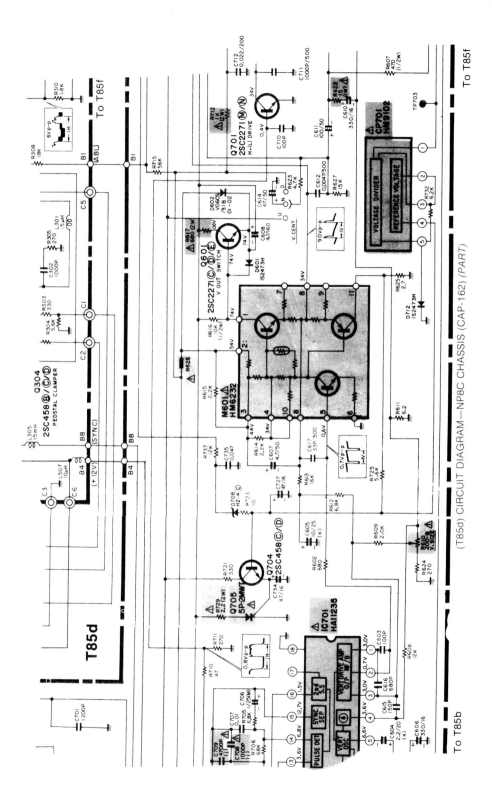

(T85d) CIRCUIT DIAGRAM—NP8C CHASSIS (CAP-162) (PART)

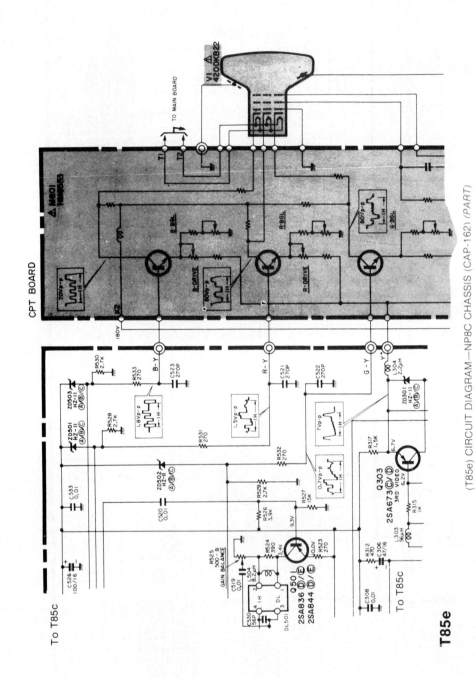

(T85e) CIRCUIT DIAGRAM—NP8C CHASSIS (CAP-162) (PART)

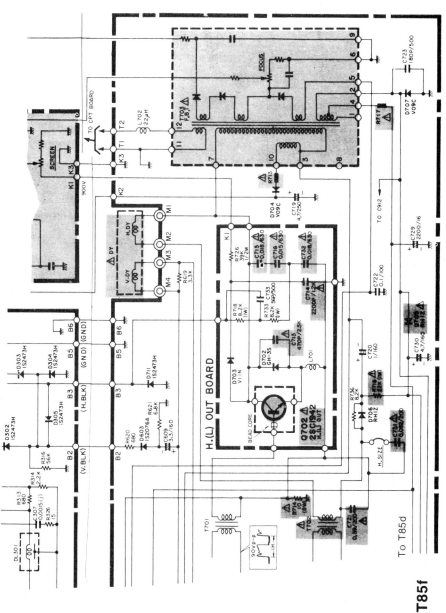

(T85I) CIRCUIT DIAGRAM—NP8C CHASSIS (CAP-162) (CONTINUED)

T85f

To T85d

HITACHI   Model F-41

General Description: A portable monochrome receiver operating from mains or battery supplies and featuring an electronic channel seeking circuit. The chassis is isolated by mains transformer and a socket is provided for the connection of an earphone.

Mains Supply: 240 volts, 50Hz.

Battery: 12 volts, 16W.

Cathode Ray Tube: 340AMB4.

Adjustments

H.T. (+B): If less than 11.1 volts, cut R908; If more than 11.7 volts cut R906.

Line Hold: Short C704. Adjust R709 for drifting picture. Remove short.

Picture Centre: Rotate rectangular magnet attached to deflection assembly.

Circuit Description (Manual Seeking Circuit)

The manual seeking circuit is a circuit which indicates the tuned band and channel by means of bars appearing on the screen. The manual seeking circuit consists of IC301, Q304 ~ Q306.

An I.C., which incorportes four 2-input NAND gates is used for IC301.

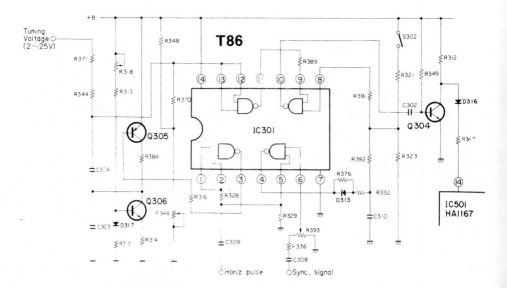

(T86) CIRCUIT DIAGRAM (MANUAL SEEKING)—MODEL F-41

64

The basic circuit is shown in Fig. T86. IC301 generates the reset signal. It is required to discriminate whether or not the signal entering through the antenna is the video carrier wave of a broadcast signal. This is done by judging whether the correct synchronising signal is output to the synchronisation separation circuit. Pins 4 5 6 of IC301 is the circuit which judges whether or not the normal synchronising signal is present; when the synchronising signal is present with the same timing as the horizontal pulse, pin 4 of IC301 becomes 'L' periodically and C310 is discharged through R332 and D313, so the voltge at pin 9 of IC301 becomes lower than the input threshold voltage.

When a normal synchronising signal is not present, pin 4 of IC301 becomes 'H', so C310 is charged through R376 and R332 and pin 9 of IC104 is set to 'H'.

Screen Indicator Circuit: The screen indication circuit is composed of IC301, Q304 ~ Q305. The principle of the screen indication circuit is as follows.

The saw-tooth wave, which synchronizes to the horizontal pulse, is superimposed on the D.C. current divided from the tuning voltage, and by comparing this with the input threshold voltage of the I.C. and amplifying it, the waveform, whose pulse width changes according to the tuning voltage during the horizontal period, is produced. This pulse is passed through the differential circuit to make a pulse with a specified width at the rise section of the pulse, and bar indication is done by adding to pin 14 of IC501.

In Fig. T86, pins 1~3 of IC301, Q305 and Q306 compose the circuit producing the horizontal period saw-tooth wave. The horizontal pulse turns on Q305 and charges C303. By charging and discharging C303 at constant current by Q306 the saw-tooth wave shown in Fig. T87C is produced. R318 change the amplitude of this saw-tooth wave; the range of the bar indication on the screen is changed by adjusting them.

This saw-tooth wave is A.C.-connected with pins 12, 13 of IC301 by means of C304. D.C. bias of pins 12 and 13 of IC301 is determined by the voltage divided from the tuning voltage by R371, R344 and R370 and the adjusting position of R346. R346 absorbs unevenness in the input threshold voltage of pins 12, 13 of IC301 by adjusting R346, the position of the bar indication on the screen can be changed. The saw-tooth wave at pins 12 and 13 of IC301 forms the waveform shown in Fig. T87-D.

To indicate the bar on the screen, pin 9 of IC301 is set to 'L'. In this case, pin 10 of IC301 becomes the pulse waveform shown in Fig. T87-F, which is obtained by comparing the input threshold voltage with the waveform as shown in Fig. T87-D.

The period of this pulse waveform is the horizontal period and is constant, but the pulse width T is determined by the width of the saw-tooth wave at pins 12 and 13 of IC301 cut by the input threshold voltage of pins 12 and 13 of IC301, and when the tuning voltage is high the average D.C. level of the saw-tooth wave rises, so the pulse width becomes larger, and when the tuning voltage is low, the pulse width becomes smaller. The pulse waveform appearing at pin 10 of IC301 is differentiated by C302 and R349 and input to

(continued on p.70)

65

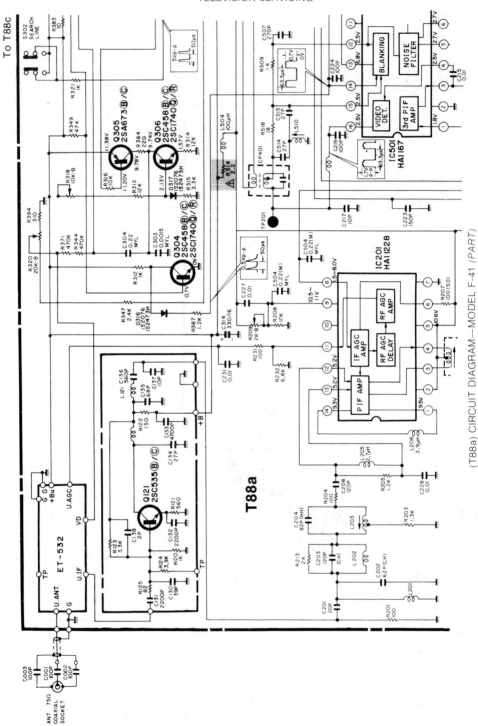

(T88a) CIRCUIT DIAGRAM—MODEL F-41 (PART)

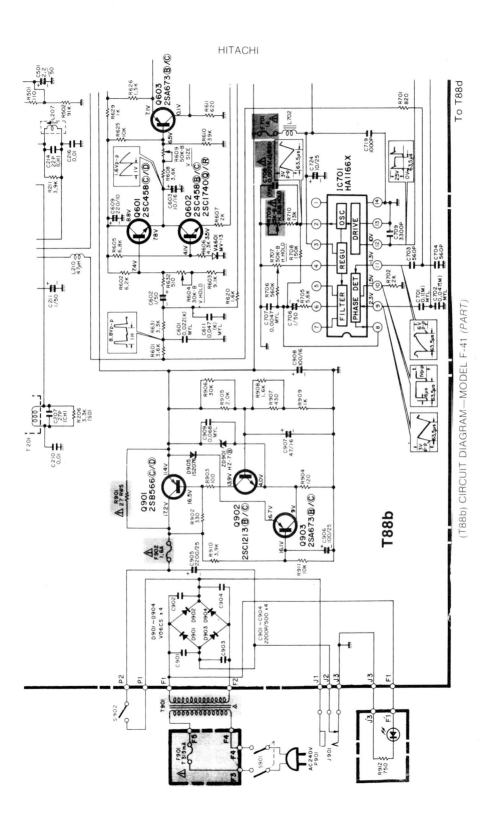

HITACHI

(T88b) CIRCUIT DIAGRAM—MODEL F-41 (PART)

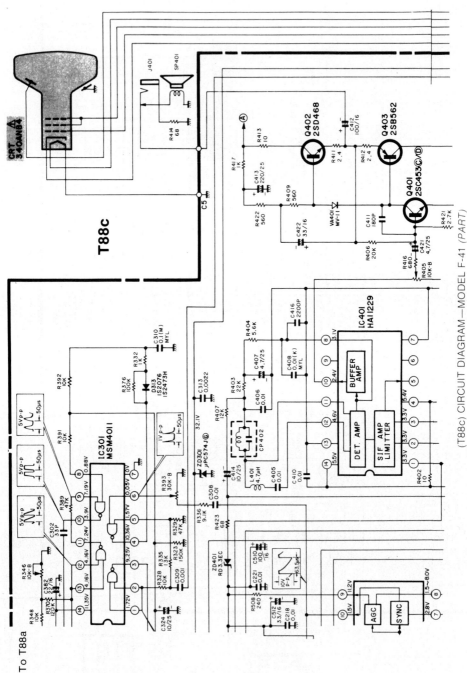

(T88c) CIRCUIT DIAGRAM—MODEL F-41 (PART)

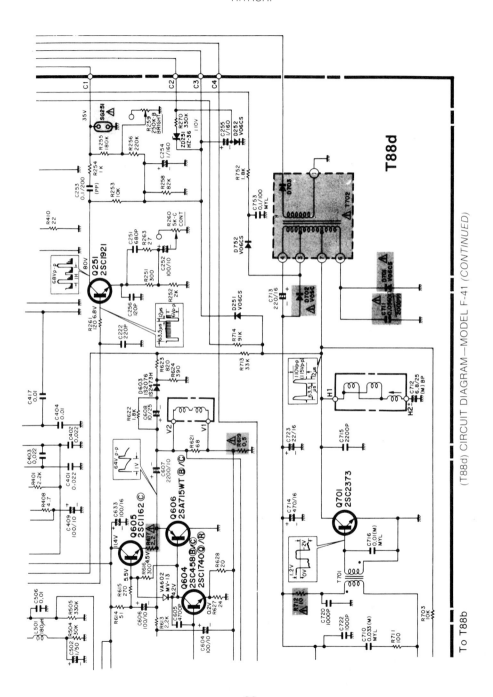

HITACHI

T88d

(T88d) CIRCUIT DIAGRAM—MODEL F-41 (CONTINUED)

To T88b

69

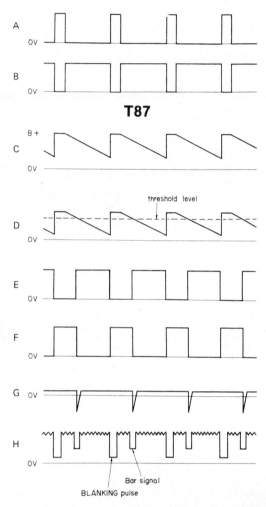

(T87) CIRCUIT WAVEFORMS (MANUAL SEEKING)—MODEL F-41

the base of Q304, so the waveform Q304's base is as shown in Fig. T87-D, and Q304 is cut for a certain time after pulse width 'T'.

Pin 8 of IC301 is the circuit which controls whether or not the bar indication is output. When pin 8 of IC301 is 'L', the pulse from pin 1 of IC301 is transmitted to pin 10 of IC301 and the bar indication disappears, but when pin 8 of IC301 is 'H', pin 11 of IC301 is always set to 'L' and the bar indication appears. When the search line (S302) is pressed (pin 8 of IC301 is set to 'H'), pin 10 of IC301 is set to H, so the bar indication appears.

When the synchronising signal is not present (Pin 5 of IC301 is set to 'H').

It is designed so that in cases, the indication is held for a while (approx. 1.5 sec) from the time when the search mode is finished or the indicator switch is released.

70

HITACHI   Model P-26

General Description: A portable monochrome receiver operating from mains or battery supplies. The chassis is isolated by a mains transformer and a socket is provided for the connection of an earphone. Integrated circuits are used in the signal processing stages.

Mains Supply: 240 volts, 50Hz.

Battery: 12 volts, 14W.

Cathode Ray Tube: 12VCAP4 or 310EUB4.

Adjustments

H.T. Voltage: (D.C. at Q901 collector). If less than 11.1 volts, cut off R908; if more than 11.7 volts, cut off R906.

Line Hold: T701.

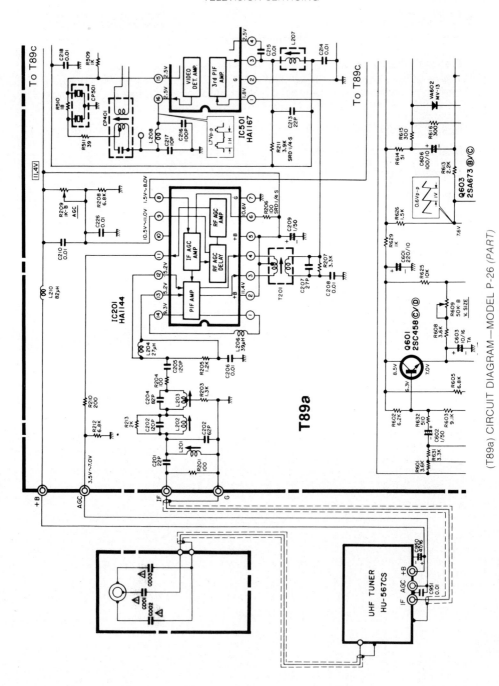

(T89a) CIRCUIT DIAGRAM—MODEL P-26 (PART)

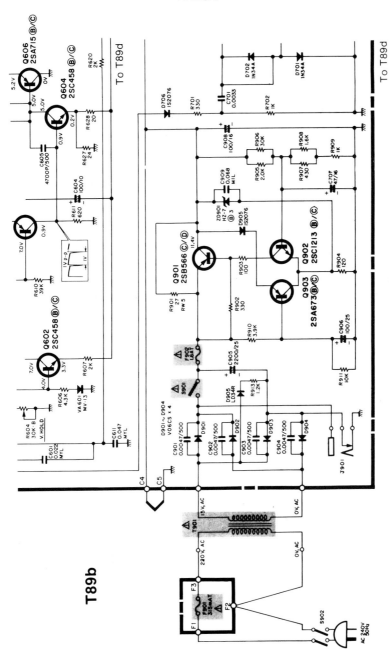

(T89b) CIRCUIT DIAGRAM—MODEL P-26 (PART)

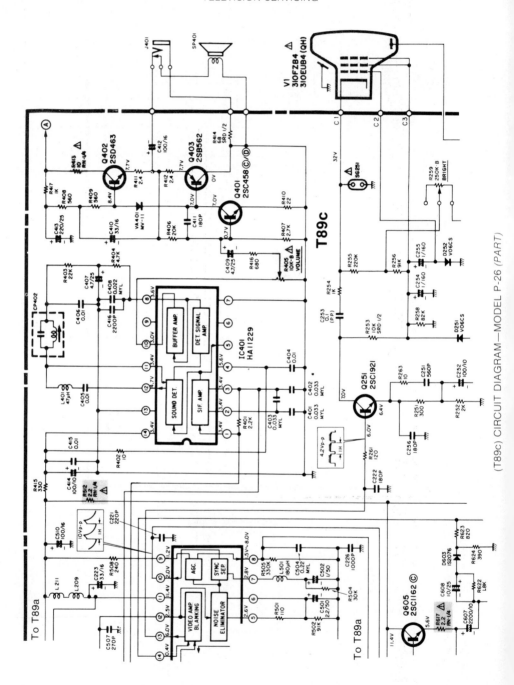

(T89c) CIRCUIT DIAGRAM—MODEL P-26 (PART)

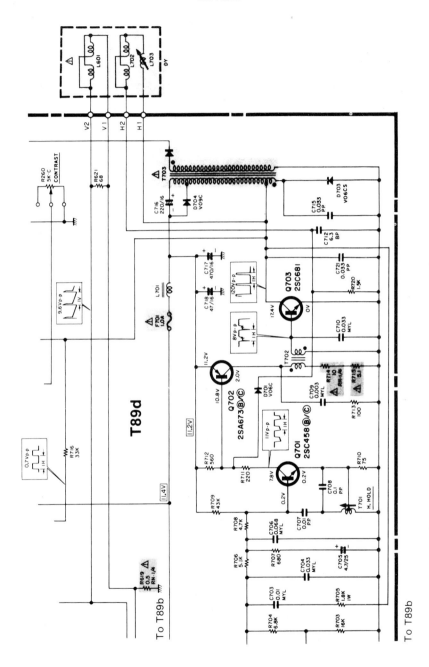

(T89d) CIRCUIT DIAGRAM—MODEL P-26 (CONTINUED)

I.T.T.

Models CB9504, CB9602, CB9604, CB9704

General Description: This information covers the latest range of 20", 22" and 26" colour T.V. models using simple push-button channel selection. Existing chassis are used for the 20" and 26" tubes. The 22" tube is driven by a modified CVC 40 chassis but the modifications are minimal.

The basic CVC 30, 40 and 45/1 chassis have been covered in previous volumes of *Radio and Television Servicing*. Information on the new control panels and tuner control units, showing chassis inter-connections, is included together with the changes made to the CVC 40 to enable it to drive the larger 22" tube. Setting-up instructions are also included in full for each chassis and information should be used with that given previously.

Model	Tube	Chassis
CB9504	(20") 510 RCB 22	CVC 45/1
CB9604	(22") 560 CGB 22	CVC 40/1
CB9602	(22") 560 CGB 22	CVC 40/1
CB9704	(26") Mullard 20 AX	CVC 30/1

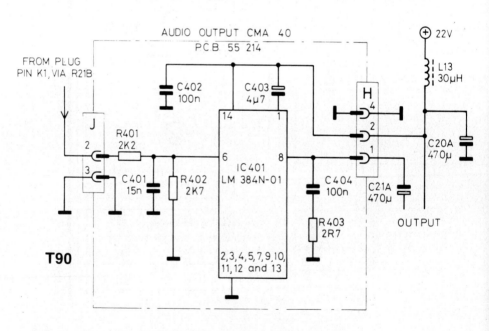

(T90) CIRCUIT DIAGRAM—CMA40 MODULE

76

Removal of Control Panels: For models CB9504, CB9604, CB9704 remove all inter-connecting plugs and sockets, undo the four screws at each corner and withdraw the panel. Remove the separately mounted tuner control unit in the same manner after unplugging socket 'T'.

For the CB9602 proceed as above, except that in this case the tuner unit and control panel are all in one piece. To separate the tuner unit from the control panel simply undo the two cross slotted screws from the two mounting lugs at either side.

Setting-up Instructions for CVC 30/1

Warning. The chassis is always live regardless of the mains polarity and it is essential that a mains isolation transformer of at least 500 watt rating be used when carrying out the setting-up. The power supply pre-sets R810, R817 are sealed with an I.T.T. approved glue to comply with safety requirements and should not normally need adjustment. If it becomes necessary to reset these components after, for example, major servicing work on the horizontal output and E.H.T. stages of the receiver, they should be replaced by components of the correct type as approved by I.T.T. Consumer Products (U.K.) Ltd.; after setting-up they should be sealed with suitable cement such as fast setting Araldite, in the same manner as the original components. For completeness, the following instructions include the setting for the supply trips, R810, R817.

Initial Settings: With the CMP 30 module removed from the main board, turn R810, R817 (see warning notice) fully clockwise and R808 fully anti-clockwise viewed from the component side of the module with the pins facing

(T91) CIRCUIT DIAGRAM—CMC67 CONTROL PANEL

T91

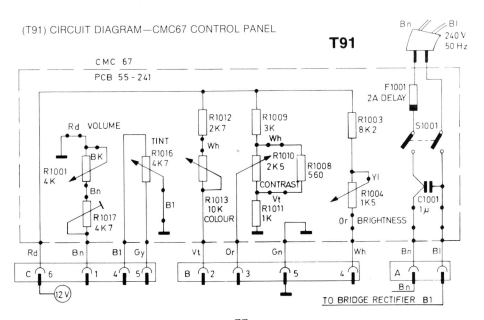

77

downwards. Through the hole provided in the main board, turn the horizontal frequency control, R710 approx. a quarter turn from fully clockwise. Turn the sound pre-set R1017 on the control panel fully anti-clockwise viewed 'in situ' from the rear of the receiver.

Remove R1* from the CMP 30 power supply module and plug the module into its servicing position on the print side of the main board. Connect the bias supply positive to TP 801 (large solder pad connected to R1) and negative to TP 802 (large solder pad connected to R2). Set the brightness control to minimum. Ensure that the blue and green guns are on (B and G switches fully clockwise from the print side of the tube base). Connect the Avo 8 across C52 (HT 3 to earth) and the E.H.T. meter to the tube anode socket. Set the bias supply to 4.0V.

Switch on the receiver and adjust R810 until the power supply trips out. IMMEDIATELY reduce the bias potential until the power supply switches on again. This must be done quickly or the power supply will trip out permanently. The receiver will then have to be switched off for at least 10 seconds and switched on again to reset the protection circuit before proceeding.

Slowly increase the biasing potential and check that the power supply trips out when the biasing potential reaches 4V ± 0.1V.

Remove the biasing potential and re-connect pin R1 to the module (or resolder the service link if provided). Adjust R808 to give an E.H.T. of 29kV. Adjust R817 until the power supply trips out. IMMEDIATELY reduce R808 (if necessary switching off and on again as in the previous step) and then slowly

*On some sets a service link, WL 803, will be found on the CMP 30 module in series with pin R1 in which case unsolder the end of this link connected to R1. The bias supply positive may then be connected to the free end.

(T92) CIRCUIT DIAGRAM—CMC68 CONTROL PANEL

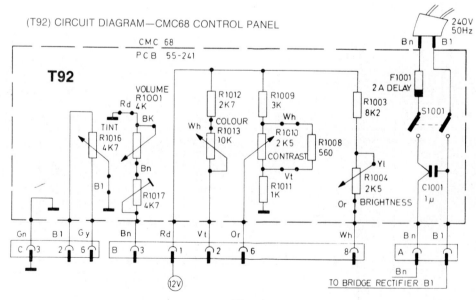

78

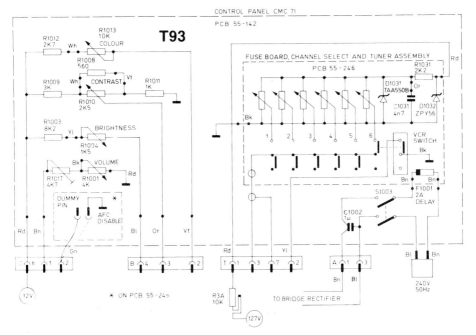

(T93) CIRCUIT DIAGRAM—CMC71 CONTROL UNIT

increase until the power supply trips out between 28.5 and 29.5kV. Reset R808 to give a reading of 25kV on the E.H.T. meter. Check that HT3 is 163V ± 0.5V. Seal R810, R817 with suitable cement, such as fast setting Araldite, and replace the CMP 30 module in its normal operating position.

Connect the Avo to the collector of T14 (pin F1 near the top left of the main board) and adjust R104, 'Set 12V', for a reading of 12V ± 0.1V.

Connect the cross-hatch pattern to the receiver. Set the Brightness, Contrast, and Colour controls to mid-range. If the vertical timebase is out of lock adjust the Vertical Hold control, R30, to obtain a stable picture. Adjust the Focus control, R100 for optimum focus in the centre of the picture.

Adjust the Height control, R2011, so that the top and bottom of the cross-hatch pattern may just be seen. Adjust R2017 for correct N/S linearity. Turn the N/S amplitude control, R111, to maximum (fully anti-clockwise). Adjust the N/S phase coil, L36 for maximum N/S barrel distortion. Reduce N/S amplitude, R111, until the horizontal lines at the top and the bottom of the picture are as straight as possible.

Adjust L25 for optimum horizontal linearity.

Adjust the width, R901, trapezium, R904 and pincushion, R905 to obtain vertical edges.

Connect test card 'F' in place of the cross-hatch pattern. Short pin G3 to earth (a small bladed screwdriver from pin G3 to the adjacent chassis point may be used) to disable the flywheel circuit. Adjust the horizontal frequency control, R710 until the picture is as stable as possible. Remove short.

Centre the picture by adjusting the Video/sync. phase control, R27.

Adjust the height, R2011 and the width, R901, controls until approx. ¾ of the castellations are excluded.

Degaussing and Purity: Manually degauss the tube and chassis as follows. Connect the manual degaussing coil to the mains supply and pass the coil over the top, bottom, and sides of the cabinet, but avoid the back and particularly the tube neck components. Finish with the front of the receiver and finally withdraw slowly to a distance of about eight feet before switching off the current.

If the convergence at the centre of the picture is very bad, proceed to the instructions given under 'Static Convergence' and reduce the error before attempting purity adjustments.

Lower the chassis to its horizontal position. Adjust the A1 pre-sets on the tube base, R604, R605, R606 to their mid-position. Reduce the ambient lighting as far as is practical. Switch-off the blue and green guns—S602 S601 respectively. Switch S501 on the decoder to give a blank raster. Note—this switch has three positions. (1) Fully clockwise viewed from the copper side of the decoder, normal operating position. (2) Half anti-clockwise giving a blank raster. (3) Fully anti-clockwise giving a collapsed frame. Adjust R604 to give a low brightness raster with Brightness control at minimum.

Release the deflection yoke fixing clips and move the yoke to its most forward position by rotating the adjustment ring fully clockwise.

Centre the area of red raster with respect to the discoloured areas by rotating the purity ring.

Turn the yoke adjustment ring anti-clockwise until the red raster is as pure as possible.

Trim the purity ring until any remaining discolouration is equal on either side of the screen. Re-adjust the Deflector Yoke until any discolouration just disappears.

Switch on the green gun and adjust R605 for a pure yellow raster. Switch on the blue gun and adjust R606 for a pure white raster. If any discolouration remains adjust the yoke ring slightly anti-clockwise until the raster is as white as possible. Turn S501 back to its normal operation position.

Note: Moving the deflector yoke back too far will reduce beam landing margins and may cause impurity at high beam currents.

Grey Scale Tracking:

Lowlights: Turn the A1s, R604, R605, R606 to minimum (fully clockwise viewed in situ from the rear of the receiver). Turn S501/502 fully anti-clockwise to collapse the frame. Turn the drive pre-sets, R554, R564, R574 to maximum (fully anti-clockwise from the copper side of the decoder. Set the brightness control to mid-position. Connect the Avo to TP 511 (the pin adjacent to R557 on the copper side) and connect test card F to the receiver.

Adjust the brightness preset R518 to give 2.4V ± 0.1V at TP511. Adjust the Brightness control to give 2.8V ± 0.1V at TP511.

Reduce the ambient lighting to as low a level as practicable. Adjust R604 to obtain a clearly visible red line. Adjust R605, R606 to obtain a white line. Do NOT re-adjust the Brightness control.

Highlights: Return S501/502 to its normal position. De-tune the receiver to give a monochrome picture with the Colour control set to maximum to ensure complete loss of any colour information. To achieve this it may be necessary to connect a 270pF capacitor between TP501 and earth.

Adjust the Contrast control until the brightness of the white in the test card grey scale matches the brightness of the brightest window of the grey scale reference.

Adjust the drive pre-sets, R554, R564, R574 for a correct grey scale match throughout the range. Colour bars may be used with advantage in place of test card 'F' for this operation. *Note:* After this adjustment at least one of the drive pre-sets must be at a maximum (fully anti-clockwise from the copper side of the decoder).

Turn down the Contrast control until the darkest area of grey on the test card (blue on colour bars) is equal in brightness to the darkest area of grey on the reference. If necessary re-adjust the A1s slightly for a correct match. Remove the 270pF capacitor from TP501 to earth if fitted.

Saturation: Connect the colour bar pattern and re-tune the receiver for correct colour. Turn the Colour control to minimum. Connect the oscilloscope to TP511 in place of the Avo. Adjust the Brightness control to give a black level 0.2V above blanking thus ensuring that the beam current limiter is rendered inoperative for the following adjustments.

Adjust the Contrast control to give 3.2V black to white signal. Adjust the saturation pre-set, R527 until the top extremities of the cyan (3rd) and magenta (5th) bars are equal. If this is not possible adjust R527 for maximum saturation.

Audio Module and Sound Pre-set: Unplug the Audio module and remove pin H3. Set R407 to mid-range and plug the module back into the board. Connect the Avo between TP1 and TP401 and connect a 0.1mF low voltage non-polarised capacitor across the terminals of the Avo. Adjust R407 to give a reading of 7mA ignoring any downward drift of the current after making this adjustment.

Set the Volume control to minimum. Listen close to the speaker and adjust R1017 on the control panel circuit board until sound can just be heard. Re-adjust R1017 until the sound JUST disappears. It is preferable to use test card 'F' 1kHz sine wave for this purpose.

Static Convergence: Connect the cross-hatch pattern to the receiver and switch-off the green gun.

Adjust the 4 pole magnet strength and direction levers for optimum convergence of blue and red at the centre section of the screen.

Switch-on the green gun. Adjust the 6 pole magnet strength and direction levers to obtain the best possible white cross-hatch near the screen centre.

Adjust the raster symmetry magnet to obtain the straightest possible central horizontal line.

Dynamic Convergence: Adjust R1302 to converge horizontal lines at the top of the raster.

Adjust R1307 to converge horizontal lines at the bottom of the raster.

Adjust L1305/6 to converge central horizontal lines.

Adjust L1301-4 for optimum vertical convergence at 3 o'clock and 9 o'clock.

Switch-off the green gun. Turn R1304 fully clockwise (viewed in situ from the rear of the receiver). Adjust R1305 for optimum symmetry of red and blue vertical error at 6 o'clock and 12 o'clock.

Re-adjust R1304 for zero red/blue vertical error at 6 o'clock and 12 o'clock.

Turn-on the green gun. If necessary re-adjust the static controls in conjunction with the dynamic controls to remove any small residual errors.

Setting-up Instructions for CVC 40/1 and CVC 45/1 Chassis

Warning: *This chassis is always live regardless of mains polarity and it is essential that a mains isolation transformer of at least 250 watt rating be used during this procedure.*

The power supply pre-set R824* is sealed with an I.T.T. approved glue to comply with safety requirements and should not normally need adjustment. If it becomes necessary to re-set this component after, for example, major servicing work on the horizontal output and E.H.T. stages of the receiver, it should be replaced by a component of the correct type as specified in the parts list or as approved by I.T.T. Consumer Products (U.K.) Ltd.; after setting-up it should be sealed with suitable cement, such as fast setting Araldite in the same manner as original component.

*Note: This instruction applies to earlier chassis only (pre July 1979). On later models, the power supply trip is permanently set.

Do not attempt to adjust the tube neck ring components as this will invalidate the tube guarantee. For this reason, no convergence instructions are included for these two chassis.

Initial Settings: Adjust 127V: connect meter to any 127V test point and rotate R828 to give a reading of 127V ± 0.5V on the D.V.M.

Set 12V: transfer meter to any 12V test point, and rotate R61 to give a reading of 12V ± 0.1V, disconnect meter.

Connect test card 'F'.

Set horizontal frequency: short pin G3 to ground in order to disable the 'fly-wheel' circuit. Rotate R708 until picture is as stable as possible. Remove short to ground.

Set vertical frequency: rotate R2003 for stable picture.

Set focus: rotate R55 to give optimum focusing one-third of the way across the screen.

Picture Geometry: Adjust height: rotate R2016 so that the Teletext signal is visible at the top of the picture.

Set field blanking: rotate R37 so that the Teletext signal is eliminated from the screen without cutting off the tops of the castellations.

Set vertical linearity: rotate R2017 to obtain optimum linearity up and down the screen.

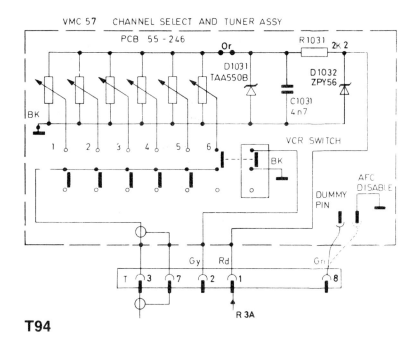

T94

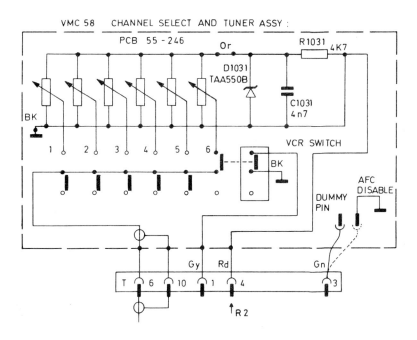

(T94) CIRCUIT DIAGRAM—VMC57, VMC58 CONTROL UNITS

Set vertical shift: rotate R32 to centralise picture on the screen.

Set horizontal linearity: rotate L9 to obtain optimum linearity across the screen.

Set horizontal shift: rotate R65 to centralise picture on the screen.

Set E-W pincushion: rotate R75 to give straight, vertical lines at the sides of the picture.

Set width: rotate L8 until approximately three-quarters of the castellations are excluded from the sides of the screen.

Set height: adjust R2016 to give a correct circle on the test card. Re-adjust the pincushion control R75, if necessary, ignoring the top castellations.

Grey Scale: Manually degauss the tube: connect the manual degaussing coil to the mains supply and pass the coil over the top, bottom, and sides of the cabinet, being careful to avoid the back and particularly the tube neck components. Finish with the front of the receiver and finally withdraw slowly to a distance of about eight feet before switching off the current.

Reduce black levels: rotate R23, R25 and R27 fully anti-clockwise from copper side of board.

Collapse frame: turn service switch S501/S502 fully anti-clockwise (from copper side of board).

Increase RGB drives: rotate R554, R564 and R574 fully anti-clockwise from copper side of board.

Adjust brightness: set Brightness control to its mid-position.

Connect meter to TP511.

Set brightness pre-set: rotate R518 to give reading of 2.4V ± 0.1V on meter.

Adjust Brightness control: set Brightness control to give reading of 2.8V ± 0.1V on meter.

Adjust black level (red): transfer meter to TP512 and rotate R23 to give 165V ± 2V.

Adjust black level (green): transfer meter to TP513 and rotate R25 to give 165V ± 2V.

Adjust black level (blue): transfer meter to TP514 and rotate R27 to give 165V ± 2V, disconnect meter.

Reduce ambient lighting: dim all lighting to as low a level as practicable.

Set A1 volts: increase voltage by rotating R47A until a coloured line just becomes clearly visible on the screen.

Set black levels: by careful adjustment of the black-level pre-sets, increase the two deficient colours until a white line is obtained. The third black-level adjustment (corresponding to the colour of the original line on the screen) must remain at 165 volts.

Return service-switch to normal position: turn S501/S502 to fully clockwise position.

Adjust colour: set Colour control to maximum position.

De-tune receiver: slightly de-tune the set to produce a monochrome picture.

Adjust contrast: set Contrast control until the brightest area of white in the test card grey scale matches the brightest window of the reference grey scale.

Set drive pre-sets: alter R554, R564 and R574 for correct grey scale matching throughout the range, bearing in mind that at least one of these pre-sets must be at maximum after this adjustment.

Adjust contrast: set Contrast control until the darkest area of grey in the test card grey scale matches the darkest window of the reference grey scale.

Reset pre-sets: if necessary fractionally re-adjust the appropriate black-level pre-set to obtain correct colour match for darkest grey.

Saturation: Connect colour-bar pattern.

Retune receiver: tune-in to receive correct colour picture again.

Switch-in A.F.C.

Adjust colour: set Colour control to minimum position.

Connect oscilloscope: attach the probe to TP511 on the decoder module.

Adjust brightness: set Brightness control so that black-level is just above blanking level.

Adjust contrast: set Contrast control to give 3.2V 'Black to White' signal.

Set saturation pre-set: rotate R527 until the top extremities of the cyan (3rd) and magenta (5th) bars are equal. If this is not possible, set R527 for maximum saturation. Disconnect oscilloscope.

Sound: Adjust volume: set Volume control to minimum position.

Connect test card 'F'.

Set Volume pre-set: listen close to the speaker and rotate pre-set R1017 until sound can just be heard, then turn R1017 until sound just becomes inaudible. (If greater objectivity is desired, use the 1kHz tone on test card 'F'. Set R1017 to give 1mV ± 0.2mV R.M.S. across the speaker, with the Volume control at minimum.)

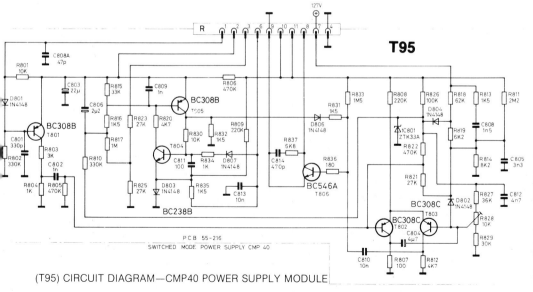

(T95) CIRCUIT DIAGRAM—CMP40 POWER SUPPLY MODULE

Power Supply Trip*: Reduce brightness: set Brightness control to the minimum position.

Reduce A1 volts: rotate R47A to the minimum position.

Connect E.H.T. meter: with the earth lead connected to the aquadag earthing braid, slide the probe of the meter under the E.H.T. cap on the tube. Measure E.H.T. volts and note reading.

Adjust E.H.T. volts:

CVC 40/1. Adjust R828 to give a reading of 3kV above previous value on E.H.T. meter.

CVC 45/1. Adjust R828 to give a reading of 28kV on E.H.T. meter.

Set over-volts trip: rotate R824 anti-clockwise until power supply just trips out.

Check over-volts trip:

CVC 40/1. Rapidly reduce R828, then slowly increase, checking that power supply trips out between 2.5kV and 3.5kV above the value measured in step 3.

CVC 45/1. As above, but power supply should trip out between 25.5kV and 28.5kV.

Set 127V: reset R828 to give reading of 127V ± 0.25V on the D.V.M., connected to any 127V test point.

Check E.H.T. volts:

CVC 40/1. Check reading on E.H.T. meter is correct to 23kV ± 1.5kV. Disconnect meter.

CVC 45/1. Check reading on E.H.T. meter is correct to 24kV ± 1kV.

*It will be found on later models that the potentiometer R824 has been deleted, the power supply trip on these models being permanently set. To check that the power supply is within specification, make sure that the voltage on plug pin R3 falls between the value —90V to —115V.

(T96) CIRCUIT DIAGRAM (E/W MODULATOR)—
CVC40/1 CHASSIS

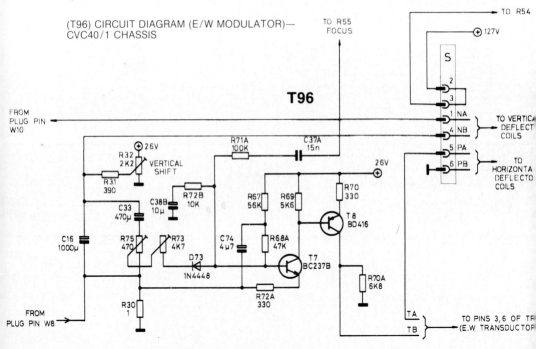

I.T.T.   Model CP9350

General Description: A remote control version portable colour television receiver using the CVC40 chassis which is described in the 1978-79 volume of *Radio and Television Servicing*. This addendum describes the remote control transmitter, the revised control unit, and the mains input and audio isolation module.

Mains Supplies: 220-240 volts, 50Hz.

Cathode Ray Tube: Hitachi 420CS B22-TC01 16-in.

Circuit Description—Remote Control System

Connection of Mains Voltage to T.V. Receiver: It is important to remember that the remote control system will not work until the mains switch is on, and that the remote commands Ideal or Channel Select cause the connection of mains voltage between the control panel and the T.V. receiver via the relay switch S1001. The command Standby will break this connection.

Use of Terms 'High' and 'Low' Explanatory Note: In the text that follows the words 'High' and 'Low' indicate the logic states which can be expected at various points in the circuit. The following table quantifies them in terms of D.C. voltage.

	Pin No.	Low	High		Pin No.	Low	High
IC1201	3	1V	5.6V	IC1202	2	0.7V	5.0V
	4	1V	5.6V		3	0.5V	5.0V
	5	1V	5.6V		4	0.5V	5.0V
	1	0.1V	33.0V		5	0.5V	5.0V
	10	0.1V	33.0V		6	0.25V	12.0V
	11	0.1V	33.0V		9	0.5V	12.0V
	12	0.1V	33.0V		10	0.7V	8.0V
	13	0.1V	33.0V		11	0.7V	8.0V
	16	0.1V	33.0V		14	0.7V	8.0V
	17	0.1V	33.0V		15	0.7V	8.0V
	18	0.1V	33.0V		20	0.8V	5.0V

RG922: The RG922 is a remote control infra-red transmitter powered by a 6 volt battery.

The heart of the transmitter is the transmitter encoder integrated circuit SAA5000. When a push-button on the keypad is depressed, one of pins 4-9 on the I.C. is connected to one of pins 10-14, or pin 4 or 5 is connected to pin 15, and a coded train of binary pulses is produced at pin 16. Different pin combinations will produce different code trains. There are 32 possible combinations, though only 19 are used in this application. The 32 transmitted commands and the corresponding binary codes are shown in Table 1.

To ensure that the receiver responds correctly to commands received under adverse transmission path conditions, the 5 bit command code is incorporated in a 24 bit code which consists of a 7 bit framing code, the 5 bit command code, the complementary of the framing code and the complementary of the command code. This 24 bit sequence is transmitted twice with an extra bit at the end of each sequence. The bit period is determined by the capacitor on pin 2 of the I.C. In this case it is 470p and the period is 3.9ms.

The I.C. output is at pin 16 and it is here that the coded pulse train appears. When no command is transmitted pin 16 is at V_{dd} potential (6 volts) and Tr1801 is held cut-off. It follows that Tr1802 is also cut-off and no current is flowing through the light emitting diodes. When a command is selected, the output at pin 16 will consist of a voltage at V_{dd} potential with brief interruptions corresponding to what would be the rise and fall times of digital waveforms for the 24 bit sequences. It is during these brief interruptions that Tr1801 conducts and forward biases Tr1802. Tr1802 collector current causes the light emitting diodes to radiate. The three 1.5 ohm resistors set the maximum current through the diodes.

CMC 42: Binary encoded infra-red radiation will cause D1201 to vary the collector voltage of Tr1201. This voltage is coupled via C1201 and developed across R1205 and C1204 before being applied to the base of Tr1202 which, together with Tr1203, forms a Darlington Pair. The signal is then directly coupled to the bases of Tr1204 (PNP) and Tr1205 (NPN) in turn and, from the collector of the latter, via R1214 to the base of Tr1206. The signal at this point is negative going. Tr1206 is a data slicer and is normally conducting. The biasing components R1213, R1214, and R1215 are chosen so that only the negative spikes of the coded signal are passed through to the collector. From the collector of Tr1206 the signal is passed to pin 22 of IC1202 whose function is to decode the binary signal presented to it.

Table 2 shows the responses to the various coded inputs.

D1202-D1204 form a bridge rectifier and provide 5 volts across D1207 for the operation of IC1202 and 12 volts across D1206 for use in various parts of the circuit. It should be noted that an external source of 12 volts is also present at connector 6 on plug C.

Transmission of either a channel select command or the ideal command will put a High on pin 6 of IC1202 and this will turn on Tr1207 and activate the relay in its collector circuit. The closed contacts of this relay will connect mains voltage to the T.V. receiver. D1001 is the back E.M.F. suppressor. Transmission of the standby code will of course put a Low on pin 6, turn off Tr1207, open the relay contacts and remove mains voltage from the receiver.

The operation of the sequence switch on the control panel puts a Low on pin 2 of IC1202 and, since it biases off Tr1208, puts a High on pin 20. These conditions cause the I.C.'s internal tuning selection counter to step up one, the I.C.'s analogue outputs at pins 10, 11, 14, and 15 revert to their mid-range levels, the mute output at pin 6 will change to the 'unmute' state, and the On/Standby output at pin 6 will change to On, if in the Standby mode. Continuous operation of the sequence switch will cause the station selection to progress through 1-8 and through 1 again.

When the T.V. set is placed into operation with the mains switch, a contact on that same switch will put a Low on pin 2 of IC1202 to ensure that the remote control circuitry is in the On and not the Standby mode.

The components connected to pins 18 and 19 of IC1202 set the frequency of the oscillator which controls the timing of all the I.C.'s functions.

Pin 9 will go Low whenever a remote programme selection command is being executed or for a period of 2 seconds when such a selection is made with the remote control in the Standby mode. This will cut off Tr1212 and mute the T.V. sound output.

Operation of the remote control analogue functions of contrast, colour, brilliance, and volume produce variable mark/space voltage waveforms at pins 15, 14, 11 and 10 respectively of IC1202. The waveforms are integrated to produce D.C. voltage levels and these voltages are presented to the bases of the emitter follower transistors Tr1209, Tr1210, Tr1211, and Tr1212. The resultant voltage levels at the emitters of the transistors control the contrast, colour, brilliance, and volume.

Here follows an explanation of the integration circuitry in the base of Tr1209—the other three analogue controls are similar. It can be seen from the circuit diagram that when pin 15 is High, C15 is charged via D11 and the top half of R1238. When pin 15 is Low, C15 is discharged via D12, R37 and the bottom half of R1238. This means that the setting of the potentiometer R1238 together with the mark/space voltage waveform at pin 15 determine the base voltage at Tr1209. When the Ideal command is selected, a 1:1 mark/space ratio waveform appears at pin 15 and therefore the only factor controlling the voltage on the base of Tr1209 is the setting of R1238.

The A.F.C. switch S2 is mounted on the CMC 42 control panel.

Depending upon which binary code is present at the input pins 3, 4, and 5 of IC1201, so a Low will appear at the output pin corresponding to the channel selected. If channel 2 is selected then the output of IC1202 will be such that at IC1201 pin 3 will be Low, pin 4 will be Low and pin 5 will be High. This input pattern will cause pin 16 of IC1201 to go Low and current will pass through R1258 to the 33 volt supply rail. Tr1213 will be forward biased via D1221 and the voltage at the emitter of the transistor, which is dependent upon the setting of the potentiometer R1258, will be applied to the tuner and thus determine the received frequency.

A Low at pin 1 of IC1201 will allow R1264 to set the receiver frequency for channel 8. As this is the channel which has been allocated for V.C.R. operation, its selection will also put a Low on pin 3 of plug T from whence it is fed to the sync. phase comparator on the CMS40 board.

The binary code present at pins 3, 4, and 8 of IC1202 is also fed to IC1203, the display driver, whose function is to supply channel display information to the seven segment LED display DL304.

D1231 will illuminate whenever the T.V. is in the Standby mode and also when the push-buttons on the remote control gun are depressed.

Table 1

Key No.	Command	Binary Code	Key No.	Command	Binary Code
1	Ideal	00000	17	Channel 1	10000
2	Not used	00001	18	Channel 2	10001
3	Standby	00010	19	Channel 3	10010
4	On	00011	20	Channel 4	10011
5	Not used	00100	21	Channel 5	10100
6	Not used	00101	22	Channel 6	10101
7	Not used	00110	23	Channel 7	10110
8	Not used	00111	24	Channel 8	10111
9	Vol +	01000	25	Not used	11000
10	Vol —	01001	26	Not used	11001
11	Bri +	01010	27	Not used	11010
12	Bri —	01011	28	Not used	11011
13	Col +	01100	29	Not used	11100
14	Col —	01101	30	Not used	11101
15	Con +	01110	31	Not used	11110
16	Con —	01111	32	Not used	11111

Table 2

Code Received	Command	Response
00000	Ideal	High on pin 6. Sets mark/space ratios on analogue outputs 10, 11, 14, and 15 to 1:1.
00010	Standby	Low on pin 6.
01000	Volume +	Increasing mark/space ratio waveform at pin 10.
01001	Volume —	Decreasing mark/space ratio waveform at pin 10.
01010	Brilliance +	Increasing mark/space ratio waveform at pin 11.
01011	Brilliance —	Decreasing mark/space ratio waveform at pin 11.
01100	Colour +	Increasing mark/space ratio waveform at pin 14.
01101	Colour —	Decreasing mark/space ratio waveform at pin 14.
01110	Contrast +	Increasing mark/space ratio waveform at pin 15
01111	Contrast —	Decreasing mark/space ratio waveform at pin 15.
10000	Channel 1	Low pin 8. Low pin 4. Low pin 3.
10001	Channel 2	Low pin 8. Low pin 4. High pin 3.
10010	Channel 3	Low pin 8. High pin 4. Low pin 3.
10011	Channel 4	Low pin 8. High pin 4. High pin 3.
10100	Channel 5	High pin 8. Low pin 4. Low pin 3.
10101	Channel 6	High pin 8. Low pin 4. High pin 3.
10111	Channel 7	High pin 8. High pin 4. Low pin 3.
11000	Channel 8	High pin 8. High pin 4. High pin 3.

Module Access: Remove the back cover.

Slacken the two bolts which secure the left hand lip of the motherboard to the left-hand mounting bracket assembly. Do the same to the bolts on the right-hand side.

Curl fingers under the top lip of the motherboard. Ease upwards and swivel back so that the board is horizontal.

Remove the slider control knobs from the control panel.

Disconnect sockets B, C, and T from the plugs on the motherboard. Disconnect sockets A, AA, E, and Y from the plugs on the mains input panel. Disconnect the two tags on the rear of the speaker.

Un-do the four screws securing the cabinet front and shell to the cabinet centre section. Ease the cabinet front and shell forward until it is detached from the rest of the television set.

Un-do the six screws which hold the cabinet front and shell together.

Un-do the three screws securing the control panel to the cabinet front and separate the two by gently prising the outside edge of the control panel.

The control unit is secured to the cabinet front by a screw at centre top and another at centre bottom.

Servicing Notes—Remote Control System

The following checks will assist in pointing toward any defective area of the remote control system.

Equipment required: Digital Multimeter, or an Analogue Multimeter with a sensitivity of at least 20,000 ohms per volt.

RG 922 (Remote Control Transmitter): Check the current consumption. It should be 40mA ± 10% when any one of the buttons is depressed and a maximum of 30μA when the button is released. When the gun is pointed directly at the sensor on the T.V. receiver it should be effective from a distance of up to 10 metres.

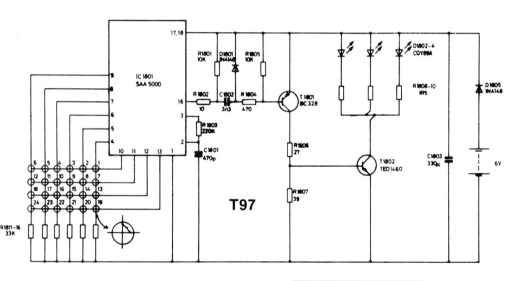

KEYPAD CODE:–

NO.	OPERATION	NO.	OPERATION
1	IDEAL	13	COLOUR+
2	MUTE	14	COLOUR−
3	STANDBY	15	CONTRAST+
4	NOT USED	16	CONTRAST−
5	NOT USED	17	CHANNEL 1
6	NOT USED	18	CHANNEL 2
7	NOT USED	19	CHANNEL 3
8	NOT USED	20	CHANNEL 4
9	VOLUME+	21	CHANNEL 5
10	VOLUME−	22	CHANNEL 6
11	BRIGHTNESS+	23	CHANNEL 7
12	BRIGHTNESS−	24	CHANNEL 8

(T97) CIRCUIT DIAGRAM (REMOTE CONTROL TRANSMITTER RG922)—MODEL CP9350

91

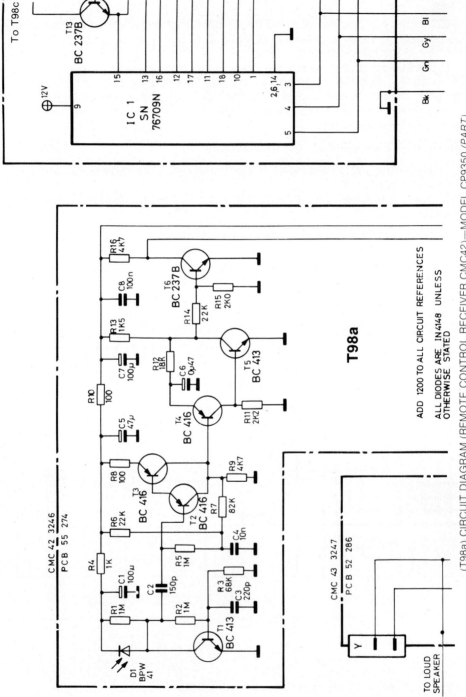

(T98a) CIRCUIT DIAGRAM (REMOTE CONTROL RECEIVER CMC42)—MODEL CP9350 (PART)

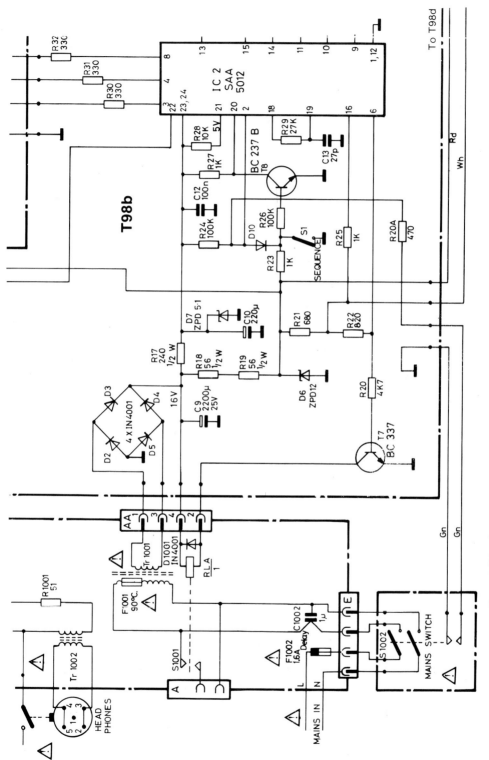

(T98b) CIRCUIT DIAGRAM (REMOTE CONTROL RECEIVER CMC42)—MODEL CP9350 (PART)

(T98c) CIRCUIT DIAGRAM (REMOTE CONTROL RECEIVER CMC42)—MODEL CP9350 (PART)

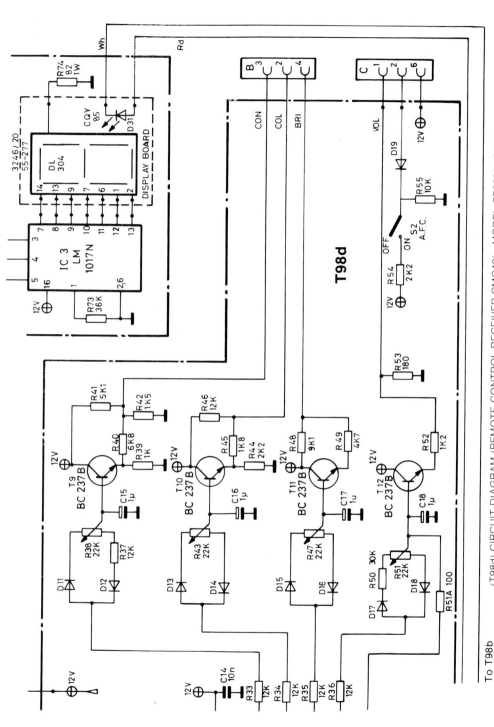

(T98d) CIRCUIT DIAGRAM (REMOTE CONTROL RECEIVER CMC42)—MODEL CP9350 (CONTINUED)

To T98b

CMC 42:

Check Operation of	Connect DVM to	Conditions	Result or Approximate Reading
Mains rectification	Pin 4 Plug AA	Mains switch on	16V D.C.
Tuning voltage	Pin 3 Plug T	Select each channel in turn	0.6-28V D.C., depending upon position of tuning control.
V.C.R.	Pin 2 Plug T	10K resistor connected between Pin 2 Plug T and 12 volt supply.	1V D.C. max. when channel 8 selected, 5V D.C. min. when channels 1-7 selected.
A.F.C.	Pin 2 Plug C	100K resistor connected between Pin 2 Plug C and 12 volt supply.	A.F.C. on (button depressed) 10V D.C. min. A.F.C. off —2 D.C. max.
Volume	Pin 1 Plug C	R1251 mid travel: With RG922 turn volume to max. With RG922 turn volume to min. With RG922 select Reset (Ideal) Turn R1251 to max. Turn R1251 to min. R1251 mid travel: With RG922 select Mute With RG922 re-select Mute	1.1-1.4V D.C. 0-6V D.C. 0.3-0.5V D.C. 0.45-0.6V D.C. 0.1-0.3V D.C. 0-0.1V D.C. 0.3-0.5V D.C.
Brightness	Pin 4 Plug B	1K2 resistor connected between Pin 4 Plug B and ground. R1247 mid travel: With RG922 turn bright. to max. With RG922 turn bright. to min. With RG922 select Reset (Ideal) Turn R1247 to max. Turn R1247 to min.	1.5-1.7V D.C. 1.3-1.4V D.C. 1.3-1.6V D.C. 1.5-1.6V D.C. 1.3-1.5V D.C.
Colour	Pin 2 Plug B	4K7 resistor connected between Pin 2 Plug B and ground. R1243 mid travel: With RG9022 turn colour to max. With RG922 turn colour to min. With RG922 select Reset (Ideal) Turn R1243 to max. Turn R1243 to min.	7.6-8.0V D.C. 1.7-1.9V D.C. 4.3-4.6V D.C. 5.7-6.0V D.C. 2.9-3.1V D.C.
Contrast	Pin 3 Plug B	R1238 mid travel With RG922 turn contrast to max. With RG922 turn contrast to min. With RG922 select Reset (Ideal) Turn R1238 to max. Turn R1238 to min.	3.6-3.8V D.C. 2.2-2.5V D.C. 2.9-3.2V D.C. 3.2-3.5V D.C. 2.7-2.9V D.C.
Standby		Use RG922 to select Standby	The T.V. receiver should shut-down and the standby light should illuminate.
Standby light		Select any remote command	The Standby light should illuminate during any remote control operation.

J.V.C.   Model P-100 UKC

General Description: A portable monochrome television receiver incorporating a 2-in. cathode ray tube and A.M./F.M. radio. The instrument is powered by internal batteries or from A.C. mains by the power adaptor supplied. A socket is provided for the connection of an earphone.

Batteries: 6 volts (4×1.5 volts), 1.7W.

Mains Adaptor: 240 volts, 50Hz.

Cathode Ray Tube: C2054P4.

Loudspeaker: 16 ohms impedance.

Access for Service

Front Panel Removal: Pull off T.V., Radio, and Vol. knobs. Remove 3 screws (1 left side, 2 right side) from front panel.

Bottom Board Removal: Take out battery case and remove the 2 screws revealed in the side of the case.

Top Panel Removal: Dismantle as described previously. Position the rod aerial vertically and pull the top panel up over the rod.

Adjustments

H.T.: Connect a 6 volt supply to P5. Adjust R503 to obtain a reading of 4.5 volts at TP52 (Collector of X501).

Drive Cord Assembly: (See Fig. T136):

The dial cord length is 70.5cm.
Tie up the spring and drum with the dial cord as illustrated.
After tightening, the cord B length is cut to approx. 3m/m.

Procedure	Illustration No.	Remarks
1. Put the spring on the drum A.	1	
2. Draw the dial cord in arrow direction.	2~5	
3. Wind the dial cord on the tuning shaft three and a half times	5~6	Wind the dial cord on under-slot of the drum A.
4. Draw the dial cord in arrow direction.	6~9	
5. Wind the dial cord on the setting screw one and a half times.	10	After winding on, screw down and supply a rock paint.
6. Draw the dial cord in arrow direction.	11~13	Wind the dial cord on upper slot of the drum A.
7. Draw the cord upward through the roller.	14~16	
8. Wind the dial cord on the drum B four times.	16	
9. Insert the spring and drum supporter into the drum B opening.	17	Insert one end of the spring in the drum supporter.
10. After rotating the drum supporter five times with a screwdriver, set the drum B into the tuning base.	18~20	

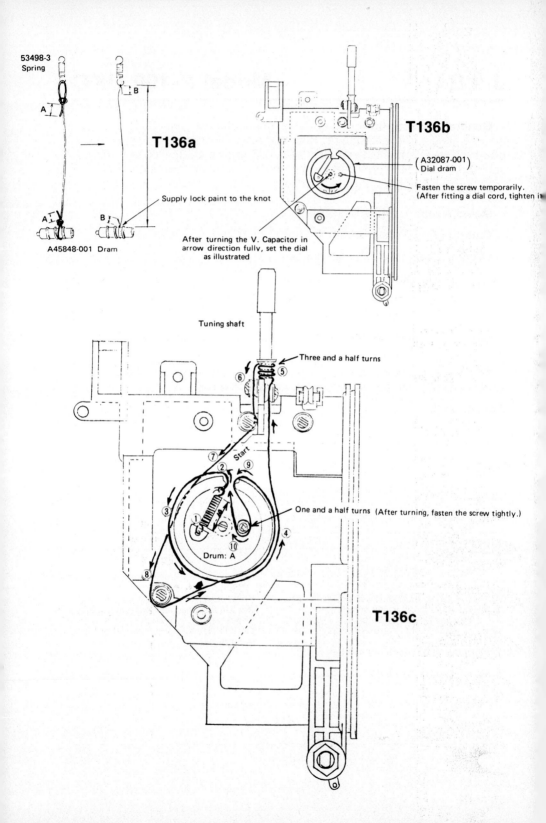

53498-3
Spring

T136a

A

B

A

B

Supply lock paint to the knot

A45848-001 Dram

T136b

$\left(\begin{matrix}A32087\text{-}001\\ Dial\ dram\end{matrix}\right)$

Fasten the screw temporarily.
(After fitting a dial cord, tighten it)

After turning the V. Capacitor in
arrow direction fully, set the dial
as illustrated

Tuning shaft

Three and a half turns

⑥ ⑤

⑦ Start
② ⑨

③

One and a half turns (After turning, fasten the screw tightly.)

①

④

⑩

Drum: A

⑧

T136c

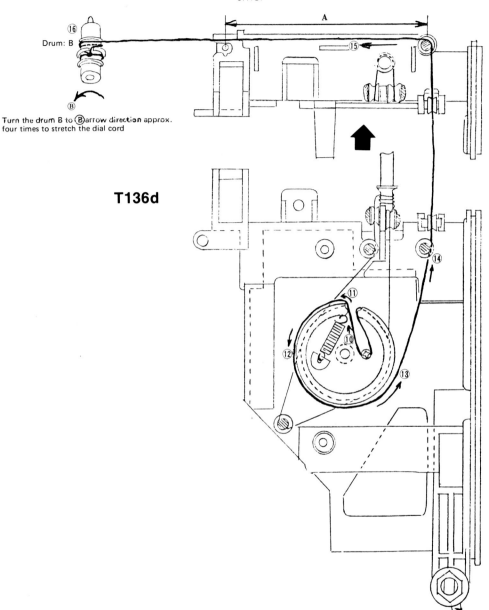

T136d

Drum: B

Turn the drum B to ⒷArrow direction approx.
four times to stretch the dial cord

(T136a-d) TUNING DRIVE ASSEMBLIES (SEE TEXT)—MODEL P-100 UKC

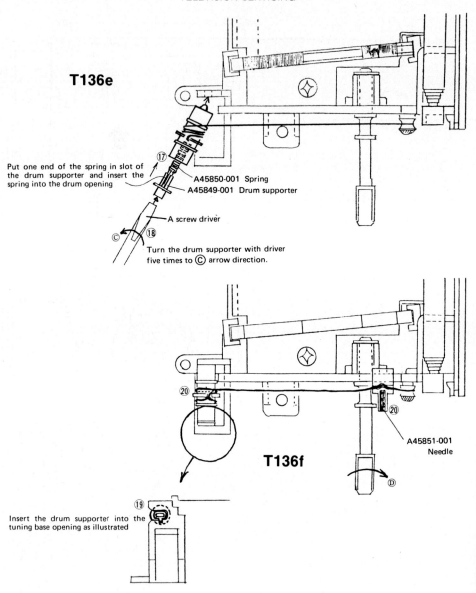

T136e

Put one end of the spring in slot of the drum supporter and insert the spring into the drum opening

A45850-001 Spring

A45849-001 Drum supporter

A screw driver

Turn the drum supporter with driver five times to Ⓒ arrow direction.

T136f

A45851-001 Needle

Insert the drum supporter into the tuning base opening as illustrated

(T136e-f) TUNING DRIVE ASSEMBLIES—MODEL P-100 UKC

On completion, check for smooth dial cord running and confirm that one or more turns of dial cord remain on the drum B when turning the tuning shaft to D arrow direction fully.

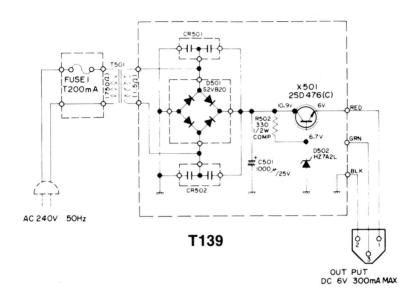

T139

OUT PUT
DC 6V 300mA MAX

(T139) CIRCUIT DIAGRAM (POWER ADAPTOR AA-24LUK)—MODEL P-100 UKC

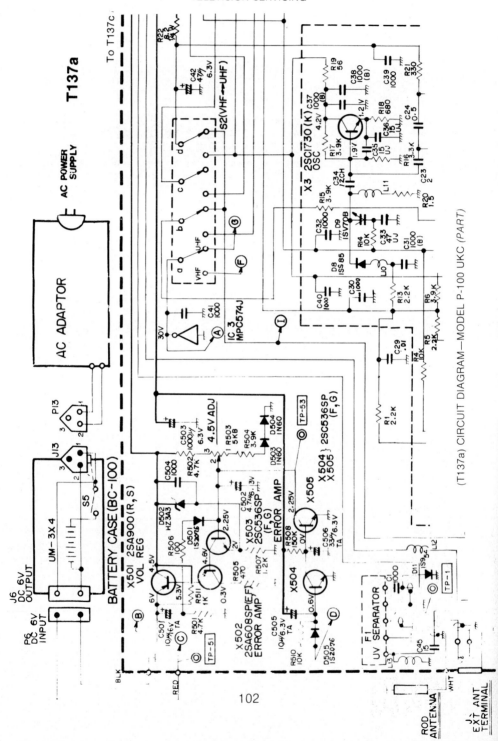

(T137a) CIRCUIT DIAGRAM—MODEL P-100 UKC (PART)

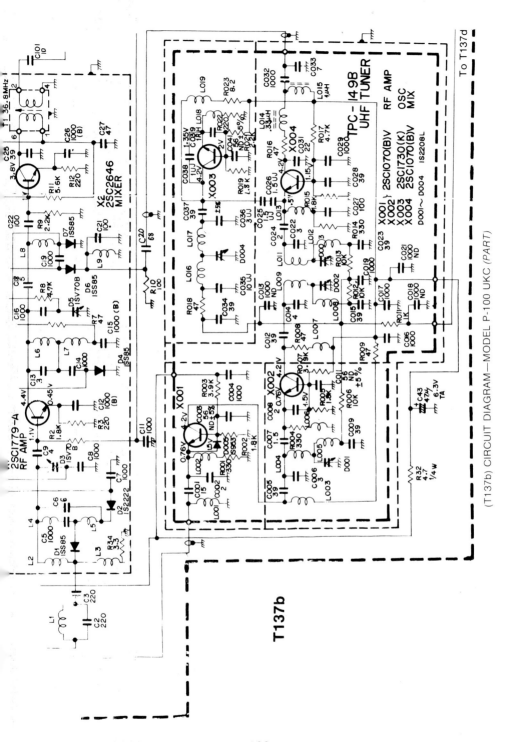

(T137b) CIRCUIT DIAGRAM—MODEL P-100 UKC (PART)

(T137c) CIRCUIT DIAGRAM—MODEL P-100 UKC (PART)

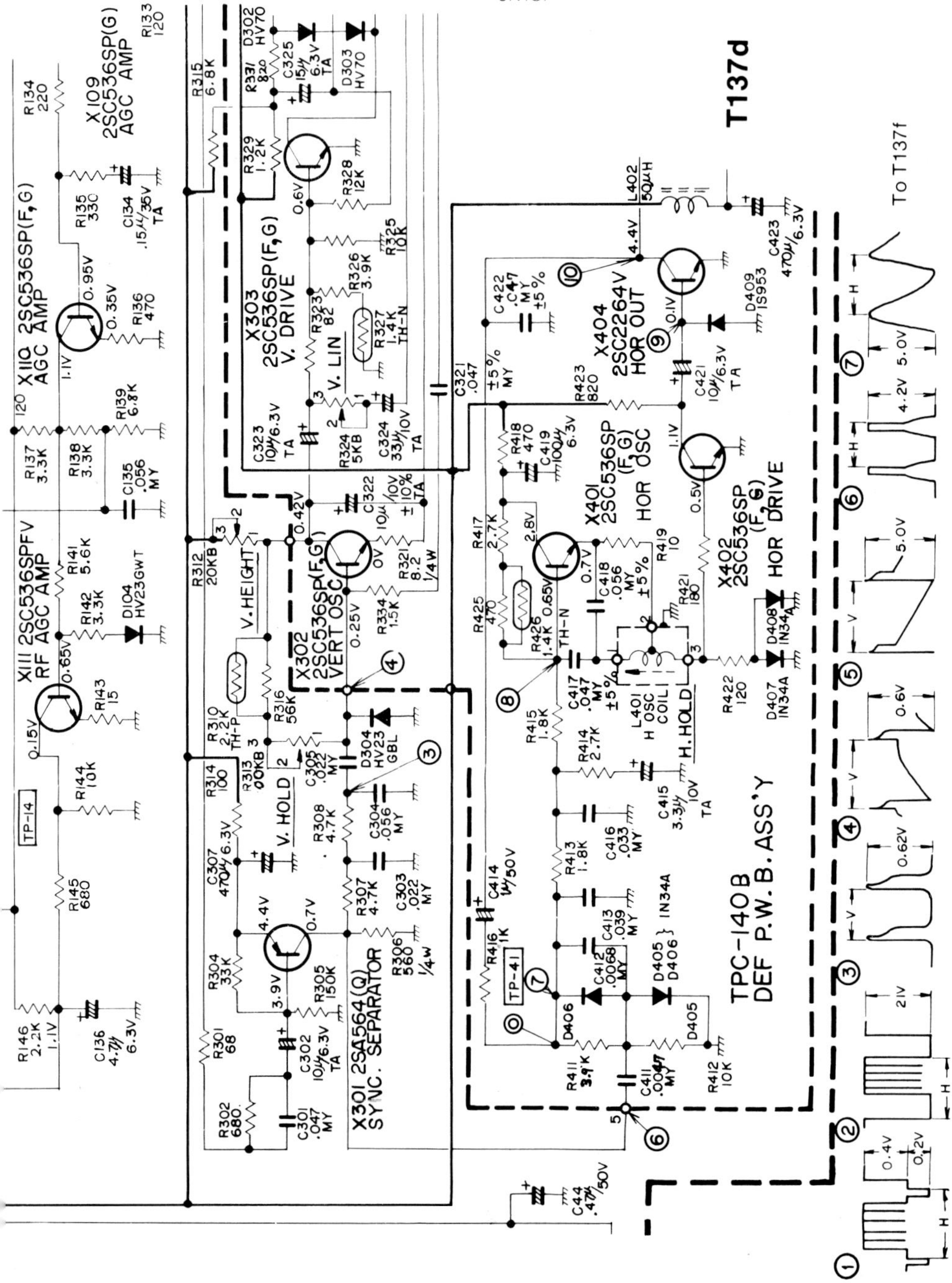

(T137d) CIRCUIT DIAGRAM—MODEL P-100 UKC (PART)

T137d

TPC-140B DEF P.W.B. ASS'Y

X301 2SA564(Q) SYNC. SEPARATOR

To T137f

To T137b

(T137e) CIRCUIT DIAGRAM—MODEL P-100 UKC (PART)

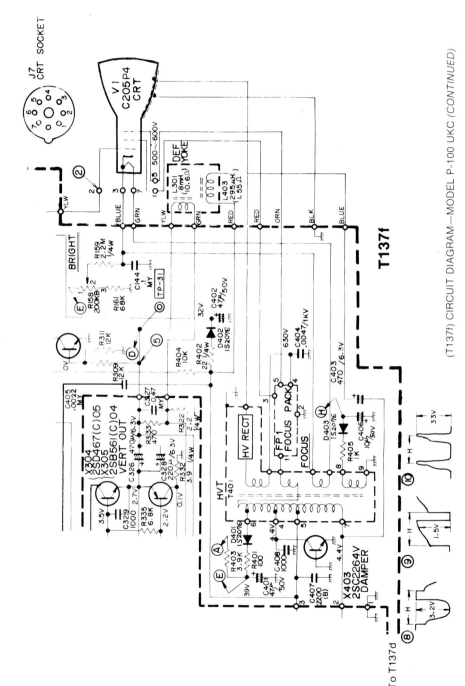

(T137f) CIRCUIT DIAGRAM—MODEL P-100 UKC (CONTINUED)

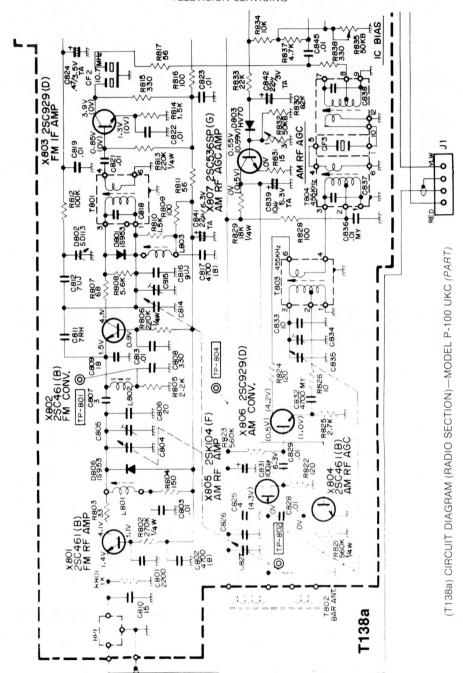

(T138a) CIRCUIT DIAGRAM (RADIO SECTION)—MODEL P-100 UKC *(PART)*

T138a

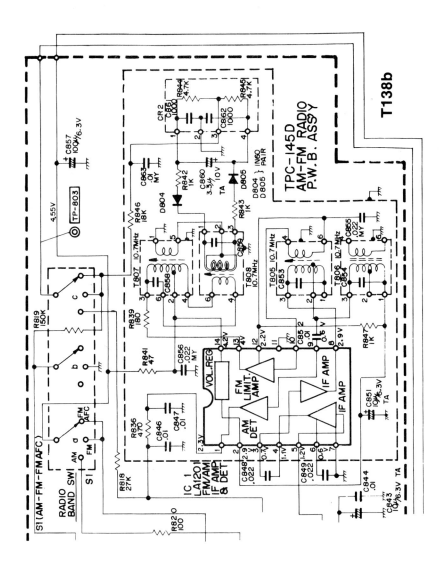

(T138b) CIRCUIT DIAGRAM (RADIO SECTION)—MODEL P-100 UKC (CONTINUED)

NATIONAL U-1 Chassis, Models TC2203, TC2204

General Description: A mains-operated colour television receiver chassis with standard or pre-aligned cathode ray tube. The circuit for Model TC2203 is given here. Model TC2204 is similar with the omission of convergence components.

Mains Supply: 240 volts, 50Hz.

Cathode Ray Tube: A56-500X, 510X (TC2203); 560CXB22-TC02 (TC2204).

Important! This chassis is 'live' irrespective of mains connection. A suitable isolating transformer must be used when any servicing is performed on these receivers.

Adjustments (TC2203)

Using Philips PM5509 pattern generator or similar equipment.

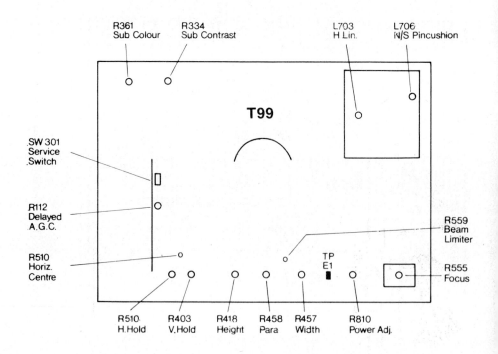

(T99) COMPONENT LOCATION (INSTALLATION ADJUSTMENTS)—MODEL TC2203

A.B.L. Adjustment: Receive colour bar signal.

Turn the Brightness and Contrast controls to maximum and Colour control to minimum. Connect micro-ammeter between TPE3 (Positive) and TPE2 (Negative) on 'E' circuit board. Adjust A.B.L. control (R559) for 1200 ± 100 A.

Focus Adjustment: Receive colour bar signal.

Set Contrast and Brightness controls to middle position.

Adjust Focus control (R555) to obtain the best focus.

Sub-contrast Adjustment: Select colour bar signal and switch A.F.C. on.

Turn Brightness and Colour controls to minimum and Contrast control to maximum.

Connect resistor jumper (12k) between TPA17 and A4.

Connect oscilloscope to TPA20 and adjust sub-contrast VR (R334) so that waveform becomes 100 ± 5V p-p.

Sub-colour Adjustment: Receive colour bar signal.

Set Brightness control to minimum and Contrast, Colour controls to maximum.

Connect resistor jumper (12k) between TPA17 and A4.

Connect oscilloscope probe to TPA19. Adjust Sub-colour control (R631) so that waveform is 2.7 ± 0.2V p-p.

Power Line Adjustment: Select colour bar signal.

Set service switch on.

Connect digital voltmeter to TPE1 and adjust R810 for 160 ± 1V.

Connect D.V.M. to C010EP Pin 3 and confirm voltage is 195 ± 20V.

Connect D.V.M. to C03EP Pin 5 and confirm voltage is 800 ± 90V.

Connect D.V.M. to TPE4 and confirm voltage is 37 ± 5V.

Connect D.V.M. to TPE6 and confirm voltage is 20 ± 2V.

Connect D.V.M. to C08EP Pin 3 and confirm voltage is 16.5 ± 2V.

Connect D.V.M. to TPE5 and confirm voltage is 11.7 ± 0.5V.

Set service switch off, confirm C.R.T. heater voltage (Y4, Y6) is 6.3 ± 0.24V R.M.S.

Magic Line Adjustment:

Note: Controls are situated within screened can on vertically mounted circuit board 'A'. Receive normal picture signal and adjust local frequency.

Set the A.F.C. magic line selector to magic line on position to make green belt appear on the screen.

Turn L901 to the point where magic line width becomes narrowest.

When magic line disappears, adjust R902 to make it appear on the screen.

Adjust R905 to the point where magic line is at the centre of the screen.

Adjust R902 to the point where magic line width is approximately 6cm.

Horizontal Circuit Adjustment: Receive test card pattern and A.F.C. on.

Short TPE7 to ground.

Turn H. Hold control to stabilize pattern and remove shorting jumper.

Adjust horizontal centre control (R511) so that centre of pattern is located at centre of screen.

Adjust parabola control (R458) so that vertical lines on pattern are straight.

Adjust width control (R457) for correct picture size.

Adjust H. Linearity control (L703) for linear picture.

Vertical Circuit Adjustment: Receive test card pattern.

Adjust vertical centre plug so that pattern centre is located at screen centre.

Adjust Height control (R418) and V. Linearity control (R411) for linear picture of correct size.

Adjust L706 for best N/S pincushion.

R.F. (Delayed) A.G.C. Control Adjustment: Receive normal picture signals. (Middle strength channel available.)

Slowly turn the R.F. A.G.C. control (R112) clockwise from where it was fully turned counter-clockwise and set it at a point where noise is minimised.

Receive picture on all channels and make sure that neither synchronism distortion nor cross modulation takes place.

Sound Leakage Adjustment: Receive constant tone sound signal.

Set Sound control (R205) at minimum position.

Connect oscilloscope probe across speaker terminals.

Adjust sound leakage pre-set (R216) for minimum sound leakage.

Purity, Static and Dynamic Convergence Adjustments (TC2203)

Before all adjustments described below are attempted, V. Hold, H. Hold, V. Height, V. Linearity, B+ voltage and Focusing adjustments must be completed.

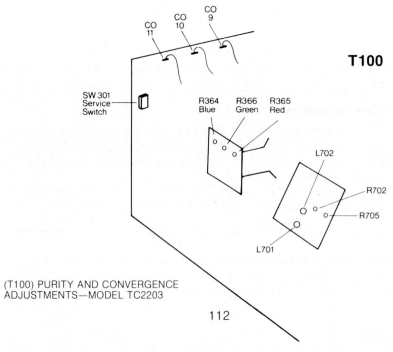

(T100) PURITY AND CONVERGENCE
ADJUSTMENTS—MODEL TC2203

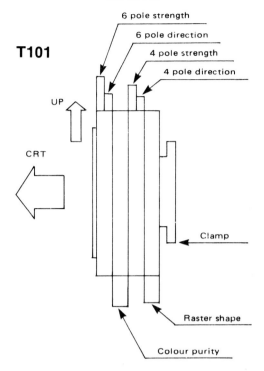

NATIONAL

T101

6 pole strength

6 pole direction

4 pole strength

4 pole direction

UP

CRT

Clamp

Raster shape

Colour purity

(T101) C.R.T. MAGNET ASSEMBLY—MODEL TC2203

Preparation: Switch the T.V. receiver on and thoroughly degauss the C.R.T. Set rough white balance, by setting service switch (SW301) to on (this collapses the frame and removes video information). Turn the screen controls (R364, R365 and R366) completely off, then increase each one in turn (R.G.B.) to produce a white line that is just visible. Set the service switch to off.

Caution: Do not operate the C.R.T. at beam currents higher than 600 A until the purity adjustment is completed.

Adjustment: On white pattern, at low level of brightness, move deflection coil to obtain rough purity of raster. (Blue and green guns can be switched off if necessary by disconnecting plugs CO9AS and CO10AS.)

Select X-hatch, adjust the tilt of the picture by rotating the deflection coils inside the housing, when correctly adjusted move the DY clamps to half way position. This will prevent the DY from turning inside its housing, but still allow movement of the DY in an axial direction.

Using cross-hatch pattern, with green gun off (maintaining lowest brightness consistent with adjustment) obtain convergence of red and blue statics using simultaneous adjustment of 4 pole direction and strength levers. Switch green gun on and converge green with red/blue by using 6 pole direction and strength levers. Adjust raster shape magnet lever so that horizontal centre line of test pattern becomes straight. This will optimise raster shape and symmetry.

Move the deflection coils fully forward in their housing. Switch-off green and blue guns and using medium brightness, adjust purity lever until pure red region is centralised. Pull back the deflection coil until the raster becomes pure.

Caution: When pulling back the deflection coil, as soon as pure raster is obtained, do not move the coil back any further (this is to allow for changes in beam landing due to expansion of shadow mask when operating at high beam currents).

Check purity using green and then blue rasters, and make any slight adjustment as necessary. Lock the deflection coil by moving the DY clamps fully forward.

Obtain cross-hatch pattern and reduce brightness and increase contrast until sharply defined lines of cross-hatch are obtained. Switch-off green gun and using 4 pole direction and strength levers complete adjustment of red/blue static convergence.

Display a cross-hatch pattern and adjust L702 to converge vertical lines at left and right of screen.

Adjust R702 so that red and blue vertical lines at top and bottom of screen converge. Adjust L701 so that red and blue horizontal lines at left and right of screen converge. (Red and blue will cross over about centre of screen.)

Adjust R705 so that red and blue horizontal lines converge at the top and bottom of screen.

Switch-on green gun and complete adjustment of static convergence by registering the green beams precisely with the red/blue beams by using the 6 pole direction and strength levers.

Grey Scale Adjustment: Select colour bar signal.

Turn screen controls fully to anti-clockwise. Set service switch on and slowly turn screen controls clockwise to the point where beams just illuminate and white horizontal line is obtained.

Set service switch to normal and confirm uniform white picture.

Adjustments (TC2204)

Switch the T.V. receiver on and thoroughly degauss the C.R.T.

Set rough white balance, by setting service switch (SW301) to on (this collapses the frame and removes video information). Turn the screen controls (R364, R365 and R366) completely off (C.R.T. Base) then increase each one in turn (R.G.B.) to produce a white line which is just visible. Set service switch to off.

Convergence and Purity: The picture tube employed in the TC-2204 is supplied complete with deflection yoke and multipole unit pre-aligned by the C.R.T. manufacturer.

No further alignment of purity or convergence is necessary. Should replacement of the C.R.T. be necessary it will be supplied complete with

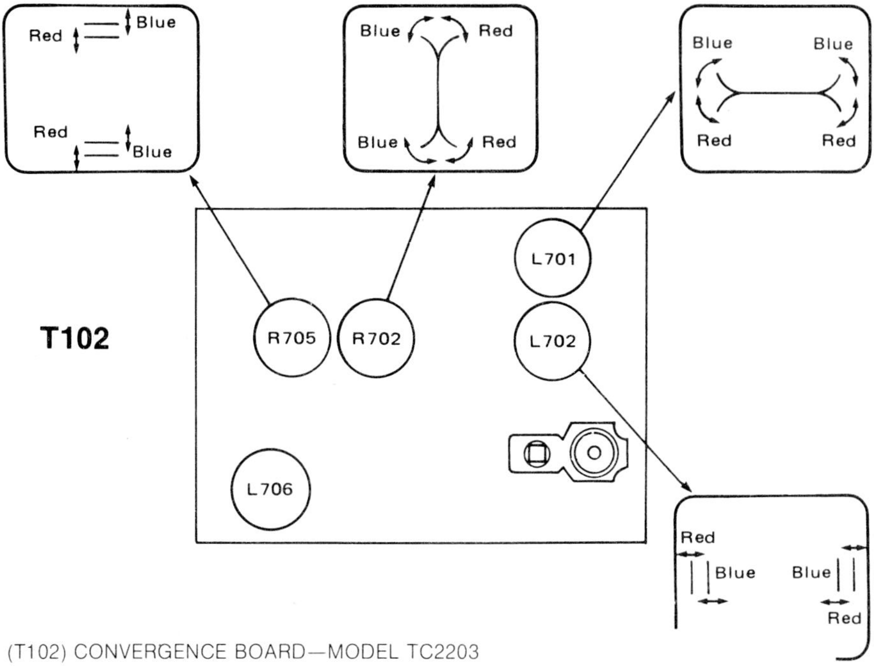

Red ⇕ ≡ ⇕ Blue

Red ≡ ⇕ Blue

Blue ⤵ ⤴ Red

Blue ⤴ ⤵ Red

Blue   Blue

Red   Red

T102

L701

R705 R702

L702

L706

Red

Blue Blue

Red

(T102) CONVERGENCE BOARD—MODEL TC2203

deflection yoke and multipole unit which will have been pre-aligned at manufacture.

Circuit Diagram Notes

All voltages and waveforms taken on a studio colour bar reception at 1mV input. Measurements made with Philips digital multimeter type PM2513 (DC 100K /V) and Philips oscilloscope type PM3234, with A.C. mains input at 240V (r.m.s.).

Control Settings: Normal adjustment specification of all pre-set controls. Brightness, Contrast and Colour controls at maximum. Picture and Sound controls at mid-position. A.F.C./Magic Line switch to A.F.C. position (except where noted).

Corrections

Q819 should read D819.
In IC601 and IC602 block shown as A.A.C. should read: A.C.C.

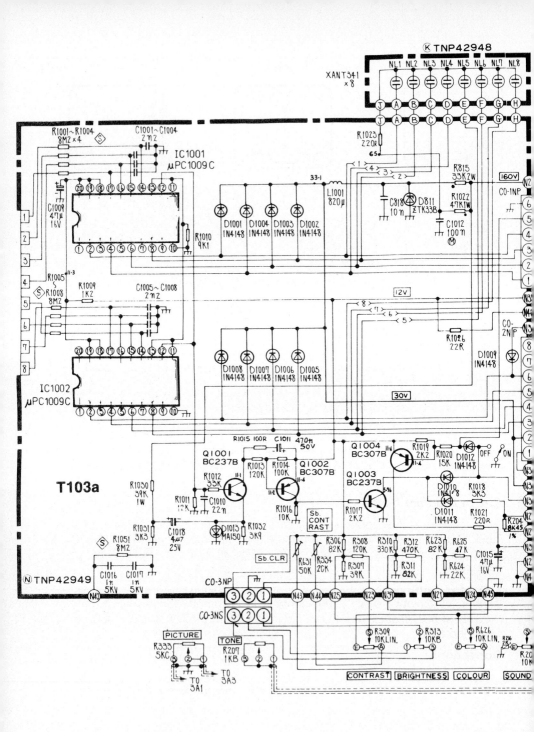

(T103a) CIRCUIT DIAGRAM (SIGNAL STAGES)—MODEL TC2203 *(PART)*

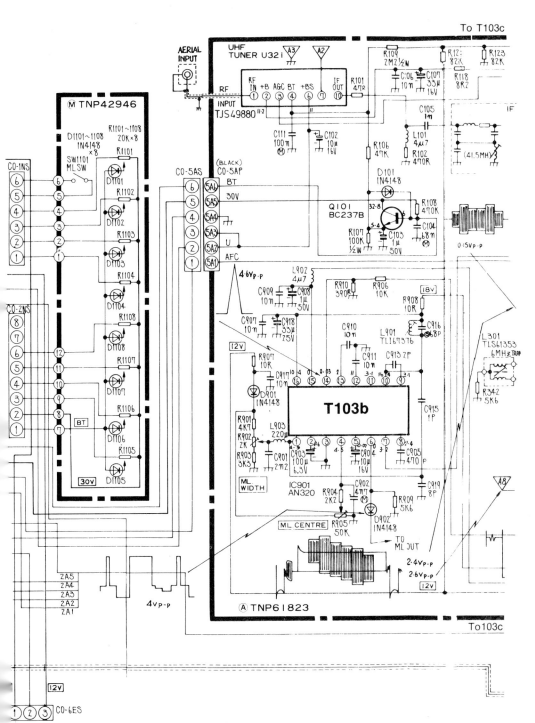

(T103b) CIRCUIT DIAGRAM (SIGNAL STAGES)—MODEL TC2203 *(PART)*

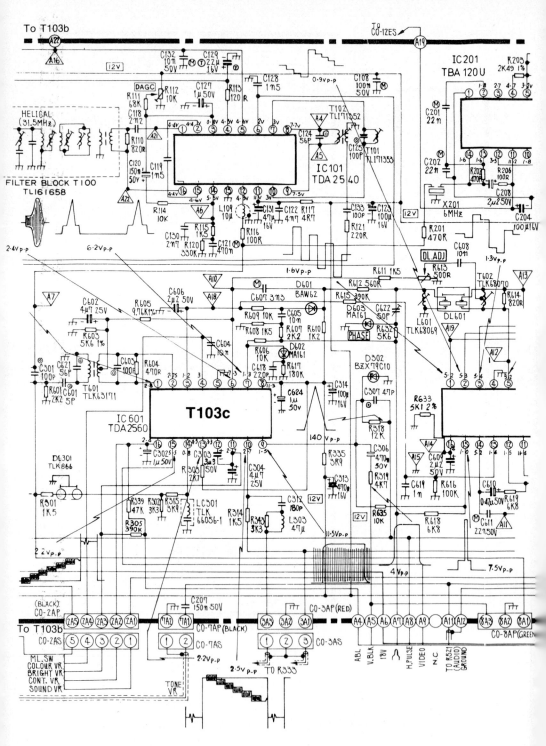

(T103c) CIRCUIT DIAGRAM (SIGNAL STAGES)—MODEL TC2203 *(PART)*

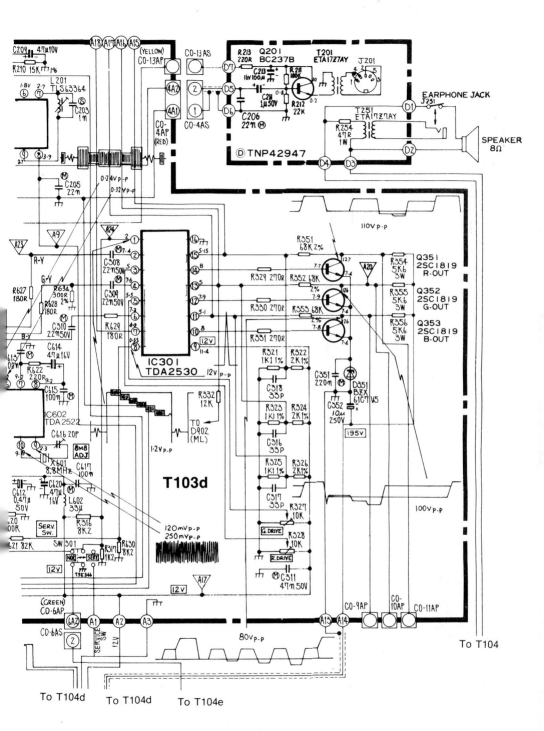

(T103d) CIRCUIT DIAGRAM (SIGNAL STAGES)—MODEL TC2203 *(CONTINUED)*

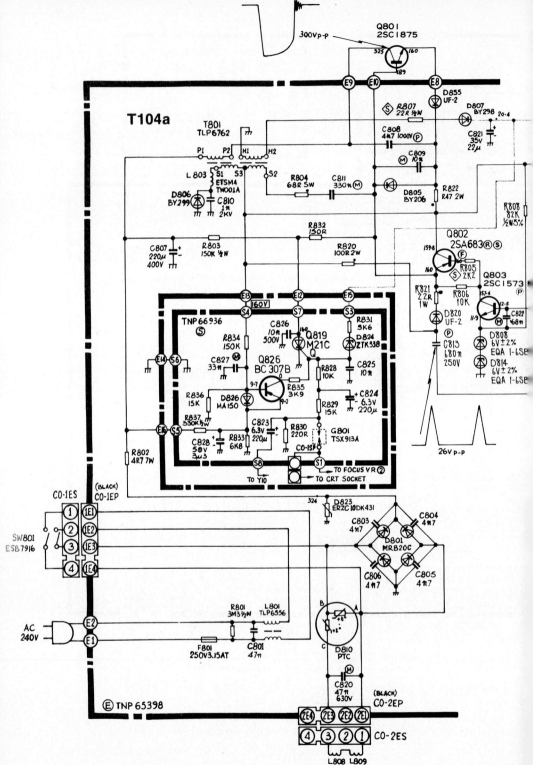

(T104a) CIRCUIT DIAGRAM (POWER SUPPLY)—MODEL TC2203 *(PART)*

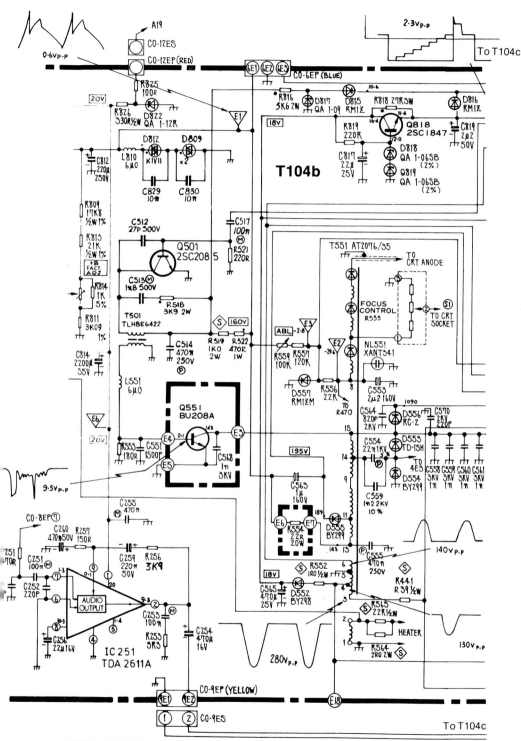

(T104b) CIRCUIT DIAGRAM (TIMEBASE PANEL)—MODEL TC2203 *(PART)*

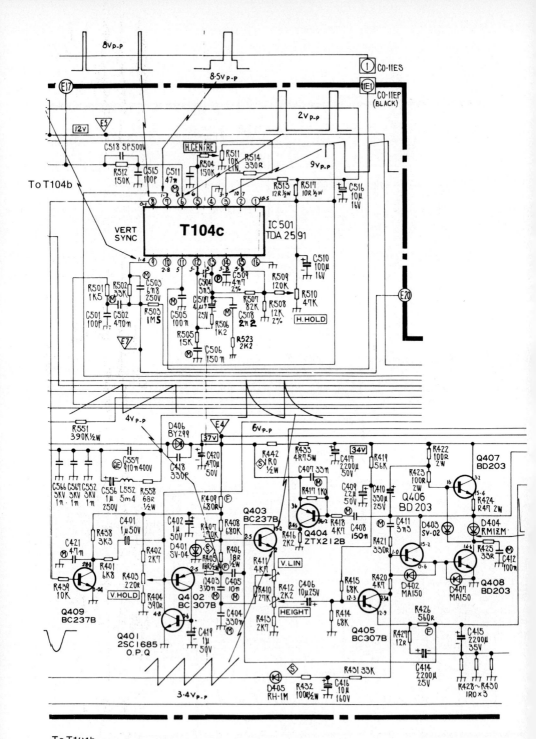

(T104c) CIRCUIT DIAGRAM (TIMEBASE PANEL)—MODEL TC2203 *(PART)*

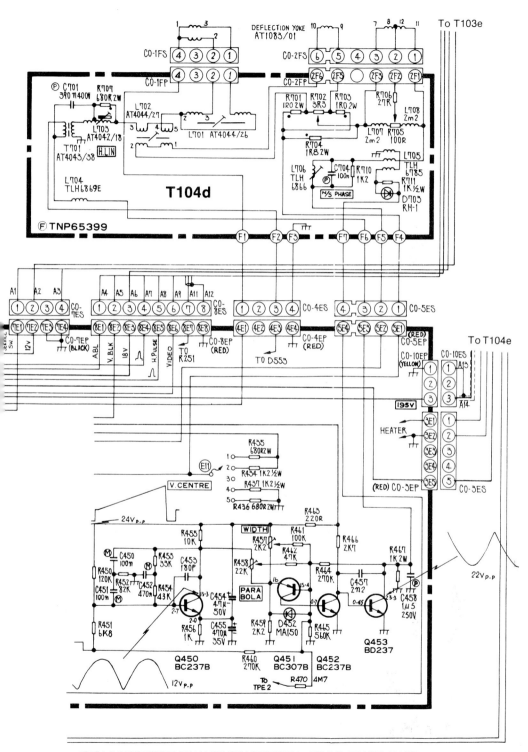

(T104d) CIRCUIT DIAGRAM (TIMEBASE PANEL)—MODEL TC2203 *(PART)*

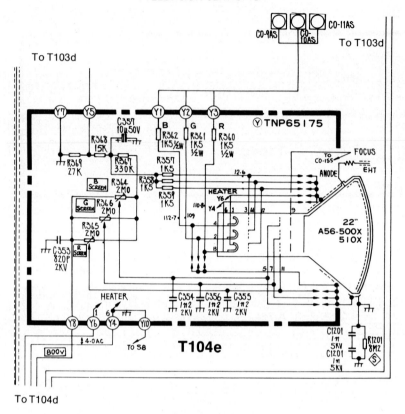

(T104e) CIRCUIT DIAGRAM (C.R.T. BASE)—MODEL TC2203 *(CONTINUED)*

NATIONAL   Model TR-3000G

General Description: A portable monochrome television and radio receiver incorporating a 3-in. cathode ray tube and operating from mains or battery supplies. Integrated circuits are used in the radio I.F. and A.F. stages and the chassis is isolated by mains transformer.

Mains Supply: 230 volts, 50Hz.

Batteries: 9 volts (6×1.5 volts).

Cathode Ray Tube: 85VB4.

E.H.T.: 7KV.

Radio Wavebands: M.W. 525-1605kHz; F.M. 87.5-108MHz.

Loudspeaker: 8 ohms impedance.

Access for Service

Remove Radio Tuning knob and Battery cover. Remove 4 screws from the left-side (looked at from the rear) and unclip the side case.

Adjustments

Automatic Voltage Regulator: Connect a voltmeter across TP71 and chassis. Set the B+ supply voltage to 6V±0.05V by Adjust the A.V.R. control VR71 if necessary.

Yoke Position: The yoke is secured to the neck of the picture tube, with an angular clamp and screw. To adjust the yoke and correct for picture tilt, loosen the clamp, correct tilt, and re-tighten the clamp.

Centring: The picture centring device consists of two rings located at the rear of the yoke assembly. Each ring has a tab for ease of adjustment. The tabs should be rotated and moved towards or away from each other until the picture is properly centred on the picture tube screen.

A.G.C.: The adjustment of the A.G.C. control effectively changes the operating point of the A.G.C. amplifier. Tune the I.F. A.G.C. control fully clockwise to set it for maximum gain. In some areas this may cause clipping of the sync. pulses, a wiggle in the picture and unstable sync. Turning the I.F. A.G.C. control counter-clockwise to decrease the gain of the receiver.
Set the channel selector to a station transmitting a strong signal.
Turn the R.F. A.G.C. control VR19 fully clockwise from the component side.
Adjust the I.F. A.G.C. control VR18 to obtain a sharp and clear picture.
If I.F. A.G.C. control VR18 is turned fully clockwise, the input signal strength will be maximum.
Observe the input signal, turn the R.F. A.G.C. control VR19 clockwise to the point where the snow noise disappears in the picture.
Readjust I.F. A.G.C. VR18 as above.
Check the reception on all channels. If the set does not get a good clear picture on all channels re-adjust the R.F. A.G.C. and I.F. A.G.C.
(Assuming of course that all channels have sufficient signal strength and are essentially free from interference.)

Vertical Linearity and Vertical Height: These controls VR32 and VR33 should be adjusted simultaneously to give proper vertical size consistent with good vertical linearity approximately $\frac{3}{16}''$ (5mm) beyond the top and bottom edges of the mask.

125

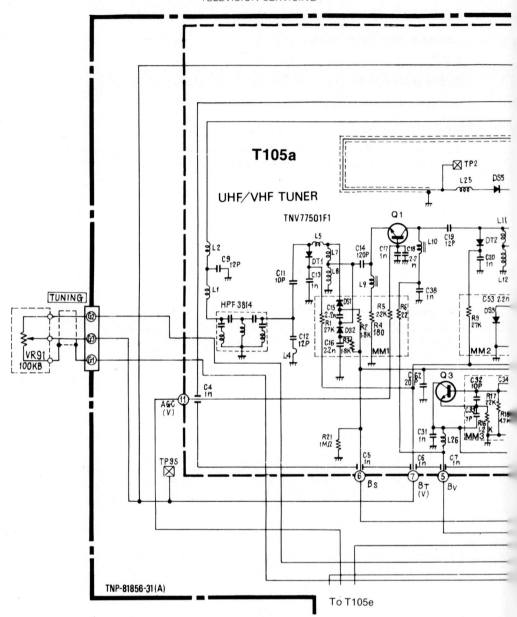

(T105a) CIRCUIT DIAGRAM—MODEL TR-3000G *(PART)*

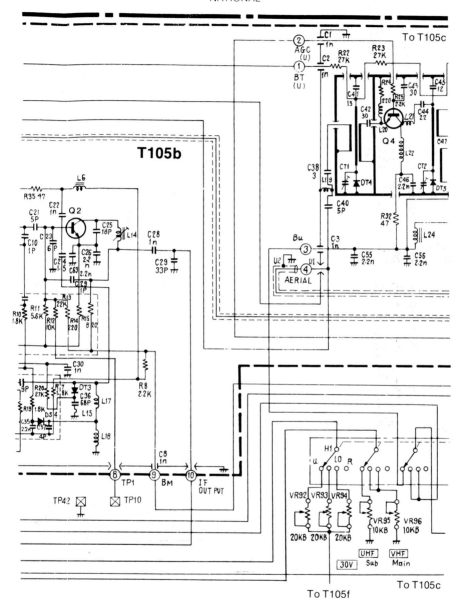

(T105b) CIRCUIT DIAGRAM—MODEL TR-3000G *(PART)*

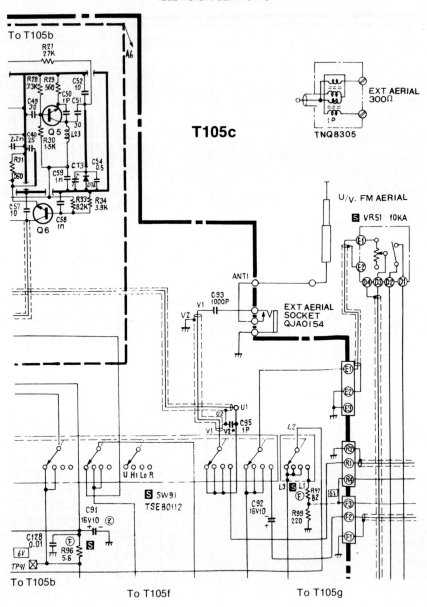

(T105c) CIRCUIT DIAGRAM—MODEL TR-3000G *(PART)*

Radio

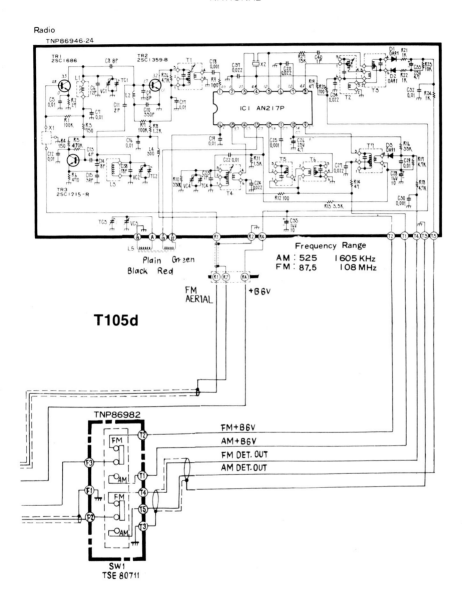

T105d

Frequency Range

AM : 525   1605 KHz
FM : 87,5   108 MHz

Plain Green
Black Red

FM
AERIAL   +B6V

TNP86982

FM+B6V
AM+B6V
FM DET. OUT
AM DET.OUT

SW1
TSE 80711

(T105d) CIRCUIT DIAGRAM—MODEL TR-3000G *(PART)*

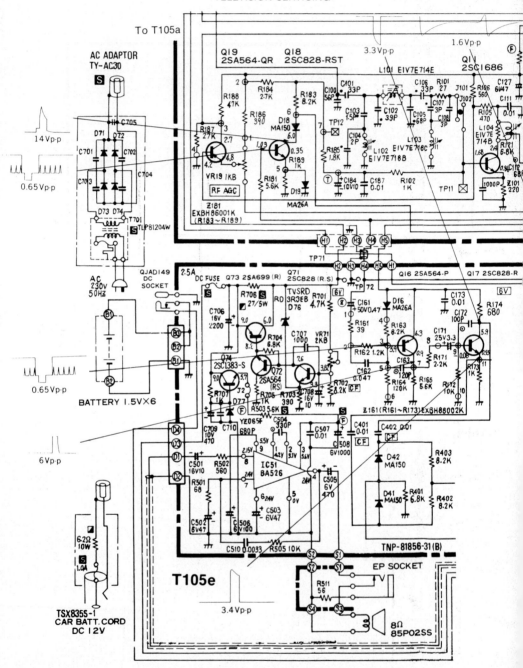

(T105e) CIRCUIT DIAGRAM—MODEL TR-3000G *(PART)*

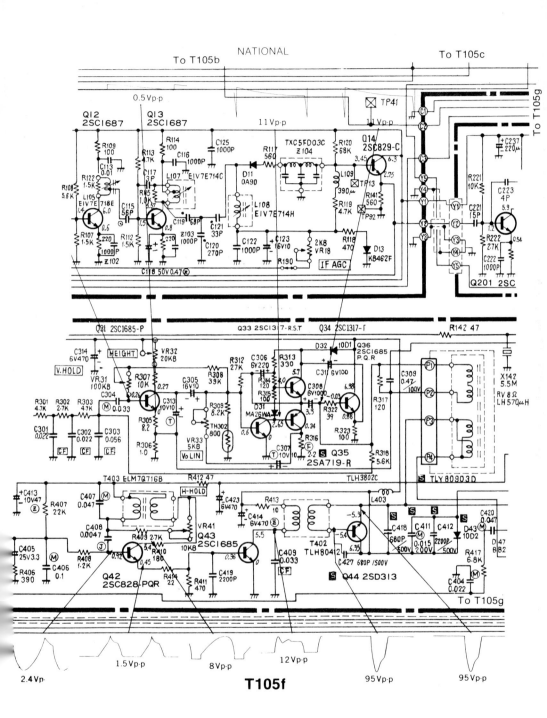

T105f

(T105f) CIRCUIT DIAGRAM—MODEL TR-3000G *(PART)*

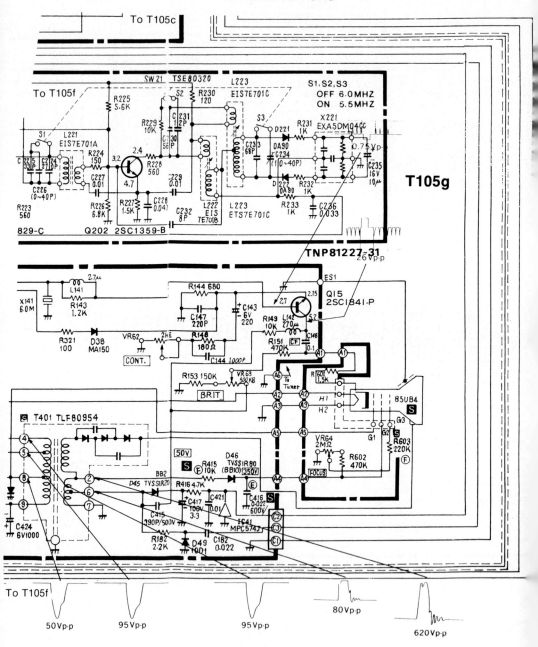

(T105g) CIRCUIT DIAGRAM—MODEL TR-3000G *(CONTINUED)*

NATIONAL   Model TR-5001G

General Description: A portable entertainment centre comprising a monochrome television receiver with 5-in. cathode ray tube, four waveband A.M./F.M. radio and two-track cassette tape-recorder. The instrument may be operated from mains or battery supplies and sockets are provided for the connection of an external battery, auxiliary tape signals, microphone, and earphone.

Mains Supplies: 220-240 volts, 50Hz.

Batteries: 13.5 volts (9×1.5 volts), 8W.

Cathode Ray Tube: 140BEB4.

E.H.T.: 7.6KV.

Wavebands: L.W. 145-285kHz; M.W. 525-1605kHz; S.W. 5.9-18MHz; F.M. 87.5-108MHz.

Loudspeaker: 8 ohms impedance.

Access for Service

Remove Horizontal and Vertical Hold knobs from the rear of the case. Remove 7 screws (2 left-side, 1 right-side, 1 top front, 3 bottom rear). Disconnect loudspeaker connection and remove cover upward.

Adjustments

Voltage Regulator: Connect voltmeter between TP91 and chassis. Set the B+ voltage to 11.5 by adjusting VR91.

Other adjustments are similar to the procedures outlined for Model TR-3000 described previously.

Bias Frequency: 33 ± 5kHz (L1).

Bias Current: Connect V.T.V.M. between TP3 and 4. Adjust VR3 for a reading of 4mV.

Drive Cords (See Fig. T106)

A-Block: Turn the tuning pulley A fully clockwise.
Arrows 1-9 indicate correct order and direction of dial threading.

B-Block: Turn the tuning pulley B fully anti-clockwise.
Arrows 1-9 indicate correct order and direction of dial threading.

C-Block: Turn the tuning shaft fully anti-clockwise.
Thread and set rope knot as shown.

Circuit Voltages

T.V.: See Circuit Diagram.

A-BLOCK

T106

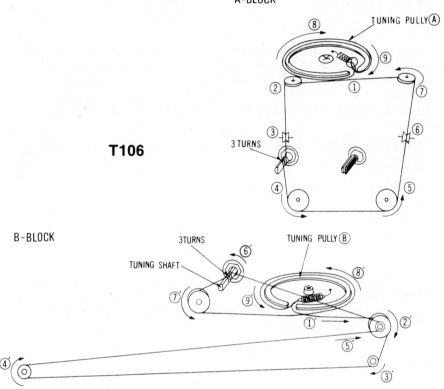

B-BLOCK

C-BLOCK

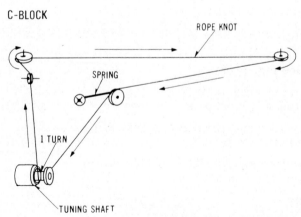

(T106) DRIVE CORD ASSEMBLIES—MODEL TR-5001G

Radio:

	M.W., S.W., L.W.						**F.M.**				
	Q101	Q102	Q103	Q104	Q105		Q101	Q102	Q103	Q104	Q105
C	0.35V	0.35V	0.35V	1.86V	1.86V	C	1.86V	1.86V	1.86V	0.56V	1.86V
B	0.35V	0.35V	0.35V	0.96V	1.1V	B	0.83V	0.74V	1.18V	0.56V	1.1V
E	0V	0V	0V	0V	0.48V	E	0V	0V	0.46V	0V	0.48V

	IC101						IC101		
1	0.78V	9	1.84V			1	0.78V	9	0.82V
2	0V	10	1.49V			2	0V	10	0.58V
3	1.84V	11	0.76V			3	1.86V	11	0.76V
4	1.84V	12	1.84V			4	1.86V	12	0.56V
5	1.04V	13	1.84V			5	1.06V	13	0.36V
6	0V	14	1.59V			6	0V	14	0.58V
7	1.04V	15	1.84V			7	1.06V	15	0.59V
8	1.84V	16	0.73V			8	1.86V	16	0.46V

Tape:

		TR1	TR2	TR3	TR4	TR5	TR6	TR7	TR8	TR9	TR10	TR11	TR12	TR51
	E	0.03	0.03	0.9	0	0	0	0	6.2	0.13	0.14	5.5	5.5	0.05
Play	B	0.3	0.64	1.6	0.35	0	0.1	0	6.8	0.64	0.74	6.1	4.9	0.64
	C	1.4	1.6	5.1	5.4	0	5.4	0	17.5	4.2	4.9	13	0	5
	E	0.03	0.03	0.9	0	0	0	0.2	6.2	0.13	0.14	5.5	5.5	0.05
Rec	B	0.3	0.64	1.6	0.05	0	0.1	0.77	6.8	0.64	0.74	6.1	4.9	0.64
	C	1.4	1.6	5.1	5.6	0	5.4	7	17.5	4.2	4.9	13	0	5

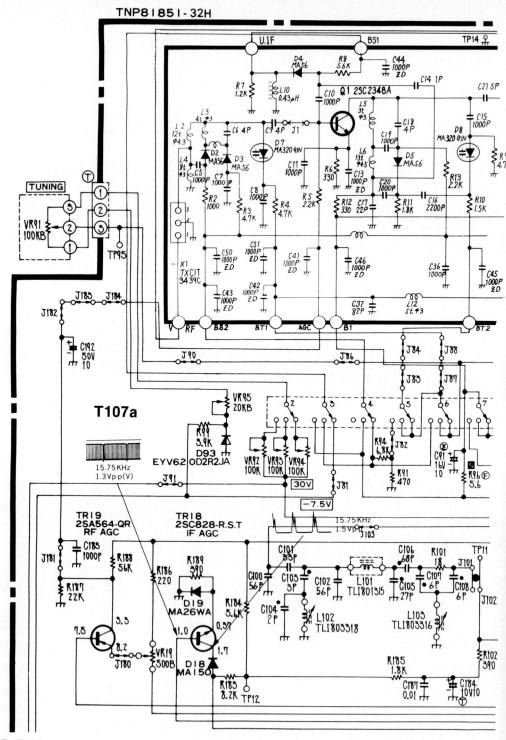

TNP81851-32H

(T107a) CIRCUIT DIAGRAM (T.V. SIGNAL SECTION)—MODEL TR-5001G *(PART)*

To T108a

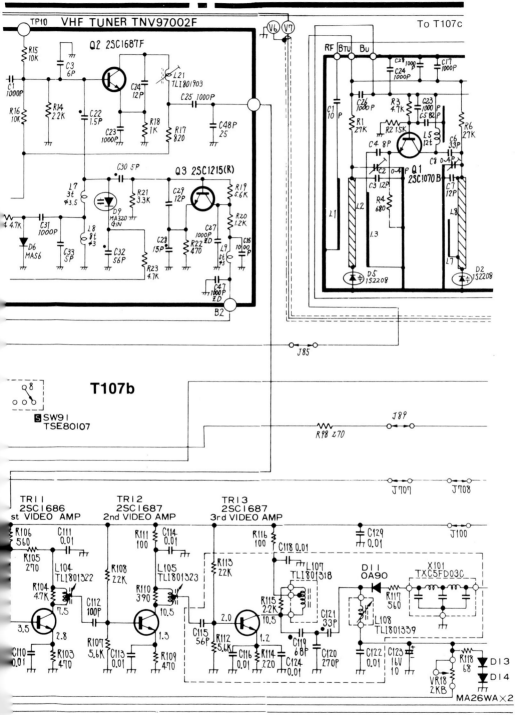

(T107b) CIRCUIT DIAGRAM (T.V. SIGNAL SECTION)—MODEL TR-5001G *(PART)*

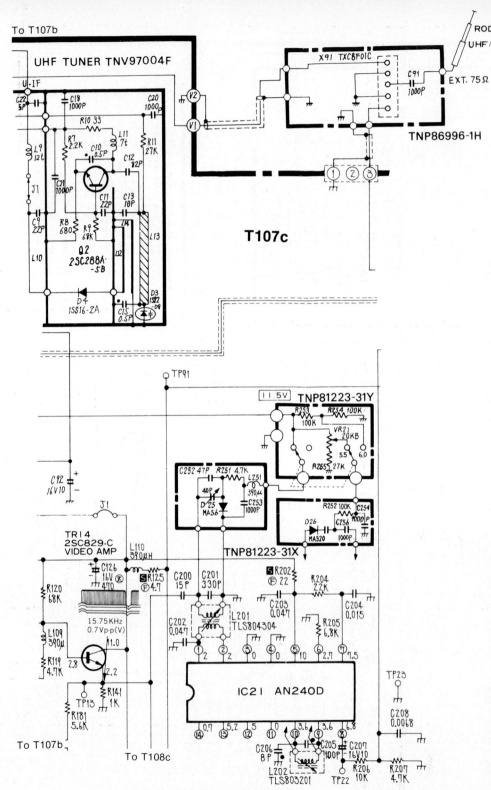

(T107c) CIRCUIT DIAGRAM (T.V. SIGNAL SECTION)—MODEL TR-5001G *(PART)*

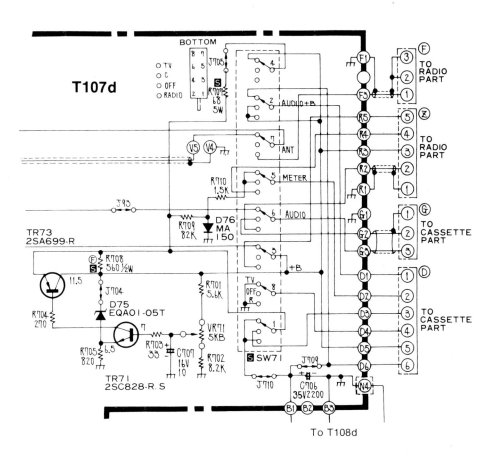

(T107d) CIRCUIT DIAGRAM (T.V. SIGNAL SECTION)—MODEL TR-5001G *(CONTINUED)*

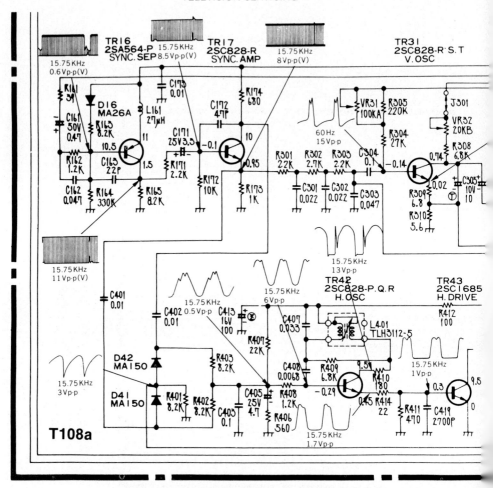

(T108a) CIRCUIT DIAGRAM (TIMEBASES AND POWER)—MODEL TR-5001G *(PART)*

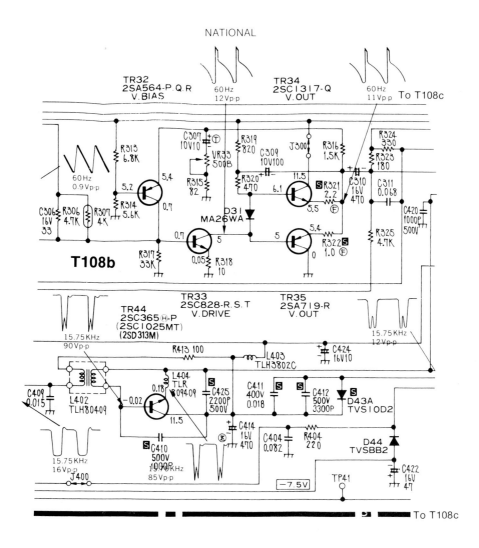

(T108b) CIRCUIT DIAGRAM (TIMEBASES AND POWER)—MODEL TR-5001G *(PART)*

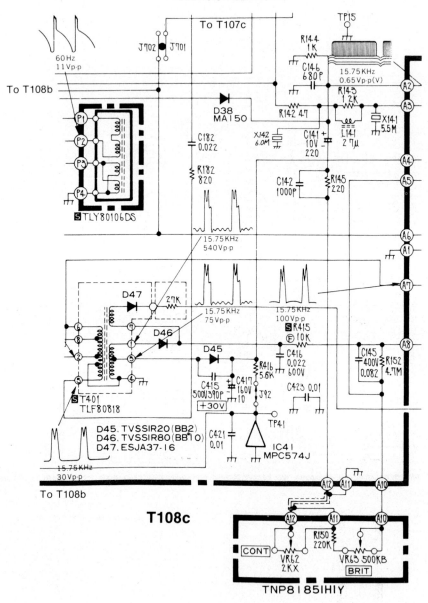

T108c

(T108c) CIRCUIT DIAGRAM (TIMEBASES AND POWER)—MODEL TR-5001G *(PART)*

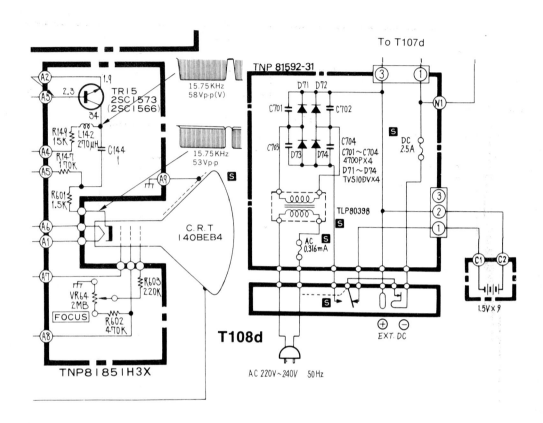

(T108d) CIRCUIT DIAGRAM (TIMEBASES AND POWER)—MODEL TR-5001G *(CONTINUED)*

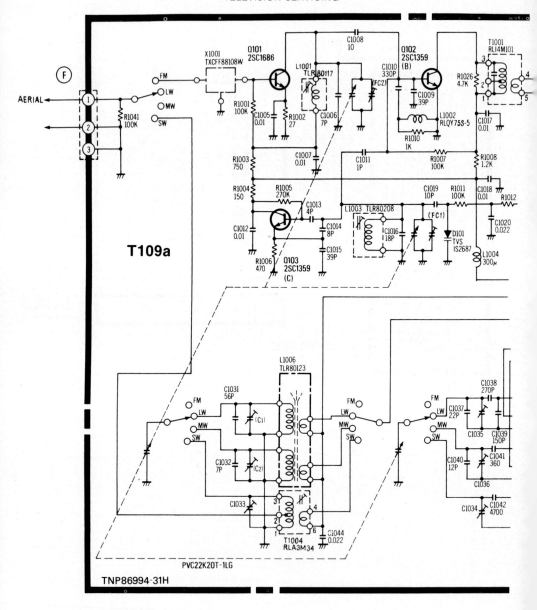

(T109a) CIRCUIT DIAGRAM (RADIO SECTION)—MODEL TR-5001G *(PART)*

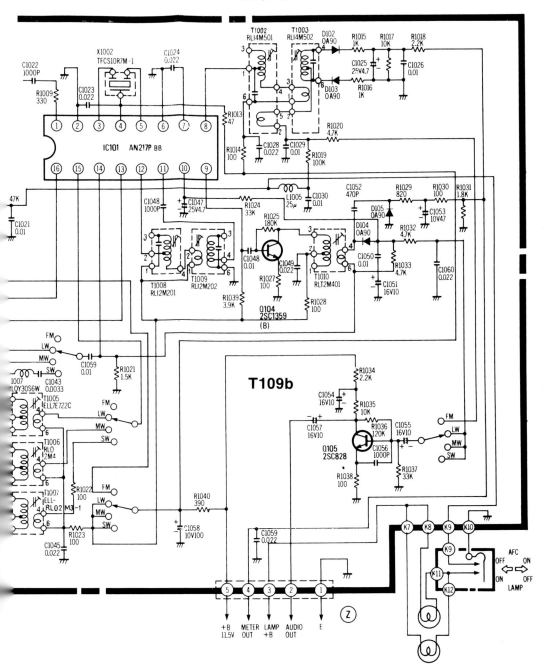

(T109b) CIRCUIT DIAGRAM (RADIO SECTION)—MODEL TR-5001G *(CONTINUED)*

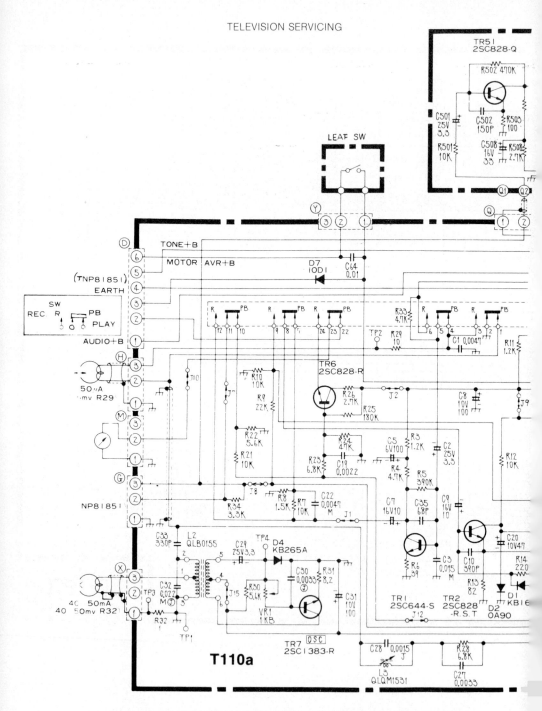

(T110a) CIRCUIT DIAGRAM (TAPE SECTION)—MODEL TR-5001G *(PART)*

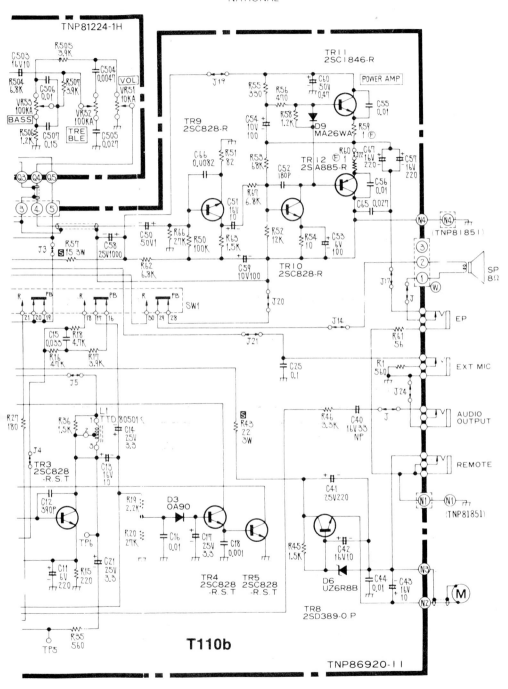

T110b

TNP86920-11

(T110b) CIRCUIT DIAGRAM (TAPE SECTION)—MODEL TR-5001G *(CONTINUED)*

NATIONAL Model TR-5001G

General Description: A portable monochrome receiver incorporating an A.M./F.M. radio and operating from mains or battery supplies.

Mains Supply: 240 volts, 50Hz.

Battery: 12 volts, 6.5W.

Cathode Ray Tube: 140BRB4 5-in.

E.H.T.: 7.6KV.

Wavebands: M.W. 525-1605kHz; F.M. 88-108MHz; Aircraft 108-136MHz.

Loudspeakers: 8 ohms impedance.

Dismantling

Remove 1 screw from the handle-side and 5 from the rear of the cabinet. Disconnect loudspeaker as upper cabinet is lifted off.

Adjustments

Follow the procedure outlined for Model TR-5001G given previously.

Circuit Voltages

T.V.: See Circuit Diagram (Fig. T112).

Radio:

F.M. and Air Bands

IC101															
1	2	3	4	5	6	7	8	9	10	11	12	13	14	15	16
0.72V	0V	2.2V	4.3V	1.0V	0V	1.0V	4.5V	0.76V	0.24V	0.66V	0.74V	0.30V	0.72V	0.72V	0.3V

Q101		*Q102*		*Q103*	
C	3.2V	C	0V	C	0.12V
B	0.71V	B	0.66V	B	0.68V
E	0.06V	E	2.5V	E	4.2V

M.W. Band

IC101															
1	2	3	4	5	6	7	8	9	10	11	12	13	14	15	16
0.72V	0V	2.2V	5.2V	1.0V	0V	1.0V	5.7V	5.7V	0.5V	0.72V	5.8V	0.72V	1.5V	5.7V	0.72V

Q101		*Q102*		*Q103*	
C	3.2V	C	0V	C	0.12V
B	0.71V	B	0.66V	B	0.68V
E	0.06V	E	2.5V	E	4.2V

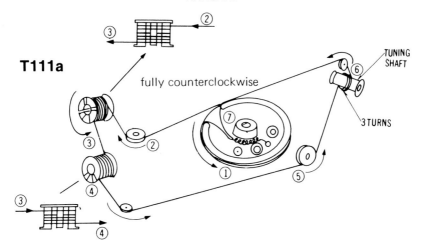

(T111a) DRIVE CORD (T.V. TUNER)—MODEL TR-5010G

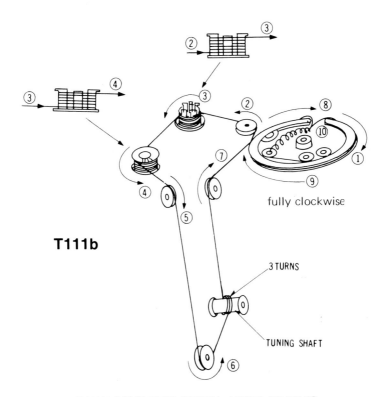

(T111b) DRIVE CORD (RADIO)—MODEL TR-5010G

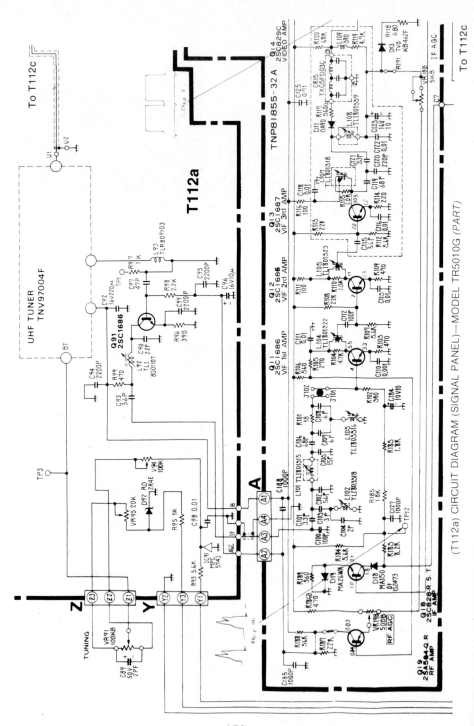

(T112a) CIRCUIT DIAGRAM (SIGNAL PANEL)—MODEL TR5010G *(PART)*

(T112b) CIRCUIT DIAGRAM (TIMEBASE PANEL)—MODEL TR5010G (PART)

151

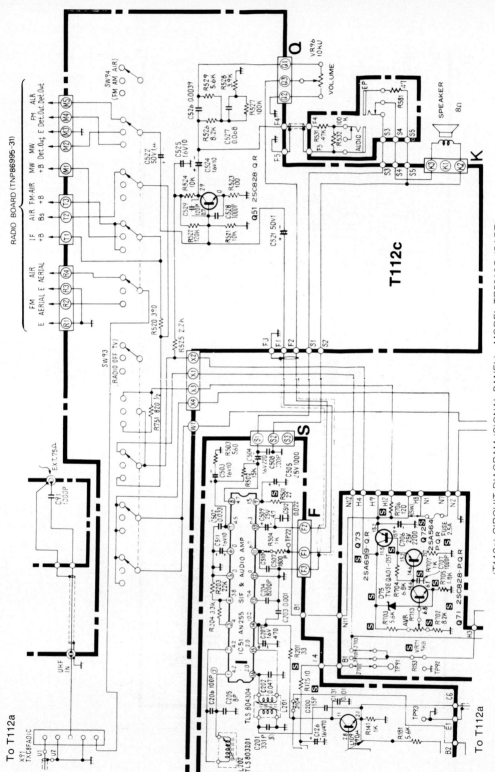

(T112c) CIRCUIT DIAGRAM (SIGNAL PANEL)—MODEL TR5010G *(PART)*

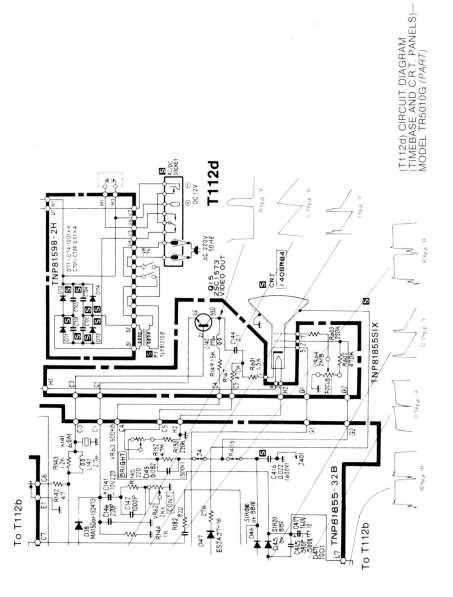

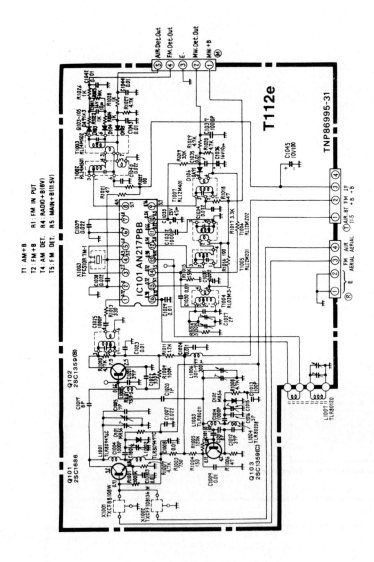

(T112e) CIRCUIT DIAGRAM (RADIO SECTION)—MODEL TR5010G CONTINUED)

PHILIPS   E2 Chassis

General Description: A mains-operated monochrome television chassis for various screen sizes. Integrated circuits are widely used in small-signal stages and a bridge rectifier across the mains supply renders the chassis 'live' irrespective of mains connection. An isolation transformer is necessary when service work is undertaken.

Mains Supply: 240 volts, 50Hz.

E.H.T.: 17KV.

Loudspeaker: 25 ohms impedance.

Circuit Notes

The D.C. voltages specified in the circuit diagram are average voltages. They have been measured under the following conditions: No signal applied to the aerial input. Brightness adjusted to minimum and contrast to maximum.

The oscillograms have been measured under the following conditions: A signal from a generator on grey scale has been applied to the aerial input. Contrast control R210 has been so adjusted that on the base of TS550 a signal of 1.5 V_{pp} is present.

When the picture tube is being replaced safety goggles must be worn.

If it is necessary to replace a safety resistor, never use another type.

Safety regulations require that the set be restored to the original condition and that spare parts applied should be identical to those specified.

Removing the Rear Panel: Remove the rear panel after having pressed downwards the plastic clamps with a screwdriver.

Hinging out the Chassis: Remove the rear panel. Swing the cassette backwards after having slightly bent the plastic clamps on the left and right sides of the chassis.

Adjustments

Supply Voltage: Connect a voltmeter between +215 and chassis. Adjust the meter reading to 217 volts with R318.

A.G.C.: Supply a signal from a pattern generator to the aerial input. Connect an oscilloscope between point 7-U510 and chassis. With R006 (in U510), adjust for minimum noise on the oscillogram.

Horizontal Time Base: Supply a signal to the aerial input. Make a short-circuit between point 6-IC820 and chassis. Adjust R830 so that the picture is drifting. Remove short.

F.M.-Sound Detector: Supply a sound modulated signal from a pattern generator to the aerial input. (Continued on page 162.)

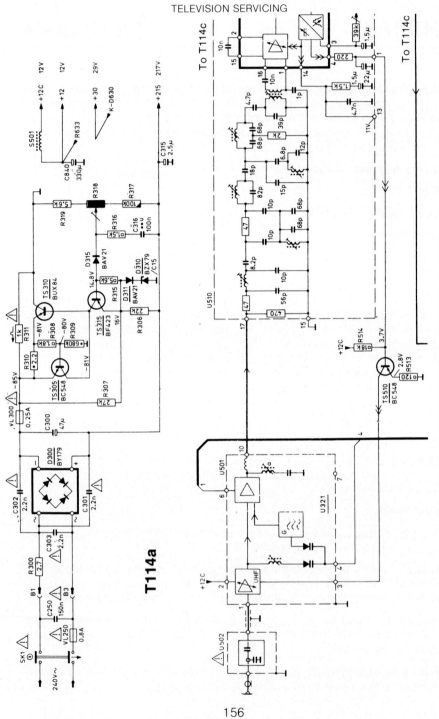

(T114a) CIRCUIT DIAGRAM—E2 CHASSIS (PART)

156

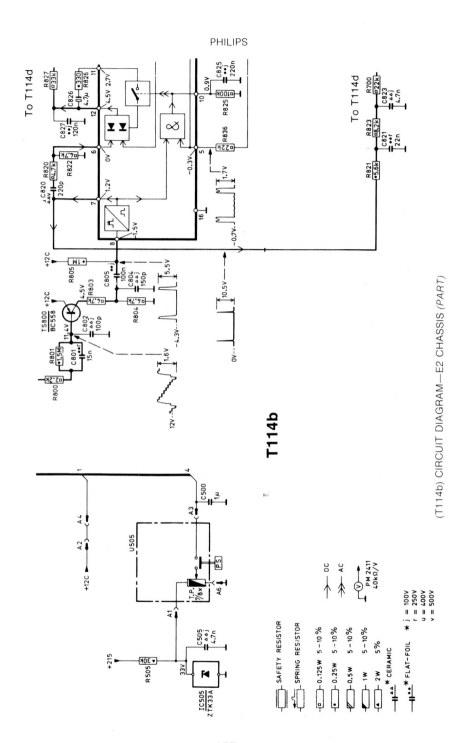

PHILIPS

(T114b) CIRCUIT DIAGRAM—E2 CHASSIS (PART)

157

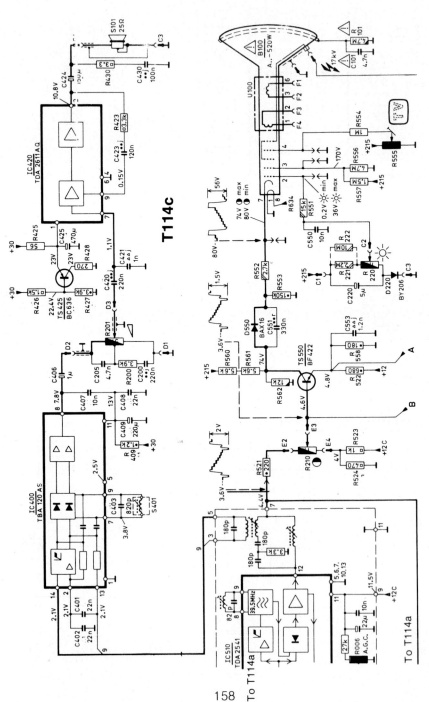

T114c

(T114c) CIRCUIT DIAGRAM—E2 CHASSIS (PART)

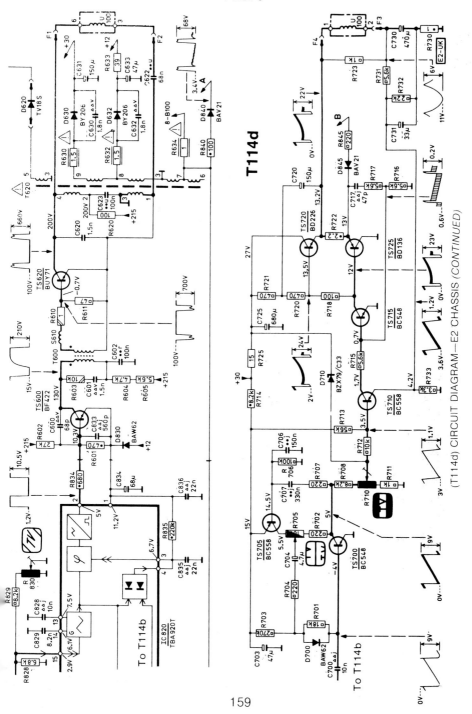

T114d

(T114d) CIRCUIT DIAGRAM—E2 CHASSIS (CONTINUED)

Turn up the volume control slightly so that the sound modulation is audible. Connect a sensitive A.C. voltmeter across the loudspeaker. Adjust S401 at maximum meter reading.

V.C.R. Reproduction: To make the chassis fit for V.C.R. reproduction, point 10-IC820 must be connected to chassis via a switch. For this switching function, the non-connected switch of push-button unit U504 may be used.

For apparatus with a combined push-button tuning unit U505, an auxiliary switch (4822 278 90372) has to be fitted in parallel with the last switch of U505, see Fig. T113.

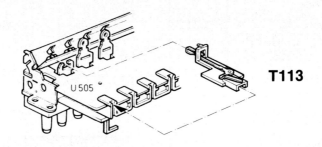

(T113) SWITCH MODIFICATION FOR V.C.R.—E2 CHASSIS

PHILIPS

K12 Chassis, Model 26C797

General Description: A mains-operated colour television chassis with 20AX picture tube. A switch-mode power supply is used and an isolation transformer should be used when carrying out service work as the chassis is 'live' irrespective of mains connection.

Mains Supply: 240 volts, 50Hz.

Access for Service

Removing the Back Cover: It can be removed after pushing away 4 locking tags at the corners.

Hinging out the Chassis: After pushing away locking tags the chassis can be hinged out. When doing so, slightly lift the chassis.

Removing the Mounting Blocks of the Chassis: Push locking tag away from the mounting block using a screwdriver.
Next, slide the block from the holder in the cabinet.

Replacing the Aerial Input U429: Remove the 2 screws. Unsolder connection from the aerial input to the channel selector. This connection is visible underneath the channel selectors on the component side. Next, remove the soldered joint between the housing of the aerial input and chassis.
After straightening the two twist lugs H, the aerial input may be removed.

Removing and Relocating Modules: Slightly lift the upper fixing arm of the module holder.
The easiest way to remove the module from its holder is by making a rotating movement in downward direction with the module. When remounting the module, place it straight in the holder. To prevent the module from being wrongly replaced in the module holder, a plate is fitted so that the module can be inserted in one way only.
When modules are re-inserted, the monopanel should be supported at the back.

Removing the Pre-selection Drawer: If present, the drawer may be removed as follows:
Pull out the drawer. Remove the cover plate by pushing it upward.
Push the drawer to its stop into the cabinet and slide the metal pin as far as possible to the right.

Replacing Plugs: To connect wires to the plug, the bushes have to be slid out of the housing. This can be done after depressing the circlip on the open side.

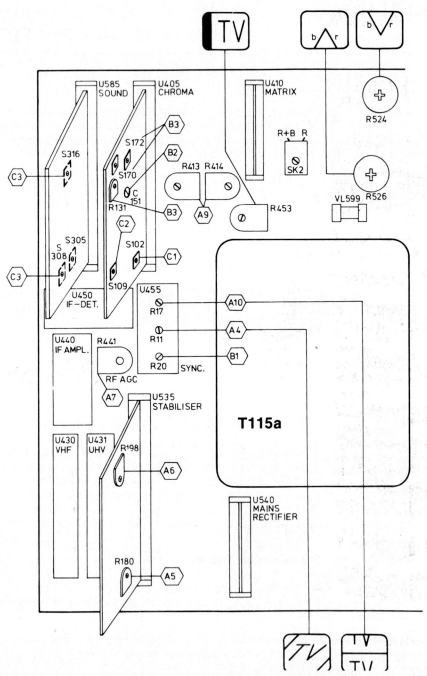

(T115a) ADJUSTMENTS—K12 CHASSIS *(PART)*

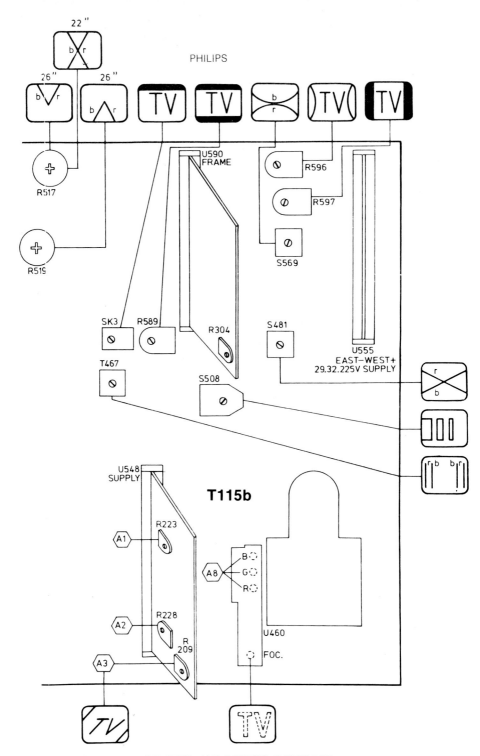

PHILIPS

22"

26"   26"

U590
FRAME

R596

R597

S569

SK3   R589   R304   S481

T467   U555
                                        EAST—WEST+
          S508   29.32.225V SUPPLY

R517

R519

U548
SUPPLY

T115b

A1 — R223

A2 — R228   A8 — B
                        G
                        R

A3 — R
      209   U460
                    FOC.

(T115b) ADJUSTMENTS—K12 CHASSIS *(CONTINUED)*

Adjustments

+145V Supply Voltage: Connect a voltmeter (position D.C.) between junction 1-T525/C571b (M2) and chassis. With R223 on the supply module U548, adjust the meter reading to 145V (tolerance ± 1%).

Overvoltage Protection: Brightness and contrast to minimum. Connect a voltmeter (position D.C.) between junction 1-TS25/C571b (M2) and chassis. Turn R228 on the supply module U548 (seen from the component side) clockwise to its full amount. With R223 on U548, adjust the meter reading to 155V. Adjust R228 on U548 so that the supply voltage just starts hiccuping. Next, re-adjust the +145V supply voltage.

Oscillator in the Supply Section: Supply an aerial signal. Interconnect points 14 and 15 of IC201 on the supply module U548 and adjust R209 on U548 until the picture stands upright.
Remove the interconnection.

Horizontal Synchronisation: Supply an aerial signal. Interconnect points 15 and 16 of U455. Adjust R11 in this unit until the picture stands straight.
Remove the interconnection.

Varicap Voltage (No Aerial Signal): Connect a voltmeter (position D.C.) between junction 13-U535/plug L42 and chassis. Interconnect points 6 and 7 of U450. Switch the set to position V.H.F.
With R180 on the stabiliser module U535, adjust the meter reading to 28.5V.
If the set is not equipped with V.H.F. channel selector, switch the set to position U.H.F. Adjust R180 on U535 to 30.2V.
Remove the interconnection.

+12V Supply Voltage: Connect a voltmeter (position D.C.) between junction 19-U535/C542 (M6) and chassis. With R198 on the stabiliser module U535, adjust the meter reading to 12V (tolerance ± 1½%).

H.F./A.G.C.: Comes into operation only in case of very strong aerial signals. If the picture of a local transmitter is distorted, adjust R441 until the picture is undistorted.

Cut-off Point Picture Tube: Apply an aerial signal. Set Brightness, Contrast and saturation to minimum.
Remove plug L7 if it is connected. Interconnect points 11 and 6 of U405.
Connect an oscilloscope (position D.C. and frame-frequent) to 17-U611. With the Vg2 control for green in U460, adjust to 65V amplitude.
Now connect the oscilloscope to 17-U615 and adjust with the Vg2 control for blue, the measuring line to 65V.
Next, connect the oscilloscope to 17-U608 and adjust with the Vg2 control for red, the measuring line to 65V. Remove the interconnection and connect plug L7 again.
If no oscilloscope is available, the following approximating procedure may be followed:

164

No aerial signal. Set Brightness, Contrast and saturation to minimum. Connect a voltmeter (position D.C.) to point 17-U611.

With Vg2 control for green in U460, adjust the meter reading to 44V. Now connect the voltmeter to point 17-U615.

With Vg2 control for blue, adjust the meter reading to 44V. Next connect the voltmeter to point 17-U608. With Vg2 control for red, adjust the meter reading to 44V.

Adjusting the Grey Scale: Apply a test pattern signal. The T.V. set is normally adjusted. Allow the set to warm-up for 10 minutes.

Adjust R413 and R414 to the grey scale desired in the bright sections of the picture.

Vertical Synchronisation: Adjust R17 in U455 to a still picture.

Connect an oscilloscope to point 1-U590, adjusting the oscilloscope in such a manner that one period of the pulse voltage has a width of 5cm. Next, connect point 14-U455 to chassis and adjust R17 so that one period becomes 5.5cm wide. Remove the connections.

If no oscilloscope is available, the following approximating procedure may be followed:

Adjust R17 in U455 in such a manner that the receiver locks in quickly when switching over from a channel on which no transmitter is received to a channel on which a transmitter is received.

Purity and Convergence Adjustments (Fig. T116)

Securing the Deflection Unit: Loosen screw L a few turns and slide the deflection unit on the neck of the colour picture tube.

Place notch B of the housing opposite the mark on the picture tube and make sure that the housing overlaps the centring edge on the picture tube. Then, fix the deflection unit with screw L.

Securing the Multipole Unit: Rotate handle K of the unit counter-clockwise, and slide the unit on the neck of the colour picture tube. Place the unit in the locating recesses of the deflection unit; see to it that notch H is at the upper-side exactly opposite recess B of the deflection unit and the mark on the picture tube. Then, rotate handle K clockwise so that the unit is locked.

Setting the Picture Straight: Tune in a cross-hatched or a dot pattern. Set the picture straight by setting the handles A to position 3 and rotating the deflection unit with notch C. Then, set the handles again to position 1.

Static Convergence (Fig. T116): Tune in a cross-hatched pattern and allow the set to warm-up for 20 minutes.

Switch-off the green gun with SK2 in position 4 and remove the adhesive tape from the multipole unit.

Set handle F to one of the extreme positions.

Make the red and the blue cross-hatched pattern coincide, with handle G, along a vertical or horizontal line in the centre of the screen. Then, make coincide, with handles F and G, the red and the blue cross-hatched pattern in the centre of the screen.

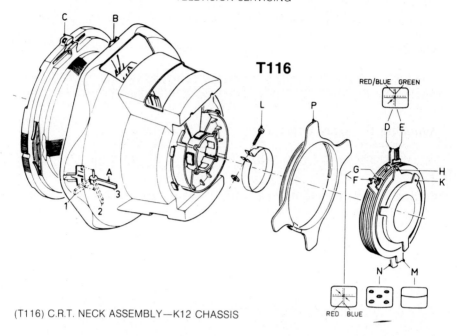

(T116) C.R.T. NECK ASSEMBLY—K12 CHASSIS

Switch-on the green gun with SK2 in position 3.

Set handle D to one of the extreme positions.

Make coincide, with handle E, the red/blue and the green cross-hatched pattern along a vertical or horizontal line in the centre of the screen. Then, make coincide, with handles D and E, the blue/red and the green cross-hatched pattern in the centre of the screen. Make the horizontal line with handle M in the centre of the screen as straight as possible. Carefully affix the adhesive tape again to the rings of the multipole-unit.

Colour Purity (Fig. T116): Place the cold receiver with its front to the East or the West. Swinging the chassis completely out; switch on the receiver and allow it to warm up for 15 minutes.

Check the static convergence.

Tune in a white pattern signal.

Adjust brightness and contrast to obtain a normal picture.

Switch-off the green and the blue gun with SK2 in position 2. Set the handles A to position 2 and rotate handle P clockwise so that the deflection unit slides in the direction of the screen, and discolouration appears on the sides of the screen. The flame pattern on the left and right hand side should be made symmetrical using handle N. Next, using handle P, slide back the deflection unit again to exactly that point where the two flame patterns become uniformly red. Next, switch-on the green and the blue guns again (SK2 in position 3). Now a uniformly white picture should be obtained. In this picture no colour marks

166

should be visible. If necessary, make a slight correction by sliding handle N and/or handle P.

Set the handles A again to position 1 and check the static and the dynamic convergence.

Dynamic Convergence (Fig. T115): Tune in a cross-hatched pattern. Adjust brightness and contrast to obtain a normal picture and allow the receiver to warm-up for 20 minutes. Swing out the chassis completely and check the static convergence. Switch-off the green gun with SK2 in position 4. Adjust S481 so that the middle blue and red horizontal lines coincide as much as possible. Then, adjust with S469 so that these lines coincide completely.

Adjust R524 so that the blue and red horizontal lines at the upper side of the picture coincide. Adjust R526 so that the blue and red horizontal lines at the underside of the picture coincide.

Adjust T467 so that the blue and the red vertical lines at the left and the right side of the picture coincide.

Adjust R517 so that the blue and the red vertical lines at the upper side of the picture coincide.

Adjust R519 so that the blue and the red vertical lines at the underside of the picture coincide.

Switch-on the green gun with SK2 in position 3 and check the static convergence.

If necessary, adjust the East-West-correction with R596.

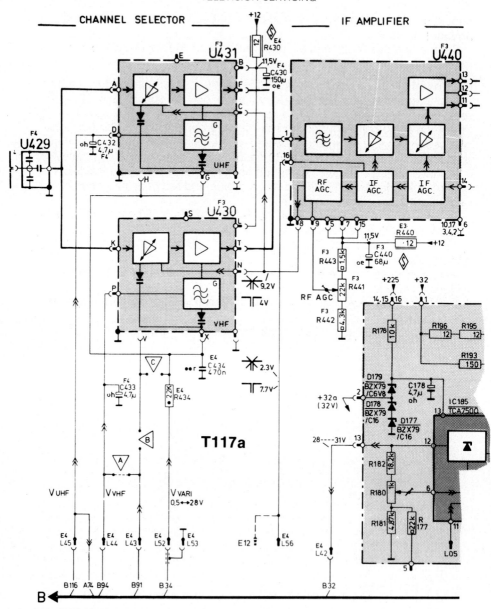

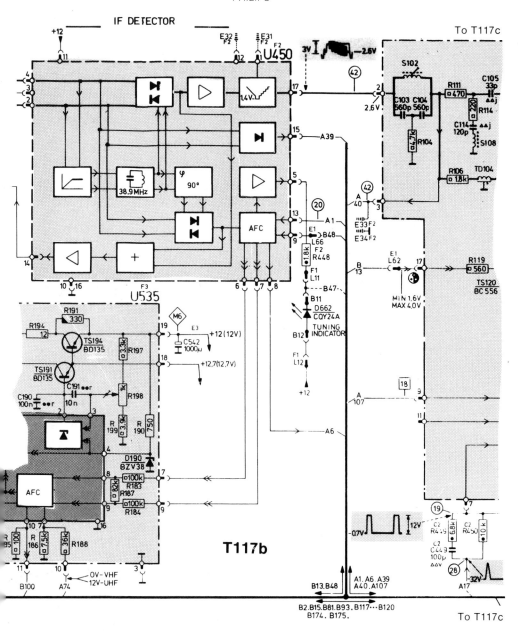

T117b

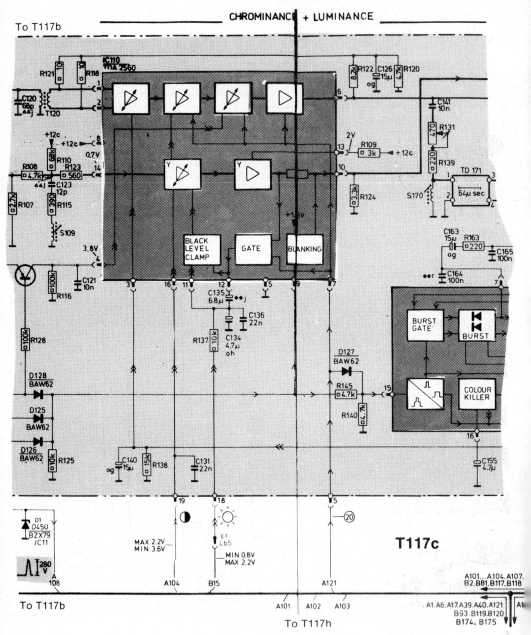

(T117c) CIRCUIT DIAGRAM—K12 CHASSIS *(PART)*

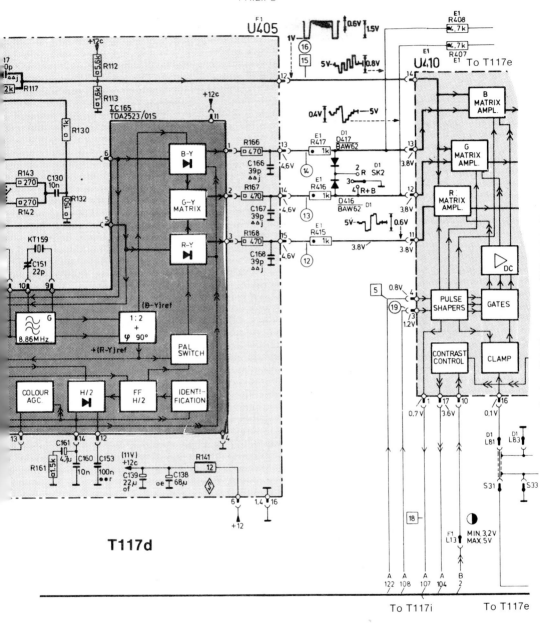

T117d

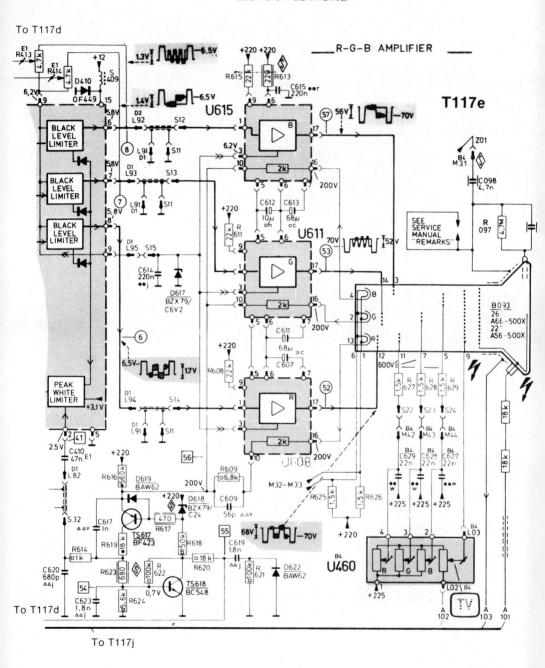

(T117e) CIRCUIT DIAGRAM—K12 CHASSIS *(PART)*

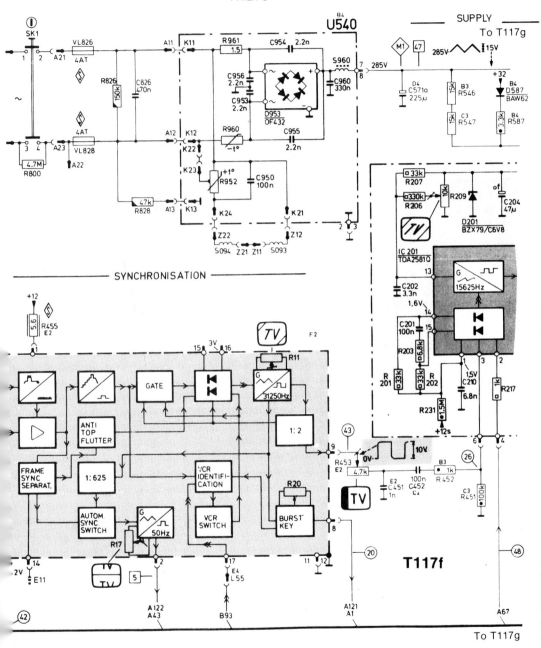

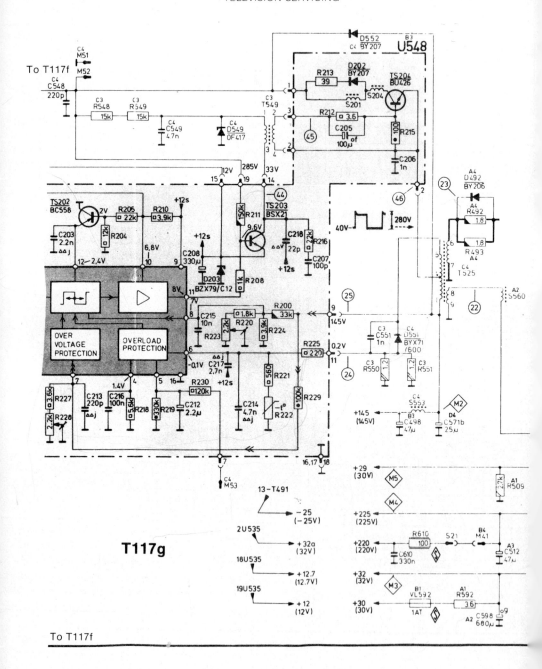

T117g

To T117f

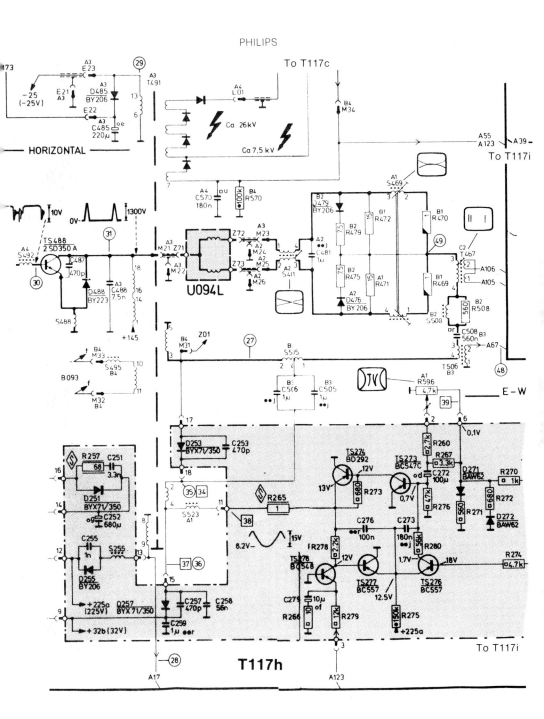

(T117h) CIRCUIT DIAGRAM—K12 CHASSIS *(PART)*

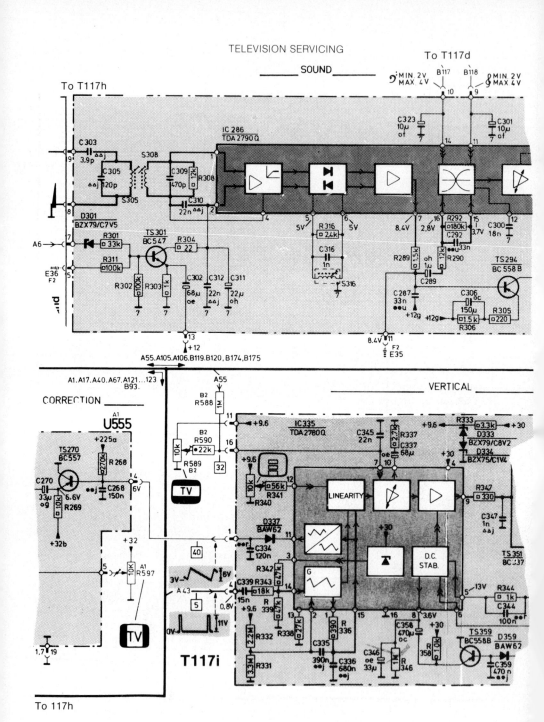

(T117i) CIRCUIT DIAGRAM—K12 CHASSIS *(PART)*

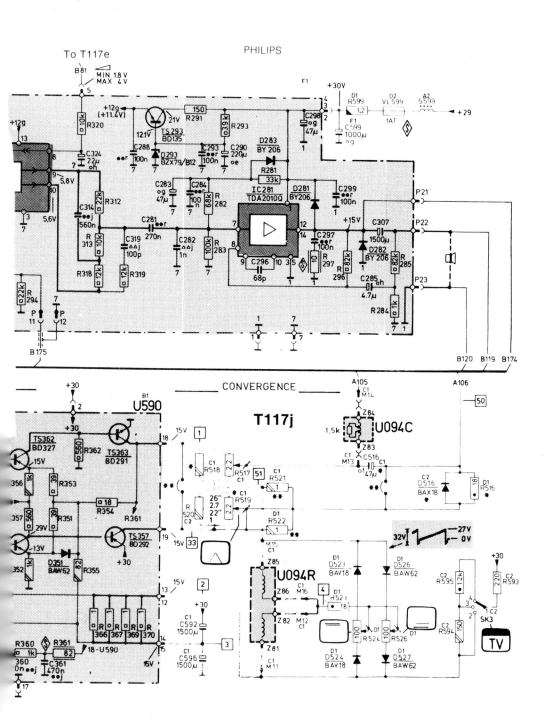

(T117j) CIRCUIT DIAGRAM—K12 CHASSIS *(CONTINUED)*

PHILIPS

KT3 Chassis, 14C925 16C927, 16C928, 20C933, 20C934

General Description: The 'KT3' is a solid-state colour television chassis designed for both colour and monochrome reception on 625 lines U.H.F. The 90° deflection in line picture tube with quick vision guns produces sharply defined pictures within about five seconds of switching on. It consists of a single 'motherboard' printed panel vertically mounted around the neck of the picture tube which carries eight plug-in 'daughter' modules (including the tuner). The 'motherboard' is mounted on special pivots which allow it to be easily unclipped and lowered into the horizontal position for servicing.

Mains Supply: 240 volts, 50Hz.

E.H.T.: 24kv.

Loudspeaker Impedance: 16 ohms impedance (or 25 ohms).

Adjustments

Pre-set Adjustments:

Set H.T.2 (R7317): Adjust the receiver for a normal picture and connect a D.C. voltmeter between the junction of S1466/C1460C and chassis. Adjust R7317 on the supply panel U7470 for a reading of 129 volts (± 1%).

Line Hold (R8371): Tune the receiver to a transmission. Connect a shorting link between pins 14 and 17 of the sync panel U8475 and adjust R8371 for minimum line slip. Disconnect the shorting link, the picture should lock.

Field Hold (R8390): Tune the receiver to a transmission. Connect a shorting link between pin 7 of the sync panel U8475 and adjust R8390 for minimum vertical slip. Disconnect the shorting link, the picture should lock.

Contrast (R1422): Adjust for optimum results with R1422 on the main panel.

A.G.C. (R1414): Connect a D.C. voltmeter between pin 11 of the I.F. panel and chassis, turn the A.G.C. control fully clockwise (as viewed from the print side) and with no aerial input, check for a nominal voltage between 1.2 and 1.3 volts. Inject a 2mV R.F. signal into the aerial socket and adjust R1414 until the meter reading has increased by 0.2 volt.

Volume Pre-set (R5166): With the receiver tuned to a transmnission and the customer Volume control at minimum, adjust R5166 on the sound panel U5420 such that the sound in the loudspeaker is barely audible (2mV).

Grey Scale:

C.R.T. Cut-off (1581) and Dark Grey Tones: With no aerial signal, turn the red, blue and green gun controls, R1445, R1454 and R1451, fully clockwise (viewed from the component side of the panel) and switch-off SK9014, SK9015 and SK9016. Adjust R1581 to obtain a barely visible raster.

Switch-on SK9014, SK9015 and SK9016 and adjust the Brightness control to obtain a barely visible raster. The Brightness control must then be left undisturbed during the following adjustments.

Because the barely visible raster obtained *may* be produced by only one gun it is necessary to check and equalise the three C.R.T. guns as follows:

Switch-off SK9015 and SK9016, check and adjust if necessary with R1454 for a barely visible blue raster.

Switch-off SK9014, switch-on SK9015, check and adjust if necessary with R1445 for a barely visible red raster.

Switch-off SK9015, switch-on SK9016, check and adjust if necessary with R1451 for a barely visible green raster.

White Tones (R1443 and R1452): The controls for setting the 'white tone' in the grey scale tracking are accurately adjusted during the manufacture of the receiver, and should not normally require further adjustment.

The following instruction is given for guidance only since it is necessary to use special equipment to obtain precise results.

Tune the receiver to a pattern generator and display a pattern containing a large area of white. Adjust the green drive control R1443 and/or the blue drive control R1452 to obtain a neutral white.

N.B.: R1445, R1451, R1454 may be slightly re-adjusted if necessary if the above adjustment has impaired the grey scale at low brightness levels.

Convergence and Purity (See Fig. T1): The following adjustments are carried out during the manufacture of the receiver and no subsequent adjustments are normally required unless the C.R.T., deflection coils, multi-pole unit or dynamic correction components have been replaced. Unless the deflection unit has been replaced it is not necessary to remove the rubber wedges (G in Fig. T1), adjustment of the multi-pole unit should be sufficient. Before attempting the following adjustments ensure that the pre-set adjustments (above) have been completed. During the adjustments, let the receiver face either the East or West—this ensures optimum results in all subsequent positions of the receiver.

Static Convergence (See Fig. T1): Tune the receiver to a cross-hatch pattern from a pattern generator and allow the receiver to warm-up for ten minutes.

Switch-off the green gun with SK9016 and turn locking ring B anti-clockwise.

With tags C adjust the four-pole rings so that the red and blue cross-hatch patterns are superimposed at the centre of the screen.

Switch-on the green gun with SK9014 and switch-off the blue gun with SK9014.

With tags D adjust the six-pole rings so that the red and green cross-hatch pattern are superimposed at the centre of the screen.

Switch-on the blue gun with SK9014 and tighten ring B.

Purity (See Fig. T1): Loosen fixing screw F on the deflection unit, move the deflection coils enough to remove the rubber wedges (G in Fig. T1).

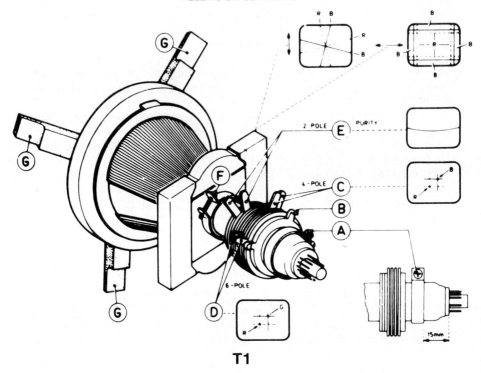

T1

(T1) CONVERGENCE ADJUSTMENTS—KT3 CHASSIS

Slide the deflection coils forward as far as possible against the C.R.T. and tighten screw F such that the deflection unit can still be moved but with some friction.

Set the multipole unit as shown in Fig. T1, tighten screw A and turn securing ring B anti-clockwise.

Set the purity tags E so that a rounded and a flat tag cover each other.

Tune to a cross-hatch pattern and turn the Brightness control to maximum and allow the receiver to warm-up for ten minutes.

Turn the field shift switch SK1002 to its mid-position. Switch-off the blue gun (with SK9014) and the green gun (with SK9016).

With tags E adjust the purity rings so that the vertical red band is as close to the centre of the screen consistent with the central horizontal line of the cross-hatch remaining as straight as possible.

Change the pattern generator to 'white' and check that the red band is in the centre of the screen and if necessary switch the pattern generator back to cross-hatch and move the red band in the correct direction whilst ensuring that the picture does not move too much in the vertical direction.

Switch the pattern generator to 'white' and move the deflection unit back until the whole raster is uniformly red.

Switch-on the green and blue guns and there should be no colour patches on the white screen. If necessary slightly adjust the colour purity rings E and/or the position of the deflection unit.

Tighten fixing screw F.

Adjust the field shift if necessary with SK1002.

Switch the pattern generator to cross-hatch, check and re-adjust if necessary the static convergence (described above).

N.B.: The static convergence and purity adjustments are interdependent, and if initially they are too far from the correct setting, purity adjustments adversely affect the static convergence adjustments. Ideally, they should both be set approximately before carrying out all the adjustments in the above order.

Dynamic Convergence (See Figs. T2 and T3): Dynamic convergence is achieved by vertically and horizontally tilting the deflection unit. To secure the correct position, three rubber wedges (G in Fig. T1) are fitted between the C.R.T. and the deflection unit as shown in Figs. T2 and T3. Two wedge thicknesses are available, one 7mm thick, code number 462 40356, the other 11mm thick, code number 462 40357. Spare wedges are needed to carry out dynamic convergence adjustments.

First check the colour purity and static convergence.

Tune the receiver to a cross-hatch pattern from a pattern generator and switch off the green gun with SK9016.

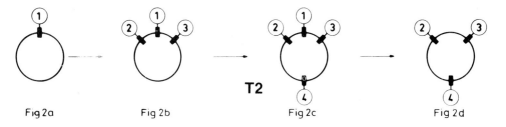

Fig 2a   Fig 2b   **T2**   Fig 2c   Fig 2d

(T2) DYNAMIC CONVERGENCE—KT3 CHASSIS

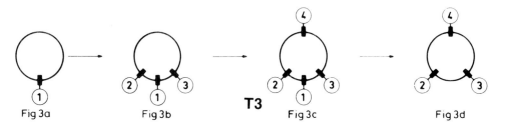

Fig 3a   Fig 3b   **T3**   Fig 3c   Fig 3d

(T3) DYNAMIC CONVERGENCE—KT3 CHASSIS

Vertically tilt the deflection unit so that the central horizontal red and blue lines are superimposed together with the central vertical red and blue lines being superimposed. Having ensured that the position of the deflection unit is correct insert a rubber wedge (1) with the backing strip not removed, either at the top (Fig. T2a) *or* at the bottom (Fig. T3a).

N.B.: Fig. 2a is applicable if the deflection unit is tilted upwards and Fig. T3a if the unit is tilted downwards. Now horizontally tilt the deflection unit such that the horizontal red and blue lines in the upper and lower halves of the picture and the vertical red and blue lines on the left and right side of the picture are superimposed. Insert wedges with backing strips removed in positions (2) and (3) as shown in Fig. T2b *or* Fig. T3b firmly pressing the adhesive sides against the glass of the C.R.T.

Now place a wedge with the backing strip removed in position (4) as shown in Fig. T2c *or* Fig. T3c firmly pressing the adhesive side against the glass of the C.R.T. Remove the wedge (1) so that the setting-up is as shown in either Fig. T2d or T3d.

Finally switch-on the green gun with SK9016.

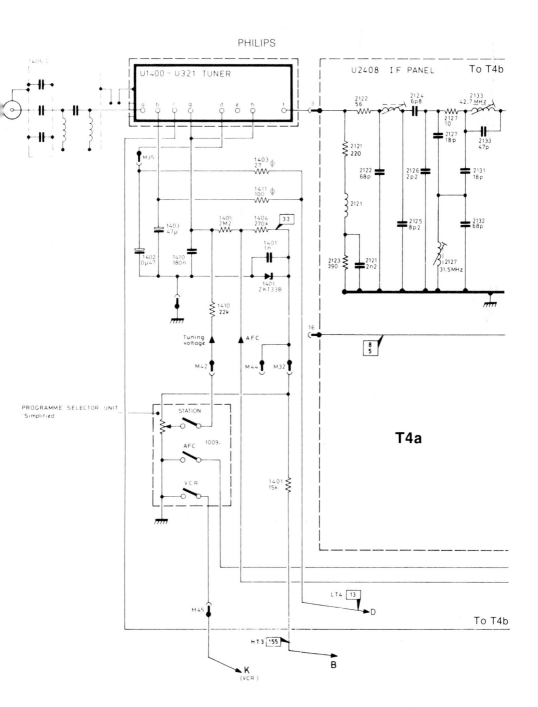

PHILIPS

(T4a) CIRCUIT DIAGRAM—KT3 CHASSIS *(PART)*

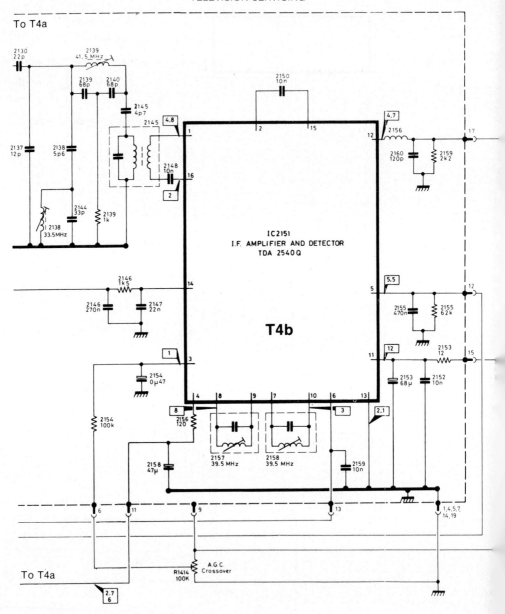

(T4b) CIRCUIT DIAGRAM—KT3 CHASSIS *(PART)*

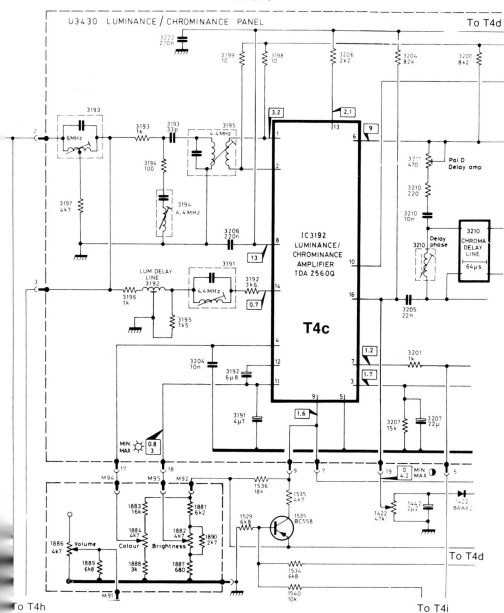

(T4c) CIRCUIT DIAGRAM—KT3 CHASSIS *(PART)*

(T4d) CIRCUIT DIAGRAM—KT3 CHASSIS *(PART)*

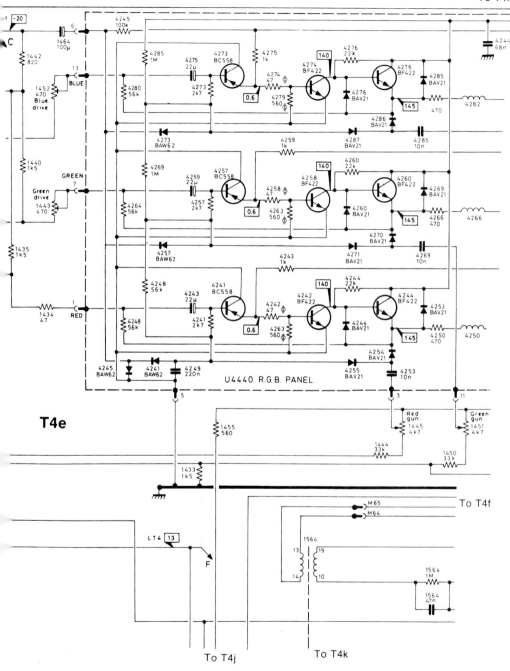

(T4e) CIRCUIT DIAGRAM—KT3 CHASSIS *(PART)*

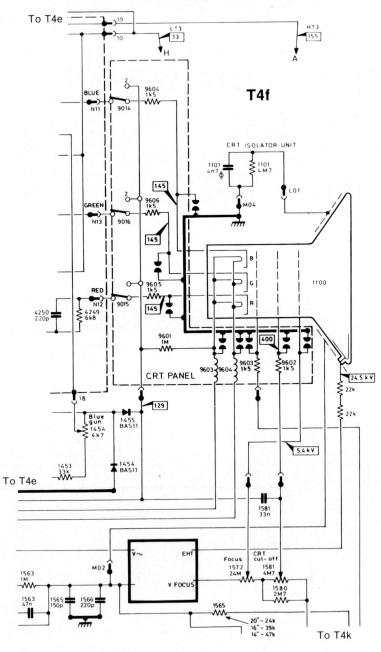

(T4f) CIRCUIT DIAGRAM—KT3 CHASSIS *(PART)*

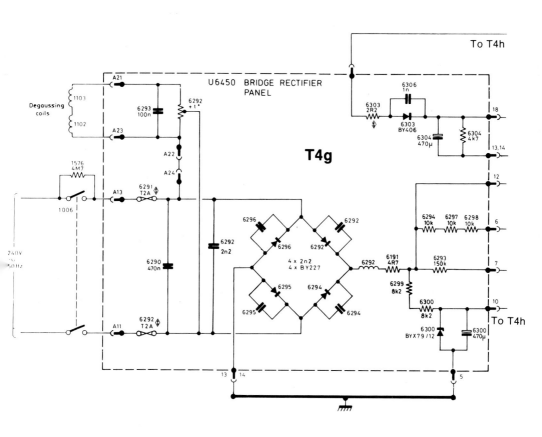

CIRCUIT NOTES

Special safety component
Refer to Safety Section in Manual
before replacing

Indicates local earth on panel or
unit

M3.2

Denotes contact 2 of connector M3

VOLTAGES

Except where stated, voltages are measured
with respect to chassis, with no signal input,
the brightness control at minimum and the
saturation control at maximum

1.7 = No signal input except where
indicated by min/max condition,
where two voltages are shown

3
9 = No signal input
= Receiver tuned to colour bars
and adjusted for normal picture

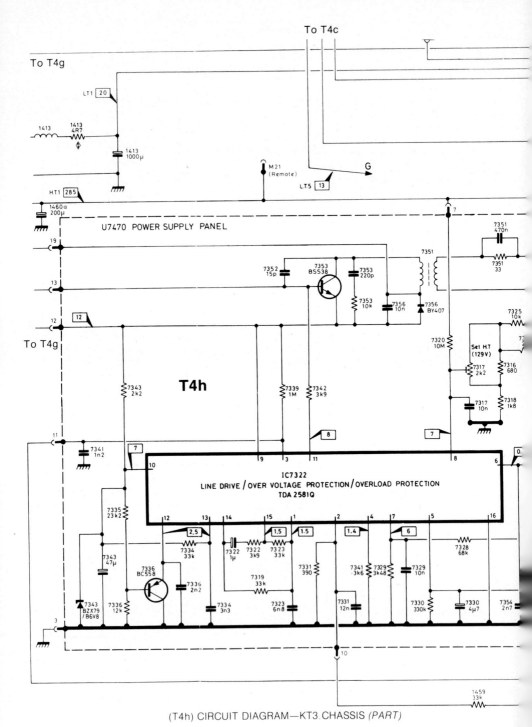

(T4h) CIRCUIT DIAGRAM—KT3 CHASSIS *(PART)*

190

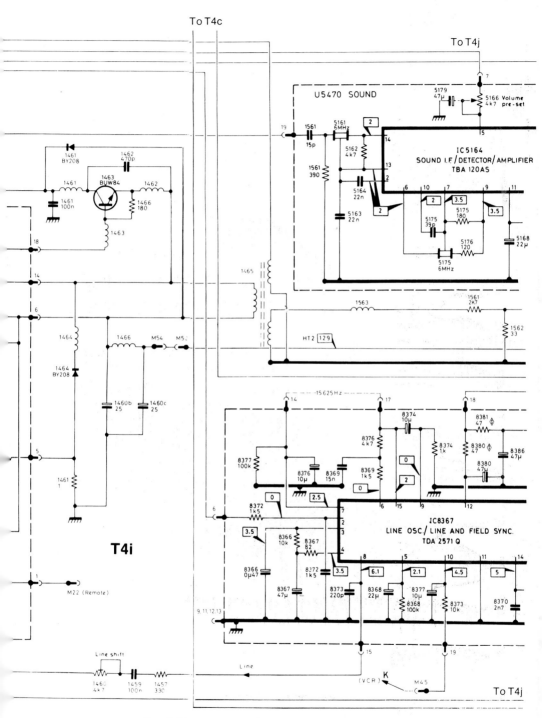

(T4i) CIRCUIT DIAGRAM—KT3 CHASSIS *(PART)*

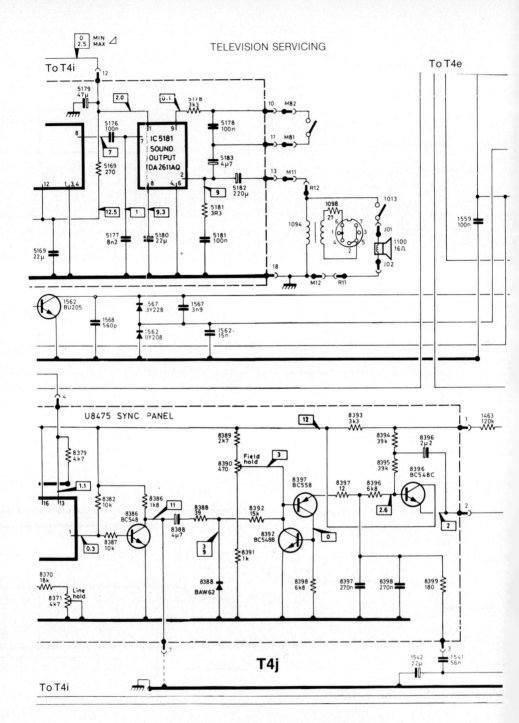

(T4j) CIRCUIT DIAGRAM—KT3 CHASSIS *(PART)*

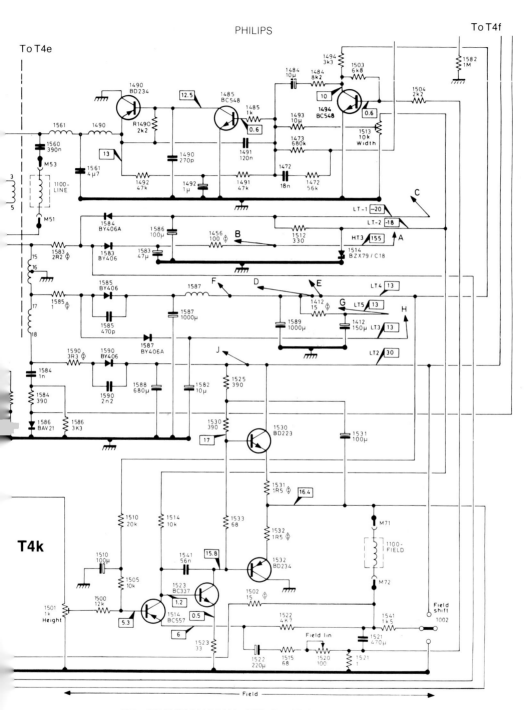

(T4k) CIRCUIT DIAGRAM—KT3 CHASSIS *(CONTINUED)*

PLUSTRON   Model TV14

General Description: A portable 14-in. monochrome television receiver for mains or battery operation. The chassis is isolated by mains transformer and a socket is provided for the connection of an earphone.

Mains Supply: 240 volts, 50Hz.

Battery: 12 volts, 15W.

Cathode Ray Tube: 340AMB4.

Loudspeaker: 16 ohms impedance.

Access for Service

Disconnect mains supply and unplug loop aerial. Remove 9 screws from the rear cover which may now be withdrawn.

Adjustment

H.T.: Operate from mains supplies and connect a voltmeter between pins 3 and 4 of C.R.T. socket. Adjust VR901 for a reading of 11.5 ± 0.05 volts.

(T118a) CIRCUIT DIAGRAM—MODEL TV14 (PART)

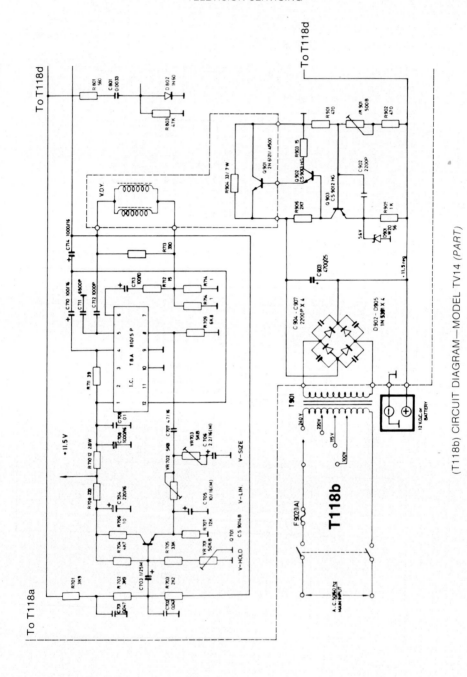

(T118b) CIRCUIT DIAGRAM—MODEL TV14 *(PART)*

(T118c) CIRCUIT DIAGRAM—MODEL TV14 (PART)

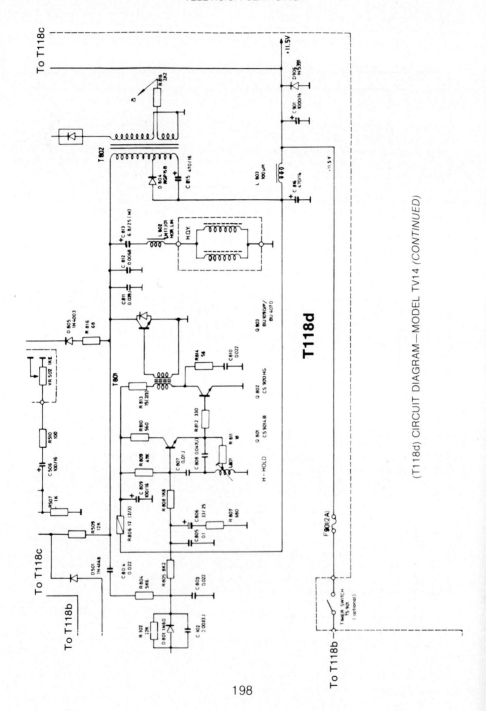

(T118d) CIRCUIT DIAGRAM—MODEL TV14 (CONTINUED)

PLUSTRON

Models TVR5D, TVRC5D, TVR7C

General Description: A series of miniature portable monochrome television receivers incorporating A.M./F.M. radio and cassette tape-recorder (Models TVRC5D, TVR7C). Power Supply is from A.C. mains or battery supplies internally or externally.

Mains Supply: 240 volts, 50Hz.

Batteries: 13.5 volts (9×1.5 volts) or 12 volts car battery.

Wavebands: L.W. 150-250kHz; M.W. 150-250kHz; F.M. 88-108MHz.

Dismantling: See Figs. T120-122.
Although sections of these models are generally similar, many small variations of value and interconnection necessitate the inclusion of separate circuits for each model. Variations of alignment allow the use of these receivers on other transmission standards.

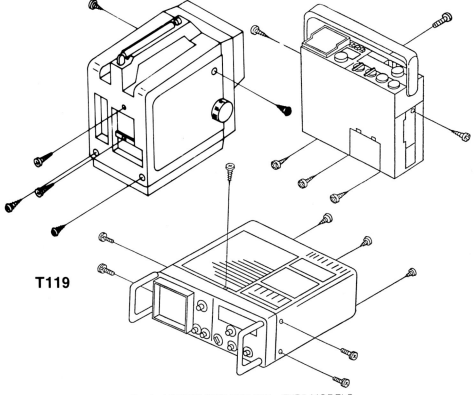

T119

(T119) ACCESS FOR SERVICE—TVR5 MODELS

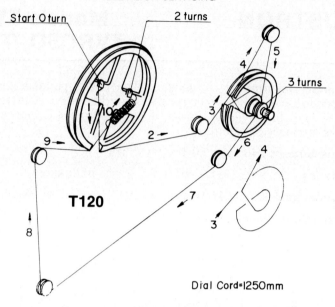

T120

(T120) DRIVE CORD—MODEL TVR5D

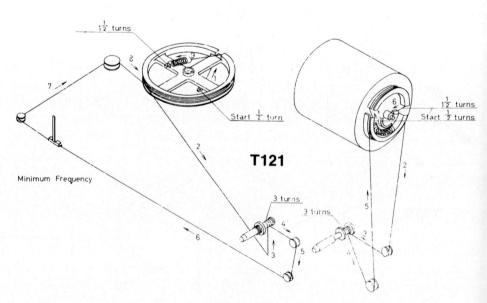

T121

(T121) DRIVE CORD—MODEL TVRC5D

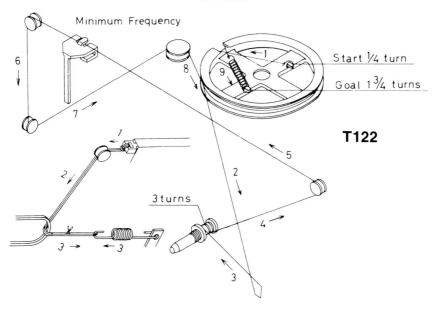

Minimum Frequency

Start ¼ turn

Goal 1¾ turns

T122

3 turns

(T122) DRIVE CORD—MODEL TVR7C

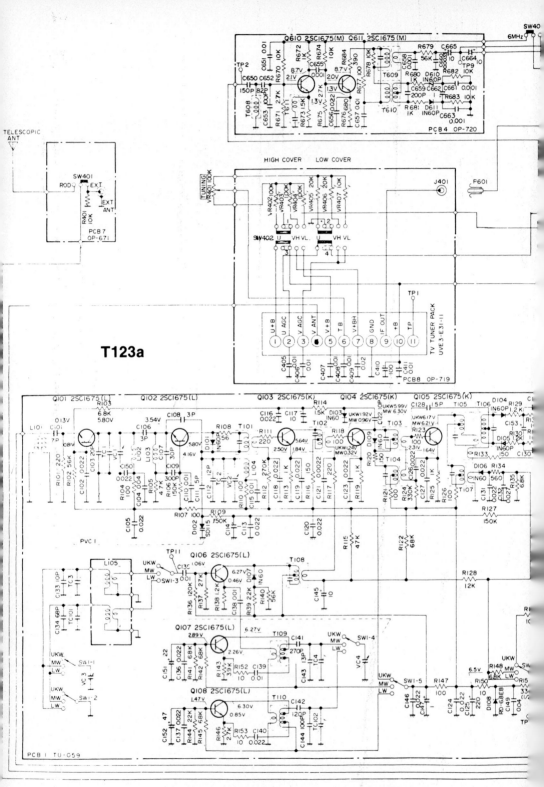

(T123a) CIRCUIT DIAGRAM—MODEL TVR5D *(PART)*

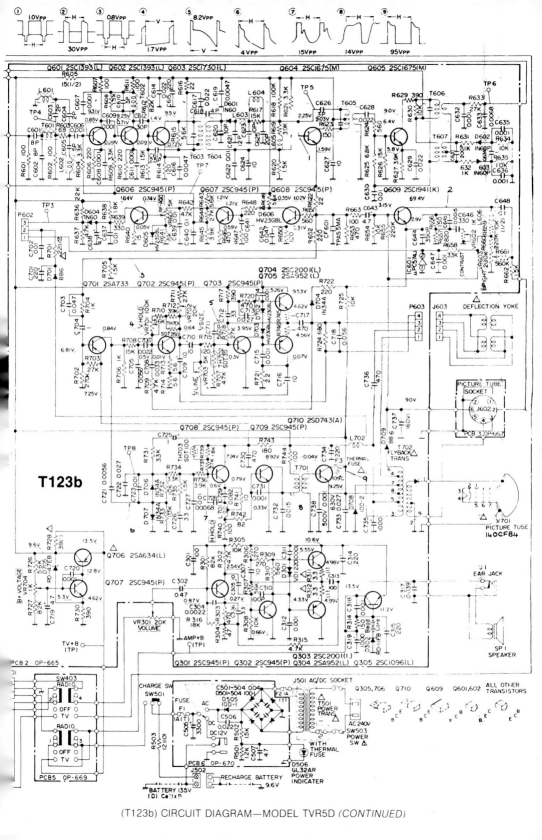

(T123b) CIRCUIT DIAGRAM—MODEL TVR5D *(CONTINUED)*

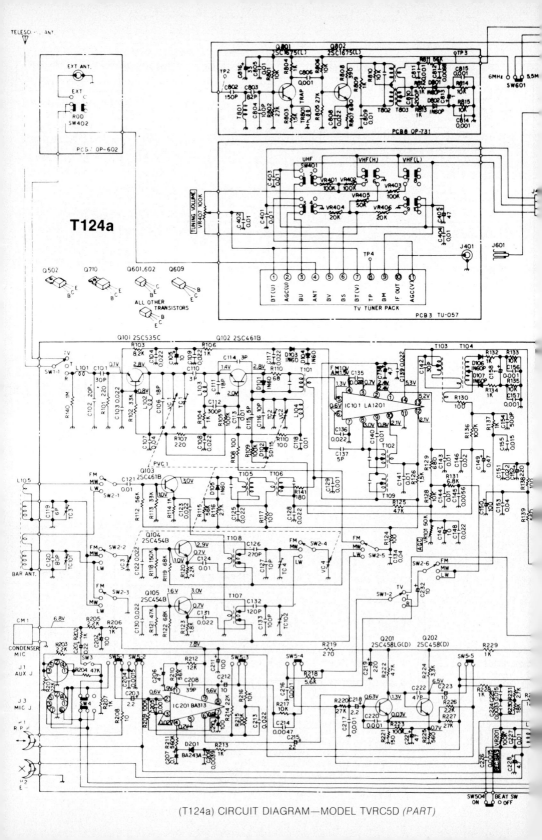

(T124a) CIRCUIT DIAGRAM—MODEL TVRC5D *(PART)*

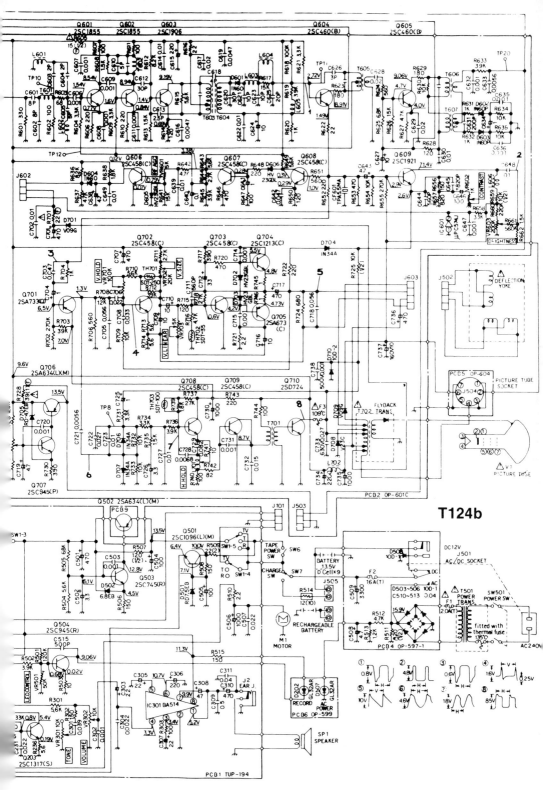

T124b

(T124b) CIRCUIT DIAGRAM—MODEL TVRC5D *(CONTINUED)*

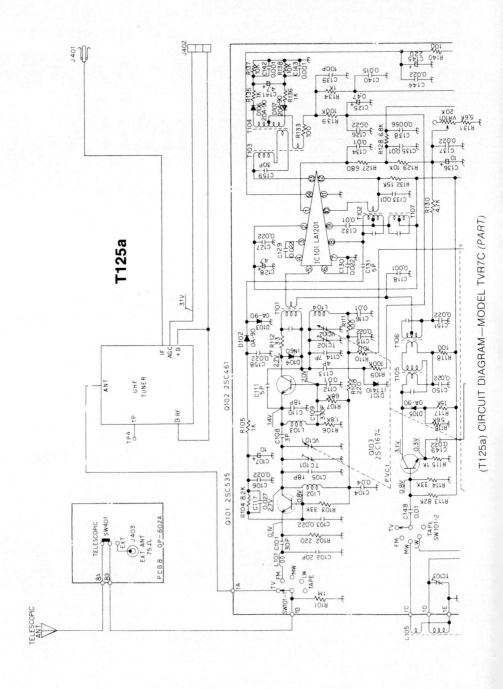

(T125a) CIRCUIT DIAGRAM—MODEL TVR7C (PART)

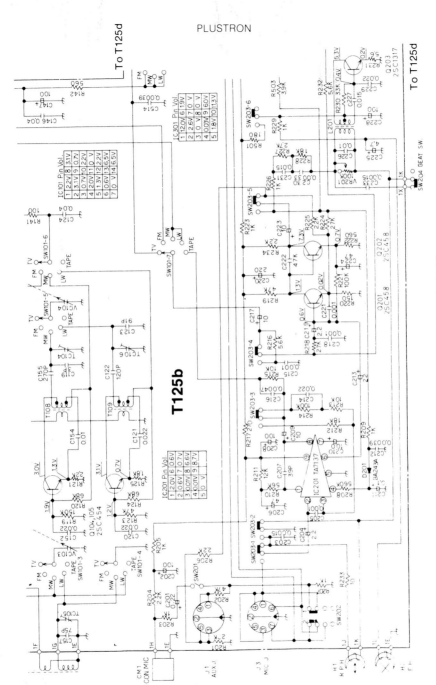

(T125b) CIRCUIT DIAGRAM—MODEL TVR7C (PART)

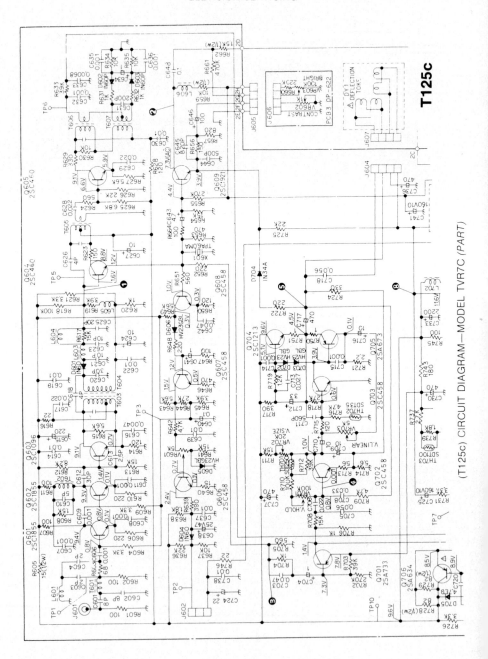

(T125c) CIRCUIT DIAGRAM—MODEL TVR7C (PART)

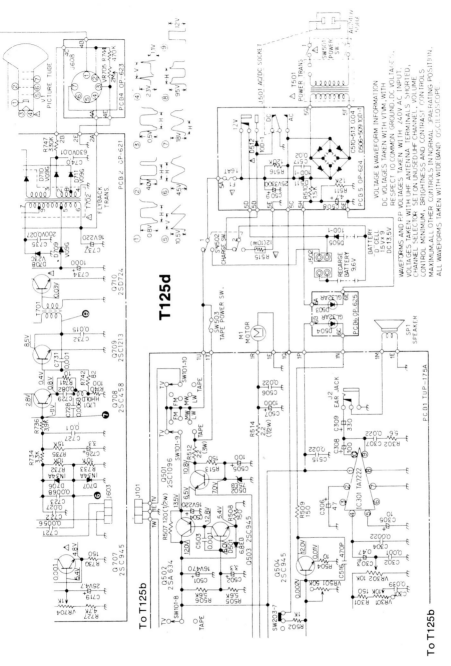

(T125c) CIRCUIT DIAGRAM—MODEL TVR7C (CONTINUED)

SANYO   Model 12-T280

General Description: A mains or battery operated monochrome television receiver incorporating a 12-in. cathode ray tube. The chassis is isolated by mains transformer and a socket is provided for the connection of an earphone. Integrated circuits are used in I.F., Sound and Field circuits.

Mains Supply: 240 volts, 50Hz.

Battery: 12 volts, 13W.

Loudspeaker: 8 ohms impedance.

Cathode Ray Tube: 310GAB4, 310KCB4 or 12VCGP4.

Dismantling

Remove 3 screws (1 either side, 1 under handle) and loosen aerial panel screws. Detach aerial panel as the cabinet back is withdrawn.

Adjustments

H.T.: Adjust VR701 to obtain 10.5 ± 0.1 volts at TP91.

Picture Focus (See Fig. T126): Focus adjustment jumper wire is located near picture tube socket. If focus is inadequate clip the jumper wire (J901).

Picture Width: If picture is too wide, cut the jumper wire (J601). This jumper wire may have been opened in some chassis as a result of factory adjustment.
If picture is still too wide, cut the jumper wire (J602).

Deflection Yoke and Centring Rings: Loosen the Deflection Yoke clamp and carefully move the yoke on the neck of the picture tube as far forward as possible. Rotate the yoke until the top and bottom edges of the raster are straight. Tighten the clamp.
Centre the raster and eliminate shaded corners by rotating the centring rings until the best effect is obtained.

Vertical Height and Linearity:

Preliminary: Adjust the set as soon as possible after switch 'ON'.
Set V. Hold (VR501), and V. Linearity (VR503) controls to the mid-position, and Contrast (VR201), Brightness (VR202) controls to the fully clockwise.
Adjustment Procedure: Set Height (VR502) to 80% of the screen.
Adjust V. Linearity control to obtain the best linearity.
Adjust Height control to obtain proper picture height.
Rotate V. Hold control completely clockwise or anti-clockwise to confirm the picture rolls up or down at both extreme positions.

SANYO

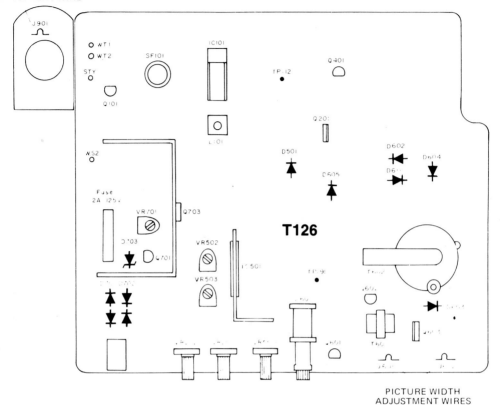

PICTURE FOCUS ADJUSTMENT WIRE

PICTURE WIDTH ADJUSTMENT WIRES

(T126) LOCATION OF ADJUSTMENTS—MODEL 12-T280

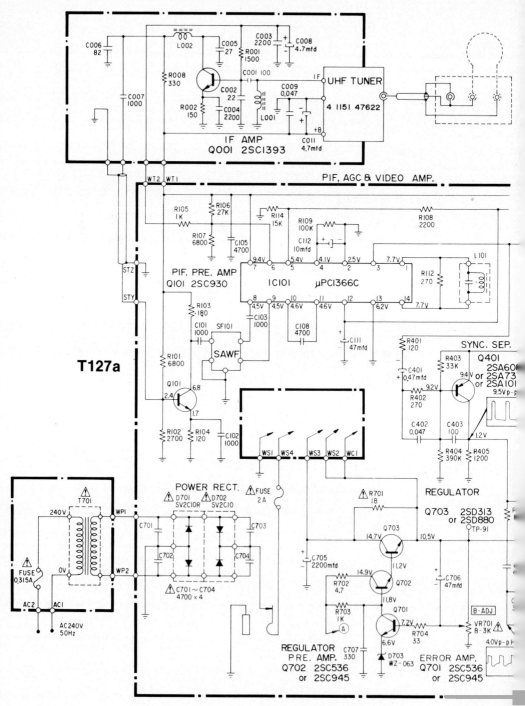

(T127a) CIRCUIT DIAGRAM—MODEL 12-T280 *(PART)*

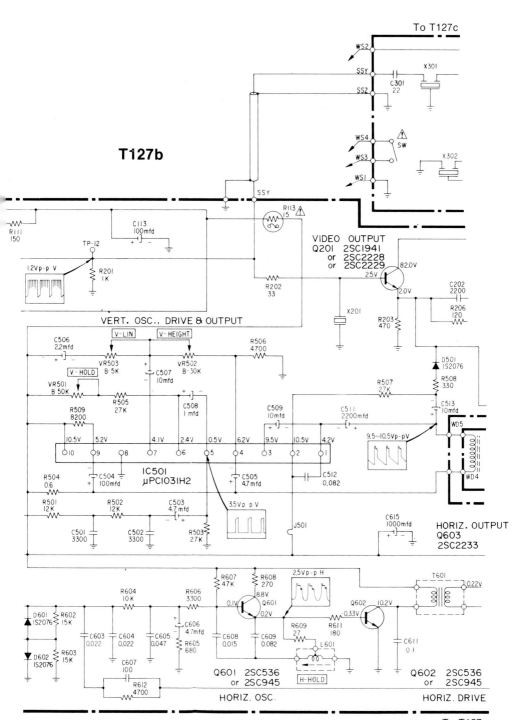

T127b

To T127c

VERT. OSC., DRIVE & OUTPUT

VIDEO OUTPUT
Q201 2SC1941
or 2SC2228
or 2SC2229

HORIZ. OUTPUT
Q603
2SC2233

Q601 2SC536
or 2SC945

Q602 2SC536
or 2SC945

HORIZ. OSC.

HORIZ. DRIVE

IC501
μPC1031H2

(T127b) CIRCUIT DIAGRAM—MODEL 12-T280 *(PART)*

To T127c

SIF AMP., DET & AUDIO AMP., OUTPUT

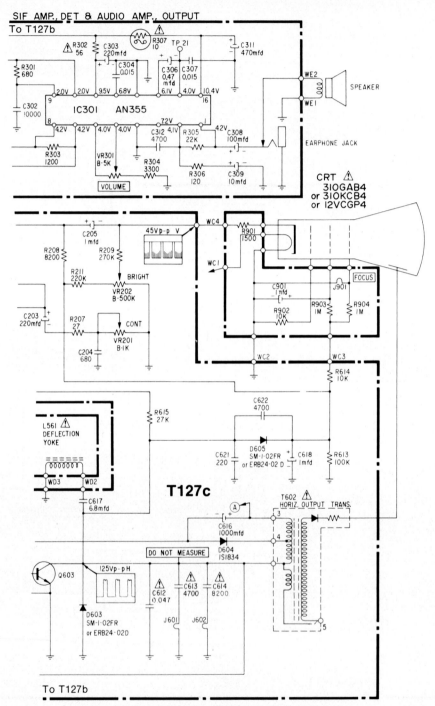

SANYO   Model 14-T408

General Description: A portable monochrome television receiver incorporating a 14-in. cathode ray tube and operating from mains or battery supplies. Integrated circuits are used in the sound stages and an isolating mains transformer allows the connection of an earphone.

Mains Supply: 240 volts, 50Hz.

Battery: 12 volts, 18W.

Cathode Ray Tube: 340AUB4 or 340RB4.

Loudspeaker: 8 ohms impedance.

Access for service may be obtained by removing 8 screws and lifting the back away from the chassis assembly.

Adjustments

H.T. Supply: Set VR701 to obtain 11.5 ± 0.1 volts at P6.

Focus Adjustment: Connect the wire lead from picture tube socket to one of the two terminals (P19, P20) for the best focus.

Width: If picture is too wide, cut the jumper wire J2. This wire may have been opened in some chassis as a result of factory adjustment.

If picture is still too wide, cut the jumper wire J1.

Deflection Yoke and Centring Rings: Loosen the deflection yoke clamp and carefully move the yoke on the neck of the picture tube as far forward as possible.

Rotate the yoke until the top and bottom edges of the raster are straight. Tighten the clamp.

Centre the raster and eliminate shaded corners by rotating the centring rings until the best effect is obtained.

Vertical Height and Linearity: Check the picture width before adjustment.

Adjust A.C. power to the rated voltage with a voltage regulator.

Set V. Hold (VR501), Height (VR503) and V. Lin (VR502) controls to the mid-position, contrast (VR202) and Brightness (VR201) to maximum.

Leave the receiver 'on' for about 5 minutes before proceeding with the adjustments.

Adjust the Vertical Linearity control (VR502) to obtain the best linearity.

Adjust the Height control (VR503) to obtain proper picture height.

Adjust the voltage at TP-30 to 5.6 ± 0.4V D.C. with Vertical Balance control (VR504).

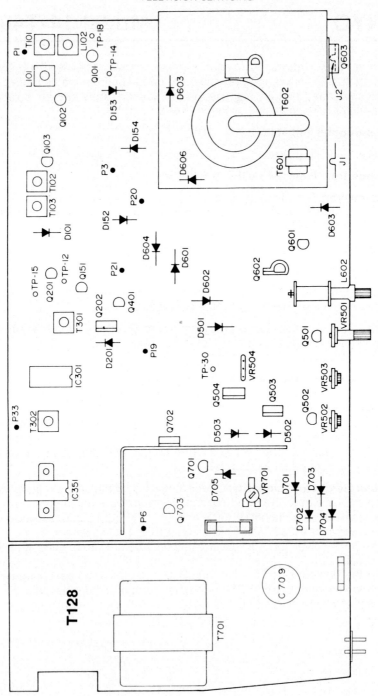

(T128) LOCATION OF ADJUSTMENTS—MODEL 14T-408

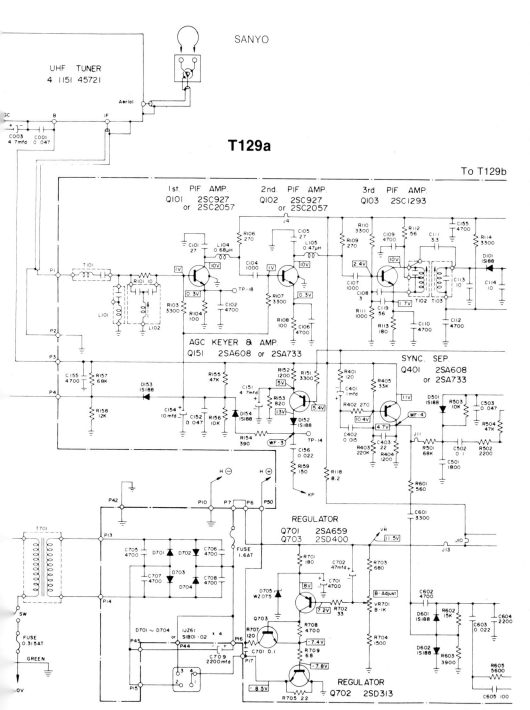

SANYO

T129a

To T129b

(T129a) CIRCUIT DIAGRAM—MODEL 14T-408 *(PART)*

217

To T129b

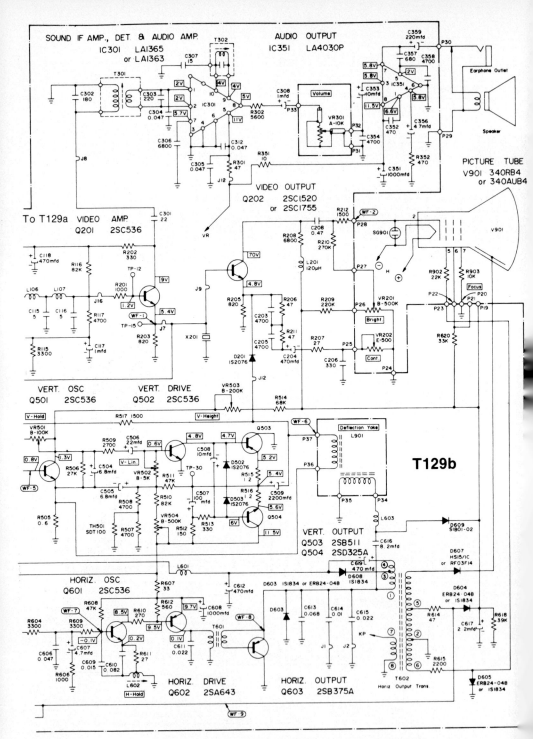

To T129a   (T129b) CIRCUIT DIAGRAM—MODEL 14T-408 *(CONTINUED)*

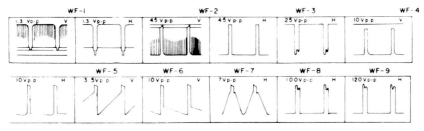

T130 (T130) CIRCUIT WAVEFORMS—MODEL 14T-408

SANYO   79P Chassis, Models CTP3104, CTP3105, CTP4100, CTP6118

General Description: A basic solid-state colour television chassis operating from mains supplies and fitted with a variety of tube sizes. The basic circuit for Model CTP6118 is given here with details of variations for other presentations. Model CTP4100 is fitted with remote control facility.

Mains Supply: 240 volts, 50Hz.

Adjustments (See Figs. T327a/b)

Sub-brightness Adjustment:

Note: +220V power supply, A.G.C. and grey scale tracking should be adjusted before attempting this adjustment.
Tune the receiver to colour bar pattern.
Set brightness to maximum and colour and contrast to minimum.
Connect D.C. meter between test points 'TP-J' (+ lead) and 'TP-K' (— lead).
Adjust VR181 for 0.25V.

+220V (+B1) Power Supply Adjustment: Set brightness and contrast to maximum, and colour to mid-range.
Connect voltmeter to terminal 'B1'.
Adjust VR321 for +220V.

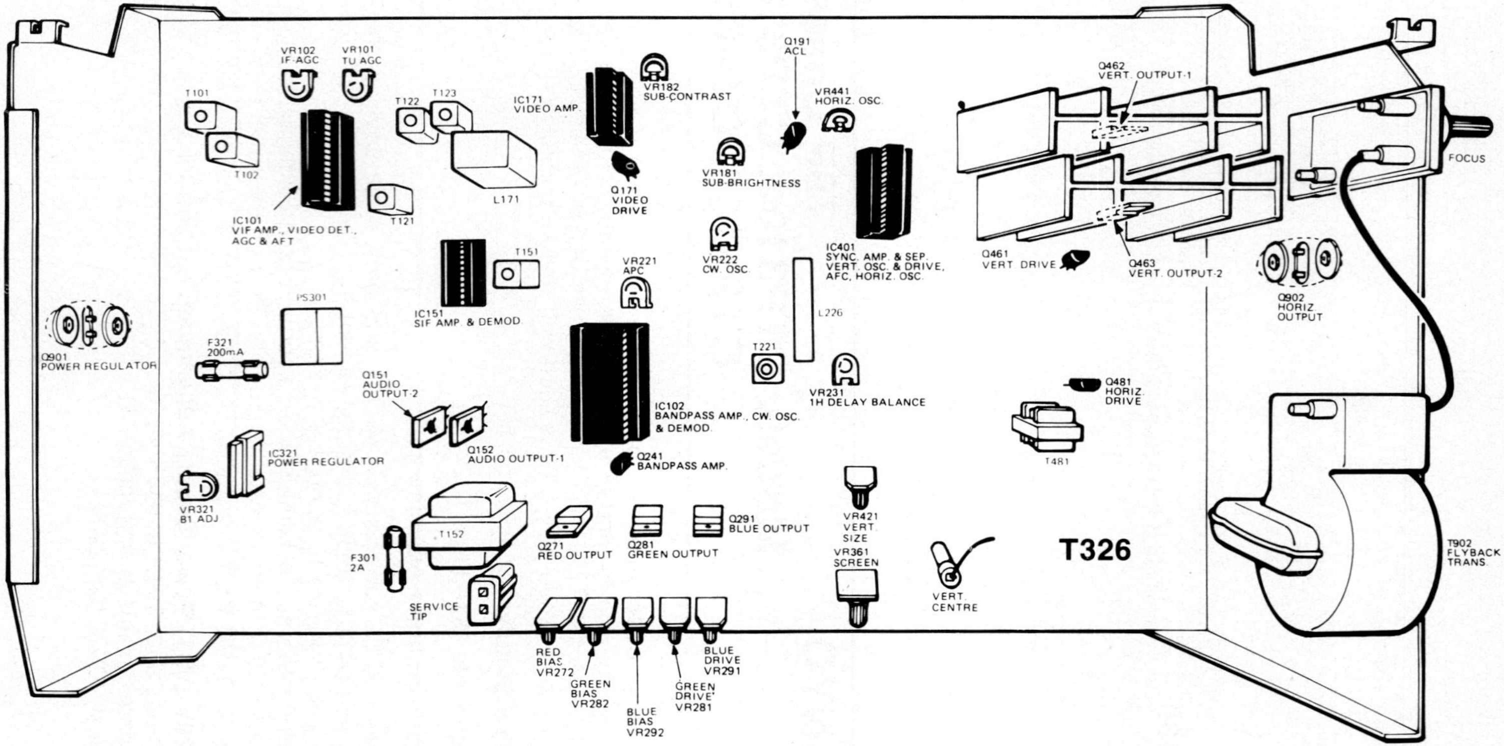

(T326) COMPONENT LOCATION—79P CHASSIS

FOCUS

T902 FLYBACK TRANS

Q902 HORIZ OUTPUT

Q462 VERT OUTPUT-1

Q463 VERT OUTPUT 2

Q481 HORIZ DRIVE

T481

Q461 VERT DRIVE

T326

VERT CENTRE

VR441 HORIZ OSC

IC401 SYNC. AMP. & SEP. VERT. OSC. & DRIVE. AFC. HORIZ. OSC.

L226

VR231 1H DELAY BALANCE

VR421 VERT SIZE

VR361 SCREEN

Q191 ACL

VR181 SUB-BRIGHTNESS

T221

Q241 BANDPASS AMP.

IC102 BANDPASS AMP. CW OSC. & DEMOD.

Q291 BLUE OUTPUT

BLUE DRIVE VR291

GREEN DRIVE VR281

VR222 CW OSC

VR182 SUB-CONTRAST

VR221 APC

Q281 GREEN OUTPUT

BLUE BIAS VR292

Q171 VIDEO DRIVE

Q271 RED OUTPUT

GREEN BIAS VR282

IC171 VIDEO AMP

L171

T151

RED BIAS VR272

RED DRIVE VR271

T123

T122

T121

IC151 SIF AMP. & DEMOD

Q152 AUDIO OUTPUT-1

T152

SERVICE TIP

VR101 TU AGC

Q151 AUDIO OUTPUT-2

T102

T101

VR102 IF-AGC

F301 2A

IC101 VIF AMP. VIDEO DET. AGC & AFT

IS301

IC321 POWER REGULATOR

F321 200mA

VR321 B1 ADJ

Q901 POWER REGULATOR

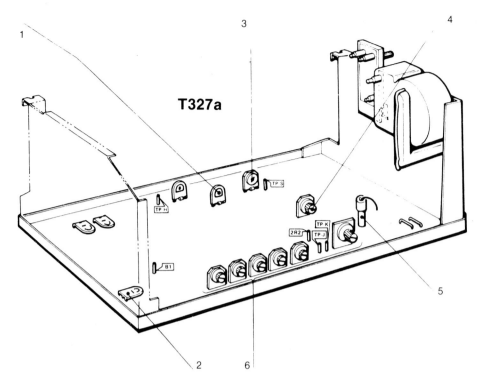

T327a

(T327a) INSTALLATION ADJUSTMENTS—79P CHASSIS

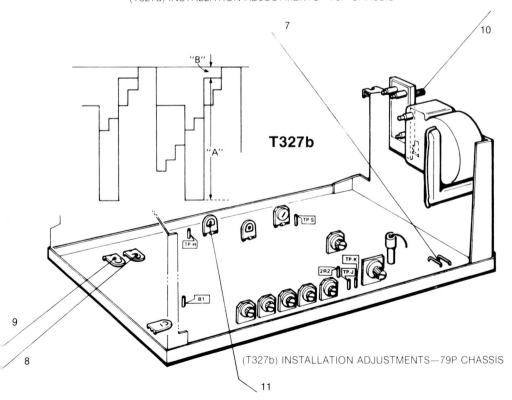

T327b

(T327b) INSTALLATION ADJUSTMENTS—79P CHASSIS

Horizontal Oscillation Adjustment: Set horizontal hold (VR907) to mechanical centre of its range.

Connect a short jumper between test points 'TP-S' and ground.

Adjust VR441 to momentarily synchronise picture.

Vertical Size Adjustment: Tune the receiver to circular pattern.

Adjust VR421 to obtain proper picture.

Vertical Centring Adjustment: Set the Vertical and Horizontal hold controls for a properly synchronised picture.

Vertical centring can be adjusted by connecting vertical tap to any one of the three terminals.

Grey Scale Tracking Adjustment: Set brightness and contrast to maximum, and colour to minimum.

Disconnect service tap.

Set green (VR281) and blue (VR291) drive controls to mid-range.

Set red (VR272), green (VR282) and blue (VR292) bias controls to minimum.

Adjust screen control (VR361) to obtain a just visible one coloured line.

Advance each bias control to obtain just visible three coloured lines.

Reconnect service tap.

Adjust green and blue drive controls alternately to produce normal black and white picture.

Check for proper grey scale tracking at all brightness levels.

Horizontal Width and High-voltage Adjustment:

Note: +220V power supply, A.G.C. and grey scale tracking should be adjusted before attempting this adjustment.

Tune the receiver to circular pattern.

Set brightness and contrast to maximum and colour to minimum.

Check picture width. If picture is too wide or narrow, cut or shorten the leads (AJ1, AJ2). In case the lead is cut, horizontal width will be decreased, and the lead is shorted, it will be increased.

Connect a high-voltage meter to anode on picture tube.

Check high-voltage. High-voltage must measure 19KV ± 1.0KV. If high-voltage is lower than 18KV, clip the leads (AJ1, AJ2). (By attempting this, the high-voltage is increased approx. 0.5KV.)

Remarks: This adjustment affects sub-brightness. Therefore, re-check Sub-brightness adjustment.

T.U.-A.G.C. Adjustment: Tune the receiver to clearest station.

Rotate VR101 fully anti-clockwise and then clockwise slowly until the snow just disappears.

I.F.-A.G.C. Adjustment: Tune the receiver to colour bar pattern.

Set brightness and contrast to maximum, and colour to minimum.

Connect oscilloscope to test point 'TP-H'.

Adjust VR102 for 1.35Vp-p amplitude.

Focus Adjustment: Adjust focus control on the right side of the chassis for clear scanning lines.

Sub-contrast Adjustment: Tune the receiver to colour bar pattern.
Set contrast to maximum and colour to minimum.
Connect oscilloscope to terminal '2R2'.
Set brightness for 5Vp-p at 'B' as illustrated.
Adjust VR182 for 100Vp-p at 'A' as illustrated.

Purity Adjustment (Fig. T328):

1. Place the picture tube face North or South and demagnetise the picture tube and receiver using an external degaussing coil. When replacing picture tube or Deflection Yoke, mount Deflection Yoke and Purity-convergence Magnets assembly properly.

2. Turn red and blue guns off to provide only green raster by rotating red and blue bias controls fully counter-clockwise. Slowly rotate green bias control clockwise to produce green raster.

3. Loosen the screw holding the Deflection Yoke and slide the Deflection Yoke backward as far as possible, and remove the 3 spacers.

4. Rotate the tabs of the two Purity Magnets to centre the vertical green belt on the picture screen. The Purity Magnets are also adjusted to obtain vertical centring of the raster.

5. Slowly slide the Deflection Yoke forward until a uniform green screen is obtained.

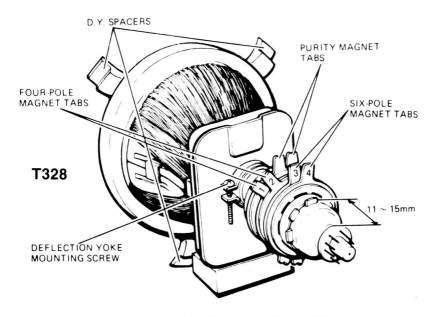

(T328) C.R.T. ADJUSTMENTS—79P CHASSIS

6. Check the purity of the red and blue screens for uniformity, turn-off other colours to check this (use Bias controls). Re-adjust the yoke position if necessary until all screens are pure.

7. Adjust each Bias control and screen control to obtain white raster. Refer to Grey Scale Adjustment. If part of the picture screen is coloured, adjust the Deflection Yoke position forward or backward slightly.

8. Fasten the screw of the Deflection Yoke. Adjust Convergence next.

Convergence Adjustment (Fig. T329):

1. Use a dot-cross-hatch pattern signal.

2. Turn red and blue guns on and turn-off green gun, refer to Purity Adjustment step 2. Adjust the angle between the tabs of the Four Pole Magnet 1 and 2, and superimpose the red and blue vertical lines in the centre area of the picture screen.

3. Keeping the mutual angle of the tabs of the Four Pole Magnet turn them together to superimpose the blue and red horizontal lines in the centre area of the picture screen.

4. Turn green gun on and adjust Six Pole Magnet 3 and 4 so that the green line superimposes on the red/blue lines. This is the same procedure used in steps 2 and 3.

Outer Convergence Adjustment: If mis-convergence appears in the outer area, follow the procedure shown in Fig. T330.

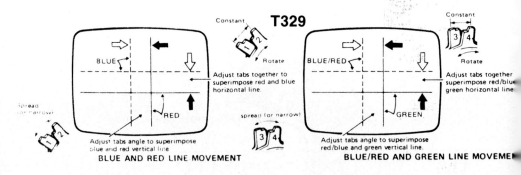

(T329) CONVERGENCE ADJUSTMENTS—79P CHASSIS

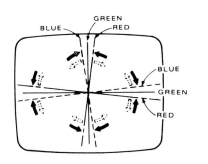 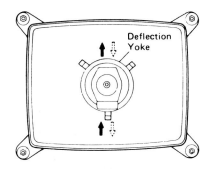

Swing the Deflection Yoke the ← direction, Red/Blue lines on the screen move the ← direction.
Swing the Deflection Yoke the ∷ direction, Red/Blue lines on the screen move the ∷ direction.

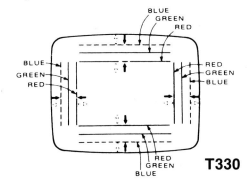 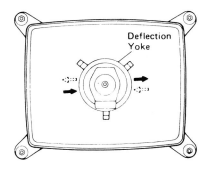

T330

Swing the Deflection Yoke the ← direction, Red/Blue lines on the screen move the ← direction.
Swing the Deflection Yoke the ∷ direction, Red/Blue lines on the screen move the ∷ direction.
To fasten the Deflection Yoke, Insert and fix the D.Y. spacer.

(T330) OUTER AREA CONVERGENCE—79P CHASSIS

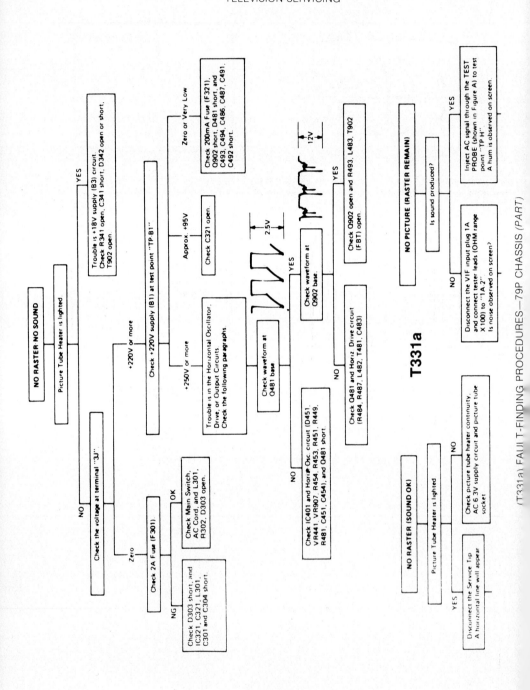

NO RASTER NO SOUND

Picture Tube Heater is lighted.

YES → Trouble is +18V supply (B3) circuit. Check R341 open, C341 short, D342 open or short, T902 open.

NO → Check the voltage at terminal "3".

+220V or more → Check +220V supply (B1) at test point "TP.B1"

+250V or more → Trouble is in the Horizontal Oscillator, Drive, or Output Circuits. Check the following paragraphs.

Approx. +95V → Check C321 open.

Zero or Very Low → Check 200mA Fuse (F321), Q902 short, D481 short, and C493, C494, C486, C487, C491, C492 short.

Zero → Check 2A Fuse (F301)

OK → Check Main Switch, AC Cord, and L301, R302, D303 open.

NG → Check D303 short, and IC321, C321, L301, C301 and C304 short.

Check waveform at Q481 base. — 2.5V

YES → Check waveform at Q902 base. — 12V

YES → Check Q902 open and R493, L483, T902 (FBT) open.

NO → Check Q481 and Horiz Drive circuit (R484, R487, L482, T481, C483)

NO → Check IC401 and Horiz Osc circuit (D451, VR441, VR907, R454, R453, R451, R449, R481, C451, C454), and Q481 short.

T331a

NO RASTER (SOUND OK)

Picture Tube Heater is lighted.

YES → Disconnect the Service Tap. A horizontal line will appear.

NO → Check picture tube heater continuity, AC 6.3V supply circuit and picture tube socket.

NO PICTURE (RASTER REMAIN)

Is sound produced?

YES → Inject AC signal through the TEST PROBE (shown in Figure A) to test point "TP H". A hum is observed on screen

NO → Disconnect the VIF input plug 1A and connect tester leads (OHM range X100) to "1A.2". Is noise observed on screen?

(T331a) FAULT FINDING PROCEDURES—79P CHASSIS *(PART)*

226

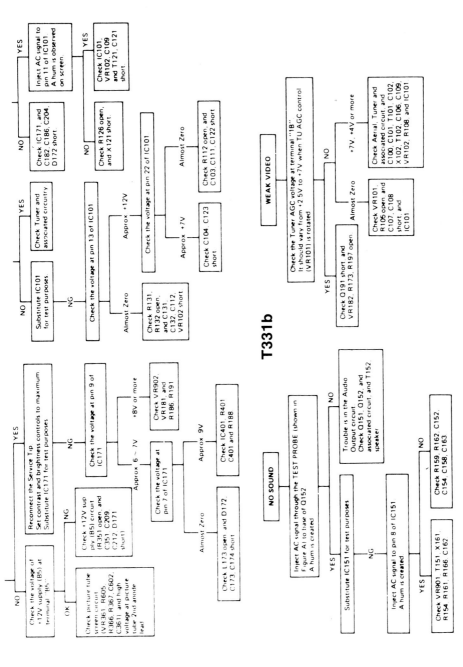

T331b

(T331b) FAULT-FINDING PROCEDURES—79P CHASSIS *(PART)*

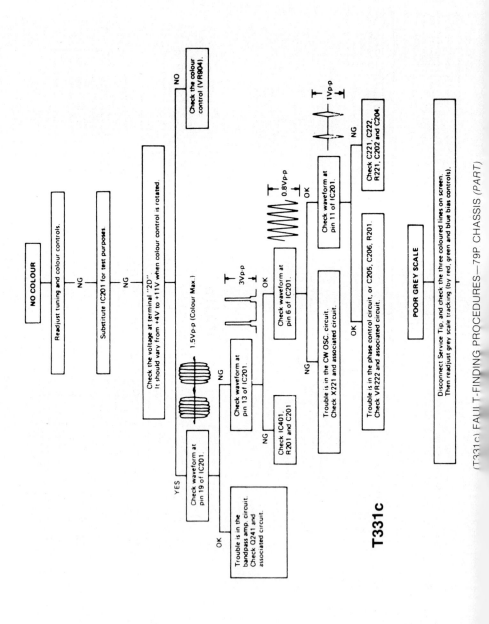

T331c

(T331c) FAULT-FINDING PROCEDURES—79P CHASSIS (PART)

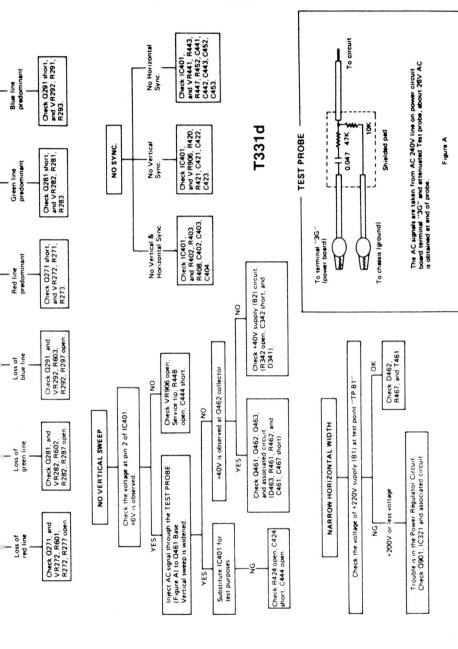

T331d

TEST PROBE

To terminal "3G" (power board)

To chassis (ground)

0.047 47K

10K

Shielded pad

To circuit

The AC signals are taken from AC 240V line on power circuit board terminal "3G" and attenuated Test probe, about 26V AC is obtained at end of probe.

Figure A

NO SYNC.

No Vertical & Horizontal Sync.

Check IC401, and R402, R403, R408, C402, C403, C404.

No Vertical Sync.

Check IC401, and VR906, R420, R421, C421, C422, C423.

No Horizontal Sync.

Check IC401, and VR441, R443, R447, R452, C441, C442, C443, C452, C453.

Red line predominant

Check Q271, short, and VR272, R271, R273.

Green line predominant

Check Q281 short, and VR282, R281, R283

Blue line predominant

Check Q291 short, and VR292, R291, R293.

Loss of red line

Check Q271, and VR272, R601, R272, R277 open.

Loss of green line

Check Q281, and VR282, R602, R282, R287 open.

Loss of blue line

Check Q291, and VR292, R603, R292, R297 open.

NO VERTICAL SWEEP

Check the voltage at pin 2 of IC401. +6V is observed.

Inject AC signal through the TEST PROBE (Figure A) to Q461 Base. Vertical sweep is widened.

YES

Substitute IC401 for test purposes.

NG

Check R424 open, C424 short, C444 open.

NO

Check VR906 open, Service tip, R448 open, C444 short.

YES

+40V is observed at Q462 collector.

NO

Check +40V supply (B2) circuit (R342 open, C342 short, and D341).

YES

Check Q461, Q462, Q463, and associated circuit (D463, R461, R462, and C461, C467 short).

NARROW HORIZONTAL WIDTH

Check the voltage of +220V supply (B1) at test point "TP-B1"

NG

+200V or less voltage

Trouble is in the Power Regulator Circuit. Check Q901, IC321 and associated circuit.

OK

Check D462, R467, and T461

(T331d) FAULT-FINDING PROCEDURES—79P CHASSIS (CONTINUED)

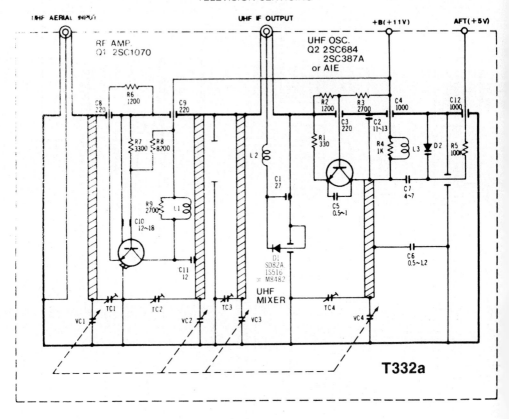

(T332a) CIRCUIT DIAGRAM (U.H.F. TUNER)—MODEL CTP3104

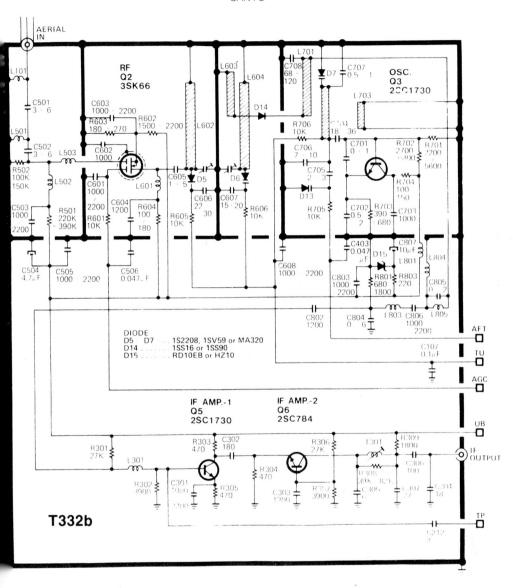

(T332b) CIRCUIT DIAGRAM (U.H.F. TUNER)—MODELS CTP3105, CTP4100, CTP6118

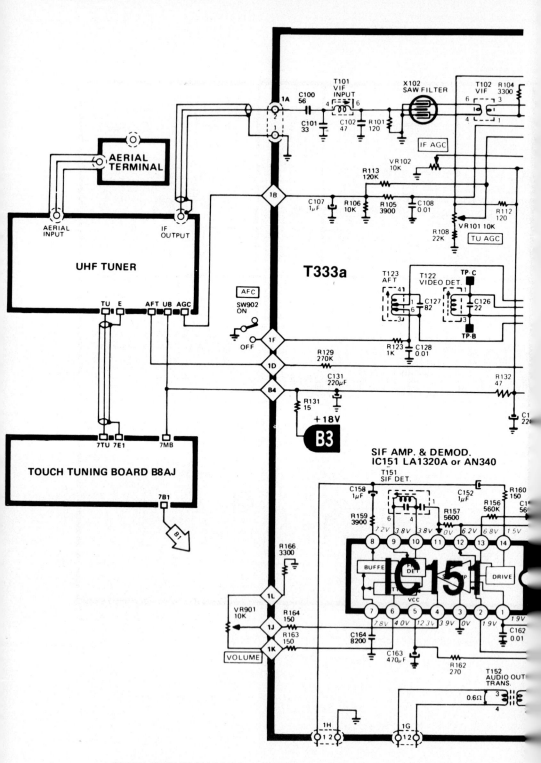

(T333a) CIRCUIT DIAGRAM—79P CHASSIS, MODEL CTP6118 *(PART)*

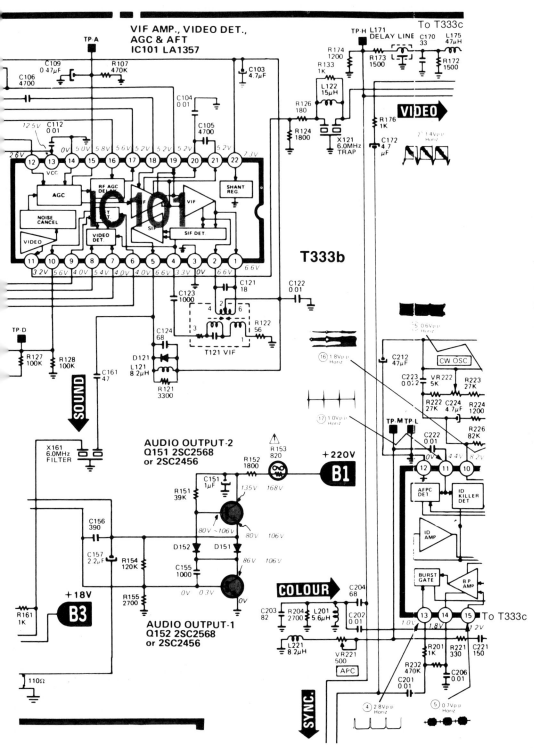

(T333b) CIRCUIT DIAGRAM—79P CHASSIS, MODEL CTP6118 *(PART)*

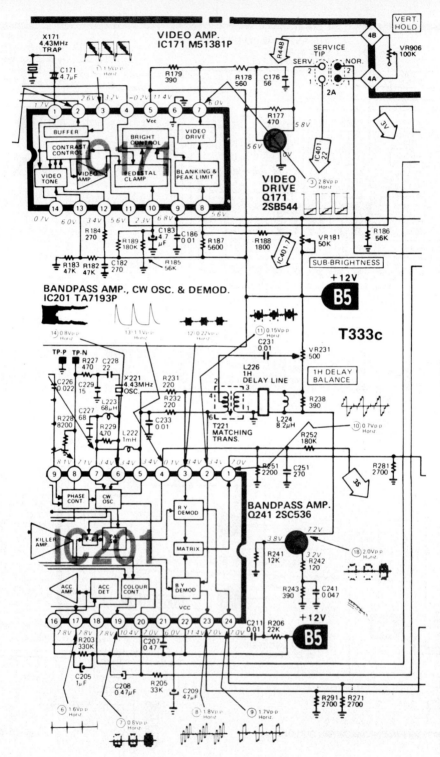

(T333c) CIRCUIT DIAGRAM—79P CHASSIS, MODEL CTP6118 *(PART)*

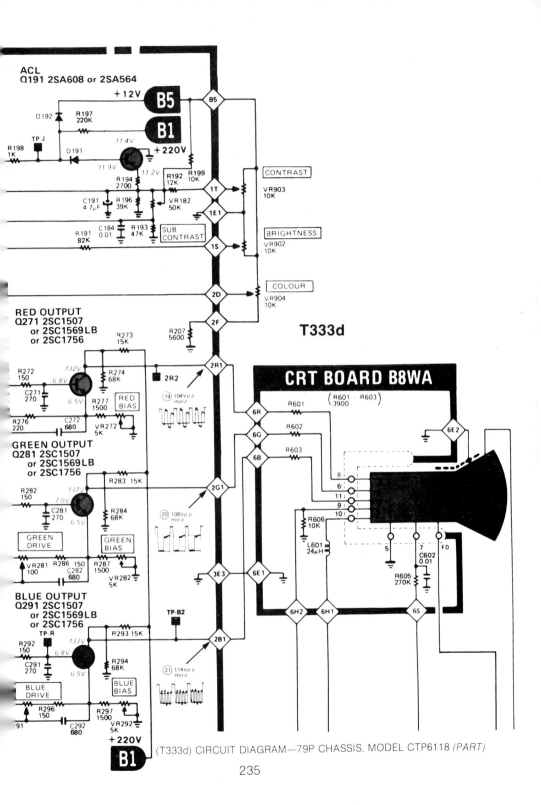

ACL
Q191 2SA608 or 2SA564

RED OUTPUT
Q271 2SC1507
or 2SC1569LB
or 2SC1756

GREEN OUTPUT
Q281 2SC1507
or 2SC1569LB
or 2SC1756

BLUE OUTPUT
Q291 2SC1507
or 2SC1569LB
or 2SC1756

T333d

CRT BOARD B8WA

(T333d) CIRCUIT DIAGRAM—79P CHASSIS, MODEL CTP6118 *(PART)*

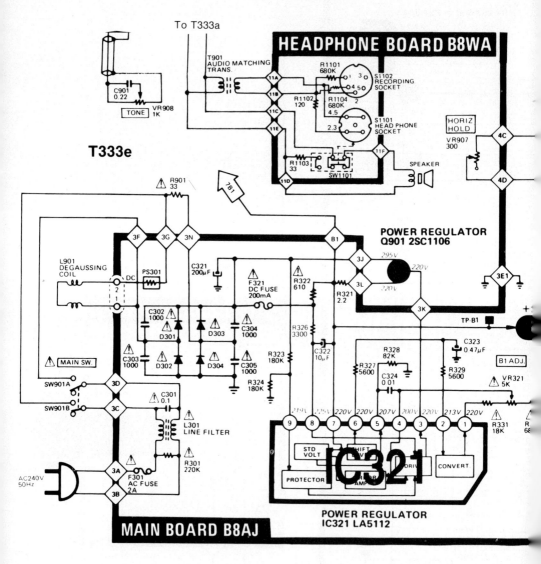

(T333e) CIRCUIT DIAGRAM—79P CHASSIS, MODEL CTP6118 *(PART)*

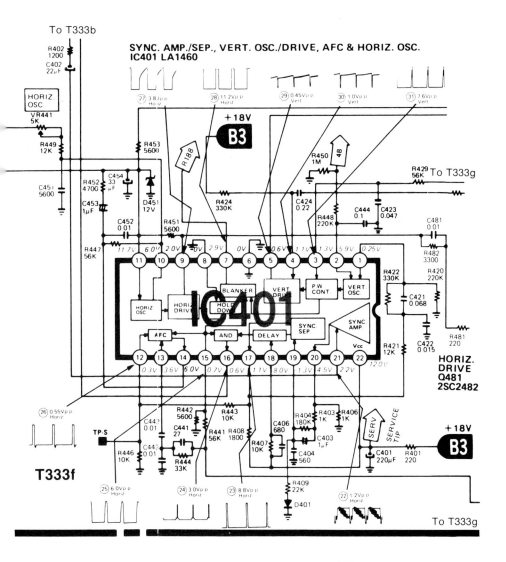

(T333f) CIRCUIT DIAGRAM—79P CHASSIS, MODEL CTP6118 *(PART)*

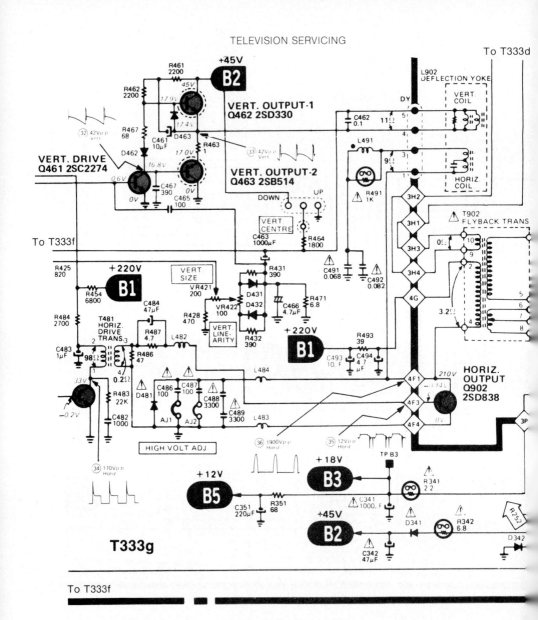

(T333g) CIRCUIT DIAGRAM—79P CHASSIS, MODEL CTP6118 *(PART)*

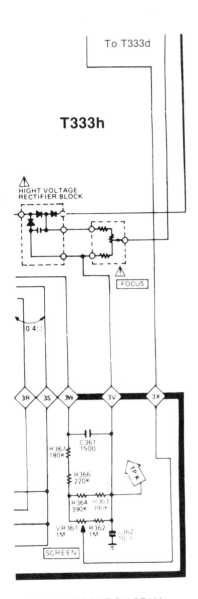

(T333h) CIRCUIT DIAGRAM—
79P CHASSIS, MODEL CTP6118
(CONTINUED)

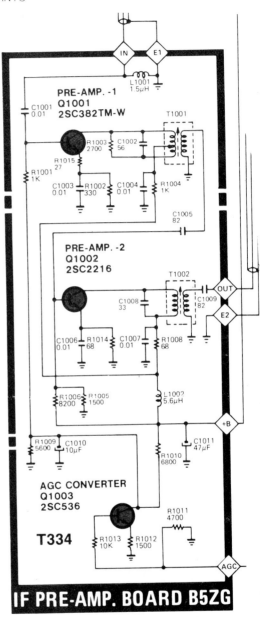

(T334) CIRCUIT DIAGRAM (I.F. PRE-AMP)—
MODEL CTP3104

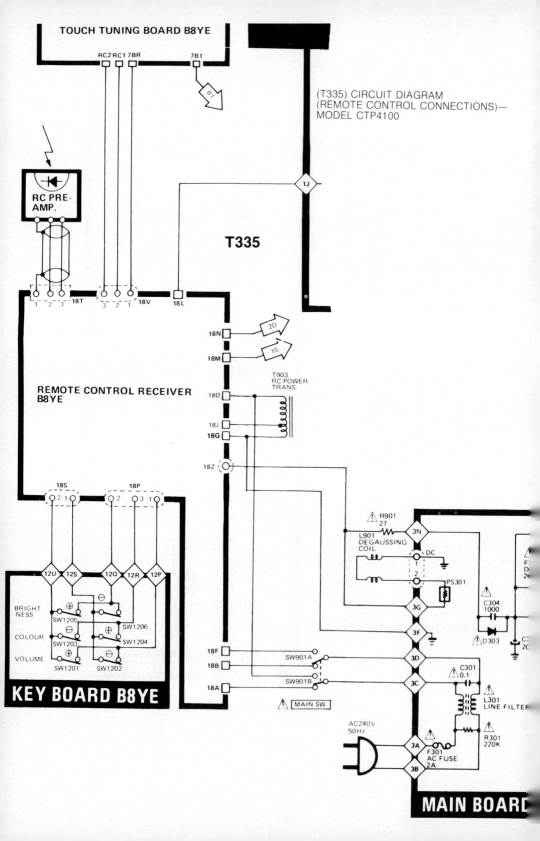

TOUCH TUNING BOARD B8YE

(T335) CIRCUIT DIAGRAM
(REMOTE CONTROL CONNECTIONS)—
MODEL CTP4100

T335

RC PRE-
AMP.

REMOTE CONTROL RECEIVER
B8YE

T903
RC POWER
TRANS.

KEY BOARD B8YE

BRIGHT
-NESS

COLOUR

VOLUME

R901
27

L901
DEGAUSSING
COIL

DC

PS301

MAIN SW.

SW901A

SW901B

C301
0.1

C304
1000

D303

L301
LINE FILTER

AC240V
50Hz

F301
AC FUSE
2A

R301
220K

MAIN BOARD

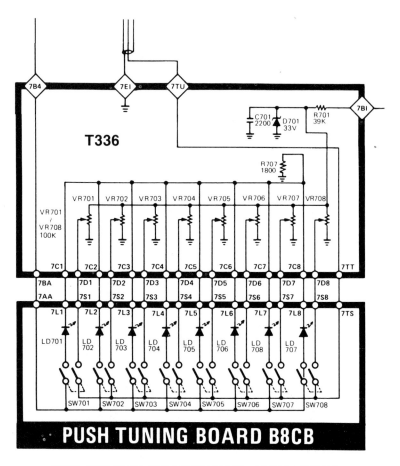

(T336) CIRCUIT DIAGRAM (PUSH-TUNE)—MODEL CTP3105

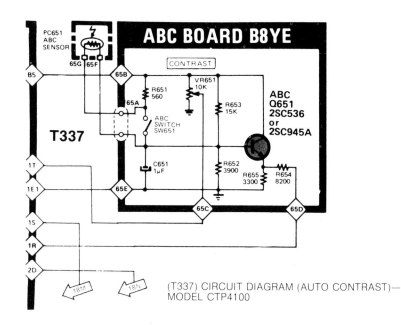

(T337) CIRCUIT DIAGRAM (AUTO CONTRAST)—
MODEL CTP4100

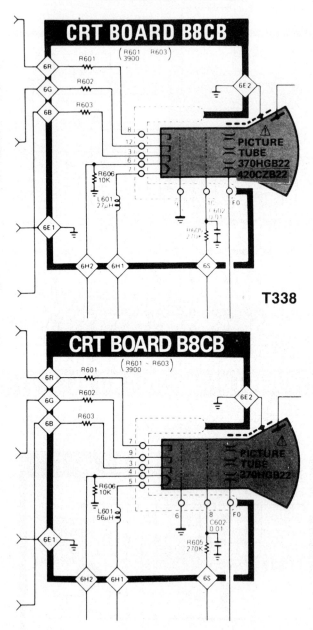

(T338) CIRCUIT DIAGRAM (C.R.T. BASES)—
TOP: MODELS CTP3105, CTP4100;
BOTTOM: MODEL CTP3104

General Description: A mains operated colour television receiver incorporating an 18-in. cathode ray tube of the self-converging type. Integrated circuits are widely used and vision band-pass characteristics are achieved by S.A.W. filter.

Mains Supply: 240 volts, 50Hz.

Loudspeaker: 8 ohms impedance.

Dismantling

Chassis Removal: Remove back cover by releasing the three retaining screws and pressing up the two plastics retainers at the top part of the cover.

Note: Easier removal can be attained by withdrawing the lower half of the back cover before raising the plastic retainers.

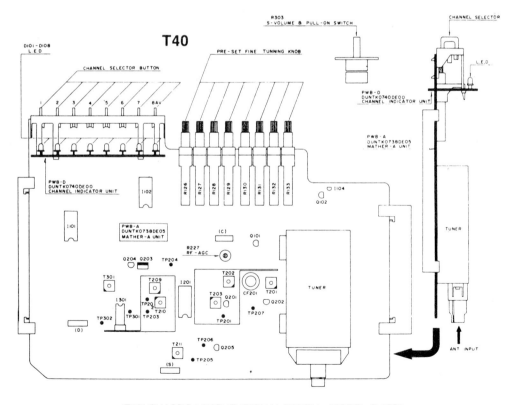

(T40) CHASSIS LAYOUT (SIGNAL PANEL)—MODEL C-1891

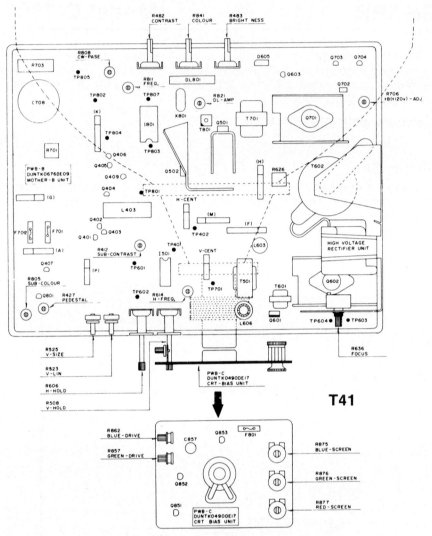

(T41) CHASSIS LAYOUT (MAIN PANEL)—MODEL C-1891

In this position the chassis can be inspected from all sides. After all plug connection on PWB-B chassis and picture tube anode cap have been disconnected the PWB-B chassis can be pulled out of the front cabinet completely. When removing the PWB-A chassis, pull out the connections on PWB-A first.

Picture Tube Assembly Removal and Replacement: Remove PWB-B chassis from cabinet.

244

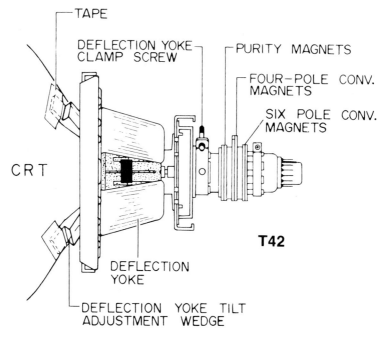

(T42) C.R.T. ASSEMBLY—MODEL T-1891

Disconnect picture tube coating earth tap from the PWB-C.

Unplug picture tube socket board (PWB-C) from tube.

Spread a blanket on the work surface to be used to prevent scratching the cabinet and carefully place cabinet face down on this protective covering.

Remove the four screws that secure the picture tube mounting tabs to the cabinet front.

Carefully grasp the picture tube assembly by its mounting tabs and lift from the cabinet front.

The picture tube must be handled with care.

Remove the picture tube ground harness assembly.

Pull out the four plastic retainers from picture tube mounting tabs.

Carefully seat the new picture tube assembly in place on the cabinet front and install all hardware in reverse sequence.

E.H.T. Check: The E.H.T. voltage is not adjustable but must be checked to verify that the receiver is operating within safe and efficient design limitations as specified:

Remove cabinet back.

Operate receiver for at least 15 minutes at 240V A.C. line, with strong air signal or test signal properly tuned in.

Set Brightness and Contrast controls to maximum position.

Connect an accurate high voltage meter to C.R.T. anode. Reading should be 23kV ± 1.5kV (at Beam 1.1mA).

If correct reading cannot be obtained, check circuitry for malfunctioning components.

Focus: Adjust the Focus control (R636), located on the rear of the T.V. chassis, for maximum over-all definition and fine picture detail with Brightness and Contrast controls set at normal viewing levels.

Vertical Size and Linearity: The Vertical Linearity control (R523) primarily affects the top of the raster while the Vertical Size control (R525) primarily affects the bottom of the raster. However, there is some interaction between these two controls. With receiver operating at 240V A.C. line, Vertical Centring properly positioned and Brightness and Contrast controls adjusted for normal picture, alternately adjust Vertical Linearity and Vertical Size controls to obtain a linear picture.

+120V Adjustment: The +120V Adj. control (706) is adjusted at the factory. However, should re-adjustment be required, proceed as follows:

Rotate the R706 (120V Adjust control) fully anti-clockwise.

Rotate the R614 (Horizontal Frequency control) fully clockwise.

Turn on the power switch.

Rotate the Horizontal control to anti-clockwise and adjust the Frequency control to attain synchronisation of picture. (Receive signal.)

Set the Brightness control (R483) and Contrast control (R482) to min.

Connect D.C. voltmeter to the test point TP701.

If, however, voltmeter indication exceeds 125V, do the same (120V adjustment) as above only after cutting off the R707.

If voltmeter indication does not reach 116V, first cut off the R705 and then make 120V adjustment.

H-Cent Tap Adjustment: Receive round pattern.

Set the Contrast control and Brightness control to 10/10 position. (H. centre tap centre.)

Adjust the H. centre adjust tap so that a pattern centre of the picture will be at the centre of C.R.T. frame (H. centre, +1.5 ± 3mm).

Grey Scale Adjustment: The purpose of this procedure is to optimise the picture tube to obtain good black and white picture at all brightness levels while at the same time achieving maximum usable brightness. Normal R.F. A.G.C. setting and purity adjustments must precede this procedure.

This adjustment is to be made only after a warm-up operation is provided for 5 minutes at least.

With antenna connected to the receiver, tune in picture on a strong channel.

Rotate the Colour control (R841) to maximum CCW position and misadjust pre-set Tuning so that the receiver will not produce a colour picture while the following adjustments are being performed.

Remove short clip of service tap.

Connect an ammeter (3mA full scale) between TP603 and TP604.

Connect the positive (+) side of the ammeter to the test point TP604.

Set the Brightness control to 10/10 position.

Check whether beam current between the test points TP603 and TP604 is within the range of 700μA to 800μA. If otherwise, correct it by using the sub-contrast control (R412).

Adjust the green Drive control (R858) and blue Drive control to white balance.

Rotate the Contrast control (R482) to darken the picture on screen and check for its background. Correct by using the Bias controls (R875), (R876) and (R877).

Beam Current Adjustment (Sub-contrast): Black and white tracking procedure must have been completed before attempting this adjustment.

Operate receiver for at least 15 minutes at 240V A.C. line and with antenna connected to the receiver, tune in picture on a strong channel.

Connect an ammeter between TP603 and TP604.

Connect the positive (+) side of the ammeter to the test point TP604.

Set the Brightness control and Contrast control to 10/10.

Adjust the Sub-contrast control (R412) to beam current of 1.1mA.

Colour Purity Adjustment: For best results, it is recommended that the purity adjustment be made in final receiver location. The receiver must have been operating 15 minutes prior to this procedure and the faceplate of the C.R.T. must be at room temperature. The receiver is equipped with an automatic degaussing circuit. However, if the C.R.T. shadow mask has become excessively magnetised, it may be necessary to degauss it with manual coil.

The following procedure is recommended while using a Dot Generator.

Check for correct location of all neck components. (See Fig. T42.)

Rough-in the static convergence at the centre of the C.R.T. as explained in the static convergence procedure.

Rotate the picture control to centre of its rotation range and rotate Brightness control to maximum clockwise position.

To obtain a blank raster, disconnect P201 from J201, on PWB-A. Then, rotate screen control clockwise until normal raster is obtained.

Rotate the red Bias and blue Bias controls to maximum anti-clockwise position. Rotate the green Bias control sufficiently in a clockwise direction to produce a green raster.

Loosen the Deflection Yoke tilt adjustment wedges (three), loosen the Deflection Yoke clamp screw and push the Deflection Yoke as close as possible to the C.R.T. screen.

Begin the following adjustment with the tabs on the round purity magnet rings set together, initially move the tabs on the round purity magnet rings to the side of the C.R.T. neck. Then, slowly separate the two tabs while at the same time rotating them to adjust for a uniform green vertical band at the centre of the C.R.T. screen.

247

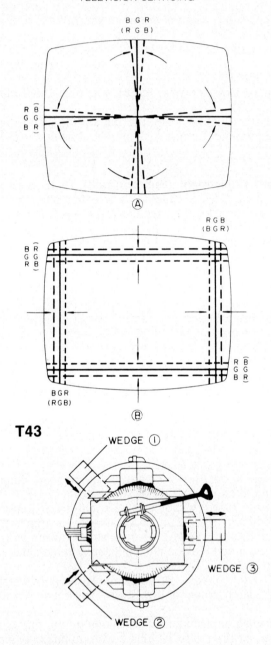

DEFLECTION YOKE REAR VIEW

(T43) CONVERGENCE ADJUSTMENTS—MODEL C-1891

Carefully slide the Deflection Yoke backward to achieve green purity (uniform green screen). Tighten the Deflection Yoke clamp screw.

Check for red and blue field purity by reducing the output of the green Bias control and alternately increasing output of red and blue Bias controls and touch up adjustments, if required.

Install P201 into J201, if disconnected previously.

Perform BLACK AND WHITE TRACKING procedure.

Static (Centre) Convergence Adjustment: Switch the Receiver ON and allow it to warm-up for 15 minutes.

Connect the output of a Cross-hatch Generator to the Receiver and, concentrating on the centre of the C.R.T. screen, proceed as follows:

Locate the pair of 4 pole magnet rings. Rotate individual rings (change spacing between tabs) to converge the vertical red and blue lines. Rotate the pair of rings (maintaining spacing between tabs) to converge the horizontal red and blue lines.

After completing red and blue centre convergence, locate the pair of 6 pole magnet rings. Rotate individual rings (change spacing between tabs) to converge the vertical red and blue (magenta) and green lines. Rotate the pair of rings (maintaining spacing between tabs) to converge the horizontal red and blue (magenta) and green lines.

Dynamic Convergence Adjustment (Fig. T43): Dynamic convergence (convergence of the three colour fields at the edges of the C.R.T. screen) is accomplished by proper insertion and positioning of three rubber wedges between the edge of the deflection yoke and the funnel of the C.R.T.

Switch receiver ON and allow it to warm-up for 15 minutes.

Apply cross-hatch pattern from Dot/Bar Generator to receiver. Observe spacing between lines around edges of C.R.T. screen.

Tilt the Deflection Yoke up and down, and insert tilt adjustment wedges 1 and 2 between the Deflection Yoke and the C.R.T. until the mis-convergence illustrated in Fig. T43 A has been corrected.

Tilt the Deflection Yoke right and left, and insert tilt adjustment wedge 3 between the Deflection Yoke and the C.R.T. until the mis-convergence illustrated in Fig. T43 B has been corrected.

Alternately change spacing between, and depth of insertion of, the three wedges until proper dynamic convergence is obtained.

Use a strong adhesive tape to firmly secure each of the three rubber wedges to the funnel of the C.R.T.

Check purity and re-adjust if necessary.

Checked Circuits
· Power Regulator Circuit
· Horizontal Deflection Circuit
· Picture Tube Bias Circuit
· Protector
· Video Circuit
· Picture Tube

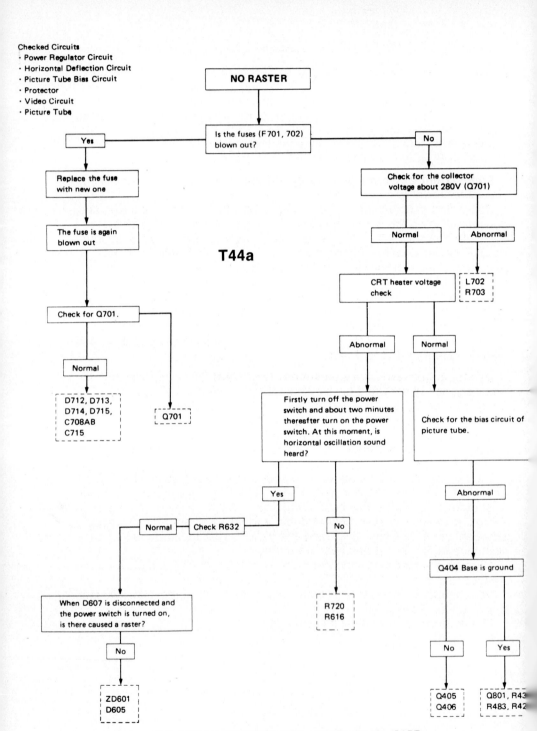

(T44a) FAULT-FINDING CHART—MODEL C-1891 *(PART)*

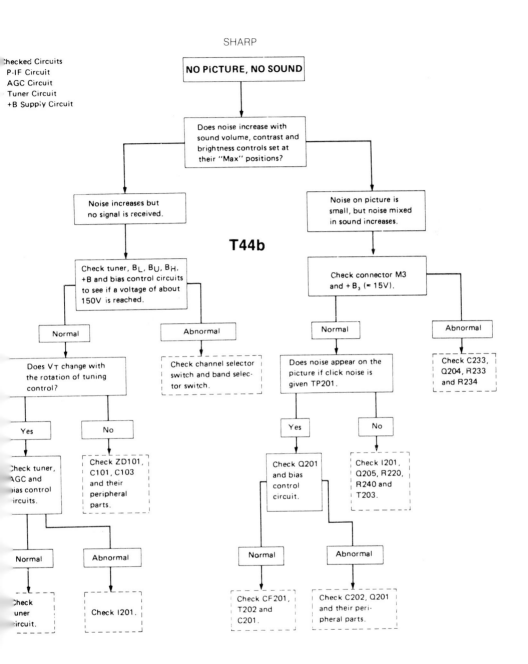

Checked Circuits
P-IF Circuit
AGC Circuit
Tuner Circuit
+B Supply Circuit

NO PICTURE, NO SOUND

Does noise increase with sound volume, contrast and brightness controls set at their "Max" positions?

Noise increases but no signal is received.

Noise on picture is small, but noise mixed in sound increases.

T44b

Check tuner, B_L, B_U, B_H, +B and bias control circuits to see if a voltage of about 150V is reached.

Check connector M3 and +B_3 (≈ 15V).

Normal

Abnormal

Normal

Abnormal

Does V_T change with the rotation of tuning control?

Check channel selector switch and band selector switch.

Does noise appear on the picture if click noise is given TP201.

Check C233, Q204, R233 and R234

Yes

No

Yes

No

Check tuner, AGC and bias control circuits.

Check ZD101, C101, C103 and their peripheral parts.

Check Q201 and bias control circuit.

Check I201, Q205, R220, R240 and T203.

Normal

Abnormal

Normal

Abnormal

Check tuner circuit.

Check I201.

Check CF201, T202 and C201.

Check C202, Q201 and their peripheral parts.

(T44b) FAULT-FINDING CHART—MODEL C-1891 *(PART)*

251

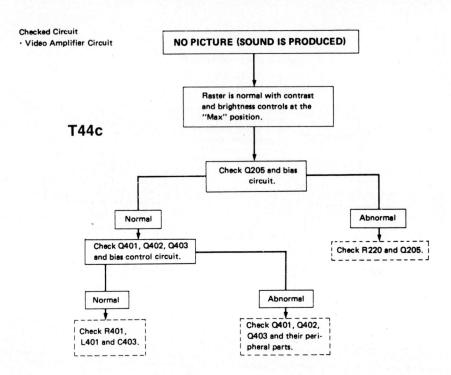

T44c

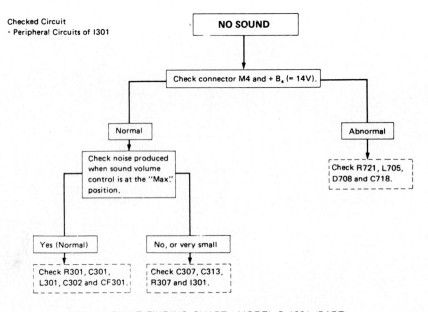

(T44c) FAULT-FINDING CHART—MODEL C-1891 *(PART)*

Checked Circuits
· I501
· Q501
· Q502

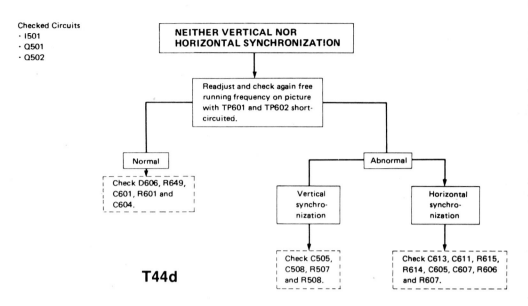

NEITHER VERTICAL NOR HORIZONTAL SYNCHRONIZATION

Readjust and check again free running frequency on picture with TP601 and TP602 short-circuited.

Normal

Check D606, R649, C601, R601 and C604.

Abnormal

Vertical synchro-nization

Check C505, C508, R507 and R508.

Horizontal synchro-nization

Check C613, C611, R615, R614, C605, C607, R606 and R607.

T44d

Checked Circuits
· I501 and its peripheral parts
· Q501 and its peripheral parts
· Q502 and its peripheral parts

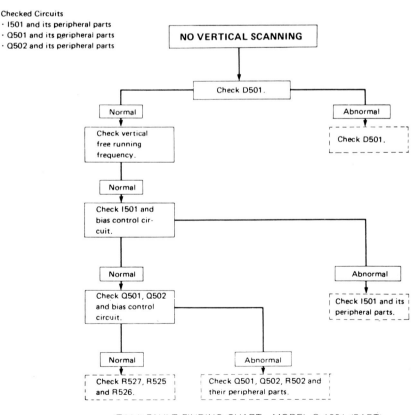

NO VERTICAL SCANNING

Check D501.

Normal

Check vertical free running frequency.

Normal

Check I501 and bias control cir-cuit.

Normal

Check Q501, Q502 and bias control circuit.

Normal

Check R527, R525 and R526.

Abnormal

Check D501.

Abnormal

Check I501 and its peripheral parts.

Abnormal

Check Q501, Q502, R502 and their peripheral parts.

(T44d) FAULT-FINDING CHART—MODEL C-1891 *(PART)*

Checked Circuit
· I501

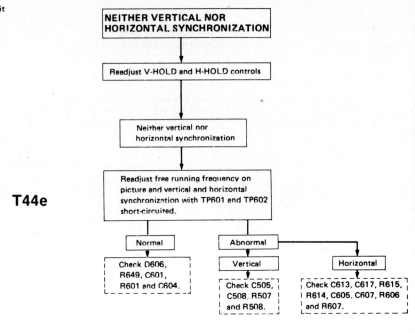

NEITHER VERTICAL NOR HORIZONTAL SYNCHRONIZATION

Readjust V-HOLD and H-HOLD controls

Neither vertical nor horizontal synchronization

T44e

Readjust free running frequency on picture and vertical and horizontal synchronization with TP601 and TP602 short-circuited.

Normal

Check D606, R649, C601, R601 and C604.

Abnormal

Vertical

Check C505, C508, R507 and R508.

Horizontal

Check C613, C617, R615, R614, C605, C607, R606 and R607.

Checked Circuits
· I501 and its peripheral parts
· Q501 and its peripheral parts
· Q502 and its peripheral parts

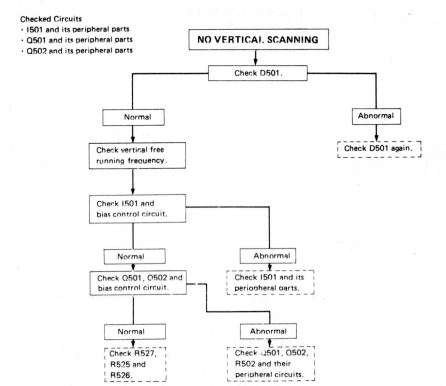

NO VERTICAL SCANNING

Check D501.

Normal

Check vertical free running frequency.

Check I501 and bias control circuit.

Abnormal

Check D501 again.

Normal

Check Q501, Q502 and bias control circuit.

Abnormal

Check I501 and its peripheral parts.

Normal

Check R527, R525 and R526.

Abnormal

Check Q501, Q502, R502 and their peripheral circuits.

(T44e) FAULT-FINDING CHART—MODEL C-1891 *(PART)*

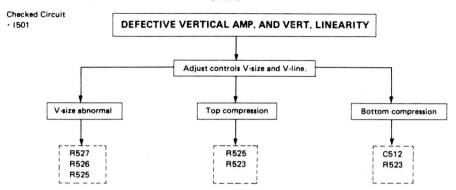

Checked Circuit
· I501

DEFECTIVE VERTICAL AMP. AND VERT. LINEARITY

Adjust controls V-size and V-line.

| V-size abnormal | Top compression | Bottom compression |

| R527 R526 R525 | R525 R523 | C512 R523 |

T44f

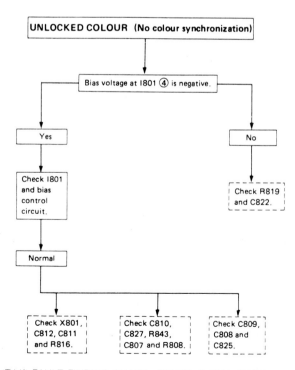

Checked Circuit
· I801

UNLOCKED COLOUR (No colour synchronization)

Bias voltage at I801 ④ is negative.

Yes — No

Check I801 and bias control circuit. — Check R819 and C822.

Normal

Check X801, C812, C811 and R816. — Check C810, C827, R843, C807 and R808. — Check C809, C808 and C825.

(T44f) FAULT-FINDING CHART—MODEL C-1891 *(PART)*

255

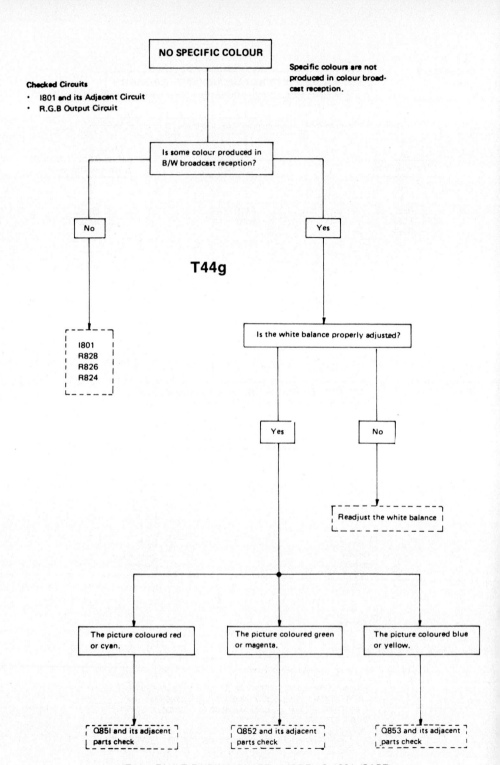

(T44g) FAULT-FINDING CHART—MODEL C-1891 *(PART)*

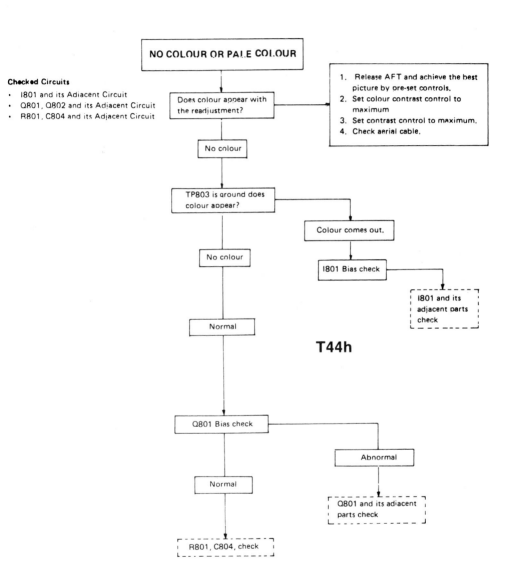

NO COLOUR OR PALE COLOUR

Checked Circuits

- I801 and its Adjacent Circuit
- Q801, Q802 and its Adjacent Circuit
- R801, C804 and its Adjacent Circuit

Does colour appear with the readjustment?

1. Release AFT and achieve the best picture by pre-set controls.
2. Set colour contrast control to maximum
3. Set contrast control to maximum.
4. Check aerial cable.

No colour

TP803 is ground does colour appear?

Colour comes out.

No colour

I801 Bias check

I801 and its adjacent parts check

Normal

T44h

Q801 Bias check

Abnormal

Normal

Q801 and its adjacent parts check

R801, C804, check

(T44h) FAULT-FINDING CHART—MODEL C-1891 *(CONTINUED)*

SHARP

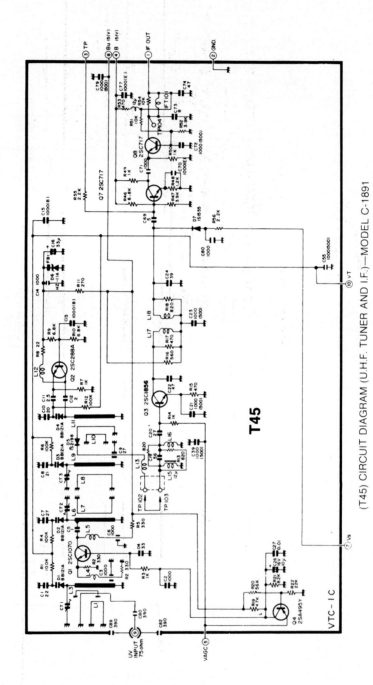

(T45) CIRCUIT DIAGRAM (U.H.F. TUNER AND I.F.)—MODEL C-1891

258

(T46) CIRCUIT DIAGRAM (VISION AND SOUND I.F.)—MODEL C-1891

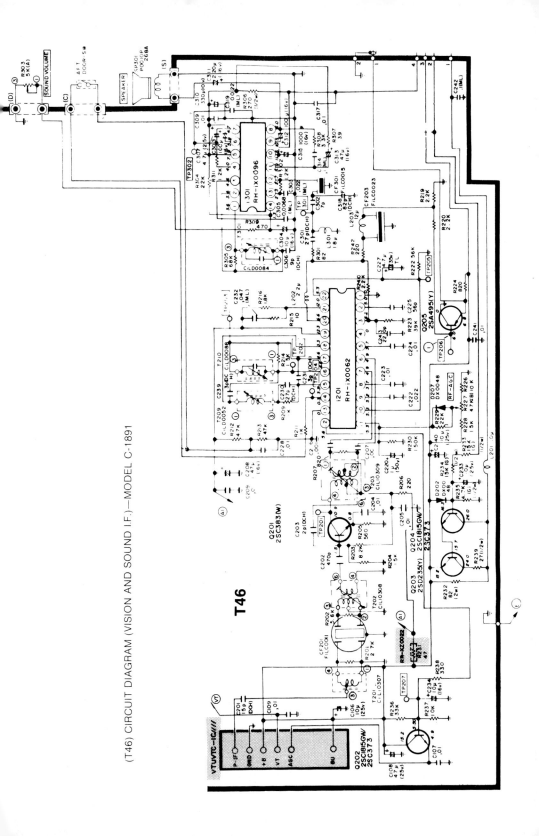

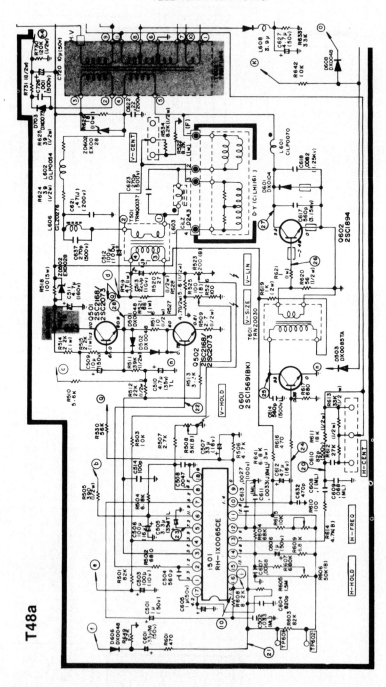

(T48a) CIRCUIT DIAGRAM (TIMEBASES)—MODEL C-1891 (PART)

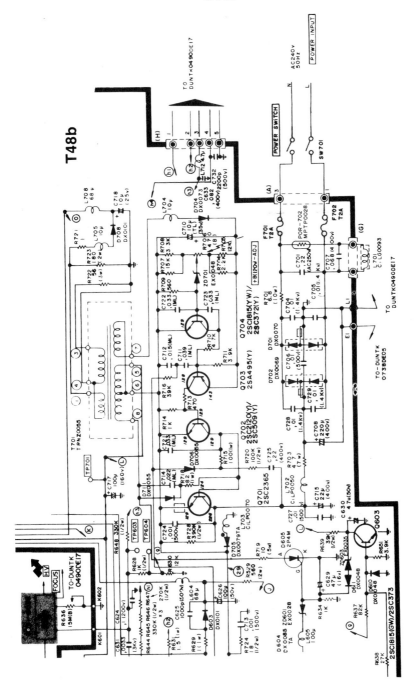

(T48b) CIRCUIT DIAGRAM (TIMEBASES)—MODEL C-1891 (CONTINUED)

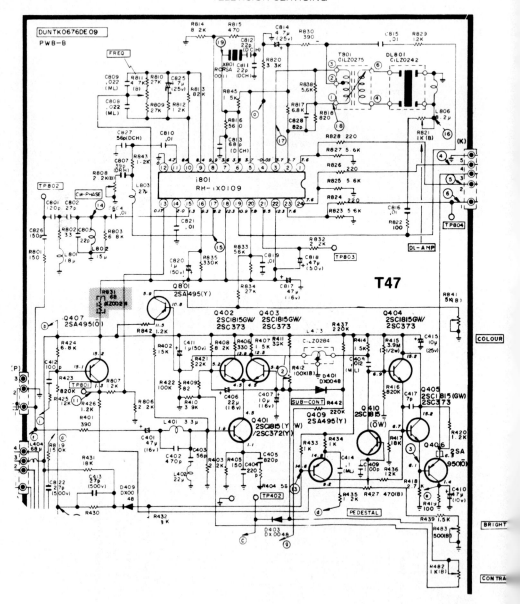

(T47) CIRCUIT DIAGRAM (DECODER)—MODEL C-1891

SHARP

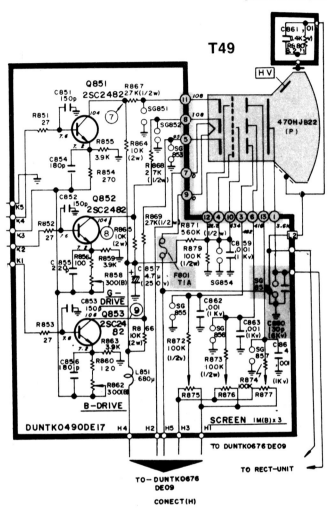

(T49) CIRCUIT DIAGRAM (R.G.B. DRIVE)—MODEL C-1891

263

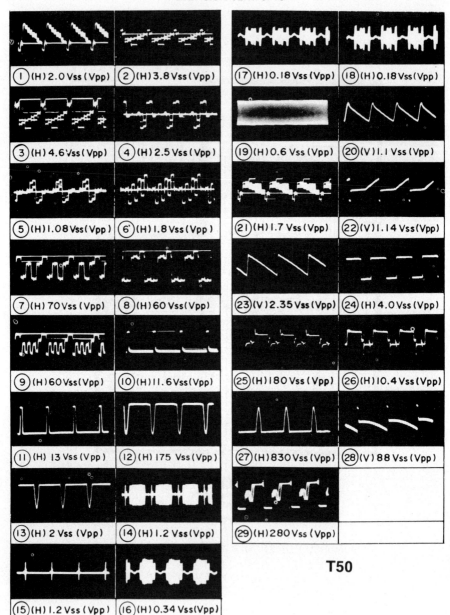

① (H) 2.0 Vss (Vpp) ② (H) 3.8 Vss (Vpp) ⑰ (H) 0.18 Vss (Vpp) ⑱ (H) 0.18 Vss (Vpp)

③ (H) 4.6 Vss (Vpp) ④ (H) 2.5 Vss (Vpp) ⑲ (H) 0.6 Vss (Vpp) ⑳ (V) 1.1 Vss (Vpp)

⑤ (H) 1.08 Vss (Vpp) ⑥ (H) 1.8 Vss (Vpp) ㉑ (H) 1.7 Vss (Vpp) ㉒ (V) 1.14 Vss (Vpp)

⑦ (H) 70 Vss (Vpp) ⑧ (H) 60 Vss (Vpp) ㉓ (V) 2.35 Vss (Vpp) ㉔ (H) 4.0 Vss (Vpp)

⑨ (H) 60 Vss (Vpp) ⑩ (H) 11.6 Vss (Vpp) ㉕ (H) 180 Vss (Vpp) ㉖ (H) 10.4 Vss (Vpp)

⑪ (H) 13 Vss (Vpp) ⑫ (H) 175 Vss (Vpp) ㉗ (H) 830 Vss (Vpp) ㉘ (V) 88 Vss (Vpp)

⑬ (H) 2 Vss (Vpp) ⑭ (H) 1.2 Vss (Vpp) ㉙ (H) 280 Vss (Vpp)

T50

⑮ (H) 1.2 Vss (Vpp) ⑯ (H) 0.34 Vss (Vpp)

(T50) CIRCUIT WAVEFORMS—MODEL C-1891

264

SHARP   Models 12P-37H, 14P-53H

General Description: Portable monochrome receivers incorporating a 12-in. or 14-in. cathode ray tube and operating from mains or battery supplies. The chassis is isolated by mains transformer and should be earthed. A socket is provided for the connection of an earphone.

Mains Supply: 240 volts, 50Hz.

Battery: 12 volts.

Fuses: 315mAT (mains); 2.5AT (battery).

Access for Service

Remove back screws and back. Pull off channel selector and tuning knob. Pull out main chassis and transformer. Remove one screw from tuner bracket. Disconnect speaker leads, C.R.T. socket and earth lead, also anode cap. Loosen deflection yoke screw and slide off the deflection coils.

Adjustments:

Set the A.C. line voltage to 240 volts and verify the D.C. output voltage is 11.5 ± 0.5 volts.

Receive a test pattern in normal operating receiver condition.

Rotate the Brightness and Contrast controls to maximum clockwise.

Adjust the H. Hold coil (L701) to synchronise the picture horizontally.

Adjust the V. Hold control (R610) to synchronise the picture vertically.

Adjust the V. Lin (R608) and V. Size (R605) controls to the best vertical linearity and pictures size.

Both horizontal and vertical are accomplished by rotating the centring ring mounted on the rear of the Deflection Yoke assembly.

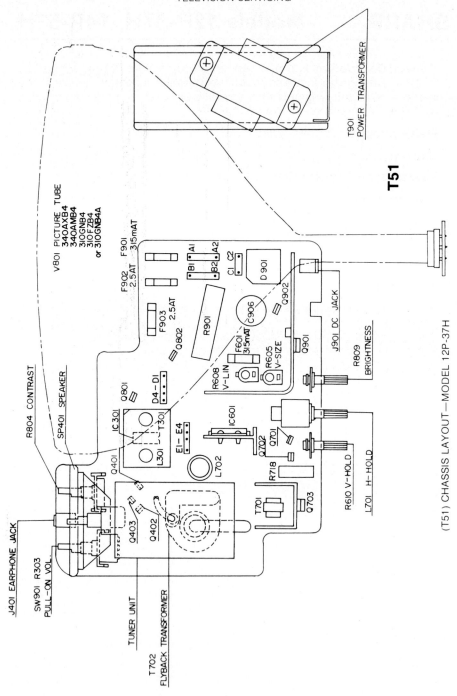

(T51) CHASSIS LAYOUT—MODEL 12P-37H

T51

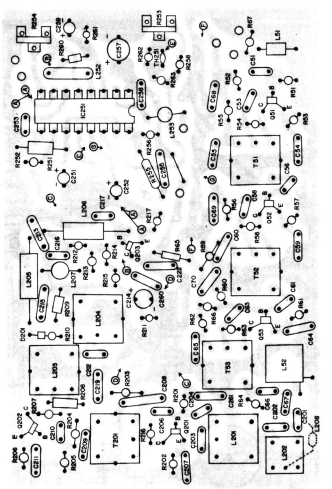

T52

(T52) COMPONENT LAYOUT (I.F. BOARD)—MODEL 12P-37H

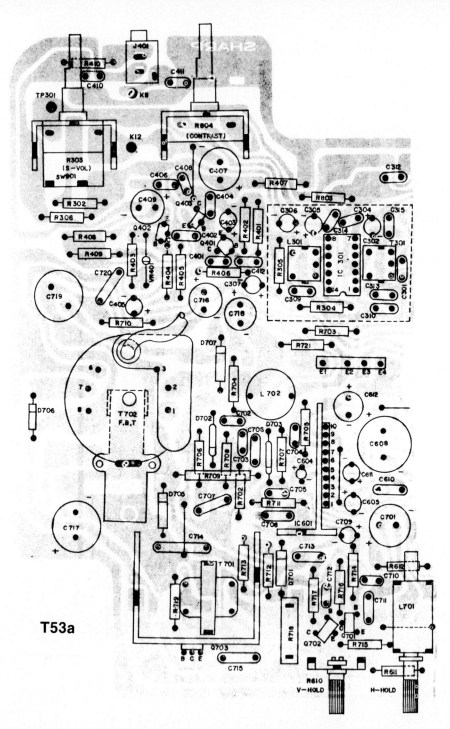

T53a

(T53a) COMPONENT LAYOUT (MAIN BOARD)—MODEL 12P-37H *(PART)*

T53b

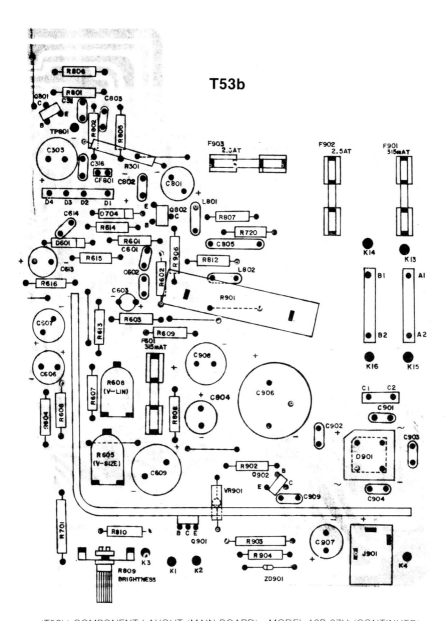

(T53b) COMPONENT LAYOUT (MAIN BOARD)—MODEL 12P-37H *(CONTINUED)*

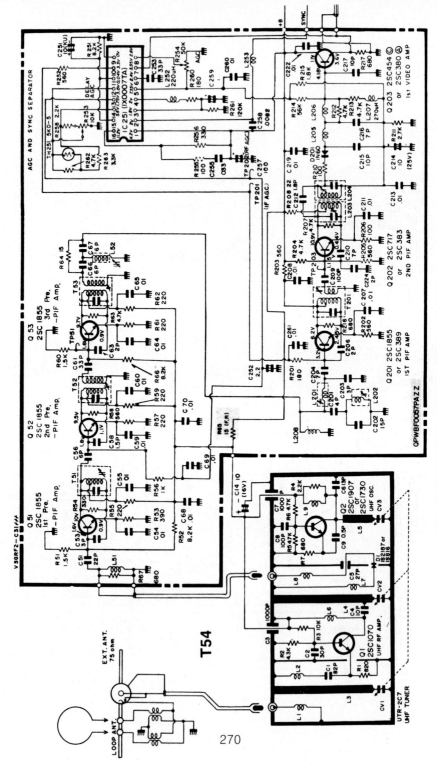

(T54) CIRCUIT DIAGRAM (SIGNAL PANEL)—MODEL 12P-37H

270

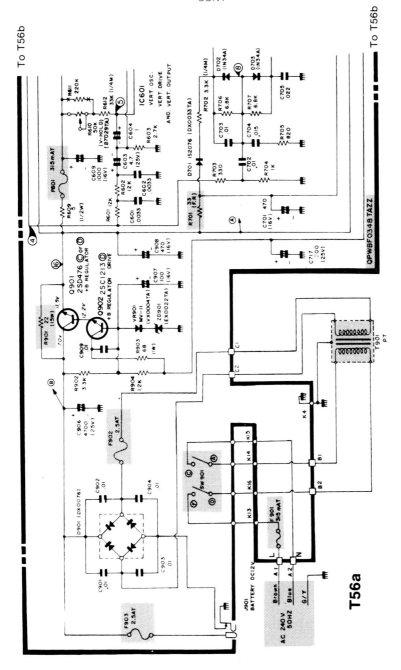

(T56a) CIRCUIT DIAGRAM (POWER SUPPLY)—MODEL 12P-37H

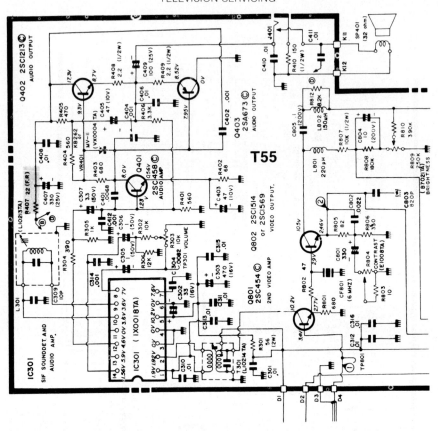

(T55) CIRCUIT DIAGRAM (VIDEO AND A.F.)—MODEL 12P-37H

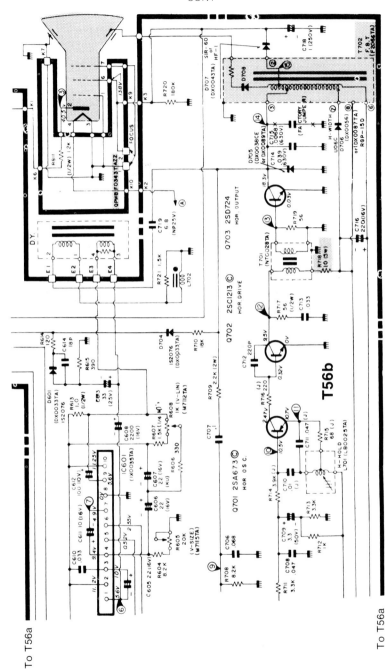

(T56b) CIRCUIT DIAGRAM (TIMEBASES)—MODEL 12P-37H (CONTINUED)

To T56a

To T56a

T56b

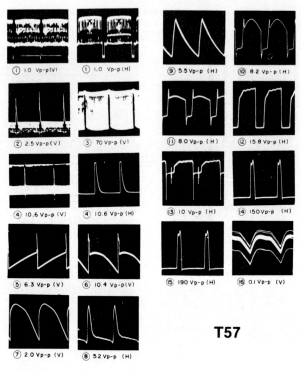

T57

(T57) CIRCUIT WAVEFORMS—MODEL 12P-37H

SONY   Model FX-414BE

General Description: A portable entertainment centre comprising a monochrome television receiver with 4-in. cathode ray tube, A.M./F.M. radio and stereo cassette-recorder. The instrument may be operated from mains or battery supplies.

Mains Supplies: 220-240 volts, 50Hz.

Batteries: 10.5 volts (7×1.5 volts) or 12 volt car battery, 18W.

E.H.T.: 6.7KV.

Radio Wavebands: L.W. 150-350kHz; M.W. 530-1605kHz; F.M. 87.5-108MHz.

Location of Circuit Board (see 286)

Dismantling

Access for service may be obtained by removing 6 screws from the base of the cabinet allowing the top and bottom section to be taken off.

Adjustments

T.V. Hold, Brightness and Contrast are accessible at the rear of the cabinet.

+25 Volt Rail: Adjust RV151 for 25.0 ± 0.2 volts at the collector of Q153.

+6 Volt Rail: Apply 12 volts D.C. to the input jack and set function switch S701 to T.V. position. Tune into a programme and set Brightness and Contrast controls to maximum. Adjust RV601 for 6.2 ± 0.05 volts at the collector of Q601.

Width: Select a value between 0.0022 and 0.0082uf for C816 which is situated on the scan coil assembly.

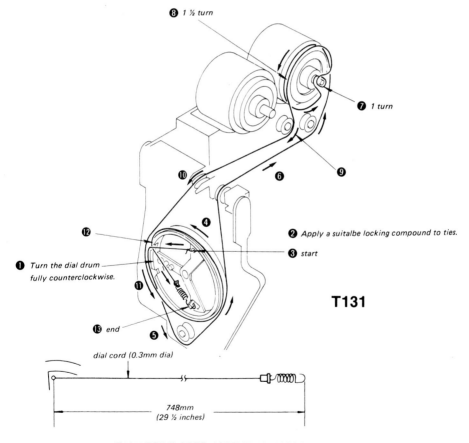

❽ 1 ½ turn

❼ 1 turn

❷ Apply a suitalbe locking compound to ties.

❸ start

❶ Turn the dial drum fully counterclockwise.

T131

⓭ end

dial cord (0.3mm dia)

748mm
(29 ½ inches)

(T131) DRIVE CORD ASSEMBLY—MODEL FX-414BE

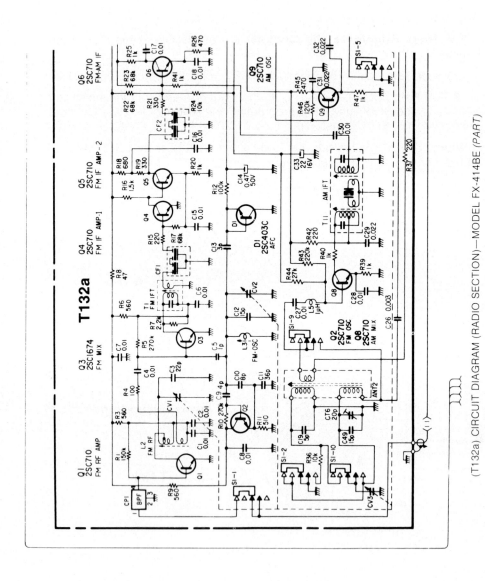

(T132a) CIRCUIT DIAGRAM (RADIO SECTION)—MODEL FX-414BE *(PART)*

SONY

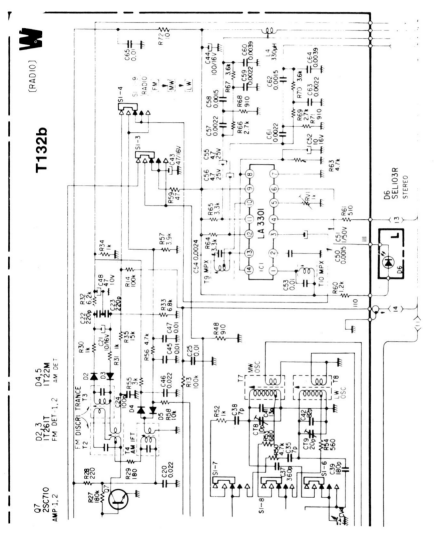

(T132b) CIRCUIT DIAGRAM (RADIO SECTION)—MODEL FX-414BE (PART)

277

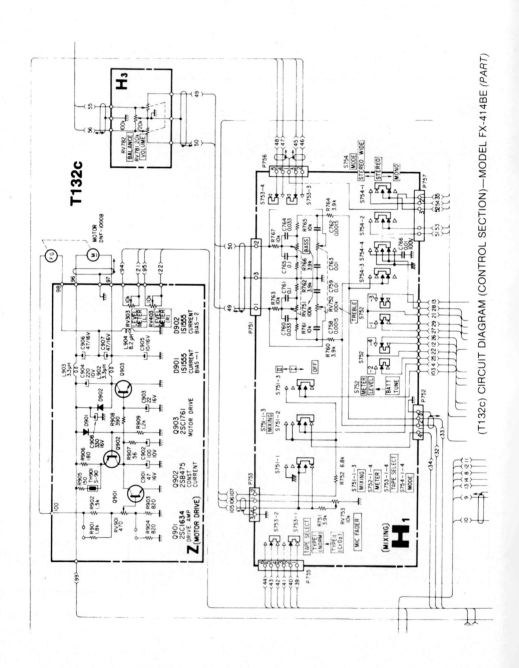

(T132c) CIRCUIT DIAGRAM (CONTROL SECTION)—MODEL FX-414BE *(PART)*

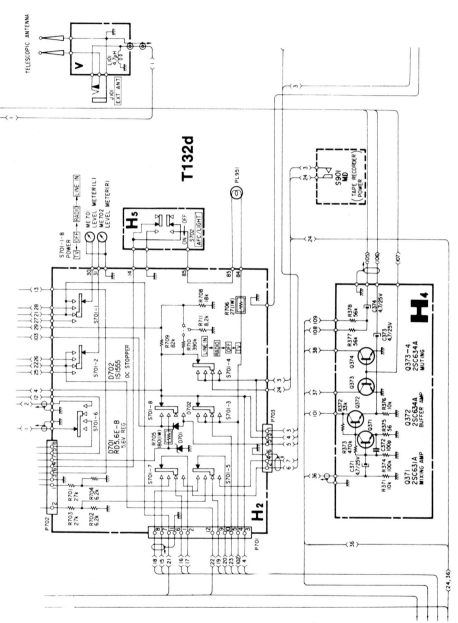

(T132d) CIRCUIT DIAGRAM (CONTROL SECTION)—MODEL FX-414BE (PART)

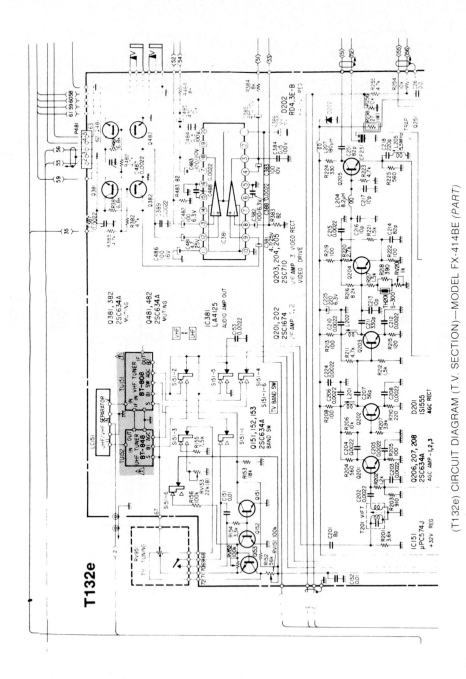

(T132e) CIRCUIT DIAGRAM (T.V. SECTION)—MODEL FX-414BE (PART)

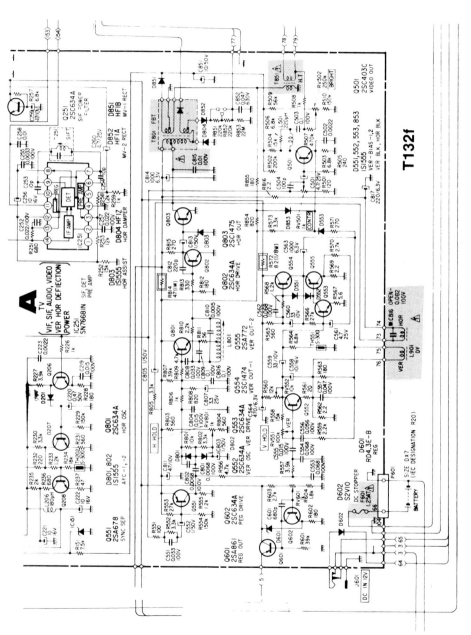

(T132f) CIRCUIT DIAGRAM (T.V. SECTION)—MODEL FX-414BE (PART)

T132f

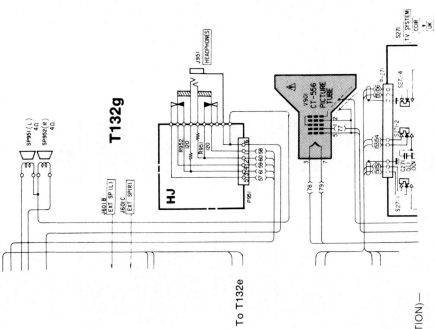

(T132g) CIRCUIT DIAGRAM (T.V. SECTION)—
MODEL FX-414BE (PART)

SONY

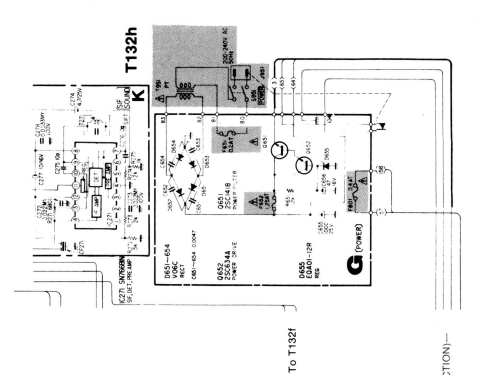

To T132f

(T132h) CIRCUIT DIAGRAM (T.V. SECTION)—
MODEL FX-414BE (PART)

283

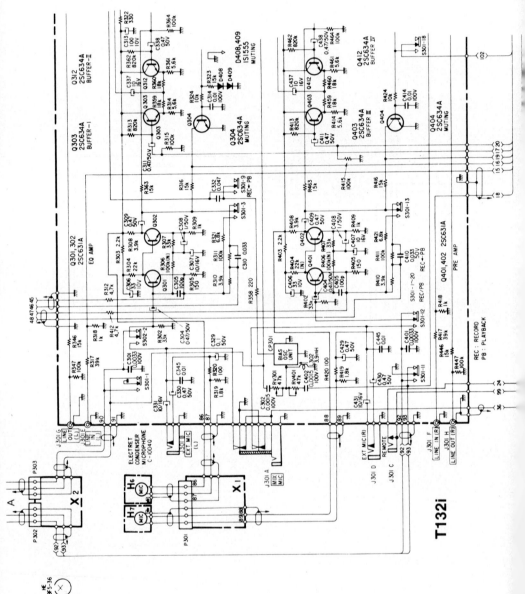

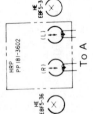

T132i

284

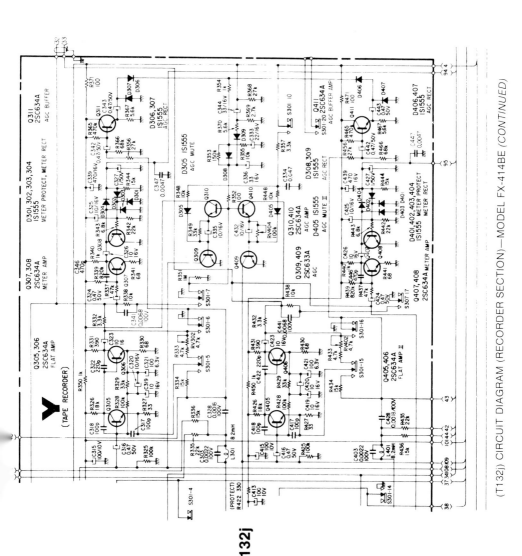

(T132j) CIRCUIT DIAGRAM (RECORDER SECTION)—MODEL FX-414BE (CONTINUED)

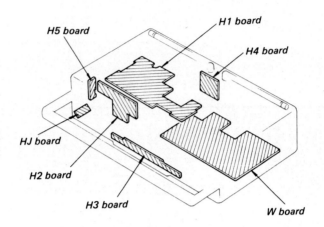

T140

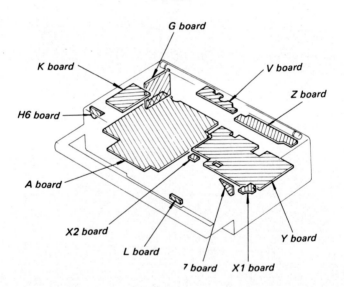

(T140) LOCATION OF CIRCUIT BOARDS—MODEL FX-414BE

286

SONY Models KV-1612, KV-2020, KV-2022

General Description: A series of mains operated colour television receivers containing basically similar chassis and offering the options of manual or remote control. Model KV-1612 is a 16-in. portable version, Models KV-2020 and KV-2022 incorporate a 20-in. cathode ray tube. The circuit given here is for the KV-1612 version which will serve as a guide for the other models.

Mains Supplies: 200-240 volts, 50Hz.

E.H.T.: 23KV (KV-1612); 23.7KV (KV-2020, KV-2022).

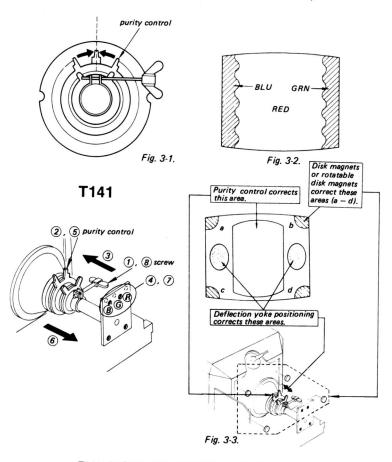

Fig. 3-1.

Fig. 3-2.

Fig. 3-3.

(T141) PURITY ADJUSTMENTS—MODELS KV-1612 ETC.

287

Adjustments

Beam Landing—Purity (Fig. T141): Feed in the white pattern and degauss the entire screen.

1. Loosen Deflection Yoke screw.
2. Adjust Purity control as shown in Fig. T141 (3-1).
3. Slide Deflection Yoke as far forward as it will go.
4. Disconnect leads G and B on the C board.
5. Adjust Purity control to centre vertical red band as shown in Fig. T141 (3-2).
6. Slide Deflection Yoke back for a uniform red screen.
7. Check green and blue rasters for uniformity by performing the same way as steps 4, 5 and 6.

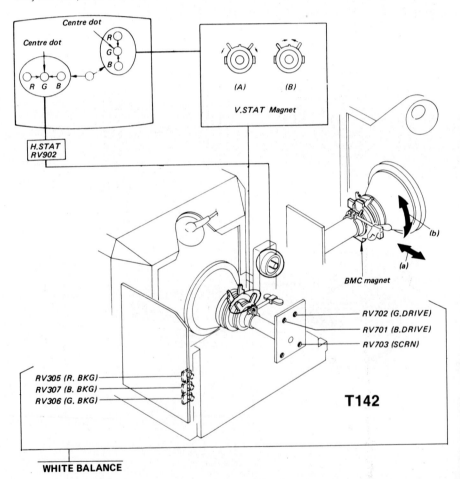

(T142) STATIC CONVERGENCE ADJUSTMENTS—MODELS KV-1612 ETC.

To get a uniform green screen, connect lead G on the C board and disconnect leads R and B.

To get a uniform blue screen, connect lead B on the C board and disconnect leads R and G.

After these checks, connect the leads R, G and B.

8. Tighten the Deflection Yoke screw.

9. Check if mislanding appears at corners a-d as shown in Fig. T141 (3-3). If mislanding is observed, correct it as shown in Fig. T141 (3-3).

10. Confirm that beam landing is correct when the receiver is faced in all directions.

Static Convergence (Fig. T142): Before starting, perform Focus, H. Size, V. Size and V. Lin adjustments.

Set Brightness control fully anti-clockwise.

If blue dot does not coincide with red and green dots, perform following steps.

Move B.M.C. magnet (a) to correct insufficient H. static convergence.

Rotate B.M.C. magnet (b) to correct insufficient V. static convergence.

In either case, repeat Beam Landing Adjustment.

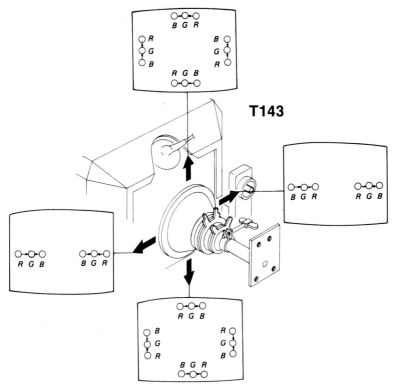

(T143) DYNAMIC CONVERGENCE ADJUSTMENTS—MODELS KV-1612 ETC.

Grey Scale (Fig. T142): Feed in the cross-hatch pattern.

Press picture-button to obtain the minimum picture, and set Brightness control to fully anti-clockwise.

Turn RV701 (B. Drive) and RV702 (G. Drive) fully clockwise.

Set RV305 (R.BKG), RV306 (G.BKG), and RV307 (B.BKG) to mechanical centre.

Turn RV703 (SCRN) slowly to obtain a faintly visible cross-hatch. Note the colour that first becomes visible by turning RV703. Do not turn a BKG control for this colour.

Adjust the other two BKG controls for best white balance (neutral grey) of the faint cross-hatch.

Turn Brightness control fully clockwise and press picture + button to maximum picture position. Observe the screen and adjust the Drive controls for best white balance.

Dynamic Convergence Adjustment (Fig. T143): Before starting, perform Horizontal and Vertical Static Convergence adjustment.

Loosen Deflection Yoke screw.

Remove Deflection Yoke spacers.

Move the Deflection Yoke for best convergence as shown below.

Tighten the Deflection Yoke screw.

Install the Deflection Yoke spacers.

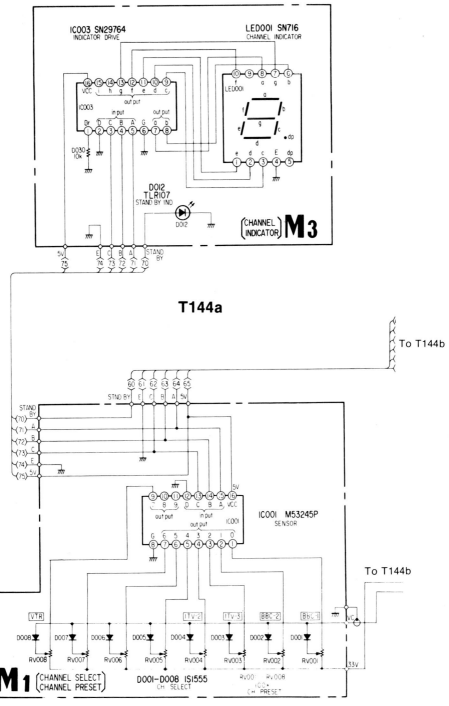

(T144a) CIRCUIT DIAGRAM—MODELS KV-1612 ETC. (PART)

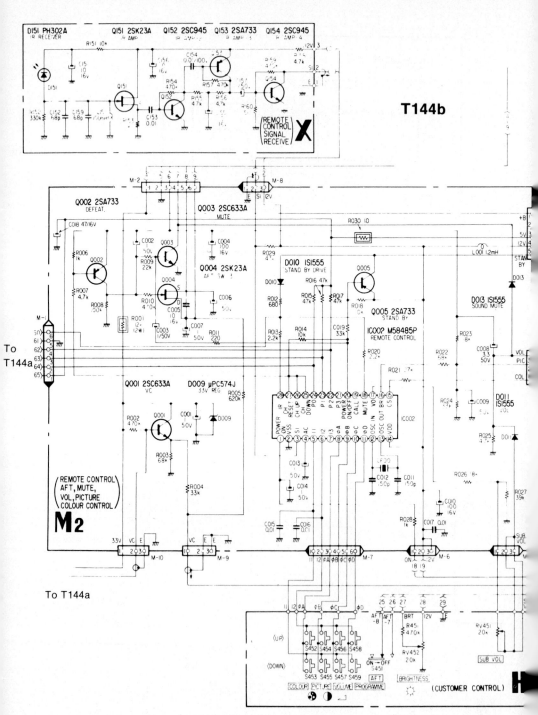

(T144b) CIRCUIT DIAGRAM—MODELS KV-1612 ETC. *(PART)*

SONY

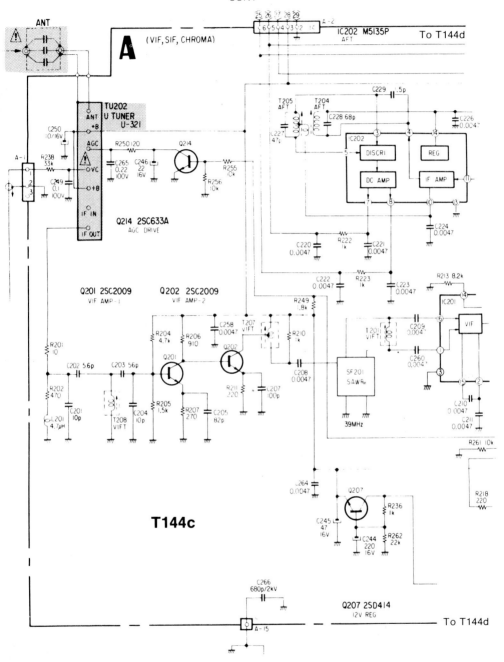

T144c

(T144c) CIRCUIT DIAGRAM—MODELS KV-1612 ETC. *(PART)*

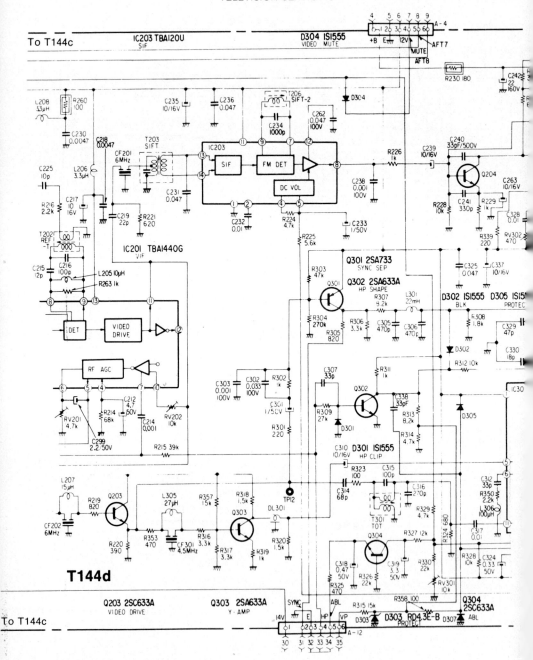

T144d

(T144d) CIRCUIT DIAGRAM—MODELS KV-1612 ETC. *(PART)*

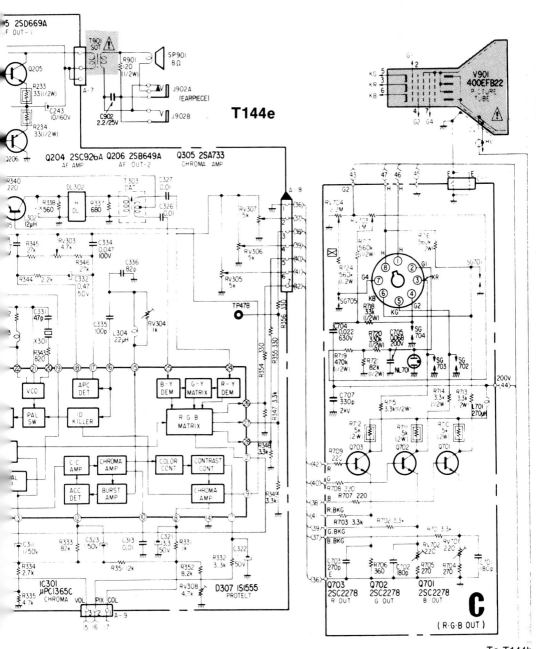

T144e

(T144e) CIRCUIT DIAGRAM—MODELS KV-1612 ETC. *(PART)* (see also 299)

To T144h

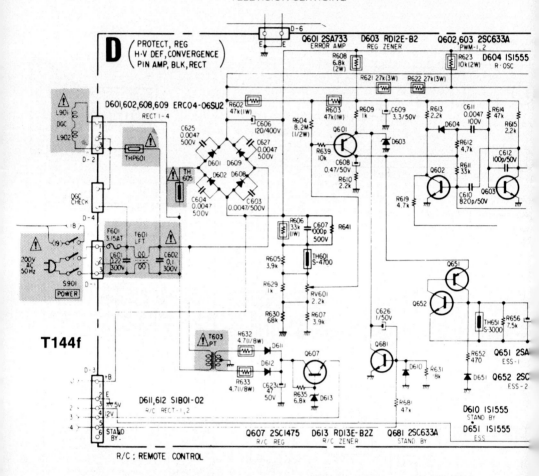

T144f

(T144f) CIRCUIT DIAGRAM—MODELS KV-1612 ETC. *(PART)*

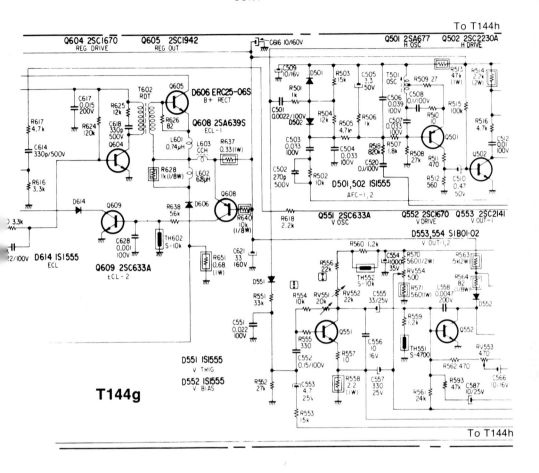

(T144g) CIRCUIT DIAGRAM—MODELS KV-1612 ETC. *(PART)*

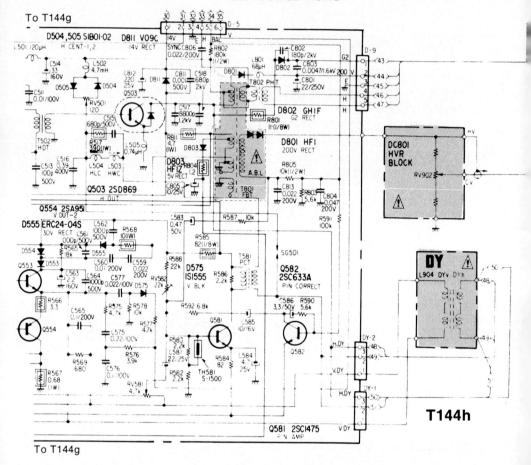

(T144h) CIRCUIT DIAGRAM—MODELS KV-1612 ETC. *(CONTINUED)*

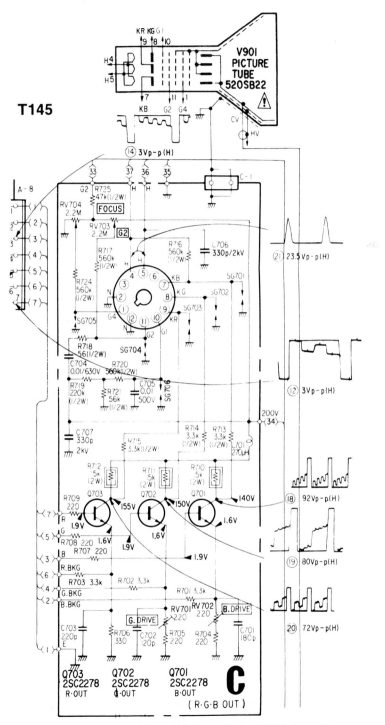

T145

(T145) CIRCUIT DIAGRAM (C.R.T. PANEL)—MODEL KV-2022

SONY   Model KV-2204

General Description: A mains operated colour television receiver incorporating a 22-in. cathode ray tube with functions operated by remote control. The signal circuits are similar to those employed in Model KV-1612 described previously and to which reference should be made. Power Supply and Timebases differ to allow the use of a larger screen area and the circuits for these sections are given here together with modified convergence procedures.

Mains Supplies: 200-240 volts, 50Hz.

E.H.T.: 24.5KV.

Loudspeaker: 8 ohms impedance.

Adjustments

Purity and Static Convergence procedures are similar to those outlined for Model KV-1612.

Dynamic Convergence (Fig. T146): (Misconvergence at Both Sides of Screen).
Set RV509 and RV510 to mechanical centre.
Adjust H. Stat control so that green and blue dots coincide at centre of screen.
Adjust RV510 so that X1 is equal to X3.
Adjust RV509 so that X2 is equal to X3.

Side Pincushion: Adjust RV504 and RV511 to obtain vertical lines.

Top and Bottom Pincushions: Adjust L508 to obtain horizontal cross-hatch lines.

SONY

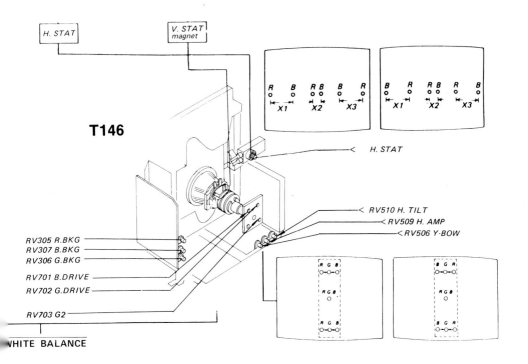

T146

WHITE BALANCE

(T146) CONVERGENCE ADJUSTMENTS—MODEL KV-2204

T147a

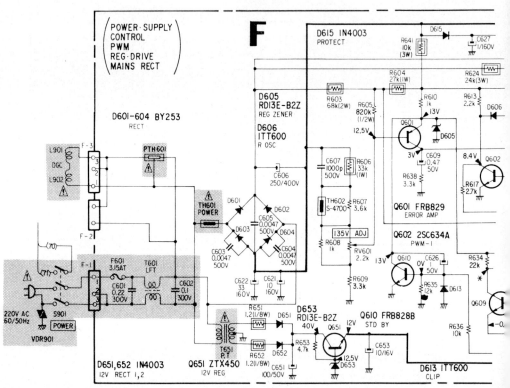

(T147a) CIRCUIT DIAGRAM (POWER SUPPLY)—MODEL KV-2204 *(PART)*

T147b

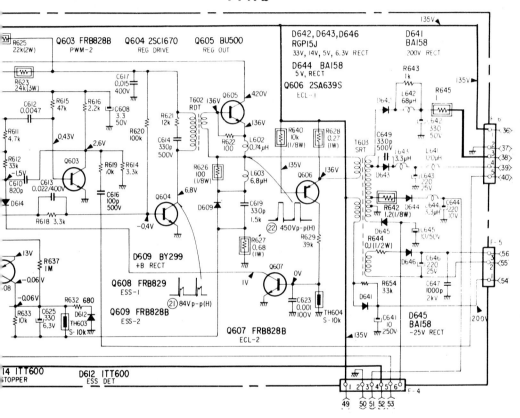

(T147b) CIRCUIT DIAGRAM (POWER SUPPLY)—MODEL KV-2204 *(CONTINUED)*

T148a

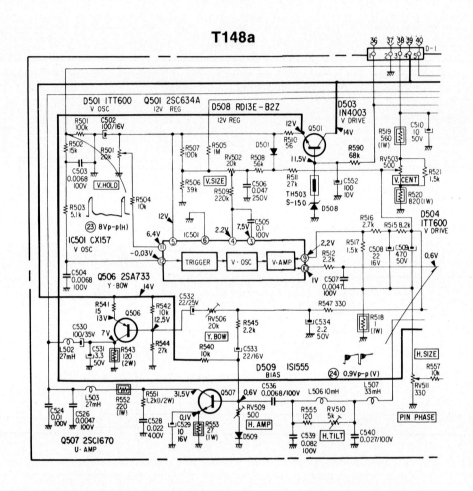

(T148a) CIRCUIT DIAGRAM (FIELD TIMEBASE)—MODEL KV-2204 *(PART)*

SONY

T148b

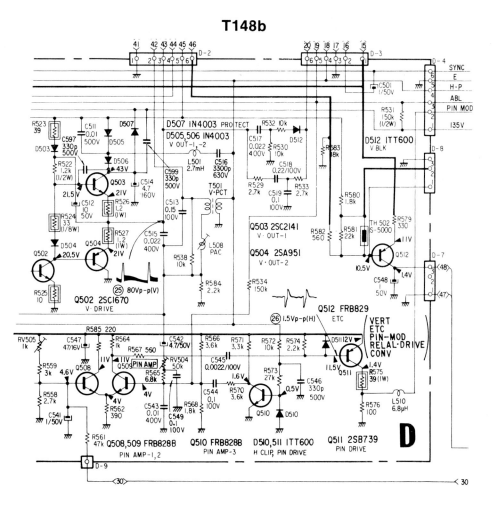

(T148b) CIRCUIT DIAGRAM (FIELD TIMEBASE)—MODEL KV-2204 (CONTINUED)

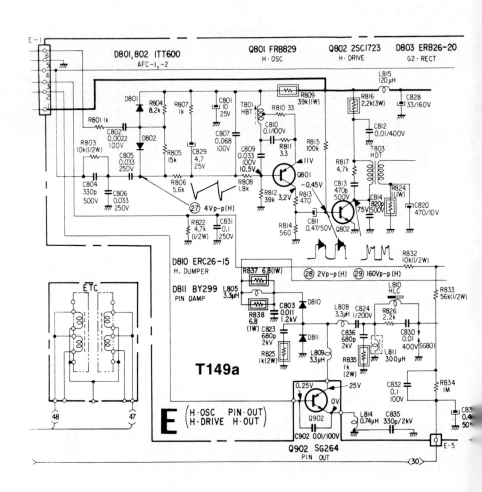

(T149a) CIRCUIT DIAGRAM (LINE TIMEBASE)—MODEL KV-2204 *(PART)*

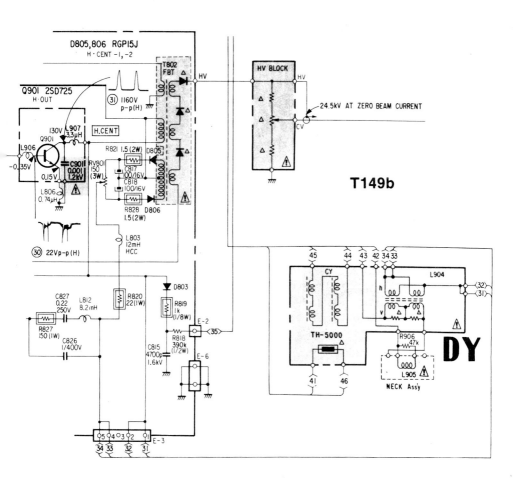

(T149b) CIRCUIT DIAGRAM (LINE TIMEBASE)—MODEL KV-2204 *(CONTINUED)*

General Description: A portable monochrome television receiver incorporating a 12-in. cathode ray tube and operating from mains or battery supplies. The chassis is isolated by mains transformer and a socket is provided for the connection of an earphone.

Mains Supply: 240 volts, 50Hz.

Battery: 12 volts, 14W.

Cathode Ray Tube: 310GBN4A.

E.H.T.: 11KV.

Loudspeaker: 8 ohms impedance.

Access for Service

The rear cover may be removed after taking 4 screws out of the back and 2 screws from the aerial socket which should be fed through the aperture.

Adjustments

H.T.: Set RV601 to obtain 11.6 ± 0.2 volts at the emitter of Q601.

Line Hold: T501.

Width: Select a suitable value between 0.0022 and 0.0082uf.

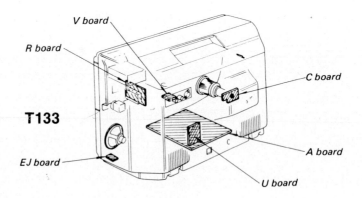

(T133) CIRCUIT BOARDS LOCATION—MODEL TV-122UK

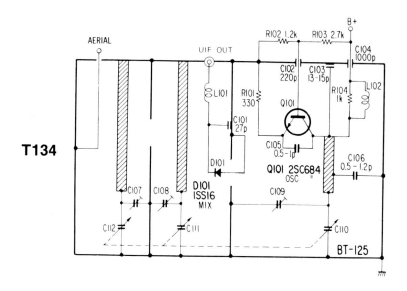

T134

(T134) CIRCUIT DIAGRAM (U.H.F. TUNER)--MODEL TV-122UK

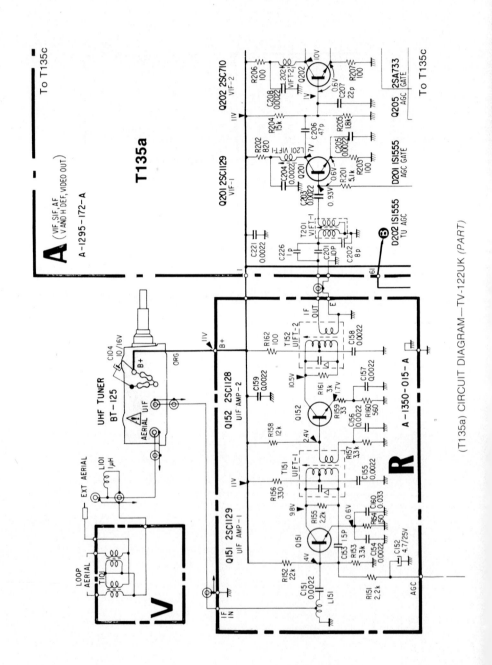

(T135a) CIRCUIT DIAGRAM—TV-122UK *(PART)*

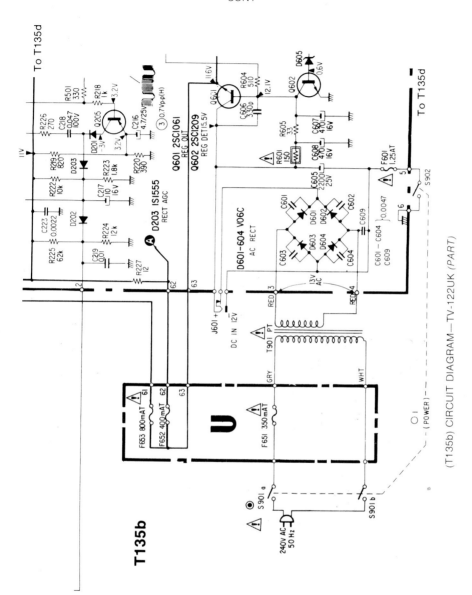

(T135b) CIRCUIT DIAGRAM—TV-122UK *(PART)*

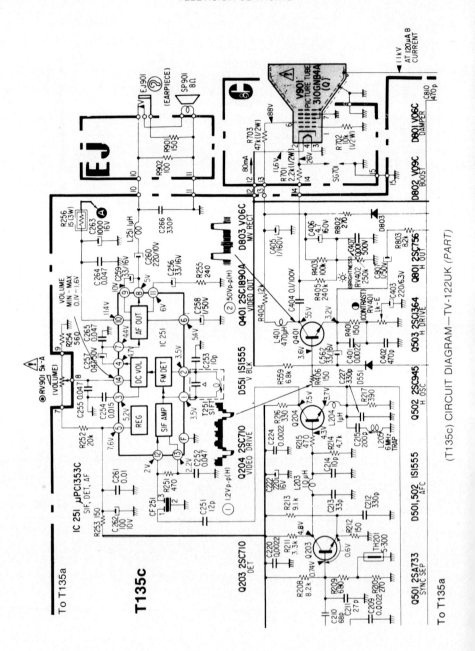

(T135c) CIRCUIT DIAGRAM—TV-122UK (PART)

SONY

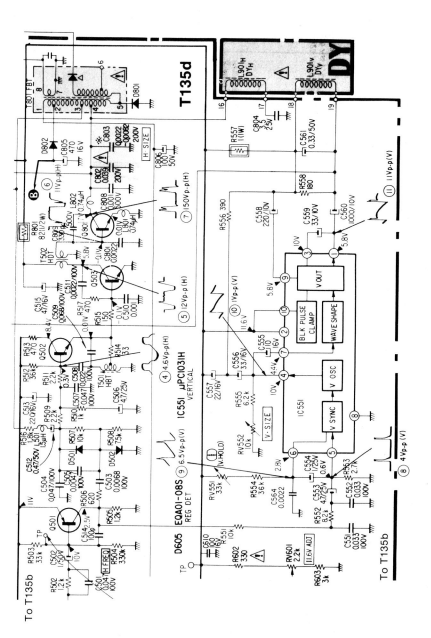

(T135d) CIRCUIT DIAGRAM—TV-122UK (CONTINUED)

313

General Description: A mains operated monochrome television receiver for international distribution and adjustable in the I.F. stages for local transmission standards. Integrated circuits are used in Detector, and Sound Stages.

Mains Supply: 220 volts, 50Hz.

Cathode Ray Tube: A50-120W/R (20-in.); A61-120W/R (24-in.).

E.H.T.: 18KV.

Loudspeaker: 35 ohms impedance.

Fuses: The mains rectifier is protected by a 1A Timelag fuse (F1) at the input side and by a fusible resistor link (R110) at the output side. Fusible resistor links are also employed in the audio output and line driver D.C. supplies (R74 and R142). The links may be renewed with ordinary solder (60/40) after eliminating any overload condition.

Adjustments

Horizontal Hold (L19): Normally this pre-set should not require adjustment on installation but if the need for adjustment arises proceed as follows:

Connect a 1μF non-polarised capacitor between TP6 and chassis. Adjust L19 for a floating but resolved picture. On removal of the capacitor the picture should lock.

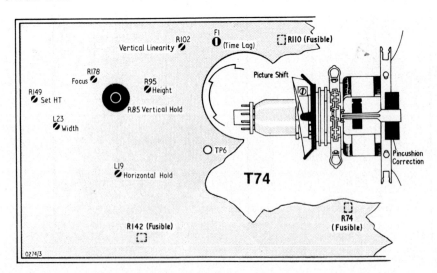

(T74) LOCATION OF ADJUSTMENTS—1715 SERIES CHASSIS

After adjustment, check for correct setting by interrupting the signal, i.e. withdraw the aerial connector or select another channel.

Horizontal Linearity: Component tolerances are chosen to ensure correct linearity without an adjustable element.

Vertical Hold (R85): Where more than one channel is available, make the adjustment on the channel with the weakest signal. The adjustment is externally accessible.

Vertical Linearity (R102): Adjust in conjunction with the Height control (R95) for a correctly proportioned picture.

Picture Shift: The picture can be moved in any direction by rotating both the control rings together around the tube neck. The position of the rings relative to one another alters the extent of the picture movement.

Set HT (R149): Normally this pre-set should not require adjustment on installation. If necessary check as follows: With a mains input of exactly 220V A.C. turn Brightness, Volume and Contrast controls to minimum settings and connect a 20,000Ω/volt meter (250V D.C. range) between junction R158-C130 and cathode of W34 with the negative lead to W34 cathode. If necessary, adjust R149 for a reading of 140V.

Picture Size (L23 and R95): Unless it is known that the picture size pre-sets have been disturbed it is advisable to check S.E.T. H.T. (R149) before re-adjustment. Height R95 and Width L23 should be adjusted for the correct aspect ratio whilst viewing a picture on a low brightness setting.

Pincushion Correction Magnets: The magnets are mounted on flexible arms on the deflection unit. To remove curvature from the sides of the picture, the positions of the magnets can be altered by bending the arms.

Focus (R178): Adjust whilst observing a test card for best overall focus.

Circuit Alignment (Fig. T75)

Note: The I.F. Carrier Regeneration and Sound Intercarrier frequencies referred to during the circuit alignment procedure vary according to which country the receiver is intended for. The first figure given in each case is for the Irish model suffix 'E' followed by both the General European model suffix 'V' and the Semi-tropical model suffix 'M' figure given in brackets.

The receiver should not normally require re-alignment after transistor substitution or general servicing. Unless a tuneable coil assembly is replaced or it is definitely known that alignment settings have been disturbed, all other possible causes of poor response or low gain should be checked before attempting to re-align the circuits.

Equipment Required:

1. An A.M./F.M. signal generator of 75Ω output impedance capable of

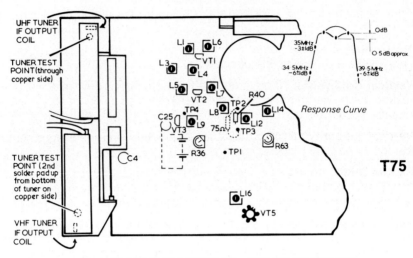

(T75) ALIGNMENT ADJUSTMENTS—1715 SERIES CHASSIS

providing 5.5MHz and 6MHz in addition to the vision I.F. and trap frequencies and having an output greater than 200mV terminated.

2. A wobbulator providing a 30-45MHz sweep and preferably incorporating a display unit, or alternatively, a separate oscilloscope may be used for display purposes.

3. An oscilloscope capable of resolving 6MHz.

4. A general-purpose meter, minimum sensitivity 20,000Ω/volt.

5. A bias source such as a bias battery.

Rejectors:

(a). Connect the terminated signal generator (set for minimum output) to the V.H.F. tuner test point (the second solder pad up from the bottom of P.C.B.).

(b). Connect the D.C. bias source across C25 with positive to positive side of C25. The bias voltage should be 2.5V. If it is necessary to decrease the gain of the I.F. strip this voltage may be increased to a maximum of 3.5V.

(c). Connect the oscilloscope or meter positive to TP1 with negative to chassis. Connect a 75Ω damping resistor across R40.

(d). Select Band 3 (channels 5-12) on one of the pre-set tuning potentiometers mounted on the front control panel and tune so that there is no 'off air' signal present. Select the frequency required on the signal generator, and increase the output until the voltage on TP1 falls from approximately 6V to 5.5V.

Tune each coil for a maximum voltage, increasing the input as necessary to keep the output at approximately 5.5V: L5, 31.5MHz (31.9MHz); L3, 41.5MHz (40.4MHz); L1, 33.5MHz (33.4MHz); L8, 44.4MHz (44.4MHz).

Note: If the input to the tuner is too high the I.C. (IC1) will 'invert' causing the output to jump from approximately +3V to approximately +7V.

I.F. Passband: Wobbulator alignment is simplified by making preliminary spot frequency adjustments as follows:

With conditions as for rejector alignment, connect the signal generator via a 0.5pF capacitor to the V.H.F. tuner test point.

Set signal generator to 37MHz (36.5MHz) and adjust L4 for minimum voltage at TP1.

Transfer the signal generator connection to VT1 base (connect on copper side of panel via 1000pF capacitor).

With the input adjusted to give approximately 5V at TP1, adjust L6 for minimum voltage at 36MHz (35.5MHz).

Transfer the generator (with the same termination) to VT2 base and adjust L7 for minimum voltage at 38MHz (37.5MHz).

Transfer generator to VT3 base and adjust L9 for minimum voltage at 37MHz (36.5MHz).

Disconnect generator.

Select V.H.F. Band III. Connect a wobbulator (terminated 75Ω) to the V.H.F. tuner test point via a 0.5pF capacitor, and a display unit to TP1. Apply a 3.5V bias across C25. Initially, adjust L4 for a correct response curve shape as shown, this may be the only adjustment required. If further adjustment is necessary, adjust L6, L7 and V.H.F. tuner I.F. output coil for optimum response. Select U.H.F. and transfer the wobbulator to the U.H.F. tuner test point via 0.5pF capacitor. Adjust U.H.F. tuner I.F. output coil for optimum response. If the tilt on the response curve shape is excessive L4 may be re-adjusted to distribute the tilt between V.H.F. and U.H.F. either side of the ideal response curve shape. Remove all test connections including the 75Ω resistor across R40.

Carrier Regeneration Filter (L12): Connect the terminated signal generator via 1000pF capacitor to TP4 (signal input level approximately 1-2mV).

Short-circuit C25 and connect the oscilloscope or meter to TP1.

Tune L12 for minimum voltage at TP1 with generator at 39.5MHz (38.9MHz). Remove all test connections.

6MHz (5.5MHz) Intercarrier Rejector (L14): Short-circuit C25. Inject a high level 6MHz (5.5MHz) unmodulated carrier via a 0.47μF capacitor into TP1. Connect the oscilloscope to the C.R.T. cathode (pin 7) and tune L14 for minimum 6MHz (5.5MHz) display.

6MHz (5.5MHz) Intercarrier Coil (L16): With test connections as for L14 adjustment, transfer oscilloscope to loudspeaker terminals. Switch generator to 24kHz deviation. Adjusting the Volume control as necessary, tune L16 for maximum audio output.

Remove all test connections.

Video D.C. Level Adjustment (R63): Carefully tune the receiver to a test card signal.

Turn Contrast to maximum and Brightness to minimum.

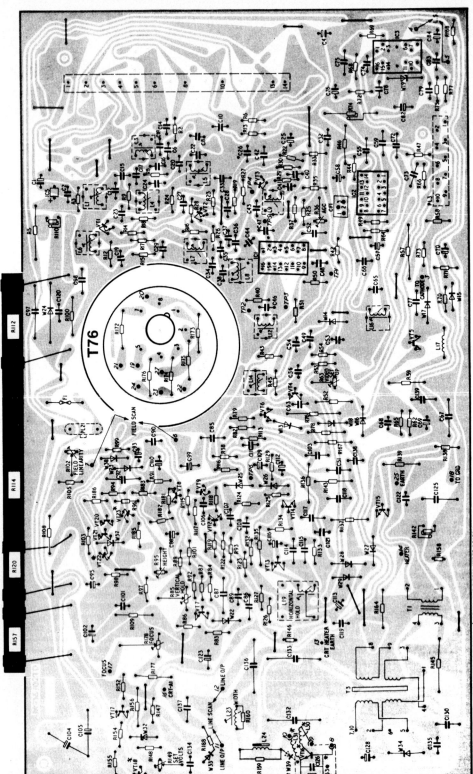

(T76) COMPONENT LAYOUT —1715 SERIES CHASSIS (PART)

* FITTED ON HEAT SINK   † COMPONENT FITTED UNDER BOARD

Modifications

The following modifications have been introduced during the course of production.

Reference	Early Chassis	Later Chassis	Remarks
C66	4k7pF	0.01	Reduces 6MHz radiation causing audio instability.
R112			
R114 } Mains Dropper	06E5-043-001	06E5-043-002	To prevent movement during transit. The dropper mountings have also changed.
R120			
R157			
R158	56R	33R	To improve audio response at low mains input.
VT9	BC237-5	BC237	
VT13	BC149	BC148B	
VT15	BF259	T6037V	
VT18	TIP31	T6028V	
VT21	BC327	BC327-5	
VT22	BD222	T6038V	
VT23	BD225	T6039V	
DIODES	1S44	F425	
W13	1S44	1S923	
W24	BY127	BY133GP	
W33	BA159	RGP10M (T6013W)	
LOPT	06D3-059-001	06D3-065-001	
Deflection unit	06D2-019 or 06D2-020	06D2-052-001 }	To produce more width and better use of width control.
R164	3.3R	5.6R	
C132 and C133	5k6pF	4k7pF	
R51	—	100	
C48	—	68pF }	To correct Band 1 instability.
C121	—	220pF	
W39	—	BY208-1200	
L30	—	90D0-063-001 }	To overcome line radiation (striations).
L31	—	90D0-063-001	
IC1	TCA270SQ	TCA270SB	

Connect the oscilloscope to VT5 collector. Adjust R63 to set the black level of the video waveform at 130V D.C.

Alternatively, using a 20,000 /voltmeter instead of the oscilloscope, adjust R63 for a reading of 110V on the collector.

A.G.C. Crossover (R36): Tune the receiver carefully to a strong clean 'off air' Channel 2-4 (Band 1) signal. Rotate the A.G.C. potentiometer (R36) fully clockwise, viewed from the copper side of the printed board. Using a continuously variable attenuator reduce the signal strength until noise just appears on the picture. Connect a 20,000Ω/V meter, set to a suitable range (10V range) across C4, with negative to chassis, to give a standing reading of 2.5V to 3.5V approximately. Adjust R36 for a fractional increase of 0.1V to 0.2V above the meter reading.

Circuit Diagram Notes

Voltages: Figures in rectangles are D.C. voltage measurements. They were taken on a mains input of 240V A.C. using a 20,000Ω/voltmeter (electrostatic meter for E.H.T.) with all controls set for normal operation; timebase circuits on a locked picture; signal circuits (except audio) with no signal input.

The figures may be considered as average and variations of 10% to 20% do not necessarily indicate fault conditions.

The D.C. resistance of inductors is shown where these exceed 1Ω. Ringed figures indicate printed board connecting points.

The I.F. Coils, Carrier Regeneration coil and Intercarrier coil frequencies quoted on the circuit diagram vary according to which country the receiver is intended for. The first figure given in each case is for the Irish model suffix 'E', followed by both the General European model suffix 'V' and the semi-tropical model suffix 'M' figure given in brackets.

Circuit Description

Both the 20-inch and 24-inch receivers are designed to operate from 220V A.C. mains supply, and employ basically the same chassis apart from a few component differences associated with tube size and presentation. The 20-inch model has a combined On-Off Volume control whereas the 24-inch model has a separate On-Off switch and a third slider control for Volume. Both models have a rear mounted Vertical Hold control. The chassis includes a main printed circuit panel assembly and a smaller printed circuit board which contains the U.H.F. and V.H.F. tuners. The main printed circuit panel and the tuner panel are hinged to allow easy access for servicing.

General: Two H.T. rails provide the power for the receiver circuits. Both the U.H.F. and V.H.F. tuners are A.G.C. controlled with an I.C. Voltage Stabiliser supplying the tuning diodes. The three stage I.F. Amplifier feeds an I.C. synchronous detector which also provides video amplification, A.G.C. amplification and noise inversion. The first two stages of the I.F. Amp are A.G.C. controlled. A ceramic filter is used to tune the input circuit of a high gain I.C. which processes the audio I.F. A D.C. operated Volume control is employed. An audio amp I.C. feeds a 35 ohm loudspeaker. Both timebases use silicon transistors throughout and are stabilised to compensate for mains supply fluctuations. The line timebase employs a balanced flywheel circuit including a sinewave oscillator and a reactance control. The field timebase contains six transistors with a class B output.

Power Supplies: Two D.C. supply rails at 185V (HT1) and 30V (HT2) are used to power the receiver circuits. The 185V rail supplies the line driver and line output stages, video and Brilliance control. All other supplies are derived from a stabilised 30V rail which is obtained via a shunt regulator from the emitter current of the line output stage. Voltage for the shunt regulator is supplied via diode W34 which, during the line scan period, rectifies a pulse derived from a winding on the line output transformer. Start-up current is achieved by ensuring that at switch-on VT15 is turned ON by pull-up resistor R138. With current through VT15, 11V is established across W28 which ensures start-up of the sinewave oscillator. High voltages for the C.R.T. are obtained by rectified line flyback pulses using a silicon diode high voltage rectifier and a vacuum impregnated line output transformer.

Safety Circuits: Fuse F1 or fusible resistor R110 will open if the 185V (HT1) rail goes short circuit or a short circuit occurs in the line stage. Fusible resistor R142 will open if VT15 goes short circuit. R109 will open if a short occurs in the field output stage. R164 opens if the C.R.T. heaters short, similarly R74 is designed to open should a short occur within its associated circuit.

R.F. and I.F. Circuits: The U.H.F. and V.H.F. tuners are mounted on a common printed circuit panel. Tuning is by means of six fascia mounted Band and Channel selector switches S400a to S400f and associated tuning potentiometers R421 to R426. To ensure stable tuning an integrated circuit voltage stabiliser IC5 is used to supply the tuning diodes. The tuners are A.G.C. controlled with the feedback taken from pin 4 of IC1. The three stage VT1-VT3 tuned I.F. strip has a bandpass coupled L4, R9, input. The input circuit also has a 'block filter' arrangement L1, L3, L5 which provides trapping of adjacent channel sound and vision signals and own channel sound. The first two stages VT1 and VT2 of the I.F. strip are forward A.G.C. controlled, the feedback being taken from pin 5 of IC1 and applied to the collector of VT1. The line gated fast action A.G.C. minimises the effects of aircraft interference. The I.F. signal is then taken from VT3 to the integrated circuit low level synchronous detector IC1 which provides video amplification, the A.G.C. detector and noise inversion.

Video: The positive going composite video signal is taken from pin 9 of IC1 passed via a 'Bridge T' intercarrier sound rejector, L14, and applied to the base of the video driver VT4. The signal is then fed from the emitter of VT4 to the Contrast Control R56, the wiper of which is connected to the base of the video output transistor VT5. The video signal is negative going at the collector of VT5 for application to the cathode of the C.R.T. The video amplifier VT4 and VT5 stages from the video detector output to the C.R.T. cathode are entirely D.C. coupled. Set video level R63 sets the correct bias level for VT5. Beam current limiting is effected by W17, R73 and protects the C.R.T. system and E.H.T. rectifier from being over run in the event of 'no signal' input. During the period of flyback the blanking transistor VT6 and its associated isolation diode W18 effect a positive pulse on the emitter of VT5 thus biasing it off. VT5 collector volts then rise so raising the volts on the C.R.T. cathode very positive and blanking the tube.

Sound: The intercarrier sound signal is obtained via a low value capacitor from across L14. The signal then passes through a ceramic filter CF1, which provides the main selectivity, to pin 14 of IC2 (intercarrier amp). IC2 provides eight stages of amplification and limiting as well as demodulating the signal by the balanced coincidence detector. After being demodulated the audio signal passes through an internal variable gain pre-amp. The Volume control R48 operates by changing the D.C. conditions of this stage. The audio signal is then taken from pin 8 of IC2 and applied to the pre-amp section of IC3 (audio output) which then feeds an internal driver and class B (audio) power output stage.

Field Timebase: The timebase uses silicon transistors throughout which are stabilised to compensate for mains supply fluctuations. There are six transistors VT7, VT8, VT20 to VT23, in the circuit with a class B output stage for low power consumption. Sync. pulses from the Sync. separator, VT9 are integrated by R93, C89 and coupled by C86 to the field oscillator VT7, VT8, via isolating diode W22. The field oscillator is self oscillating, an astable multivibrator, and provides a pulse for the initiation of flyback. During the scan period C92 charges up to produce a ramp waveform at the base of VT20. Because C92 only charges to a small proportion of its maximum a very linear ramp is produced. The ramp waveform is then fed into a three stage amplifier, the output of which drives a current ramp through the scan coils. During flyback the voltage at the base of VT20 is reduced which switches VT21, VT22 OFF and VT23 ON. This grounds the output and C99 discharges to chassis causing a rapid reversal of current in the scan coils. Scan begins again when this process has finished.

Sync. Separator, Phase Splitter and Flywheel Discriminator: Negative going video is taken from the collector of VT4, the video driver, and is fed to the sync. separator VT9 which is a low feedback capacitance transistor. The sync. separator is of the partly self biased, partly fixed biased type. It is slightly forward biased by R115 with the mean level bias being set by C103, R115/R116 time constant. On weak signals the self bias level drops and weaker signals still bottom the transistor on sync. tips. R113, C111 improve the 'rag' performance of the set under weak signal conditions, by integrating out H.F. spikes. The separated sync. is then fed to the field oscillator and via R118, C106 to the phase splitter, VT12. In order that the receiver's line oscillator is kept 'in-step' with the incoming line sync. pulses, a phase splitter, flywheel discriminator and reactance stage is employed.

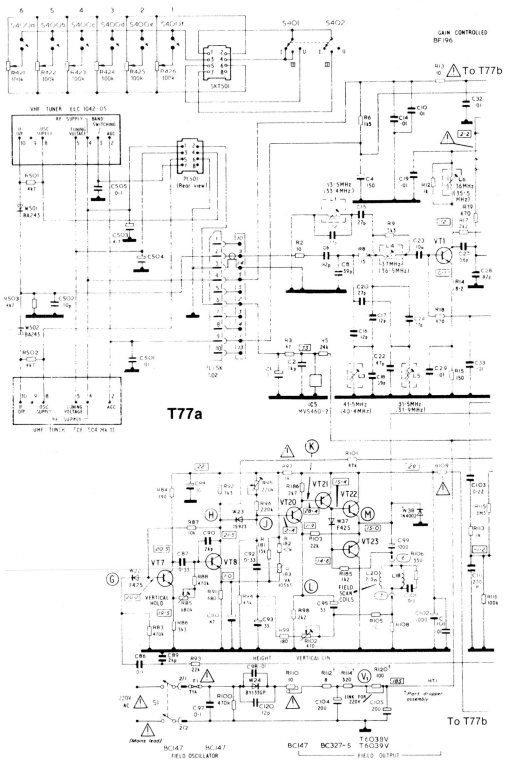

(T77a) CIRCUIT DIAGRAM—1715 SERIES CHASSIS *(PART)*

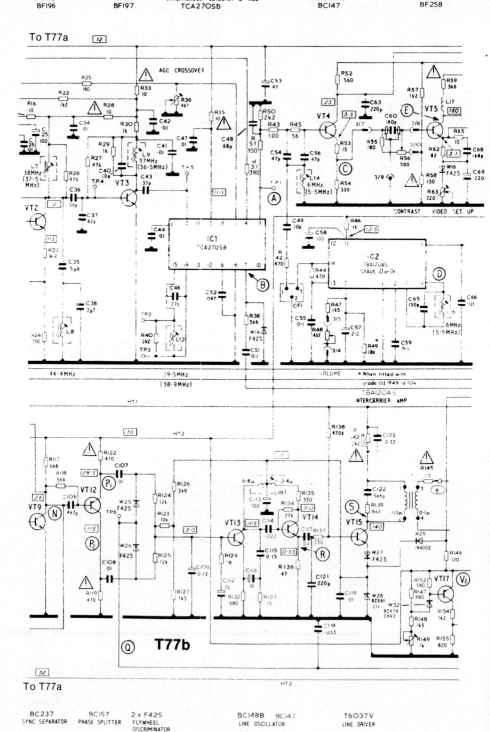

T77b

To T77a

To T77a

(T77b) CIRCUIT DIAGRAM—1715 SERIES CHASSIS *(PART)*

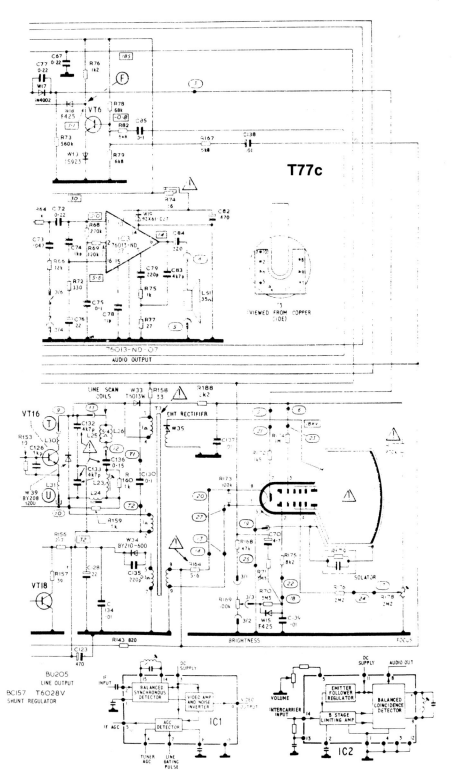

(T77c) CIRCUIT DIAGRAM—1715 SERIES CHASSIS *(CONTINUED)*

TOSHIBA   Model B1201

General Description: A portable monochrome receiver incorporating a 12-in. cathode ray tube and operating from mains or battery supplies. An integrated circuit is used for sound I.F. processing and a mains transformer isolates the chassis to allow the connection of an earphone. The chassis must be earthed.

Mains Supplies: 240-250 volts, 50Hz.

Battery: 12-17 volts, 16W.

Cathode Ray Tube: 310EUB4.

Power Supply Cord

The three core supply cord connected to the receiver is for use on A.C. mains only. The two core supply cord provided with the set is for D.C. 12-17V use.
If incorrect cord is used, damage will occur to the receiver.
The receiver is automatically switched from A.C. mains operation to D.C. battery operation by inserting the D.C. supply plug.
The D.C. plug should not be inserted into the D.C. supply socket during A.C. operation.
The A.C. mains cord should not be plugged in during D.C. operation.

Access for Service

The rear cover may be withdrawn after taking out the 6 screws which retain it in position.

Adjustments

Width: L402 may be shorted if necessary to increase width.

Height: Set the Height control R315 to mid-position.
Adjust the Vertical Linearity control R316 to obtain the best linearity.
Adjust the Height control to obtain correct picture height.

Horizontal Frequency: If there is an indication of unstable horizontal sync. adjust the Horizontal Hold coil (T401) so that the setting is in the centre of the pull-in range of the coil.

Det. Bias: Make the 'no signal' operating condition by applying +5V D.C. bias to terminal TP-14 (or remove +B lead of U.H.F. tuner) before adjustment. Adjust Det. Bias control (R110) so that the reading on V.T.V.M. is +4 volt D.C. between TP-12 and chassis ground.
Note: After adjustment of Det. Bias, it is necessary to adjust A.G.C.

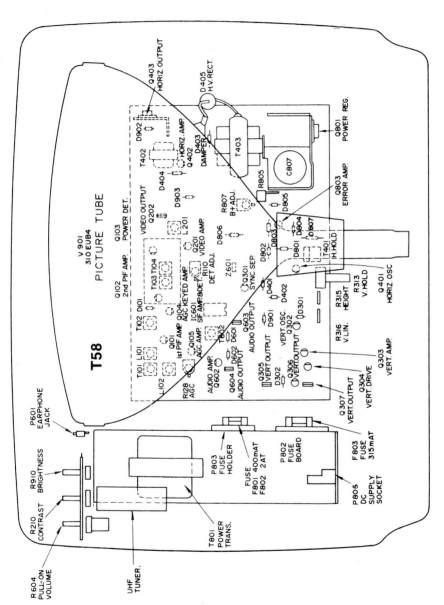

(T58) CHASSIS LAYOUT—MODEL B1201

A.G.C.: Set channel selector to the strongest station and turn contrast control about midway. Adjust A.G.C. control (R128) in the clockwise direction until the noise disappears from the picture. If buzz is heard, turn the A.G.C. control in the opposite direction until no buzz is present.

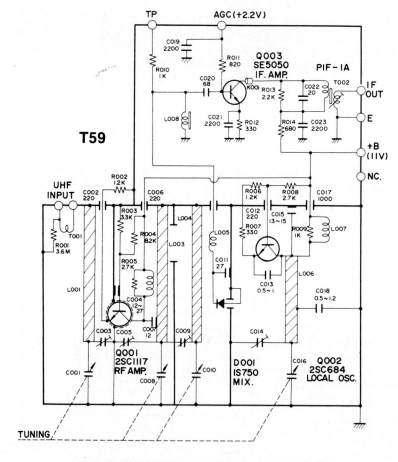

(T59) CIRCUIT DIAGRAM (U.H.F. TUNER)—MODEL B1201

328

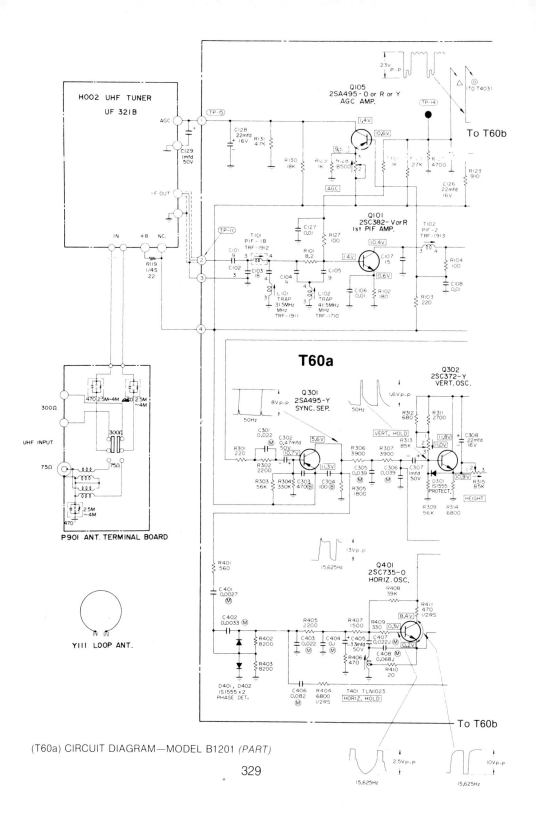

(T60a) CIRCUIT DIAGRAM—MODEL B1201 *(PART)*

329

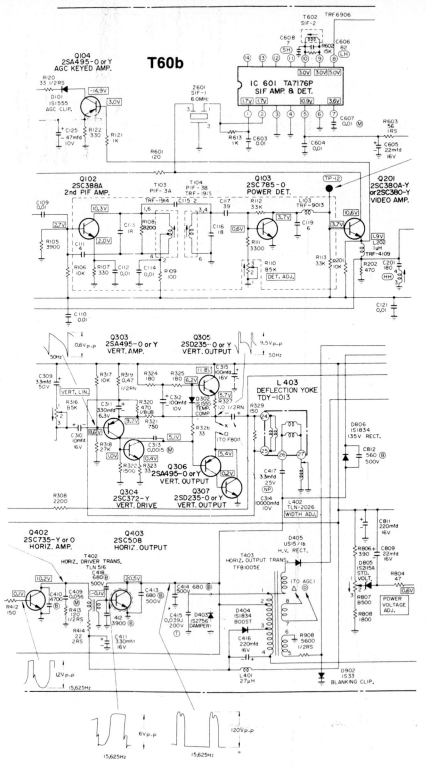

(T60b) CIRCUIT DIAGRAM—MODEL B1201 *(PART)*

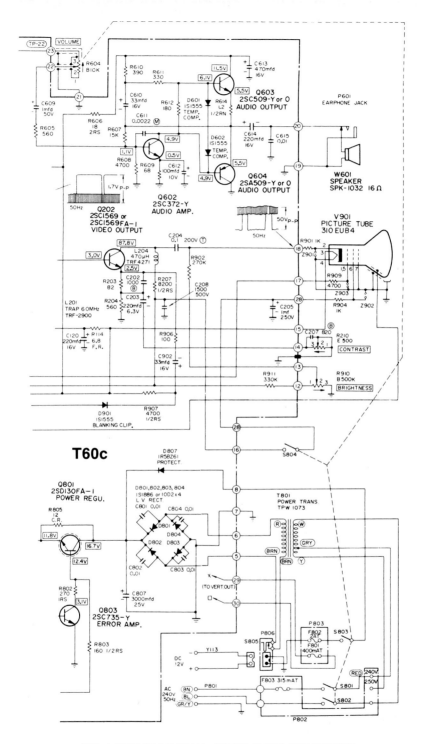

T60c

(T60c) CIRCUIT DIAGRAM—MODEL B1201 *(CONTINUED)*

TOSHIBA Models C-2090, C2095, C2295, C2695

General Description: These models are mains-operated colour television receivers incorporating a main chassis with various options for manual and remote control. The basic circuit common to all models is given here and features a S.A.W. filter for band-pass shaping, R.G.B. drive and auto-transformer power supply (live chassis). The main signal circuits are accommodated on a single board with other functions mounted as separate modules.

Mains Supply: 240 volts, 50Hz.

Cathode Ray Tubes: 510RJB22 (C-2090, C-2095, BC7200) 20-in. 560ETB22 (C-2295) 22-in. 670CZB22 (C-2695) 26-in.

Note: C.R.T. base connections for models C-2295, C-2695 differ from those shown in the circuit diagram and should be: (1) Focus, (6) K green, (7) A1, (8) K red, (9) (10) H, (11) K blue.

Circuit Diagram Notes

Components marked with the International Hazard Symbol must, if changed, be replaced by an approved type and must be mounted as the original. This will ensure that the safety standards adhered to during manufacture will be maintained following any servicing procedure.

Certain integrated circuits are susceptible to damage from the discharge of static electricity. To avoid such damage, observe the usual handling precautions for such devices.

Adjustments

+112V Power Supply Adjustment:
Caution: The setting of the +112V supply affects the amount of E.H.T. generated. To prevent the generation of hazardous X-ray radiation the 'B+' voltage line must be accurately adjusted to +112V.

Tune in an active channel. Adjust the Brightness and Contrast controls for a normal picture.

Check that the mains input to the receiver is correct: 240V 50Hz.

Connect a high impedance voltmeter between test point TP-91 on the main panel and chassis (e.g. Pin 8).

Adjust the Set +112V control, R851, on the Main panel for +112V reading on the meter. Disconnect the meter.

High Voltage Check:
Caution: There is no High Voltage adjustment on this chassis. The +112V power supply must be correctly adjusted to ensure that the E.H.T. generated remains within the stated limit.

Connect an accurate E.H.T. meter to the final anode of the C.R.T.

Switch the receiver on and set the Brightness and Contrast controls to minimum (zero beam current).

Observe the voltage meter. The E.H.T. must not at any time exceed 27.5kV.

Rotate the Brightness control to both extremes to ensure that the E.H.T. does not exceed the limit of 27.5kV.

Fail Safe Circuit Check: The Fail Safe (F.S.) circuit check must be performed at the completion of any servicing. Proceed as follows: Temporarily short-circuit terminals A and B on the Main panel with a jumper wire; the raster and sound will disappear. If the short-circuit is now removed, the raster and sound should remain off, this provides evidence that the F.S. circuit is functioning correctly.

To restore the raster and sound, switch off the receiver and allow 30 seconds to reset the F.S. circuit to its stand-by state. Now switch the receiver on again and the raster and sound should be restored.

Horizontal Oscillator Adjustment: If the horizontal sync. is unstable, adjust the Horizontal Hold control R451 to stabilise, ensuring that the control is set to the centre of the pull-in range.

Vertical Oscillator Adjustment: If the picture 'rolls' or jitters vertically, adjust the Vertical Hold control R351 to stabilise.

Height Adjustment: To adjust the vertical amplitude of the picture reset the Height control R352, making the final adjustment to overscan the mask 2cm at the top and bottom of the display.

Focus Control: Adjust the Focus control (M002) for well defined scanning lines in the central area of the screen.

Delayed R.F. A.G.C. Adjustment: Tune the receiver to the strongest local station. Turn the A.G.C. Delay control R151 fully counter-clockwise, and the Tuner A.G.C. Crossover control 1RV30 (on T139A) fully clockwise.

Adjust the A.G.C. Delay control clockwise until the noise (snow) is reduced to minimum on the picture. Adjust the Tuner A.G.C. Crossover control to finally eliminate any noise on the picture.

A.F.C. (Automatic Frequency Control) Field Alignment: Place A.F.C. Switch in the 'off' position. Tune the receiver to an active channel and adjust the tuning to obtain a good picture.

Switch the A.F.C. on and adjust coil T172 for the best picture. The picture quality should be as in 10.1 above, when the A.F.C. Switch was off.

Check the A.F.C. action by turning the Tuning control RA51 clockwise and anti-clockwise, returning it to its set position.

Colour Sync. Adjustment: Tune to a colour programme and allow the receiver to warm-up for five minutes.

Connect Test Point TP-43 (on the Chroma Module) to the module earth by a short jumper wire.

Connect pin 21 of IC501 to the module earth via a 10k ohm resistor, this will

333

disable the colour killer. Coloured stripes will run across the screen if the sync. requires adjustment. To correct, adjust R552 until the stripes remain stationary or drift slowly across the screen.

Remove the 10k ohm resistor and jumper wire.

PAL Matrix Adjustment: Inject a colour bar test signal.

Adjust the Colour control to obtain the correct colours.

If the PAL matrixing is incorrect a 'venetian blind' effect will appear on the screen.

If incorrect first adjust the Delay Line Phase coil T501 to minimise the venetian blind effect.

Next, connect TP-43 via a capacitor (30 to 50pF) to the module earth; if the venetian blind effect increases, adjust the Direct Path Gain control R551 to minimise the effect.

If, after removing the capacitor, the effect persists, repeat until it is eliminated, even when the capacitor is connected.

Sound I.F. Detector Coil Adjustment: Tune in a signal which uses a continuous tone for sound (e.g. 400Hz or 1kHz).

Connect the probe of the oscilloscope to point M on the Main panel.

Adjust the Sound I.F. Detector coil T601 for maximum detected signal amplitude on the oscilloscope.

Colour Purity Adjustments: Before attempting any purity adjustments it should be remembered that the Purity Magnets and the Deflection Yoke form part of the 'integrated tube components' assembly. As these were aligned and fixed during manufacture it is advisable that the sealing compound should not

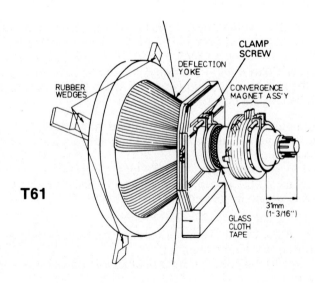

(T61) C.R.T. NECK ASSEMBLY—MODEL C-2090 ETC.

be broken unless absolutely necessary. If the Purity does require re-adjustment, allow the receiver at least fifteen minutes to warm-up.

Thoroughly demagnetise the picture tube and the surrounding metalwork using an external degaussing coil.

Turn the Brightness and Contrast controls to maximum.

Adjust the red and blue Cut-off controls (R557 and R559 on the C.R.T. Base panel) to provide a green raster only. If necessary, advance the green Cut-off control R558 to enhance the green.

Loosen the Deflection Yoke clamp screw (see Fig. T61) and slide the yoke backwards or forwards to provide a vertical green zone on the picture tube.

Remove the three rubber wedges.

Rotate and spread the tabs of the Purity Magnets (see Fig. T62a) until a green area is obtained about the centre of the screen, and at the same time centre the raster vertically by further adjustment of the magnets.

Move the yoke slowly forward or backward until a uniformly green display is obtained. Tighten the clamp screw.

Check the purity of the red and blue rasters by individual adjustment of the appropriate Cut-off controls (R557 and R559).

Temporarily tighten the Deflection Yoke clamp screw.

Adjust the three Cut-off controls to obtain a white raster and proceed with the C.R.T. Grey Scale Adjustments below.

Having set the grey scale, proceed with the Convergence Adjustments below.

C.R.T. Grey Scale Adjustments: Tune to an active channel.

Turn the Colour control to minimum.

Turn the Screen control (R951 on the C.R.T. Base panel) fully counter-clockwise.

Rotate the red, green and blue Cut-off controls (R557, R558 and R559) clockwise from the maximum, setting them so that the flat section of each knob lies parallel to the surface of the panel. Set the green and blue Drive controls (R252 and R253 on the C.R.T. Base panel) to their mid-positions.

Disconnect the luminance output at P520 (Set white) on the Main panel.

Short circuit pins J and H on the Main panel with a crocodile clip, this action reduces the vertical scan to a single line.

Observing the centre of the screen closely, gradually turn the Screen control R951 clockwise until a single coloured line appears, continue turning until a second colour is just introduced alongside the first. Now turn the two Cut-off controls corresponding to these two colours fully counter-clockwise, thus removing them from the screen.

Gradually turn the Screen control until the third colour just appears on the screen.

Adjust the two Cut-off controls to bring the levels of these two colours up to the level of the third. The resulting line will be white if the Cut-off controls are adjusted correctly.

Remove the crocodile clip between pins J and H and reconnect the luminance output at P520.

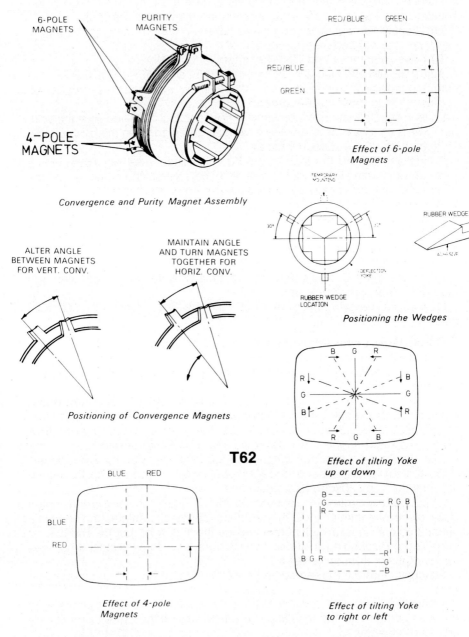

6-POLE MAGNETS

PURITY MAGNETS

4-POLE MAGNETS

Convergence and Purity Magnet Assembly

RED/BLUE   GREEN

RED/BLUE

GREEN

Effect of 6-pole Magnets

ALTER ANGLE BETWEEN MAGNETS FOR VERT. CONV.

MAINTAIN ANGLE AND TURN MAGNETS TOGETHER FOR HORIZ. CONV.

TEMPORARY MOUNTING

90°

45°

DEFLECTION YOKE

RUBBER WEDGE

ADHESIVE

RUBBER WEDGE LOCATION

Positioning the Wedges

Positioning of Convergence Magnets

B G R

R   B

G   G

B   R

R G B

T62

Effect of tilting Yoke up or down

BLUE   RED

BLUE

RED

Effect of 4-pole Magnets

B
G
R

R G B

B G R

R
G
B

Effect of tilting Yoke to right or left

(T62) CONVERGENCE AND PURITY ADJUSTMENTS—MODEL C-2090 ETC.

Turn the Brightness and Contrast controls to maximum.

Adjust the blue and green Drive controls R253 and R252 to obtain the correct white-balance in the high-light areas of the picture.

Adjust the Brightness and Contrast controls to produce a dark grey raster, then check the white balance in the low brightness areas. If the white balance is not correct, adjust the appropriate Cut-off and Drive controls to obtain a good white balance in both the low- and high-light areas.

If a pattern has been used for these adjustments, select a channel showing a normal colour picture and adjust the Colour control for normal viewing.

Pre-set Brightness Adjustment: Tune to a colour programme.

Set the Contrast control to maximum and the Brightness to its mid-point. Set the Colour control to its mid-point.

Set the Pre-set Brightness control R255 to its mid-point and allow the receiver to operate for five minutes in this state.

Observing the picture closely, adjust the Pre-set Brightness control to a position where the picture does not show evidence of 'blooming' in the high brightness areas or is too dark in the low brightness areas.

Check that the Brightness and Contrast controls provide the correct variations in picture tones from one extreme to the other.

If the picture is not dark with the Brightness and Contrast controls set to minimum; or not sufficiently light with these controls at maximum, adjust the Pre-set Brightness control again to achieve acceptable limits.

Convergence (Fig. T62)

This receiver is fitted with a picture tube which had the neck mounted assemblies adjusted and fixed permanently during manufacture. In the event of a C.R.T. Deflection Yoke or Convergence Magnet Assembly becoming faulty, it is possible to replace these components separately, but it is emphasised that great care must be taken when removing the neck mounted units from the C.R.T.

When the units are re-assembled it will be necessary to re-converge the red and blue beams of the C.R.T. Before attempting to begin the following procedure, switch-on the receiver and allow it to warm-up for at least fifteen minutes.

Central Area Convergence Adjustments: With the neck components refitted and the Deflection Yoke temporarily fixed, inject a cross-hatch pattern from a signal generator at the aerial socket.

Adjust the Brightness and Contrast controls for a well defined pattern.

Adjust the two tabs of the 4-pole magnets to change the angle between them (see Fig. T62) and superimpose the red and blue vertical lines in the central area of the screen (see Fig. T62c).

Turning the tabs of the 4-pole magnets and at the same time keeping the angle between them constant, superimpose the red and blue horizontal lines in the central area of the screen (see Fig. T62c).

Adjust the tabs of the 6-pole magnets to superimpose the red/blue lines over the green lines. Adjusting the angle between the magnets affects the vertical lines and rotating them, but maintaining the angle between them, affects the horizontal lines (see Fig. T62d).

Owing to the interaction between the fields of the 4- and 6-pole magnets, it will be necessary to repeat operations 3, 4 and 5 until optimum convergence is achieved about the centre of the screen.

Outer Area Convergence Adjustments: Loosen the clamping screw of the Deflection Yoke to allow the yoke to tilt.

Tilt the front of the yoke up or down to obtain convergence in the outer area of the screen; for the effect of this adjustment see Fig. T62f. When a satisfactory point has been found, temporarily insert a wedge (part. no. R6960 1094) between the cone and the top of the yoke to fix this position (see Fig. T62e). Do not remove the backing paper for the adhesive patch on the wedge at this stage.

Place another wedge as shown in the bottom space between yoke and C.R.T. and remove the backing paper to finally fix this position.

Twist the yoke to right or left to further improve the convergence of the outer areas (see Fig. T62g).

Maintaining the yoke in position, place another wedge into either of the upper positions as shown. Remove backing paper and fix permanently. Remove the temporarily mounted wedge and insert into the other upper position, removing the backing paper to fix permanently.

Having fitted the three wedges, check the overall convergence. If the convergence is satisfactory, tighten the yoke clamp screw ensuring that the yoke is firm but not overtightened.

I.C. Voltages:

IC101		IC301		IC501		IC601	
Pin 1	5.0	Pin 1	4.1	Pin 1	7.5	Pin 1	1.6
2	5.0	2	4.1	2	3.5	2	5.9
3	9.5	3	0	3	3.5	3	0
4	1.5	4	0.5	4	0.3	4	0
5	6.5	5	0	5	0.6	5	3.8
6	6.5	6	0	6	3.5	6	0.6
7	4.4	7	0.6	7	3.5	7	6.4
8	8.4	8	7.0	8	9.5	8	7.0
9	8.3	9	7.3	9	8.5	9	4.9
10	4.4	10	2.7	10	8.5	10	11.7
11	12.0	11	12.0	11	4.5	11	N.C.
12	3.7	12	−0.25	12	0	12	0.01
13	0	13	2.6	13	−2.3	13	1.8
14	7.5	14	−0.85	14	1.9	14	1.8
15	5.0	15	9.9	15	1.2		
16	5.0	16	0.75	16	9.0		
				17	8.0		
				18	12.0		
				19	11.0		
				20	6.5		
				21	6.5		
				22	12.0		
				23	7.5		
				24	7.5		

Fault-finding Charts (Fig. T63a-f)

The following charts provide a guide to trouble-shooting which, if followed carefully, will assist in tracking down a fault to the correct stage or area of the circuit.

In order to utilise the charts first establish the type of fault, i.e. No raster, no sound.

Locate the chart applicable to this condition and then progress through the various steps until the block is reached which indicates the offending stage or component.

NO RASTER AND NO SOUND

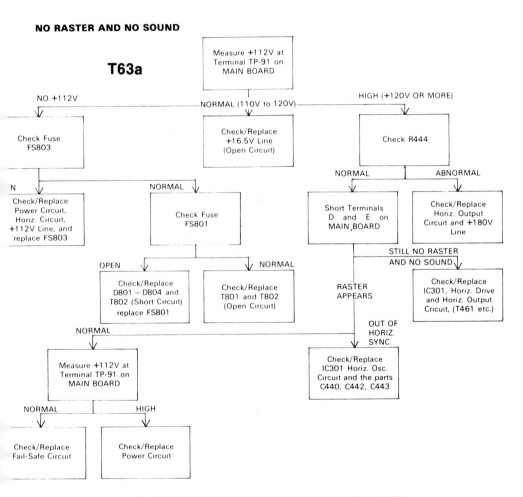

(T63a) FAULT-FINDING CHART—MODELS C-2090 ETC. *(PART)*

NO RASTER (SOUND NOISY OR WEAK)

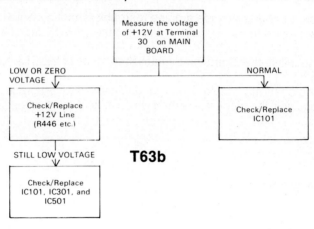

(T63b) FAULT-FINDING CHART—MODELS C-2090 ETC. *(PART)*

TOSHIBA

NO RASTER (SOUND OK)

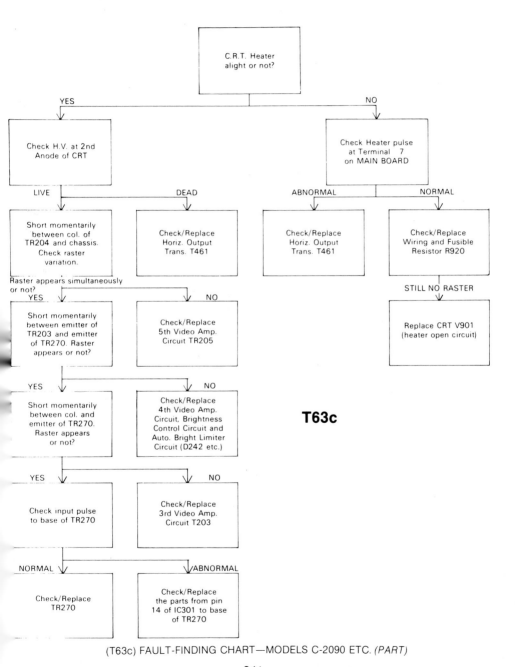

(T63c) FAULT-FINDING CHART—MODELS C-2090 ETC. *(PART)*

341

NO PICTURE (RASTER REMAINS) AND NO SOUND

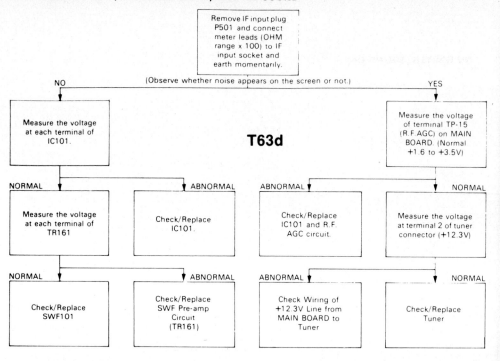

T63d

Remove IF input plug P501 and connect meter leads (OHM range x 100) to IF input socket and earth momentarily.

(Observe whether noise appears on the screen or not.)

NO

Measure the voltage at each terminal of IC101.

NORMAL — Measure the voltage at each terminal of TR161.

ABNORMAL — Check/Replace IC101.

NORMAL — Check/Replace SWF101

ABNORMAL — Check/Replace SWF Pre-amp Circuit (TR161)

YES

Measure the voltage of terminal TP-15 (R.F. AGC) on MAIN BOARD. (Normal +1.6 to +3.5V)

ABNORMAL — Check/Replace IC101 and R.F. AGC circuit.

NORMAL — Measure the voltage at terminal 2 of tuner connector (+12.3V)

ABNORMAL — Check Wiring of +12.3V Line from MAIN BOARD to Tuner

NORMAL — Check/Replace Tuner

NO PICTURE (RASTER AND SOUND OK)

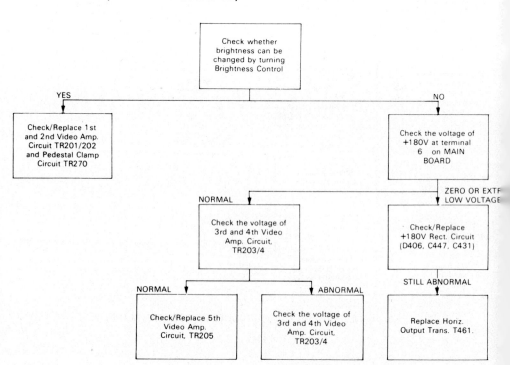

Check whether brightness can be changed by turning Brightness Control

YES

Check/Replace 1st and 2nd Video Amp. Circuit TR201/202 and Pedestal Clamp Circuit TR270

NO

Check the voltage of +180V at terminal 6 on MAIN BOARD

NORMAL — Check the voltage of 3rd and 4th Video Amp. Circuit, TR203/4

ZERO OR EXTR LOW VOLTAGE — Check/Replace +180V Rect. Circuit (D406, C447, C431)

NORMAL — Check/Replace 5th Video Amp. Circuit, TR205

ABNORMAL — Check the voltage of 3rd and 4th Video Amp. Circuit, TR203/4

STILL ABNORMAL — Replace Horiz. Output Trans. T461.

(T63d) FAULT-FINDING CHART—MODELS C-2090 ETC. *(PART)*

NO COLOUR

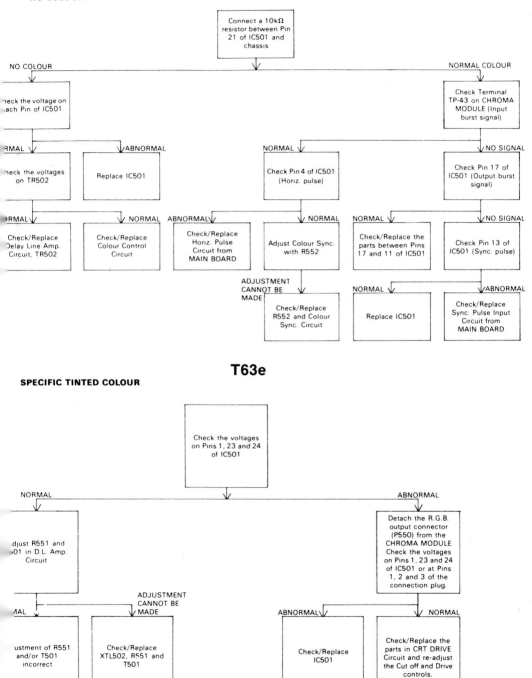

Connect a 10kΩ resistor between Pin 21 of IC501 and chassis

NO COLOUR — NORMAL COLOUR

Check the voltage on each Pin of IC501

Check Terminal TP-43 on CHROMA MODULE (Input burst signal)

NORMAL — ABNORMAL
Replace IC501

Check the voltages on TR502

NORMAL — Check Pin 4 of IC501 (Horiz. pulse)

NO SIGNAL — Check Pin 17 of IC501 (Output burst signal)

NORMAL — Check/Replace Delay Line Amp. Circuit, TR502

NORMAL — Check/Replace Colour Control Circuit

ABNORMAL — Check/Replace Horiz. Pulse Circuit from MAIN BOARD

NORMAL — Adjust Colour Sync. with R552

NORMAL — Check/Replace the parts between Pins 17 and 11 of IC501

NO SIGNAL — Check Pin 13 of IC501 (Sync. pulse)

ADJUSTMENT CANNOT BE MADE — Check/Replace R552 and Colour Sync. Circuit

NORMAL — Replace IC501

ABNORMAL — Check/Replace Sync. Pulse Input Circuit from MAIN BOARD

T63e

SPECIFIC TINTED COLOUR

Check the voltages on Pins 1, 23 and 24 of IC501

NORMAL — ABNORMAL

Adjust R551 and 501 in D.L. Amp. Circuit

Detach the R.G.B. output connector (P550) from the CHROMA MODULE Check the voltages on Pins 1, 23 and 24 of IC501 or at Pins 1, 2 and 3 of the connection plug.

ADJUSTMENT CANNOT BE MADE — Check/Replace XTL502, R551 and T501

NAL — ustment of R551 and/or T501 incorrect

ABNORMAL — Check/Replace IC501

NORMAL — Check/Replace the parts in CRT DRIVE Circuit and re-adjust the Cut off and Drive controls.

(T63e) FAULT-FINDING CHART—MODELS C-2090 ETC. *(PART)*

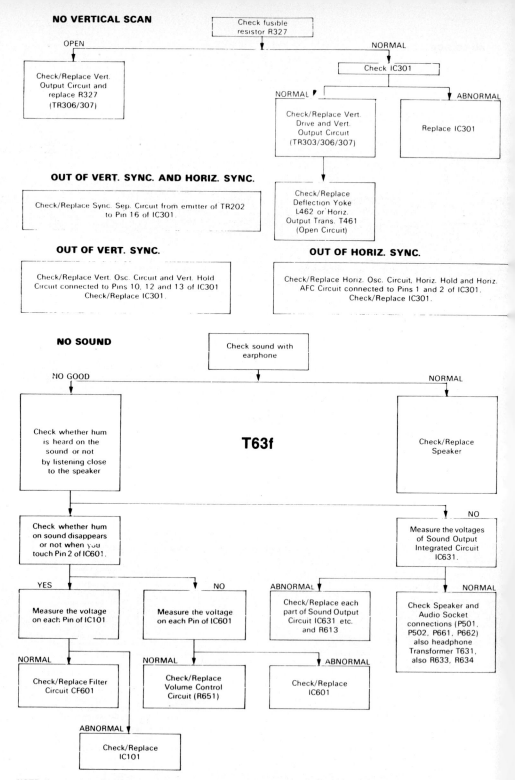

NO VERTICAL SCAN

Check fusible resistor R327

OPEN — NORMAL

Check/Replace Vert. Output Circuit and replace R327 (TR306/307)

Check IC301

NORMAL — ABNORMAL

Check/Replace Vert. Drive and Vert. Output Circuit (TR303/306/307)

Replace IC301

OUT OF VERT. SYNC. AND HORIZ. SYNC.

Check/Replace Sync. Sep. Circuit from emitter of TR202 to Pin 16 of IC301.

Check/Replace Deflection Yoke L462 or Horiz. Output Trans. T461 (Open Circuit)

OUT OF VERT. SYNC.

Check/Replace Vert. Osc. Circuit and Vert. Hold Circuit connected to Pins 10, 12 and 13 of IC301. Check/Replace IC301.

OUT OF HORIZ. SYNC.

Check/Replace Horiz. Osc. Circuit, Horiz. Hold and Horiz. AFC Circuit connected to Pins 1 and 2 of IC301. Check/Replace IC301.

NO SOUND

Check sound with earphone

NO GOOD — NORMAL

Check whether hum is heard on the sound or not by listening close to the speaker

T63f

Check/Replace Speaker

Check whether hum on sound disappears or not when you touch Pin 2 of IC601.

NO — Measure the voltages of Sound Output Integrated Circuit IC631.

YES — NO — ABNORMAL — NORMAL

Measure the voltage on each Pin of IC101

Measure the voltage on each Pin of IC601

Check/Replace each part of Sound Output Circuit IC631 etc. and R613

Check Speaker and Audio Socket connections (P501, P502, P661, P662) also headphone Transformer T631, also R633, R634

NORMAL — NORMAL — ABNORMAL

Check/Replace Filter Circuit CF601

Check/Replace Volume Control Circuit (R651)

Check/Replace IC601

ABNORMAL

Check/Replace IC101

NOTE: If a part of the Sound Output or Feedback Circuit is damaged, only weak or distorted sound may be heard.

(T63f) FAULT-FINDING CHART—MODELS C-2090 ETC. *(CONTINUED)*

TOSHIBA

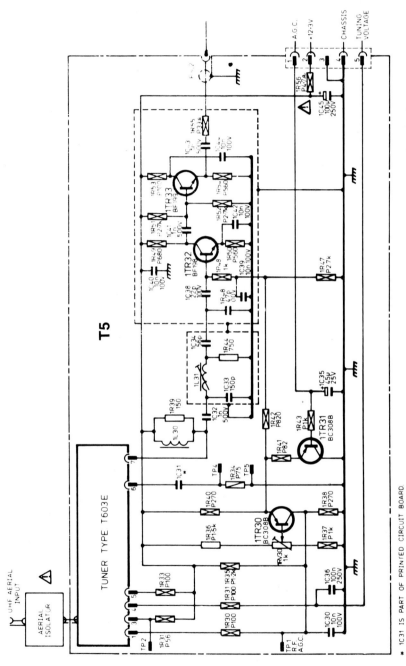

(T5) CIRCUIT DIAGRAM (T139A TUNER AND INTERFACE PANEL)—MODEL C-2090

* 1C31 IS PART OF PRINTED CIRCUIT BOARD.

(T6) CIRCUIT DIAGRAM (CUSTOMER CONTROLS—BUSH)—MODEL C-2090

346

TOSHIBA

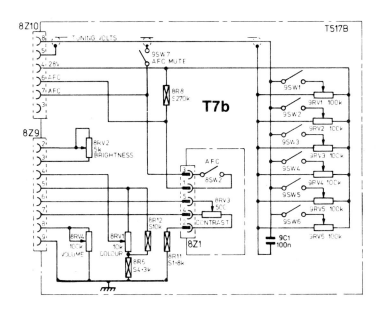

T7a

(T7a) CIRCUIT DIAGRAM (CUSTOMER CONTROLS—MURPHY)—MODEL MC7240

T7b

(T7b) CIRCUIT DIAGRAM (POWER SUPPLY BOARD)—MODEL C-2090

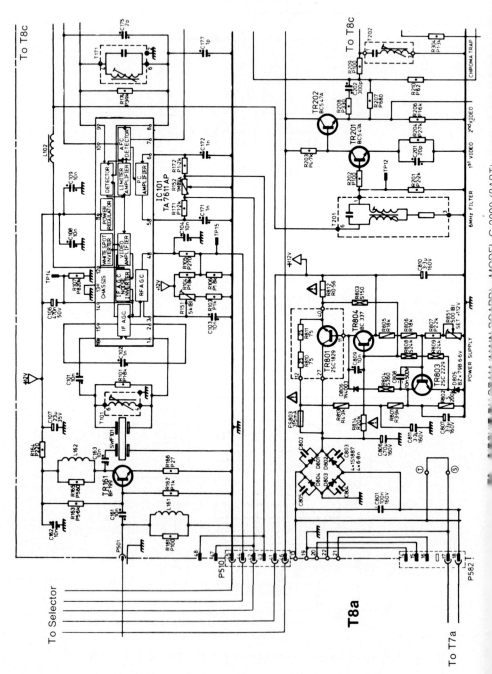

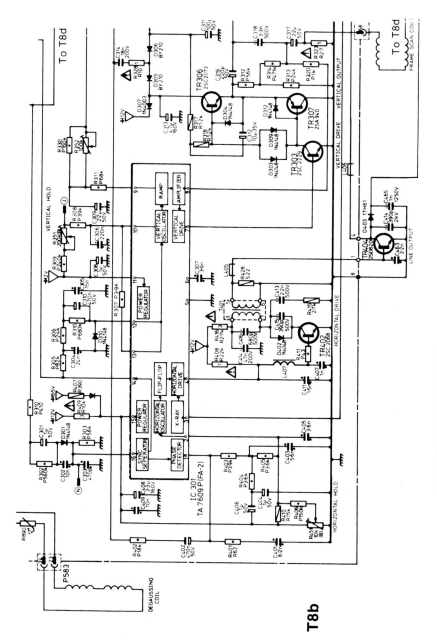

(T8b) CIRCUIT DIAGRAM (MAIN BOARD)—MODEL C-2090 (PART)

T8b

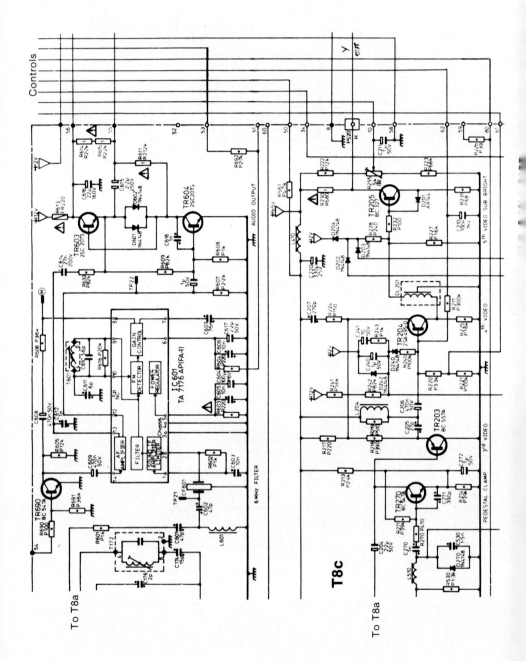

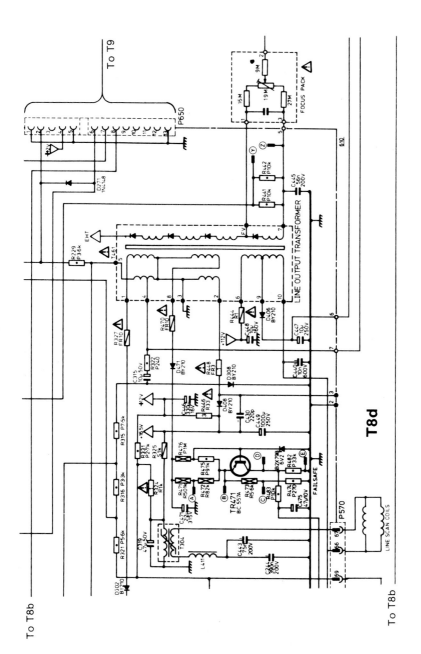

(T8d) CIRCUIT DIAGRAM (MAIN BOARD)—MODEL C-2090 *(CONTINUED)*

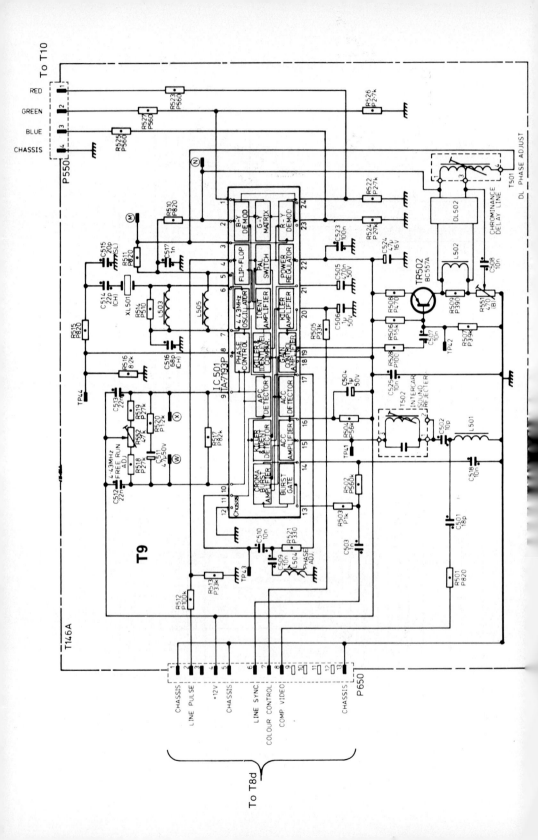

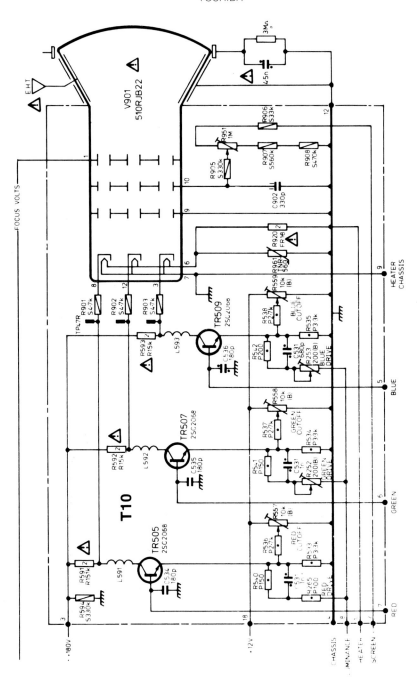

(T10) CIRCUIT DIAGRAM (C.R.T. PANEL)—MODEL C-1290 (CONTINUED)

General Description: A compact 625-line portable monochrome T.V. receiver for U.H.F. reception, using solid-state techniques, and incorporating a 6-in. C.R.T., a continuous-tuning varicap U.H.F. tuner, and operated from mains A.C. or 12V D.C. supplies.

For mains operation a converter unit is attached to the receiver back. This converter is removed for 12V D.C. operation and the supply plugged in direct.

Features include automatic line scanning and frequency control, a D.C. stabiliser circuit with short-circuit protection and protection against incorrect polarity D.C. connection.

Mains Supplies: 220-240 volts, 50Hz.

Battery: 12 volts, 7.5W.

Cathode Ray Tube: 16NK1B.

Loudspeaker: 30 ohms impedance.

Important: The 12V D.C. battery lead supplied is wired for a negative earth supply with a diode connected to the negative lead with the cathode to battery negative.

This diode is to protect the receiver against wrong polarity connection. Therefore, if removing the adaptor to allow the receiver to be operated directly

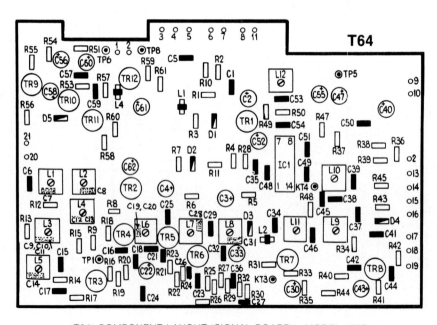

(T64) COMPONENT LAYOUT (SIGNAL BOARD)—MODEL 402D

from a 12V supply, the diode or a suitable equivalent MUST be inserted into the negative lead. See Diagram.

Dismantling

Important: Carefully keep all screws and removed fittings together. Where connections need to be unsoldered, make a note of their locations for refitting.

The Fiesta 402D comprises four main sections—cabinet front with C.R.T., main chassis assembly, main cabinet, and the mains power supply unit.

Disconnect mains lead from supply, and remove mains power unit from receiver after slackening captive long screws (1). If the receiver has been used from a 12V D.C. supply, remove battery connector from plug.

To remove the main chassis from the cabinet:

(a) Remove the portable U.H.F. aerial, if fitted, and unscrew the aerial mounting and turn it until the lug on the mounting coincides with the keyway in the cabinet top. Remove mounting.

(b) Remove four screws from cabinet front top and bottom, and two screws from cabinet back. Note that these screws must be re-sealed after refitting.

(c) Remove horizontal and vertical hold control knobs.

(d) Carefully ease chassis with attached cabinet front out from cabinet. Access to cabinet assemblies.

Receiver board—releases two screws with washers and hinge board upward.

Timebase board—release to screws with washers and hinge board down.

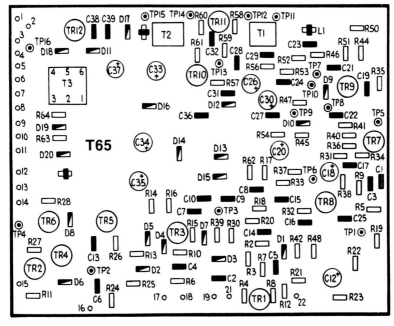

(T65) COMPONENT LAYOUT (TIMEBASE BOARD)—MODEL 402D

Stabiliser board—remove two screws, and ease out board to extent of leads.

U.H.F. tuner and I.F. amplifier. These are both mounted on the bracket which can be freed from the chassis after releasing three screws.

Loudspeaker is held by four screws to chassis side.

Removal of other chassis assemblies should be self-evident on inspection.

Removing C.R.T. First detach the cabinet front assembly from the main chassis as follows:

(a) Remove E.H.T. connector from C.R.T. (the connector is accessible through the hole in the chassis side), then remove the U.H.F. tuner and front control knobs.

(b) Remove the C.R.T. base protective cover (shown in dotted outline) after releasing the two screws. This also frees the C.R.T. neck grommet but do NOT free the grommet from the chassis yet.

(c) Release three screws from the top and bottom edges of the cabinet front and ease the cabinet front out of the main chassis after removing the C.R.T. base connector.

Important: The connection pins on the C.R.T. base are very fine—be particularly careful not to distort them when removing the base connector.

(d) Carefully turn the cabinet front with the C.R.T. to gain access to the deflection coils tagboard and disconnect the leads from the chassis components. Also unsolder the earth bonding lead and the line scan braiding from the deflection coils clamp.

(e) Free the C.R.T. neck grommet and *very carefully* ease the cabinet front complete with the C.R.T. from the main chassis.

To remove the C.R.T. from the cabinet front:

(a) Unhook the four holding springs from the cabinet front. Lift out the C.R.T. complete with the deflection coils.

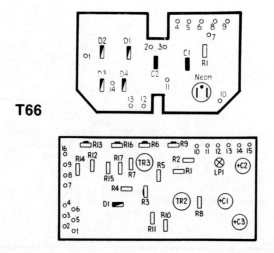

(T66) COMPONENT LAYOUT (POWER SUPPLY BOARDS)—MODEL 402D

(b) Release the clamp and withdraw the deflection coils from the C.R.T. neck.

Important: It is NOT recommended that either the U.H.F. tuner or the I.F. pre-amplifier units be dismantled. If a fault is suspected in either of these units, they should be replaced complete.

Setting-up Adjustments

D.C. Supplies (D.C. Stabiliser): Connect meter between board pin 2, 6 and 15. Adjust pre-set R6 on stabiliser board to obtain 10.5V ± 0.1V on load.

Check that, when the mains input supply voltage is varied between 5% and 10% (i.e. ±12V, ±24V on 240V on 240V A.C.) that the D.C. output voltage does not vary by more than 0.5V%.

Horizontal (Line) Scan: Use pattern generator or a transmitted test card display.

Earth the base of Tr7 (line oscillator) and connect a shorting link across tuned circuit L1, C23 on the timebase board.

Set Horizontal Hold control R49 to mid-point, and adjust Line Hold pre-set R50 for a steady picture horizontally.

If a steady picture cannot be obtained, change critical value resistors R51, R56, and, in particularly difficult cases, capacitor C29.

Remove short-circuit link across L1, C23 and adjust L1 core for a horizontally stationary picture.

Disconnect Tr7 base from earth.

Width and Line Linearity: Adjust core of linearity coil (located adjacent to the line output transformer on the main chassis) for optimum width and linearity. Note that this adjustment may affect the picture brightness and focus.

Frame (Vertical) Scan: Adjust User Line and Frame Hold controls R49, R1 to synchronise with a transmitted picture.

If proper vertical hold cannot be obtained, or is only obtainable with R1 control slider at either extreme of its travel, then replace R6 (nominal value 270 ohms) on the timebase board; select a value which brings the vertical locking point to the centre of R1 vertical hold travel.

Equipment Required: U.H.F. pattern generator, Audio generator, Multimeter or V.T.V.M., Oscilloscope.

Allow T.V. receiver and test equipment to warm up for about 20 minutes before starting adjustments.

Adjust height and vertical linearity by means of pre-sets R22 and R19 respectively. Access to these pre-sets can be gained with the cabinet fitted via two holes located below the loudspeaker at the R.H. side.

Picture Centring: Adjust deflection coil assembly to position picture horizontally with the top and bottom edges parallel with the tube sides. Then adjust the picture centring rings at the rear of the deflection coils to position the picture at the tube centre.

Setting-up C.R.T. Working Conditions:

Tune to a no-signal point, set contrast control to maximum.

Connect meter between pin 21 on timebase board and earth and check for variation of 14 to 30V D.C. as Brightness control is varied between its limits.

Check for 150 to 550V D.C. at pin 9 on stabiliser board.

Check for 300 to 350V D.C. at pin 8 on stabiliser board.

Check for 40V D.C. on pin 17 of receiver board.

Connect kilovoltmeter to E.H.T. connector to measure final anode potential which, at minimum brightness and contrast should be within 7.5 to 10kV.

Check picture centring and re-adjust as necessary.

Inject and tune receiver to a 1mV pattern generator signal. With brightness control R29 on timebase board and contrast R46 on receiver board set at maximum, check the C.R.T. cathode current with a micro-ammeter inserted into the cathode circuit. This current should not exceed 45uA.

Focus: Adjust pre-set R13 on stabiliser board for optimum focus and picture resolution. Then adjust A2 focus anode voltage for 300 to 350V D.C. measured at pin 8 on the stabiliser board for best focus.

A.G.C. Pre-set: With no aerial connected, tune the receiver to a no-signal point.

Connect multimeter or V.T.V.M. to the collector of Tr2 on the receiver board, and adjust pre-set R1 to give 9.8V D.C.

Transfer the meter lead to pin 8 on the receiver board (junction of D2, R10, R11) and adjust pre-set R11 on receiver board for 8V D.C.

Transfer meter lead to junction of R8, R9 on receiver board and adjust pre-set R8 to give 7V D.C.

Component List

Receiver Board Y1

Resistors							
R1	1k ohm*	R23	3.9k ohm	R46	1k ohm*	C3	10μF
R2	1k ohm	R24	1.2k ohm		Contrast	C4	1μF
R3	1.5k ohm	R25	560 ohm	R47	27 ohm	C5	100μF
R4	3.3k ohm	R26	120 ohm	R48	3.9k ohm	C6	39pF
R5	10k ohm	R27	560 ohm	R49	5.6k ohm	C7	15pF
R6	3.3k ohm	R28	4.7k ohm	R50	1.5k ohm	C8	4.7pF
R7	1.2k ohm	R29	820 ohm	R51	15k ohm	C9	7.5pF
R8	10k ohm*	R30	3.9k ohm	R52	22k ohm*	C10	100pF
R9	10k ohm	R31	470 ohm*		Volume	C11	100pF
R10	10k ohm	R32	470 ohm	R53	220k ohm	C12	8.2pF
R11	6.8k ohm*	R33	220 ohm	R54	47k ohm	C13	15pF
R12	27 ohm	R34	47 ohm	R55	68k ohm*	C14	5.6pF
R13	180 ohm	R35	1k ohm	R56	5.6k ohm	C15	0.01μF
R14	180 ohm	R36	100 ohm	R57	22k ohm	C16	18pF
R15	510 ohm	R37	2.7k ohm	R58	470 ohm	C17	0.01μF
R16	560 ohm	R38	2.7k ohm	R59	470 ohm	C18	0.01μF
R17	820 ohm	R39	100 ohm	R60	1.2k ohm	C19	15pF
R18	3.9k ohm	R40	68 ohm	R61	10 ohm	C20	68pF
R19	3.9k ohm	R41	470 ohm	*potentiometer		C21	0.01μF
R20	1.1k ohm	R42	2k ohm			C22	30μF
R21	510 ohm	R43	4.7k ohm	**Capacitors**		C23	0.01μF
R22	3.9k ohm	R44	470 ohm*	C1	0.01μF	C24	0.01μF
		R45	330k ohm*	C2	10μF	C25	5.1pF

C26	0.01μF	C41	0.1μF	C56	1μF	Tr7	KT315B
C27	0.01μF	C42	2200pF	C57	120pF	Tr8	KT601A
C28	18pF	C43	100μF	C58	1μF	Tr9	KT315B
C29	3.3pF	C44	220pF	C59	10μF	Tr10	KT315B
C30	100μF	C45	15pF	C60	1μF	Tr11	RT402B
C31	20pF	C46	270pF	C61	500μF	Tr12	RT402B
C32	0.01μF	C47	100μF	C62	500μF	Integrated circuit	
C33	10μF	C48	0.022μF			IC1	K174YP—1
C34	10pF	C49	0.022μF	**Transistors**			
C35	0.01μF	C50	0.022μF	Tr1	KT209A	**Diodes**	
C36	0.01μF	C51	0.022μF	Tr2	KT315B	D1	D223A
C37	0.01μF	C52	20μF	Tr3	RT328B	D2	D9B
C38	270pF	C53	510pF	Tr4	KT315A	D3	D20
C39	560pF	C54	510pF	Tr5	RT313B	D4	D223
C40	30μF	C55	5μF	Tr6	RT313B	D5	D310

Timebase Board Y2:

Resistors

R1	220k ohm* Frame hold	R37	2.2k ohm	C4	0.022μF	**Transistors**	
		R38	8.2k ohm	C5	0.047μF	Tr1	KT315A
		R39	1.8k ohm	C6	0.01μF	Tr2	KT315B
R2	820 ohm	R40	8.2k ohm	C7	0.1μF	Tr3	KT601A
R3	2.2k ohm	R41	1k ohm	C8	180pF	Tr4	KT315B
R4	220 ohm	R42	27 ohm	C9	10pF	Tr5	RT402B
R5	3.3k ohm	R43	68k ohm	C10	10pF	Tr6	RT402B
R6	270 ohm		Chassis, by R49	C11		Tr7	KT315R
R7	1.2k ohm	R44	1k ohm†	C12	300μF	Tr8	P416B
R8	47k ohm	R45	1.8k ohm	C13	0.01μF	Tr9	KY209A
R9	3.3k ohm	R46	51k ohm	C14	0.1μF	Tr10	KY209A
R10	22k ohm	R47	51k ohm	C15	1μF	Tr11	KT315A
R11	100k ohm	R48	1.2k ohm*	C16	2200pF	Tr12	RT905A
R12	22k ohm	R49	4.7k ohm* Line hold	C17	0.01μF		
R13	510 ohm			C18	1μF	**Diodes**	
R14	56k ohm	R50	68k ohm*	C19	2700pF	D1	D9E
R15	15k ohm	R51	47k ohm	C20	100μF	D2	D9B
R16	10k ohm	R52	10k ohm	C21	2200pF	D3	D9E
R17	56k ohm†	R53	3.9k ohm	C22	2200pF	D4	D223
R18	820 ohm	R54	3.3k ohm	C23	0.047μF†	D5	D9E
R19	10k ohm*	R55	22k ohm	C24	0.047μF	D6	D310
R20	6.8k ohm		Chassis, by R49	C25	0.033μF	D7	D9E
R21	1.2k ohm	R56	2.2k ohm	C26	1μF†	D8	D310
R22	68k ohm*	R57	10k ohm	C27	0.033μF	D9	D223
R23	15 ohm	R58	1k ohm	C28	1000pF	D10	D223
D24	100 ohm	R59	27k ohm	C29	0.033μF†	D11	D223A
R25	220 ohm†	R60	100 ohm	C30	50μF	D12	D818R
R26	220 ohm	R61	1k ohm	C31	1000pF	D13	D818R
R27	470 ohm	R62	3k ohm	C32	0.01μF	D14	D818R
R28	220 ohm	R63	68k ohm†	C33	20μF	D15	D818R
R29	220k ohm* Brightness	R64	2.2 ohm†	C34	500μF	D16	MD217
			*potentiometer	C35	5μF	D17	D7R
R30	560k ohm		†critical;	C36	0.01μF	D18	D223A
R31	3.3k ohm		selected on test	C37	2μF	D19	D9HC
R32	12k ohm			C38	0.015μF†	D20	D223A
R33	680k ohm†	**Capacitors**		C39	0.05μF†		
R34	3.3k ohm	C1	0.022μF	C40			
R35	2.2k ohm	C2	0.1μF	†critical:			
R36	8.2k ohm	C3	0.022μF	selected on test			

I.F. Pre-amplifier Y174

Resistors		Capacitors					
R5	3.6k	C12	10pF	C18	39pF	Tr2	KT209E
R6	8.2k	C13	3.9pF			Tr3	KT315R
R7	1.8k	C14	3.9pF	**Transistor**			
R8	1k	C15	1500pF	Tr2	RT328B	**Diodes**	
R9	560	C16	1000pF			D1	KC182A
		C17	10pF	**Transistors**		(Car adaptor diode	
				Tr1	N216	D1 KD202B)	

Stabilised Power Supply Y4

Resistors						Capacitors	
R1	1.2k	R7	220	R14	470k	C1	500uF
R2	120	R8	0.1	R15	1.5M	C2	20uF
R3	100†	R9	33k*	R16	1M*	C3 10uF	
R4	560	R10	22k	R17	2.2M		
R5	1k	R11	22k	†critical: selected			
R6	470*	R12	2.2M	on test.			
		R13	1M				

Mains Power Unit Y3:

R1	150k
R2	20
C1	0.01uF
C2	0.047uF
C3	2000uF
D1 to D4	KD202B

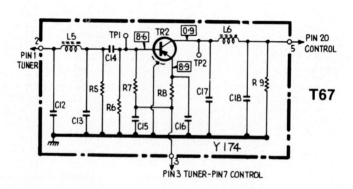

(T67) CIRCUIT DIAGRAM (I.F. PRE-AMPLIFIER)—MODEL 402D

VEGA

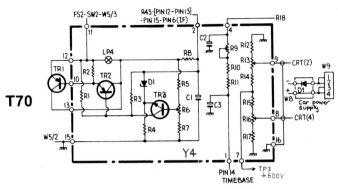

(T70) CIRCUIT DIAGRAM (STABILISER PANEL)—MODEL 402D

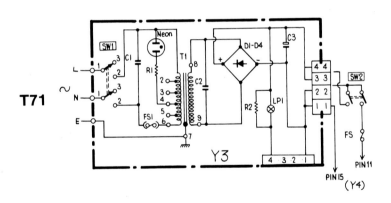

(T71) CIRCUIT DIAGRAM (P.S.U.)—MODEL 402D

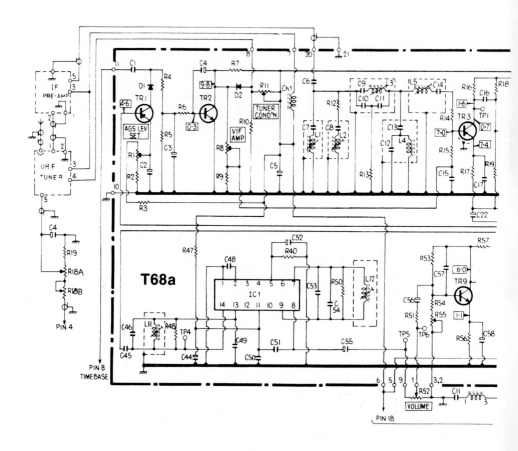

(T68a) CIRCUIT DIAGRAM (SIGNAL PANEL)—MODEL 402D *(PART)*

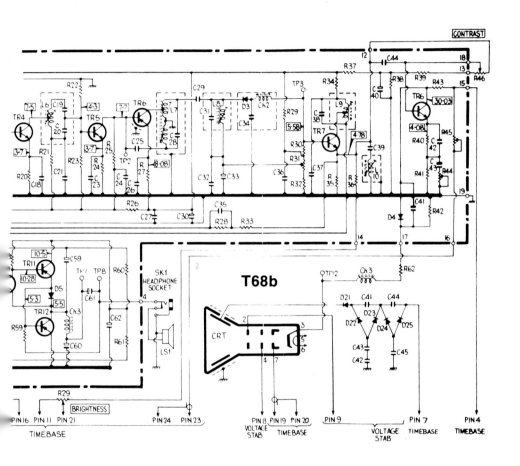

(T68b) CIRCUIT DIAGRAM (SIGNAL PANEL)—MODEL 402D *(CONTINUED)*

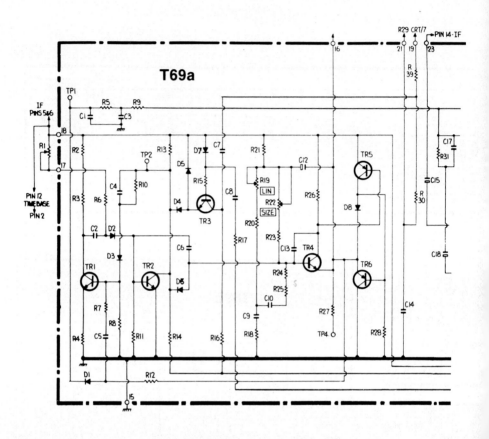

(T69a) CIRCUIT DIAGRAM (TIMEBASE PANEL)—MODEL 402D *(PART)*

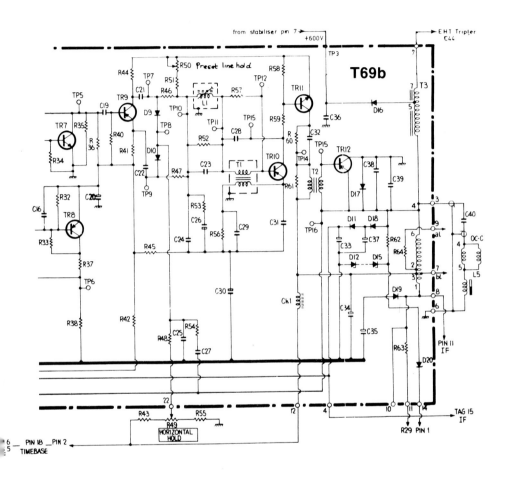

(T69b) CIRCUIT DIAGRAM (TIMEBASE PANEL)—MODEL 402D *(CONTINUED)*

WALTHAM   Model W154

General Description: A portable entertainment centre comprising 5-in. monochrome television, A.M./F.M. radio and cassette tape-recorder operating from mains or battery supplies.

Mains Supplies: 220-240 volts, 50Hz.

D.C. Supplies: 13.5 volts (9×HP2); 12 volt car battery.

Wavebands: T.V. (Ch. 21-69); L.W. 150-250kHz; M.W. 535-1605kHz; F.M. 88-108MHz.

Dismantling

Remove 3 screws from the base and 1 from each side of the cabinet.

Adjustments

U.H.F. Coverage: Input 471.25MHz, Adjust VR402; Input 855.25MHz, Adjust VR403.

Field: VR701 (Hold), VR702 (Height), VR703 (Lin.).

Line Hold: (L701).

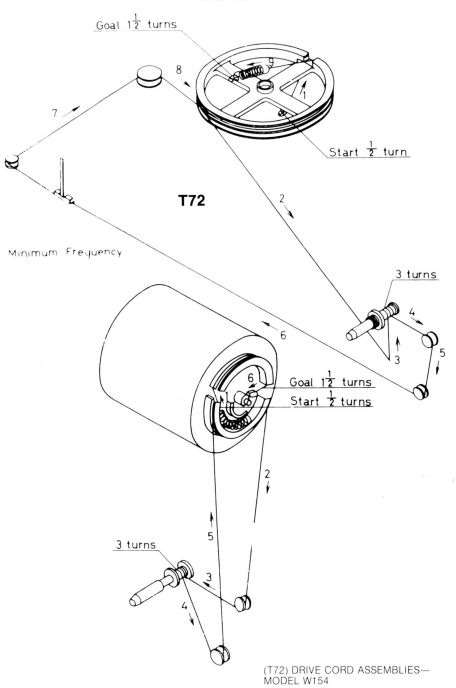

WALTHAM

Goal 1½ turns

T72

Minimum Frequency

Start ½ turn

3 turns

Goal 1½ turns
Start ½ turns

3 turns

(T72) DRIVE CORD ASSEMBLIES—
MODEL W154

367

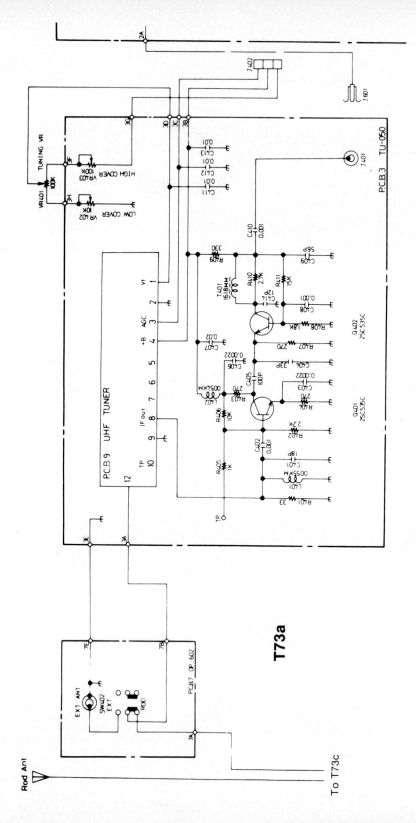

(T73a) CIRCUIT DIAGRAM (TUNER AND I.F. STAGES)—MODEL W154 (PART)

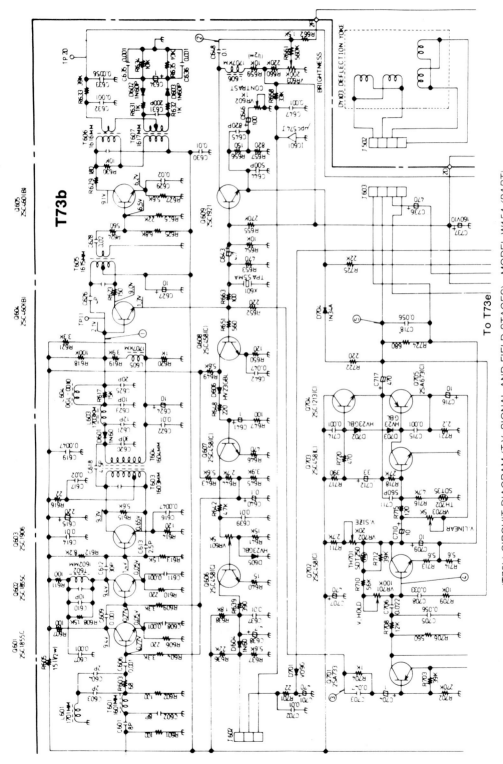

(T73b) CIRCUIT DIAGRAM (T.V. SIGNAL AND FIELD STAGES)—MODEL W154 (PART)

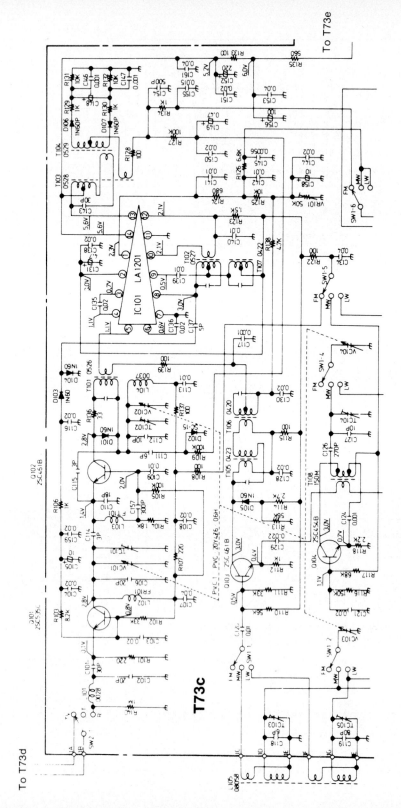

(T73c) CIRCUIT DIAGRAM (RADIO AND TAPE STAGES) — MODEL W154 (PART)

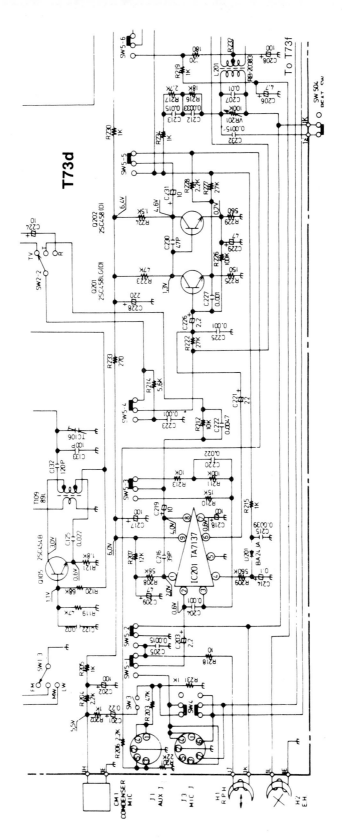

(T73d) CIRCUIT DIAGRAM (RADIO AND TAPE STAGES)—MODEL W154 (PART)

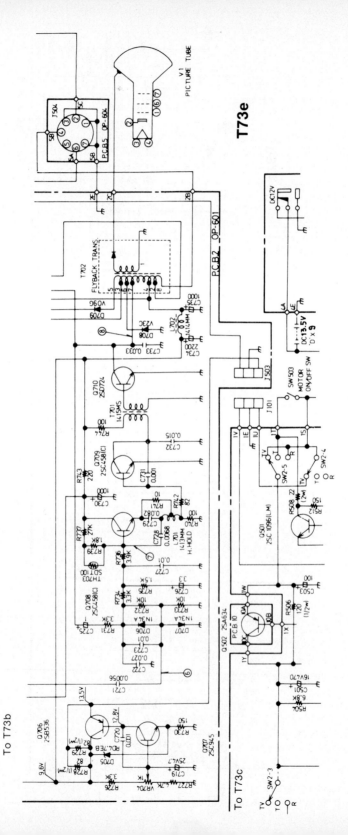

(T73e) CIRCUIT DIAGRAM (L.O.P. AND POWER STAGES)—MODEL W154 (PART)

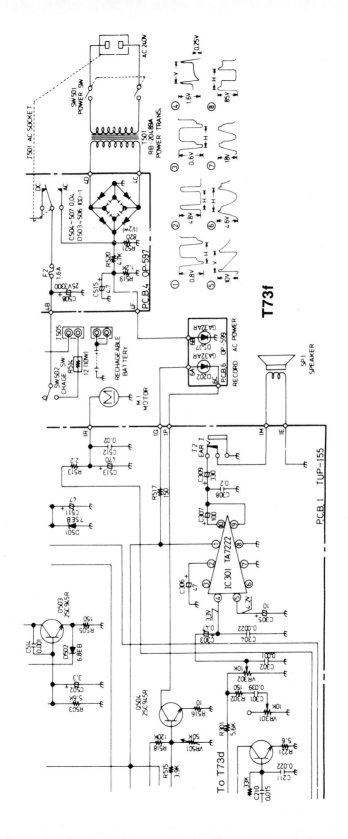

(T73i) CIRCUIT DIAGRAM (A.F. AND POWER STAGES)—MODEL W154 (CONTINUED)

RADIO SERVICING
(Including Tape Recorders, Record Players, etc.)

ACKNOWLEDGEMENTS
Alba (Radio and Television) Ltd.
Binatone International Ltd.
Crown Radio Ltd.
Fidelity Radio Ltd.
Hacker Sound
Hitachi Sales (U.K.) Ltd.
J.V.C. (U.K.) Ltd.
Philips Service
Rank Radio International
Roberts Radio Company Ltd.
Sanyo Marubeni (U.K.) Ltd.
Sharp Electronics (U.K.) Ltd.
Sony (U.K.) Ltd.
Thorn Consumer Electronics
Technical and Optical Equipment (London) Ltd.
Waltham Electronics (U.K.) Ltd.

ALBA   Model 945

General Description: A three-waveband A.M./F.M. portable radio receiver operating on mains or battery supplies. A socket is provided for the connection of an earphone.

Mains Supply: 240 volts, 50Hz.

Batteries: 6 volts (4×HP7).

Fuse: 500mA.

Wavebands: L.W. 150-270kHz; M.W. 510-1620kHz; F.M. 87-109MHz.

Loudspeaker: 8 ohms impedance.

Dismantling

Remove the two screws from the bottom of the cabinet. The two sections of the cabinet may then be separated. Pull off the clip on the telescopic aerial and this will allow the two sections to be laid side by side (limited to the extent of the interconnecting leads) for servicing. The handle will be free from its runners.

The p.c.b. scale assembly and fuse panel may be removed complete by taking out the following five screws from the p.c.b.—(1) top left-hand corner. (2) between the Volume and Tuning control knobs, (3) bottom left-hand of panel, (4) bottom right-hand corner, also serving to secure cable tag, (5) adjacent to D10.

Components List

Resistors		R25	10kΩ	C3	30pF	C27	2nF	C51	110pF
R1	5kΩ	R26	2.2kΩ	C4	15pF	C28	5nF	C52	10nF
R2	3.9kΩ	R27	470Ω	C5	1nF	C29	2nF		
R3	330KΩ	R28	10kΩ	C6	22pF	C30	20nF	**Transistors**	
R4	3.9kΩ	R29	27kΩ	C7	1pF	C31	10nF	Q1	ED1502B
R5	220kΩ	R30	3.9kΩ	C8	20nF	C32	150pF	Q2	ED1502B
R6	100Ω	R31	33Ω	C9	20pF	C33	1pF	Q3	ED1502C
R7	220kΩ	R32	2.2kΩ	C10	500pF	C34	10μF	Q4	ED1502C
R8	1kΩ	R33	270kΩ	C11	1nF	C35	20nF	Q5	ED1502C
R9	220Ω	R34	5.6kΩ	C12	3pF	C36	100nF	Q6	ED1502B
R11	330Ω	R35	5Ω	C13	25pF	C37	470nF	Q7	ED1602C
R12	100Ω	R36	6.8kΩ	C14	10nF	C38	10pF	Q8	ED1602C
R13	22Ω	R37	22kΩ	C15	20nF	C39	500pF	Q9	ED1802K
R14	330kΩ	R38	27kΩ	C16	20nF	C40	470μF	Q10	ED1802K
R15	470Ω	R39	5Ω	C17	20nF	C41	10nF		
R16	470Ω	R40	150Ω	C18	20nF	C42	10nF	**Diodes**	
R17	5.6kΩ	R41	680Ω	C19	20nF	C43	220μF	D1	1N4148
R18	1kΩ	R42	680Ω	C20	20nF	C44	470nF	D2	1N4148
R19	1kΩ	R43	220Ω	C21	3pF	C45	1000μF	D3	1N60
R20	1kΩ	R44	1.5kΩ	C22	100μF	C46	10nF	D4	1N4148
R2	13.3kΩ			C23	20nF	C47	10nF	D5	1N60
R22	3.3kΩ	**Capacitors**		C24	20nF	C48	0-20pF	D6	1N60
R23	1kΩ	C1	tuning	C25	10μF	C49	1nF	D7	1N4148
R24	6.8kΩ	C2	25pF	C26	2nF	C50	0-20pF	D8	1N4148

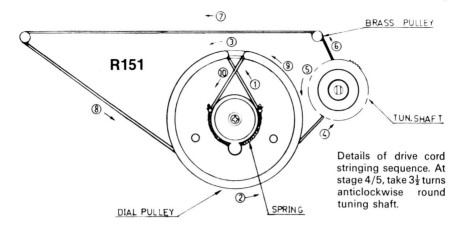

Details of drive cord stringing sequence. At stage 4/5, take $3\frac{1}{2}$ turns anticlockwise round tuning shaft.

(R151) DRIVE CORD—MODEL 945

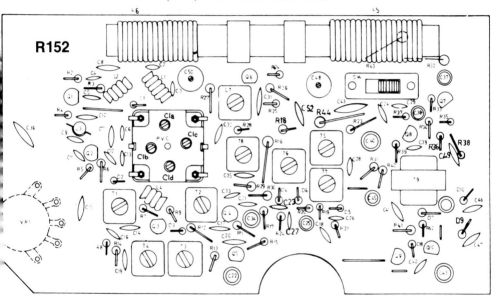

(R152) COMPONENT LAYOUT—MODEL 945

Transistor Voltages:

Transistor		Emitter	Base	Collector
Q1	ED1502B	1.2V	1.7V	4.1V
Q2	ED1502B	1.75V	2.25V	3.9V
Q3	ED1502C	0.75V	1.4V	3.8V
Q4	ED1502C	0.29V	0.99V	4.0V
Q5	ED1502C	0.3V	0.95V	3.8V
Q6	ED1502B	0.85V	1.5V	4.0V
Q7	ED1602C	4.2V	3.6V	2.76V
Q8	ED1602C	4.2V	3.5V	0.73V
Q9	ED1802K	3.0V	2.4V	0
Q10	ED1802K	5.9V	5.25V	3.0V

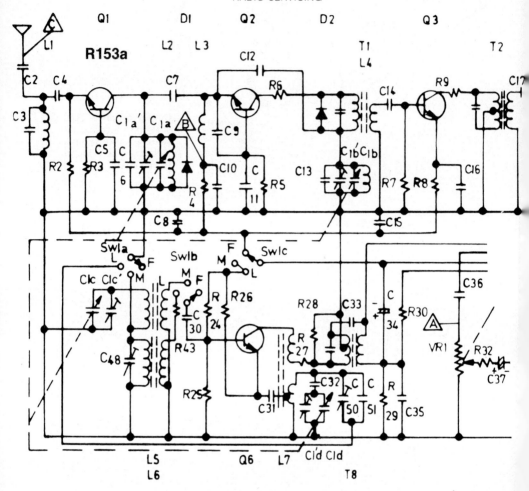

(R153a) CIRCUIT DIAGRAM—MODEL 945 *(PART)*

Alignment

A.M. Alignment: Connect output meter across the loudspeaker terminals. Connect A.M. signal generator to standard coupling loop placed near to, and coaxial with, the ferrite rod aerial.

Switch Receiver to M.W. and turn the Volume control to maximum. The output from the signal generator should be progressively reduced, as alignment proceeds, to the lowest level consistent with useable output readings on the meter.

378

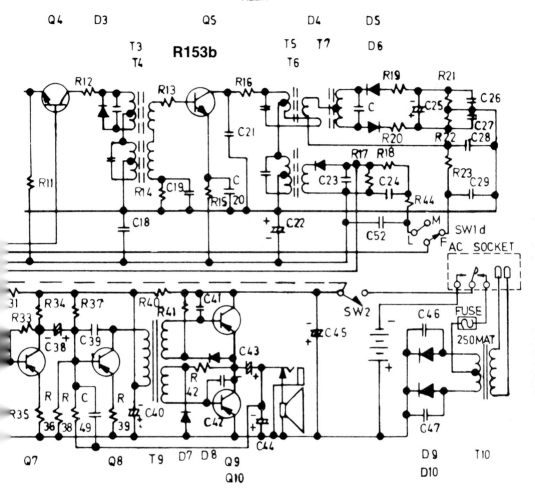

(R153b) CIRCUIT DIAGRAM—MODEL 945 *(CONTINUED)*

Tune to extreme high frequency end of scale. Inject a signal of 470kHz, modulated to 30% A.M. at 400Hz, and adjust the cores of T8, T6 and T4 for maximum output. Repeat these steps for optimum results.

Retune receiver to extreme low frequency end of scale, inject a signal of 510kHz, then tune the core of L7 for maximum output. Retune receiver to extreme high frequency end of scale, inject a signal of 1620kHz, then adjust C1d for maximum output.

Repeat the L7/C1d steps.

Retune receiver to 600 mark, inject a signal of 600kHz, then adjust position of L5 on ferrite rod for maximum output. Retune receiver to 1400 mark, inject a signal of 1400kHz then adjust trimmer C1c for maximum output.

Repeat the L5/C1c steps.

Switch receiver to L.W. and tune to extreme high frequency end of scale. Inject a signal of 270kHz and adjust trimmer C50 for maximum output. Retune receiver to 260 mark, inject a signal of 260kHz, then adjust trimmer C48 for maximum output. Retune receiver to 170, inject a signal of 170kHz, then adjust position of L6 on ferrite rod for maximum output.

Repeat the C48 and L6 steps. Repeat the C50, C48 and L6 steps.

F.M. Alignment: Switch radio to F.M., tune to extreme high frequency end of scale and turn the Volume control to minimum. Connect F.M. sweep generator to test point B (junction R4/C10) and connect Oscilloscope to test point A (junction VR1/C36). Inject a signal of 10.7MHz, deviation 250kHz, and adjust the cores of T1, T2, T3, T5 and T7 to obtain maximum gain and symmetry of S curve centred on 10.7MHz.

Transfer F.M. generator to test point C (F.M. aerial). Retune receiver to extreme low frequency end of scale, inject a signal of 87MHz and adjust L4 (altering spacing of coil turns) for maximum output. Retune receiver to extreme high frequency end of scale, inject a signal of 109MHz, then adjust C1b for maximum output.

Repeat L4 and C1b steps until no further improvement can be obtained.

Tune Radio to 90 mark, inject a signal of 90MHz and adjust L2 (altering spacing of coil turns) for maximum output. Retune radio to 106, inject a signal of 106MHz, then adjust C1a for maximum output.

Repeat the L2/C1a and then the L4/C1b/L2/C1a steps until no further improvement can be obtained.

General Description: A two waveband car radio operating from a positive or negative earthed system by means of an internal switch.

Battery: 12 volts.

Fuse: 2 amps.

Wavebands: L.W. 150-272kHz; M.W. 545-1515kHz.

Loudspeaker: 4 ohms impedance.

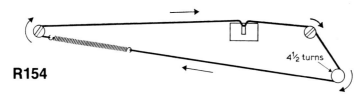

R154

CORD DRIVE SHOWN WITH CORES FULLY IN.

(R154) DRIVE CORD—MODELS ACR1, ACR4

Dismantling

To obtain access to the component side of the printed circuit board and the drive cord, remove two screws, one each side of the casing metalwork, when the U-shaped top plate can be removed.

To obtain access to the copper side of the printed circuit board, remove the two screws on the cover plate on underside of case; cover plate can then be removed.

To remove escutcheon plate, pull off the two control knobs and remove the hexagon nuts and washers from control spindles; the plate will then lift off. The removal of its two fixing screws will allow the scale moulding to be removed. Note that in replacing the escutcheon plate, that a thick washer is placed on each control spindle behind the plate and a thin washer in front of it.

Alignment

Removal of casing top plate will provide access to all alignment adjustments. Connect A.C. output meter ($4\,\Omega$ impedance) across loudspeaker terminals. Connect A.M. signal generator, via dummy aerial, across aerial socket. Turn receiver Volume control to maximum.

During alignment, progressively reduce signal generator output level to maintain useful output indication on 50mW range of meter.

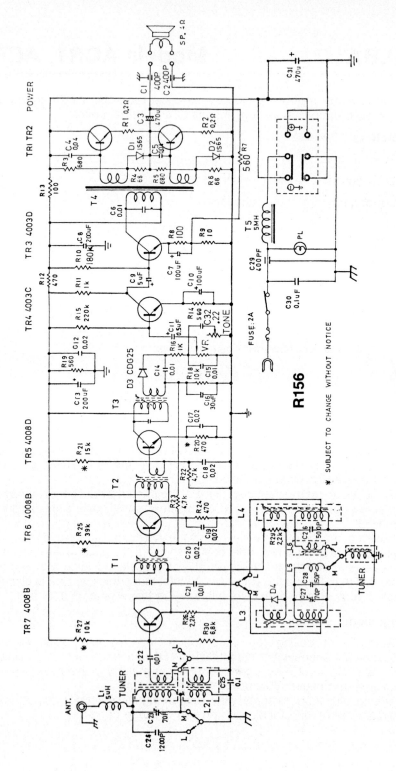

(R156) CIRCUIT DIAGRAM—MODELS ACR1, ACR4

R156

* SUBJECT TO CHANGE WITHOUT NOTICE

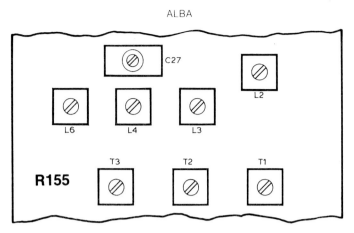

(R155) ALIGNMENT ADJUSTMENTS—MODELS ACR1, ACR4

Switch receiver to M.W. Tune to a signal-free position at low frequency end of waveband. Inject signal of 470kHz and adjust cores of T3, T2 and T1, in that order, for maximum output. Repeat for optimum sensitivity.

Check that scale pointer is correctly positioned; it should line up with the centre of the 2000 mark on L.W. scale. Tune to 500m (mid-way between 450 and 550 marks), inject signal of 600kHz and adjust core of L3 for maximum output. Retune receiver to 200m, inject signal of 1500kHz and adjust trimmer C27 for maximum output. Repeat these adjustments.

Tune to 300m, inject signal of 1kHz and adjust trimmer C23 for maximum output. This trimmer should be re-adjusted on installation when connected to car aerial.

Switch to L.W. Tune to 1500m, inject signal of 200kHz and adjust core of L4 for maximum output. Also peak core of L2. Retune receiver to 200m, inject signal of 150kHz and adjust core of L6 for maximum output. Repeat these adjustments.

ALBA   Models ACR2, ACR5

General Description: A two-waveband A.M. car radio adjustable for positive or negative chassis supply by a switch accessible through the case back. Model ACR5 has no tone control.

Battery: 12 volts D.C.

Fuse: 2 amp. (in battery lead).

Wavebands: L.W. 150-272kHz; M.W. 545-1515kHz.

In addition to continuous tuning, facilities are provided for preset tuning one L.W. channel and four M.W. channels. To set a preset button, tune in required station (push L or any M button as appropriate). Pull fully out L or M button as required, then push in again firmly. The channel is then preset.

Loudspeaker: 4 ohms impedance.

Dismantling

To obtain access to component side of circuit board, remove the two x-head screws securing the top plate to the back of the casing. The top plate may then be slid out. Alignment can be carried out without further dismantling.

To obtain access to the copper side of the circuit board, remove the two x-head screws securing the bottom plate to the back of the casing. The cover plate may then be removed.

Alignment

Removal of the case top plate will provide access to all alignment adjustments. Connect an A.C. output meter (4Ω impedance) across the loudspeaker terminals. Connect an A.M. signal generator, via dummy aerial, across the aerial socket. Turn receiver Volume control to maximum. During alignment, progressively reduce signal generator output level to maintain useful output indication on 50mW range of output meter.

Switch receiver to M.W. by depressing one of the M buttons and tune to a signal-free position at the low frequency end of the scale. Inject signal of 470kHz and adjust cores of T3, T2 and T1, in that order, for maximum output. Repeat for optimum sensitivity.

Tune receiver to 500m (mid-way between 450 and 550 markings), inject signal of 600kHz and adjust core of L9 for maximum output. Retune receiver to 200m, inject signal of 1500kHz and adjust trimmer C13 for maximum output. Repeat for optimum tracking.

Tune receiver to 300m, inject signal of 1000kHz and adjust trimmer C6 for maximum output.

Switch to L.W. by depressing the L button. Tune receiver to 2000m, inject signal of 150kHz and adjust core of L7 for maximum output. Retune receiver to 1500m, inject signal of 200kHz and adjust core of L8 for maximum output. Repeat for optimum tracking. Inject signal of 175kHz, tune in signal on receiver, then adjust L6 and L5 for maximum output.

Remove signal generator, connect aerial. Switch to M.W. and tune to a weak station around 200m. Then adjust trimmer C1 (accessible through hole in side of case) for maximum output.

(R157) ALIGNMENT ADJUSTMENTS—MODELS ACR2, ACR5

384

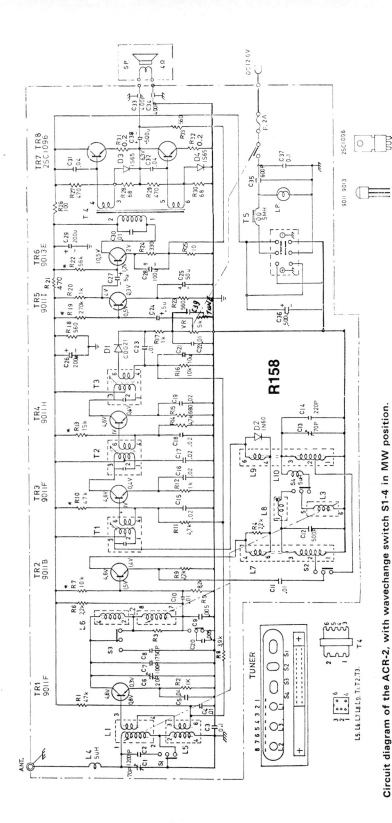

Circuit diagram of the ACR-2, with wavechange switch S1-4 in MW position.

(R158) CIRCUIT DIAGRAM—MODELS ACR2, ACR5

General Description: A mains-operated electronic digital clock radio covering A.M. and F.M. wavebands. Alarm facilities are included in the timing integrated circuit.

Mains Supply: 240 volts, 50Hz.

Fuse: 500mA.

Wavebands: L.W. 150-270kHz; M.W. 515-1620kHz; F.M. 88-108MHz.

Press Buttons: *Time, fast, slow:* To set the time, press and hold down Time button, then advance the display to obtain correct hours and minutes A.M. or P.M. by pressing either Fast or Slow buttons. Depressing Fast button will advance display by 60 minutes per second: Slow button by 2 min/s.

Note: On first switching on, the display will flash on and off and will not function as a clock until the time has been set. After a break in power, a flashing display will indicate that actual time and alarm time must be reset.

Sleep: Depress Sleep button; real time will disappear from the display and a time between 00 and 59 minutes will be shown. While still holding down the Sleep button, depress the Slow button also; when the required 'sleep time' appears, release the Slow button then the Sleep button, when the display will return to real time.

Set function selector to Off for the radio to switch off completely at the end of sleep time; to switch off before the total number of minutes has passed, press the Snooze button. Set the function switch to Auto if it is required for an alarm call (radio or buzzer) to be made at the end of sleep time.

Alarm: Depress the Alarm button, hold it down, and depress Fast or Slow button to display the required call time. Release Fast or Slow button, then Alarm button; the clock will revert to displaying real time. Function switch should be set to Auto and the Alarm/Music switch set to required position. Switch-on of radio/buzzer will continue for one hour unless cancelled by turning function switch to Off.

Snooze: Apart from shutting off the sleep cycle (see above) this allows an extra 'Oversleep' period to be selected after a call has been given. Pressing the button shuts off the radio or buzzer for 8/9 minutes, after which the call will sound again. This can be repeated 6 or 7 times until the call time is exhausted or the function switch turned to Off.

Loudspeaker: 8 ohms impedance.

Dismantling

To obtain access to the component sides of the printed circuit boards, the top of the case can be separated from the lower section, to the extent of the speaker lead, by removing three screws in deep holes in the bottom of the cabinet. Viewing the bottom with the scale at the top, the screws are located as

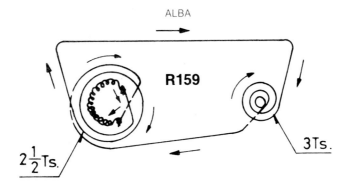

(R159) DRIVE CORD—MODEL C6

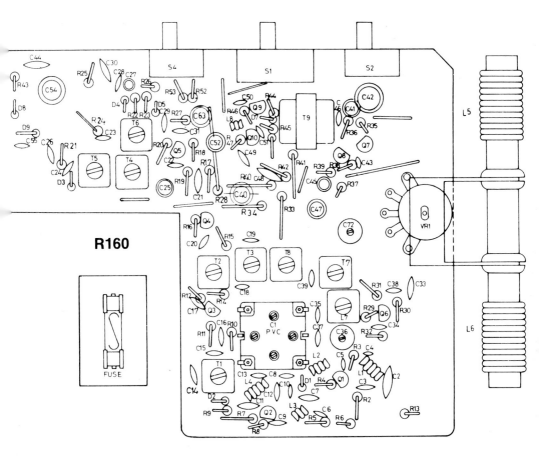

(R160) COMPONENT LAYOUT—MODEL C6

follows: (1) left of and below top left rubber foot, (2) right of and below top right rubber foot, (3) central between bottom two rubber feet.

To obtain access to the copper side of the main p.c.b. it is first necessary to detach the front panel assembly by taking out the three short securing screws fixing it to the cabinet base. The main p.c.b. is secured to the cabinet by 4 x-head screws, the removal of which will enable the complete p.c.b./drive assembly to be lifted away, gently flexing the cabinet side to enable the tuning and volume knobs to be cleared.

Transistor Voltages:

	Q1	Q2	Q3	Q4	Q5	Q6	Q7	Q8	Q9	Q10	Q11	Q12
B	—3.9V	—3.6V	—3.5V	—5.3V	—3.6V	—4.2V	—0.6V	—1.25V	—4.7V	—0.6V	—7.6V	—8.1V
E	—4.5V	—4.1V	—4.1V	—5.9V	—4.2V	—4.8V	0	—0.65V	—4.1V	0	—8.3V	—7.5V
C	0	0	0	0	0	0	—1.3V	—6.5V	—8.3V	—4.1V	—8.1V	—8.3V

Alignment

M.W./L.W. Alignment: Connect output meter across the speaker terminals. Connect an A.M. signal generator output leads to a standard coupling coil placed near to, and coaxial with, the ferrite rod aerial. Throughout alignment, keep signal output level as low as possible consistent with clear indication, reducing signal level as the circuits come into alignment.

I.F. Alignment: Switch to M.W. and tune to extreme high frequency end of scale. Turn volume control to maximum. Inject a signal of 470kHz and adjust the cores of T5, T8 and T7 for maximum output. Repeat for optimum gain.

R.F. Alignment (M.W.): With the receiver and test equipment set as above, inject a signal of 1630kHz and adjust oscillator trimmer C1d' for maximum output. Return receiver to extreme low frequency end of scale, inject a signal of 507kHz and adjust oscillator coil L7 for maximum output. Repeat the C1d' and L7 adjustments for optimum results.

Return receiver to centre of 130 scale mark, inject a signal of 1300kHz and adjust aerial trimmer C1C' a for maximum output. Return receiver to 60 scale mark, inject a signal of 600kHz and adjust L5 on ferrite rod for maximum output.

Repeat in sequence C1c'/L5, C1d'/L7, C1c'/L5 until no further improvement can be obtained.

R.F. Alignment (L.W.): Switch to L.W. and tune receiver to extreme high frequency end of scale. Inject a signal of 270kHz and adjust trimmer C36 for maximum output. Retune receiver to 260 mark, inject a signal of 260kHz and adjust trimmer C72 for maximum output.

Retune receiver to 170 mark, inject a signal of 170kHz and adjust L6 on ferrite rod for maximum output.

Repeat in sequence C72/L6 and C72/C36/L6 until no further improvement can be obtained.

F.M. Alignment:

I.F. Alignment: Switch to F.M. and tune to extreme high frequency end of scale. Turn Volume control to minimum. Connect the output terminal of a F.M. Genescope to the F.M. mixer transistor (02) emitter and its input terminal to F.M. detector output (C63). Inject a signal of 10.7MHz centre frequency with a 10.7MHz marker and adjust the cores of T6, T4, T3, T2 and T1 for Symmetric 'S' curve. Repeat for optimum 'S' curve.

R.F. Alignment: Connect output meter across the speaker terminals. Turn Volume control to maximum. Connect the output leads of a F.M. signal generator to the F.M. antenna terminal. Throughout alignment, keep signal output level as low as possible, consistent with clear indication, reducing signal level as the circuits come into alignment.

Inject a signal of 108.75MHz and adjust oscillator trimmer C1b' for maximum output. Retune receiver to extreme low frequency end of scale, inject a signal of 87.25MHz and adjust oscillator coil L4 for maximum output. Repeat the C1b' and L4 adjustments for optimum results.

Retune receiver to centre of 106 scale mark, inject a signal of 106MHz and adjust aerial trimmer C1a' for maximum output. Retune receiver to the centre between 88 and 92 scale mark, inject a signal of 90MHz and adjust aerial coil L2 for maximum output.

Repeat in sequence C1a'/L2, C1b'/L4, C1a'/C2 until no further improvement can be obtained.

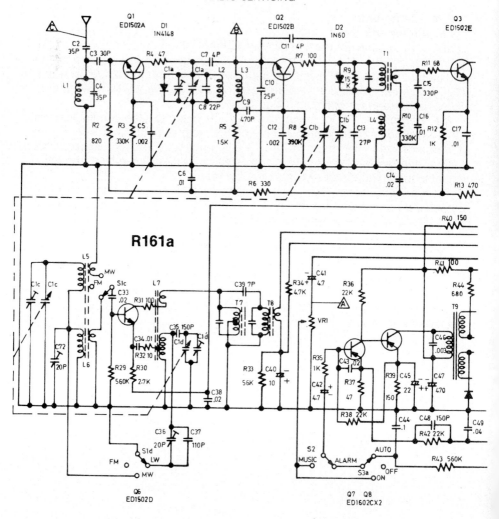

(R161a) CIRCUIT DIAGRAM—MODEL C6 *(PART)*

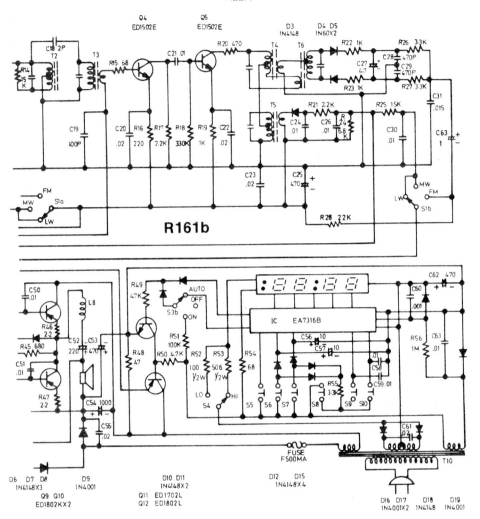

R161b

(R161b) CIRCUIT DIAGRAM—MODEL C6 *(CONTINUED)*

ALBA   Model CR27

General Description: A mains or battery-operated A.M./F.M. radio with cassette tape-recorder. A built-in microphone is fitted and sockets are provided for auxiliary inputs and earphone.

Mains Supply: 240 volts, 50Hz.

Batteries: 6 volts (4×HP11).

Wavebands: M.W. 505-1650kHz; F.M. 87.5-110MHz.

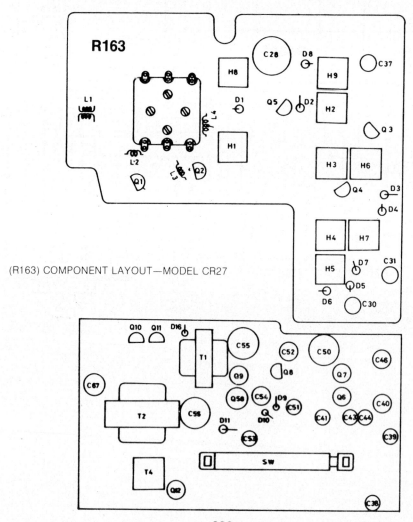

(R163) COMPONENT LAYOUT—MODEL CR27

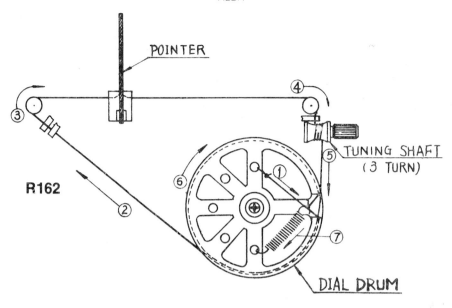

(R162) DRIVE CORD—MODEL CR27

Alignment

A.M. Section:

Control Setting A.M./F.M. Selector Switch . . . . A.M.   Volume . . . . Max.

Circuit Alignment	Instrument connection	Step	Gen. freq.	Dial setting	Adjustment
I.F.	**A.M. Signal Generator** Radiated Signal	1	470kHz (Mod.)	Tuning gang fully open	A.M. I.F.T. H6, H7 & H9 Adjust for max. output
	Output Meter (V.T.V.M.) Connect across speaker voice coil.	2			Repeat until no further improvement can be made.
Oscillator		3	600kHz (Mod.)	Tuning gang fully open	H8: (A.M. Osc. coil) Adjust for max. output
		4	1500kHz (Mod.)	Tuning gang fully open	A.M. Osc. trimmer Adjust for max. output
		5	—	—	Repeat steps 3 & 4
R.F. Tracking		6	600kHz (Mod.)	Tune to Signal	L5 (A.M. Ant. coil) Adjust coil on ferrite core for max. output
		7	1400kHz (Mod.)	Tune to Signal	A.M. Antenna trimmer Adjust for max. output
		8	—	—	Repeat steps 6 & 7

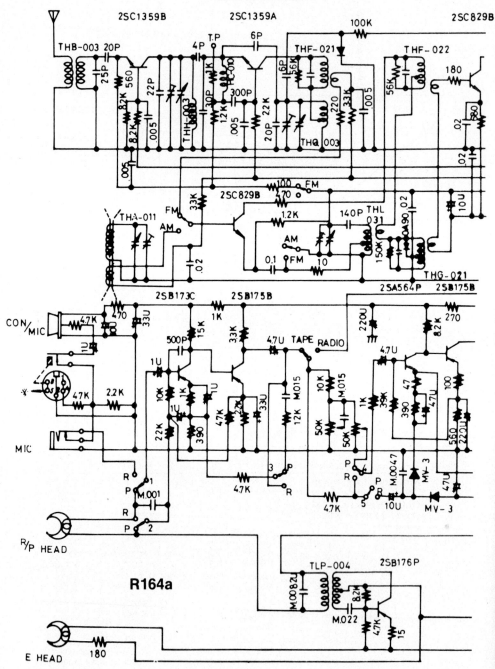

(R164a) CIRCUIT DIAGRAM—MODEL CR27 *(PART)*

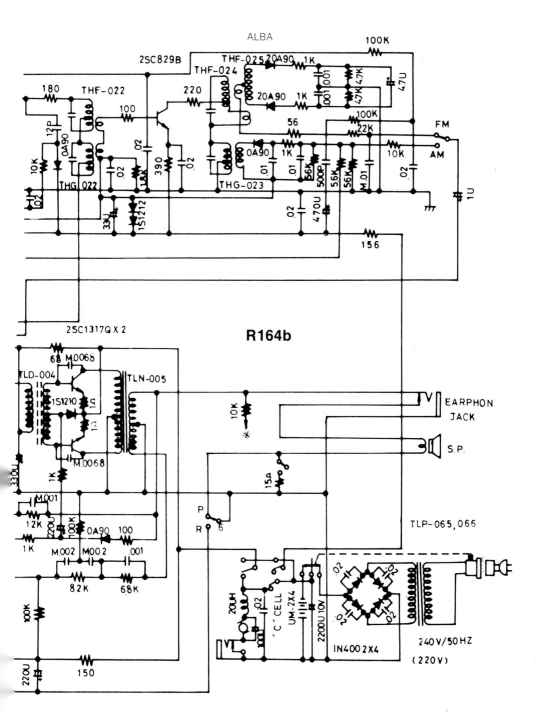

(R164b) CIRCUIT DIAGRAM—MODEL CR27 *(CONTINUED)*

F.M. Section:

Control Setting A.M./F.M. Selector Switch . . . . F.M.   Volume . . . . Max.

Circuit Alignment	Instrument connection	Step	Gen. freq.	Dial setting	Adjustment
	F.M. I.F. Sweep Generator Connect across test point TP—1	1	10.7MHz (Mod.)	Tuning gang fully open	F.M. I.F.T. H1, H2, H3 & H4 Adjust for max.
I.F.	**Oscilloscope** Connect across test point TP—2	2	—	—	symmetrical response Repeat step 1
Ratio det.	**Oscilloscope** Connect across TP—3 and ground	3	10.7MHz (Mod.)	Tuning gang fully open	F.M. I.F.T. H5 Adjust for symmetrical 'S' curve entered 10.7MHz
	F.M. Signal Generator Connect L1	4	86.5MHz (Mod.)	Tuning gang fully closed	L4 (F.M. Osc. coil) Adjust for max. output
Oscillator	**Output meter (V.T.V.M.)** Connect across speaker voice coil	5	110MHz (Mod.)	Tuning gang fully open	F.M. Osc. trimmer Adjust for max. output
		6	—	—	Repeat step 4 & 5
		7	90MHz (Mod.)	Tune to signal	L2 (F.M. R.F. coil) Adjust for max. output
R.F. Tracking		8	106MHz (Mod.)	Tune to signal	F.M. R.F. trimmer Adjust for max. output
		9	—	—	Repeat steps 7 & 8

Tape Section:

Control Setting Tape/Radio Selector Switch Tape Volume . . . Min. Tape Condition Recording

Circuit alignment	Instrument connection	Adjustment
Oscillator	Digital counter	Adjust T4 for frequency 40KHz

ALBA   Model CR28

General Description: A mains or battery-operated A.M./F.M. radio with cassette tape-recorder. A microphone is 'built-in', and sockets are provided for the connection of auxiliary inputs and an earphone.

Mains Supply: 240 volts, 50Hz.

Batteries: 6 volts (4×1.5 volts).

Wavebands: 145-285kHz; M.W. 520-1620kHz; F.M. 88-108MHz.

Components List

Resistors		R22	390	R46	47K	R69	120	Transistors	
R1	820	R23	56	R47	3.3K	R70	330	Q1	2SC1359B
R2	15K	R24	3.9K	R48	1K	R71	68	Q2	2SC1359A
R3	12K	R25	120	R49	470K	R72	33K	Q3-6	2SC829B
R4	1K	R26	56	R50	1.8K	R73	1.5K	Q7	2SC644R
R5	3.3K	R27,28	1.5K	R51	2.7K	R74	3.3K	Q8-10	2SC828R
R6	2.2K	R29	1K	R52	2.2K	R75	2.7K	Q11,12	2SC1788
R7	15K	R30	82K	R53	120K	R76	3.9K	Q13	2SC828Q,P
R8	100K	R31	39K	R54	1.8K	R77	100	Q14	2SC828R
R9	180	R32	6.8K	R55	220	R78	1		
R10	3.3K	R33	15K	R56	18K	R79	470K	Diodes	
R11	390	R34	2.2K	R57	1K	R80	1.2K	D1	IS2139B
R12	560	R35	68K	R58	5.6K	R81	33K	D2-4	QA90
R13	120	R36	82K	R59	8.2K	R82	8	D5,6	VD1222
R14	150	R37	1K	R60,61	15K	R83	820	D7,8	OA90
R15	27K	R38	120K	R62	3.3K	R84	150K	D9,10	20A90
R16	68	R39	10K	R63	120K	R85	10K	D11	1S1212
R17	270	R40	12K	R64	680	R86	27K	D12	1S1210
R18	470	R41	4.7K	R65	390	R87	22	D13,14	OA90
R19	100	R42	3.3K	R66	120	R88	1K	D15-18	1N4002
R20	470K	R43	22K	R67	6.8K	R89	22		
R21	100	R44,45	1.5K	R68	270K				

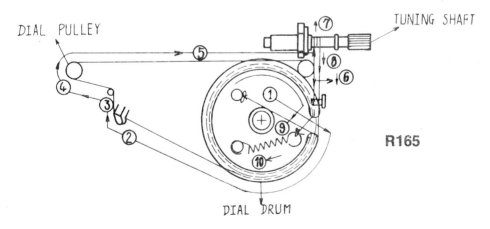

(R165) DRIVE CORD—MODEL CR28

Alignment

L.W. Section:

Control Setting F.M./M.W./L.W. Selector Slide Switch . . . . L.W.

Circuit Alignment	Instrument connection	Step	Gen. freq.	Dial setting	Adjustment
	L.W. Signal Generator radiated signal	1	465kHz (Mod.)	Tuning gang fully open	L.W. I.F.T. H3, H5, H7 Adjust for max. output
I.F.	Output meter (V.T.V.M.) connect across speaker voice coil	2			Repeat until no further improvement can be made
		3	145kHz (Mod.)	Tuning gang fully closed	L8 (L.W. Osc. coil) Adjust for max. output
Oscillator	''	4	285kHz (Mod.)	Tuning gang fully open	L.W. Osc. trimmer Adjust for max. output
		5	—	—	Repeat steps 3 & 4
		6	175kHz (Mod.)	Tuning to signal	L_6 (L.W. Ant. coil) Adjust coil on ferrite core for max. output
R.F. Tracking	''	7	250kHz (Mod.)	Tuning to signal	L.W. Antenna trimmer Adjust for max. output
		8	—	—	Repeat steps 6 & 7

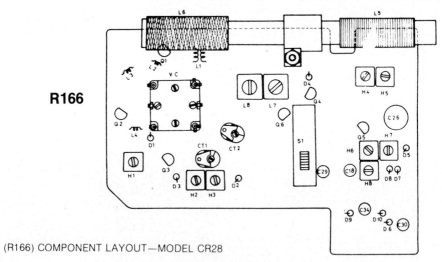

R166

(R166) COMPONENT LAYOUT—MODEL CR28

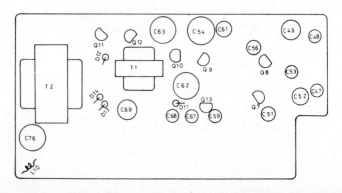

M.W. Section:

Control Setting F.W./M.W./L.W. Selector Slide Switch . . . . M.W.

Circuit Alignment	Instrument connection	Step	Gen. freq.	Dial setting	Adjustment
I.F.	A.M. Signal Generator radiated signal	1	465kHz (Mod.)	Tuning gang fully open	M.W. I.F.T. H3, H5, H7 Adjust for max. output
	Output Meter (V.T.V.M.) connect across speaker voice coil	2			Repeat until no further improvement can be made
Oscillator	''	3	520kHz (Mod.)	Tuning gang fully closed	L7 (M.W. Osc. coil) Adjust for max. output
		4	1620kHz (Mod.)	Tuning gang fully open	M.W. Osc. trimmer Adjust for max. output
		5	—	—	Repeat steps 3 & 4
R.F. Tracking	''	6	600kHz (Mod.)	Tune to signal	L5 (M.W. Ant. coil) Adjust coil on ferrite core for max. output
		7	1400kHz (Mod.)	Tune to signal	M.W. Antenna trimmer Adjust for max. output
		8	—	—	Repeat steps 6 & 7

F.M. Section

Control Setting F.M./M.W./L.W. Selector Slide Switch . . . . F.M.

Circuit alignment	Instrument connection	Step	Gen. freq.	Dial setting	Adjustment
I.F.	F.M. I.F. Sweep Generator connect across test point TP-1	1	10.7MHz (Mod.)	Tuning gang fully open	F.M. I.F.T. H1, H2, H4 & H6 Adjust for max. symmetrical response
	Oscilloscope Connect across test point TP-2	2	— —	—	Repeat step 1
	Oscilloscope connect across TP-3 and ground	3	10.7MHz (Mod.)	Tuning gang fully open	F.M. I.F.T. H8 Adjust for symmetrical 'S' curve entered 10.7MHz
Oscillator	F.M. Signal Generator connect L1	4	88MHz (Mod.)	Tuning gang fully closed	L_4 (F.M. Osc. coil) Adjust for max. output
	Output Meter (V.T.V.M.) connect across speaker voice coil	5	108MHz (Mod.)	Tuning gang fully open	F.M. Osc. trimmer Adjust for max. output
		6	—	—	Repeat steps 4 & 5
R.F. tracking	''	7	90MHz (Mod)	Tuning to signal	L2 (F.M. R.F. coil) Adjust for max. output
		8	106MHz (Mod.)	Tuning to signal	F.M. R.F. trimmer Adjust for max. output
		9	—	—	Repeat steps 7 & 8

Tape Section:

Control Setting Tape/Radio Selector Switch . . . Tape   Volume . . . Min.   Tape Condition . . . Recording

Circuit Alignment	Instrument Connection	Adjustment
Oscillator	Digital counter	Adjust T3 for frequency 43KHz

399

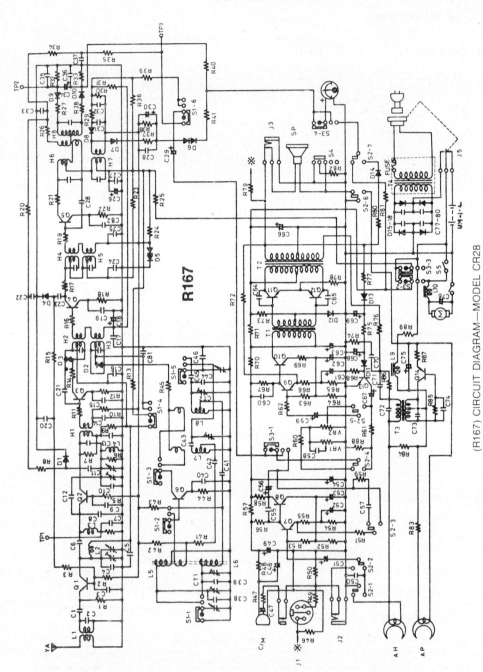

(R167) CIRCUIT DIAGRAM—MODEL CR28

BINATONE   Model 'Calendar' 01/6373

General Description: A mains-operated electronic clock with A.M./F.M. stereo radio. Automatic alarm is included and a socket is provided for the connection of stereo headphones.

Mains Supply: 240 volts, 50Hz.

Wavebands: L.W. 156-285kHz; M.W. 525-1620kHz; F.M. 88-108MHz.

Loudspeaker: 8 ohms impedance.

Transistor Voltages:

Item	Type	Function	Ve(V)	Vb(V)	Vc(V)
Q1	FCS9016F	V.H.F. R.F.	0.46	1.21	5.61
Q2	FCS9018F	V.H.F. Convertor	1.37	2.07	5.60
Q3	FCS9018F	L.W.-M.W.-V.H.F. I.F.	0.29	1.02	5.63
Q4	FCS9018G	L.W.-M.W.-V.H.F. I.F.	1.5	2.24	4.86
Q5	FCS9018G	V.H.F. I.F.	0.4	1.08	5.24
Q6	FCS9016F	L.W.-M.W. Mixer	1.04	1.68	5.64
Q7	FCS9014C	Audio Pre-Amp. (L)	4.72	5.32	7.45
Q8	FCS9014C	Audio Pre-Amp. (R)	4.72	5.32	7.45
Q9	FCS9015C	Audio Driver (L)	8.13	7.45	4.34
Q10	FCS9015C	Audio Driver (R)	8.13	7.45	4.34
Q11	JE9013H	Power-Switching	9.8	10.6	10.5
Q12	JE9013F	Power-Amp. (L)	3.71	4.35	10.5
Q13	JE9013F	Power-Amp. (R)	3.71	4.35	10.5
Q14	JE9012F	Power-Amp. (L)	3.70	3.07	0
Q15	JE9012F	Power-Amp. (R)	3.70	3.07	0
Q16	LM9015D	Snooze Sensor	18.2		0.51
Q17	JE9012H	Brightness Control	10.5	6.98	10.4

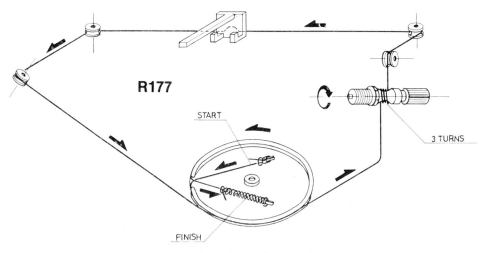

(R177) DRIVE CORD—MODEL 'CALENDAR'

Alignment:

Step	Signal source connect to	Set signal at	Set radio to	Output indication connect to	Adjust	Adjust for
1.	Set Band switch to M.W. section					
2.	M.W. I.F. sweep generator through TP9 & TP10	465kHz	High end (Gang open)	Oscilloscope through TP5 & TP6	T6 T7 T8	Maximum output and symmetrical V curve
3.	M.W. R.F. signal generator through radiating antenna loop	525kHz	Low End (Gang close)	V.T.V.M. across speaker output	L7	
4.		1650kHz	High end (Gang open)		CT3	Maximum output
5.	Repeat steps 3 and 4 to get the correct band coverage					
6.	M.W. R.F. signal generator through radiating antenna loop	600kHz	600kHz	V.T.V.M. across speaker output	L5	
7.		1400kHz	1400kHz		CT4	Maximum output
8.	Repeat steps 6 and 7 to get the correct tracking					
9.	Set Band switch to L.W. section					
10.	L.W. R.F. signal generator through radiating antenna loop	285kHz	High end (Gang open)	V.T.V.M. across speaker output	CT5	Maximum output
11.		180kHz	180kHz		L6	
12.		245kHz	245kHz		CT6	
13.	Repeat steps 10, 11 and 12 to get the correct band coverage and tracking					
14.	Set Band switch to V.H.F. section					
15.	V.H.F. I.F. sweep generator through TP3 & TP4	10.7MHz	High end (Gang open)	Oscilloscope through TP7 & TP8	T1 T2 T3 T4 T5	Maximum amplitude and symmetrical 'S' curve
16.	Repeat step 15 to get the maximum amplitude waveform					
17.	V.H.F. signal generator through V.H.F. ant. input TP1 & TP2	87MHz	Low end (Gang close)	V.T.V.M. across speaker output	L4	Maximum output
18.		109MHz	High end (Gang open)		CT1	
19.	Repeat steps 17 and 18 to get the correct band coverage					
20.	V.H.F. signal generator through V.H.F. ant. input TP1 & TP2	90MHz	90MHz	V.T.V.M. across speaker output	L2	
21.		106MHz	106MHz		CT2	Maximum output
22.	Repeat steps 20 and 21 to get the correct tracking					
23.	V.H.F. Stereo generator through TP1 & TP2	98MHz	98MHz	V.T.V.M. across speaker output	SFR34	Maximum channel separation and maximum stereo indicator

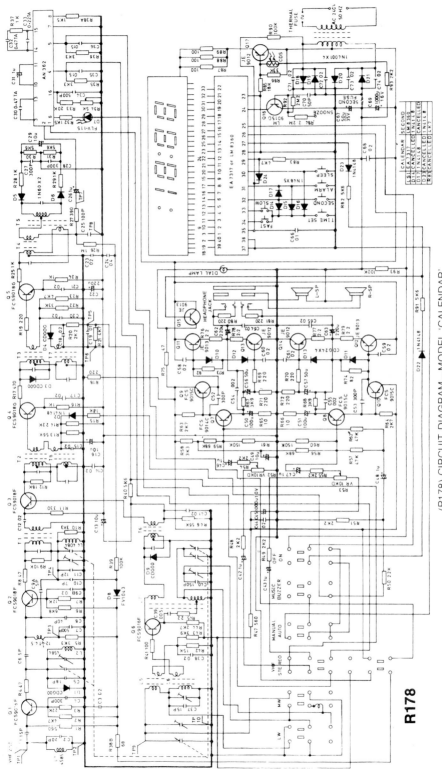

(R178) CIRCUIT DIAGRAM—MODEL 'CALENDAR'

R178

BINATONE — Model 'Mirage' 01/2971

General Description: A mains-operated electronic digital clock radio covering A.M. and F.M. wavebands. Alarm facilities are fitted and a socket is provided for the connection of an earphone.

Mains Supply: 240 volts, 50Hz.

Wavebands: Long, Medium, and V.H.F.

Loudspeaker: 8 ohms impedance.

Transistor Voltages and Types

Transistor	Type	Application	V_c	V_b	V_e
Q_1	9018F	F.M. R.F. amp.	4.5	2	1.35
Q_2	9018F	F.M. Conv.	4.6	1.4	1
Q_3	9018G	A.M. F.M. I.F. amp.	4.6	0.8	0.25
Q_4	9018G	A.M. F.M. I.F. amp.	4.3	0.75	0.3
Q_5	9018G	F.M. I.F. amp.	4.2	2.05	2.1
Q_6	9011F	A.M. conv.	5	1.75	1.35
Q_7	9015C	Audio pre-amp.	4.3	0.755	0.35
Q_8	9015C	Audio driver	4.4	1.25	0.75
Q_9	2SB178N	Power	5.9	3.2	3.1
Q_{10}	2SB178N	Power	3	0.2	0.1

Components List:

Resistors

R_1	1.5K	R_{25}	680	R_{49}	150
R_2	10K	R_{26}	1K	R_{50}	470
R_3	12K	R_{27}	1K	R_{51}	10K
R_4	100	R_{28}	47K	R_{52}	820
R_5	1.5K	R_{29}	47K	R_{53}	56
R_6	10K	R_{30}	100	R_{54}	56
R_7	18K	R_{31}	1.5K	R_{55}	820
R_8	100	R_{32}	470K	R_{56}	2.7-3
R_9	330	R_{33}	100	R_{57}	2.7-3
R_{10}	330	R_{34}	10K	R_{58}	470
R_{11}	3.3K	R_{35}	15K	R_{59}	100K
R_{12}		R_{36}	2.2K	R_{60}	100K
R_{13}	100	R_{37}	10	R_{61}	
R_{14}	27K	R_{38}	100K	R_{62}	1M
R_{15}	6.8K	R_{39}	47K	R_{63}	4.7K
R_{16}	220	R_{40}	1.5K	R_{64}	5.6K
R_{17}	470	R_{41}	47K	R_{65}	5.6K
R_{18}		R_{42}	10K	R_{66}	47K
R_{19}	100	R_{43}	3.3K	R_{67}	2.2K
R_{20}	2.2K	R_{44}	2.2K	R_{68}	330
R_{21}	5.6K	R_{45}	6.8K	R_{69}	2.2K
R_{22}	56K	R_{46}	15K	R_{70}	680K
R_{23}	33K	R_{47}	5.6K	R_{71}	82K
R_{24}	2.2K	R_{48}	10	R_{72}	330K

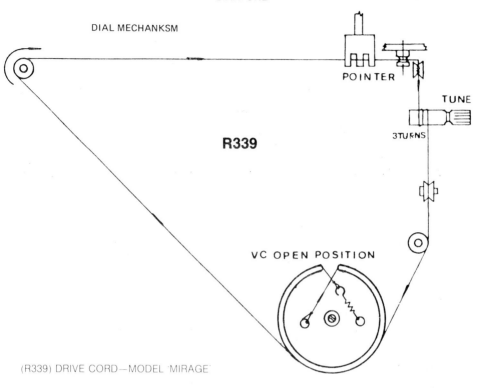

BINATONE

DIAL MECHANKSM

R339

POINTER

TUNE

3TURNS

VC OPEN POSITION

(R339) DRIVE CORD—MODEL 'MIRAGE'

Capacitors

C_1	30p	C_{21}	1000p		
C_2	30p	C_{22}	0.01uf	C_{40}	47uf/10V
C_3	25p	C_{23}	300p	C_{41}	220uf/10V
C_4	5000p	C_{24}	300p	C_{42}	5000p
C_5	22p	C_{25}	0.04uf	C_{43}	5000p
C_6	5p	C_{26}	20p (Trim)	C_{44}	220uf/10V
C_7	30p	C_{27}	20p	C_{45}	470uf/10V
C_8	300p	C_{28}	0.02uf	C_{46}	100uf/10V
C_9	5p	C_{29}	0.02uf	C_{47}	470uf/10V
C_{10}	50000p	C_{11}	18p	C_{48}	0.01uf
C_{12}	5p	C_{30}	20p (Trim)	C_{49}	
C_{13}	0.04uf	C_{31}	120p	C_{50}	0.01uf
C_{14}	0.02uf	C_{32}	150p	C_{51}	0.01uf
C_{15}	0.02uf	C_{33}	0.02uf	C_{52}	0.01uf
C_{16}	0.01uf	C_{34}	4.7uf/10V	C_{53}	100uf125V
C_{17}	0.02uf	C_{35}	47uf/10V	C_{54}	0.01uf
C_{18}	2p	C_{36}	10uf/10V	C_{55}	0.01uf
C_{19}	0.02uf	C_{37}	10uf/10V	C_{56}	0.01uf
C_{20}	0.02uf	C_{38}	200uf/10V	C_{57}	0.01uf
		C_{39}	1uf/10V	C_{58}	0.1uf

405

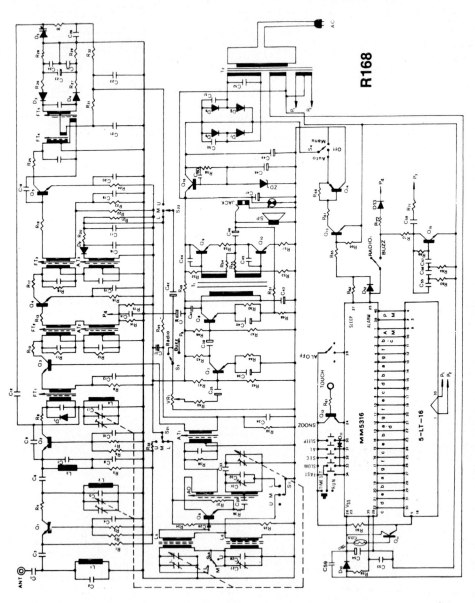

(R168) CIRCUIT DIAGRAM—MODEL 'MIRAGE'

BINATONE   Model 'Digitron' 01/6071

General Description: A mains-operated 3-waveband electronic clock radio. A.F. amplification is by integrated circuit and no provision is made for the connection of an earphone.

Mains Supply: 240 volts, 50Hz.

Fuse: 500mA.

Wavebands: L.W. 160-285kHz; M.W. 520-1640kHz; F.M. 87-109MHz.

Loudspeaker: 8 ohms impedance.

Alignment

L.W. Section:

Control Setting V.H.F./M.W./L.W. Selector Slide Switch . . . . L.W.   Volume . . . . Max.

Circuit alignment	Instrument connection	Step	Gen. freq.	Dial setting	Adjustment
Osc.	Signal gen. radiated signal output meter (V.T.V.M.) connect across speaker voice coil	1	160kHz (Mod.)	Tuning gang fully closed	L6 (L.W. Ant. coil) Adjust for max. output
		2	285kHz	Tuning gang fully open	L.W. trimmer (Osc.) Adjust for max. output
		3			Repeat steps 1 & 2
		4	185kHz (Mod.)	Tune to signal	L6 (L.W. Ant. coil) Adjust for max. output
R.F. tracking	Same as above	5	245kHz (Mod.)	Tune to signal	L.W. trimmer ant. adjust for max. output
		6			Repeat steps 4 & 5

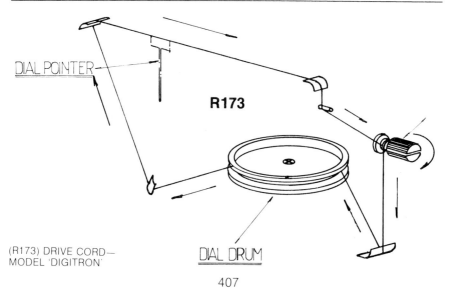

DIAL POINTER

R173

(R173) DRIVE CORD—
MODEL 'DIGITRON'

DIAL DRUM

M.W. Section:

Control Setting V.H.F./M.W./L.W. Selector Slide Switch . . . . M.W.   Volume . . . . Max.

Circuit Alignment	Instrument connection	Step	Gen. freq.	Dial setting	Adjustment
	A.M. Signal gen. radiated signal	1	465kHz (Mod.)	Tuning gang fully closed	A.M. I.F.T. T1, T2, T3 adjust for max. output
I.F.	Output Meter (V.T.V.M.) connect across speaker voice coil	2			Repeat until no further improvement can be made
		3	520kHz (Mod.)	Tuning gang fully closed	L.T. (M.W. Osc. coil) adjust for max. output
Osc.	Same as above	4	1640kHz (Mod.)	Tuning gang fully open	M.W. Osc. trimmer adjust for max. output
		5			Repeat steps 3 & 4
		6	600kHz (Mod.)	Tune to signal	L5 (M.W. Ant. coil) adjust coil on ferrite core for max. output
R.F. tracking	Same as above	7	1400kHz	Tune to signal	M.W. Antenna trimmer adjust for max. output
		8			Repeat steps 6 & 7

V.H.F. Section:

Control Setting V.H.F./M.W./L.W. Selector Slide Switch . . . . V.H.F.   Volume . . . . Max.

Circuit alignment	Instrument connection	Step	Gen. freq.	Dial setting	Adjustment
2F	F.M. I.F. Sweep gen. connect across test point TP-1	1	10.7MHz (Mod.)	Tuning gang fully open	F.M. I.F.T. T1, T2, T3, T4, T5 Adjust for max. symmetrical response 'S' curve
	Oscilloscope connect across test point TP-2	2			Repeat step 1
	F.M. Signal gen. connect L1	3	87MHz	Tuning gang fully closed	L4 (F.M. Osc. coil) Adjust for max. output
Osc.	Output meter (V.T.V.M.) connect across speaker voice coil	4	109MHz (Mod.)	Tuning gang fully open	F.M. Osc. trimmer Adjust for max. output
		5			Repeat steps 3 & 4
		6	90MHz (Mod.)	Tune to signal	L2 (F.M. R.F. coil) Adjust for max. output
R.F. tracking	Same as above	7	106MHz (Mod.)	Tune to signal	F.M. R.F. trimmer Adjust for max. output
		8			Repeat steps 6 & 7

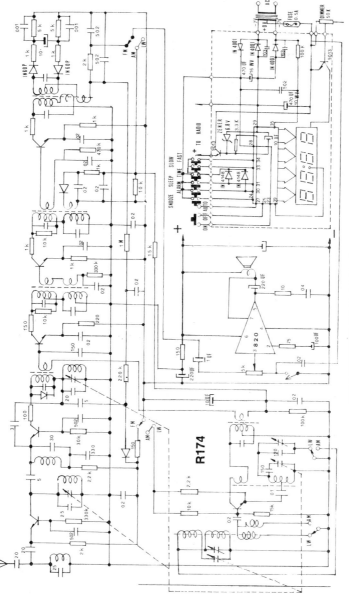

(R174) CIRCUIT DIAGRAM—MODEL 'DIGITRON'

BINATONE   Model 'Majestic' 01/6187

General Description: A 3-waveband stereo radio with electronic digital clock operating from mains supplies. Alarm facilities are fitted and a socket is provided for the connection of stereo headphones.

Mains Supply: 240 volts, 50Hz.

Wavebands: L.W. 165-280kHz; M.W. 535-1605kHz; F.M. 88-108MHz.

Loudspeakers: 8 ohms impedance.

Alignment

M.W./L.W./I.F. Alignment:

Step	Signal source connector	Set signal to	Alignment indicator connector	Set radio dial to	Adjust	Adjust for
1	A.M. R.F. sweep generator	470kHz	V.T.V.M. Oscilloscope across speaker voice coil (8 ohm)	Max. freq. (Tuning gang open)	T1 IF:A	Maximum output symmetrical curve shape
2	To a standard radiation loop	470kHz	V.T.V.M. Oscilloscope across speaker voice coil (8 ohm)	Max. freq.	T4 IF:B	Maximum IF:B
3	To a standard radiation loop	470kHz	V.T.V.M. Oscilloscope across speaker voice coil (8 ohm)	Max. freq.	T6 IF:C	Maximum

V.H.F./I.F. Alignment:

Step	Signal source connector	Set signal to	Alignment indicator connector	Set radio dial to	Adjust	Adjust for
1	F.M. I.F. sweep generator	Sweep centred 10.7MHz	Oscilloscope discriminator output terminal—junction R26 and R31	Max. freq.	T2 IF:A	Volume control Min. position
2	F.M. I.F. sweep generator	Sweep centred 10.7MHz	Oscilloscope discriminator output terminal—junction R26 and R31	Max. freq.	T3 IF:B	Volume control Min. position
3	F.M. I.F. sweep generator	Sweep centred 10.7MHz	Oscilloscope discriminator output terminal— junction R26 and R31	Max. freq.	T5 IF:C	Volume control Min. position
4	F.M. I.F. sweep generator	Sweep centred 10.7MHz	Oscilloscope discriminator output terminal—junction R26 and R31	Max. freq.	T7, 8	Symmetrical 'S' response centred on 10.7MHz

M.W./R.F. Alignment:

Step	Signal source connector	Set signal to	Alignment indicator connector	Set radio dial to	Adjust	Adjust for
1	A.M. signal generator a standard radiation loop antenna	520kHz (low end)	V.T.V.M. oscilloscope connect across voice coil (8 ohm)	520kHz (modulated)	L4 (osc. coil)	Maximum output
2	A.M. signal generator a standard radiation loop antenna	1650kHz (modulated)	V.T.V.M. oscilloscope connect across voice coil (8 ohm)	1650kHz (high end)	TC4 (osc. trimmer)	Maximum output
3	A.M. signal generator a standard radiation loop antenna	600kHz (modulated)	V.T.V.M. oscilloscope connect across voice coil (8 ohm)	600kHz	L6 (ant. coil)	Maximum output
4	A.M. signal generator a standard radiation loop antenna	1400kHz	V.T.V.M. oscilloscope connect across voice coil (8 ohm)	1400kHz (modulated)	TC3 (ant. trimmer)	Maximum output

V.H.F./R.F. Alignment:

Step	Signal source connector	Set signal to	Alignment indicator connector	Set radio dial to	Adjust	Adjust for
1	F.M. signal generator (F.M. ant.) 75 ohm	86.5MHz (modulated)	V.T.V.M. oscilloscope connect across speaker voice coil (8 ohm)	86.5MHz (low end)	L3 (osc. coil)	Maximum
2	F.M. signal generator (F.M. ant.) 75 ohm dummy antenna	108MHz (modulated)	"	108MHz (high end)	TC6 (osc. trimmer)	
3	F.M. signal generator (F.M. ant.) 75 ohm dummy antenna	90MHz (modulated)	"	90MHz	L2 (R.F. coil)	
4	F.M. signal generator (F.M. ant.) 75 ohm dummy antenna	106MHz (modulated)	"	106MHz	TC5 (R.F. trimmer)	

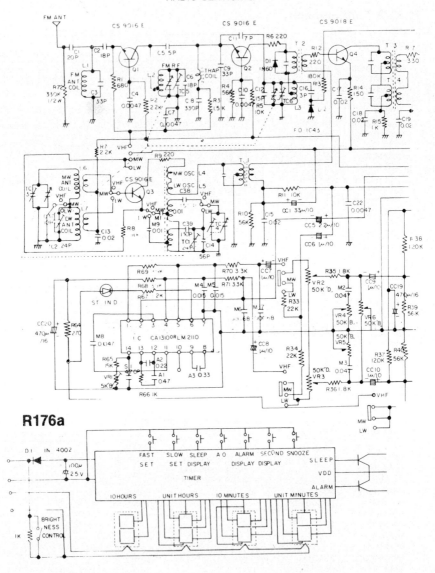

R176a

(R176a) CIRCUIT DIAGRAM—MODEL 'MAJESTIC' *(PART)*

BINATONE

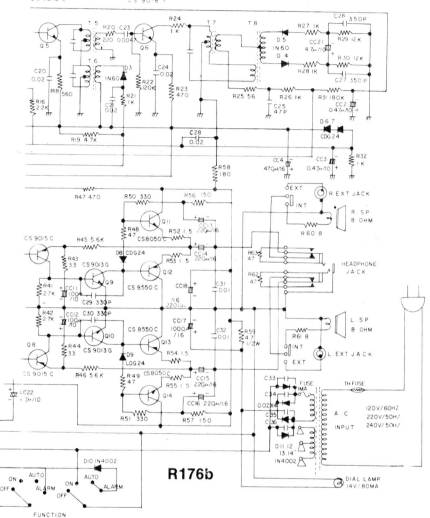

R176b

(R176b) CIRCUIT DIAGRAM—MODEL 'MAJESTIC' *(CONTINUED)*

413

F.M./Multiplex Alignment:

Step	Signal source connector	Set radio dial to	Output indicator connector	Set signal to	Adjust	Adjust for
	F.M. MPX standard signal generator F.M. Ant. input	98MHz		98MHz	VR1 5K 'B'	Maximum stereo lamp intensity

L.W./R.F. Alignment:

Step	Signal source equipment	Set frequency to	Augment indicator 8 connection	Set radio dial to	Adjust	Adjust for
1	A.M. signal generator a standard radiation loop antenna	150kHz (30% modulation)	V.T.V.M. oscilloscope connector across speaker voice coil 8 ohm	150kHz (Low end)	L5 (Osc. coil)	Max. output
2	A.M. signal generator a standard radiation loop antenna	290kHz (30% modulation)	,,	290kHz (high end)	TC1 (Osc. trimmer)	Max. output
3	A.M. signal generator a standard radiation loop antenna	170kHz (30% modulation)	,,	170kHz	L7 (ant. coil)	Max. output
4	A.M. signal generator a standard radiation loop antenna	270kHz (30% modulation)	,,	270kHz	TC2 (ant. trimmer)	Max. output

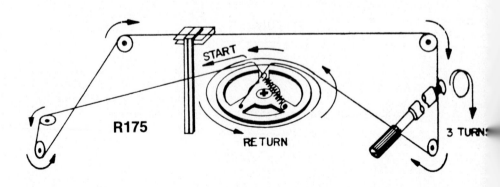

(R175) DRIVE CORD—MODEL 'MAJESTIC'

BINATONE

Model 'Symphony' 01/6063

General Description: A 3-waveband mains-operated stereo radio with electronic digital clock. Alarm facilities are fitted and a socket is provided for the connection of stereo headphones.

Mains Supply: 240 volts, 50Hz.

Fuse: 1 amp. and thermal.

Wavebands: L.W. 156-285kHz; M.W. 520-1620kHz; F.M. 88-108MHz.

Loudspeakers: 8 ohms impedance.

Transistor Voltages

Item no.	Type no.	Function	Ve	Vb	Vc
Q1	FCS 9016F	F.M. R.F.	0.5	1.1	7.8
Q2	FCS 9018F	F.M. convertor	2.2	2.8	7.8
Q3	FCS 9018F	A.M.-F.M. I.F.	0.35	0.95	7.8
Q4	FCS 9018G	A.M.-F.M. I.F.	1.40	1.95	7.8
Q5	FCS 9018G	F.M. I.F.	0.43	1.05	7.4
Q6	FCS 9016F	A.M. mixer	1.15	1.65	8.6
Q7	FCS 9014B	Audio pre-amp (L)	5.4	4.8	8.4
Q8	FCS 9014B	Audio pre-amp (R)	5.4	4.8	8.4
Q9	FCS 9015C	Audio driver (L)	9.1	8.4	5.1
Q10	FCS 9015C	Audio driver (R)	9.1	8.4	5.1
Q11	NEC 9013	Power (L)	4.5	5.1	11
Q12	NEC 9013	Power (R)	4.5	5.1	11
Q13	NEC 9012	Power (L)	4.4	3.8	0
Q14	NEC 9012	Power (R)	4.4	3.8	0
Q15	NEC 9112	Switching power		−0.65	−0.7
Q16	FCS 9014B	Switching	−0.7		−0.65
Q17	NEC 9014C	Snooze sensor	−7.8		8.2
Q18	FCS 9015B	Brightness control	−9	−9	−9

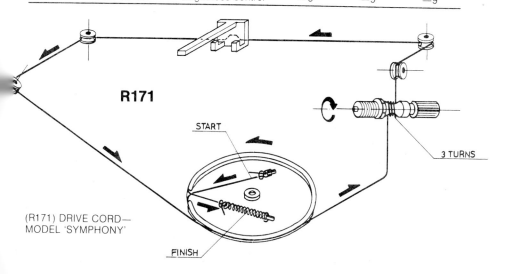

R171

START

3 TURNS

(R171) DRIVE CORD—
MODEL 'SYMPHONY'

FINISH

Alignment Procedure

Step	Signal source connect to	Set signal at	Set radio to	Output indication connect to	Adjust	Adjust for
1	Set Band Switch to A.M. section					
2	A.M. I.F. Sweep generator through TP9 & TP10	465kHz	High end (Gang open)	Oscilloscope through TP5 & TP6	T6 T7 T8	Maximum output and symmetrical 'V' curve
3	A.M. R.F. signal generator through radiating antenna loop	510kHz	Low end (Gang close)	V.T.V.M. across speaker output	L7	
4		1650kHz	High end (Gang open)		CT3	Maximum output
5	Repeat steps 3 and 4 to get the correct band coverage					
6	A.M. R.F. signal generator through radiating antenna loop	600kHz	600kHz	V.T.V.M. across speaker output	L5	
7		1400kHz	1400kHz		CT4	Maximum output
8	Repeat steps 6 and 7 to get the correct tracking					
9	Set band switch to L.W. section					
10	L.W. R.F. signal generator through radiating antenna loop	285kHz	High end (Gang open)	V.T.V.M. across speaker output	CT5	Maximum output
11		180kHz	180kHz		L6	
12		245kHz	245kHz		CT6	
13	Repeat steps 10, 11 and 12 to get the correct band coverage and tracking					
14	Set band switch to F.M. section					
15	F.M. I.F. Sweep generator through TP3 & TP4	10.7MHz	High end (Gang open)	Oscilloscope through TP7 & TP8	T1 T2 T3 T4 T5	Maximum amplitude and symmetrical 'S' curve
16	Repeat step 15 to get the maximum amplitude waveform					
17	F.M. Signal generator through F.M. ant. input TP1 & TP2	87MHz	Low end (Gang close)	V.T.V.M. across speaker output	L4	
18		109MHz	High end (Gang open)		CT1	Maximum output
19	Repeat steps 12 and 13 to get the correct band coverage					
20	F.M. Signal generator through F.M. ant. input TP1 & TP2	90MHz	90MHz	V.T.V.M. across speaker output	L2	
21		106MHz	106MHz		CT2	Maximum output
22	Repeat steps 15 and 16 to get the correct tracking					
23	F.M. Stereo generator through TP1 & TP2	98MHz	98MHz	V.T.V.M. across speaker output	SFR32	Maximum channel separation and maximum stereo indicator sensitivity

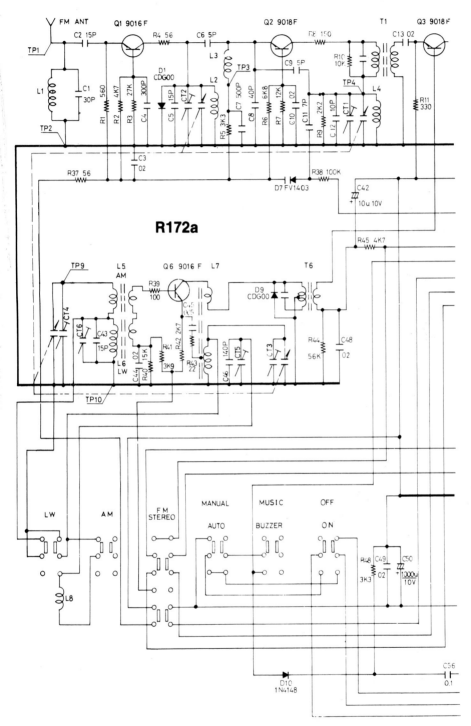

(R172a) CIRCUIT DIAGRAM—MODEL 'SYMPHONY' *(PART)*

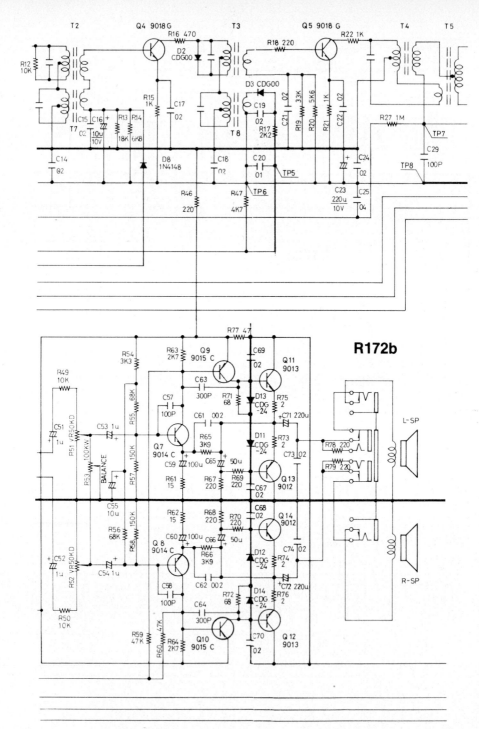

(R172b) CIRCUIT DIAGRAM—MODEL 'SYMPHONY' *(PART)*

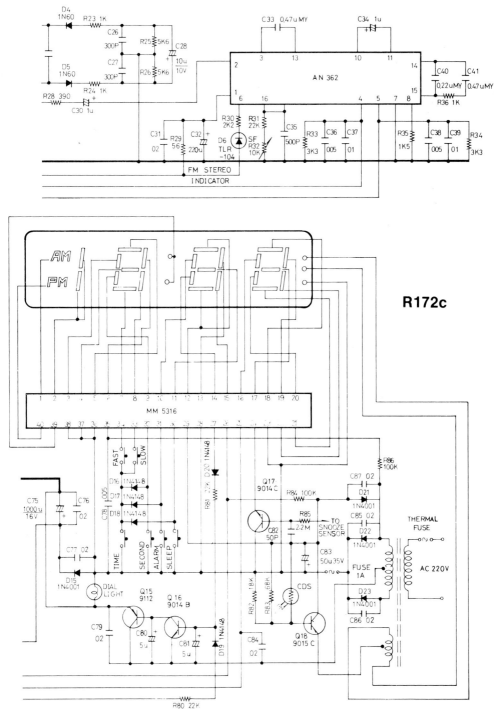

R172c

(R172c) CIRCUIT DIAGRAM—MODEL 'SYMPHONY' *(CONTINUED)*

BINATONE   Model 'Worldstar' 01/4451

General Description: A multi-band portable radio receiver operating from mains or battery supplies. A socket is provided for the connection of an earphone.

Mains Supply: 240 volts, 50Hz.

Battery: 6 volts.

Wavebands: L.W. 150-300kHz; M.W. 535-1605kHz; Marine 1.5-4.4MHz; F.M. 88-108MHz; V.H.F. 108-174MHz.

Loudspeaker: 8 ohms impedance.

Transistor Voltages

Tran-sistor	Q1	Q2	Q3	Q4	Q5	Q6	Q7	Q8	Q9	Q10	Q11	Q12	Q13	Q14	Q15	Q16	Q17
C	4.4	4.4	4.4	4.4	4.4	4.4	4.4	4.4	0.2	4	5.6	0.7	4.4	3	4.4	6	6
B	1.3	1.3	1.3	0.65	0.65	1.3	1.3	1.3	0.7	0.2	4.8	0.4	1.3	0.6	1.5	0.6	0.6
E	1	1.2	1.1	0.2	0.2	1	1	1.2	0.1	0.1	4.8	0	1.2	0.2	1.25	0	0

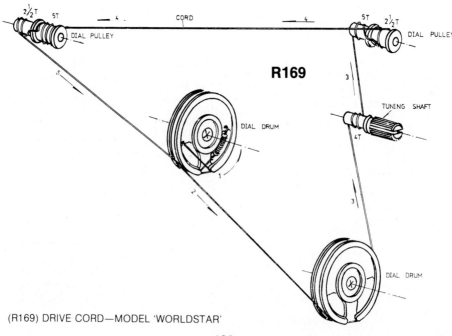

R169

(R169) DRIVE CORD—MODEL 'WORLDSTAR'

Semiconductors

Q1—4006B		D1—IN60 Diode V.H.F. Overload	
Q2—9018H		D2—IN60 Diode A.M. Det.	
Q3—9018G		D3 D4—IN60 Diode F.M. Det.	
Q4—9018G		D5 D6 D7—CDG22 Bias Voltage	
Q5—1402A		D8—IN60 F.M. Overload	
Q6—1502E		D9—Diode F.M. A.F.C.	
Q7—4006B		D10—IN60 Diode Squelch	
Q8—9018H		D11—IN60 Diode Squelch	
Q9—1402B		D12—LED Diode	
Q10—1402B		D13—D14—IN60 Diode———LED	
Q11—1602E		D15—LW—Diode CDG—21	
Q12—1402E		D16—MB—Diode CDG—21	
Q13—9016G		D17—CDG22 Diode Thermistor Temperature	
Q14—1402B			
Q15—1402B			
Q16—Q17—1702N			

Resistors

R1	1	kohm	R18	6.8	kohm	R35	6.8	kohm	R52	220	kohm
R2	6.8	kohm	R19	1	kohm	R36	6.8	kohm	R53	10	ohm
R3	100	ohm	R20	330	ohm	R37	1	kohm	R54	3.3	kohm
R4	1	kohm	R21	3.3	kohm	R38	47	kohm	R55	100	kohm
R5	6.8	kohm	R22	1	kohm	R39	2.2	kohm	R56	10	kohm
R6	100	ohm	R23	10	kohm	R40	100	ohm	R57	3.3	kohm
R7	56	ohm	R24	1	kohm	R41	100	kohm	R58	1	kohm
R8	220	ohm	R25	1	kohm	R42	100	ohm	R59	56	ohm
R9	1	kohm	R26	3.3	kohm	R43	1.5	kohm	R60	18	kohm
R10	56	ohm	R27	10	kohm	R44	V.R.		R61	10	kohm
R11	47	kohm	R28	10	kohm	R45	15	kohm	R62	560	ohm
R12	15	kohm	R29	220	kohm	R46	150	ohm	R63	10	ohm
R13	220	kohm	R30	1	kohm	R47	33	ohm	R64	100	ohm
R14	220	ohm	R31	6.8	kohm	R48	33	ohm	R65	2.2	kohm
R15	470	ohm	R32	100	ohm	R49	100	kohm	R66	680	
R16	330	ohm	R33	1.5	kohm	R50	6.8	kohm	R67	680	
R17	100	ohm	R34	100	ohm	R51	1	kohm	R68	1	ohm

Capacitor

C1	15p	C19	50f	C37	35p	C55	1000p
C2	50p	C20	0.02	C38	200p	C56	500p
C3	15p	C21	5p	C39	0.005p	C57	300p
C4	0.02pf	C22	0.04	C40	5p	C58	500uf
C5	0.005pf	C23	0.02	C41	0.02	C59	0.02
C6	5pf	C24	300	C42	3p	C60	0.1uf
C7	15pf	C25	0.02	C43	0.02	C61	0.005uf
C8	200pf	C26	10uf	C44	5uf	C62	0.002uf
C9	0.02pf	C27	500	C45	30uf	C63	1uf
C10	0.005pf	C28	500p	C46	1uf	C64	0.1
C11	5pf	C29	0.01	C47	0.04	C65	30uf
C12	0.02pf	C30	0.02	C48	0.04	C66	50uf
C13	10uf	C31	35p	C49	0.02	C67	500uf
C14	50pf	C32	50p	C50	0.02	C68	0.005uf
C15	0.02pf	C33	100p	C51	0.02	C69	0.005
C16	0.02	C34	0.005p	C52	0.01	C70	0.01
C17	0.02	C35	0.02	C53	0.02	C71	0.01
C18	0.02	C36	5p	C54	0.005		

Alignment:

Equipment required: 1. R.F. Signal generator. 2. Electronic voltmeter.
General
1. Signal input must be as low as possible to avoid overload and clipping. (Use highest sensitivity of output indicator.)
2. Volume control at maximum.
3. Standard modulation is 400Hz at 30%.
4. Connect A.C. V.T.V.M. across voice coil.

Step	Connect signal source to	Connect output indicator to	Set signal generator to	Set radio dial to	Adjust	Adjust for
			Set band selector switch to M.W.			
1	Loop of several turns of wire		465kHz A.M. mod.	Tuning gang closed	T6 T7 T8	
2	connected across gen. leads.	A.C. V.T.V.M. across voice coil	520kHz A.M. mod.	Tuning gang closed	L11	Maximum output on V.T.V.M.
3	Place loop close to the A.M. antenna.		1620kHz A.M. mod.	Tuning gang open	TC7	
4			Repeat steps 2 and 3 for optimum sensitivity			
5	Same as above	A.C. V.T.V.M. across voice coil	600kHz A.M. mod. 1400kHz	Tune for signal	L8	Maximum output on V.T.V.M.
6			A.M. mod.		TC5	
7			Repeat steps 5 and 6 for optimum sensitivity			
			Set band selector switch to L.W.			
1	Same as above	A.C. V.T.V.M. across voice coil	148kHz A.M. mod. 310kHz	Tuning gang closed	L12	Maximum output on V.T.V.M.
2			A.M. mod.	Tuning gang open	TC8	
3			Repeat steps 1 and 2 for optimum sensitivity			
4	Same as above	A.C. V.T.V.M. across voice coil	180kHz A.M. mod. 250kHz	Tune for signal	L9	Maximum output on V.T.V.M.
5			A.M. mod.		TC6	
6			Repeat steps 4 and 5 for optimum sensitivity			
			Set band selector switch to MB			
1	Same as above	A.C. V.T.V.M. across voice coil	1.5MHz A.M. mod. 4.5MHz	Tune for signal	L13	Maximum output on V.T.V.M.
2			A.M. mod.	Tune for signal	TC9	
3			Repeat steps 1 and 2 for optimum sensitivity			
4	Same as above	A.C. V.T.V.M. across voice coil	2MHz 4MHz A.M. mod.	Tune for signal	L10 TC10	Maximum output on V.T.V.M.
5			Repeat steps 4 and 5 for optimum sensitivity			

Step	Connect signal source to	Connect output indicator to	Set signal generator to	Set radio dial to	Adjust	Adjust for
		Set band selector switch to F.M.				
1		A.C. V.T.V.M. across voice coil	10.7MHz F.M. mod.		T1 T2 T3 T4	Maximum output on V.T.V.M.
2	Place gen. leads across F.M. ant. terminals.	D.C. probe across C24	10.7MHz (Unmod.)	Tuning gang closed	T5	Zero reading, a positive or negative reading will be obtained on either side of correct setting.
3		Repeat steps 1 and 2 for optimum sensitivity				
4	Same as above	A.C. V.T.V.M. across voice coil	87MHz F.M. mod.	Tuning gang closed	L6	Maximum output on V.T.V.M.
5			109.5MHz F.M. mod.	Tuning gang open	TC4	
6		Repeat steps 4 and 5 for optimum sensitivity				
7	Same as above	A.C. V.T.V.M. across voice coil	90MHz F.M. mod.	Tune for signal	L4	Maximum output on V.T.V.M.
8			106MHz F.M. mod.		TC2	
9		Repeat steps 7 and 8 for optimum sensitivity				
		Set band selector switch to V.H.F.				
1	Same as above	A.C. V.T.V.M. across voice coil	108MHz F.M. mod.	Tuning gang closed	L5	Maximum output on V.T.V.M.
2			176MHz F.M. mod.	Tuning gang open	TC3	
3		Repeat steps 1 and 2 for optimum sensitivity				
4	Same as above	A.C. V.T.V.M. across voice coil	110MHz F.M. mod.	Tune for signal	L3	Maximum output on V.T.V.M.
5			175MHz F.M. mod.		TC1	
6		Repeat steps 4 and 5 for optimum sensitivity				

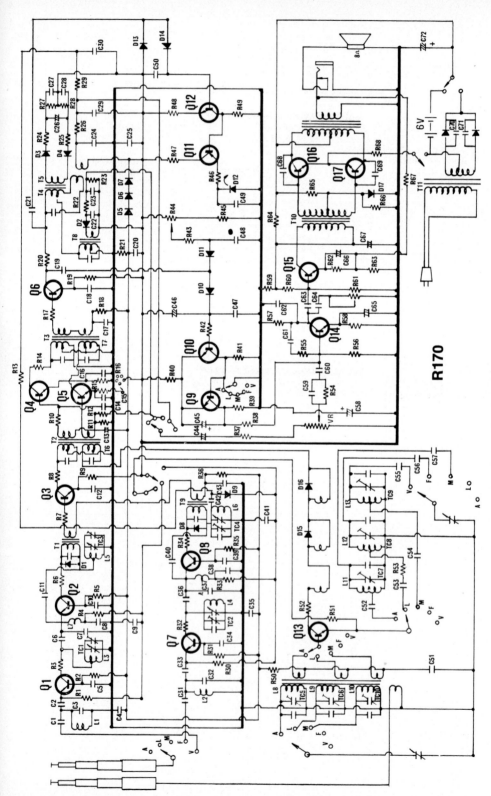

(R170) CIRCUIT DIAGRAM—MODEL 'WORLDSTAR'

R170

BUSH   Model BB5400

General Description: A 3-waveband A.M./F.M. radio receiver incorporating cassette tape-recorder and electronic digital clock operating from mains
supplies. Integrated circuits are used in the A.F. and timer stages and sockets
are provided for the connection of auxiliary inputs and outputs.

Mains Supplies: 240 volts, 50Hz.

Fuses: 2×315mA.

Wavebands: L.W. 145-350kHz; M.W. 530-1620kHz; F.M. 87.5-108MHz.

Loudspeakers: 8 ohms impedance.

Semiconductors

IC1	Integrated Circuit UPC 1350 C
IC2	Integrated Circuit HD38991A
Q1	Transistor 2SC1417H
Q2	Transistor 2SC1417H
Q3	Transistor 2SC1417H
Q4	Transistor 2SC1417H
Q5	Transistor 2SC1417H
Q6	Transistor 2SC1417H
Q101	Transistor 2SC1390J
Q102	Transistor 2SB561C
Q103	Transistor 2SC4581G
Q104	Transistor 2SD467C
Q105	Transistor NA217H
D101	Diode 1N4148
D102	Diode 1N4148
D103	Diode 1N4148
D104	Diode 1N4148
D106	Zener Diode 1N5240 10V
D107	Diode 1N4001
D108	Diode 1N4001
D109	Diode 1N4001
D110	Diode 1N4001
D111	Diode 1N4148
D112	Diode 1N4148
D113	Diode 1N4148
D201	Diode 1N60 (P)
D202	Diode 1S2638
D203	Diode CDG00
D204	Diode 1N60 (P)
D205	Diode 1N60 (P)
D206	Zener Diode 1N5238 6V2
D207	Diode 1N60 (P)

Tape Recording A.C. Bias Frequency Adjustment

Frequency counter	Adjustment	Purpose	Remark
To TP1	L101	Align 40kHz oscillator	Repeat adjustment of L101 until 40kHz is obtained

Alignment

A.M., F.M., I.F. Alignment:

Opera-tion	Generator connection	Input signal frequency	Band	Position of P.V.C.	Meter or oscilloscope	Adjustment	Purpose
1	Coupling to A.M. aerial coil	470kHz	A.M.	Close	P.1	T5,3,8	Align. A.M. I.F.
2	To T.C.	10.7MHz	F.M.	Closed	To T.P.	T1,2,4,6,7	Align. A.M. I.F.
3	To T.C.	Sweep marker at 10.7MHz	F.M.	Closed	To T.P.	T6,7	Align. 'S' curve

A.M. Band Alignment:

Opera-tion	Generator connection	Input signal frequency	Band	Position of P.V.C.	Meter or oscilloscope	Adjustment	Purpose
4	Loop aerial	530kHz	A.M.	Close	A.F. output terminal	L8	Adjust band coverage
5	Loop aerial	1620kHz	A.M.	Open	A.F. output terminal	TC6	Adjust band coverage
6	Loop aerial	600kHz	A.M.	Tuned to 600kHz	A.F. output terminal	L6	For maximum sensitivity
7	Loop aerial	1400kHz	A.M.	Tuned to 1400kHz	A.F. output terminal	TC3	For maximum sensitivity
8	Repeat adjustments 4, 5, 6 & 7 in sequence until no further change is noted						

L.M. Band Alignment:

Opera-tion	Generator connection	Input signal frequency	Band	Position of P.V.C.	Meter or oscilloscope	Adjustment	Purpose
9	Loop aerial	145kHz	L.W.	Close	A.F. output terminal	L7	Adjust band coverage
10	Loop aerial	350kHz	L.W.	Open	A.F. output terminal	TC5	Adjust band coverage
11	Loop aerial	175kHz	L.W.	Tuned to 175kHz	A.F. output terminal	L5	For maximum sensitivity
12	Loop aerial	300kHz	L.W.	Tuned to 300kHz	A.F. output terminal	TC4	For maximum sensitivity
13	Repeat adjustments 9, 10, 11 & 12 in sequence until no further change is noted						

F.M. Band Alignment:

Opera-tion	Generator connection	Input signal frequency	Band	Position of P.V.C.	Meter or oscilloscope	Adjustment	Purpose
14	Dummy aerial	87.5MHz	F.M.	Close	A.F. output terminal	L4	Adjust band coverage
15	Dummy aerial	108MHz	F.M.	Open	A.F. output terminal	TC2	Adjust band coverage
16	Dummy aerial	90MHz	F.M.	Tuned to 90MHz	A.F. output terminal	L2	For maximum sensitivity
17	Dummy aerial	106MHz	F.M.	Tuned to 106MHz	A.F. output terminal	TC1	For maximum sensitivity
18	Repeat adjustments 14, 15, 16 & 17 in sequence until no further change is noted						

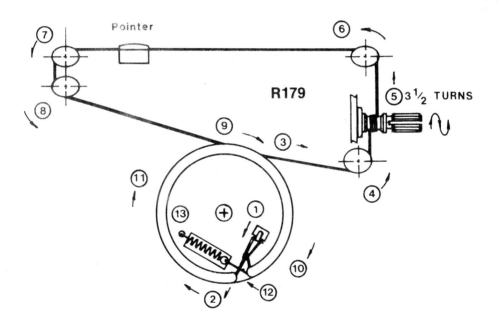

(R179) DRIVE CORD—MODEL BB5400

427

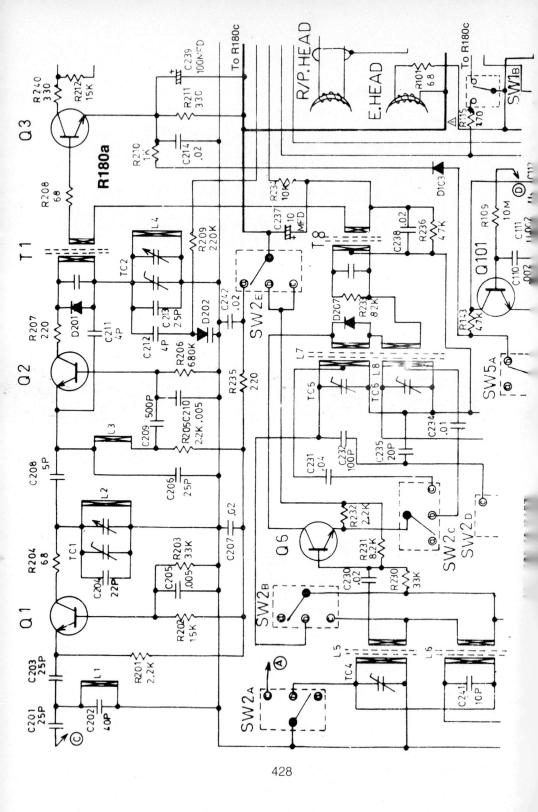

428

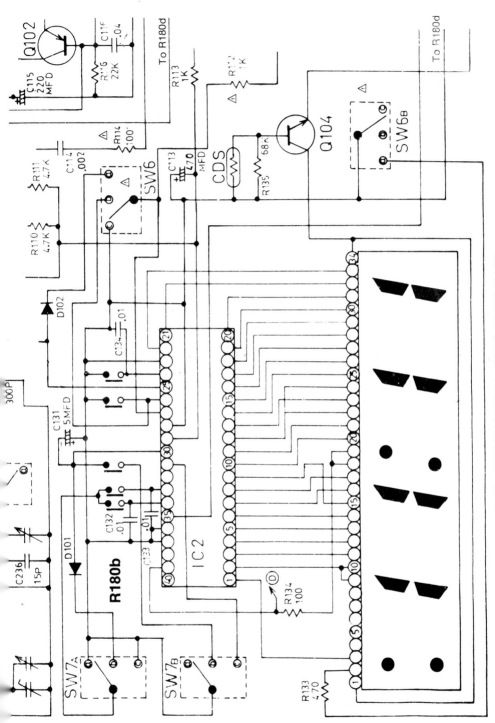

(R180b) CIRCUIT DIAGRAM—MODEL BB5400 (PART)

429

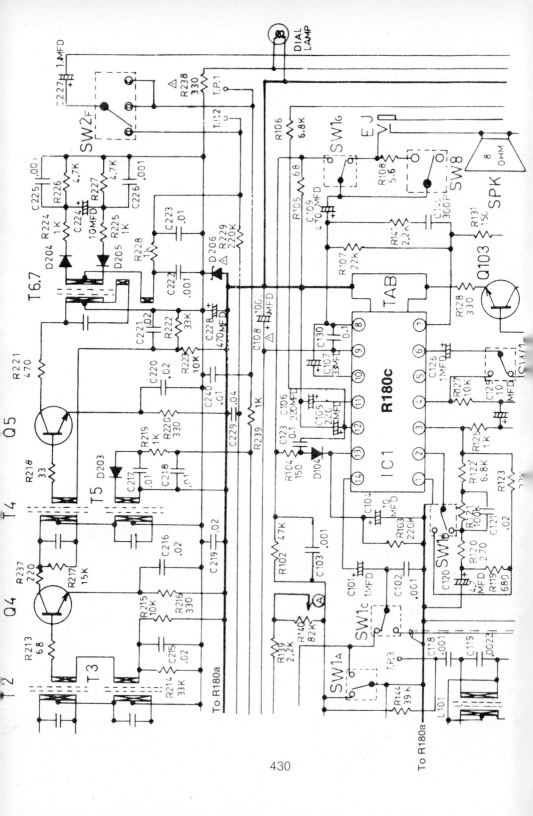

430

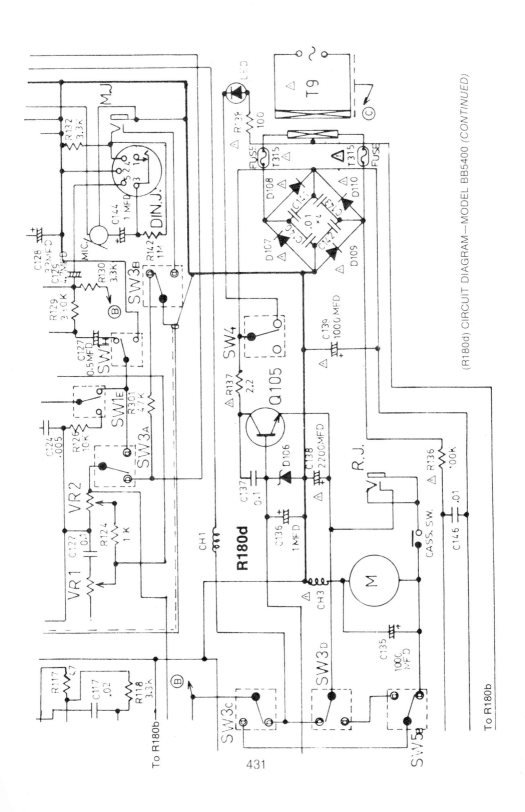

(R180d) CIRCUIT DIAGRAM—MODEL BB5400 (CONTINUED)

431

BUSH

Model BB5401

General Description: A 3-waveband mains-operated electronic digital clock radio. Alarm facilities are provided and a socket is provided for the connection of an earphone.

Mains Supply: 240 volts, 50Hz.

Wavebands: L.W. 140-360kHz; M.W. 520-1640kHz; F.M. 87.5-104MHz.

Alignment

V.H.F., L.W., M.W., I.F. Alignment:

Opera-tion	Generator connection	Input signal frequency	Band Position		Meter or oscilloscope	Adjust	Purpose
1	Coupling to A.M. aerial coil	470kHz	A.M.	Closed	To T.P.1	T8,3,5	Align A.M. I.F.
2	To T.C.2	10.7MHz	F.M.	Closed	To T.P.2	T1,2,4,6,7	Align A.M. I.F.
3	To T.C.2	10.7MHz	F.M.	Closed	To T.P.2	T67	Align 'S' curve

L.W. Alignment:

Opera-tion	Generator connection	Input signal frequency	Band Position		Meter or oscilloscope	Adjust	Purpose
4	Coupling to L.W. aerial coil	140kHz	L.W.	Close	A.F. output terminal	L6	Adjust band coverage
5	Coupling to L.W. aerial coil	360kHz	L.W.	Open	A.F. output terminal	TC4	Adjust band coverage
6	Coupling to L.W. aerial coil	165kHz	L.W.	Tuned to 165kHz	A.F. output terminal	L5	For maximum sensitivity
7	Coupling to L.W. aerial coil	320kHz	L.W.	Tuned to 320kHz	A.F. output terminal	TC3	For maximum sensitivity
8	Repeat steps 4, 5, 6 & 7 in sequence until no further improvement is noted						

V.H.F. Alignment:

Opera-tion	Generator connection	Input signal frequency	Band Position	Meter or oscilloscope	Adjust	Purpose
9	Direct to V.H.F. aerial terminal	87.5MHz	V.H.F. Close	A.F. output terminal	L4	Adjust band coverage
10	Direct to V.H.F. aerial terminal	104MHz	V.H.F. Open	A.F. output terminal	TC2	Adjust band coverage
11	Direct to V.H.F. aerial terminal	88MHz	V.H.F. Tuned to 88MHz	A.F. output terminal	L2	For maximum sensitivity
12	Direct to V.H.F. aerial terminal	101MHz	V.H.F. Tuned to 101MHz	A.F. output terminal	TC1	For maximum sensitivity
13	Repeat steps 9, 10, 11 & 12 in sequence until no further improvement is noted					

M.W. Alignment:

Opera-tion	Generator connection	Input signal frequency	Band Position	Meter or oscilloscope	Adjust	Purpose
14	Coupling to M.W. aerial coil	520kHz	M.W. Close	A.F. output terminal	L8	Adjust band coverage
15	Coupling to M.W. aerial coil	1640kHz	M.W. Open	A.F. output terminal	TC6	Adjust band coverage
16	Coupling to M.W. aerial coil	600kHz	M.W. Tuned to 600kHz	A.F. output terminal	L7	For maximum sensitivity
17	Coupling to M.W. aerial coil	1400kHz	M.W. Tuned to 1400kHz	A.F. output terminal	TC5	For maximum sensitivity
18	Repeat steps 14, 15, 16 & 17 in sequence until no further improvement is noted					

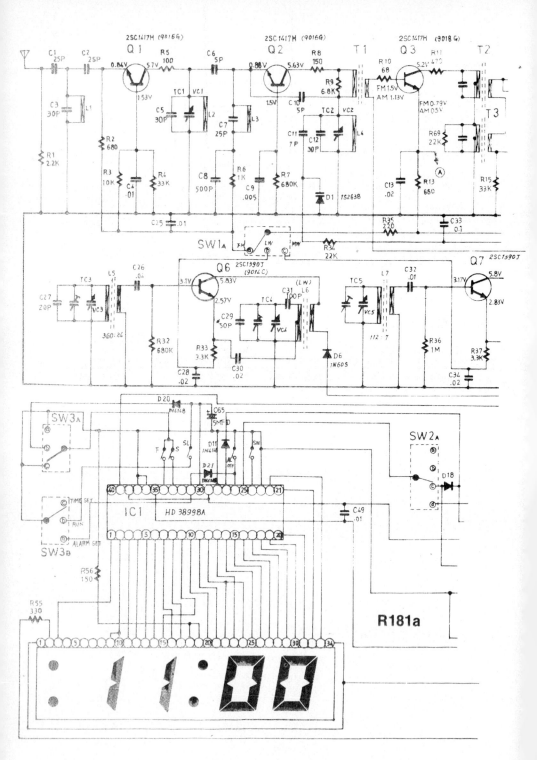

(R181a) CIRCUIT DIAGRAM—MODEL BB5401 *(PART)*

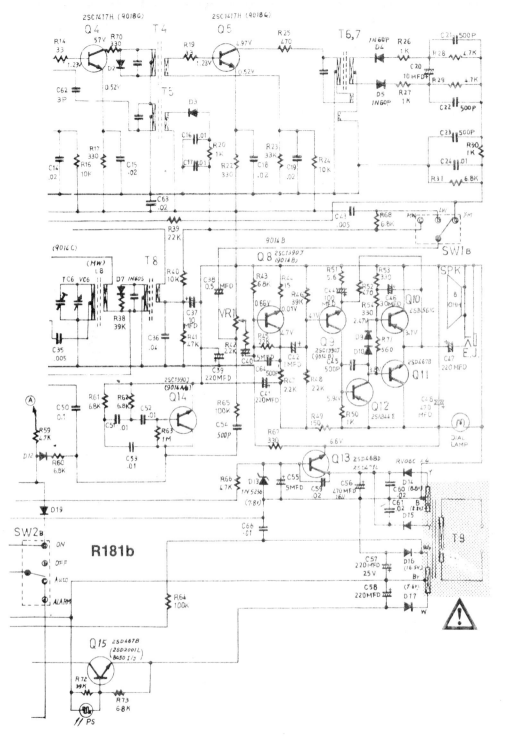

(R181b) CIRCUIT DIAGRAM—MODEL BB5401 (CONTINUED)

BUSH

Model BB5507A

General Description: A 3-waveband A.M./F.M. stereo radio receiver with electronic digital clock operating from mains supplies. A socket is provided for the connection of stereo headphones.

Mains Supply: 240 volts, 50Hz.

Wavebands: L.W. 175-275kHz; M.W. 515-1640kHz; F.M. 87-105MHz.

Loudspeakers: 16 ohms impedance.

Alignment

A.M. Section:

Step	Alignment frequency	Test equipment	Signal-in	Signal-out	Dial setting	Adjust	Remarks
1	470kHz	1 A.M. I.F. Sweep gen. with ant. 2 Oscilloscope 3 Power supply	Set the A.M. ant. coil close to gen. ant.	Signal taken out from point TP6	Tune gang capacitor to high-end	Adjust T205 T206 T207 to get max. output at 470kHz +—3kHz	1 Band switch in A.M. position 2 Volume control in min. position
2	515kHz	1 A.M. Sweep gen. with ant. 2 Oscilloscope 3 Power supply	Same as step 1	Same as step 1	Tune gang capacitor to low-end	Adjust T101 to get max output at 515kHz +—3kHz	Same as step 1
3	1640kHz	Same as step 2	Same as step 1	Same as step 1	Tune gang capacitor to high-end	Adjust C20 h to get max. output at 1640kHz +—10kHz	Same as step 1
4	Repeat 2 and 3						
5	600kHz	Same as step 2	Same as step 1	Same as step 1	Tune gang capacitor to 600kHz	Adjust L101 to get max. output at 600kHz	Same as step 1
6	1400kHz	Same as step 2	Same as step 1	Same as step 1	Tune gang capacitor to 1400kHz	Adjust C20 f to get max. output at 1400kHz	Same as step 1
7	Repeat 5 and 6 until no further improvement can be made						

L.W. Section:

Step	Alignment frequency	Test equipment	Signal-in	Signal-out	Dial setting	Adjust	Remarks
1	470kHz	1 A.M. I.F. Sweep gen. with ant. 2 Oscilloscope 3 Power supply	Set the L.W. ant. coil close to gen. ant.	Signal taken out from point TP6	Tune gang capacitor to high-end	Adjust T205 T206 T207 to get max. output at 470kHz +—3kHz	1 Band switch in A.M. position 2 Volume control in min. position
2	275kHz	1 A.M. Sweep gen. with ant. 2 Oscilloscope 3 Power supply	Same as step 1	Same as step 1	Tune gang capacitor to high-end	Adjust C105 to get max. output at 275kHz +—5kHz	Same as step 1
3	175kHz	Same as step 2	Same as step 1	Same as step 1	Tune gang capacitor to 175kHz	Adjust L102 to get max. output at 175kHz	Same as step 1
4	245kHz	Same as step 2	Same as step 1	Same as step 1	Tune gang capacitor to 245kHz	Adjust C107 to get max. output at 245kHz	Same as step 1
5	Repeat 3 and 4 until no further improvement can be made						

F.M. Section:

Alignment frequency	Test equipment	Signal-in	Signal-out	Dial setting	Adjust	Remarks
10.7MHz	1 F.M. I.F. Sweep generator 2 Oscilloscope 3 Power supply	Set the F.M. I.F. marker signal close to point TP3	Signal taken out from point TP4	Tune gang capacitor to high-end	Adjust T1 T201 T202 to get max. output at 10.7MHz +—0.2MHz	1 Band switch in F.M. position 2 T203 Primary coil should be short circuit
10.7MHz	Same as step 1	Same as step 1	Signal taken out from point TP5	Tune gang capacitor to high-end	Adjust T203 T204 to get the best 'S' curve with centre freq. 10.7MHz	1 Band switch in F.M. position 2 T203 Primary coil should be open circuit 3 Volume control in min. position
Repeat 1 and 2						
87MHz	1 F.M. I.F. Sweep generator 2 Oscilloscope 3 Power supply	Connected to ant. terminals point TP1 and point TP2	Signal taken out from point TP5	Tune gang capacitor to low-end	Adjust L4 to get max. output at 87MHz +—0.3MHz	1 Band switch in F.M. position 2 Volume control in min. position
105MHz	Same as step 4	Same as step 4	Same as step 4	Tune gang capacitor to high-end +—0.3MHz	Adjust C20d to get max. output at 105MHz +0.3MHz —0.5MHz	Same as step 4
Repeat 4 and 5						
90MHz	Same as step 4	Same as step 4	Same as step 4	Tune gang capacitor to 90MHz	Adjust L2 to get max. output	Same as step 4
102MHz	Same as step 4	Same as step 4	Same as step 4	Tune gang capacitor to 102MHz	Adjust C20b to get max. output	Same as step 4
Repeat 4, 5, 7, 8 until no further improvement can be made						

F.M. Stereo Section:

Alignment frequency	Test equipment	Signal-in	Signal-out	Dial setting	Adjust	Remarks
19.05kHz	1 F.M. stereo signal generator 2 Frequency counter 3 Power supply	Set the F.M. stereo generator freq. at 98MHz switch-off pilot signal and modulation. Close to F.M. Ant. terminal.	Connection frequency counter to point TP7	Tune gang capacitor to 98 MHz	Adjust R308 to get the centre frequency at 19.05kHz +5Hz —30Hz	Band switch in F.M.-stereo position

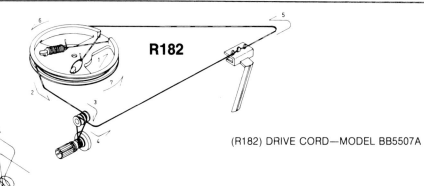

R182

(R182) DRIVE CORD—MODEL BB5507A

$3\frac{3}{4}$ TURNS

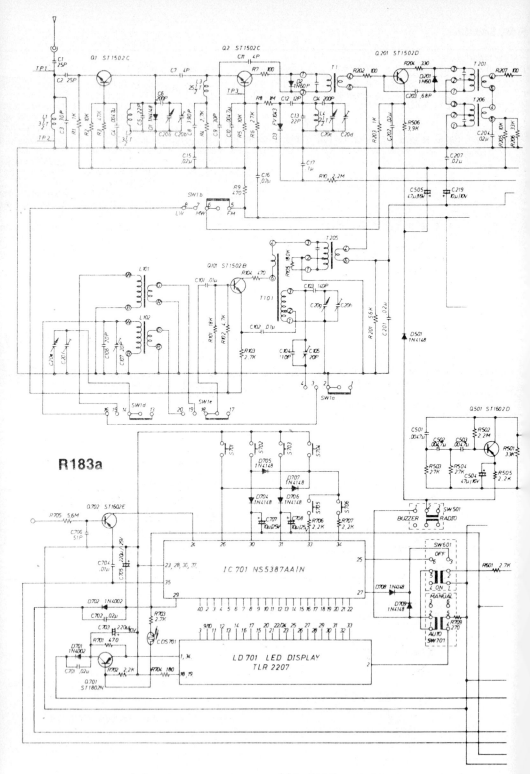

(R183a) CIRCUIT DIAGRAM—MODEL BB5507A (PART)

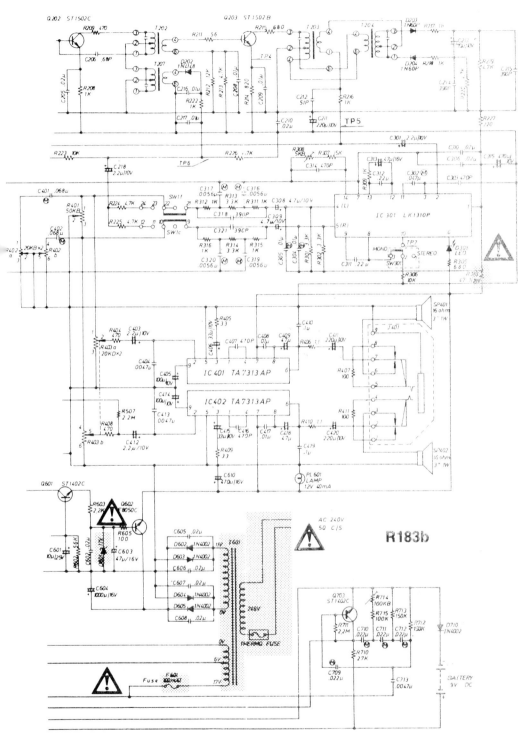

(R183b) CIRCUIT DIAGRAM—MODEL BB5507A *(CONTINUED)*

BUSH
Model BR8428AA

General Description: A portable A.M./F.M. stereo radio receiver with stereo cassette-recorder operating from mains or battery supplies. Integrated circuits are used for stereo decoder and A.F. power stages. A microphone is built-in and sockets are provided for auxiliary inputs and outputs.

Mains Supply: 240 volts, 50Hz.

Fuse: 1 amp.

Wavebands: L.W. 145-360kHz; M.W. 515-1650kHz; F.M. 87-109MHz.

Tape Adjustments

Azimuth Alignment:
(a) Tone control at max.
(b) Function Switch at tape.
(c) Stereo/Mono switch at stereo.
10kHz standard tape must be used for these adjustments. Connect a V.T.V.M. or an oscilloscope to Monitor jack and adjust the azimuth height so that the input voltage is max.

Bias Frequency Adjustment: Set for recording and position beat selector switch at RIF1 (S106) obtain frequency.
Connect test point 4 (TP4) to a frequency counter.
Adjust Osc. coil (T301) until the counter indicates 56kHz.

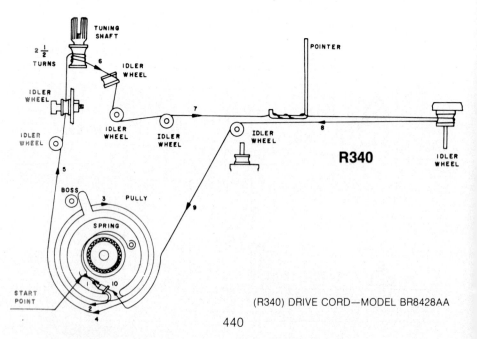

(R340) DRIVE CORD—MODEL BR8428AA

Semiconductors:

IC1	LA3301	TR104	2SC733BL	TR302	2SC735Y
IC101	LA4102	TR105	2SC733BL	D1	HV80
IC201	LA4102	TR106	2SC374BL	D2	S3073C
TR1	MPS9426B	TR107	2SC374BL	D3	1S188FM-1
TR2	2SC785R	TR201	2SC1000BL	D4	1S188FM-1
TR3	2SC380A-O	TR202	2SC374BL	D5	1S188FM-1
TR4	2SC380A-O	TR203	2SC374BL	D6	1S188FM-2
TR5	2SC380A-O	TR204	2SC733BL	D7	1S188FM-2
TR6	2SC372-O	TR205	2SC733BL	D101	1S188FM-1
TR101	2SC1000BL	TR206	2SC374BL	D201	1S188FM-1
TR102	2SC374BL	TR207	2SC374BL	D301	Zener diode HX6-C
TR103	2SC374BL	TR301	2SC735Y	D302	Bridge rectifier KPB005

F.M. R.F. and I.F. Alignment Procedure Using F.M. Sweep Generator and Scope:

Step	Connect scope	Connect generator	Dummy aerial	Input signal frequency	Band	Tune to	Adjust	Purpose
	Note: For F.M. alignment use a 400Hz sinewave signal at 75kHz deviation							
1							T5	Detune secondary of ratio detector
2				10.7MHz	F.M.	Gang closed	T1	Align I.F. and primary of
3							T2 T3 T4	ratio detector for maximum output and symmetry.
4	Test point 'TP3' with detector probe	Test point 'TP1'		Repeat steps 1 to 3 for minimum change			T5	Align secondary of ratio detector for for maximum amplitude and symmetry of 'S' curve.
5			Standard Dummy aerial	87MHz	F.M.	Gang closed	L4	
6				109MHz		Gang open	TC1	Set F.M. oscillator to end point.
7	Across speaker	Test point 'TP1' (disconnect) F.M. aerial)		Repeat steps 5 and 6 for minimum change				
8				90MHz	F.M.	90MHz	L2	Align F.M. R.F. stage for maximum.
9				106MHz		106MHz	TC2	
0				Repeat steps 8 and 9 for minimum change				

A.M. R.F. and I.F. Alignment:

Step	Connect V.T.V.M.	Connect generator	Dummy aerial	Input signal frequency	Band	Tune to	Adjust	Purpose
	Note: For A.M. alignment use a 400Hz sinewave signal at 30% modulation							
1			None	470kHz		Gang closed	T6 T7 T8	Align I.F. transformers for maximum output.
					A.M.			
2				515kHz			L9	
								Set oscillator to end point
3				1650kHz		Gang open	TC7	
4	Across speaker	(Standard loop aerial)		Repeat steps 2 and 3 for minimum change				
5				600kHz		600kHz	L6 (A.M. aerial coil if necessary)	Align aerial stage for maximum output.
					A.M.			
6				1400kHz		1400kHz	TC4	
7				Repeat steps 5 and 6 for minimum change				

L.W. R.F. Alignment:

Tone Control: max. position   Volume Control: max. position.

Step	Connect V.T.V.M.	Connect generator	Dummy load	Input signal frequency	Band	Tune to	Adjust	Purpose
	Note: For L.W. alignment use a 400Hz sinewave signal at 30% modulation.							
1				145kHz		Gang closed	L10 Osc. coil	
					L.W.			Set oscillato to end point
2				360kHz		Gang open	TC8 Osc. trimmer	
3	Across speaker	Standard loop aerial	None	Repeat steps 1 and 2 for minimum change				
4				160kHz		160kHz	L7 R.F. coil	
					L.W.			
5				330kHz		330kHz	TC3 R.F. trimmer	Align aerial stage for maximum
6				Repeat steps 4 and 5 for minimum change				output

S.W. R.F. Alignment:

Tone Control: max. position   Volume Control: max. position.

Step	Connect V.T.V.M.	Connect generator	Dummy load	Input signal frequency	Band	Tune to	Adjust	Purpose
				Note: For S.W. alignment use a 400Hz sinewave signal at 30% modulation				
1				5.7MHz		Gang closed	L8 Osc. coil	
					S.W.			Set oscillator to end point
2				18.5MHz		Gang open	TC6 Osc. trimmer	
3	Across speaker	A telescopic aerial	Standard dummy load	Repeat steps 1 and 2 for minimum change				
4				6.5MHz		6.5MHz	L5 R.F. coil	Align aerial stage for maximum output
					S.W.			
5				16MHz		16MHz	TC5	
6				Repeat steps 4 and 5 for minimum change				

MPX Stereo Alignment:

Important. 1. Frequency deviation should be set to 75kHz.
             2. Input signal should be kept at 60dB.
             3. Set Stereo/Mono switch to Stereo.

Circuit alignment	Meter and connection	Dial pointer setting	Signal generator output	Adjustments
Channel separation	Signal Generator: F.M. Stereo generator to Ext. mod. of F.M. signal generator and connect output terminal of F.M. signal generator to dummy aerial. V.T.V.M.: connect probe to Din out terminal.	98MHz	98MHz	T9 (MPX coil) T10 (MPX coil) R45 (Semi-fixed resistor) Adjust T9, 10, R45 for optimum separation. After adjustment, confirm that stereo indicator lights.

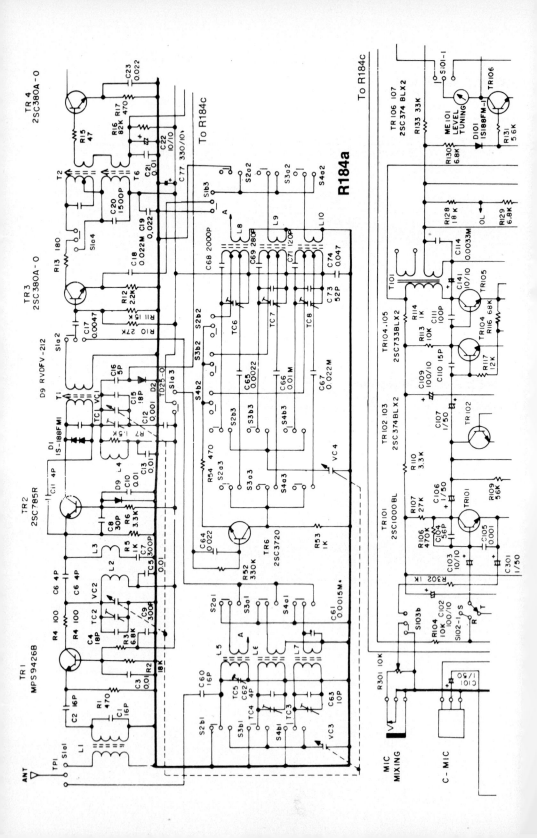

R184a

R184c

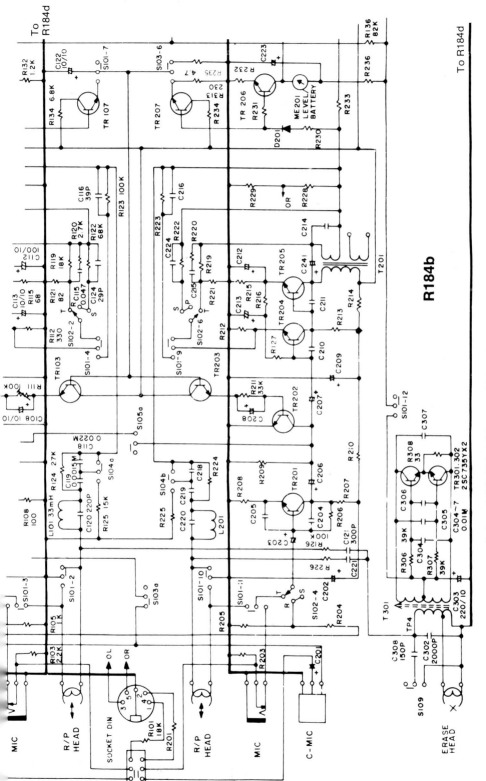

(R184b) CIRCUIT DIAGRAM—MODEL BR8428AA *(PART)*

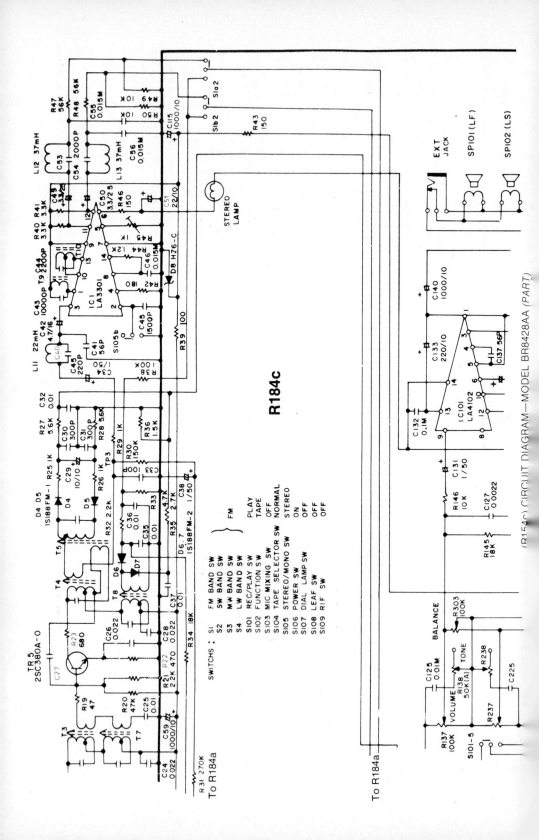

(R184c) CIRCUIT DIAGRAM—MODEL BR8428AA (PART)

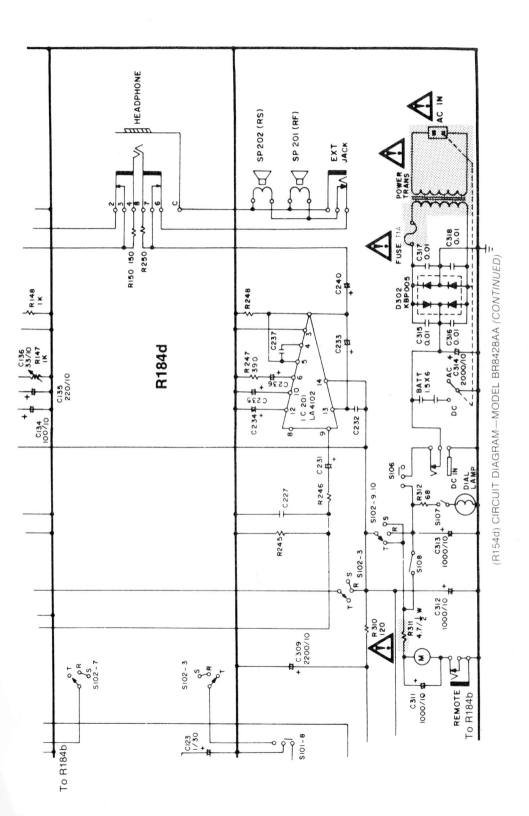

(R154d) CIRCUIT DIAGRAM—MODEL BR8428AA (CONTINUED)

BUSH

Model BW5503AH

General Description: A 3-waveband A.M./F.M. radio receiver with electronic digital clock operating from mains supplies. Two versions of this chassis are produced with the same type number and are distinguished by the A.F. output circuitry. Other changes occur mainly in the switching arrangements and components are renumbered. Both versions of the circuit are given here.

Mains Supply: 240 volts, 50Hz.

Wavebands: L.W. 140-360kHz; M.W. 520-1640kHz; F.M. 87.5-104MHz.

Loudspeaker: 8 ohms impedance.

Semiconductor Types (I.C. Version):

IC1	HA1311W	Q5	2SC1417H	D2	CDG00	D8	RV06
IC2	HD38991A	Q6	2SC1390J	D3	1N60(P)	D9	RV06
Q1	2SC1417H	Q7	2SC1390J	D4	1N60(P)	D10	1N5235
Q2	2SC1417H	Q8	2SC1390J	D5	1N60(P)	D11	1N4148
Q3	2SC1417H	Q9	2SD468D	D6	RV06	D12	1N4148
Q4	2SC1417H	D1	1S2638	D7	RV06	D13	1N4148

Semiconductor Types (Discrete Version):

Q1	2SC1417H	Q9	2SC1390J	D3	CDG00	D12	1N4148
Q2	2SC1417H	Q10	2SB561	D4	1N60(P)	D13	1N5253
Q3	2SC1417H	Q11	2SD467	D5	1N60(P)	D14	RV06
Q4	2SC1417H	Q12	2SA884D	D6	1N60(P)	D15	RV06
Q5	2SC1417H	Q13	2SD468D	D7	1N60(P)	D16	RV06
Q6	2SC1390J	Q14	2SC1390J	D9	CDG22	D17	RV06
Q7	2SC1390J	D1	1S553	D10	CDG22	D18	1N4148
Q8	2SC1390J	D2	CDG00	D11	1N4148	D19	1N4148

1 Complete Turn

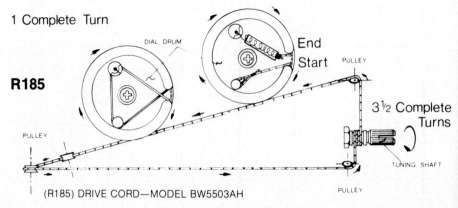

R185

(R185) DRIVE CORD—MODEL BW5503AH

Alignment

V.H.F., L.W., M.W., I.F. Alignment:

Opera-tion	Generator connection	Input signal frequency	Band Position		Meter or oscilloscope	Adjust	Purpose
1	Coupling to A.M. aerial coil	470kHz	A.M.	Closed	To T.P.1	T8,3,5	Align A.M. I.F.
2	To TC2	10.7MHz	F.M.	Closed	To T.P.2	T1,2,4,6,7	Align F.M. I.F.
3	To TC2	10.7MHz	F.M.	Closed	To T.P.2	T67	Align 'S' curve

L.W. Alignment:

Opera-tion	Generator connection	Input signal frequency	Band Position		Meter or oscilloscope	Adjust	Purpose
4	Coupling to L.W. aerial coil	140kHz	L.W.	Close	A.F. output terminal	L6	Adjust band coverage
5	Coupling to L.W. aerial coil	360kHz	L.W.	Open	A.F. output terminal	TC4	Adjust band coverage
6	Coupling to L.W. aerial coil	165kHz	L.W.	Tuned to 165kHz	A.F. output terminal	L5	For maximum sensitivity
7	Coupling to L.W. aerial coil	320kHz	L.W.	Tuned to 320kHz	A.F. output terminal	TC3	For maximum sensitivity
8	Repeat steps 4, 5, 6 & 7 in sequence until no further improvement is noted						

V.H.F. Alignment:

Opera-tion	Generator connection	Input signal frequency	Band Position		Meter or oscilloscope	Adjust	Purpose
9	Direct to V.H.F. aerial terminal	87.5MHz	V.H.F.	Close	A.F. output terminal	L4	Adjust band coverage
10	Direct to V.H.F. aerial terminal	104MHz	V.H.F.	Open	A.F. output terminal	TC2	Adjust band coverage
11	Direct to V.H.F. aerial terminal	88MHz	V.H.F.	Tuned to 88MHz	A.F. output terminal	L2	For maximum sensitivity
12	Direct to V.H.F. aerial terminal	101MHz	V.H.F.	Tuned to 101MHz	A.F. output terminal	TC1	For maximum sensitivity
13	Repeat steps 9, 10, 11 & 12 in sequence until no further improvement is noted						

M.W. Alignment:

Opera-tion	Generator connection	Input signal frequency	Band Position		Meter or oscilloscope	Adjust	Purpose
14	Coupling to M.W. aerial coil	520kHz	M.W.	Close	A.F. output terminal	L8	Adjust band coverage
15	Coupling to M.W. aerial coil	1640kHz	M.W.	Open	A.F. output terminal	TC6	Adjust band coverage
16	Coupling to M.W. aerial coil	600kHz	M.W.	Tuned to 600kHz	A.F. output terminal	L7	For maximum sensitivity
17	Coupling to M.W. aerial coil	1400kHz	M.W.	Tuned to 1400kHz	A.F. output terminal	TC5	For maximum sensitivity
18	Repeat steps 14, 15, 16 & 17 in sequence until no further improvement is noted						

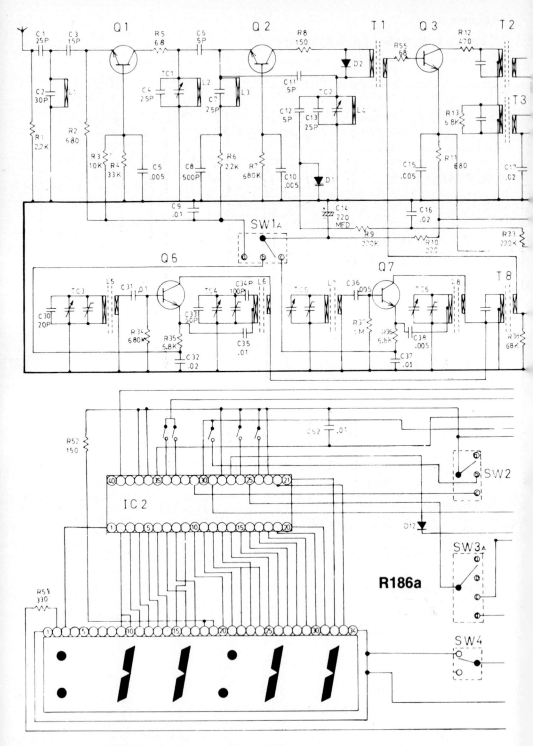

(R186a) CIRCUIT DIAGRAM—MODEL BW5503AH IC VERSION *(PART)*

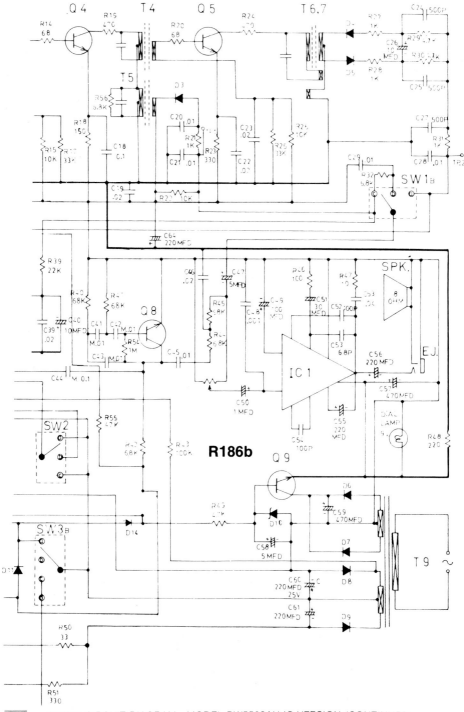

(R186b) CIRCUIT DIAGRAM—MODEL BW5503AH IC VERSION *(CONTINUED)*

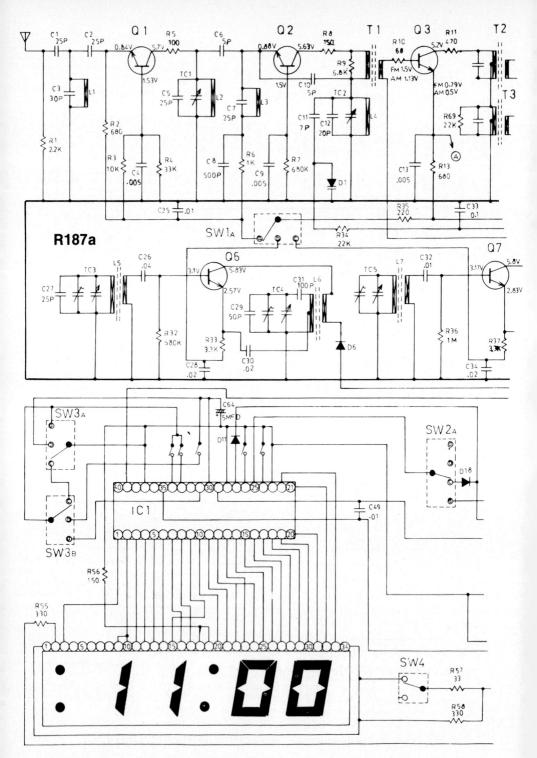

(R187a) CIRCUIT DIAGRAM—MODEL BW5503AH DISCRETE VERSION *(PART)*

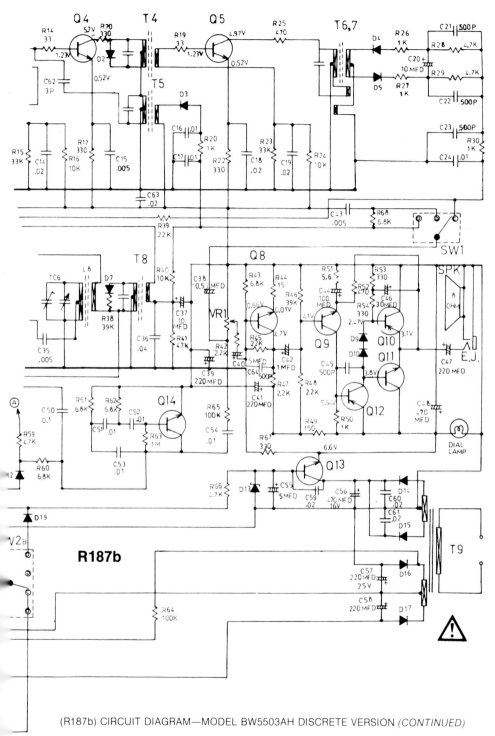

(R187b) CIRCUIT DIAGRAM—MODEL BW5503AH DISCRETE VERSION *(CONTINUED)*

BUSH   Model BW5777A

General Description: A 4-waveband A.M./F.M. portable radio receiver operating from mains or battery supplies. Sockets are provided for the connection of a tape-recorder and earphone.

Mains Supply: 240 volts, 50Hz.

Battery: 6 volts.

Wavebands: L.W. 145-300kHz; M.W. 510-1650kHz; F.M. 87.5-104MHz; Aircraft Band 114-146MHz.

Loudspeaker: 8 ohms impedance.

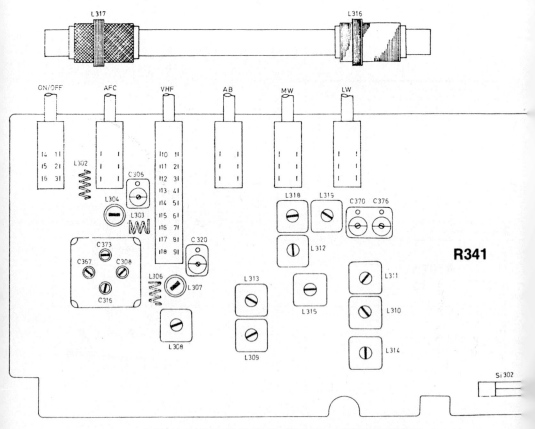

(R341) ALIGNMENT ADJUSTMENTS—MODEL BW5777A

Alignment: (See R341).

	STEP	CONNECT	FREQUENCY	SET RADIO DIAL TO	POINTS OF ALIGNMENT (MAX. OUTPUT)
AM—ALIGNMENT FR—Level Below Limiting Function					
IF	1	Signal gen. coupled by single turn coil to ferrite ant.	470 KHz	Bottom	L312
IF	2		470 KHz	Bottom	C313
IF	3				L314
IF	4		Repeat alignment 1 to 3		
MW / RF	5	Oscilloscope to AB switch no. 1	510 KHz	Top	L318
MW / RF	6		1650 KHz	Bottom	C373
MW / RF	7		Repeat alignment 5 and 6		
MW	8		600 KHz	600 KHz	L316
MW	9		1400 KHz	1400 KHz	C367
MW	10		Repeat alignment 8 and 9		
LW	11		145 KHz	Top	L319
LW	12		300 KHz	Bottom	C376
LW	13		Repeat alignment 11 and 12		
LW	14		170 KHz	170 KHz	L317
LW	15		250 KHz	250 KHz	C370
LW	16		Repeat alignment 14 and 15		

FM—ALIGNMENT

	STEP	CONNECT	FREQUENCY	SET RADIO DIAL TO	POINTS OF ALIGNMENT
IF	1	Sweep gen. via 10pf to T302 base. Oscilloscope to FM switch no. 12	10.7 KHz	Bottom	L308
IF	2				L309
IF	3				L310
IF	4				L311 s-curve
IF	5		Repeat alignment 1 to 4 until s-curve is symmetrical		
FM / RF	6	Sweep gen. connect to FM switch no. 2	87.5 MHz	Top	L306
FM / RF	7		104.5 MHz	Bottom	C316
FM / RF	8		Repeat alignment 6 and 7		
FM	9	Oscilloscope to FM switch no. 12	88 MHz	88 MHz	L303
FM	10		101 MHz	101 MHz	C308
FM	11		Repeat alignment 9 and 10		

AB—ALIGNMENT

	STEP	CONNECT	FREQUENCY	SET RADIO DIAL TO	POINTS OF ALIGNMENT
IF	1	Sweep gen. via 10pf to T302 base. Oscilloscope to FM switch no. 12	10.7 MHz	Bottom	L315
RF	2	Sweep gen. connect to FM switch no. 2	114 MHz	Top	L307
RF	3		146 MHz	Bottom	C320
RF	4		Repeat alignment 2 and 3		
AB	5	Oscilloscope to FM switch no. 12	115 MHz	ca. 115 MHz	L304
AB	6		140 MHz	ca. 140 MHz	C306
AB	7		Repeat alignment 5 and 6		

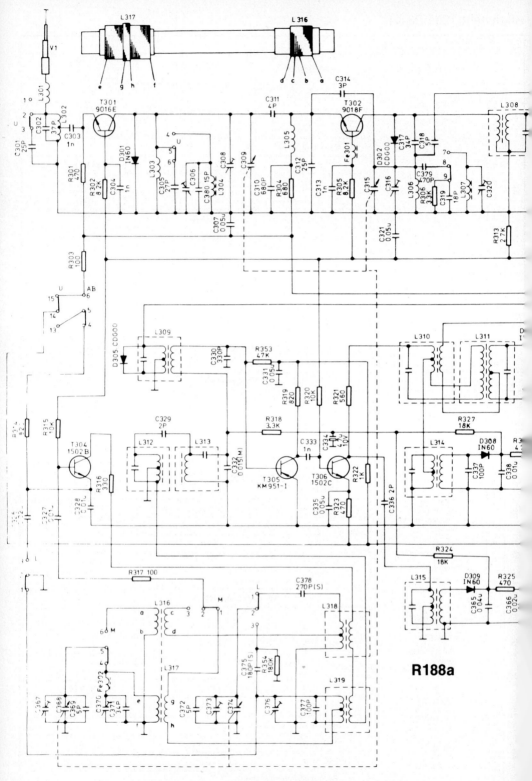

(R188a) CIRCUIT DIAGRAM—MODEL BW5777A *(PART)*

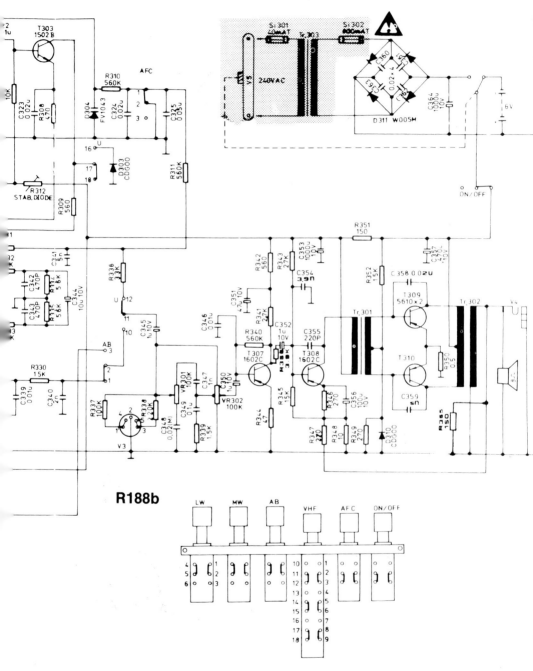

R188b

(R188b) CIRCUIT DIAGRAM—MODEL BW5777A *(CONTINUED)*

CROWN　Model CTR-375 Series

General Description: A portable monaural cassette tape-recorder operating from mains or battery supplies. Integrated circuits are used in the A.F. stages and automatic switches operate at the end of spool and for chromium tape selection. A microphone is built-in and sockets are provided for the connection of auxiliary inputs and outputs.

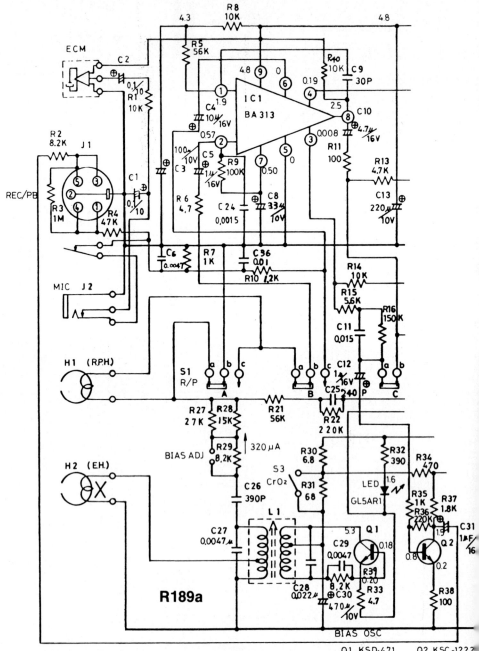

R189a

(R189a) CIRCUIT DIAGRAM—MODEL CTR-375 *(PART)*

Q1 KSD-471　　Q2 KSC-1222

Mains Supplies: 220-240 volts, 50/60Hz.

Batteries: 6 volts (4×1.5 volts).

Loudspeaker: 3.2 ohms impedance.

Access for Service: May be obtained after taking out the batteries and removing the four screws holding the bottom case.

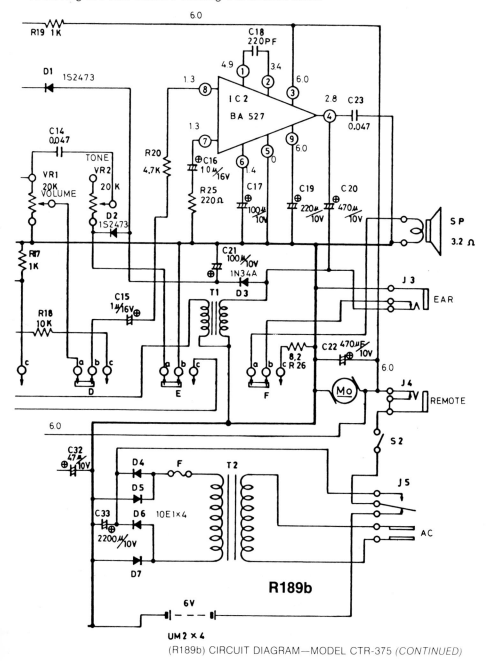

(R189b) CIRCUIT DIAGRAM—MODEL CTR-375 *(CONTINUED)*

FERGUSON   Model 3195

General Description: A 3-waveband A.M./F.M. portable radio receiver operating from mains or battery supplies. A socket is provided for the connection of an earphone.

Mains Supply: 240 volts, 50Hz.

Fuse: 160mA.

Batteries: 6 volts (4×HP7).

Wavebands: L.W. 150-270kHz; M.W. 530-1600kHz; F.M. 88-108MHz.

Loudspeaker: 8 ohms impedance.

Access for Service: Remove batteries and 2 screws securing back cover. Prise off the back cover by applying pressure under the battery compartment at the top of the case.

Alignment

Tuning indication can best be obtained by connecting a 20,000Ω/V meter, set to the 10V A.C. range, across the Loudspeaker terminals.

Throughout alignment the signal input to the receiver should be adjusted as necessary, so that the meter reading does not exceed 0.63V (50mW).

A.M. I.F. Circuits: Set the tuning capacitor to maximum capacitance, the Volume control to maximum and select M.W. Inject 470kHz signals via a loop of wire loosely coiled around the ferrite rod aerial.

Adjust T8, T7 and T6 for maximum meter reading. Repeat adjustments until no further improvement results.

A.M. R.F. Circuits: Connect test equipment as for I.F. adjustments and proceed as follows:

Range	Inject	Cursor position	Adjust for max.
M.W.	600kHz	600kHz	
			T9
			L5*
	1400kHz	1400kHz	TC3
			TC5
L.W.	150kHz	150kHz	L6*
	250kHz	250kHz	TC6
			TC4

*Adjust by sliding coils along ferrite rod.

Repeat adjustments until no further improvement results.

F.M. I.F. Circuits: Set the Volume control to minimum and connect the signal generator via a 5pF capacitor to test point TP1.

Connect the 20,000Ω/V meter (set to A.C. range) between TP2 and chassis

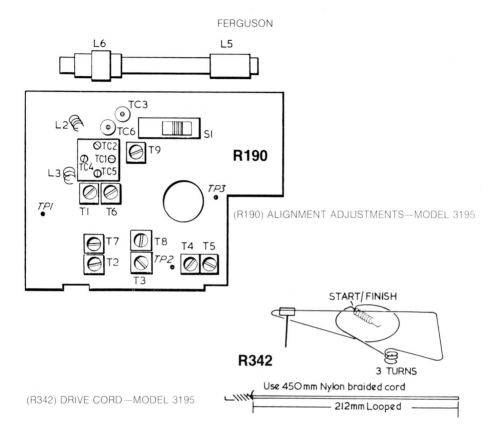

(R190) ALIGNMENT ADJUSTMENTS—MODEL 3195

(R342) DRIVE CORD—MODEL 3195

R342

START/FINISH

3 TURNS

Use 450mm Nylon braided cord

212mm Looped

earth. Inject 10.7MHz and adjust T1, T2 and T3 to give maximum meter reading.

Reconnect the meter (set to 0.1V D.C. range) between TP3 and chassis earth. Inject 10.7MHz and adjust T5 to give a meter reading of zero volts.

Set the meter to the A.C. range, inject 10.7MHz and adjust T4 for maximum meter reading.

Repeat adjustments until no further improvement results.

F.M. R.F. Circuits: Connect the 20,000Ω/V meter across the Loudspeaker terminals and set the Volume control to maximum. Connect the signal generator through a 75 ohm resistor to the F.M. aerial input and chassis earth.

Range	Inject	Cursor position	Adjust for max.
F.M.	88MHz	88MHz	L3†
			L2†
	104MHz	104MHz	TC2
			TC1

†Adjust by slightly opening or closing coil turns.

Repeat adjustments until no further improvement results.

461

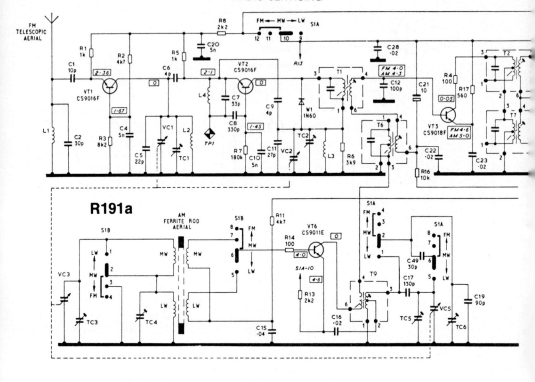

(R191a) CIRCUIT DIAGRAM—MODEL 3191 *(PART)*

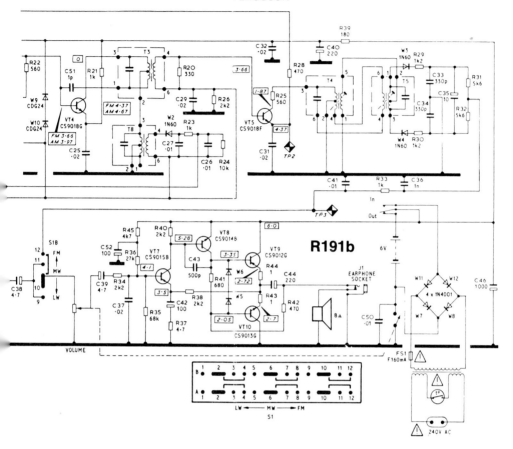

(R191b) CIRCUIT DIAGRAM—MODEL 3191 *(CONTINUED)*

FERGUSON   Model 3T09

General Description: A 3-waveband A.M./F.M. stereo radio cassette-recorder operating from mains or battery supplies. Stereo microphones are built into the case and sockets are provided for the connection of auxiliary inputs and outputs. Integrated circuits are used in decoder and A.F. stages.

Mains Supplies: 240 volts, 50Hz.

Batteries: 9 volts (6×HP2).

Wavebands: L.W. 150-350kHz; M.W. 520-1620kHz; F.M. 88-108MHz.

Loudspeakers: 4 ohms impedance.

Access for Service: To remove back cover, take out six screws from the back and one from the battery compartment. The P.C.B. may be lifted out after pulling off 3 top and 1 side knobs and the securing screw.

Alignment

IC1 Bias Alignment: Connect a D.C. voltmeter between pins 4 and 6 of IC1. Adjust variable resistor VR1 to obtain a reading of 0.5V on the voltmeter.

A.M. I.F. Alignment: Connect an A.M. sweep generator, with the sweep centred at 470kHz modulated, to the ferrite rod aerial, using a standard radiation loop. Tuning indication is best obtained by connecting an oscilloscope between TP1 and earth.

Select M.W. on the function switch, set cursor to maximum frequency end of scale (minimum capacitance), set Tone control to maximum, Volume control to minimum and turn the radio on.

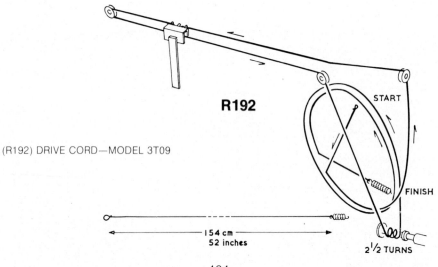

R192

(R192) DRIVE CORD—MODEL 3T09

START

FINISH

154 cm
52 inches

2½ TURNS

464

Adjust T3 to give a maximum reading on the oscilloscope, similarly adjust T4 and T5 for maximum. Repeat adjustments in sequence until no further improvement results. Disconnect all test equipment.

F.M. I.F. Alignment: Connect an F.M. sweep generator, with the sweep centred at 10.7MHz modulated, between the telescopic aerial and earth terminal. Tuning indication is best obtained by connecting an oscilloscope between TP2 and earth.

Select F.M. on the function switch, set cursor to maximum frequency end of scale (min. capacitance), set Tone control to maximum, Volume control to minimum and turn Radio on.

Adjust T1 to give maximum waveform with the 10.7MHz marker at peak and the waveform symmetrical about that peak. Similarly adjust T2, T6 and T7 for maximum symmetrical waveform.

Adjust T8 to give a symmetrical 'S' curve response above and below the base datum line, with the 10.7MHz marker at the centre of the 'S'. Repeat adjustments in sequence until no further improvement can be obtained.

Disconnect all test equipment.

A.M. R.F. Alignment: Connect an A.M. signal generator to the ferrite rod aerial via a standard radiation loop. Tuning indication is best obtained by connecting an electronic voltmeter across the loudspeaker terminals. Throughout alignment the signal input to the receiver should be adjusted, as necessary, so that the meter reading does not exceed 0.45V (50mW) into 4Ω, the loudspeaker impedance.

Set Volume and Tone controls to maximum and turn the radio on.

Range	Inject	Cursor position	Adjust for max.
L.W.	145kHz	Min. frequency end of scale (max. capacitance)	L8
	370kHz	Max. frequency end of scale (min. capacitance)	TC6
	160kHz	160kHz	L106*
	320kHz	320kHz	TC4
M.W.	505kHz	Min. frequency end of scale (max. capacitance)	L7
	1650kHz	Max. frequency end of scale (min. capacitance)	TC5
	600kHz	600kHz	L6*
	1400kHz	1400kHz	TC3

*Adjust by sliding coils along ferrite rod.

Repeat adjustments in sequence until no further improvement results.

F.M. R.F. Alignment: Connect an F.M. signal generator, terminated with a 75Ω resistor, to the telescopic aerial and earth terminal. Tuning indication is best obtained by connecting an electronic voltmeter, across the loudspeaker terminals.

Throughout alignment the signal input to the receiver should be adjusted, as necessary, to ensure that the meter reading does not exceed 0.45V (50mW) into 4Ω, the loudspeaker impedance.

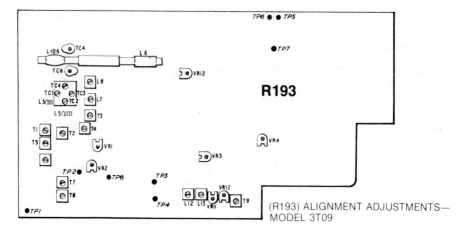

(R193) ALIGNMENT ADJUSTMENTS—
MODEL 3T09

Set Volume and Tone controls to maximum and turn radio on.

Range	Inject	Cursor position	Adjust for max.
F.M.	109MHz	Min. frequency end of scale (max. capacitance)	L5*
	90MHz	Max. frequency end of scale (min. capacitance)	TC2
	106MHz	90MHz	L3*
	87MHz	106MHz	TC1

*Adjust by slightly opening or closing coil turns.

Repeat adjustments until no further improvement results.

Stereo Decoder Alignment: Adjust the F.M. stereo generator to give an unmodulated 98MHz stereo signal at 1mV and inject between F.M. aerial terminal and earth terminal. Set the cursor to the 98MHz position. (Mid point on the frequency scale.) Connect a frequency meter between TP8 and earth and adjust VR2 until the measured frequency is 19kHz ± 100Hz.

Alternatively, tune the receiver to a strong stereo signal and adjust VR2 to establish the range over which the stereo beacon is illuminated. Adjust VR2 for the mid point of beacon illumination.

Tape Circuit Adjustments

Recording Bias Oscillator Alignment: Connect a frequency meter between TP3 and earth. With the Tape-Deck in record mode, the beat cut switch (SW6) and the tape-deck turned on, adjust T9 to give a reading on the frequency meter of 100kHz.

Recording Bias Alignment: Set the function switch to 'Tape', the tape switch to 'Chrome' and the mode switch to 'Stereo'.

L.H. Channel: Connect an electronic voltmeter between TP3 and earth. Adjust L12 to give maximum reading on the voltmeter and to provide the same reading at OFF and ON positions of the beat cut switch (SW6).

Adjust VR10 to give a bias level of 6.3mV. Repeat adjustments until no further improvement results.

R.H. Channel: Connect electronic voltmeter between TP4 and earth. Adjust L23 to give maximum reading on the voltmeter and to provide the same reading at OFF and ON positions of the beat cut switch (SW6).

Adjust VR11 to give a bias level of 6.3mV. Repeat adjustments until no further improvement results.

Azimuth Alignment: Connect an electronic voltmeter to the DIN output socket, select MONO on the mode switch and playback a standard azimuth adjustment tape. Turn the azimuth adjusting screw to give a maximum reading on the voltmeter. The screw can be reached through a small hole above the cassette flap.

Note: The output voltage shows three peaks whilst adjustment is being made. Be sure to find the maximum (centre) peak.

Automatic Level Control Balance Alignment: Connect an electronic voltmeter to the external speaker jack sockets (J1 and J2), and an audio oscillator to the external microphone input (J6 and J7). Set the function switch to TAPE, the mode switch to STEREO and depress the play and record buttons.

Determine the A.L.C. starting point, as signified on the voltmeter, by increasing or decreasing the audio input via the oscillator. Having set the A.L.C. starting point, increase the audio input by 30dB.

Adjust VR4 until the same level of output is obtained on each channel, i.e., the voltmeter reading is the same when connected to either J1 or J2.

Record Level Meter Alignment: With an audio oscillator connected as above, i.e., to external microphone jacks J6 and J7, set the input level to A.L.C. starting point plus 30dB.

Adjust VR12 so that the level meter indicates 4.

Tape Motor Speed Adjustment: The speed control is set to give correct frequency playback of a tape pre-recorded with a known signal.

Playback a 50Hz speed test tape and inject the output from the loudspeaker socket (J1 or J2) into the X amplifier of an oscilloscope. Inject the 50Hz standard mains frequency into the X amplifier, and compare the two waveforms.

Adjust the variable resistor in the motor governor circuit until a stationary image is obtained on the oscilloscope. The variable resistor can be adjusted by inserting a screwdriver through the small aperture in the base of the motor. The aperture is sealed with tape to protect the motor from dust, ensure that the aperture is re-sealed after adjustment.

Playback Output Alignment: Connect the electronic voltmeter to the external loudspeaker sockets (J1 and J2). Playback a standard test tape, pre-recorded at 333Hz (or 1kHz). Set the Balance control (VR7) to its centre (zero) position and adjust VR3 until the same level of output is obtained on each channel, i.e., the voltmeter reading for J1 is the same as that for J2.

(R194a) CIRCUIT DIAGRAM—MODEL 3T09 (PART)

468

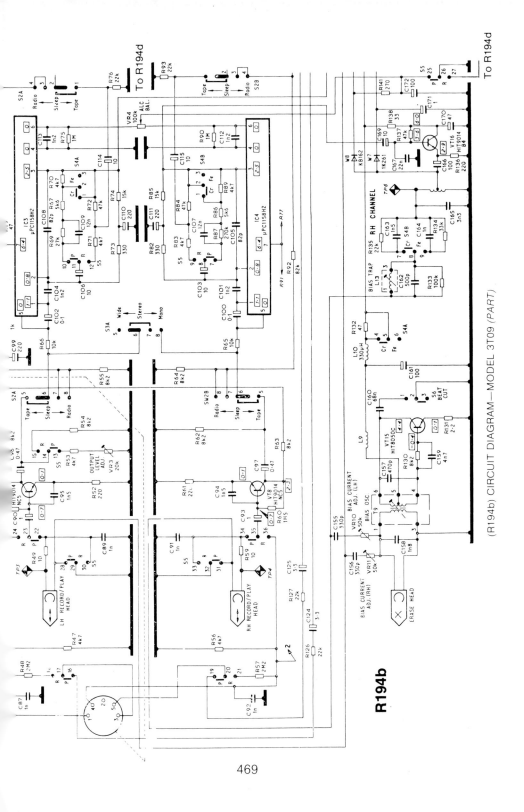

(R194b) CIRCUIT DIAGRAM—MODEL 3T09 (PART)

R194b

469

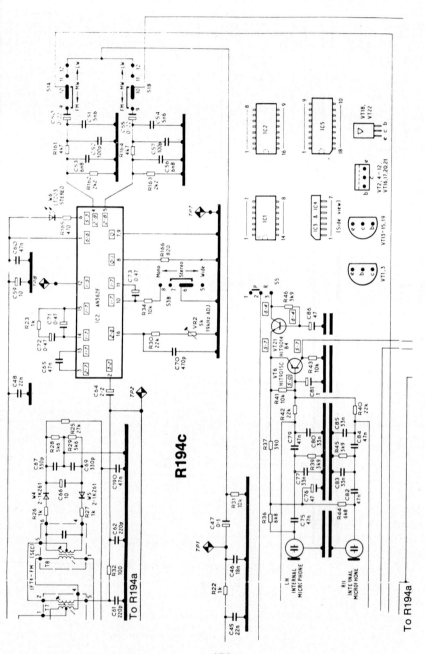

(R194c) CIRCUIT DIAGRAM—MODEL 3T09 (PART)

FERGUSON

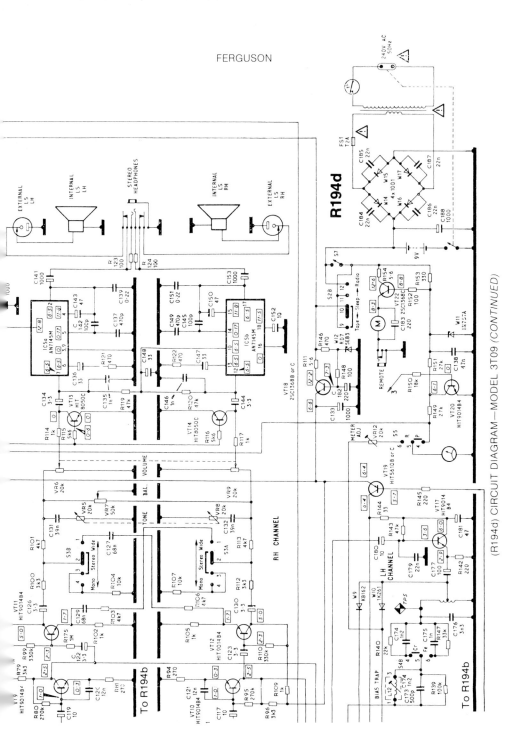

(R194d) CIRCUIT DIAGRAM—MODEL 3T09 (CONTINUED)

471

FERGUSON   Model 3T10

General Description: A 4-waveband A.M./F.M. radio with cassette tape-recorder for mains or battery operation. A microphone is built-in and sockets are provided for the connection of auxiliary inputs and outputs. Integrated circuits are used in decoder and A.F. stages.

Mains Supply: 240 volts, 50Hz.

Fuse: 800mA.

Batteries: 9 volts (6×HP2).

Wavebands: L.W. 150-260kHz; M.W. 520-1620kHz; S.W. 6-16MHz; F.M. 88-108MHz.

Loudspeaker: 4 ohms impedance.

Access for Service: The back cover is secured by 7 screws (1 in the battery compartment). The circuit board is held by self-tapping screws and may be taken out after pulling off the control knobs.

Modifications in Production

R108 1.5MΩ added; R307 4.7kΩ was 1.5kΩ; R320 10kΩ added; R409 330kΩ added; C112 3pF was 5pF; C432 0.033μF was 0.068μF; C438 3000pF was 3300pF; C446 0.001μF added; C509 0.047μF was 0.0047μF.

Alignment

A.M. I.F. Circuits: Tuning indication is best obtained by connecting a 20,000Ω/V meter, set to the 2.5V A.C. range, across the Loudspeaker terminals.

Throughout alignment signals to the receiver should be adjusted, as necessary, so that the meter reading does not exceed 0.63V (50mV) with the Tone control and Volume control at maximum, i.e., both controls advanced fully clockwise.

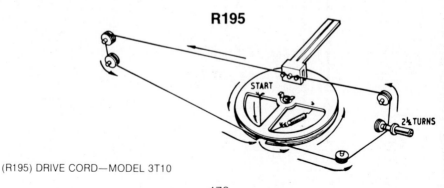

(R195) DRIVE CORD—MODEL 3T10

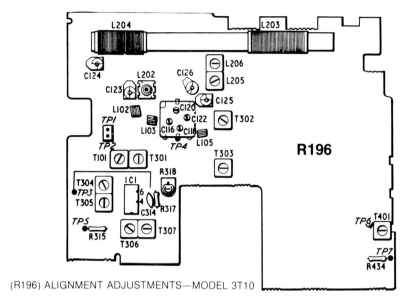

(R196) ALIGNMENT ADJUSTMENTS—MODEL 3T10

Switch receiver to M.W. and set the tuning capacitor at maximum capacitance. Inject 470kHz signals (30% modulated) via a loop loosely coupled to the ferrite rod aerial. Adjust IFT1-AM for maximum reading on voltmeter. Return tuning capacitor to minimum capacitance and adjust IFT2-AM and IFT3-AM for maximum meter reading.

Repeat adjustments until no further improvement results.

Range	Inject	Cursor position	Adjust for max.
M.W.	505kHz	Extreme left	L205
	1650kHz	Extreme right	C122
	600kHz	600kHz	L203*
	1400kHz	1400kHz	C120
L.W.	270kHz	Extreme right	C126
	170kHz	170kHz	L204*
	250kHz	250kHz	C124

*Adjust by sliding coils along ferrite rod.

Repeat adjustments until no further improvement results.

Short wave alignment is best achieved using a dummy aerial with signal injection into TP1 and TP2.

Range	Inject	Cursor position	Adjust for max.
S.W.	5.8MHz	Extreme left	L206
	16.5MHz	Extreme right	C125
	7MHz	7MHz	L202
	15MHz	15MHz	C123

Repeat adjustments until no further improvement results.

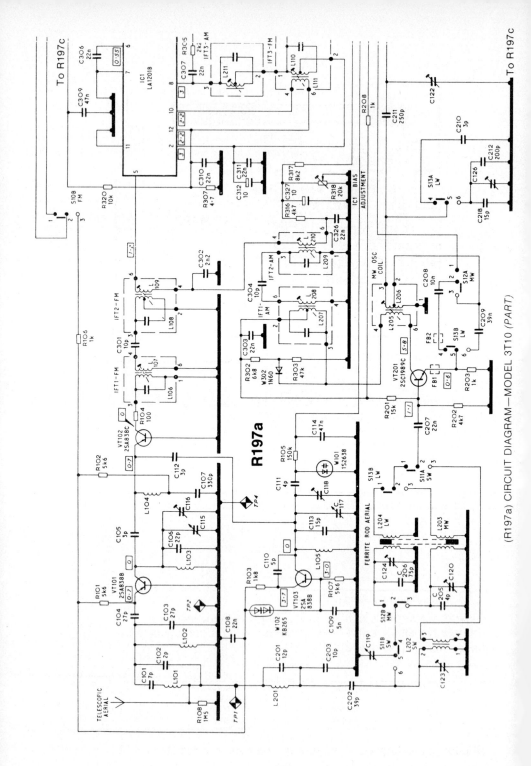

(R197a) CIRCUIT DIAGRAM—MODEL 3T10 *(PART)*

474

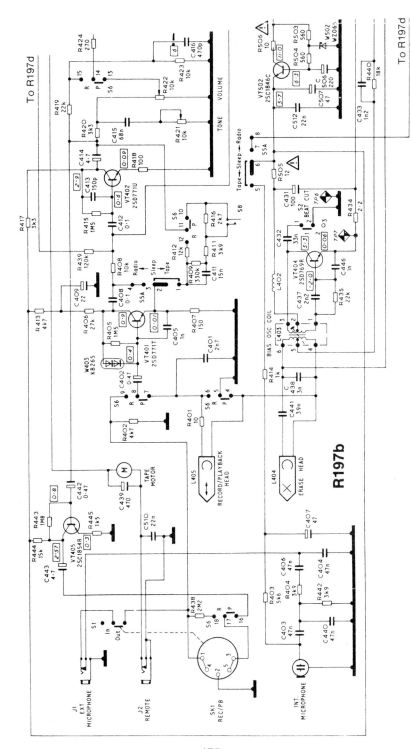

(R197b) CIRCUIT DIAGRAM—MODEL 3T10 (PART)

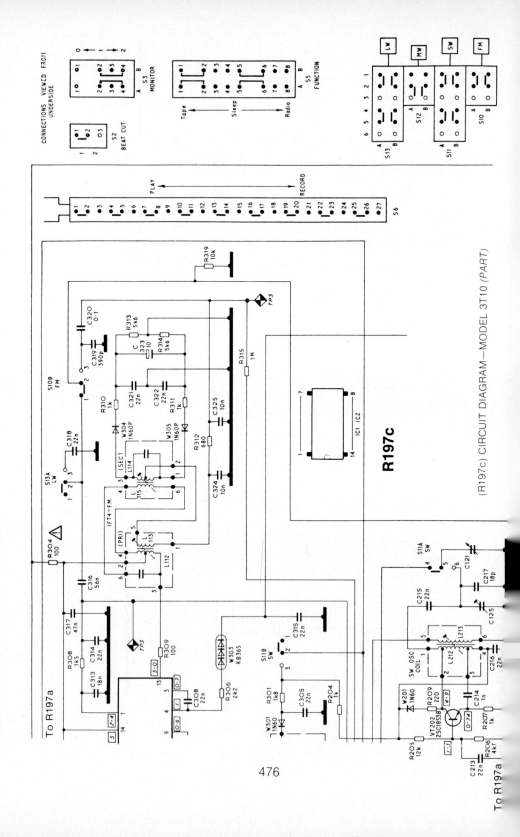

(R197c) CIRCUIT DIAGRAM—MODEL 3T10 *(PART)*

R197c

476

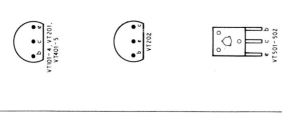

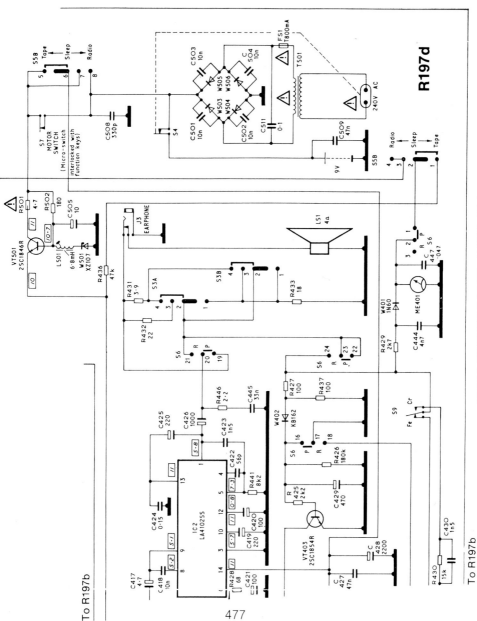

R197d

To R197b

To R197b

(R197d) CIRCUIT DIAGRAM—MODEL 3T10 (CONTINUED)

477

F.M. I.F. Circuits: Switch receiver to V.H.F./F.M. Alignment is best obtained using a wobbulator with V.H.F./F.M. and A.M. facilities and a display unit. The wobbulator should be terminated with a 75 ohm resistor across the output and a 0.01 μF capacitor in series with the 'live' lead to the injection point. Connect display unit to TP5 and TP6 and turn Volume control to minimum.

Inject 10.7MHz (22.5kHz deviation) signals between TP1 and TP2 and adjust IFT1-FM and IFT2-FM for maximum symmetrical response above and below base line, also IFT3-FM and IFT4-FM for maximum response, switch on 10.7MHz marker and adjust IFT5 for a symmetrical 'S' curve with the 10.7MHz marker at the centre of the 'S' curve.

F.M. R.F. Circuits: Defeat A.F.C. by short circuiting either end of R315 to negative supply line.

Inject signals from a V.H.F./F.M. signal generator (22.5kHz deviation) terminated with a 75 ohm resistor into TP1 and TP2.

Range	Inject	Cursor position	Adjust for max.
F.M.	87.25MHz	Extreme left	L105*
	109MHz	Extreme right	C118
	90MHz	90MHz	L103*
	106MHz	106MHz	C116

*Adjust by slightly opening or closing coil turns.

Adjusting IC1 Bias: Switch receiver to V.H.F./F.M. and connect a D.C. voltmeter between tags 4 and 6 of IC1. Adjust R318 to produce a reading of 0.5V on meter.

FERGUSON   Model 3T11

General Description: A 3-waveband A.M./F.M. radio with cassette-recorder operating from mains or battery supplies. Sockets are provided for the connection of auxiliary inputs and outputs and integrated circuits are used in radio and tape stages.

Mains Supply: 240 volts, 50Hz.

Fuse: 1A.

Wavebands: L.W. 150-350kHz; M.W. 550-1500kHz; F.M. 88-104MHz.

Loudspeaker: 8 ohms impedance.

Dismantling: Take off the battery cover, pull off three rotary control knobs and take out 5 back screws.

IC1 Voltages				IC2 Voltages		
Pin no.	*F.M.*	*A.M.*	*Rec*	*Pin no.*	*F.M.*	*Rec*
1	0.7			1	1.7	1.8
2	1.4			2	0.5	
3	0			3	0.001	
4	1.3			4	0	
5	1.4			5	0	
6	0			6	0	
7	4.8	5.0		7	0.4	
8	4.4	4.9		8	2.5	2.9
9	4.0		4.9	9	4.2	4.7
10	0.3		4.9			
11	1.0		4.9			
12	1.0		4.9			
13	4.3		4.9			
14	0.7					
15	0.4					
16	0					

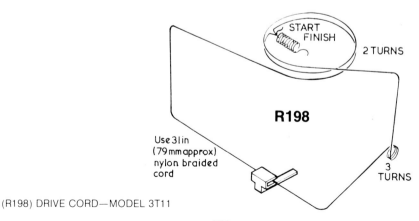

START
FINISH
2 TURNS

R198

Use 3 in
(79 mm approx)
nylon braided
cord

3
TURNS

(R198) DRIVE CORD—MODEL 3T11

479

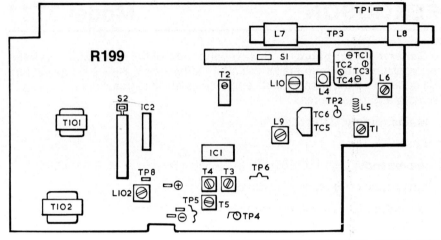

(R199) ALIGNMENT ADJUSTMENTS—MODEL 3T11

Alignment

A.M. I.F. Alignment: With the receiver Volume control at minimum, Tone control at maximum and cursor fully right (minimum capacitance), inject 470kHz from the signal generator via a loop of wire loosely coiled around the ferrite rod aerial.

Throughout alignment the signal input to the receiver should be adjusted as necessary, so that the meter reading does not exceed 0.63V (50mW).

Using a 20,000 ohms/voltmeter (set to the 10V A.C. range) connected across the Loudspeaker terminals, adjust T3 and T2 to give maximum meter reading.

Repeat adjustment until no further improvement results.

A.M. R.F. Alignment: Signals are injected via a wire loosely coiled around the ferrite rod aerial. Volume and Tone controls should be set at maximum.

Range	Inject	Cursor position	Adjust for max.
L.W.	145kHz	Fully left (max. capacitance)	L10
	360kHz	Fully right (min. capacitance)	TC6
	150kHz	150kHz	L8*
	350kHz	350kHz	TC1

Repeat adjustments until no further improvement results.

Range	Inject	Cursor position	Adjust for max.
M.W.	500kHz	Fully left (max. capacitance)	L9
	1650kHz	Fully right (min. capacitance)	TC5
	620kHz	620kHz	L7*
	1400kHz	1400kHz	TC2

*Adjust by sliding coils along ferrite rod.

480

Repeat adjustments until no further improvement results.

F.M. I.F. Alignment: Alignment is best obtained using a wobbulator with an F.M. facility and a display unit. The wobbulator should be terminated with a 75 ohm resistor across the output and a capacitor of $0.01\mu F$ in series with the 'live' lead to the injection point.

With the receiver Volume control at minimum, Tone control at maximum and cursor fully right (minimum capacitance) inject F.M. signals between TP2 and TP6.

Connect the display unit between TP5 and TP6 and de-tune T5 by unscrewing the core to just above the can. Adjust T1 and T4 for maximum output and symmetrical waveform, with the 10.7MHz marker at peak.

Adjust T5 to give an 'S' curve which is symmetrical about the 10.7MHz marker.

F.M. R.F. Alignment: Defeat A.F.C. by short circuiting C13 to earth. Connect the 20,000 ohms/voltmeter across the Loudspeaker terminals and inject F.M. signals into TP1 and TP6 as follows:

Range	Inject	Cursor position	Adjust for max.
F.M.	87.5MHz	Fully left (max. capacitance)	L6
	105MHz	Fully right (min. capacitance)	TC3
	90MHz	90MHz	L4
	104MHz	104MHz	TC4

Repeat adjustments until no further improvement results.

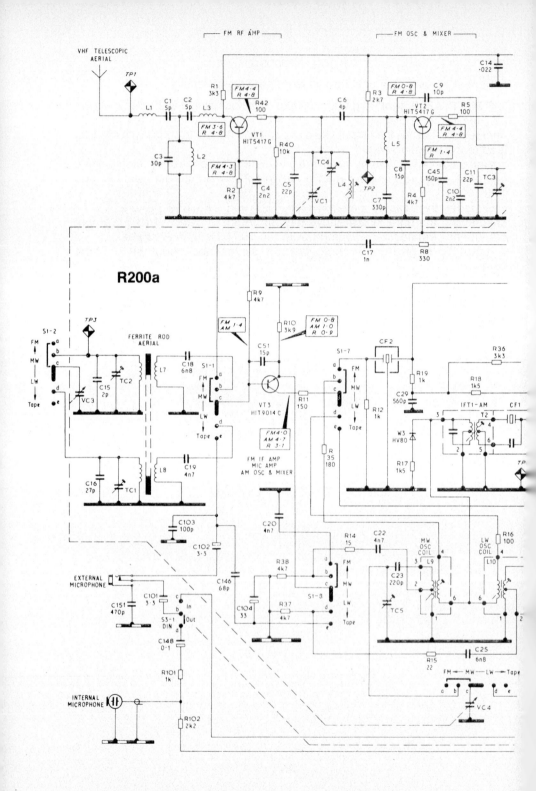

(R200a) CIRCUIT DIAGRAM—MODEL 3T11 *(PART)*

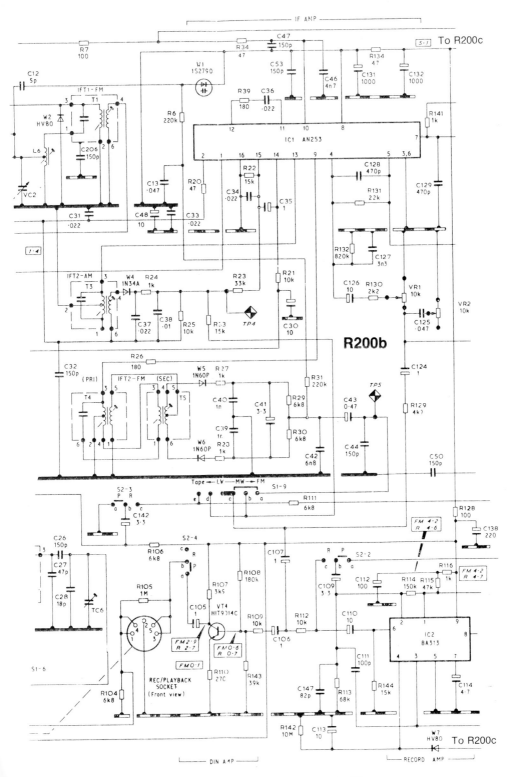

(R200b) CIRCUIT DIAGRAM—MODEL 3T11 *(PART)*

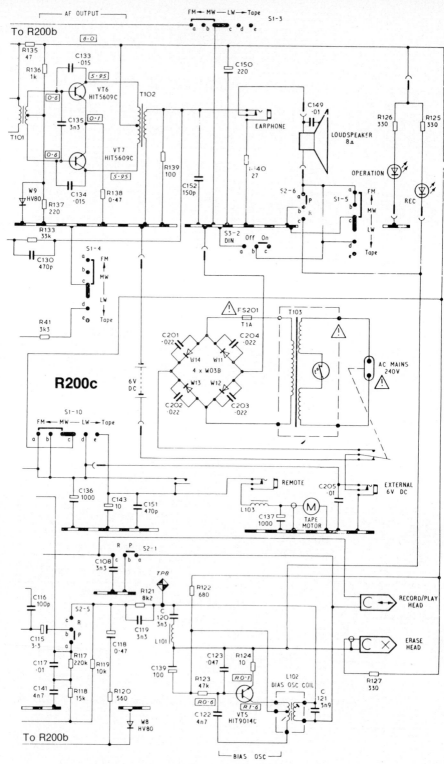

(R200c) CIRCUIT DIAGRAM—MODEL 3T11 *(CONTINUED)*

FIDELITY   Models MC3, MC5

General Description: These models which differ in the tuning section are A.M./F.M. stereo radio music-centres operating from mains supplies. The A.F. stages are common to both models and integrated circuits are used in both radio tuners and in the A.F. output stages. The loudspeakers are free-standing and a socket is provided for the connection of a tape-recorder.

Mains Supplies: 110/220, 220/250 volts, 50Hz.

Wavebands: L.W. 150-250kHz; M.W. 525-1625kHz; F.M. 87.5-108MHz.

Loudspeakers: 4 ohms impedance.

P.U. Cartridge: B.S.R. SC12H with ST16 stylus.

Dismantling Procedure (See Fig. T201)

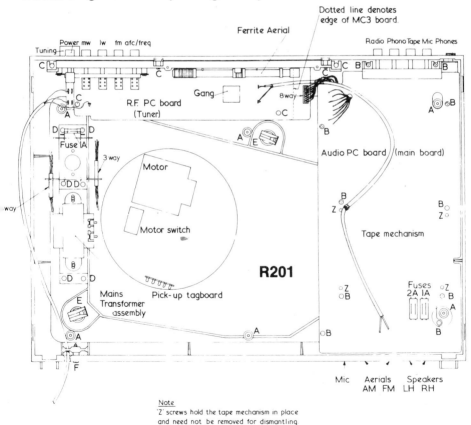

Note
'Z' screws hold the tape mechanism in place
and need not be removed for dismantling.

(R201) DISMANTLING PROCEDURE—MODELS MC3/5

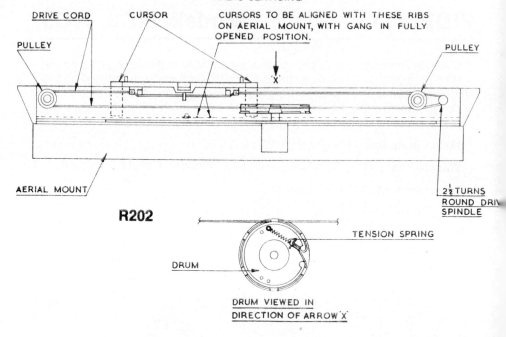

DRIVE CORD   CURSOR   CURSORS TO BE ALIGNED WITH THESE RIBS ON AERIAL MOUNT, WITH GANG IN FULLY OPENED POSITION.

PULLEY   PULLEY

AERIAL MOUNT   2½ TURNS ROUND DRIV SPINDLE

R202

TENSION SPRING

DRUM

DRUM VIEWED IN DIRECTION OF ARROW 'X'

(R202) DRIVE CORD—MODELS MC3/5

(a). Base: First clamp the record player to its mounting plate by turning the two transit screws E fully anti-clockwise then turn the music-centre upside down and carefully support it, avoiding damage to trims, controls and record-player (we suggest the use of thick foam if no other support is available). The fibre base may be taken off after removing the six black screws fixing it to the cabinet. These fixing positions are indicated A on the base view of the unit. The complete unit is now accessible for servicing and repair.

(b). Radio Chassis: The Tuning knob should be removed. The mains 3-way plug and the 8-way plug should be disconnected and the co-axial cable unsoldered. The six screws indicated C should be removed including the two fixing the front moulding to the cabinet. The D screw holding the earth link should also be removed from the transformer bracket. The chassis is now ready to be removed.

If you require the chassis to be removed completely then it will be necessary to unscrew the mains lead clamp F, unsolder the earth wire from the pick-up tag-board and the co-axial feeder. When re-assembling the tuner chassis into the cabinet, ensure that the pointer is travelling freely, before screwing it in.

(c). Tape Audio Chassis: First open the cassette flap and take off the four slider knobs then unscrew the ten screws B as indicated on the base view.

Undo the chrome headphone jack socket nut and remove 8-way connector from radio chassis. Pull the chassis up from the back first.

If you require the chassis to be removed completely then it will be necessary to unsolder the pick-up lead and co-axial aerial feed and disconnect the 4-way supply plug. The tape-deck may be dismantled from the circuit board by unscrewing the four black screws Z. Ensure that the base earthing spring if fitted is repositioned on to the B screw next to the fuse holders.

(d). Transformer Bracket: Unsolder the record-player motor leads and undo the 3-way and 4-way plugs, then remove the five fixing screws D and lift the bracket out.

(e). Record Player: Unsolder the pick-up and motor leads, then unscrew the transit screws E. The clip which sits at the end of the transit screw should be turned over vertically then the player can be removed from the cabinet.

Adjustment of the Radio Section (Indications in bold print refer to MC3 only)

Note: Always use a high frequency insulated srewdriver or trimmer to make the adjustments. These should be done very carefully.

(a). A.M. Alignment:

(1). I.F.: Place a coupling loop in proximity to the ferrite rod and radiate a 470kHz signal. Select M.W. band and with gang set to minimum capacitance at the H.F. end align IFT2 (Black) **(Mauve)** for maximum output. The 470kHz Filter (Red and Blue) should not require alignment but may be peaked if necessary.

(2). R.F.: Check that the scale pointer is correctly positioned, this should line up with the scribe lines on the front moulding. With receiver switched to M.W. at the L.F. end (maximum capacitance) radiate a signal of 525kHz. Align the oscillator coil L5 (Red) **(L10)** for the signal. Tune receiver to the H.F. end (minimum capacitance) and radiate a signal of 1625kHz and align TC104 **(TC4)** for the signal. Repeat for optimum results.

Tune receiver to 500 metres, radiate a signal of 600kHz and adjust M.W. aerial coil L8 **(L6/L8)** for maximum output.

Tune receiver to 200 metres, radiate a signal of 1500kHz and align aerial trimmer TC105 **(TC3)** for maximum output. Repeat alignment of L8 **(L6/L8)** and TC105 **(TC3)** for optimum results.

Switch receiver to L.W. and tune to 2000 metres, radiate a signal of 150kHz and adjust trimmer TC103 **(TC5)** for the signal. Tune to 1500 metres and radiate a signal of 200kHz and adjust the L.W. aerial coil L7 **(L7/L9)** for maximum output. Repeat for optimum results.

During the adjustments ensure that the output of the signal is low enough to prevent the A.G.C. of the set from coming into operation.

(b). F.M. Alignment·(set switched to F.M.):

(1). (a). I.F. for MC5: Connect a wobbulator via a 2pf capacitor to the base of T102 and earth. View the 'S' curve at pin 1 of the stereo decoder, IC2. Inject a

signal of 10.7MHz and adjust L4 (Brown) for a symmetrical 'S' curve and IFT1 (Brown) for maximum amplitude.

(b). I.F. for MC3: Connect the output of a wobbulator (75 ohm output impedance) across the F.M. oscillator section of the tuning-gang VC2. Connect the oscilloscope (Y-input) of the wobbulator to pin 1 of the stereo-decoder (IC202). Inject a signal of 10.7MHz and adjust L4 for a symmetrical 'S' curve and IFT1 for maximum amplitude. Repeat for optimum results, i.e., until a straight centre portion of the 'S' curve has been obtained which is symmetrical about the zero axis of the display.

(2). R.F.: Inject an 87.5MHz signal into the Aerial socket and with the gang at maximum capacitance (L.F. end) align the oscillator coil L3 for the signal and aerial coil L1 for maximum output. Tune to the H.F. end, i.e., minimum capacitance, and inject a 108MHz signal. Align the oscillator trimmer TC102 **(TC2)** for the signal and adjust the aerial trimmer TC101 **(TC1)** for maximum output. Repeat the above procedure (for R.F.) until no further improvement can be achieved.

(3). Decoder Alignment: Inject a stereo modulated R.F. signal at the Aerial input and adjust R146 for LED illumination. Reduce the R.F. signal whilst adusting R146 **(VR202)** to obtain the optimum setting.

(4). A.F.C. Alignment: With the A.F.C. button in the off position, inject a signal of 100MHz at 1mV. Tune receiver to the above signal. Depress A.F.C. button (on) and adjust R121 **(VR201)** to receive signal. With A.F.C. off vary signal on generator by ±200kHz and switching in the A.F.C. should lock on in either position.

Integrated Circuit Voltages (MC3):

TBA 120		CA 758		CA 3123	
1	0V	1	2V65	1	3V65
2	1V9	2	7V8	2	5V8
3	0V	3	4V7	3	5V8
4	0V	4	4V1	4	3V7
5	0V65	5	4V1	5	0V05
6	1V9	6	4V7	6	9V05
7	3V3	7	0V8	7	0V7
8	7V1	8	0V	8	0V
9	3V3	9	2V8	9	0V
10	1V9	10	2V6	10	0V65
11	11V3	11	2V	11	0V65
12	0V	12	3V	12	0V65
13	1V	13	2V95	13	3V75
14	1V	14	2V95	14	5V8
		15	3V4		
		16	11V5		

Adjustments (Tape Section)

Ensure that the record/playback and erase heads are clean by either using a head cleaning tape or by using a soft fluffless cloth or soft brush moistened with pure alcohol or methylated spirits.

Azimuth Head Alignment: Select play mode and load the cassette-deck with a 6.3kHz azimuth tape and switch unit to Tape. Monitor the output of both channels with an oscilloscope and adjust the azimuth screw (nearest the erase head) on the record/playback head for (a) maximum output and (b) the two channels to be in phase. The 21mm screw should then be sealed.

Bias Adjustment: Select Record mode. Connect a VV meter across R40 (left channel) and adjust P1 to read 3mV on the meter. Repeat the above for the Right channel by connecting the meter across R104 and adjusting P101 for 3mV. The MC3 used various types of heads thus requiring different bias settings, ranging from 3 to 6mV across R40 and R104. In order to check for this use a good quality tape to record and playback suitable material and assess the reproduction. Should the recording sound be distorted increase the bias. If the higher frequencies are suppressed decrease the bias.

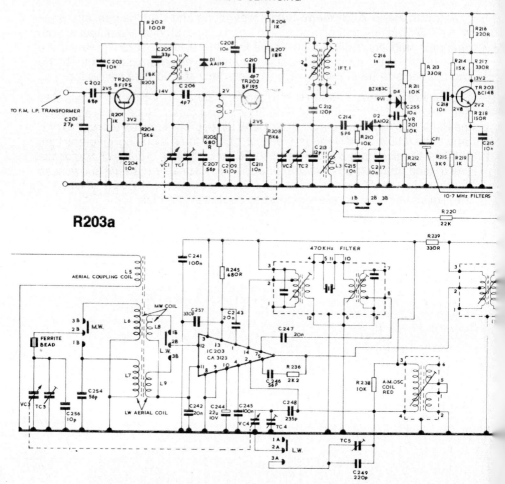

R203a

(R203a) CIRCUIT DIAGRAM (TUNER UNIT)—MODEL MC3 *(PART)*

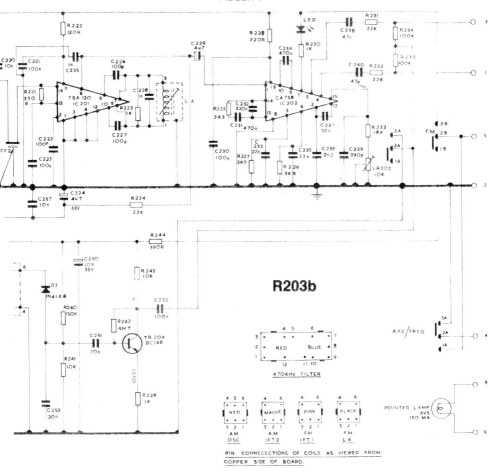

(R203b) CIRCUIT DIAGRAM (TUNER UNIT)—MODEL MC3 *(CONTINUED)*

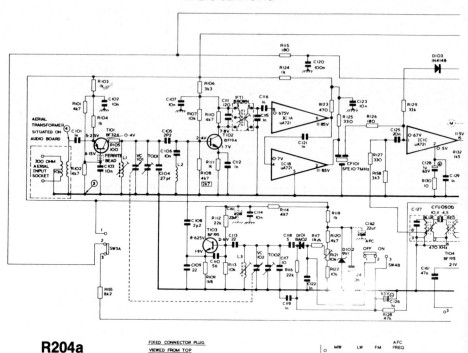

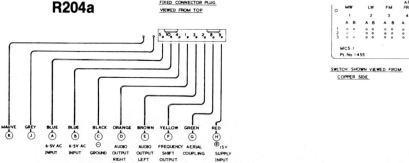

R204a

(R204a) CIRCUIT DIAGRAM (TUNER UNIT)—MODEL MC5 *(PART)*

492

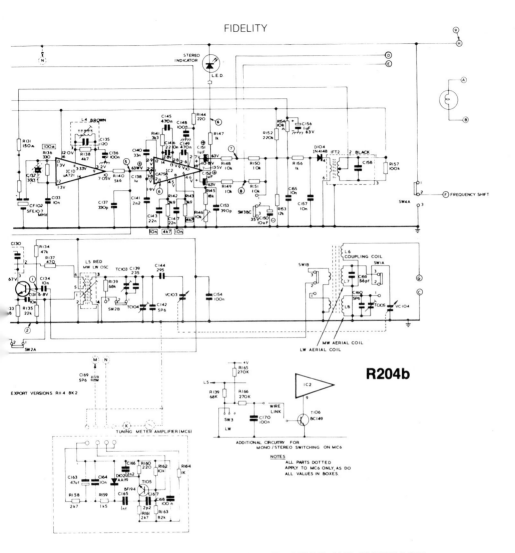

R204b

(R204b) CIRCUIT DIAGRAM (TUNER UNIT)—MODEL MC5 *(CONTINUED)*

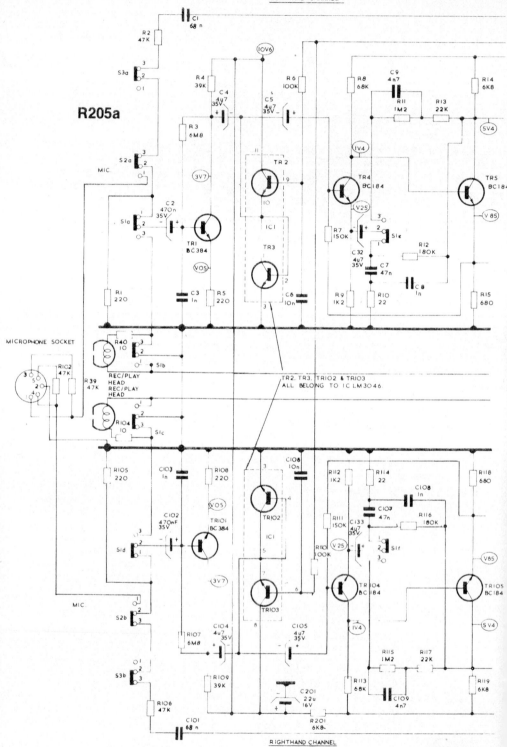

(R205a) CIRCUIT DIAGRAM (A.F. STAGES)—MODELS MC3, MC5 *(PART)*

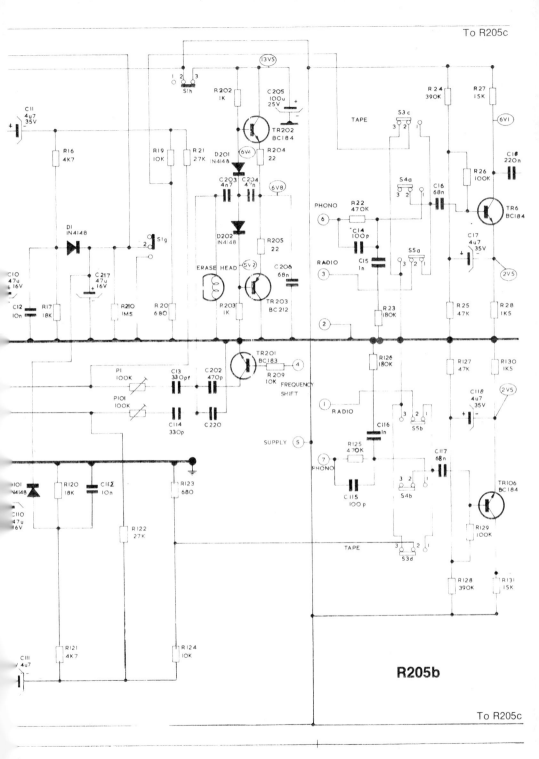

To R205c

R205b

To R205c

(R205b) CIRCUIT DIAGRAM (A.F. STAGES)—MODELS MC3, MC5 *(PART)*

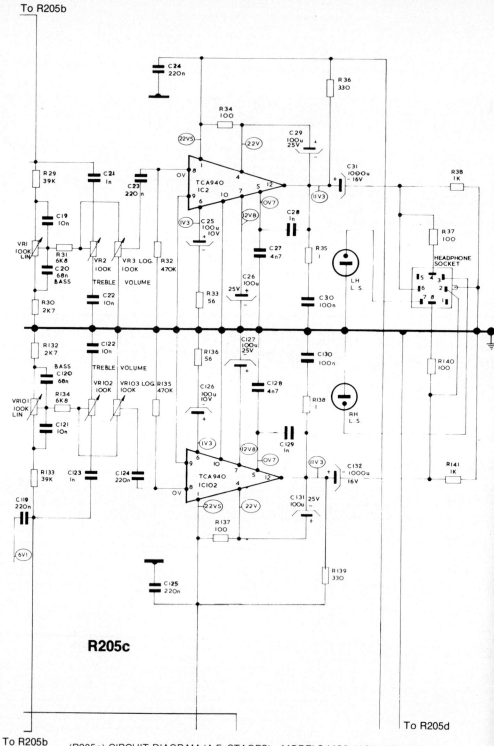

R205c

(R205c) CIRCUIT DIAGRAM (A.F. STAGES)—MODELS MC3, MC5 *(CONTINUED)*

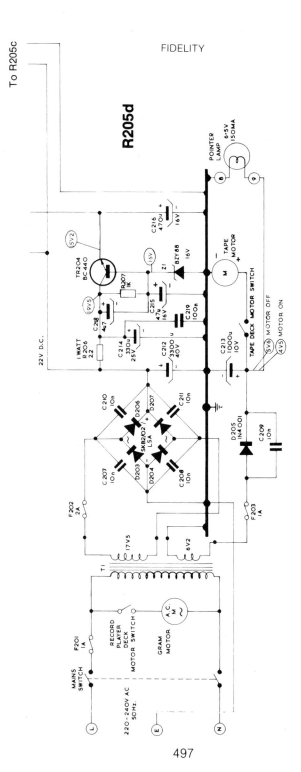

R205d

To R205c

(R205d) CIRCUIT DIAGRAM (POWER SUPPLY)—MODELS MC3, MC5

497

FIDELITY   Model 4-40

General Description: A 4-waveband stereo music-centre operating on mains supplies. Separate free-standing loudspeakers are plugged into the unit and sockets are provided for the connection of auxiliary inputs and outputs. Comprehensive tone controls are fitted and the unit contains stereo record-player and cassette tape-recorder.

Mains Supplies: 110/220, 220/250 volts, 50Hz.

Wavebands: L.W. 150-250kHz; M.W. 525-1625kHz; S.W. 5.70-15.5MHz; F.M. 87.5-108MHz.

P.U. Cartridge: A.D.C. magnetic.

Dismantling Procedure (See Fig. T206)

Base: First clamp the record-player to its mounting plate by turning the two transit screws fully anti-clockwise, then turn the music-centre upside down and carefully support it, avoiding damage to trims, controls and record player (we suggest the use of thick foam if no other support is available). The fibre base may be taken off after removing the 10 black screws fixing it to the wooden plinth. The complete unit is now accessible for servicing and repair.

Radio Chassis: The Tuning knob and the slide knobs should be taken off then the knurled Headphone socket nut and the Tuning spindle nut should be removed from the top. Then remove all screws from the chassis marked with an arrow and indicated B on the inside base view. The chassis is now ready to be removed and this should be achieved by lifting the chassis up, sliding it to the side and then up again.

If you require the chassis to be removed completely then it will be necessary to unsolder the changer pick-up tags and unplug the leads from the Tape Audio board. If it is necessary to remove the scale pan to have access to the components underneath, then undo the three screws Y and carefully pull the LED stereo indicator out of the grommet.

Tape Audio Chassis: First open the cassette flap and then unscrew the five silver screws C. Next undo all the plugs and then pull the chassis straight out. The tape-deck may be dismantled from the circuit board by unscrewing the four black screws Z.

Power Supply Board and Meters: This board is dismantled by unscrewing the four silver screws D holding the metal brackets to the cabinet moulding. Undo all the plugs and lift the chassis out. The meters are now accessible.

Transformer Bracket: Unsolder the motor leads and undo the plug then remove all six fixing screws G and lift the bracket out. It might be necessary to remove the on/off switch-button. To remove this assembly completely it will be necessary to undo the mains lead clamp H.

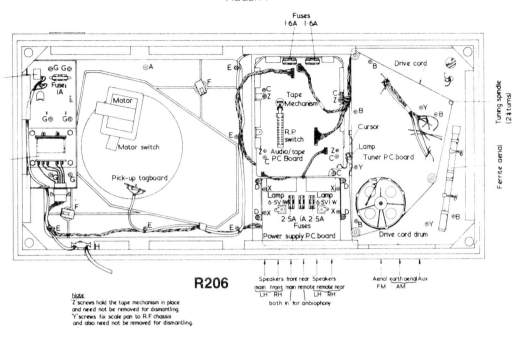

R206

Note
'Z' screws hold the tape mechanism in place and need not be removed for dismantling.
'Y' screws fix scale pan to R.F chassis and also need not be removed for dismantling.

(R206) DISMANTLING PROCEDURE—MODEL 4-40

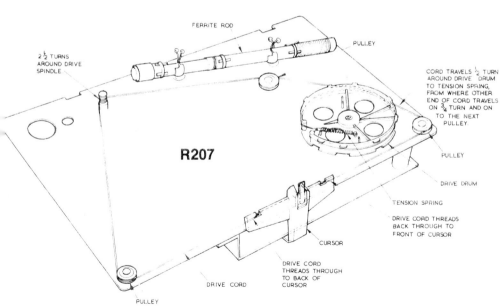

R207

(R207) DRIVE CORD—MODEL 4-40

Record-Player: Unsolder the pick-up and motor leads, then unscrew the transit screws F. The clip which sits at the end of the transit screws should be turned over vertically then the player can be removed from the cabinet.

Note: Please ensure after assembly of the unit that it is satisfactory from a performance aspect and is completely safe before returning it to the customer.

A.M. Alignment

I.F.: Place a coupling loop in proximity to the ferrite rod and radiate a 470kHz signal. Select M.W. band and with gang set to minimum capacitance at the H.F. end align IFT2 (Black) for maximum output. The 470kHz Filter (Red and Blue) should not require alignment but may be peaked if necessary.

R.F.: Check that the scale pointer is correctly positioned as indicated by the arrows on the radio chassis. With receiver switched to M.W. at the L.F. end (maximum capacitance) radiate a signal of 525kHz. Align the oscillator coil L5 (Red) for the signal. Tune receiver to the H.F. end (minimum capacitance) and radiate a signal of 1625kHz and align TC104 for the signal. Repeat for optimum results.

Tune receiver to 600kHz, radiate this signal and adjust M.W. aerial coil L9/L10 for maximum output.

Tune receiver to 1500kHz, radiate this signal and align aerial trimmer TC106 for maximum output. Repeat alignment of L9/L10 and TC106 for optimum results.

Switch receiver to L.W. and tune to 150kHz, radiate this signal and adjust trimmer TC103 for the signal. Tune to 200kHz and radiate this signal and adjust the L.W. aerial coil L11/L12 for maximum output.

Switch to S.W. and inject 5.8MHz into the aerial socket. With the gang fully closed (maximum capacitance) align L6 for the signal and L7 for maximum output. Ensure that the correct tuning point has been found by checking that the image appears on the high side, i.e., 6.74MHz. With the gang fully open, inject 15.5MHz and align TC105 for the signal. Repeat above operations until no further improvement is realised.

During the adjustments ensure that the output of the signal source is low enough to prevent the A.G.C. of the set from coming into operation.

F.M. Alignment

I.F.: Connect a wobbulator via a 2pf capacitor to the base of T102 and earth. View the 'S' curve at pin 1 of the stereo decoder, IC2. Adjust L4 (Brown) for a symmetrical 'S' curve and IFT1 (Brown) for maximum amplitude.

R.F.: Inject an 87.5MHz signal into the Aerial socket and with the gang at maximum capacitance (L.F. end) align the oscillator coil L3 for the signal and aerial coil L1 for maximum output. Tune to the H.F. end, i.e., minimum capacitance, and inject a 108MHz signal. Align the oscillator trimmer TC102 for the signal and adjust the aerial trimmer TC101 for maximum output. Repeat the above procedure (for R.F.) until no further improvement can be achieved.

Decoder Alignment: Inject a stereo modulated R.F. signal at the aerial input and adjust R146 for LED illumination. Reduce the R.F. signal whilst adjusting R146 to obtain the optimum setting.

A.F.C. Alignment: With the A.F.C. button in the off position, inject a signal of 100MHz at 1mV. Tune receiver to above signal. Depress A.F.C. button (on) and adjust R121 to receive signal. With A.F.C. off vary signal on generator by ±200kHz, and switching in the A.F.C. should lock on in either position.

Adjustments (Audio and Tape Sections)

Ensure that the record/playback and erase heads are clean by either using a head cleaning tape or by using a soft fluffless cloth or soft brush moistened with pure alcohol or methylated spirits.

Amplifier Balance Adjustment: Select auxiliary input and adjust both Volume controls to mid position. Feed a 1kHz signal through the auxiliary socket (pins 3 and 5) and monitor the speaker outputs of both channels with wattmeters or an oscilloscope, adjust P102 to give equal output levels on both channels.

Azimuth Head Alignment: Select play mode and load the cassette-deck with a 10kHz azimuth tape. Monitor the output of both channels with an oscilloscope and adjust the azimuth screw on the Record/Playback head for (a) maximum output and (b) the two channels to be in phase. The 21mm screw should then be sealed.

Bias Adjustment: Select Record mode and ferrous tape. Connect a VV meter across R1 (Left channel) and adjust P1 to read 3mV on the meter, when switching to chrome the meter should read 4.2mV. Repeat above for Right channel by connecting the meter across R101 and adjusting P101.

Oscillator Frequency Adjustment: Select Record mode and connect a frequency counter across the erase head and adjust the Tape oscillator coil L1 to read 64kHz.

Record Level Meter Adjustment: Select Record mode and feed a signal of 13mV at 1kHz through C4 and C104. Adjust P201 to read 0dB on the meter.

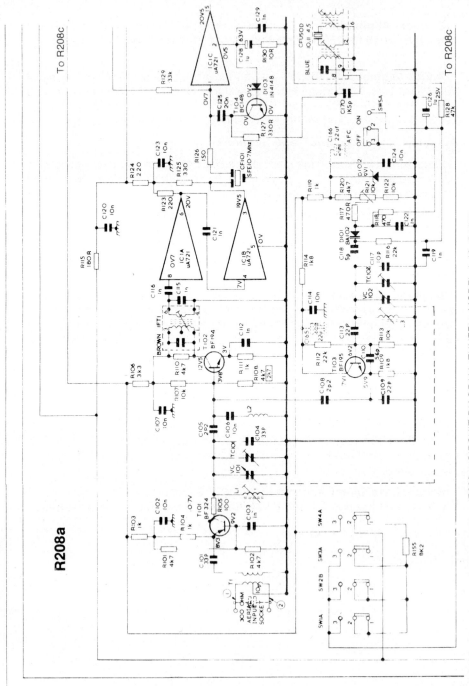

(R208a) CIRCUIT DIAGRAM (TUNER)—MODEL 4-40 (PART)

(R208b) CIRCUIT DIAGRAM (A.F. STAGES)—MODEL 4-40 (PART)

503

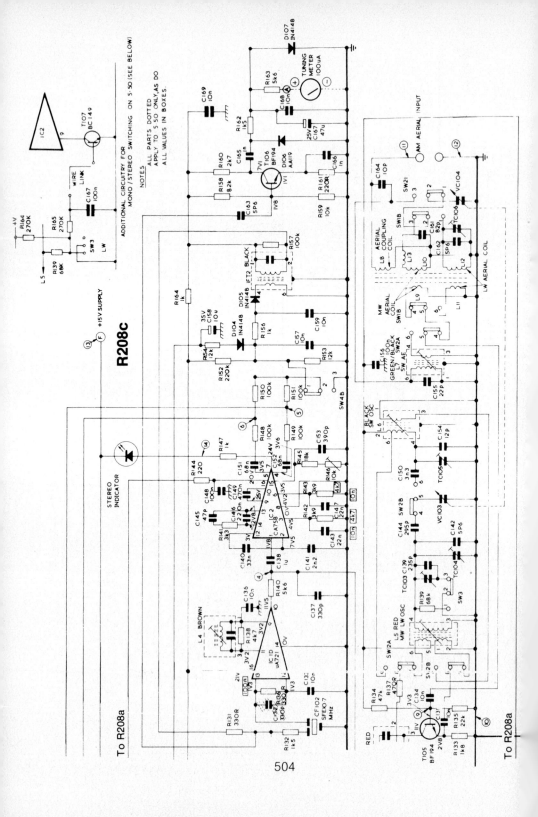

R208c

504

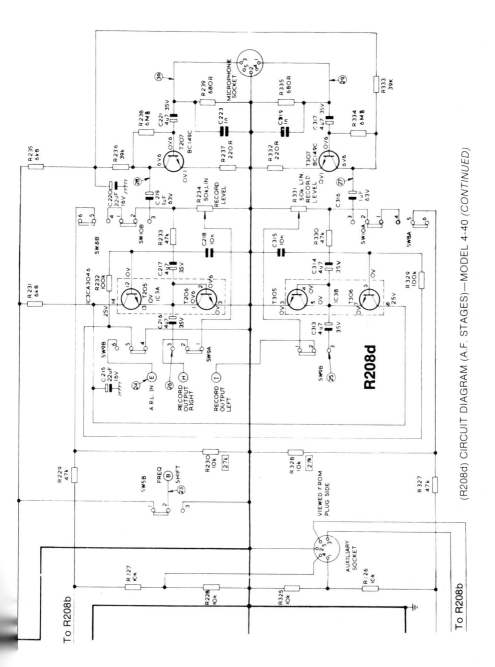

(R208d) CIRCUIT DIAGRAM (A.F. STAGES)—MODEL 4-40 (CONTINUED)

(R209a) CIRCUIT DIAGRAM (RECORDER)—MODEL 4-40 (PART)

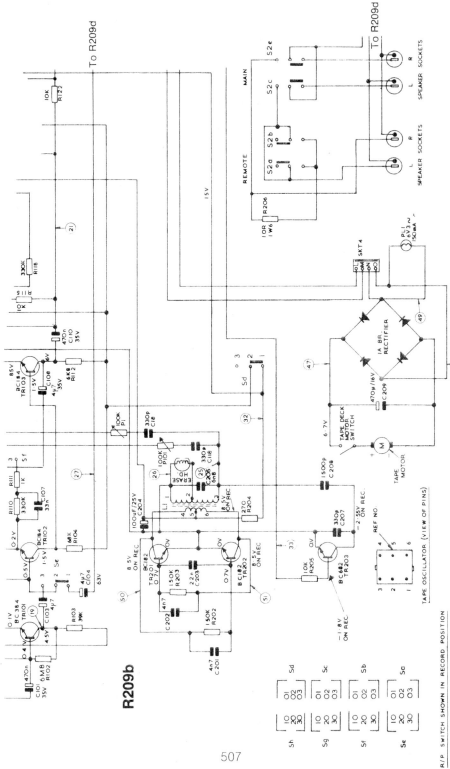

(R209b) CIRCUIT DIAGRAM (RECORDER)—MODEL 4-40 (PART)

507

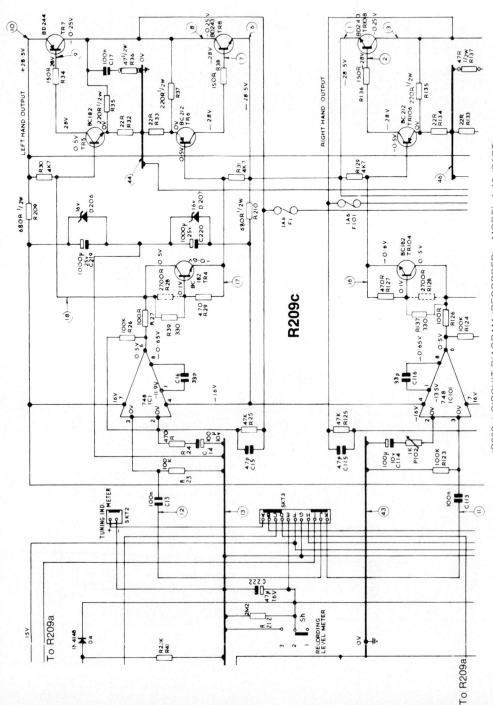

(R209c) CIRCUIT DIAGRAM (RECORDER)—MODEL 4-40 *(PART)*

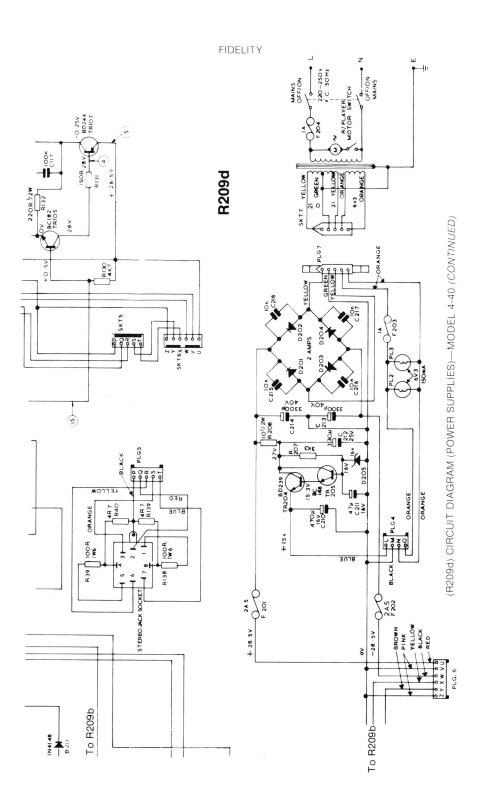

R209d

(R209d) CIRCUIT DIAGRAM (POWER SUPPLIES)—MODEL 4-40 (CONTINUED)

HACKER SOUND

Model RP79MB 'Consort'

General Description: An A.M./F.M. portable radio operating from mains or battery supplies. The modules forming the radio tuning section are of the type used in Hacker Model RP78. This is described in the 1977-8 volume of *Radio and Television Servicing*, to which reference should be made. The revised A.F. and Power Supply modules are detailed here and feature separate bass and treble controls and sockets for the connection of tape-recorder and earphone.

Mains Supplies: 220-240 volts, 50Hz.

Battery: 9 volts (PP9).

Removal of Chassis

Remove the wooden battery cover, take out and disconnect the battery, remove the battery lead from the plastic clip.

Take out the screws at the ends of the cabinet which retain the handle and remove the handle.

From underneath the cabinet remove the screw securing the telescopic aerial.

Disconnect the loudspeaker tags and the power pack connector; the complete chassis may now be withdrawn from the top of the cabinet.

Retrieve the spacer from under the end of the aerial rod and ensure that it is refitted when re-assembly is carried out.

Use care to avoid damage to the printed circuit boards when carrying out these operations.

Removal of Power Pack

Remove chassis as previously described.

Remove the screw (adjacent to connector pins) securing the power pack to the base of the cabinet.

Slide power pack towards centre of cabinet and lift out.

To gain access to components, including fuse, remove the two cross-headed screws on top of the case and the two in the printed circuit board nearest the open side of the case. Do *not* remove the two screws in the printed circuit board below the 'Warning' label.

Replacement of Speaker

Remove chassis and power pack as previously described.

Remove the four nuts securing the speaker using flat and box 2BA spanners, and lift out speaker.

Fit new speaker on to screws (with tags at end away from power pack) and secure both the nuts.

Re-fit the power pack.

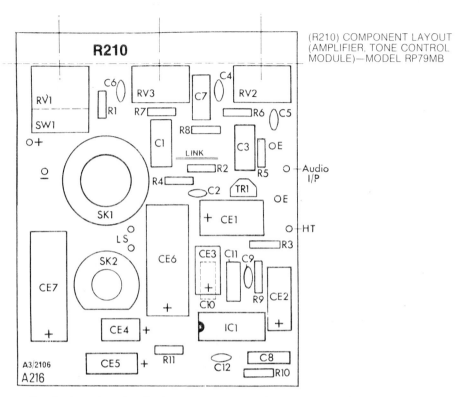

R210

(R210) COMPONENT LAYOUT
(AMPLIFIER, TONE CONTROL
MODULE)—MODEL RP79MB

Re-fit the chassis, fit the connector to the power pack and tags to the speaker.

Note: The Black lead must be connected to the tag marked Red.

Component List (A.F. Stages)

uit ref. nos.	1	2	3	4	5	6	7	8	9	10*	11	12	13†	14†
stors 'R'	10K	4M7	5K6	18K	1K	33K	56K	10K	220K	82	150		s.o.t.	s.o.t.
acitors 'C'	100n	560p	47n	330p	4n7	4n7	33n	47n	330p		100n	150p		
acitors elec. 'CE'	220	100	2μ2	47	100	1000	470							
s working	10	10	63	10	10	10	10							

10 value may vary in production.
t.=select on test.
13 or R14 may be required to achieve symmetrical clipping at full power (typical value 27K).

	RV1/SW1	47K Log	TR1	BC149
Misc.	RV2	220K Log	IC1	TBA820
	RV3	220K Log		

Component List (Power Supply)

10n	CE1	470	25V	R1	820	D1-4	IN4001	TR1	BD433	F1	50mA delayed	T1	A3/909/3
	CE2	33	16V	R2	22	ZD1	BZY79						
	CE3	33	16V	R3	4M7		C10V						

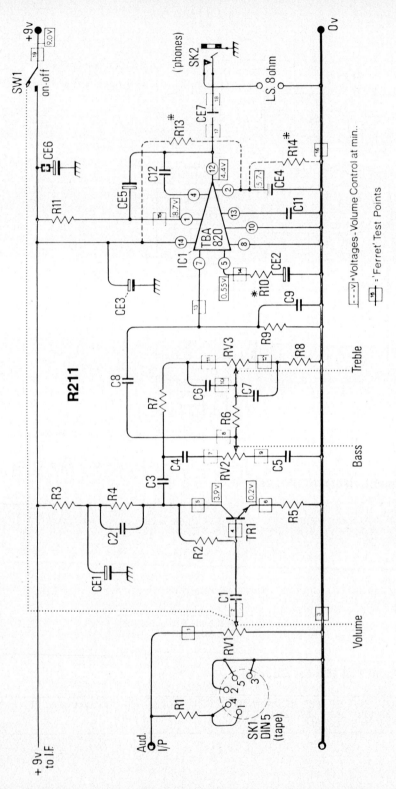

(R211) CIRCUIT DIAGRAM (A.F. MODULE A216)—MODEL RP79MB

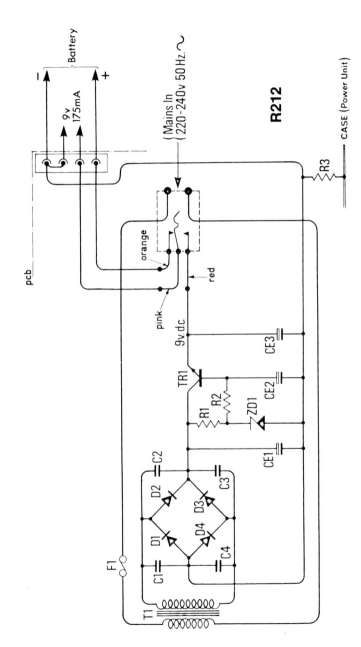

(R212) CIRCUIT DIAGRAM (POWER SUPPLY)—MODEL RP79MB

HACKER SOUND   Models RP77MB 'Sovereign IV', RPC1 'Sovereign'

General Description: A.M./F.M. radio receivers using modular construction of the main sections. The radio tuner units are similar to those used in Hacker Model RP78 and information will be found in the 1977-8 volume of *Radio and Television Servicing*. Alternative A.F. and Power Supply stages are detailed here together with the cassette unit which is fitted to Model RPC1.

Mains Supply: 240 volts, 50Hz.

Battery: 12 volts.

Dismantling

To Remove Chassis from Cabinet. RPC1:

1. Press 'Eject' button. Remove 4 screws holding front flap to cassette carriage, taking care not to damage front grille. Take off flap and press carriage back into 'closed' position.

2. Remove back cover. Disconnect and remove battery tray.

3. Release leads from plastic cable clamp and disconnect (a) leads from speaker, (b) lead from power unit to 214 P.C.B. (c) lead from internal microphone to cassette P.C.B.

4. Remove screw and clamp from wood block at bottom of cassette chassis.

5. Remove 2 screws and washers from underside of cabinet base and carefully lift chassis from cabinet.

To Re-Assemble:

6. Reverse above procedure.

7. After replacing cassette flap, check for correct operation of cassette carriage. It may be necessary to loosen the 2 bottom fixing screws and adjust positions of chassis end panels for correct positioning of flap. Check and tighten screws.

RP77: Procedure as above less instructions in Paragraphs (1) and (4) and (7).

Amplifier Adjustment: In order to set the quiescent current for the output transistors, cut the link on the amplifier circuit board and insert an 0-10mA meter. Adjust the current by means of the small pre-set RP2, to give a reading of 3mA in conjunction with adjusting RP1 for mid-rail of 5.7V with supply =12.0V. Remove meter and re-solder link.

Record Head Current: With the rec/replay head connected an input signal of 500mV, the record current =0.8mV across R9 10 ohm.

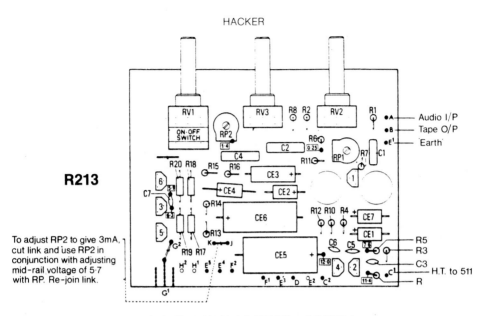

R213

To adjust RP2 to give 3mA, cut link and use RP2 in conjunction with adjusting mid-rail voltage of 5·7 with RP. Re-join link.

(R213) COMPONENT LAYOUT (A.F. STAGE)—'SOVEREIGN' MODELS

Bias: Bias trap adjustment. In record mode no signal input. Connect VV to junction to R29 L1 C8, and adjust L1 for a minimum.

Set Bias F_eO Connect VV across R9 (Note earth of VV must be connected to earth end of R9 or braid of rec/replay head, and adjust PR1 to give 5.5mV.

Set Bias CRO_2 to give 7.7mV across R9.

Erase current, connect VV across R45 1 ohm and check erase current =50mV across R45.

Component List

L.F. Module					
R1	10K	R17	}	CE1	33μ
R2	27	R18	} 1.0	CE2	2μ2
R3	3K3	R19	}	CE3	100μ
R4	1K5	R20	}	CE4	47μ
R5	6K8			CE5	} 1000μ
R6	680	RP1	} 22K	CE6	}
R7	150K	RP2	}	CE7	33
R8	} 1K			TR1	} BC149
R9	}	RV1	47K.Log	TR2	}
R10	39	RV2	4K7.R.Log	TR3	} BC158
R11	68K	RV3	47K.Log	TR4	}
R12	2K2			TR5	BC465
R13	}	C1	68n	TR6	BC464
R14	} 470	C2	220n		
R15	}	C3*	5n6 (2n2 Early Models)		
R16	150	C4	220n		
		C5	(3n3 Early Models)		
		C6	68p (56p Early Models)		
		C7	10n		

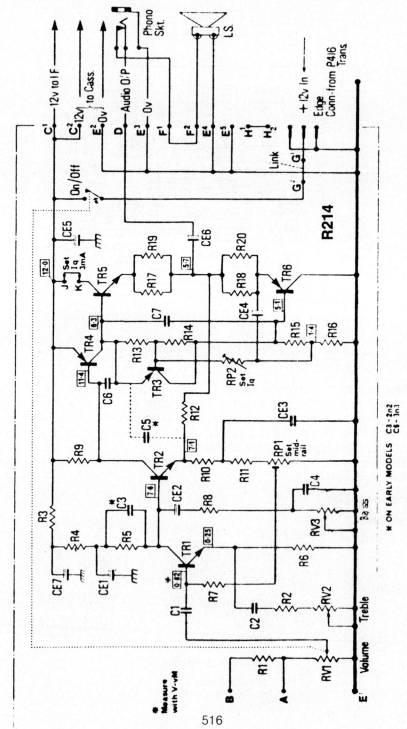

(R214) CIRCUIT DIAGRAM (A.F. STAGE)—'SOVEREIGN' MODELS

* ON EARLY MODELS   C3 = 2n2
                     C6 = 3n3

516

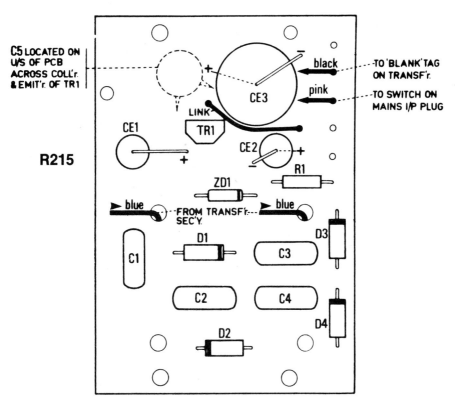

R215

black --- TO 'BLANK' TAG ON TRANSF'r.

pink --- TO SWITCH ON MAINS I/P PLUG

CE3

LINK

TR1

CE1

CE2

R1

ZD1

blue ► FROM TRANSF'r. SEC'Y ► blue

D1

D3

C1

C3

C2

C4

D4

D2

(R215) COMPONENT LAYOUT (POWER SUPPLY)—MODEL RPC1

Cassette

R1	3K3	R28	82K	C4	27p		CE15	220μ
R2	100	R29	10K	C5	10n		CE16	47μ
R3	2M2	R30 } R31 }	100	C6	150p		CE17	220μ
R4	10K	R32	1K	C7	10n			
R5	330	R33	1M	C8	330p		TR1 } TR2 }	BC149c
R6	3K3	R34	15K	C9 } C10 }	68n		TR3 }	
R7	22K	R35	220	C11	220p		TR4 } TR5 }	BC149
R8	150K	R36	100	C12	68n		TR6 }	
R9	10	R37	1K5	C13	220p		TR7	BC158
R10	220	R38	1K5	BETWEEN			TR8 } TR9 }	ZTX108
R11	22K	R39	1+1	SW5 & SW6				
R12	150K	R40	82K	C14	100n		TR10	ZTX550
R13	6K8	R41	68K				TR11	BC158
R14	100	R42	22K	CE1	6μ8			
R15	22K	R43	56K	CE2	47u			
R16	150K	R44	15K	CE3 } CE4 }	2μ2			
R17	220	R45	1.0	CE5	6μ8		D1 } D2 }	BA314
R18	10K	R46	330	CE6	100μ		D3	RL209
R19 } R20 }	2K2	R47	56K	CE7	22μ		D4	BZX79 C6V2
R21	330K	ON SW7		CE8	330μ			
R22	6K8			CE9 } CE10 } CE11 }	6μ8		D5	BA316
R23	1K5	RP1 } RP2 }	100K				D6	BA314
R24	15K			CE12	220μ		L1	22mH
R25	12K	C1	1n5	CE13	22μ		L2	5.6mH
R26	6K8	C2 } C3 }	150p	CE14	2μ2		B.Osc. {	721BOR 1021N
R27	150K							

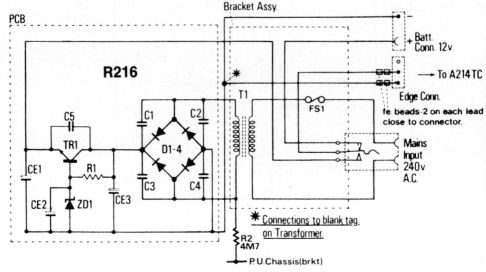

(R216) CIRCUIT DIAGRAM (POWER SUPPLY)—MODEL RPC1

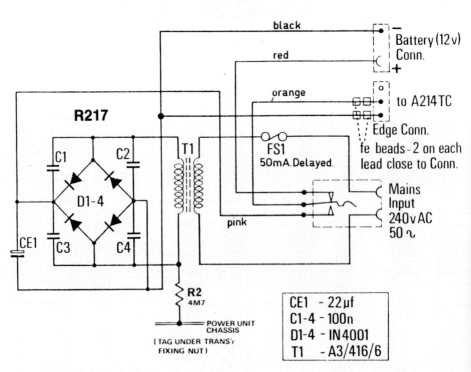

(R217) CIRCUIT DIAGRAM (POWER SUPPLY)—MODEL RP77MB

Power Unit P416

R1	680	TR1	BCX34
R2	4M7		
		D1 ⎫	
C1 ⎫		D2 ⎬ IN4001	
C2 ⎬		D3 ⎪	
C3 ⎬ 100n		D4 ⎭	
C4 ⎪			
C5 ⎭		ZD1	BZX79
CE1	33		C13
CE2	22		
CE3	470	FS1	50mA delayed

Power Unit P416E

As P416 less
R1, C5, CE1, CE3
(CE2 becomes CE1)
Used on RP77
only

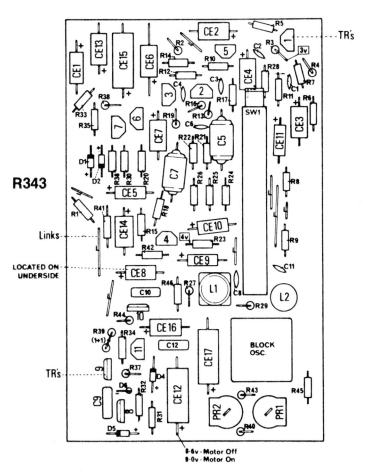

R343

Links

LOCATED ON
UNDERSIDE

TR's

(R343) COMPONENT LAYOUT (CASSETTE UNIT)—MODEL RPC1

519

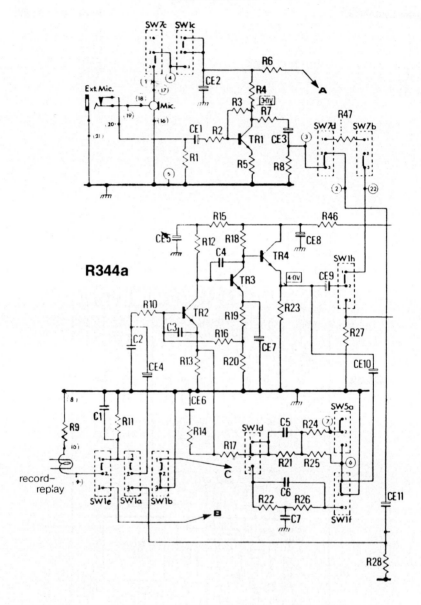

(R344a) CIRCUIT DIAGRAM (CASSETTE UNIT)—MODEL RPC1 *(PART)*

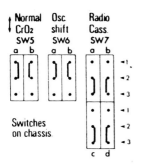

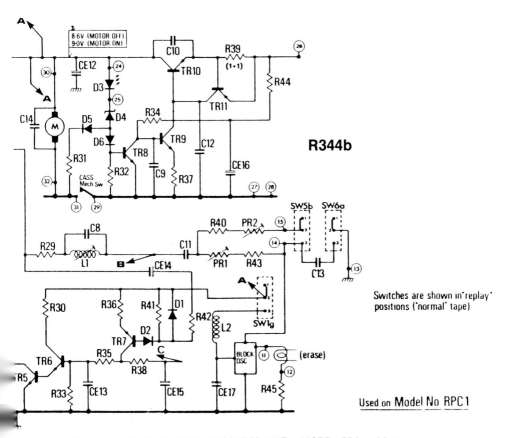

R344b

Switches are shown in 'replay' positions ('normal' tape)

(erase)

Used on Model No RPC1

(R344b) CIRCUIT DIAGRAM (CASSETTE UNIT)—MODEL RPC1 *(CONTINUED)*

HITACHI   Model KH-434E

General Description: An A.M./F.M. 2-waveband portable radio receiver operating from mains or battery supplies. A socket is provided for the connection of an earphone.

Mains Supply: 220 volts, 50Hz.

Fuse: 315mA.

Batteries: 6 volts (4×HP7).

Wavebands: M.W. 530-1605kHz; 88-108MHz.

Loudspeaker: 8 ohms impedance.

Access for Service: The back is held by one central screw. The p.c.b. may be lifted out after removing three screws.

Alignment

Genescope	Dial pointer position	Adjust	Remarks
10.7MHz		T5	Turn T5 fully anti-clockwise
		T1	Maximum
		T2	Reduce the level of the F.M. generator to make one waveform
		T3	
	Highest	T4	
		T5	Adjust T5 for a symmetrical sinewave (S curve) output
		T4	Adjust T4 for a straight reference line of the S curve

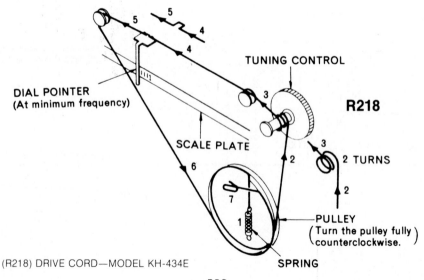

(R218) DRIVE CORD—MODEL KH-434E

522

F.M./R.F.

Item		Signal generator Frequency	Modulation	Dial pointer position	Adjust	Reading
1	Covering	87.5MHz	400Hz 30%	Lowest	L4	Max.
2		109MHz		Highest	CT2	
3	Repeat 1 and 2.					
4	Tracking	90MHz	400Hz 30%	90MHz	L2	Max.
5		106MHz		106MHz	CT1	
6	Repeat 4 and 5					

A.M./I.F.:

Signal generator Frequency	Modulation	Dial pointer position	Adjust	Reading
465kHz	—	Highest	T6 T7 T8	Max.

A.M./R.F.:

Item		Signal generator Frequency	Modulation	Dial pointer position	Adjust	Reading
1	Covering	515kHz	400Hz 30%	Lowest	L6	Max.
2		1650kHz		Highest	CT4	
3	Repeat 1 and 2					
4	Tracking	600kHz	400Hz 30%	600kHz	L5	Max.
5		1400kHz		1400kHz	CT3	
6	Repeat 4 and 5					

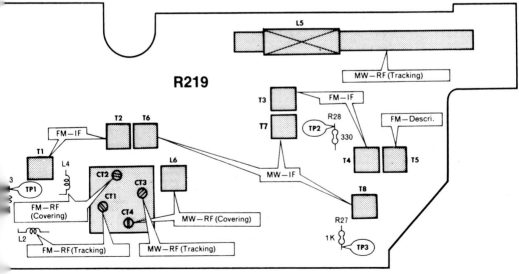

(R219) ALIGNMENT ADJUSTMENTS—MODEL KH-434E

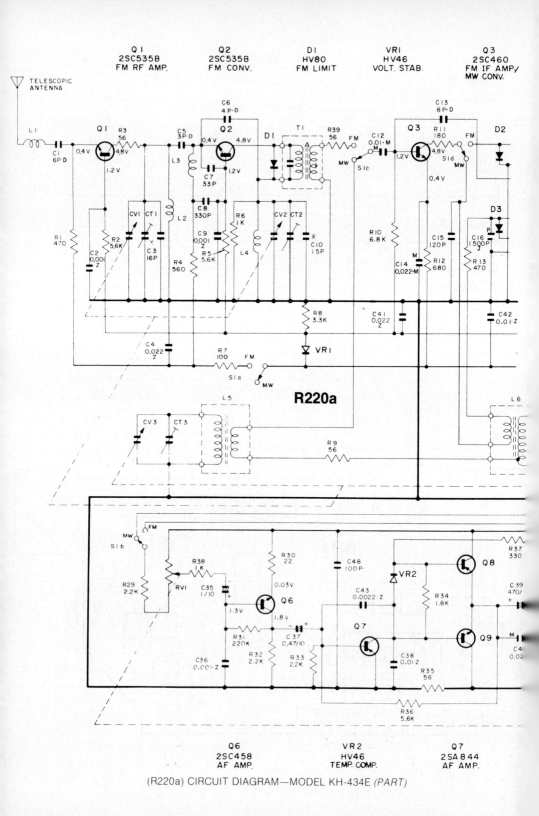

(R220a) CIRCUIT DIAGRAM—MODEL KH-434E *(PART)*

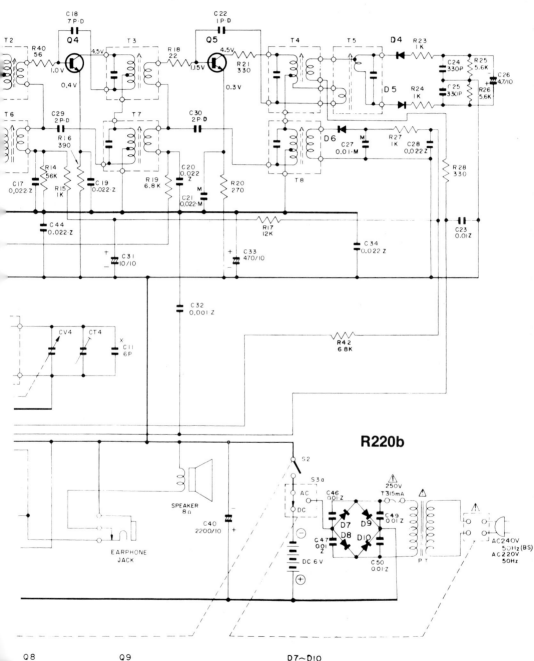

(R220b) CIRCUIT DIAGRAM—MODEL KH-434E *(CONTINUED)*

HITACHI   Model KH-924L

General Description: An A.M./F.M. 3-waveband portable radio receiver operating from mains or battery supplies. A socket is fitted for the connection of an earphone.

Mains Supply: 240 volts, 50Hz.

Fuse: 400mA.

Batteries: 6 volts (4×HP7).

Wavebands: L.W. 150-350kHz; M.W. 530-1605kHz; F.M. 87.5-108MHz.

Loudspeaker: 8 ohms impedance.

Access for Service: Remove the screw from the F.M. aerial. Remove the batteries and take out three screws securing the back cover. The p.c.b. is held by three screws.

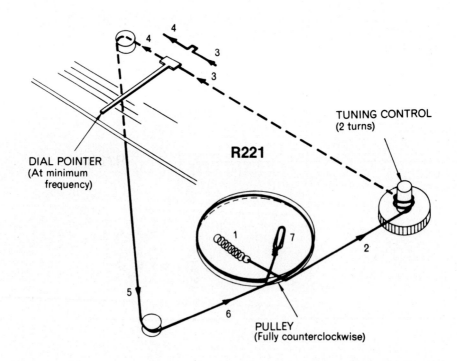

(R221) DRIVE CORD—MODEL KH-924L

526

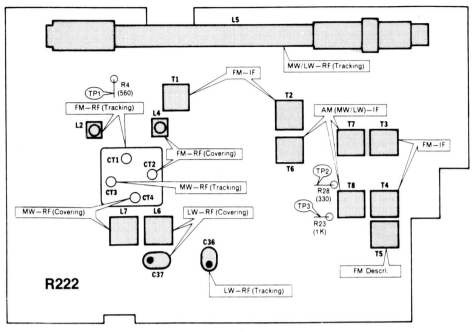

(R222) ALIGNMENT ADJUSTMENTS—MODEL KH-924L

Alignment

F.M./I.F.

F.M. Generator	Dial pointer position	Adjust	Remarks
10.7MHz		T5	Turn the T5 fully counter-clockwise.
		T1	Maximum
		T2	Reduce the level of the F.M. generator so that the waveform is
		T3	a single curve.
	Highest	T4	
		T5	Adjust the T5 so that the output (S curve) is symmetrical
		T4	Adjust the T4 so that the straight line reference of the 'S' curve can be achieved

F.M./R.F.:

	Item	Signal generator		Dial pointer position	Adjust	Reading
		Frequency	Modulation			
1	Covering	87.5MHz	400Hz 30%	Lowest	L4	Max.
2		109MHz		Highest	CT2	
3	Repeat 1 and 2					
4	Tracking	90MHz	400Hz 30%	90MHz	L2	Max.
5		106MHz		106MHz	CT1	
6	Repeat 4 and 5					

527

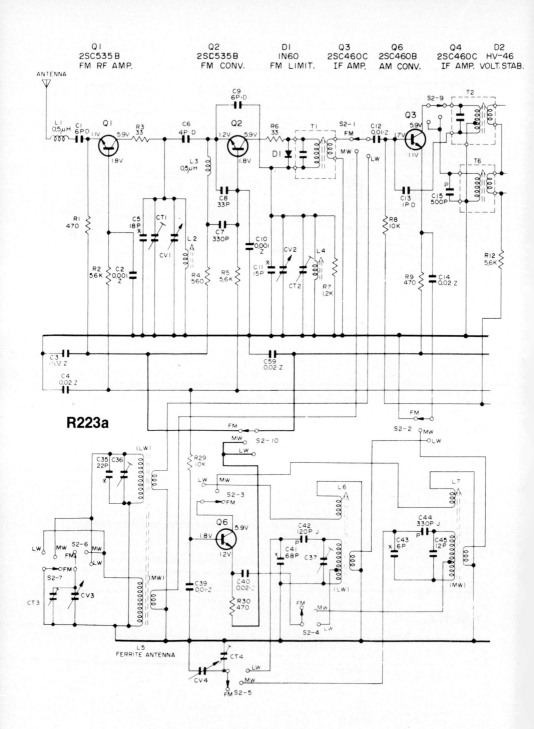

(R223a) CIRCUIT DIAGRAM—MODEL KH-924L *(PART)*

528

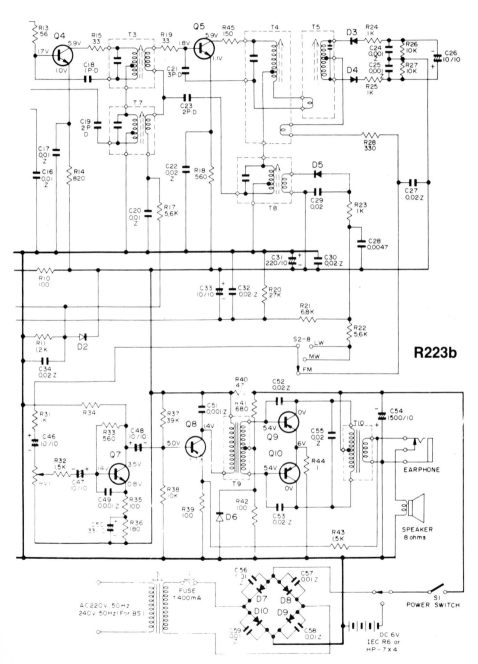

(R233b) CIRCUIT DIAGRAM—MODEL KH-924L *(CONTINUED)*

A.M./I.F.:

Signal generator Frequency	Modulation	Dial pointer position	Adjust	Reading
465kHz	—	Highest	T6 T7 T8	Max.

A.M./M.W.:

	Item	Signal generator Frequency	Modulation	Dial pointer position	Adjust	Reading
1	Covering	515kHz	400Hz 30%	Lowest	L7	Max.
2		1650kHz		Highest	CT4	
3	Repeat 1 and 2					
4	Tracking	600kHz	400Hz 30%	600kHz	L5	Max.
5		1400kHz		1400kHz	CT3	
6	Repeat 4 and 5					

A.M./L.W.:

	Item	Signal generator Frequency	Modulation	Dial pointer position	Adjust	Reading
1	Covering	145kHz	400Hz 30%	Lowest	L6	Max.
2		360kHz		Highest	C37	
3	Repeat 1 and 2					
4	Tracking	160kHz	400Hz 30%	160kHz	L5	Max.
5		330kHz		330kHz	C36	
6	Repeat 4 and 5					

HITACHI   Model TRQ-247

General Description: A small portable cassette tape-recorder operating from mains or battery supplies. Various mains supply options are available to suit local conditions and sockets are provided for auxiliary inputs and outputs. A microphone is built into the case of the instrument.

Mains Supply: 220-240 volts, 50Hz (others available).

Battery: 6 volts (4×1.5 volts).

Bias and Erase: D.C.

Loudspeaker: 4 ohms.

Access for Service: Remove four back screws to reveal the p.c.b. which is held by two screws. The cassette-deck may be removed after taking out two screws at the motor end and prising apart the two retaining lugs.

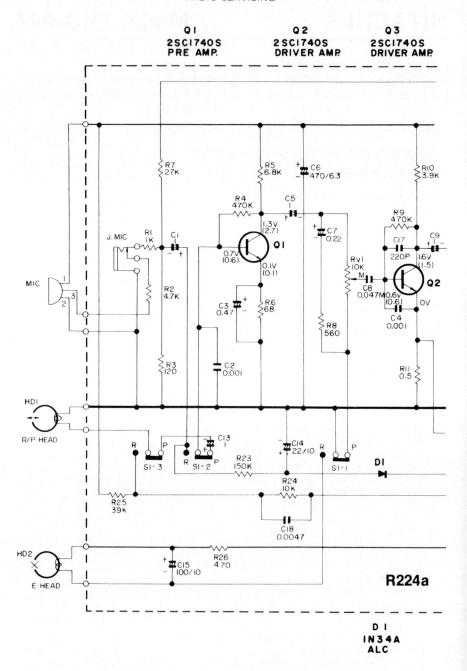

(R224a) CIRCUIT DIAGRAM—MODEL TRQ-247 (PART)

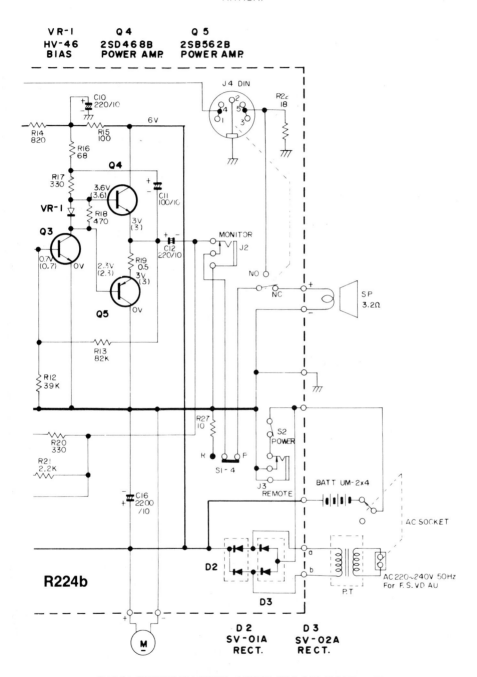

(R224b) CIRCUIT DIAGRAM—MODEL TRQ-247 *(CONTINUED)*

HITACHI   Model WM-711

General Description: A 2-waveband car radio for negative chassis operation. All active circuit elements are contained in two integrated circuits.

Battery: 12 volts (negative earth).

Fuse: 1 amp.

Wavebands: L.W. 150-300kHz; M.W. 530-1605kHz.

Dismantling

Top and bottom covers are push-lift. Remove nuts and washers securing the front escutcheon. Remove 3 side screws and unclip tuning pointer cover. Remove chassis screws.

Alignment

Connect oscilloscope or V.T.V.M. to T.P.

Sequence	Setting		Adjusting	
	Tuner	Signal	Adjust	Indication
A.M.-I.F.			T251	max.
			T252	
			T253	
	f max.	465kHz		
			L154	min.
M.W.-R.F.	f min.	520kHz	T151	
	f max.	1650kHz	CT153	
		1000kHz	CT151	V max.
L.W.-R.F.	f max.	145kHz	CT152	
	f min.	310kHz	L155	
		260kHz	L153	
Sensitivity		1000kHz	RT251	

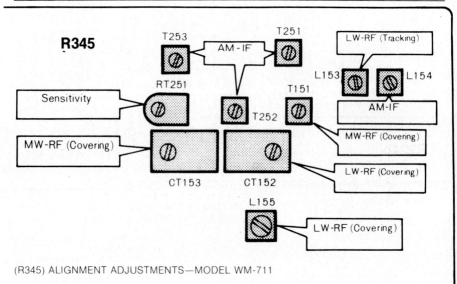

(R345) ALIGNMENT ADJUSTMENTS—MODEL WM-711

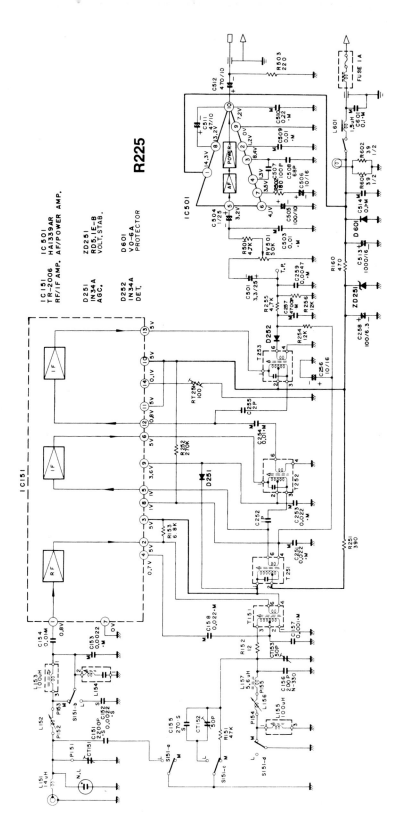

(R225) CIRCUIT DIAGRAM—MODEL WM-711

HITACHI   Model WM-865

General Description: A 2-waveband car radio receiver operating with a negative chassis. An integrated circuit is used for A.F. power amplification and a tone control is fitted.

Battery: 12-14 volts (negative chassis).

Fuse: 1 amp.

Wavebands: L.W. 150-300kHz; M.W. 530-1605kHz.

Loudspeaker: 4 ohms impedance.

Dismantling

Remove front knobs, washers and nuts to gain access to 2 screws retaining the front of the case. Take out screws at side and rear to gain access to the interior.

Alignment

I.F.: 465kHz (T252, T253, T254). M.W.: 520kHz (T251); 1650kHz (CT251); 1400kHz (CT151, CT152). L.W.: 145kHz (L253); 310kHz (CT252); 210kHz (L153, L155).

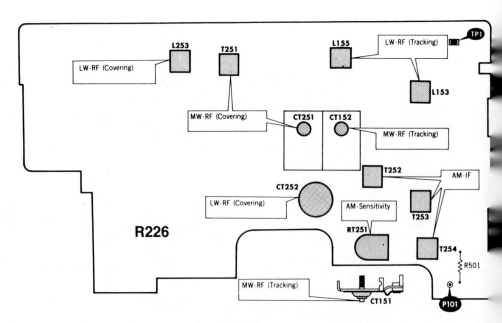

(R226) ALIGNMENT ADJUSTMENTS—MODEL WM-865

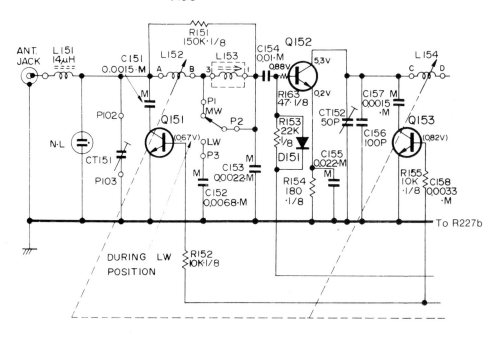

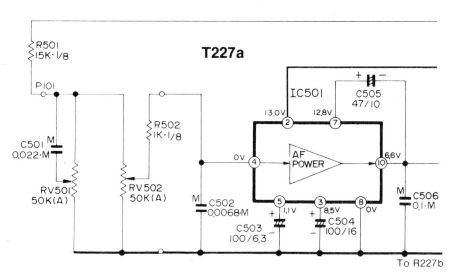

IC501
HA-1366W
AUDIO POWER AMP.

(R227a) CIRCUIT DIAGRAM—MODEL WM-865 *(PART)*

Q154
2SC460C
CONVERTER

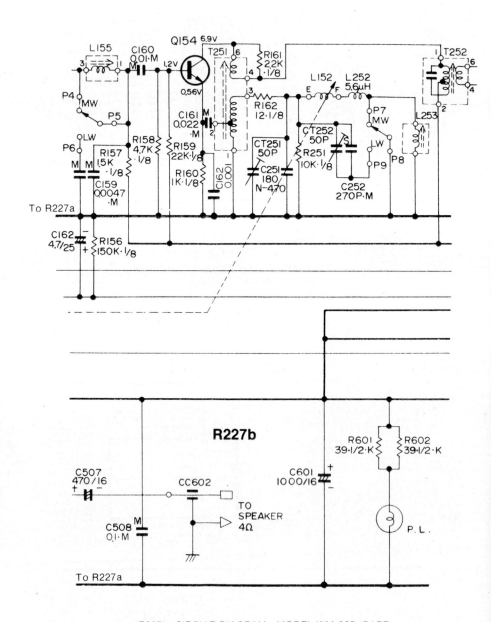

(R227b) CIRCUIT DIAGRAM—MODEL WM-865 *(PART)*

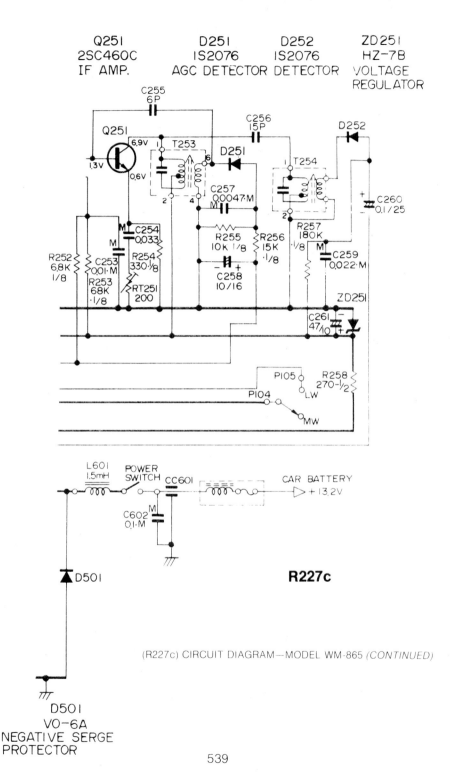

Q251
2SC460C
IF AMP.

D251
IS2076
AGC DETECTOR

D252
IS2076
DETECTOR

ZD251
HZ-7B
VOLTAGE
REGULATOR

C255
6P

Q251

6.9V

1.3V

0.6V

T253

D251

C256
15P

D252

C257
0.0047·M

T254

C260
0.1/25

C254
0.033

R252
6.8K
1/8

R253
68K
·1/8

C253
001·M

R254
330·1/8

RT251
200

R255
10k 1/8

R256
15K
·1/8

C258
10/16

R257
180K
·1/8

C259
0.022·M

ZD251

C261
47/10

P105
R258
270-1/2

P104

LW

MW

L601
1.5mH

POWER
SWITCH

CC601

CAR BATTERY
+ 13.2V

C602
0.1·M

D501

R227c

(R227c) CIRCUIT DIAGRAM—MODEL WM-865 *(CONTINUED)*

D501
VO-6A
NEGATIVE SERGE
PROTECTOR

General Description: A 3-waveband portable radio receiver with 2-track cassette tape recorder operating from mains or battery supplies. Sockets are provided for the connection of auxiliary inputs and outputs and a microphone is fitted into the case. An integrated circuit provides A.F. amplification.

Mains Supplies: 120/220 volts (RC-222L); 240 volts (RC-222LB), 50Hz.

Battery: 6 volts (4×U2).

Wavebands: L.W. 150-350kHz; M.W. 540-1600kHz; F.M. 88-108MHz.

Loudspeaker: 3.2 ohms impedance.

Dismantling

Pull off Volume, Tone and Tuning knobs and remove three screws from the back of the cabinet (one in the battery compartment). Press the bottom of the cabinet inwards to disengage the retaining lugs.

Alignment (See Fig. R346)

A.M. I.F. and R.F. Alignment:

Step	Frequency band	Frequency	Input signal Given to	Place to be aligned	Set the V. capacitor to
1	M.W. (I.F.)	455kHz	Loop antenna	L12,16	Minimum
2		Repeat the step 1, and adjust for no further improvement			
3		145kHz	Loop antenna	L10	Maximum
4		360kHz		C9	Maximum
5	L.W.	Repeat the steps 3 and 4			
6		160kHz	Loop antenna	L8	160kHz signal
7		350kHz		C7	350kHz signal
8		Repeat the steps 6 and 7, and adjust for no further improvement			
9		520kHz	Loop antenna	L11	Maximum
10		1650kHz		C10	Minimum
11	M.W.	Repeat the steps 9 and 10			
12		600kHz	Loop antenna	L9	600kHz signal
13		1400kHz		C8	1400kHz signal
14		Repeat the steps 12 and 13, and adjust for no further improvement			

F.M. I.F. and Discriminator Alignment (Using Sweep Method):

1. Set the Volume to minimum and tune in the maximum frequency where no signal is received.

2. Connect the sweep generator to the test point TP3 and the other clip to the earth.

3. Connect the Oscilloscope to the test point TP5 and TP6 (Earth).

4. I.F. Alignment

(a). De-tune L15.

(b). Align the L7 and 14 so that the maximum sensitivity and symmetrical wave mode will be obtained setting the marker 10.7MHz on the peak.

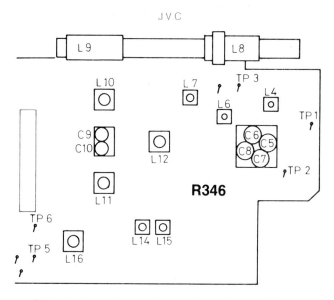

(R346) ALIGNMENT ADJUSTMENTS—MODEL RC222L/LB

5. Discriminator Alignment: Align the L15 so that the symmetrical 'S' curve will be obtained setting the marker 10.7MHz on the centre of the 'S' curve.

F.M. R.F. Alignment Input (SSG): Use 75Ω terminal modulation 400Hz modulated to 22.5kHz deviation. Connect hot side to TP1 and cold side to TP2.

Step	Frequency band	Input signal Frequency	Given to	Place to be aligned	Set the V. capacitor to
1		87.5MHz	TP1 and TP2	L6	Maximum
2		109MHz		C6	Minimum
3	F.M.	Repeat the steps 1 and 2			
4		90MHz	TP1 and TP2	L4	90MHz signal
5		106MHz		C5	106MHz signal
6		Repeat the steps 4 and 5, and adjust for no further improvement			

Circuit Diagram Notes

SA-1~8 (Radio-Tape switch), 'F.M.' position. SB-1~6 (Play-Record switch), 'Play' position. SC-1~4 (DIN switch), 'Out' position. SE-1,2 (Monitor switch), 'Off' position. Voltages are measured against minus potential with no signal using V.T.V.M. at 'F.M.' ( ) values at 'M.W.' [ ] values at 'Tape Play'.

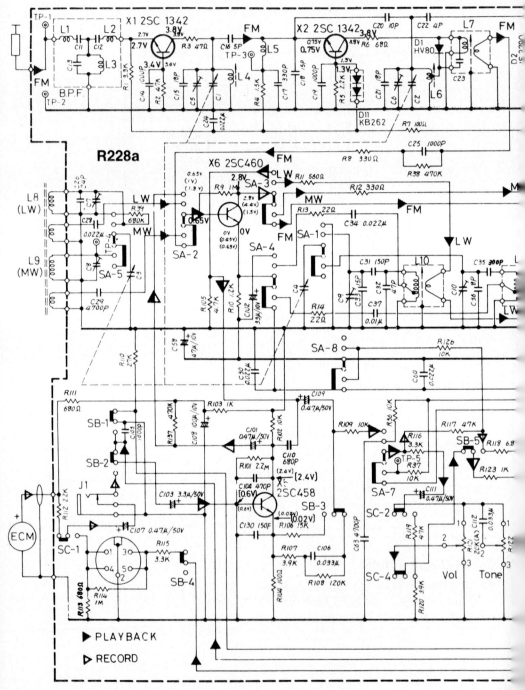

(R228a) CIRCUIT DIAGRAM—MODEL RC222-222L/B *(PART)*

542

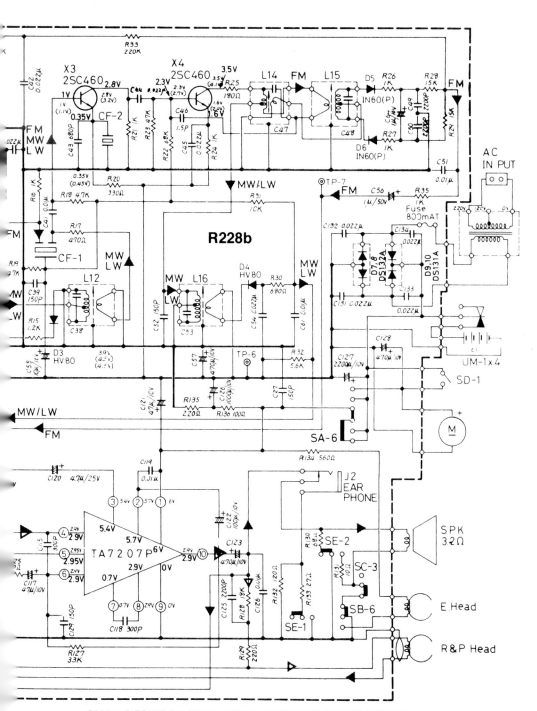

(R228b) CIRCUIT DIAGRAM—MODEL RC222-222L/LB (CONTINUED)

PHILIPS   Model N2234

General Description: A 2-track portable cassette tape recorder operating from mains or battery supplies. A microphone is fitted to the case and sockets are provided for the connection of auxiliary inputs and outputs.

Mains Supply: 127/220-240 volts, 50/60Hz.

Battery: 9 volts (6×1.5 volts).

Loudspeaker: 8 ohms impedance.

Dismantling (See Fig. R229)

To uncase the apparatus the 5 screws have to be removed from lower part of the case.

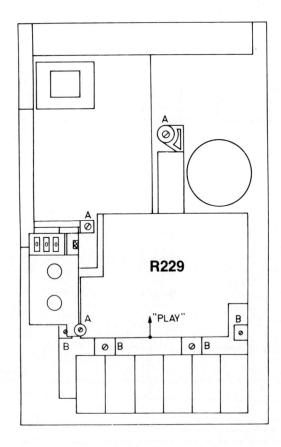

(R229) DISMANTLING PROCEDURE—MODEL R2234

544

After having removed screws A (fig. R229), the printed panel and the mechanism can be taken out of the cabinet.

Loudspeaker LS can be removed by breaking off the bending tags.

For fitting the loudspeaker the appropriate tags must be hot bent (using a soldering iron).

The delay unit has been mounted in the upper casing part using a snap-in fastening. By pressing—from inside of cassette-well—on the boss of the delay unit, the unit can be removed from upper casing part.

Cassette cover can be removed in open position by pressing the tags in the cassette cover slightly inwards.

Warning: When the apparatus is connected to the mains and the back cover has been removed, there is a risk of touching the mains voltage.

The mains voltage is then connected to the primary side of the transformer, via print tracks on the print.

The points where the mains voltage is connected to the print are marked with a warning sign.

Changing the Mains Voltage: To make the cassette recorder fit for 127V, cut the print track to point 5. For this purpose, the print has a recess.

Make a connection on the track side between the mains connection and point 6 of the transformer.

Tape Speed Adjustment

With Wow-and-Flutter Meter: Connect the set to a wow-and-flutter meter. Set in Playback position, using the 3150Hz TC-FL3.15 cassette (8945 600 14701). The speed is adjustable with R20. Maximum permissible deviation ±2%. Besides, the wow-and-flutter value can be read with this meter. It may be 0.3% maximum.

With Cassette Service Set 801/CSS: Connect the apparatus to the cassette service set, via BU1. Use the 50Hz-side from the cassette service set. Set in Start position. With R20, adjust for minimum wow-and-flutter of the test indicator.

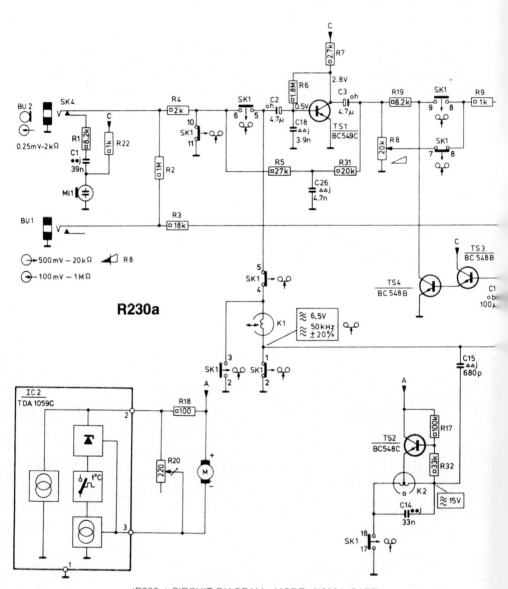

(R230a) CIRCUIT DIAGRAM—MODEL N2234 *(PART)*

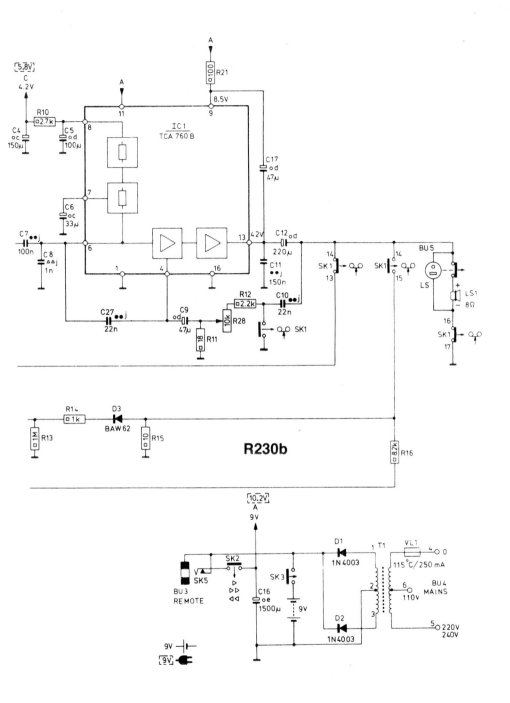

(R230b) CIRCUIT DIAGRAM—MODEL N2234 *(CONTINUED)*

General Description: A 2-waveband A.M. car radio with stereo cassette tape-player unit. Integrated circuits are used throughout with the exception of the local oscillator and head pre-amplifiers.

Battery: 14.4 volts D.C. max. (negative chassis).

Wavebands: L.W. 150-254kHz; M.W. 520-1605kHz.

Loudspeaker: 4 ohms impedance.

Note: During measurement and/or adjustments the tape deck should be connected and an extra wire should be used for connection to earth of the main set and tape-deck.

Alignment (See Fig. R231, R232).

SK						
MW/PO	468 kHz	Ⓐ	Min. ind.		5007	① Max. ~
		Ⓑ			5003	① Min. ~
MW/PO	520 kHz		Max. ind.	⊕ Ÿ 2005	1006	
	600 kHz	Ⓑ			1004	① Max. ~
	1500 kHz				1005	
LW/GO	150 kHz		Max. ind.		5005	
	165 kHz	Ⓑ		**R231**	1005	① Max. ~
	245 kHz				5002	

(R231) ALIGNMENT
PROCEDURE—
MODEL 22AC280

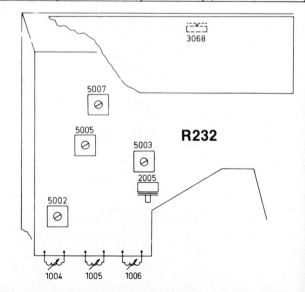

(R232) ALIGNMENT
ADJUSTMENTS—
MODEL 22AC280

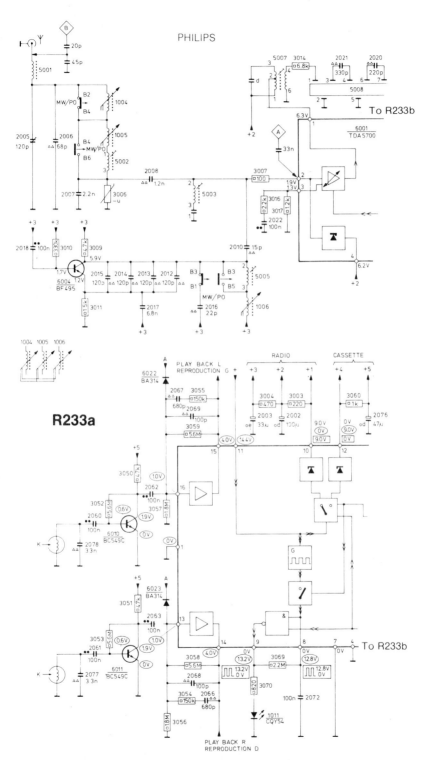

PHILIPS

R233a

(R233a) CIRCUIT DIAGRAM—MODEL 22AC280 *(PART)*

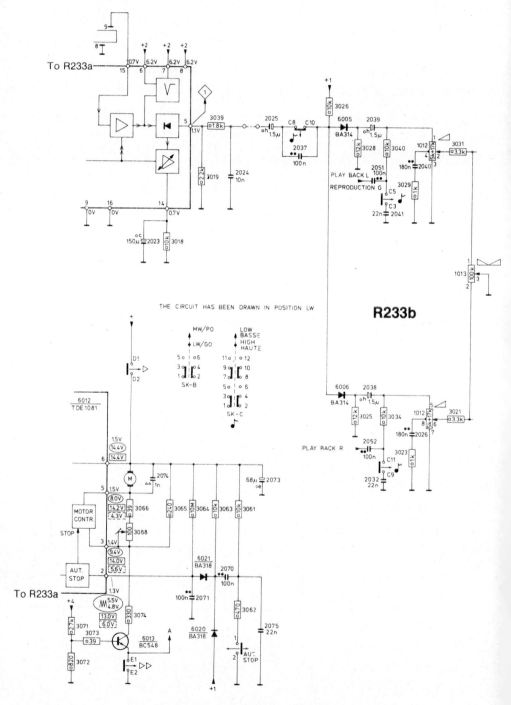

(R233b) CIRCUIT DIAGRAM—MODEL 22AC280 *(PART)*

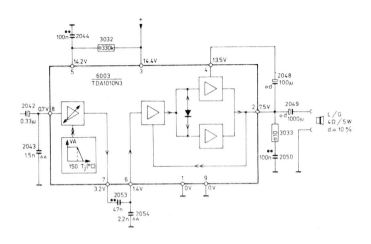

R233c

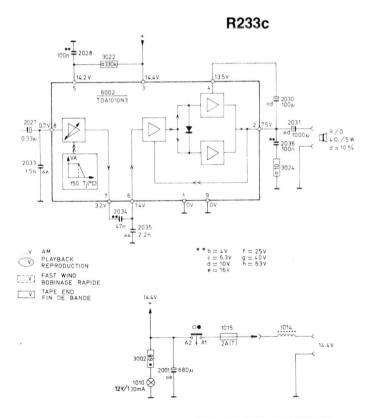

(R233c) CIRCUIT DIAGRAM—MODEL 22AC280 *(CONTINUED)*

PHILIPS   Model 22AC480

General Description: A 2-waveband A.M. car radio with stereo cassette tape player. Integrated circuits are used in the motor control and A.F. amplifier stages.

Battery: 14.4 volts max. (negative chassis).

Wavebands: L.W. 148-262kHz; M.W. 512-1620kHz.

Loudspeakers: 4 ohms impedance.

Note: During measurements and/or adjustments the tape deck should be connected. An extra wire should be used for connection to earth of the main set and tape-deck.

SK...					
	R234	◇ A		5212, 5211 5210, 5209	Max. ◇1
MW (518-1612 kHz)	468 kHz		Min. L		
		◇ B		5207	Min. ◇1
	516 kHz		Max. L	5605	
MW (518-1612 kHz)	600 kHz	◇ B	⌀	5603	
	1500 kHz			2223	Max. ◇1
	148 kHz		Max. L	5208	
LW (149-262 kHz)	165 kHz	◇ B		5604	
	245 kHz		⌀	5206	

(R234) ALIGNMENT PROCEDURE—
MODEL 22AC480

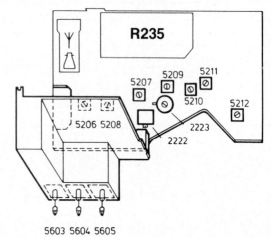

(R235) ALIGNMENT
ADJUSTMENTS—
MODEL 22AC480

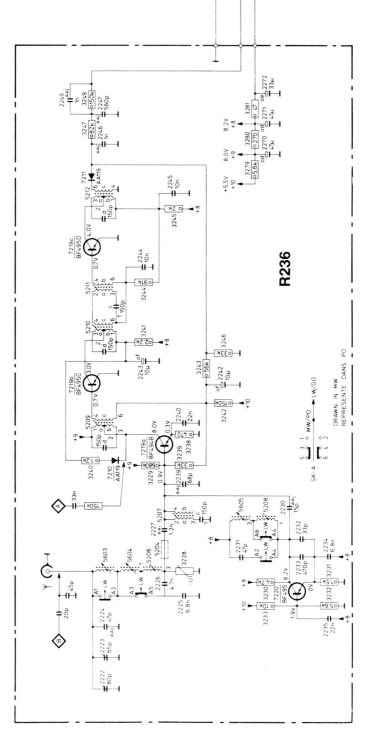

(R236) CIRCUIT DIAGRAM (TUNER SECTION)—MODEL 22AC480 (PART)

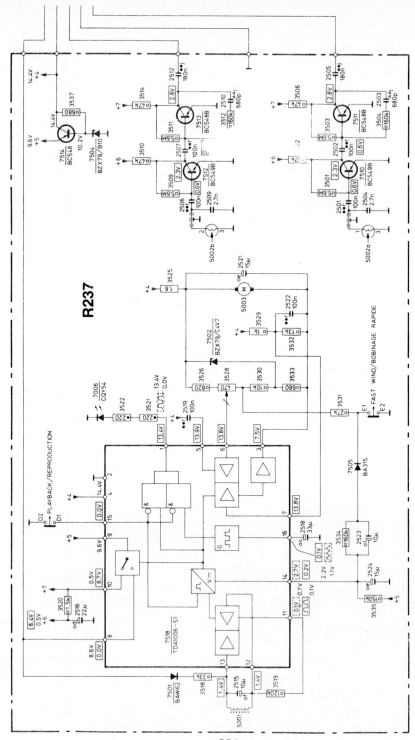

(R237) CIRCUIT DIAGRAM (MOTOR CONTROL AND TAPE PRE-AMPLIFIER)—MODEL 22AC480 (PART)

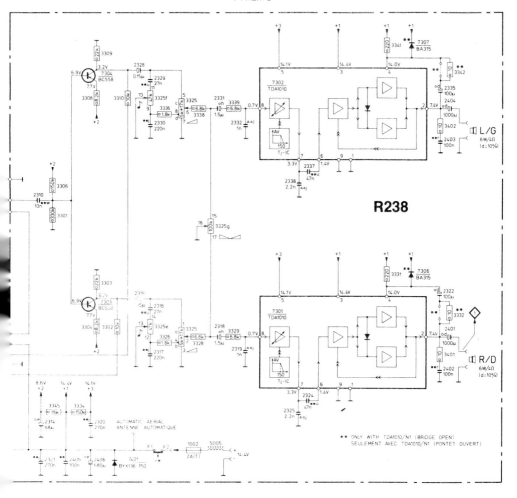

R238

** ONLY WITH TDA1010/N1 (BRIDGE OPEN)
SEULEMENT AVEC TDA1010/N1 (PONTET OUVERT)

(R238) CIRCUIT DIAGRAM (A.F. STAGES)—MODEL 22AC480 *(CONTINUED)*

General Description: A 2-speed mains or battery operated stereo record player. Amplification in both channels is performed by integrated circuit and another is used for motor speed control. A socket is provided for the connection of a tape recorder and the loudspeakers are housed in separate cabinets.

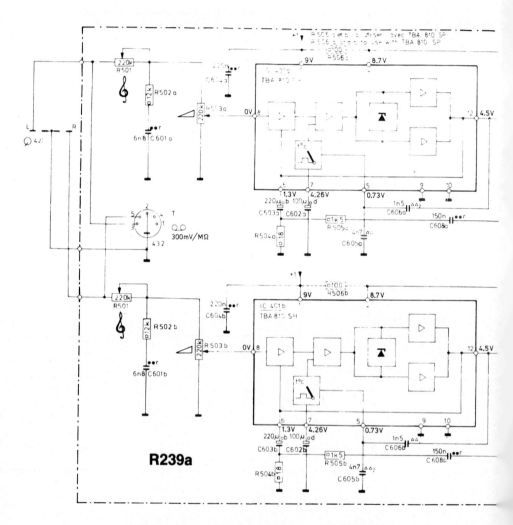

R239a

(R239a) CIRCUIT DIAGRAM—MODEL 22AF380 *(PART)*

Mains Supplies: 110/127/220/240 volts, 50/60Hz.

Battery: 9 volts (6×1.5 volts).

Loudspeakers: 4 ohms impedance.

Modifications

During production, the following parts have been changed: R504 (a and b) 47Ω-1/8W ± 5%; R505 (a and b) 2.7Ω-1/8W ± 5%; R566 220Ω; R569 390Ω-1/8W ± 5%; R570 1kΩ.

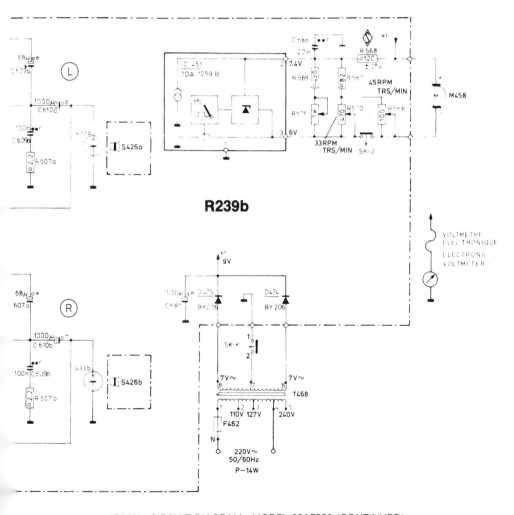

R239b

(R239b) CIRCUIT DIAGRAM—MODEL 22AF380 *(CONTINUED)*

PHILIPS   Model 22AN593

General Description: A 2-waveband A.M./F.M. car radio receiver with electronic suppression of interference signals. The interference rejector and A.F. amplifier stage use integrated circuits.

Battery: 14.4 volts (max.), negative chassis.

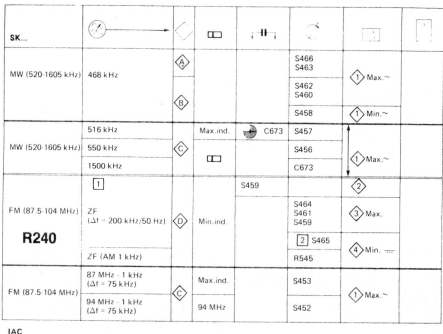

SK...						
MW (520-1605 kHz)	468 kHz	Ⓐ			S466 S463	①Max.~
					S462 S460	
		Ⓑ			S458	①Min.~
MW (520-1605 kHz)	516 kHz		Max.ind.	C673	S457	
	550 kHz	Ⓒ			S456	①Max.~
	1500 kHz				C673	
FM (87.5-104 MHz)	[1]			S459		②
	ZF (Δf = 200 kHz/50 Hz)	Ⓓ	Min.ind.		S464 S461 S459	③ Max.
R240					[2] S465	④Min.
	ZF (AM 1 kHz)				R545	
FM (87.5-104 MHz)	87 MHz - 1 kHz (Δf = 75 kHz)	Ⓒ	Max.ind.		S453	①Max.~
	94 MHz - 1 kHz (Δf = 75 kHz)		94 MHz		S452	

IAC

FM (87.5-104 MHz)	Pilot 19 kHz (250 mV) / 1·3 V / 200 μsec	Ⓔ Ⓕ			R574	⑤ [3]
	120 kHz - 22 mV				[4] R563	> 500 mV
	120 kHz - 17 mV	Ⓕ				< 50 mV

Wavebands: M.W. 520-1605kHz; F.M. 87.5-104MHz.

Loudspeaker: 4 ohms impedance.

Alignment (See Figs. R240, R241)

1. Find the resonance frequency of the Ceramic Filter. This is the frequency to which the F.M.-I.F. section is adjusted.
Connect the masses of Generator and meter to the print, as close as possible to injection point and test point respectively. Open bridge B.
2. Close B. Adjust the 'S' curve to zero-crossing.
3. I.A.C. Trigger the Oscilloscope externally with the square-wave voltage time base $20\mu sec/cm$. Adjust for minimum square wave output.
4. I.A.C.-sensitivity. Interconnect points 9 and 12 of 409 (AN101) and connect a non-earthed D.C. voltmeter between points 9 and 10 of 409.

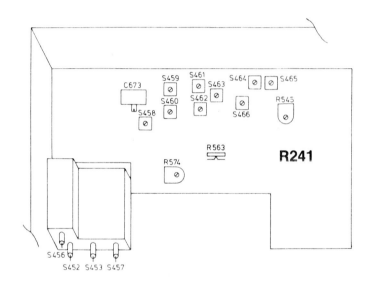

(R241) ALIGNMENT ADJUSTMENTS—MODEL 22AN593

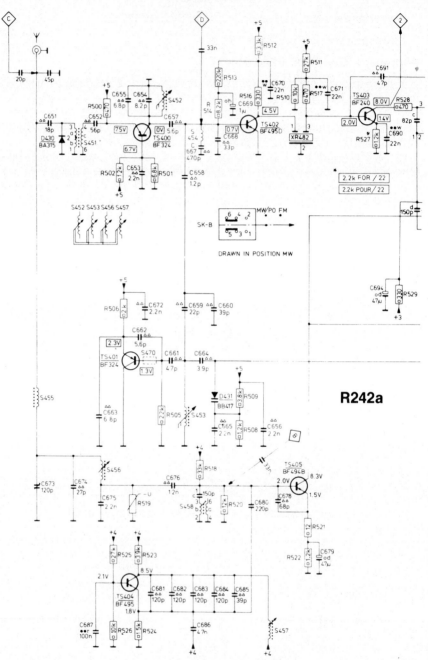

R242a

(R242a) CIRCUIT DIAGRAM—MODEL 22AN593 *(PART)*

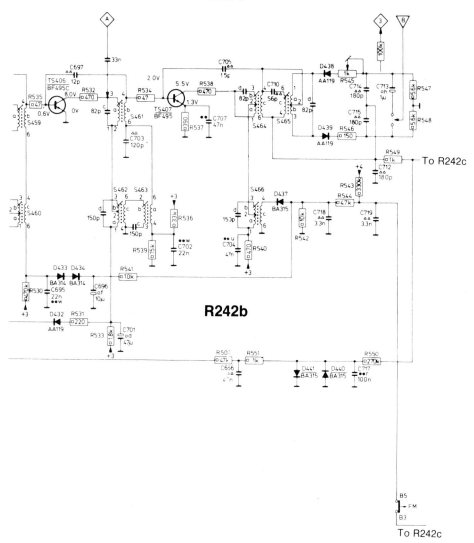

R242b

To R242c

To R242c

(R242b) CIRCUIT DIAGRAM—MODEL 22AN593 *(PART)*

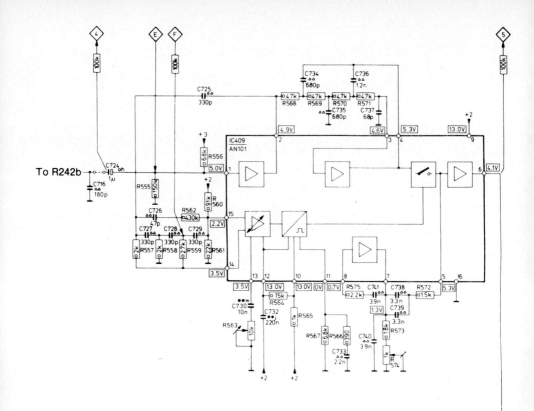

R242c

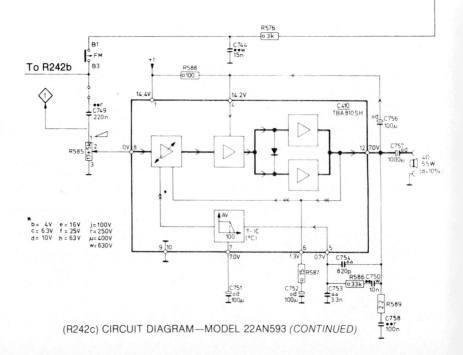

(R242c) CIRCUIT DIAGRAM—MODEL 22AN593 *(CONTINUED)*

PHILIPS

Model 90AL590

General Description: A 4-waveband portable radio receiver operating from mains or battery supplies. A socket is provided for the connection of an earphone.

Mains Supplies: 110-127/220-240 volts, 50Hz.

Battery: 6 volts (4×1.5 volts).

Wavebands: L.W. 150-255kHz; M.W. 520-1605kHz; S.W. 5.95-15.45MHz; F.M. 87.5-104MHz.

Loudspeaker: 4 ohms impedance.

Dismantling: The back cover is held by five screws (three in the battery compartment).

Alignment (See Figs. R347, R244)

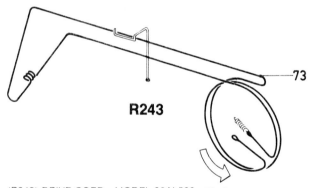

(R243) DRIVE CORD—MODEL 90AL590   **Min.Cap.**

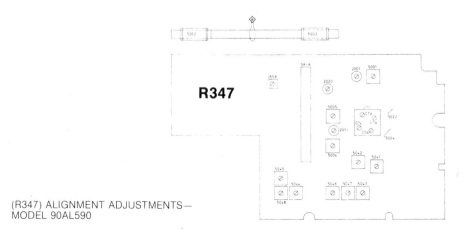

(R347) ALIGNMENT ADJUSTMENTS—
MODEL 90AL590

Wave range SK-A	Signal to	◇	Var.cap.	Detune	Adjust	Indication
	468 kHz via 39 nF	◇A	Min.cap.	5005,5046 5047,5048	5048	
					5047	⟨1⟩ Max.
					5046	
MW (520-1605 kHz)	512 kHz	◇B	Max.cap.		5005	
	1635 kHz		Min.cap.		CTc	⟨1⟩ Max.
	600 kHz		▭		5002	
	1400 kHz		Tune in		CTd	
LW (150-255 kHz)	147 kHz	◇B	Max.cap.		2020	⟨1⟩ Max.
	200 kHz		▭		5003	
			Tune in			
	5.8 MHz		Max.cap.		5004	
SW (5.95-15.45 MHz)	15.9 MHz	◇C	Min.cap.		2013	⟨1⟩ Max. [1]
	6.5 MHz		▭		5001	
	14.5 MHz		Tune in		2001	
R244	10.7 MHz via 22 nF	◇D	Min.cap.	5041,5042, 5043,5044, 5045	5044	⟨2⟩ [2]
					5043	
					5042	
					5041	
FM (87.5-104 MHz)					5045	⟨1⟩ [3]
	87.5 MHz	◇E	Max.cap.		5024	
	104 MHz		Min.cap.		CTb	⟨1⟩ Max.
	88 MHz		▭		5022	
	102 MHz		Tune in		CTa	

↕ Repeat

[1] Telescopic aerial pushed in

[2] Open bridge ▽A . Connect an oscilloscope to ⟨2⟩ via a 100 kΩ resistor. Adjust the FM-IF curve for maximum height and symmetry.

[3] Close bridge ▽A . Connect an oscilloscope to ⟨1⟩ via a 100 kΩ resistor. Adjust the S-curve for maximum symmetry and linearity.

(R244) ALIGNMENT PROCEDURE—MODEL 90AL590

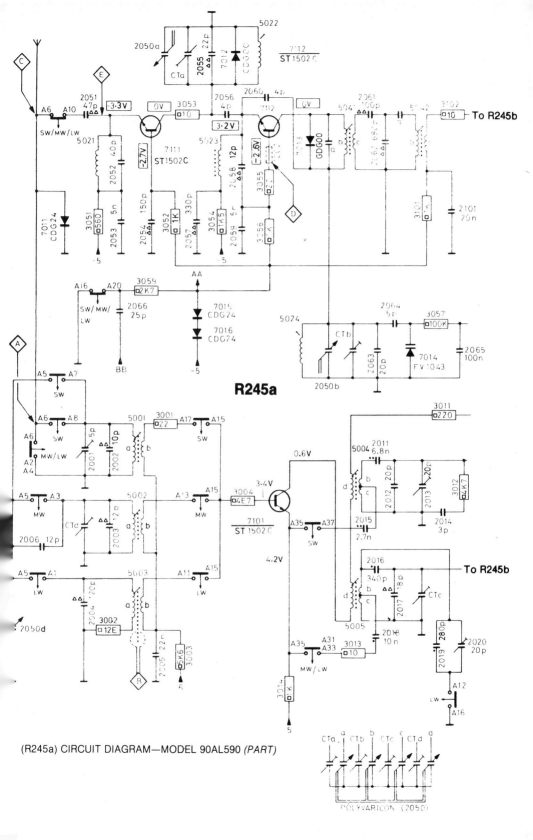

(R245a) CIRCUIT DIAGRAM—MODEL 90AL590 *(PART)*

R245a

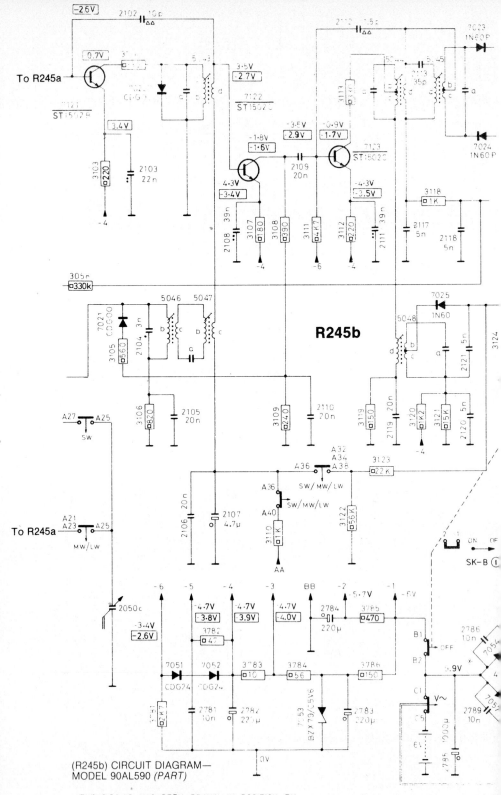

(R245b) CIRCUIT DIAGRAM—
MODEL 90AL590 *(PART)*

THE CIRCUIT HAS BEEN DRAWN IN POSITION FM

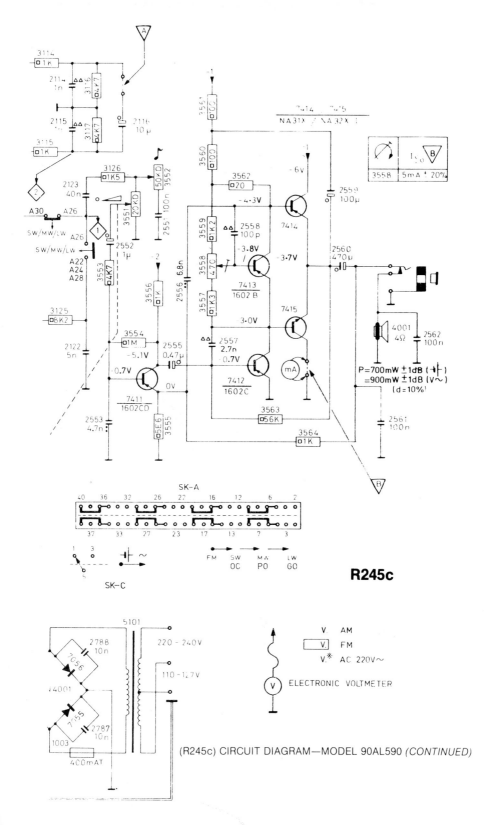

R245c

(R245c) CIRCUIT DIAGRAM—MODEL 90AL590 *(CONTINUED)*

PHILIPS   Model 90AL780

General Description: A 4-waveband portable radio receiver operating from mains or battery supplies. A bandspread adjustment is featured on Short Wave operation and a socket is provided for the connection of an earphone.

Mains Supplies: 110-127/220-240 volts, 50Hz.

Battery: 6 volts (4×1.5 volts).

Wavebands: L.W. 150-255kHz; M.W. 520-1605kHz; S.W. 5.95-15.45MHz; F.M. 87.5-104MHz.

Loudspeaker: 4 ohms impedance.

Access for Service: The back cover can be removed after withdrawing the four retaining screws.

Alignment (See Figs. R246, R247)

(R247) ALIGNMENT ADJUSTMENTS—
MODEL 90AL780

(R246) DRIVE CORD—MODEL 90AL780

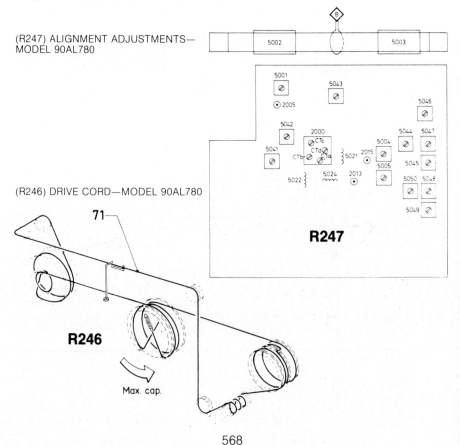

568

SK-A	⟳→	◇	≢	⌒	▱
MW/PO (520-1605 kHz)	468 kHz via 40 nF	Ⓐ	Min. cap	5049	① Max.
				5047	
				5045	
				5044	
	512 kHz	Ⓑ	Max. cap.	5005	① Max.
	1635 kHz		Min. cap.	CTd	
	600 kHz		▭	5002	
	1400 kHz			CTc	
LW/GO (150-255 kHz)	147 kHz	Ⓑ	Max. cap.	2015	① Max.
	200 kHz		▭	5003	
SW/OC (5.95-15,45 MHz)	5.8 MHz	Ⓒ Via 10 pF	Max. cap.	5004	① Max. [1]
	15.9 MHz		Min. cap.	2013	
	6.5 MHz		▭	5001	
	14.5 MHz			2005	
FM (87.5-104 MHz)	10.7 MHz Via 20 nF	Ⓓ	Min. cap.	5048 5046 5043 5042 5041	② [2]
				5050	③ [3]
	105 MHz	Ⓔ	Min. cap.	CTb	③
	86.5 MHz		Max. cap.	5022	
	86.5 MHz			5024	
	105 MHz		▭	CTa	

↕ Repeat

[1] With the telescopic aerial pulled in, set potentiometer 3008 for fine-tuning to mid-position.

R248

[2] Set the AFC switch to position "off". Open bridge ◁A▷ . Connect an oscilloscope to ② via a 100 kΩ resistor. Adjust the FM-IF curve for maximum height and symmetry.

[3] Close bridge ◁A▷ . Connect an oscilloscope to ③ . Adjust the S-curve for maximum symmetry and linearity.

(R248) ALIGNMENT PROCEDURE—MODEL 90AL780

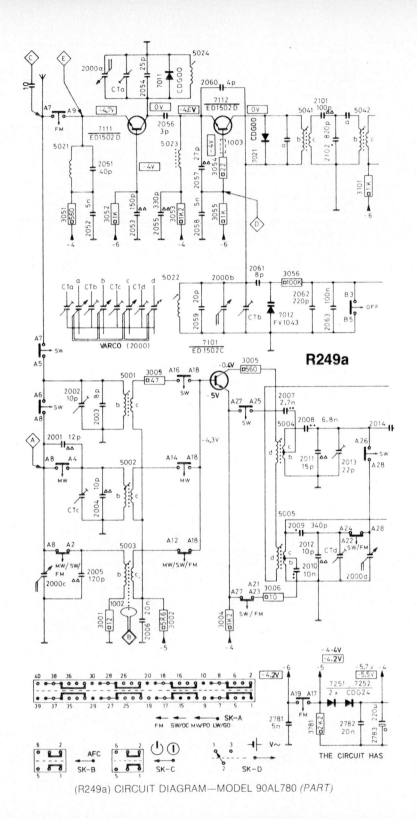

(R249a) CIRCUIT DIAGRAM—MODEL 90AL780 *(PART)*

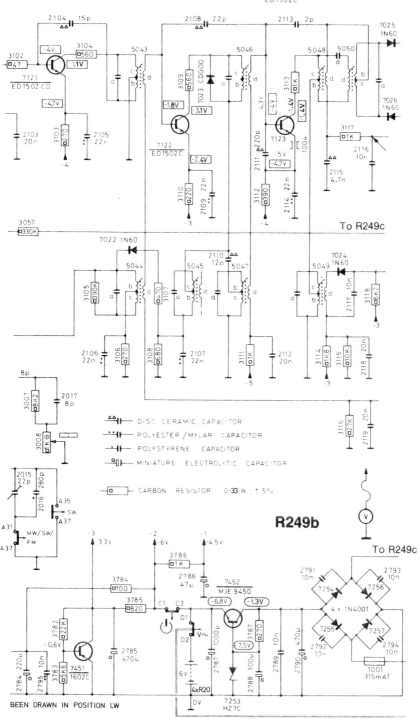

(R249b) CIRCUIT DIAGRAM—MODEL 90AL780 *(PART)*

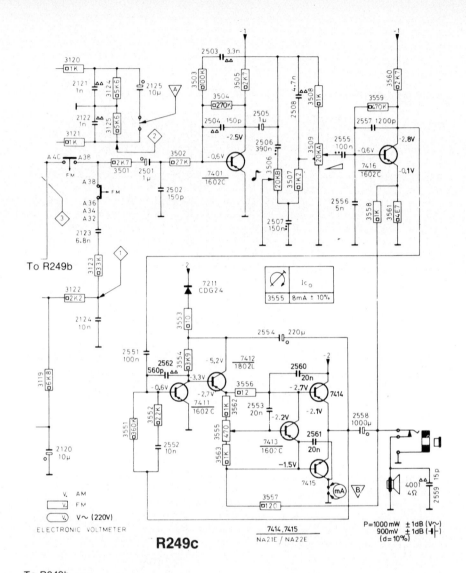

R249c

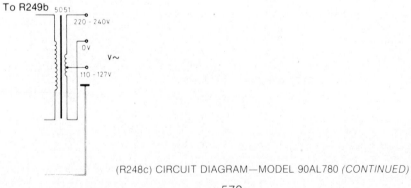

PHILIPS
Model 90AL970

General Description: A 4-waveband portable radio receiver operating from mains or battery supplies. Four pre-set F.M. frequencies can be selected by touch button with LED indication operated through an integrated circuit. Sockets are provided for the connection of tape recorder and headphones and A.F. amplification is provided by integrated circuit.

Mains Supplies: 110/220 volts, 50/60Hz.

Battery: 9 volts (6×1.5 volts).

Wavebands: L.W. 150-255kHz; M.W. 520-1605kHz; S.W.1 2.3-7.3MHz; S.W.2 9.5-21.8MHz; F.M. 87.5-108MHz.

Loudspeakers: 4 ohms (8 ohms tweeter).

Alignment (See Figs. R251, R252)

(R250) DRIVE CORD—MODEL 90AL970

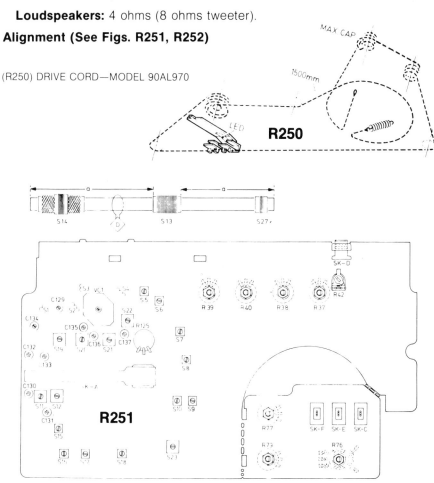

(R251) ALIGNMENT ADJUSTMENTS—MODEL 90AL970

Wave range SK-A	Signal to			Adjust	
MW/PO (520-1605 kHz)	1 via 20 nF	Ⓒ	Min. cap.	S18	
				S17	④ Max.
				S16	
				S15	
	512 kHz	Ⓓ	Max. cap.	S21	
	1635 kHz		Min. cap	C136	④ Max.
	550 kHz		▭	S27	
	1500 kHz			C132	
LW/GO (150-255 kHz)	147 kHz	Ⓓ	Max. cap.	S22	
	260 kHz		Min. cap.	C137	④ Max.
	155 kHz		▭	S14	
	255 kHz			C133	
SW1/OC1 2.3-7.3 MHz	2.25 MHz	Ⓐ	Max. cap.	S20	
	7.45 MHz		Min. cap.	C135	④ Max.
	2.5 MHz		▭	S12	
	7.2 MHz via 12 pF			C131	2
SW2/OC2 (9.5-21.75 MHz)	9.3 MHz	Ⓐ	Max. cap.	S19	
	22.2 MHz		Min. cap.	C134	④ Max.
	10 MHz		▭	S11	
	21 MHz via 12 pF			C130	2
FM (87.5-108 MHz)	10.7 MHz via 100 pF	Ⓑ	Vc-1	S9	
				S8	① 3
				S7	
				S6	
				S5	
				S10	① 4
R252	109 MHz	Ⓔ	Vc1-Min.	S4	
	86.5 MHz		Vc1-Max.	R42	① Max.
	88 MHz		▭	S2	
	106 MHz			C129	

↕ Repeat

1 The AM-IF for /00/15/28/40/51 is 468 kHz
The AM-IF for /01/45 is 455 kHz

2 With the telescopic aerial pulled in, set potentiometer R125 for fine-tuning to mid-position.

3 Set the AFC switch to position "off".
Open bridge Ⓐ . Connect an oscilloscope to ⑤ via a 100 kΩ resistor. Adjust the FM-IF curve for maximum height and symmetry.

4 Close bridge Ⓐ . Connect an oscilloscope to ① . Adjust the S-curve for maximum symmetry and linearity.

(R252) ALIGNMENT PROCEDURES—MODEL 90AL970

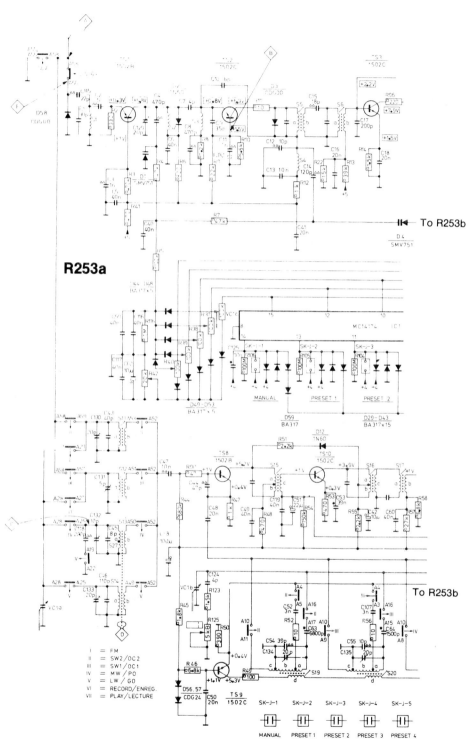

R253a

To R253b

To R253b

I = FM
II = SW2/OC2
III = SW1/OC1
IV = MW/PO
V = LW/GO
VI = RECORD/ENREG.
VII = PLAY/LECTURE

MANUAL   PRESET 1   PRESET 2   PRESET 3   PRESET 4

(R253a) CIRCUIT DIAGRAM—MODEL 90AL970 *(PART)*

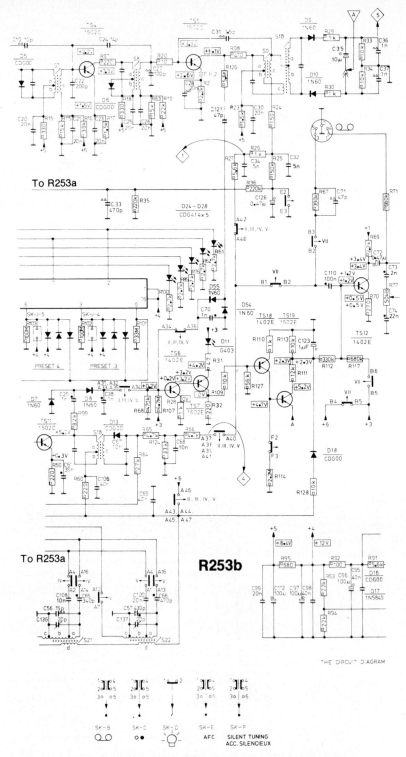

To R253a

To R253a

R253b

SK-B
SK-C
SK-D
SK-E   AFC
SK-F   SILENT TUNING
        ACC. SILENCIEUX

THE CIRCUIT DIAGRAM

(R253b) CIRCUIT DIAGRAM—MODEL 90AL970 *(PART)*

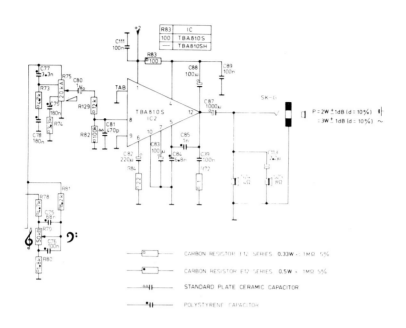

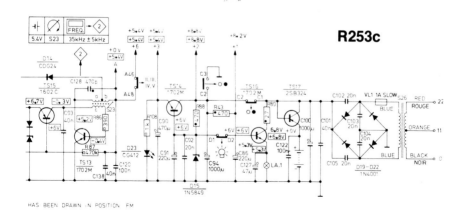

HAS BEEN DRAWN IN POSITION FM

R253c

(R253c) CIRCUIT DIAGRAM—MODEL 90AL970 *(CONTINUED)*

PHILIPS   Model 90AS300

General Description: A 2-waveband A.M./F.M. portable clock radio operating from battery supplies. Clock timing is by an integrated circuit operating from a stabilised source. Alarm facilities are included.

Battery Supplies: Radio 4.5 volts (3×1.5 volts); Clock Module 3.0 volts (2×1.5 volts).

Wavebands: M.W. 520-1605kHz; F.M. 87.5-104 or 108MHz.

Alignment: (See Figs. R255, R256).

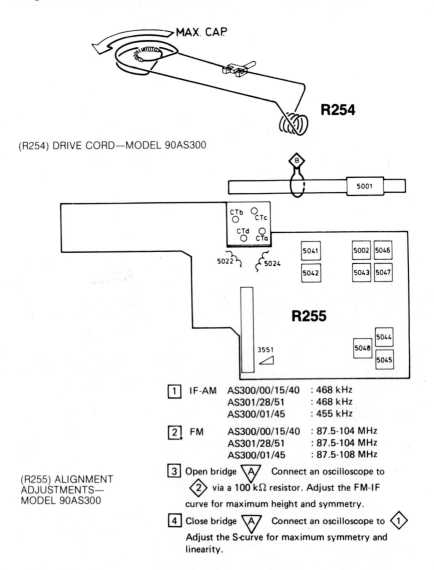

(R254) DRIVE CORD—MODEL 90AS300

(R255) ALIGNMENT ADJUSTMENTS— MODEL 90AS300

1	IF-AM	AS300/00/15/40	: 468 kHz
		AS301/28/51	: 468 kHz
		AS300/01/45	: 455 kHz
2	FM	AS300/00/15/40	: 87.5-104 MHz
		AS301/28/51	: 87.5-104 MHz
		AS300/01/45	: 87.5-108 MHz

3 Open bridge ⟨A⟩ Connect an oscilloscope to ⟨2⟩ via a 100 kΩ resistor. Adjust the FM-IF curve for maximum height and symmetry.

4 Close bridge ⟨A⟩ Connect an oscilloscope to ⟨1⟩ Adjust the S-curve for maximum symmetry and linearity.

Wave range SK-A	Signal to ⊘	◇	Var.cap. ⊬	Adjust	Indication
AS300/301 MW/PO-LW/GO	1 via 39 nF	⟨A⟩	Min.cap.	5048	
				5047	⟨1⟩ Max.
				5046	
AS300 MW/PO	512 kHz	⟨B⟩	Max.cap.	5002	
	1635 kHz		Min.cap.	CTc	⟨1⟩ Max.
	600 kHz		▭	5001	
	1400 kHz			CTd	
AS301 LW/GO	147 kHz	⟨B⟩	Max.cap.	5002	
	200 kHz		Min.cap.	CTc	⟨1⟩ Max.
	147 kHz		▭	5001	
	200 kHz			CTd	
FM 2	10.7 MHz via 20 nF	⟨D⟩	Min.cap.	5044	
				5043	⟨2⟩ 3
				5042	
				5041	
	−104 MHz	−108 MHz		5045	⟨1⟩ 4
	105 MHz	109 MHz	Min.cap.	CTb	
	86.5 MHz	86.5 MHz	Max.cap.	5024	⟨1⟩ Max.
	86.5 MHz	86.5 MHz	▭	5022	
	105 MHz	109 MHz		CTa	

(R256) ALIGNMENT PROCEDURE—MODEL 90AS300

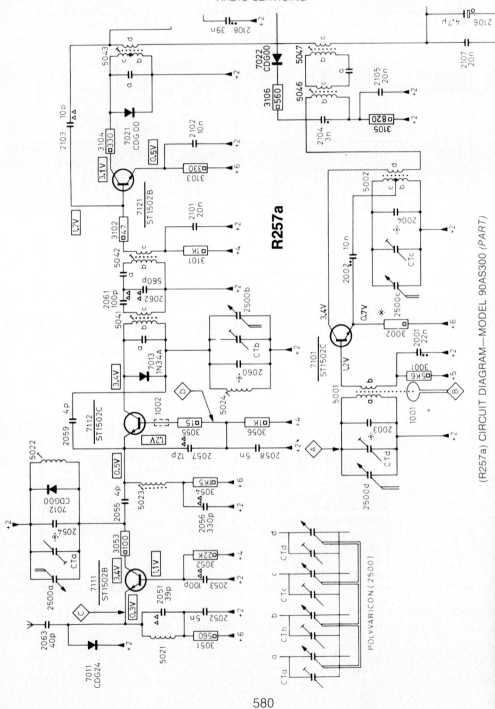

(R257a) CIRCUIT DIAGRAM—MODEL 90AS300 (PART)

R257a

PHILIPS

R257b

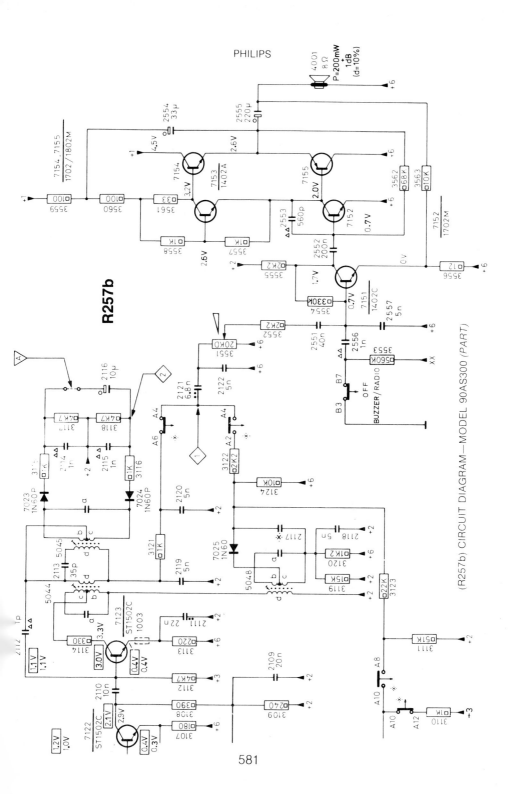

(R257b) CIRCUIT DIAGRAM—MODEL 90AS300 (PART)

581

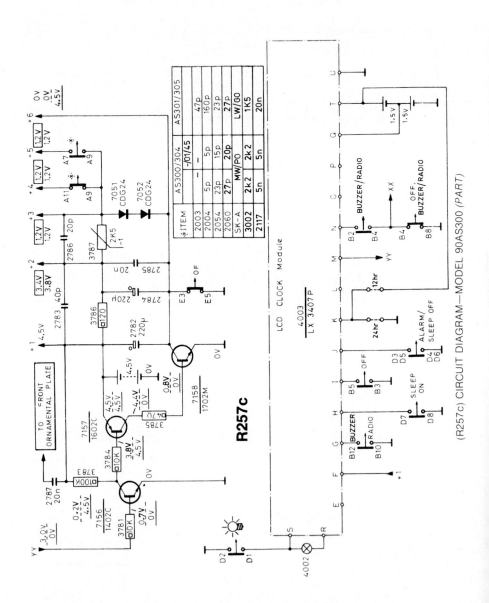

(R257c) CIRCUIT DIAGRAM—MODEL 90AS300 *(PART)*

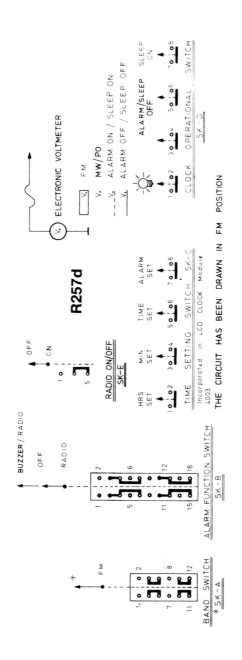

R257d

ELECTRONIC VOLTMETER

V₁ FM
V₂ MW/PO
V₃ ALARM ON / SLEEP ON
V₄ ALARM OFF / SLEEP OFF

CLOCK OPERATIONAL SWITCH SK-D

ALARM/SLEEP OFF SLEEP ON

RADIO ON/OFF SK-E

HRS SET   MIN SET   TIME SET   ALARM SET

TIME SETTING SWITCH SK-C

Incorporated in LCD CLOCK Module 4003

THE CIRCUIT HAS BEEN DRAWN IN FM POSITION

BUZZER / RADIO
OFF
RADIO

ALARM FUNCTION SWITCH SK-B

FM

BAND SWITCH *SK-A

(R257d) CIRCUIT DIAGRAM—MODEL 90AS300 (CONTINUED)

PHILIPS   Model 90AS304

General Description: A 2-waveband portable radio receiver and electronic clock with liquid crystal display operating from battery supplies. Alarm facilities are fitted.

Batteries: Radio 4.5 volts (3×1.5 volts); Clock 3 volts (2×1.5 volts).

Wavebands: M.W. 520-1605kHz; F.M. 87.5-104 or 108MHz.

Loudspeaker: 8 ohms impedance.

Drive Cord: This is similar in arrangement to that used in Model 90AS300 described previously.

Alignment: (See Figs. R258, R259).

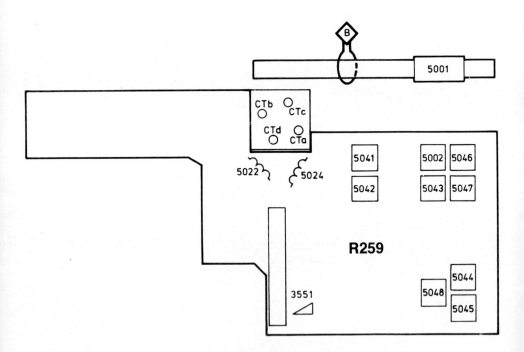

(R259) ALIGNMENT ADJUSTMENTS—MODEL 90AS304

Wave range SK-A	Signal to ⊗ →		◇	Var. cap. ≠	Adjust ⌒	Indication
AS304/305 MW/PO-LW/GO	[1] via 39 nF		⟨A⟩	Min. cap.	5048	⟨1⟩ Max.
					5047	
					5046	
AS304 MW/PO (520-1605 kHz)	512 kHz		⟨B⟩	Max. cap.	5002	⟨1⟩ Max.
	1635 kHz			Min. cap.	CTc	
	600 kHz			⊏▭⊐	5001	
	1400 kHz				CTd	
AS305 LW/GO (150-255 kHz)	147 kHz		⟨B⟩	Max. cap.	5002	⟨1⟩ Max.
	200 kHz			Min. cap.	CTc	
	147 kHz			⊏▭⊐	5001	
	200 kHz				CTd	
FM [2]	10.7 MHz via 20 nF **R258**		⟨D⟩	Min. cap.	5044	⟨2⟩ [3]
					5043	
					5042	
					5041	
	−104 MHz	−108 MHz			5045	⟨1⟩ [4]
	105 MHz	109 MHz		Min. cap.	CTb	
	86.5 MHz	86.5 MHz	⟨C⟩	Max. cap.	5024	⟨1⟩ Max.
	86.5 MHz	86.5 MHz		⊏▭⊐	5022	
	105 MHz	109 MHz			CTa	

↕ Repeat

[1] IF-AM
- AS304/00/15/40 : 468 kHz
- AS305/28/51 : 468 kHz
- AS304/01/45 : 455 kHz

[2] FM
- AS304/00/15/40 : 87,5 - 104 MHz
- AS305/28/51 : 87,5 - 104 MHz
- AS304/01/45 : 87,5 - 108 MHz

[3] Open bridge ⟨A⟩ . Connect an oscilloscope to ⟨2⟩ via a 100 kΩ resistor. Adjust the FM-IF curve for maximum height and symmetry.

[4] Close bridge ⟨A⟩ . Connect an oscilloscope to ⟨1⟩ . Adjust the S-curve for maximum symmetry and linearity.

(R258) ALIGNMENT PROCEDURE—MODEL 90AS304

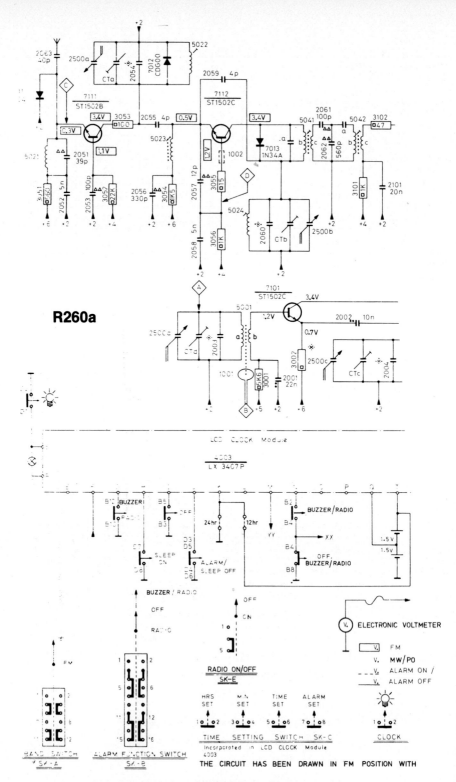

R260a

(R260a) CIRCUIT DIAGRAM—MODEL 90AS304 *(PART)*

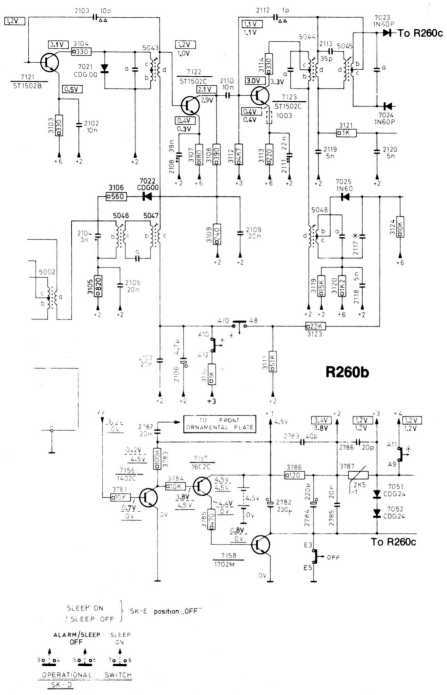

R260b

SLEEP ON
/ SLEEP OFF } SK-E position „OFF"

ALARM/SLEEP   SLEEP
OFF   ON

3 o ¦ o 4   5 o ¦ o 6   7 o ¦ o 8

OPERATIONAL   SWITCH
SK-D

CLOCK IN 24HRS. MODE & ALARM ON RADIO

(R260b) CIRCUIT DIAGRAM—MODEL 90AS304 *(PART)*

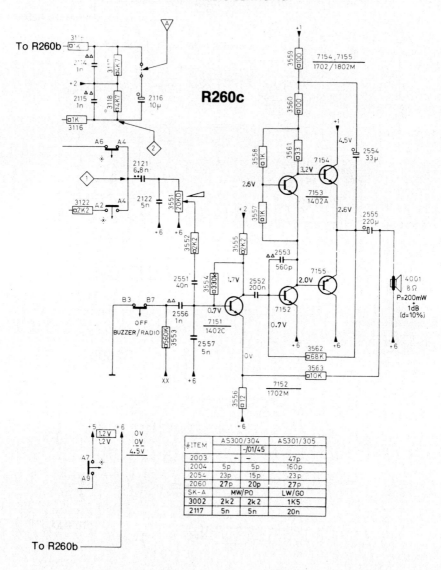

(R260c) CIRCUIT DIAGRAM—MODEL 90AS304 *(CONTINUED)*

PHILIPS   Model 90AS390

General Description: A 3-waveband A.M./F.M. clock radio receiver operating from mains supplies or back-up battery. An integrated circuit is used in the A.M. and I.F. stages and a socket is provided for the connection of an earphone. The clock section includes alarm facilities.

Mains Supplies: 110/220 volts, 50/60Hz.

Battery: 9 volts.

Wavebands: L.W. 150-255kHz; M.W. 520-1605kHz; F.M. 87.5-104MHz.

Loudspeaker: 8 ohms impedance.

Alignment: (See Figs. R262, R263).

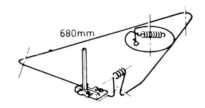

(R261) DRIVE CORD—MODEL 90AS390

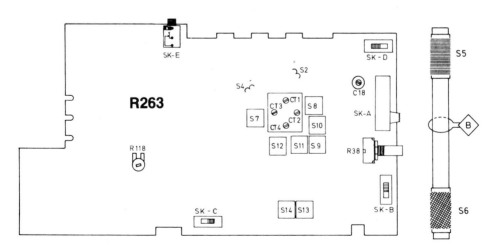

(R263) ALIGNMENT ADJUSTMENTS—MODEL 90AS390

SK........					
MW (520–1605 KHz)	468 KHz [3]	◇ D	MAX.	S12 S11	MAX. ◇1
	512 KHz	◇ B	MAX.	S8 / CT4	◇1
	1635 KHz		MIN.	S5 / CT2	
	550 KHz				
	1500 KHz				
LW (150–255 KHz)	147 KHz	◇ B	MAX.	C18 / S6	MAX. ◇1
	155 KHz				
FM (87.5–104 MHz)	10.7 MHz	◇ C	S14	S13 . S10 / S9 . S7	MAX ◇1
	86.5 MHz	◇ A	MAX.	S14	MIN ◇1
	105 MHz		MIN.		
	88 MHz				
	103 MHz			S4 / CT3 / S2 / CT1	MAX ◇1
R262					
CLOCK FREQUENCY (50 / 60 Hz)	[4]			R118	[5] ◇2

[3] Signal injected via 10 nF capacitor.

[4] 1. No mains supply from power transformer.
2. DC supply from MBB 9 V battery.

[5] Adjust to line frequency (50 or 60 Hz as specified)

(R262) ALIGNMENT PROCEDURE—MODEL 90AS390

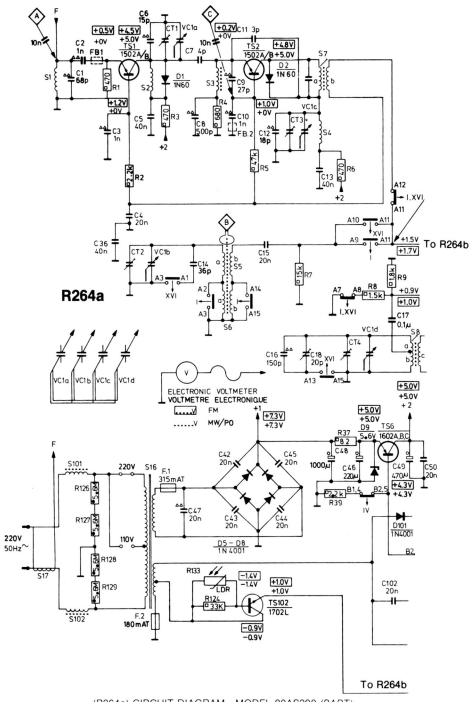

(R264a) CIRCUIT DIAGRAM—MODEL 90AS390 *(PART)*

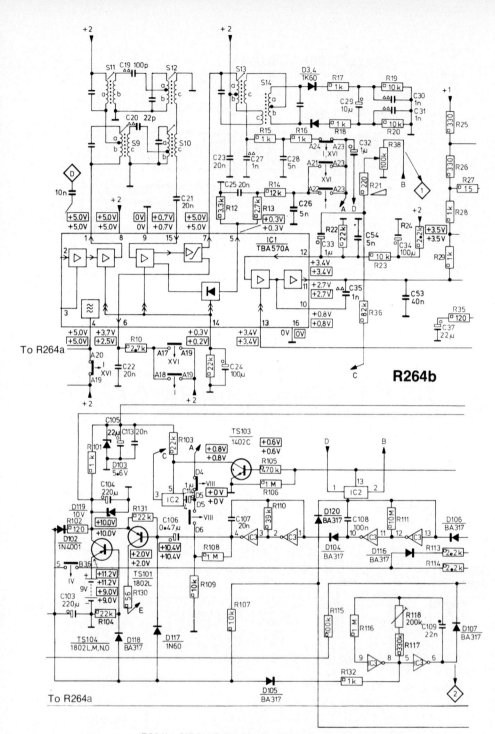

(R264b) CIRCUIT DIAGRAM—MODEL 90AS390 *(PART)*

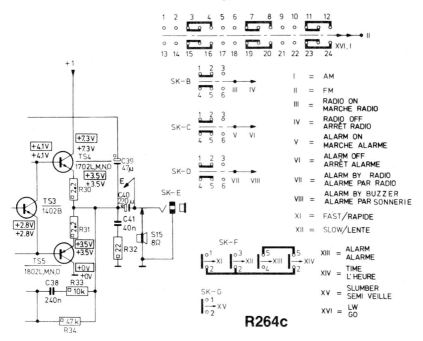

SK-A

I = AM
II = FM
III = RADIO ON / MARCHE RADIO
IV = RADIO OFF / ARRÊT RADIO
V = ALARM ON / MARCHE ALARME
VI = ALARM OFF / ARRÊT ALARME
VII = ALARM BY RADIO / ALARME PAR RADIO
VIII = ALARM BY BUZZER / ALARME PAR SONNERIE
XI = FAST / RAPIDE
XII = SLOW / LENTE
XIII = ALARM / ALARME
XIV = TIME / L'HEURE
XV = SLUMBER / SEMI VEILLE
XVI = LW / GO

R264c

THE CIRCUIT DIAGRAM HAS BEEN DRAWN IN POSITION FM

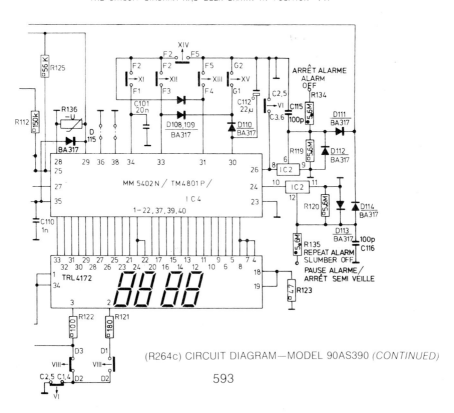

(R264c) CIRCUIT DIAGRAM—MODEL 90AS390 *(CONTINUED)*

593

General Description: A 3-waveband A.M./F.M. car stereo radio with stereo cassette tape player. Integrated circuits are used in the F.M./I.F. and decoder stages and in the tape and A.F. stages.

Battery: 12 volts (negative chassis). 140-180mA (Radio), 220-255mA (Tape).

Wavebands: L.W. 145-310kHz; M.W. 510-1620kHz; F.M. 87.5-104MHz.

Dismantling

Top Cover: Remove 2 screws from the upper surface (front) and one at the rear (centre).

A.M. and F.M./Tape Input Panels: Slacken 2 screws securing support pillars to rear of case and pull out 7-pin connector plug. Lift up panels sufficiently to enable 6-pin connector plug to be withdrawn (taking care not to damage micro-switch at rear of cassette deck).

On unscrewing the support pillars and removing the insulating plate, both panels can be lifted to the extent of connecting leads.

Note: When re-fitting these panels, ensure that the lower edge of each board engages with the locating slots in the bottom plate.

Amp. Panel: Remove the speakers/power lead clamp s/t screw: also rear fixing screw and 2 screws securing heat sink to underside of case.

Cassette Deck: Remove 2 screws on underside (one accessible through hole near A.F.C. switch); also one screw on opposite side near drive cord spring.

Tuner Unit: Remove 2 screws on underside; release aerial lead clamp.

To obtain adequate access to a particular assembly, it will usually be necessary to unsolder various leads. Refer to wiring diagram when re-assembling.

Lubrication: The flywheel shaft should be lightly oiled at intervals. A thin smear of grease can be applied, where necessary, to moving metal parts.

Cleaning: The playing head should be cleaned regularly (about 25 hour intervals), using a head-cleaning tape or a soft, non-fluffy cloth (or cotton wool bud) moistened in alcohol (not household meths).

Alcohol should also be used to keep the pinch rollers, drive belts, etc. free from dirt and grease.

Azimuth: Set balance to centre position and insert a pre-recorded 6300Hz test tape (code 8945 600 11501). Adjust the front screw for maximum output on both channels and re-seal.

Capacitors

Cct. ref.	Value	Type	Volts	Cct. ref.	Value	Type	Volts
C102	10n	M	50	C236	10n	M	100
C103	4n7	M	50	C237	6n8	M	50
C104	15n	M	50	C238	2μ2	T	35
C105	10n	C	50	C240	10n	M	100
C106	10μ	E	16	C241	6n8	M	50
C107	100p	C	50	C243	1n5	M	50
C108	10n	C	50	C244	4μ7	E	35
C109	3n3	M	50	C245	47μ	E	10
C110-111	10n	M	50	C246	330μ	E	16
C112-113	180p	C	50	C247	15n	M	50
C114	470p	P	50	C248	1n5	M	50
C115	3p	C	50	C249	4μ7	E	35
C116	1μ	T	25	C250	47μ	E	10
C117	10n	C	50	C251	15n	M	50
C118	10μ	E	16	C252-253	1μ	E	50
C119	22n	M	50	C258	33μ	E	16
C120	120p	C	50	C259	10n	C	50
C121	47n	M	50	C260	470p	P	50
C122	18p	C	50	C262	15n	M	50
C123	22n	M	50	C301	2n7	M	50
C124	33n	M	50	C302	100μ	E	10
C125	1μ	E	50	C303	47μ	E	10
C126	47μ	E	10	C304	100n	M	50
C127	1p5	C	50	C305	100n	C	50
C201	10p	C	50	C306	470μ	E	10
C202-207	22n	C	25	C307	2n7	M	50
C208	100p	C	50	C308	100μ	E	10
C209	4μ7	E	35	C309	47μ	E	10
C210	100p	C	50	C310	100n	M	50
C211	470n	E	50	C311	100n	C	50
C212	220p	C	50	C312	470μ	E	10
C213	2μ2	E	50	C313	22n	C	25
C214	220p	C	50	C314	100$\phi\mu$	E	16
C215-217	270p	C	50	C315	47μ	E	10
C218	22p	C	50	C316	22n	C	50
C219	2n2	M	50	C317-320	1n	Feedthru	
C220	1μ	E	50	C321-322	4μ7	T	10
C221	2n2	M	50	C323	330μ	E	16
C222-223	680p	C	50	C324-325	47μ	E	10
C224	1n	M	50	C326	330μ	E	16
C225	68p	C	50	C327	47n	C	50
C226	6n8	M	50	C401	4μ7	T	10
C227	1n	M	50	C501-502	33n	M	50
C228-229	560p	C	50	C601	390p	P	50
C230	10n	M	50	C701	2n	P	50
C231	1n	M	50	C702	8n2	M	50
C232	2μ2	E	50	C801	22n	C	25
C233	47n	M	50	VC101	70p	Trimmer	
C234	330n	T	35	VC102-104	100p	Trimmer	
C235	1μ	T	35	VC901	70p	Trimmer	

C—Ceramic   E—Electrolytic   M—Mylar   P—Polystyrene   T—Tantalum

595

Resistors:

Cct. ref.	Value	Cct. ref.	Value	Cct. ref.	Value
R102	3K3	R216	33K	R253	82
R103	470	R217	220K	R254	6K8
R105	1K	R218-219	2K2	R255	150K
R106	120K	R220	2K7	R258-259	3K3
R107	15K	R221	100K	R264	8K2
R108	4K7	R222	22K	R265	1K
R109	1K2	R223	33K	R266	1M
R110	47	R224	6K8	R267-268	10K
R111	220	R226-229	4K7	R269	22
R112	56K	R230	15K	R301	820
R113	27K	R231	8K2	R302	1K
R114	5K6	R232	15K	R303	390
R115	680	R233	8K2	R304	220K
R116	220	R234	2K7	R305	100K
R117	1K	R235	820	R306-307	1K
R118	10K	R236	47K	R308	27K
R119	220K	R237	15K	R309	1K5
R120	22K	R238	100	R310	2K7
R201-202	330	R239	1K	R311-312	10K
R203	12K	R240	4K7	R313	5R6
R204	3K3	R241	10K	R314	68
R206	1K	R242	22K	R315	680
R207	330	R243	100K	R401	1K
R208	47	R244	4K7	R402	18K
R209	330	R245	10K	R501-502	10K
R210	220	R247-248	22K	R601	120K
R211	1K	R249	220	R801	2K2
R212	1K2	R250	82	VR201	5K Pre-set
R213-214	10K	R251	6K8	VR501	50K×4; +100K
R215	220K	R252	150K		

Transistors:

Cct. ref.	Type
Tr101-102	2SC941TM
Tr103	2SC711
Tr201	2SC1815
Tr301	2SC711
Tr302	2SD468
Tr303-305	2SC711
Tr306	2SB525
Tr307	2SC711

Diodes:

Cct. ref.	Type
D102-103	1N60
D201-202	1N60P
D203-208	1S2075
D301	RD10EB-1
D302-303	1S2075
D304	1N4003
D801	1S2075
D901	LN-310GP (LED)
D902	TLR-124 (LED)

Alignment Procedure

Test Conditions: Signal inputs to be modulated 30% at 400Hz (A.M.) or 22.5kHz deviation at 1kHz (F.M.) and applied to aerial socket. All outputs into 4Ω resistive load at 500mW; volume at maximum, balance and tone central.

Equipment: Standard signal generator terminated by 15p series/60p shunt dummy aerial. F.M. signal generator with 75Ω termination. Output meter 0-1 watt.

Select		Inject	Tune to	Adjust for maximum	Remarks
1.	M	470kHz	Low frequency end	Cores of L111, L110, L109 & L108	
2.	M	1620kHz	High frequency end	Trimmer VC102	
3.	M	510kHz	Low frequency end	Core of L104	
4.	M	1400kHz	Signal	Trimmers VC101 & VC901	VC901 is accessible through hole in front facia panel
5.	L	310kHz	High frequency end	Trimmer VC104	
6.	L	145kHz	Low frequency end	Cores of L107, L103 & L102	
7.	V	*10.7MHz	Point of no interference	Cores of L201 & L4 (Tuner)	L201 & L202 are accessible through holes in the A.M. panel
8.	V	10.7MHz (30% A.M.)	As above	Core of L202 for *minimum* output between two maxima	

*Swing to determine resonant frequency of ceramic filters

VR201 (accessible through hole in bottom plate). Inject stereo-encoded signal and set midway between the two LED switch-on points.

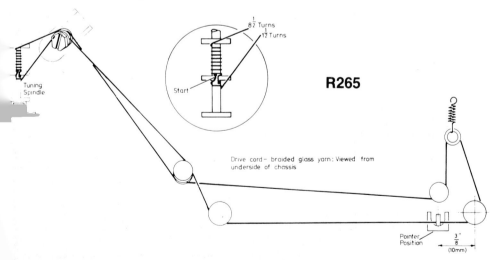

$8\frac{1}{2}$ Turns

$1\frac{1}{2}$ Turns

Tuning Spindle

Start

R265

Drive cord – braided glass yarn : Viewed from underside of chassis

Pointer Position

$\frac{3}{8}''$ (10mm)

(R265) DRIVE CORD—MODEL 2400

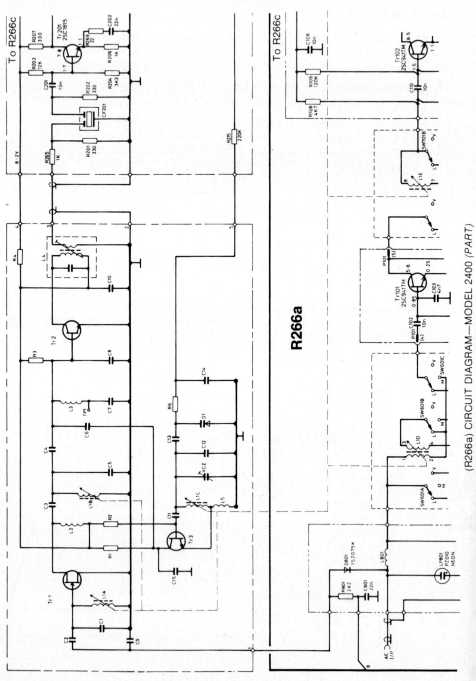

(R266a) CIRCUIT DIAGRAM—MODEL 2400 (PART)

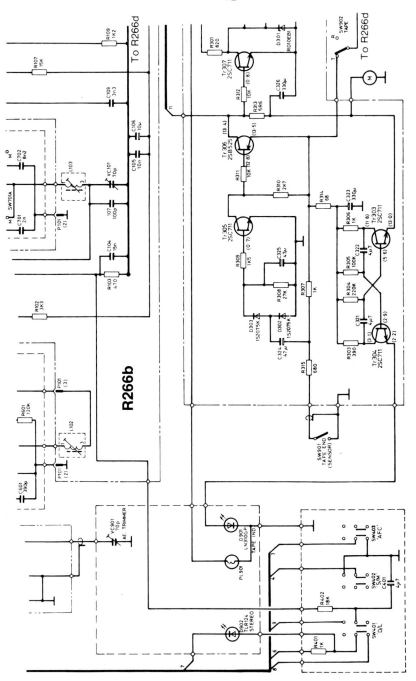

(R266b) CIRCUIT DIAGRAM—MODEL 2400 (PART)

(R266c) CIRCUIT DIAGRAM—MODEL 2400 (PART)

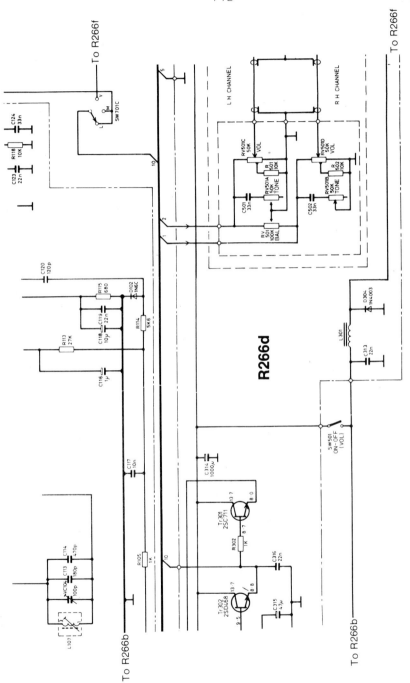

(R266d) CIRCUIT DIAGRAM—MODEL 2400 (PART)

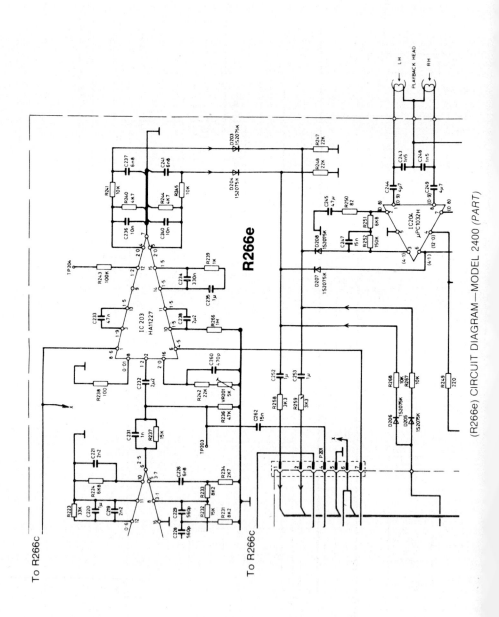

(R266e) CIRCUIT DIAGRAM—MODEL 2400 *(PART)*

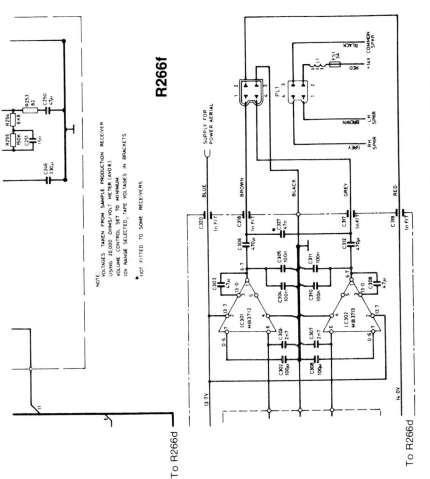

R266f

NOTE:
VOLTAGES TAKEN FROM SAMPLE PRODUCTION RECEIVER
USING 20,000 OHMS/VOLT METER (AVO 8).
VOLUME CONTROL SET TO MINIMUM.
IOV RANGE SELECTED, TAPE VOLTAGES IN BRACKETS

* NOT FITTED TO SOME RECEIVERS

To R266d

To R266d

(R266f) CIRCUIT DIAGRAM—MODEL 2400 (CONTINUED)

General Description: A two waveband digital clock radio operating from mains or back-up battery supply. The battery automatically comes into circuit should mains supplies be interrupted. A.F. amplification and clock timing is performed by integrated circuit.

Mains Supplies: 110/220 volts, 50/60Hz.

Battery: 3 volts (2×1.5 volts).

Wavebands: L.W. 150-255kHz; M.W. 520-1605kHz.

Alignment (See Figs. R267, R268)

Wave range SK-A	Signal to		Var. cap.	Adjust	Indication
MW/PO (520-1605 kHz)	468 kHz via 10 KpF	A	min. cap.	S7, 6 S5, 4	
	512 kHz		max. cap.	S3	1 max.
R267	1635 kHz	B	min. cap.	Ct2	
	600 kHz		tune in	S1	
	1400 kHz			Ct1	
LW/GO (150-255 kHz)	147 kHz	B	max. cap.	C8	1 max.
	200 kHz		tune in	S2	

(R267) ALIGNMENT PROCEDURE—
MODEL 7182

(R268) ALIGNMENT
PROCEDURE—
MODEL 7182

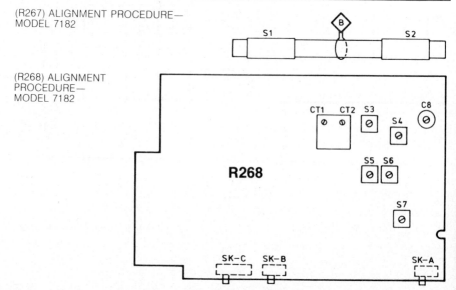

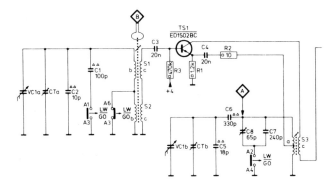

THE CIRCUIT HAS BEEN DRAWN IN POS. MW/
RADIO ON/ALARM BY BUZZER

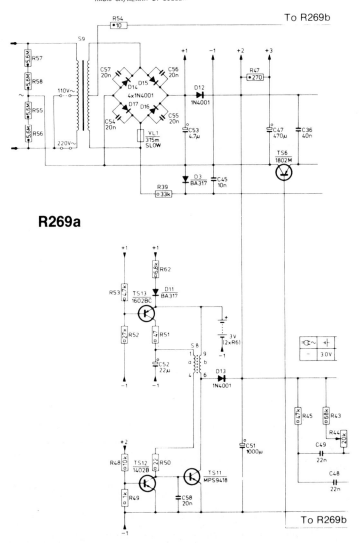

R269a

To R269b

To R269b

(R269a) CIRCUIT DIAGRAM—MODEL 7182 *(PART)*

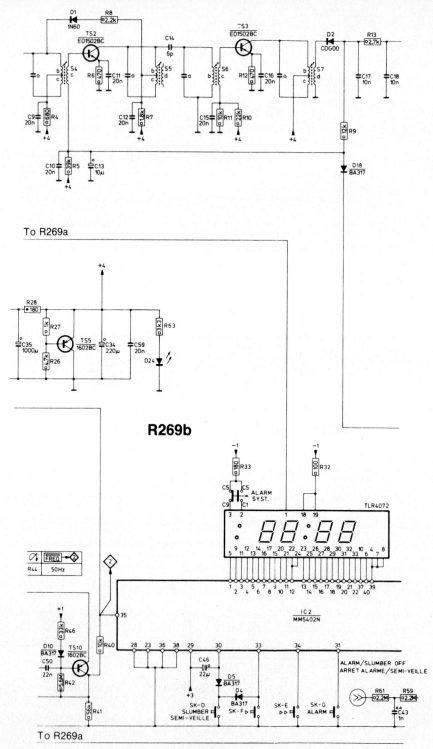

(R269b) CIRCUIT DIAGRAM—MODEL 7182 *(PART)*

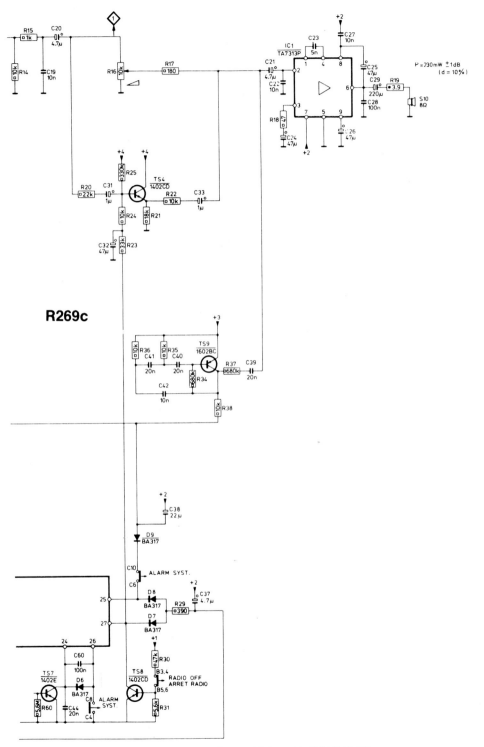

R269c

(R269c) CIRCUIT DIAGRAM—MODEL 7182 *(CONTINUED)*

ROBERTS RADIO   Model RT22

General Description: A 3-waveband A.M./F.M. portable radio operating from battery supplies. The V.H.F. tuner unit is in modular form for which no service information is available.

Battery: 9 volts (PP9).

Quiescent Current: A.M. 16mA; F.M. 19mA.

Wavebands: L.W. 150-265kHz; M.W. 530-1620kHz; F.M. 87.5-104.5MHz.

Loudspeaker: 12 ohms impedance.

Dismantling; Remove bottom cover and detach the battery. Remove screws securing fibre strips at either end of the case and screw from telescopic aerial. Ease out chassis through cabinet top.

Output Stage Adjustment: Replace Link 1 with a milli-ammeter and adjust R47 to obtain a quiescent current of 1mA. Replace link.

Alignment

Ensure: —9.0V across C45 gang to max. (Clock). Pointer coincides with datum marks at right-hand end of scale.

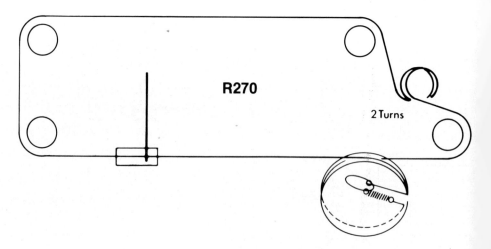

(R270) DRIVE CORD—MODEL RT22

608

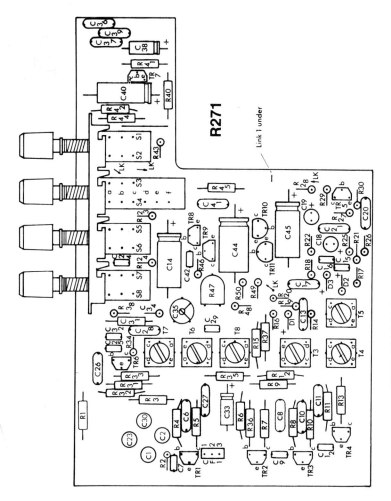

R271

(R271) COMPONENT LAYOUT—MODEL RT22

RADIO SERVICING

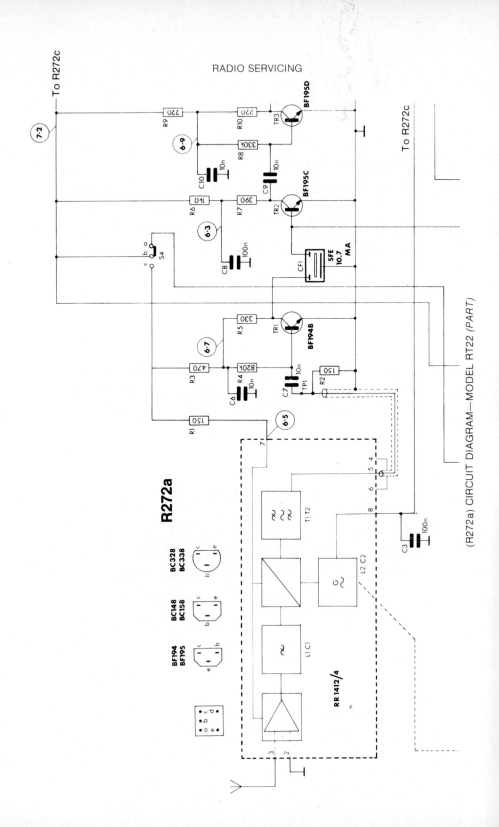

(R272a) CIRCUIT DIAGRAM—MODEL RT22 *(PART)*

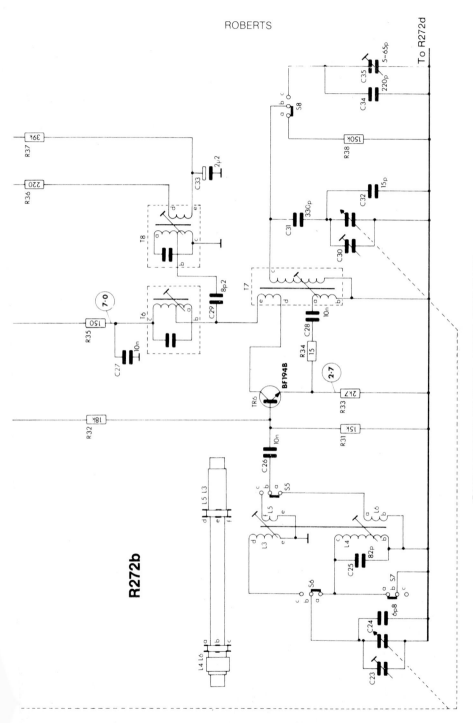

(R272b) CIRCUIT DIAGRAM—MODEL RT22 (PART)

(R272c) CIRCUIT DIAGRAM—MODEL RT22 (PART)

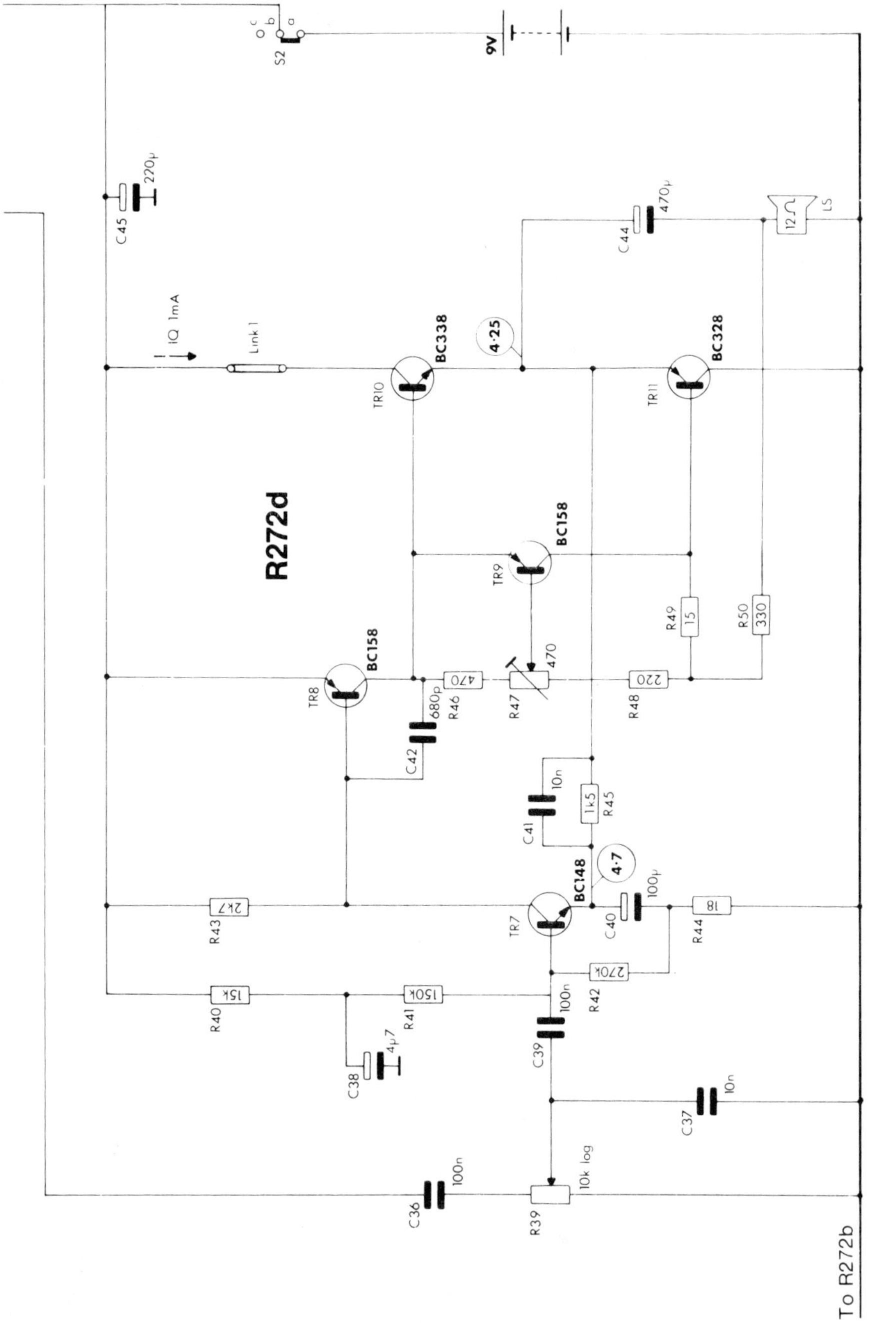

R272d

(R272d) CIRCUIT DIAGRAM—MODEL RT22 (CONTINUED)

To R272b

Wave-band	Pointer	Sweep/signal generator			Indicator	Connect	Adjust	Indication
		Inject	Frequency	Mod				
1	—	—	—	—	mA meter	In series with link 1 under print board (vol. min.)	R47	1mA after 1 min at 20°C
2 M.F.	—	Across L3	470kHz	25kHz deviation	Oscilloscope sensitivity 100mV/div.	S3a and chassis	T6, T8, T3	Max. O/P & symmetry adjust I/P to maintain display height of 5 divs
3 M.F.	H.F. cal mark	Via coupling loop	1500kHz	30% A.M.	Oscilloscope or output meter	Across loudspeaker	C30 & C23	Max. O/P
4 M.F.	L.F. cal mark	As 3	560kHz	As 3	As 3	As 3	T7 & L3	Max O/P
5 L.F.	H.F. cal mark	As 3	260kHz	As 3	As 3	As 3	C35	Max O/P
6 L.F.	L.F. cal mark	As 3	156kHz	As 3	As 3	As 3	L4	Max O/P

For 7 & 8 maintain I/P below limiting (−3dB)

Wave-band	Pointer	Inject	Frequency	Mod	Indicator	Connect	Adjust	Indication
7 V.H.F.	—	TPI remove screened lead to tuner	10.7MHz*	1MHz deviation	Oscilloscope	TP2 via diode probe	T4	Max O/P & symmetry
8 V.H.F.	—	As 7	As 7	As 7	As 7	Junction R25 & R26 & chassis	T5	'S' curve zero crossing at centre of I.F. —3dB bandwidth

*The actual I.F. is determined by the Ceramic Resonator

614

SANYO   Model M2246

General Description: A portable 2-track cassette tape recorder operating from mains or battery supplies. A microphone is fitted to the case and sockets are provided for the connection of auxiliary inputs and an earphone. D.C. bias and erase is employed.

Mains Supply: 240 volts, 50Hz.

Battery: 6 volts (4×1.5 volts).

Loudspeaker: 8 ohms impedance.

Adjustment of Head Azimuth

Connect the unit to a Power source and insert a test cassette tape (7kHz pre-recorded) in the cassette compartment.

Connect an 8 ohm dummy load with the V.T.V.M. across it to the extension speaker jack on the unit.

Set the unit into the PLAY mode.

Turn the head azimuth adjusting screw until the maximum value with reading on the V.T.V.M.

Fasten the adjusting screw securely by applying paint or glue.

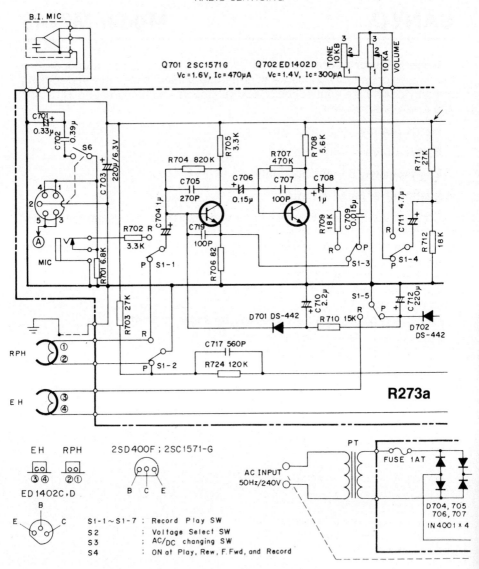

(R273a) CIRCUIT DIAGRAM—MODEL M2245 *(PART)*

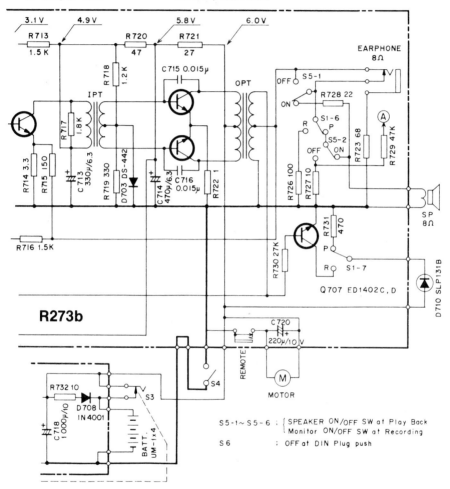

R273b

(R273b) CIRCUIT DIAGRAM—MODEL M2245 *(CONTINUED)*

General Description: A 2-track portable cassette tape recorder operating from mains or battery supplies. A.F. power amplification is by integrated circuit. A microphone is fitted to the case and sockets are provided for the connection of auxiliary inputs and an earphone.

Mains Supply: 240 volts, 50Hz.

Battery: 7 volts (5×HP2).

Loudspeaker: 8 ohms impedance.

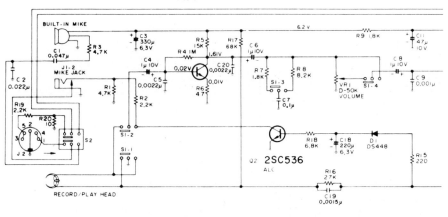

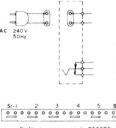

R274a

(R274a) CIRCUIT DIAGRAM—MODEL M2511 *(PART)*

Head Azimuth Adjustment

After the R.P. Head has been replaced or disassembled, its head azimuth should be adjusted by the following procedure.

Connect a V.T.V.M. with an 8 ohm dummy load to the earphone jack and play back a 6.3kHz test tape.

Turn the azimuth adjusting screw to obtain the maximum reading on the V.T.V.M.

After adjustment, secure the screw with paint or glue.

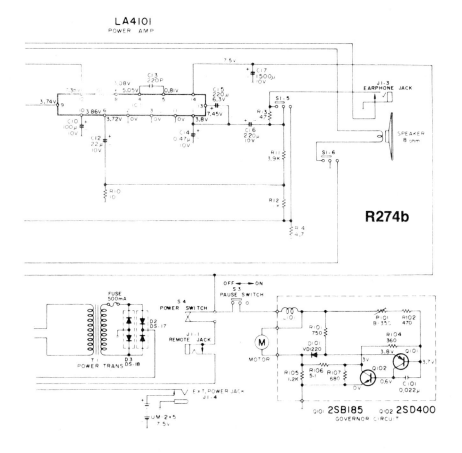

(R274b) CIRCUIT DIAGRAM—MODEL M2511 *(CONTINUED)*

SANYO   Model RM5011

General Description: A 2-waveband A.M./F.M. clock radio operating from A.C. mains supplies. On/off times may be pre-set. A socket is provided for the connection of an earphone.

Mains Supply: 240 volts, 50Hz.

Wavebands: M.W. 510-1605kHz; F.M. 87.5-108MHz.

Loudspeaker: 8 ohms impedance.

Transistor Voltages:

		Q102	Q103	Q301	Q302	Q701	Q702	Q703	Q704
Collector	A.M.	—	0.12	0.94	0.14	6.2	3.9	7.1	0
Voltage (V)	F.M.	0.028	0.45	1.2	0.14				
Base	A.M.	—	5.9	5.6	5.2	4.2	6.2	3.9	3.9
Voltage (V)	F.M.	4.2	4.9	5.55	5.6				
Emitter	A.M.	—	6.5	6.4	5.9	3.5	7.0	3.3	3.3
Voltage (V)	F.M.	4.9	5.7	6.3	5.8				

Notes:
1. All voltages are measured from common positive (+) ground.
2. Volume control is at the minimum position.

(R275) ALIGNMENT ADJUSTMENTS—MODEL RM5011

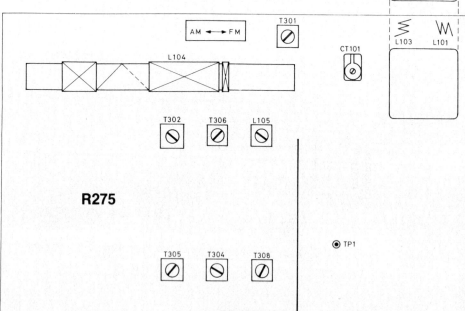

Alignment

M.W. Band: Band Selector Switch in M.W. Position

Step	Connection of signal generator	Input signal frequency	Dial setting of radio	Connection of output meter	Adjust	Remarks
1	Loop antenna	470kHz	Lowest end	Across speaker	I.F.T. T306, 308	Adjust for maximum
2	Same	505kHz	Lowest end	Same	Osc. coil L105	Same
3	Same	1650kHz	Highest end	Same	Osc. trim VCT4	Same
4	Same	600kHz	600kHz	Same	Ant. coil L104	Same
5	Same	1400kHz	1400kHz	Same	Ant. trim VCT3	Same

Repeat steps 2 to 5 to obtain maximum sensitivity.

F.M. Band: Band Selector Switch in F.M. Position

Step	Connection of signal connector	Input signal frequency	Dial setting of radio	Connection of meter or oscilloscope	Adjust	Remarks
1	Connect sweep marker generator to VCT2, ground	10.7MHz	Lowest end	Connect scope input cable through network to TP2, ground	I.F.T. T301, 302, 304	Adjust for maximum sensitivity with symmetrical curve
2	Same	10.7MHz	Lowest end	Connect scope input cable through network to R316 ground	I.F.T. T305	Adjust for symmetrical 'S' curve
3	Connect signal generator to TP1, ground	87.0MHz	Lowest end	Connect V.T.V.M. across speaker	Osc. coil L103	Adjust for maximum
4	Same	109.0MHz	Highest end	Same	Osc. trimmer CT101	Same
5	Same	90MHz	90MHz	Same	R.F. coil L101	Same
6	Same	106MHz	106MHz	Same	R.F. trimmer VCT1	Same

Repeat steps 3 to 6 to obtain maximum sensitivity.
*Note on F.M. band coverage adjustment.
Before proceeding with CT101 adjustment, VCT2 must be set at its middle-value position.
VCT2 adjustment is generally not required, but it should be made to cover 109MHz when CT101 can't provide high frequency end coverage.

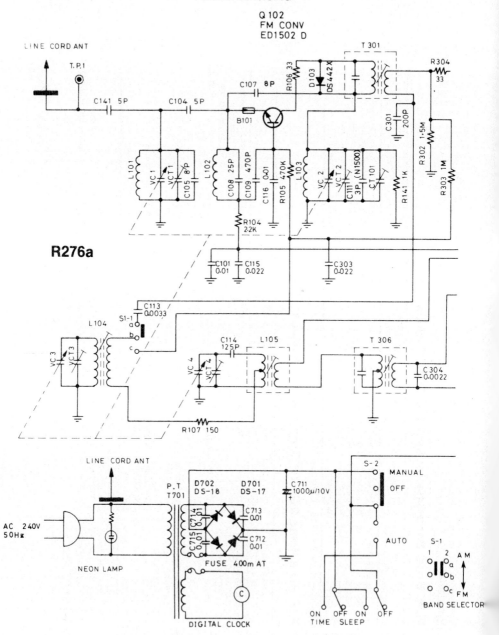

(R276a) CIRCUIT DIAGRAM—MODEL RM5011 *(PART)*

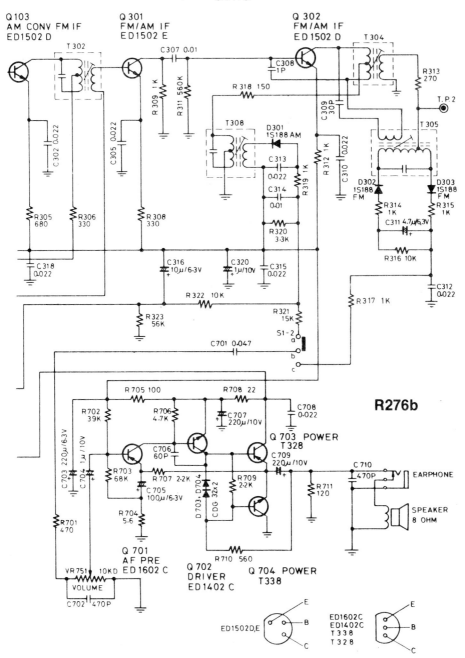

R276b

SANYO   Model RM6600

General Description: A 2-waveband A.M./F.M. digital clock radio operating from mains supplies. A socket is provided for the connection of an earphone.

Mains Supply: 240 volts, 50Hz.

Wavebands: M.W. 510-1605kHz; F.M. 87.5-108MHz.

Loudspeaker: 8 ohms impedance.

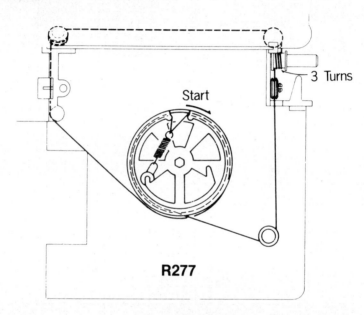

(R277) DRIVE CORD—MODEL RM6600

Handling and Repair of L.S.I. Clock Module

Handling and Storage: The L.S.I. incorporated in the clock module is very susceptible to static electricity. It may become destroyed when the voltage of static electricity is high. Due caution is required.

(a). Storage of clock module.

Keep the copper foil strip attached to the clock module until immediately before its use. (The copper foil strip has the effect of maintaining the electric potential of each terminal at the same level.)

Handling of Clock Module: Be careful not to touch the patterned surface of the module with a finger.

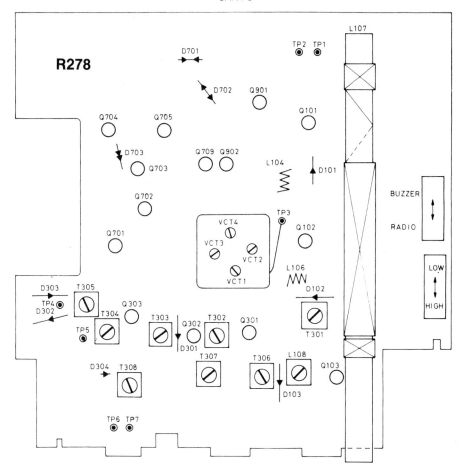

(R278) ALIGNMENT ADJUSTMENTS—MODEL RM6600

The clock module should not be stored at a place where the temperature and relative humidity are high. It should not be subjected to a strong magnetic field.

Replacement of Clock Module: Unplug the power cord of the digital clock being serviced prior to replacing its module. Short-circuit the electrolytic capacitor (C712) as well as Vss and Vdd on the P.C.B.

Connect a grounding conductor to every instrument and tool employed (either at E or G). The engineer who does the repair work should have a grounding conductor attached to his body (he should wear an arm ring connected to a grounding line having a resistance value of 1M ohms).

625

Before handling an L.S.I. he should touch the B-line and discharge into the earth static electricity charged in his body.

Place an electrically conductive sheet on the work-table and ground it.

A.C. leakage from the soldering iron being employed should be prevented. It must be less than 1V when the iron is hot. Be sure to ground it before use.

Do not wipe the clock module with a dry cloth. (Use only an antistatic cloth.)

A tester should be used only for measuring voltage and amperage. Do not use it for measuring resistance.

Transistor Voltages:

		Q101	Q102	Q103	Q301	Q302	Q303	Q701	Q702	Q703	Q704	Q705	Q709	Q901	Q902
C	A.M.			5.2	0	0		7.2	4.0	8.2	0	7.9	0.1	12.5	10.0
	F.M.	0.12	0.06		0	0	0					7.9			
B	A.M.			0.64	4.4	3.65		4.2	7.2	4.0	2.7	7.4	0.7	15.3	15.3
	F.M.	4.2	1.6		4.7	3.8	3.8					7.4			
E	A.M.			0.56	5.1	4.3		3.7	7.9	3.6	3.6	8.1	0	15.0	15.0
	F.M.	2.5	2.9		5.4	4.5	4.8					8.1			

A.M. Band: Band Selector Switch in A.M. Position

Step	Connection of signal generator	Input signal frequency	Dial setting of radio	Connection of output meter	Adjust	Remarks
1	Loop antenna	470kHz	Lowest end	Across speaker	I.F.T. T306, 307, 308	Adjust for maximum
2	Same	505kHz	Lowest end	Same	Osc. coil L108	Same
3	Same	1650kHz	Highest end	Same	Osc. trim VCT4	Same
4	Same	600kHz	600kHz	Same	Ant. coil L107	Same
5	Same	1400kHz	1400kHz	Same	Ant. trim VCT3	Same
	Repeat steps 2 to 5 to obtain maximum sensitivity					

F.M. Band: Band Selector Switch in F.M. Position

Step	Connection of signal generator	Input signal frequency	Dial setting of radio	Connection of meter or oscilloscope	Adjust	Remarks
1	Connect sweep marker generator to TP2, 3	10.7MHz	Lowest end	Connect scope input cable through network to TP4, 5	I.F.T. T301, 302 T303 & T304	Adjust for maximum sensitivity
2	Same	10.7MHz	Lowest end	Connect scope input cable through network to TP5, 6	I.F.T. T305	symmetric curve Adjust for symmetric 'S' curve
3	Connect signal generator to TP1, 2	87.0MHz	Lowest end	Connect V.T.V.M. across speaker	Osc. coil L106	Adjust for maximum
4	Same	109.0MHz	Highest end	Same	Osc. trimmer VCT2	Same
5	Same	90MHz	90MHz	Same	R.F. coil L104	Same
6	Same	106MHz	106MHz	Same	R.F. trimmer VCT1	Same
	Repeat steps 3 to 6 to obtain maximum sensitivity					

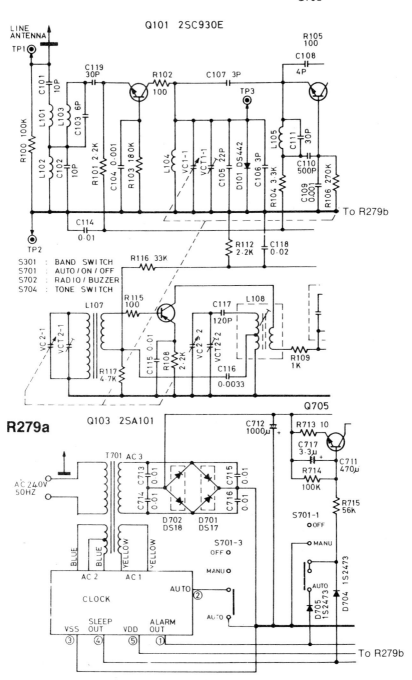

SANYO

(R279a) CIRCUIT DIAGRAM—MODEL RM6600 *(PART)*

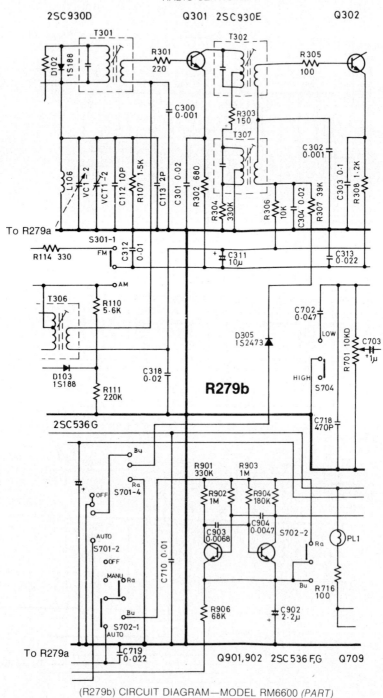

(R279b) CIRCUIT DIAGRAM—MODEL RM6600 *(PART)*

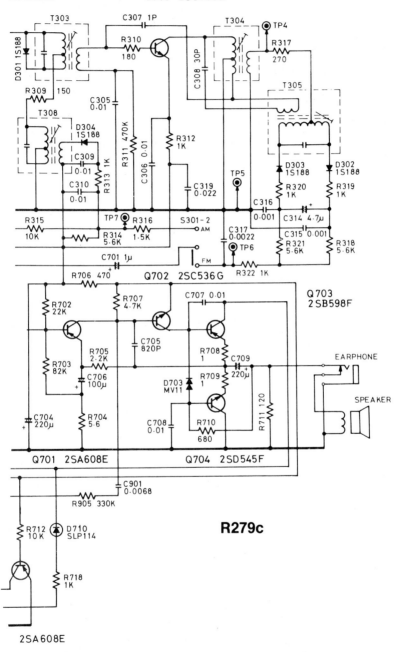

R279c

(R279c) CIRCUIT DIAGRAM—MODEL RM6600 *(CONTINUED)*

General Description: A 3-waveband A.M./F.M. digital clock radio operating from mains supplies. A socket is provided for the connection of an earphone. The clock module used in this receiver is sensitive to static voltages and the notes given for Model RM6600 should be studied before any attempt is made to handle this unit and its connections.

Mains Supply: 240 volts, 50Hz.

Wavebands: L.W. 150-350kHz; M.W. 350-1605kHz; F.M. 88-108MHz.

Loudspeaker: 8 ohms impedance.

Drive Cord (See Fig. R280)

Prepare dial cord and a tension spring as shown.

Hold the circuit board its copper-side up. First place the drum in such a position as it provides a maximum capacitance for the tuning gang.

Hook a free end of the spring to the drum at 'A' point and thread the cord as shown by starting from No. 1 through to No. 7.

Please give it four-turns around a tuning shaft at No. 4 and two-turns around the drum at No. 7.

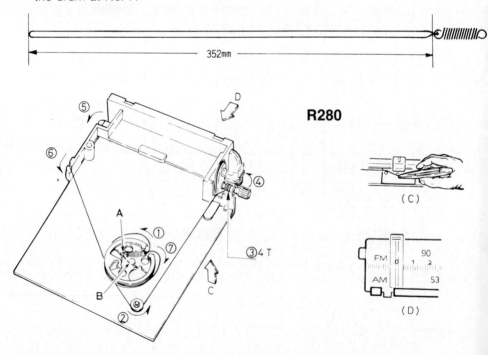

(R280) DRIVE CORD—MODEL RM7500

Change the hook point of the spring from 'A' to 'B' after completing the above threading.

Position the pointer at a centre on the dial scale and engage it with the threaded cord by using a pair of tweezers (Ref. C).

Then, locate the pointer over the letter 'O' on the scale with your fingers (Ref. D).

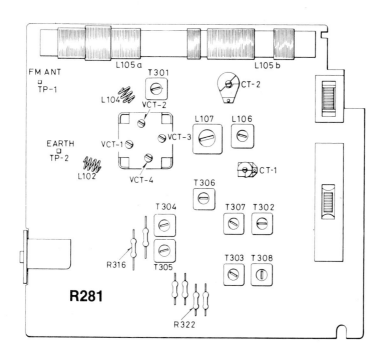

(R281) ALIGNMENT ADJUSTMENTS—MODEL RM7500

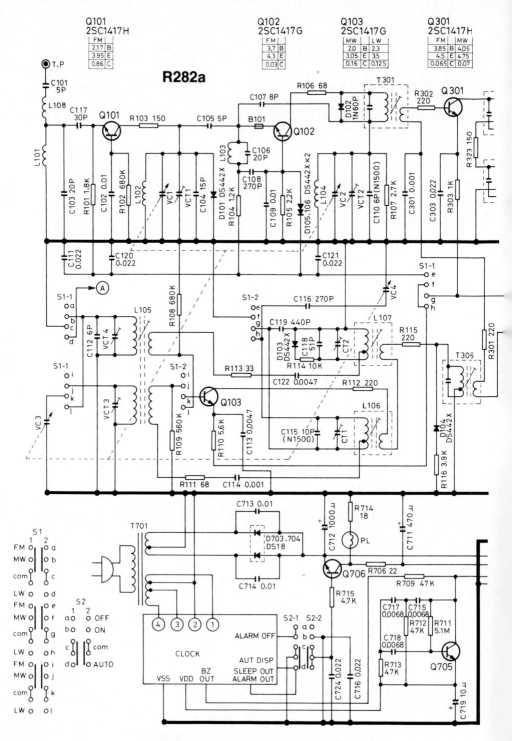

(R282a) CIRCUIT DIAGRAM—MODEL RM7500 *(PART)*

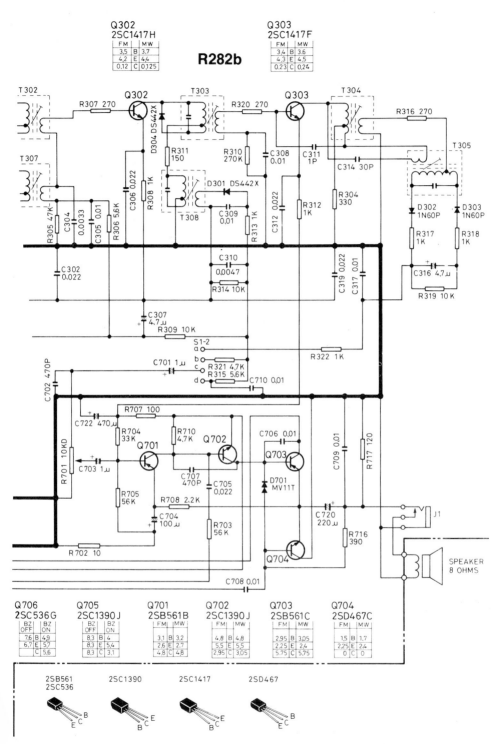

R282b

Q302 2SC1417H		
FM		MW
3,5	B	3,7
4,2	E	4,4
0,12	C	0,125

Q303 2SC1417F		
FM		MW
3,4	B	3,6
4,3	E	4,5
0,23	C	0,24

Q706 2SC536G		
BZ OFF		BZ ON
7,6	B	4,9
6,7	E	5,7
	C	5,6

Q705 2SC1390J		
BZ OFF		BZ ON
8,3	B	4
8,3	E	5,4
8,3	C	3,1

Q701 2SB561B		
FM		MW
3,1	B	3,2
2,6	E	2,7
4,8	C	4,8

Q702 2SC1390J		
FM		MW
4,8	B	4,8
5,5	E	5,5
2,95	C	3,05

Q703 2SB561C		
FM		MW
2,95	B	3,05
2,25	E	2,4
5,75	C	5,75

Q704 2SD467C		
FM		MW
1,5	B	1,7
2,25	E	2,4
0	C	0

SPEAKER 8 OHMS

(R282b) CIRCUIT DIAGRAM—MODEL RM7500 *(CONTINUED)*

Alignment

A.M. Band: Band Selector Switch in A.M. Position

Step	Connection of signal generator	Input signal frequency	Dial setting of radio	Connection of output meter	Adjust	Remarks
1	Loop antenna	470kHz	Lowest end	Across speaker	I.F.T. T306, T307 & T308	Adjust for maximum
2	Same	505kHz	Lowest end	Same	Osc. coil L106	Same
3	Same	1650kHz	Highest end	Same	Osc. trim CT1	Same
4	Same	600kHz	600kHz	Same	Ant. coil L105b	Same
5	Same	1400kHz	1400kHz	Same	Ant. trim. VCT-3	Same

Repeat steps 2 to 5 to obtain maximum sensitivity.

L.W. Band: Band Selector Switch in L.W. Position

Step	Connection of signal generator	Input signal frequency	Dial setting of radio	Connection of output meter	Adjust	Remarks
1	Loop antenna	145kHz	Lowest end	Across speaker	Osc. coil L107	Adjust for maximum
2	Same	365kHz	Highest end	Same	Osc. trim. CT2	Same
3	Same	160kHz	160kHz	Same	Ant. coil L105a	Same
4	Same	340kHz	340kHz	Same	Ant. trim VCT-4	Same

Repeat steps 1 to 4 to obtain maximum sensitivity.

F.M. Band: Selector Switch in F.M. Position

Step	Connection of signal generator	Input signal frequency	Dial setting of radio	Connection of meter or oscilloscope	Adjust	Remarks
1	Connect sweep marker generator VCT1 and TP2	10.7MHz	Lowest end	Connect osc. input cable through network to R316 and T305	I.F.T. T301, T302, T303 & T304	Adjust for maximum sensitivity with symmetrical curve
2	Same	10.7MHz	Lowest end	Connect osc. input cable through network to R322 and T305	I.F.T. T305	Adjust for symmetrical 'S' curve
3	Connect signal generator to TP1 and TP2	87.0MHz	Lowest end	Connect V.T.V.M. across speaker	Osc. coil L104	Adjust for maximum
4	Same	109MHz	Highest end	Same	Osc. trimmer VCT2	Same
5	Same	90MHz	90MHz	Same	R.F. coil L102	Same
6	Same	106MHz	106MHz	Same	R.F. trimmer VCT1	Same

Repeat steps 3 to 6 to obtain maximum sensitivity.

SANYO   Model RP6700

General Description: A 2-waveband A.M./F.M. pocket portable radio operating from battery supplies. I.F. amplification is by integrated circuit and a socket is fitted to allow the connection of an earphone.

Battery: 4.5 volts (3×1.5 volts).

Wavebands: M.W. 530-1605kHz; F.M. 87.5-108MHz.

Loudspeaker: 8 ohms impedance.

Access for Service: Remove four screws from rear cover and take out batteries. Take out the screw holding the p.c.b.

Remove the two pan head screws Y1 and the two pan head tapping screws Y2, all used for holding the chassis-pointer assembly to the printed circuit board. The former will come off the latter when the coil spring (serving also as the lead wire for power supply to the LED) is unsoldered at the connections.

Note: There is a shaft running in the centre of the coil spring. Do not lose it when changing the LED or correcting trouble involving the tuning indicator. This shaft is not included in the pointer assembly.

Dial Cord Stringing: (See Fig. R284)

Make a loop of rope 154mm in length when stretched after connecting its ends. Make a small loop and put it on the hook of the dial drum. Turn the rope around the dial drum and stretch it from (2) via (3) to (4). Wind it four turns around (4).

Pass the rope as illustrated at (5), (6) and (7) in that order of steps, and around the dial drum as shown at (8).

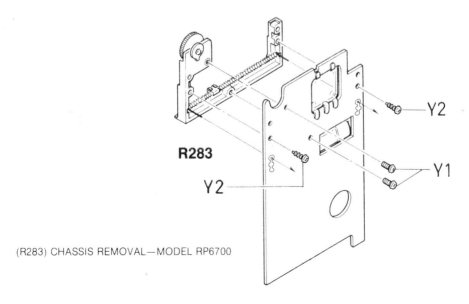

(R283) CHASSIS REMOVAL—MODEL RP6700

Alignment

A.M. Band: Band Selector Switch in A.M. Position

Step	Connection of signal generator	Input signal frequency	Dial setting of radio	Connection of output meter	Adjust	Remarks
1	Loop antenna	455kHz	Lowest end	Across speaker	I.F.T. T304, 305	Adjust for maximum
2	Same	515kHz	Lowest end	Same	Osc. coil L105	Same
3	Same	1650kHz	Highest end	Same	Osc. trim. CT4	Same
4	Same	600kHz	600kHz	Same	Ant. coil L104	Same
5	Same	1400kHz	1400kHz	Same	Ant. trim. CT3	Same

Repeat steps 2 to 5 to obtain maximum sensitivity.

F.M. Band: Band Selector Switch in F.M. Position

Step	Connection of signal generator	Input signal frequency	Dial setting of radio	Connection of meter or oscilloscope	Adjust	Remarks
1	Connect sweep marker generator to VCT2 ground	10.7MHz	Lowest end	Connect osc. input cable through network to R311 ground	I.F.T. T301, 302, 303, 304	Adjust for maximum sensitivity with symmetrical curve
2	Same	10.7MHz	Lowest end	Connect osc. input cable through network to R318 ground	I.F.T. T305	Adjust for symmetrical 'S' curve
3	Connect signal generator to TP1, TP2	87.0MHz	Lowest end	Connect V.T.V.M. across speaker	Osc. coil L103	Adjust for maximum
4	Same	109.3MHz	Highest end	Same	Osc. trimmer CT2	Same
5	Same	90MHz	90MHz	Same	R.F. coil L101	Same
6	Same	106MHz	106MHz	Same	R.F. trimmer CT1	Same

Repeat steps 3 to 6 to obtain maximum sensitivity.

SANYO

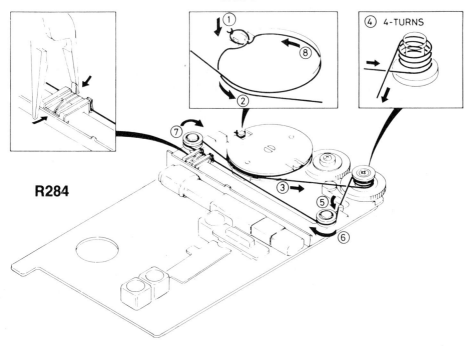

R284

(R284) DRIVE CORD—MODEL RP6700

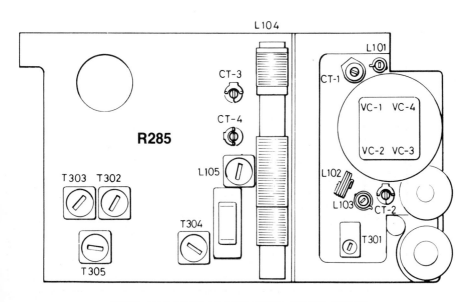

R285

(R285) ALIGNMENT ADJUSTMENTS—MODEL RP6700

637

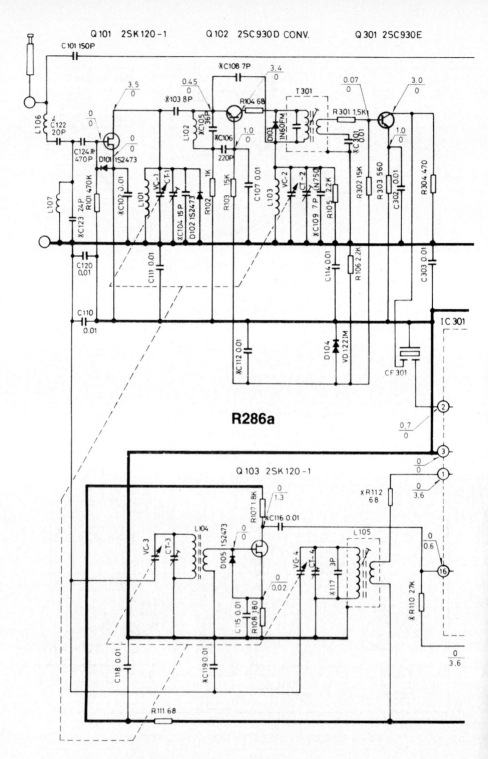

(R286a) CIRCUIT DIAGRAM—MODEL RP6700 *(PART)*

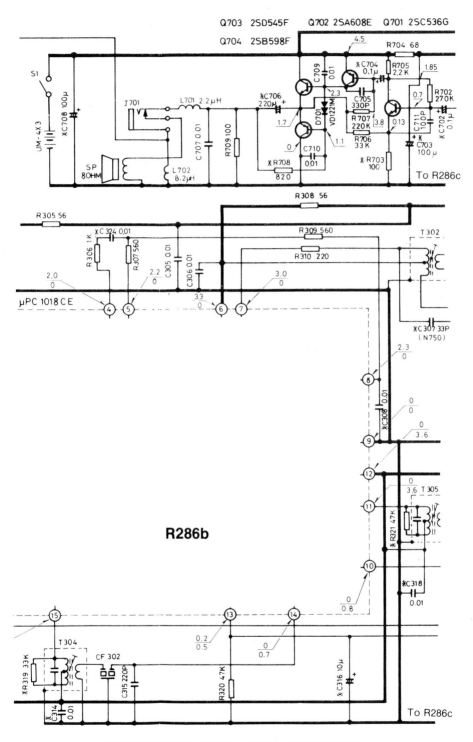

(R286b) CIRCUIT DIAGRAM—MODEL RP6700 *(PART)*

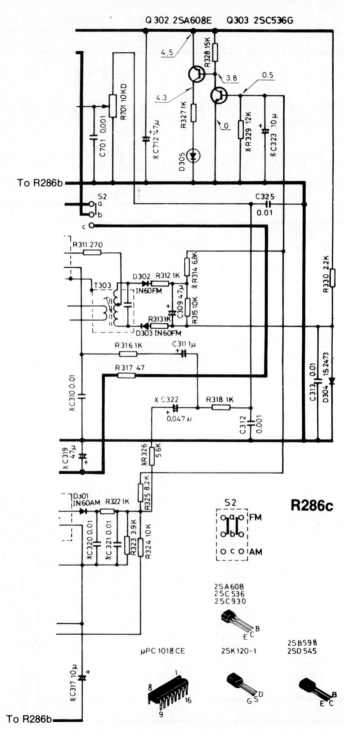

(R286c) CIRCUIT DIAGRAM—MODEL RP6700 *(CONTINUED)*

SANYO   Model RP7160

General Description: A 3-waveband A.M./F.M. portable radio receiver operating from mains or battery supplies. I.F. amplification is by means of an integrated circuit and a socket is provided for the connection of an earphone.

Mains Supply: 240 volts, 50Hz.

Battery: 6 volts (4×HP7).

Wavebands: L.W. 150-350kHz; M.W. 510-1605kHz; F.M. 87.5-108MHz.

Loudspeaker: 8 ohms impedance.

BACK LID DISASSEMBLY —————————————

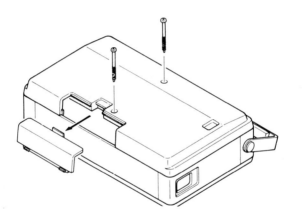

CABINET (FRONT) DISASSEMBLY ———————————

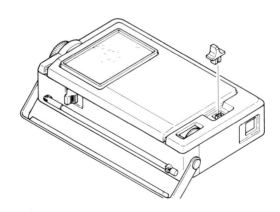

Alignment

M.W. Band: Band Selector Switch in M.W. Position

Step	Connection of signal generator	Input signal frequency	Dial setting of radio	Connection of output meter	Adjust	Remarks
1	Loop antenna	470kHz	Lowest end	Across speaker	I.F.T. T304, 305, 306	Adjust for maximum
2	Same	505kHz	Lowest end	Same	Osc. coil L105	Same
3	Same	1650kHz	Highest end	Same	Osc. trim. VCT4	Same
4	Same	600kHz	600kHz	Same	Ant. coil L104a	Same
5	Same	1400kHz	1400kHz	Same	Ant. trim. CT3	Same

Repeat steps 2 to 5 to obtain maximum sensitivity.

L.W. Band: Band Selector Switch in L.W. Position

Step	Connection of signal generator	Input signal frequency	Dial setting of radio	Connection of output meter	Adjust	Remarks
1	Loop antenna	145kHz	Lowest end	Across speaker	Osc. coil L106	Adjust for maximum
2	Same	365kHz	Highest end	Same	Osc. trim. CT2	Same
3	Same	160kHz	160kHz	Same	Ant. coil L104b	Same
4	Same	340kHz	340kHz	Same	Ant. trim. CT1	Same

Repeat steps 1 to 4 to obtain maximum sensitivity.

F.M. Band: Band Selector Switch in F.M. Position

Step	Connection of signal generator	Input signal frequency	Dial setting of radio	Connection of meter or oscilloscope	Adjust	Remarks
1	Connect sweep marker generator to TP1, TP2	10.7MHz	Lowest end	Connect osc. input cable through network to R308, ground	I.F.T. T301, 302	Adjust for maximum sensitivity with symmetrical curve
2	Same	10.7MHz	Lowest end	Connect osc. input cable through network to R311, ground	I.F.T. T303	Adjust for symmetrical 'S' curve
3	Same	87.0MHz	Lowest end	Connect V.T.V.M. across speaker	Osc. coil L103	Adjust for maximum
4	Same	109.0MHz	Highest end	Same	Osc. trimmer VCT-2	Same
5	Same	90MHz	90MHz	Same	R.F. coil L101	Same
6	Same	106MHz	106MHz	Same	R.F. trimmer VCT-1	Same

Repeat steps 3 to 6 to obtain maximum sensitivity.

SANYO

292mm

R287

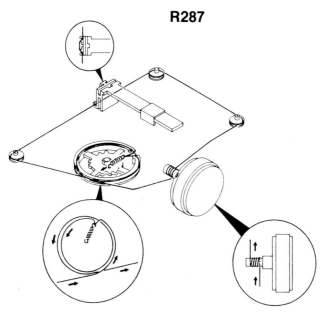

(R287) DRIVE CORD—MODEL RP7160

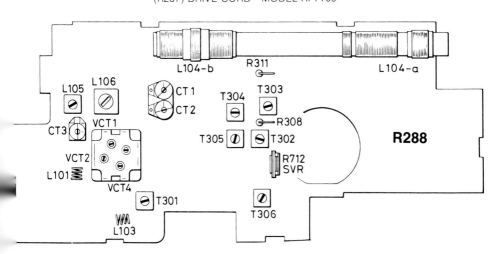

(R288) ALIGNMENT ADJUSTMENTS—MODEL RP7160

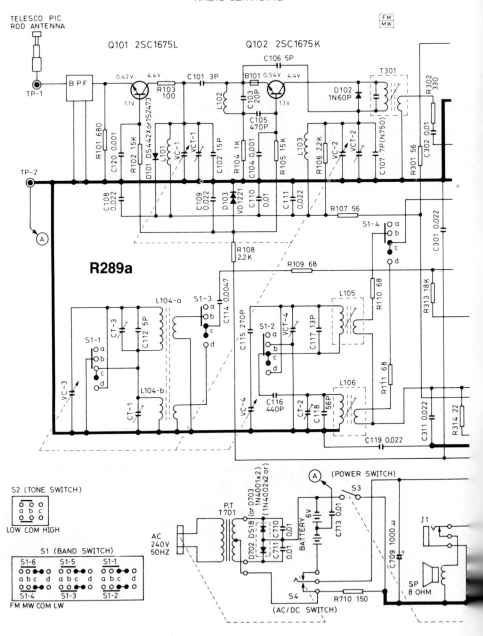

(R289a) CIRCUIT DIAGRAM—MODEL RP7160 *(PART)*

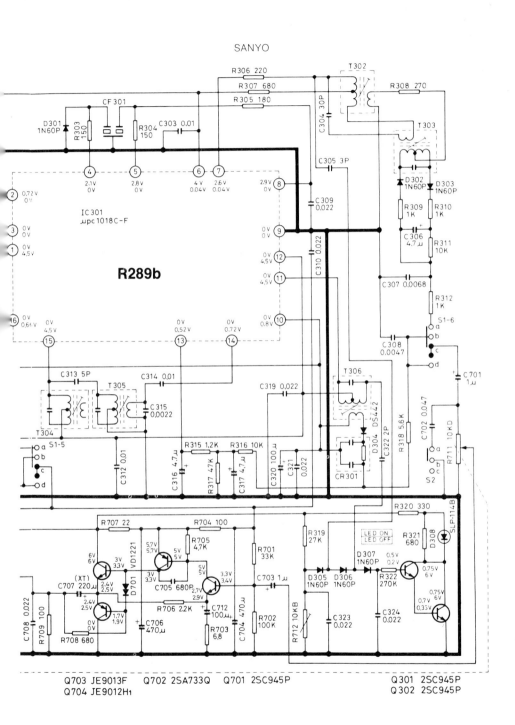

Q703 JE9013F   Q702 2SA733Q   Q701 2SC945P   Q301 2SC945P
Q704 JE9012H₁   Q302 2SC945P

(R289b) CIRCUIT DIAGRAM—MODEL RP7160 *(CONTINUED)*

General Description: A 2-waveband A.M./F.M. portable radio receiver operating from mains or battery supplies. A socket is provided for the connection of an earphone.

Mains Supply: 240 volts, 50/60Hz.

Battery: 6 volts (4×HP7).

Wavebands: M.W. 525-1605kHz; F.M. 87.6-108MHz.

Loudspeaker: 8 ohms impedance.

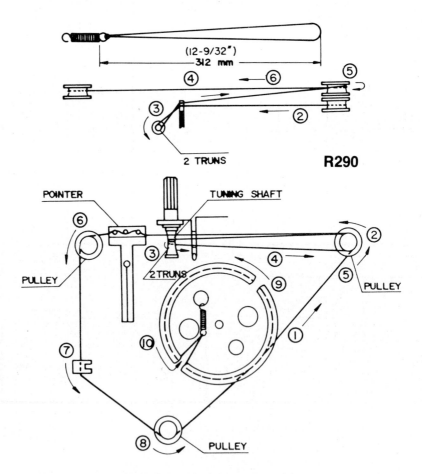

(R290) DRIVE CORD—MODEL FX-214

A.M. Alignment:

Set the band selector switch (SW2) at 'AM' position.

Step	Test stage	Signal generator		Receiver		
		Connection to receiver	Input signal frequency	Dial setting	Remarks	Adjustment
1	I.F.	Connect signal generator through a 10K ohm dummy to the antenna tuning capacitor. Ground lead to the test point TP2	Exactly 455kHz 1kHz, 30%, A.M. modulated)	High end of dial (minimum capacity)	Adjust for maximum output on speaker voice coil lugs	T4 T5 T6
2	Band coverage	Use radiation loop. Loop of several turns of wire, or place generator lead close to receiver for adequate signal pick-up. Connect generator output to one end of this wire.	Exactly 510kHz (1kHz, 30%, A.M. modulated)	Low end of dial (maximum capacity)	Same as step 1	L8
3		Same as step 2	Exactly 1650kHz (1kHz, 30%, A.M. modulated)	High end of dial (minimum capacity)	Same as step 1	TC4
4		Same as step 2	Exactly 600kHz (1kHz, 30%, A.M. modulated)	600kHz	Same as step 1	L7
5		Same as step 2	Exactly 1400kHz (1kHz, 30%, A.M. modulated)	1400kHz	Same as step 1	TC3
6	Repeat steps 2, 3, 4 and 5 until no further improvement can be made					

A.M. Alignment by using Broadcasting Station (if generator is not available)

Step	Test stage	Dial pointer setting	Indicator	Remarks	Adjustment
1	I.F.	Tune to maximum broadcasting signal around 1600kHz. Then rotate set slightly away from the maximum signal direction Repeat until no further improvement can be made	Output meter (V.T.V.M.) across voice coil	Adjust for maximum output	T4 T5 T6
2	Tracking	Tune to maximum broadcasting signal around 600kHz. Then rotate set slightly away from the maximum signal direction.	Same as step 1	Slide and adjust antenna winding for maximum output (See Note A)	Antenna coil L7
		Tune to maximum broadcasting signal around 1400kHz. Then rotate set slightly away from the maximum signal direction. Repeat until no further improvement can be made	Same as step 1	Same as step 1	Antenna trimmer TC3

F.M. Alignment:

Set the band selector switch (SW2) at 'F.M.' position.

Step	Test stage	Signal generator		Receiver		
		Connection to receiver	Input signal frequency	Dial setting	Remarks	Adjustment
1	I.F.	Connect signal generator through a 5pF capacitor to test point TP3. Connect generator ground lead to the chassis ground	Exactly 10.7MHz (1kHz, 30%, F.M. modulated)	High end of dial (minimum capacity)	Connect V.T.V.M. between test point TP4 and TP7 (chassis ground)	De-tune T3. Tune T1 and T2 for maximum indication
2	Ratio detector	Same as step 1	Exactly 10.7MHz (unmodulated)	Same as step 1	Connect V.T.V.M. (0.1 volts range D.C. scale) between test point TP5 and TP7 (chassis ground)	Adjust the T3 for 0 volt on V.T.V.M. Positive or negative reading will be obtained on either side of the correct setting
3	Band coverage	Connect signal generator through a dummy, including output impedance of signal generator to the F.M. antenna. (Refer to Fig. 2). Ground lead of generator connected to the receiver chassis.	Exactly 87.1MHz (1kHz, 30%, F.M. modulated)	Low end of dial (maximum capacity)	Adjust for maximum output on speaker voice coil lugs. Connect V.T.V.M. across the voice coil lugs	L5, L6
4		Same as step 3	Exactly 109MHz (1kHz, 30%, F.M. modulated)	High end of dial (minimum capacity)	Same as step 3	TC2
5	Tracking	Same as step 3	Exactly 88MHz (1kHz, 30%, F.M. modulated)	88MHz	Same as step 3	L3, L4
6		Same as step 3	Exactly 108MHz (1kHz, 30%, F.M. modulated)	108MHz	Same as step 3	TC1
7	Repeat steps 2, 3, 4 and 5 until no further improvements can be made.					

648

F.M. I.F. Alignment by using Broadcasting Station (if generator is not available)

Step	Test stage	Dial pointer setting	Indicator	Remarks	Adjustment
1	I.F.	Tune to maximum any broadcasting signal	Connect V.T.V.M. to point TP4 and ground (TP7). Adjust antenna for the weakest signal as possible, while still retaining a positive indication on V.T.V.M.	Adjust for maximum indication	T1 T2
		Repeat until no further improvement can be made			
2	Ratio detector	Tune to maximum any broadcasting signal	Output meter across voice coil	Adjust for maximum output	T3
		Set the pointer to low end of dial	Same as above	Adjust for minimum rushing noise	T3
		Repeat until no further improvement of maximum output and minimum rushing noise can be made			

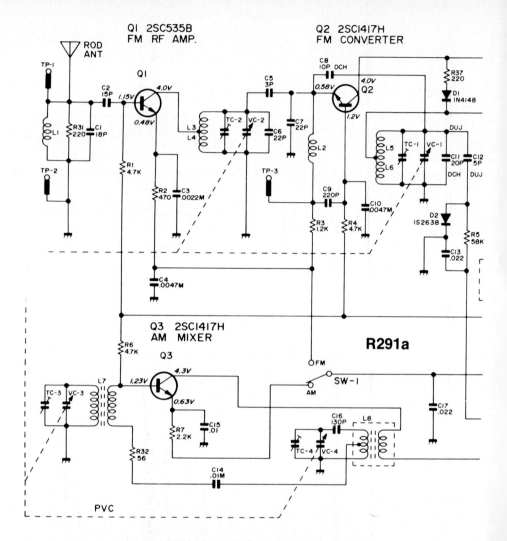

(R291a) CIRCUIT DIAGRAM—MODEL FX-214 *(PART)*

(R291b) CIRCUIT DIAGRAM—MODEL FX-214 (PART)

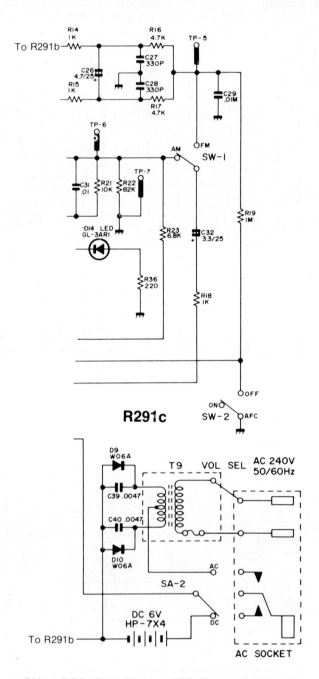

R291c

(R291c) CIRCUIT DIAGRAM—MODEL FX-214 *(CONTINUED)*

SHARP   Model FY-315

General Description: A 3-waveband A.M./F.M. portable pocket radio receiver operating from mains or battery supplies. A socket is provided for the connection of an earphone.

Mains Supply: 240 volts, 50/60Hz.

Battery: 6 volts (4×HP7).

Wavebands: L.W. 150-285kHz; M.W. 520-1620kHz; F.M. 87.6-108MHz.

Loudspeaker: 8 ohms impedance.

Alignment

A.M. Alignment (M.W. L.W.)

Step	Band	Test stage	Signal generator		Receiver		
			Connection to receiver	Input signal frequency	Dial setting	Remarks	Adjustment
1	M.W.	I.F.	Connect signal generator through a 10K ohm resistor to the antenna turning capacitor. Ground lead to the receiver chassis	Exactly 455kHz, (400Hz, 30%, A.M. modulated)	Tuning gang fully open (minimum capacity)	Adjust for maximum output on speaker voice coil lugs	T101, T102, T103
2	M.W.	Band coverage	Use radiating loop. Loop of several turns of wire, or place generator lead close to receiver for adequate signal pick-up. Connect generator output to one end of this wire	Exactly 510kHz (400Hz, 30%, A.M. modulated)	Tuning gang fully closed (maximum capacity)	Adjust for maximum output on speaker voice coil lugs	Adjust the M.W. oscillator coil (L103)
3	M.W.	Band coverage	Same as step 2	Exactly 1650kHz (400Hz, 30%, A.M. modulated)	Tuning gang fully open (minimum capacity)	Same as step 2	Adjust the M.W. oscillator trimmer (TC103)
4	M.W.	Tracking	Same as step 2	Exactly 600kHz (400Hz, 30%, A.M. modulated)	600kHz	Same as step 2	Adjust the M.W. antenna coil (L101) (Note A)
5	M.W.	Tracking	Same as step 2	Exactly 1400kHz (400Hz, 30%, A.M. modulated)	1400kHz	Same as step 2	Adjust the M.W. antenna trimmer (TC101) (Note A)
6	M.W.		Repeat steps 2, 3, 4 and 5 until no further improvement can be made				
7	L.W.	Band coverage	Same as step 2	Exactly 145kHz (400Hz, 30%, A.M. modulated)	Tuning gang fully closed (maximum capacity)	Same as step 2	Adjust the L.W. oscillator coil (L104)
8	L.W.	Band coverage	Same as step 2	Exactly 295kHz (400Hz, 30%, A.M. modulated)	Tuning gang fully open (minimum capacity)	Same as step 2	Adjust the L.W. oscillator trimmer (TC104)
9	L.W.	Tracking	Same as step 2	Exactly 160kHz (400Hz, 30%, A.M. modulated)	160kHz	Same as step 2	Adjust the L.W. antenna coil (L102) (Note A)
10	L.W.	Tracking	Same as step 2	Exactly 260kHz (400Hz, 30%, A.M. modulated)	260kHz	Same as step 2	Adjust the L.W. antenna trimmer (TC102) (Note A)
11	L.W.		Repeat steps 7, 8, 9 and 10 until no further improvement can be made				

Note A: Check the alignment of the receiver antenna coil by bringing a piece of ferrite (such as a coil slug) near the antenna loop stick, then a piece of brass. If ferrite increases output, the loop requires more inductance. If brass increases output, the loop requires less inductance. Change inductance by sliding the bobbin toward the centre of the ferrite core to increase inductance, or away to decrease inductance.

F.M. Alignment

Step	Band	Test stage	Signal generator		Receiver		
			Connection to receiver	Input signal frequency	Dial setting	Remarks	Adjustment
1	F.M.	I.F.	Connect signal generator through a 5pF capacitor to test point TP3 Connect generator ground lead to the point TP1	Exactly 10.7MHz (400Hz, 30%, F.M. modulated)	Tuning gang fully closed (maximum capacity)	Connect V.T.V.M. between test point TP4 and chassis ground	De-tune T4 Tune T1, T2, T3 for maximum indication
2	F.M.	Ratio detector	Same as step 1	Exactly 10.7MHz (unmodulated)	Same as step 1	Same as step 1 See Note B	See Note B
3	F.M.	Band coverage	Connect signal generator through a 75 ohm resistor, including output impedance of signal generator to the telescopic rod antenna. Ground lead of generator connected to the receiver chassis	Exactly 87MHz (400Hz, 30%, F.M. modulated)	Tuning gang fully closed (maximum capacity)	Adjust for the maximum output speaker voice coil lugs	Adjust the F.M. oscillator coil (L7, L8)
4	F.M.	Band coverage	Same as step 3	Exactly 109MHz (400Hz, 30%, F.M. modulated)	Tuning gang fully open (minimum capacity)	Same as step 3	Adjust the F.M. oscillator trimmer (TC2)
5	F.M.	Tracking	Same as step 3	Exactly 88MHz (400Hz, 30%, F.M. modulated)	88MHz	Same as step 3	Adjust the F.M. R.F. coil (L4, L5)
6	F.M.	Tracking	Same as step 3	Exactly 108MHz (400Hz, 30%, F.M. modulated)	108MHz	Same as step 3	Adjust the F.M. R.F. trimmer (TC1)
7	F.M.	Repeat steps 3, 4, 5 and 6 until no further improvement can be made					

Note B:
(1). Connect V.T.V.M. (0.1 volts range D.C. scale) between test point TP5 and chassis ground.
(2). Adjust secondary of T4 for 0 volts reading on V.T.V.M.
(3). Change signal generator frequency 10.7MHz + 100kHz and −100kHz approximately.
(4). Adjust primary of T4 for balanced peaks. Peak separation should be approximately 200kHz.

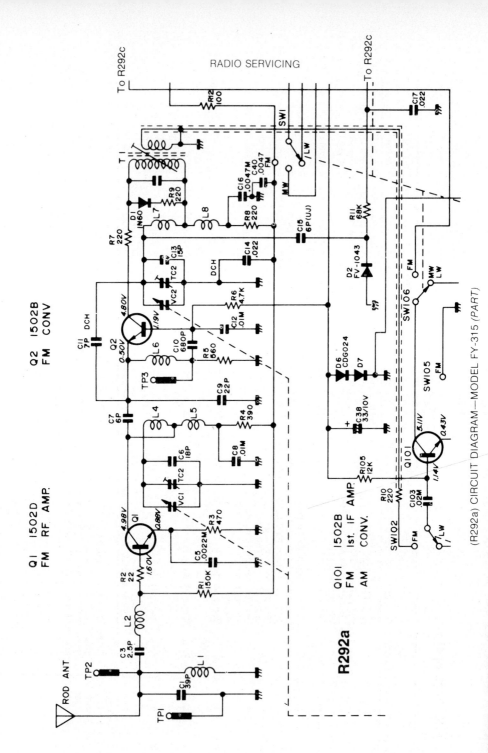

(R292a) CIRCUIT DIAGRAM—MODEL FY-315 *(PART)*

R292a

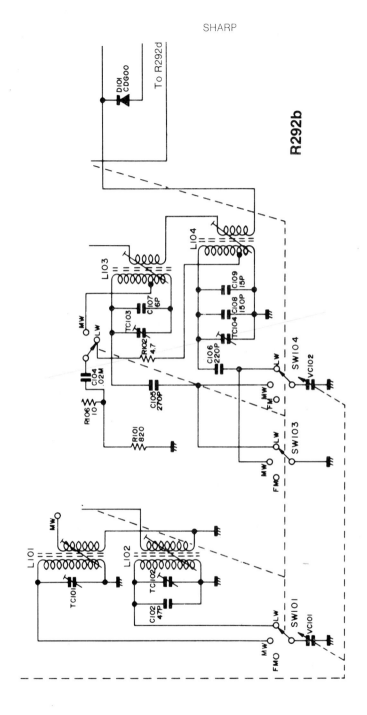

R292b

I. SW1,2 SW101~106 BAND SELECTOR SWITCH IS IN LW POSITION.

(R292b) CIRCUIT DIAGRAM—MODEL FY-315 (PART)

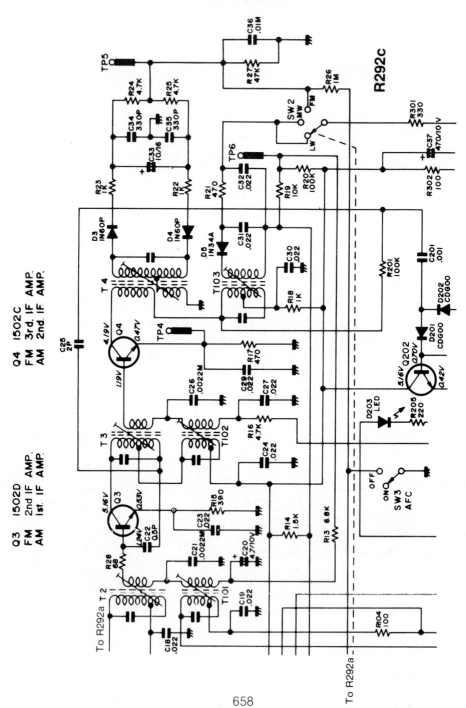

(R292c) CIRCUIT DIAGRAM—MODEL FY-315 *(PART)*

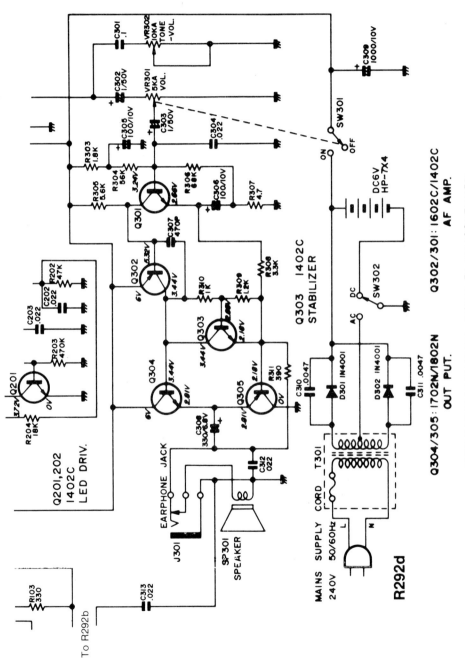

(R292d) CIRCUIT DIAGRAM—MODEL FY-315 (CONTINUED)

R292d

To R292b

General Description: A 3-waveband A.M./F.M. digital clock radio operating from mains supplies. Ceramic filters determine the I.F. bandwidth and the integrated circuit timer has alarm facilities.

Dial Cord Preparation

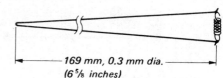

169 mm, 0.3 mm dia.
(6 ⁵⁄₈ inches)

Dial Cord Stringing

Turn TUNING Knob fully counterclockwise.
Proceed in the numerical order given.

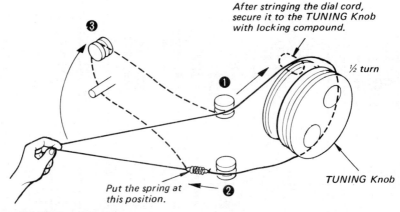

After stringing the dial cord, secure it to the TUNING Knob with locking compound.

½ turn

❸

❶

Put the spring at this position. ❷

TUNING Knob

Dial Pointer Setting

Turn TUNING Knob fully counterclockwise.

R293

Set the dial pointer to the dot on the dial scale as shown below.

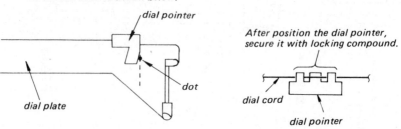

dial pointer

dot

dial plate

After position the dial pointer, secure it with locking compound.

dial cord

dial pointer

(R293) DRIVE CORD—MODEL ICF-C11L

Mains Supply: 240 volts, 50Hz.

Wavebands: L.W. 150-255kHz; M.W. 530-1605kHz; F.M. 87.5-108MHz.

Loudspeaker: 16 ohms impedance.

Alignment

A.M./I.F. 468kHz (TA1, TA2); M.W. 1680kHz (CT4), 520kHz (L5), 620kHz (L7-1), 1400kHz (CT3); L.W. 264kHz (CT6), 160kHz (L7-2), 240kHz (CT5).
F.M./I.F. 10.7MHz (TF1,2,3); R.F. 87.1MHz (L6), 108.5 (CT2), 87.1MHz (CT2, CT1).

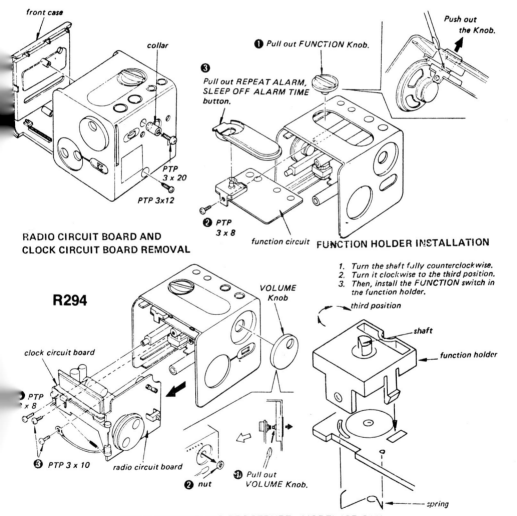

FRONT CASE REMOVAL

front case

collar

PTP 3 x 20

PTP 3x12

SWITCH CIRCUIT BOARD REMOVAL

❶ Pull out FUNCTION Knob.

❸ Pull out REPEAT ALARM, SLEEP OFF ALARM TIME button.

❷ PTP 3 x 8

function circuit

Push out the Knob.

RADIO CIRCUIT BOARD AND CLOCK CIRCUIT BOARD REMOVAL

R294

clock circuit board

❷ PTP x 8

❸ PTP 3 x 10   radio circuit board

❷ nut

❹ Pull out VOLUME Knob.

VOLUME Knob

FUNCTION HOLDER INSTALLATION

1. Turn the shaft fully counterclockwise.
2. Turn it clockwise to the third position.
3. Then, install the FUNCTION switch in the function holder.

third position

shaft

function holder

spring

(R294) DISMANTLING PROCEDURE—MODEL ICF-C11L

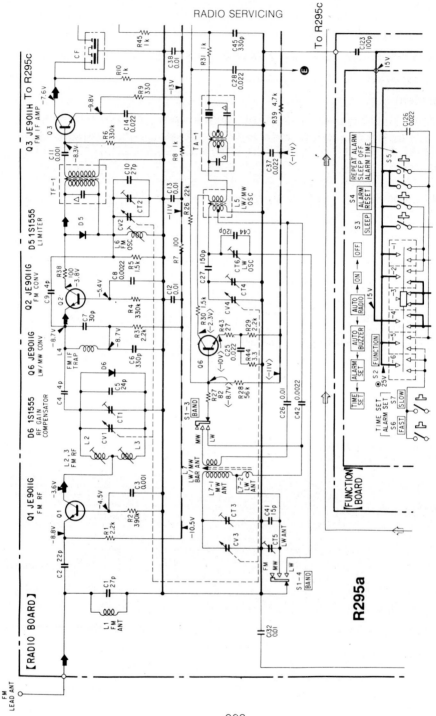

(R295a) CIRCUIT DIAGRAM—MODEL ICF-C11L (PART)

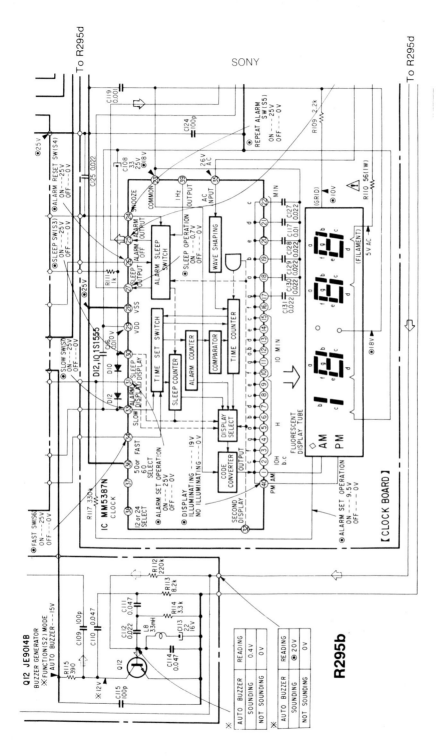

SONY

(R295b) CIRCUIT DIAGRAM—MODEL ICF-C11L *(PART)*

663

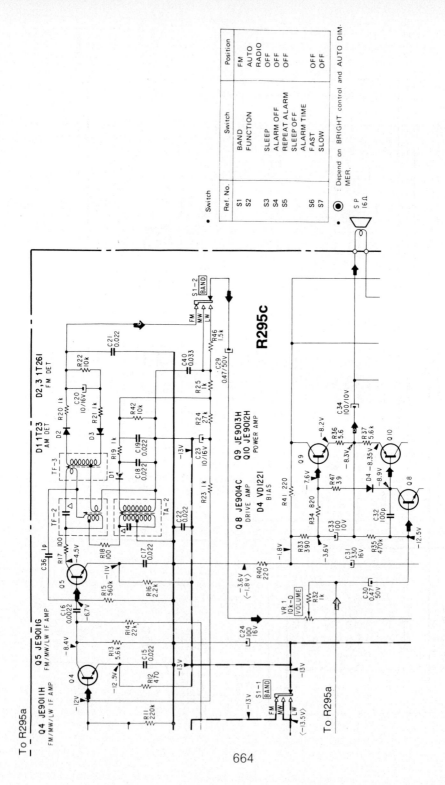

Ref. No.	Switch	Position
S1	BAND	FM
S2	FUNCTION	AUTO
		RADIO
S3	SLEEP	OFF
S4	ALARM OFF	OFF
S5	REPEAT ALARM	OFF
	SLEEP OFF	
	ALARM TIME	
S6	FAST	OFF
S7	SLOW	OFF

: Depend on BRIGHT control and AUTO DIM-MER.

(R295c) CIRCUIT DIAGRAM—MODEL ICF-C11L (PART)

664

SONY

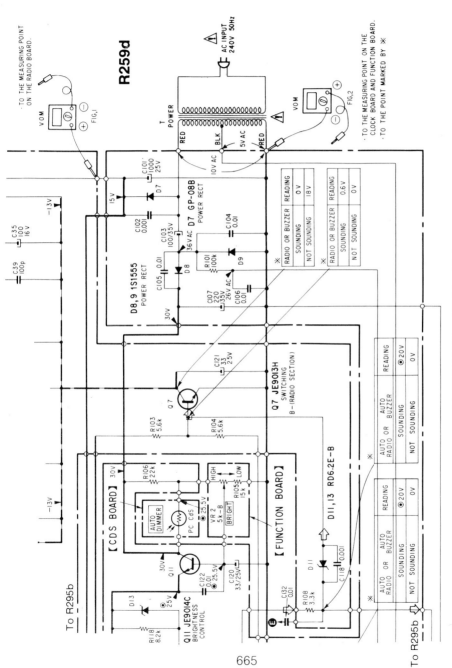

(R295d) CIRCUIT DIAGRAM—MODEL ICF-C11L (CONTINUED)

665

SONY   Model ICF-C22L

General Description: A 3-waveband A.M./F.M. digital clock radio operating from mains supplies. A 'back-up' battery is included to maintain clock accuracy in the case of mains failure. A socket is provided for the connection of an earphone.

Mains Supply: 240 volts, 50Hz.

Battery: 9 volts.

Wavebands: L.W. 150-255kHz; M.W. 530-1695kHz; F.M. 87.5-108MHz.

Loudspeaker: 8 ohms impedance.

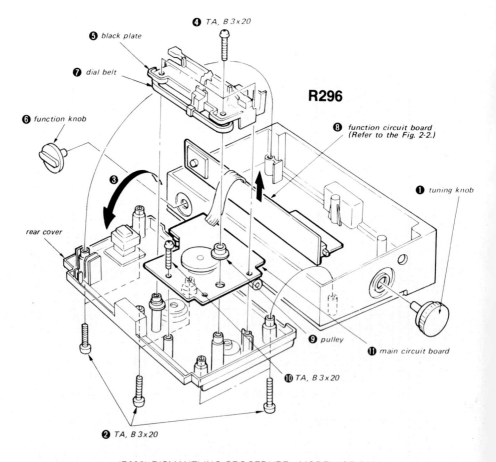

(R296) DISMANTLING PROCEDURE—MODEL ICF-C22L

Alignment

A.M./I.F. 468kHz (CFT); R.F. M.W. 1680kHz (CT4), 520kHz (L4), 1400kHz (CT3), 620kHz (L5-1); L.W. 264kHz (CT6), 240kHz (CT5), 160kHz (L5-2). F.M./I.F. 10.7MHz (T1,2,3); R.F. 87.5MHz (L1, L2), 108.5MHz (CT1, CT2).

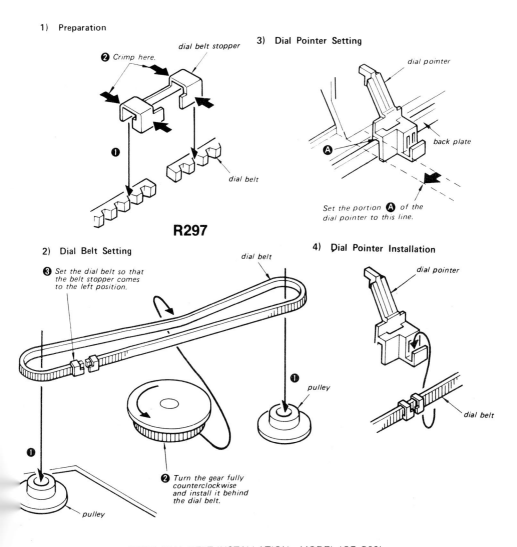

1) Preparation

dial belt stopper

❷ Crimp here.

❶

dial belt

3) Dial Pointer Setting

dial pointer

back plate

Ⓐ

Set the portion Ⓐ of the dial pointer to this line.

R297

2) Dial Belt Setting

❸ Set the dial belt so that the belt stopper comes to the left position.

dial belt

pulley

❶

❷ Turn the gear fully counterclockwise and install it behind the dial belt.

pulley

4) Dial Pointer Installation

dial pointer

dial belt

(R297) DIAL BELT INSTALLATION—MODEL ICF-C22L

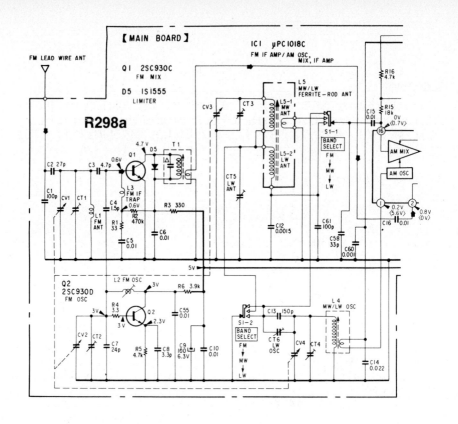

(R298a) CIRCUIT DIAGRAM—MODEL ICF-C22L *(PART)*

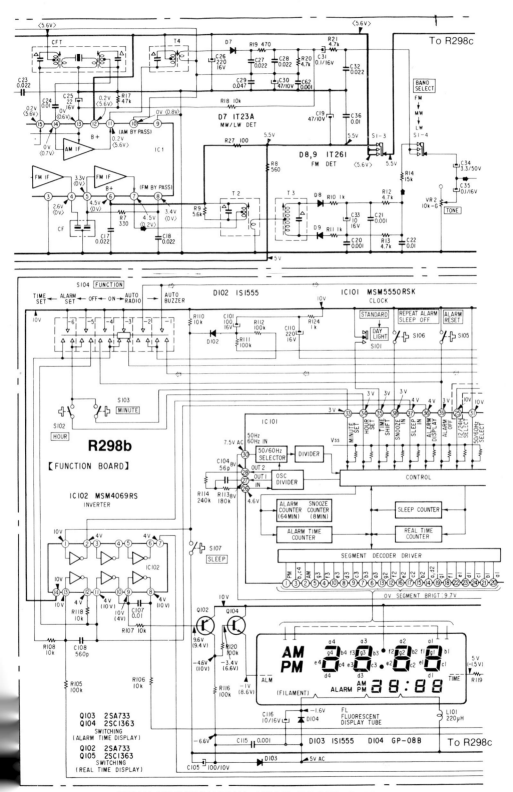

(R298b) CIRCUIT DIAGRAM—MODEL ICF-C22L *(PART)*

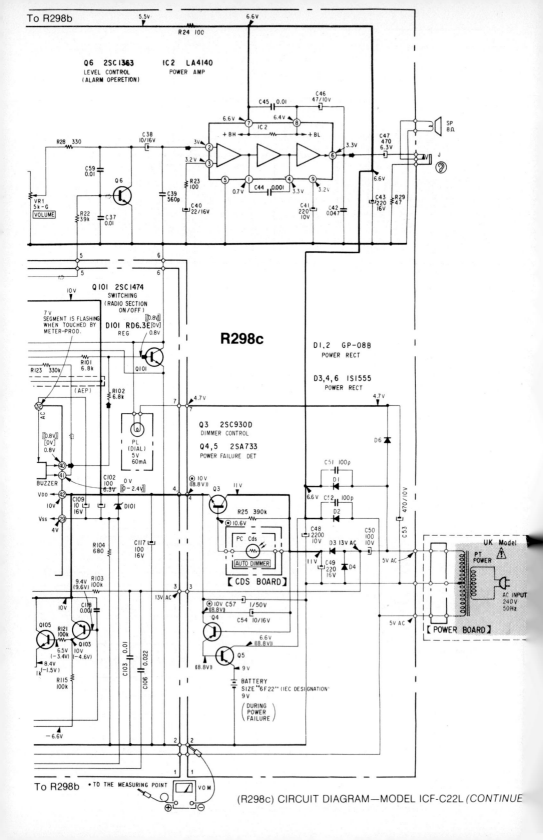

(R298c) CIRCUIT DIAGRAM—MODEL ICF-C22L *(CONTINUE*

SONY   Model ICF-C33L

General Description: A 3-waveband A.M./F.M. digital clock radio operating from mains supplies with stand-by battery in case of mains failure. A socket is provided for the connection of an earphone and the clock circuit offers alarm facilities.

Mains Supply: 240 volts, 50Hz.

Battery: 3 volts (2×1.5 volts).

Wavebands: L.W. 150-255kHz; M.W. 530-1605kHz; F.M. 87.5-108MHz.

Loudspeaker: 8 ohms impedance.

Rear Panel Assembly (See Fig. R299):

Rear Panel Installation: Remove Tone and Volume sliders from the rear panel.

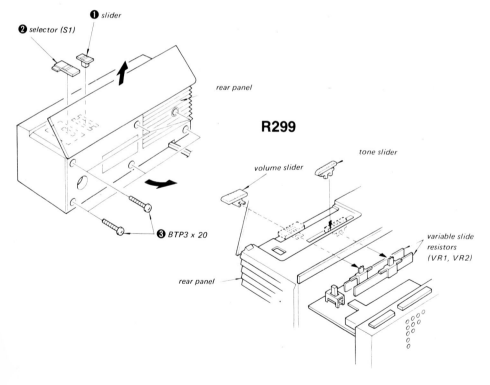

(R299) REAR PANEL ASSEMBLY—MODEL ICF-C33L

671

After installing the rear panel back to the set, install the Tone and Volume sliders.

Note: The mains transformer on this model is fitted with an overwind to provide 340 volts R.M.S. for the fluorescent light. Due care should be taken when servicing this section of the receiver.

Alignment

A.M./I.F. 468kHz (CFT); M.W. 520kHz (T2), 1680kHz (CT1-4), 1400kHz (CT1-3), 620kHz (L5); L.W. 264kHz (CT2), 240kHz (CT1), 145kHz (L7); F.M./I.F. 10.7MHz (T4, T1, T5); F.M./R.F. 87.5MHz (L3, L1), 108.5MHz (CT1-2, CT1-1).

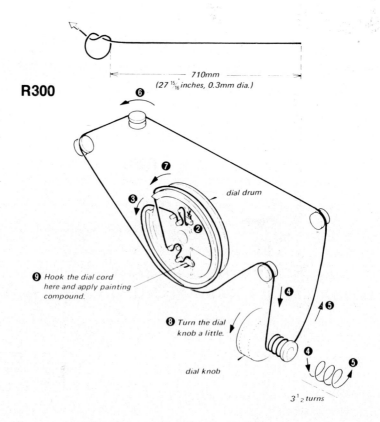

❶ *Turn the dial drum fully counterclockwise and hook the knob of the dial cord in* ❷.

R300

710mm
(27 $^{15}_{16}$ inches, 0.3mm dia.)

dial drum

❾ *Hook the dial cord here and apply painting compound.*

❽ *Turn the dial knob a little.*

dial knob

3 $^{1}_{2}$ turns

(R300) DRIVE CORD—MODEL ICF-C33L

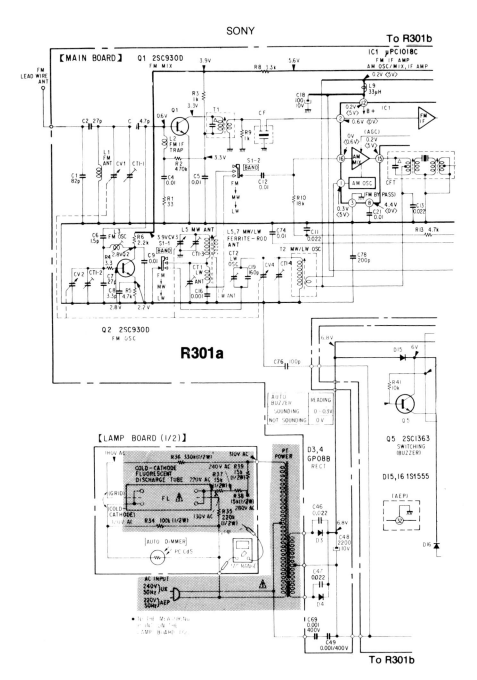

SONY

(R301a) CIRCUIT DIAGRAM—MODEL ICF-C33L *(PART)*

673

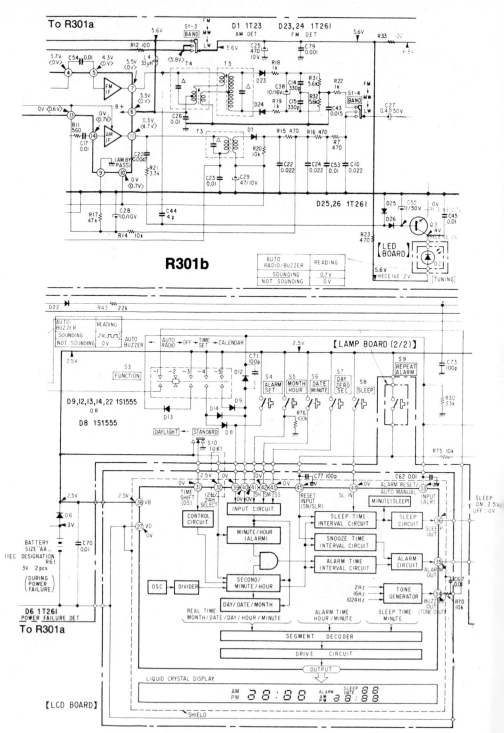

(R301b) CIRCUIT DIAGRAM—MODEL ICF-C33L *(PART)*

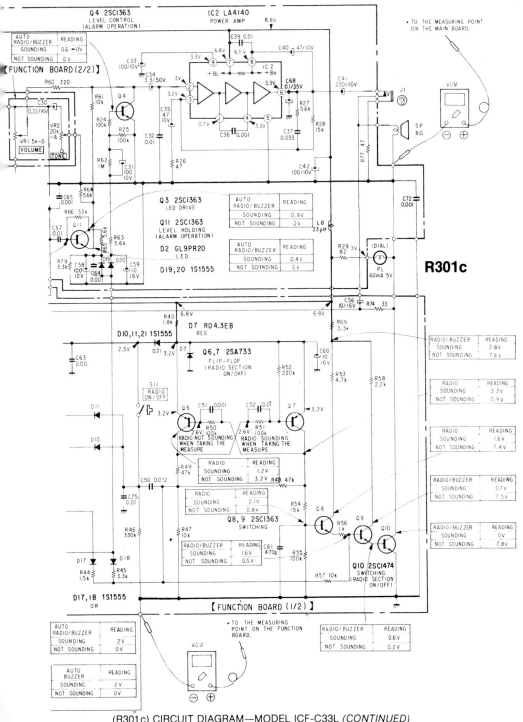

(R301c) CIRCUIT DIAGRAM—MODEL ICF-C33L *(CONTINUED)*

SONY   Model ICF-P2L

General Description: A 4-waveband A.M./F.M. portable radio receiver operating from battery supplies, external mains power unit or car battery unit. Sockets are provided for the connection of an earphone and stereo decoder unit.

Battery: 3 volts (2×1.5 volts).

Wavebands: L.W. 150-285kHz; M.W. 530-1605kHz; S.W. 5.9-18MHz; F.M. 87.5-108MHz.

Loudspeaker: 8 ohms impedance.

Dismantling: (See Fig. R302)

REAR CABINET REMOVAL

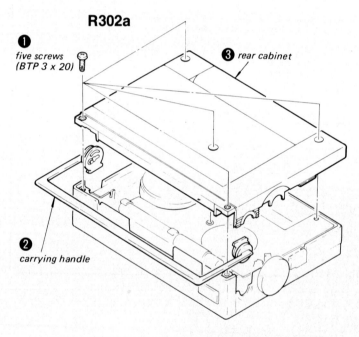

(R302a) DISMANTLING PROCEDURES—MODEL ICF-P2L

Note on Installation

Before starting to install the chassis to the front cabinet, install the POWER SAVE knob as shown.

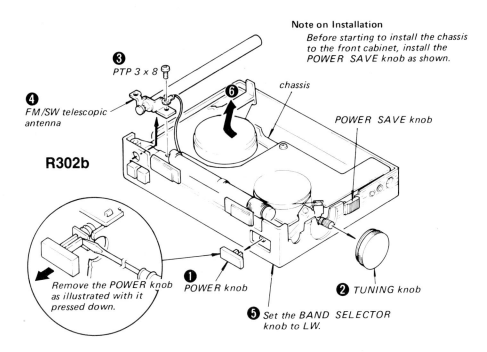

R302b

Remove the POWER knob as illustrated with it pressed down.

❸ PTP 3 x 8

❹ FM/SW telescopic antenna

❻ chassis

POWER SAVE knob

❶ POWER knob

❷ TUNING knob

❺ Set the BAND SELECTOR knob to LW.

MAIN BOARD REMOVAL

R302c

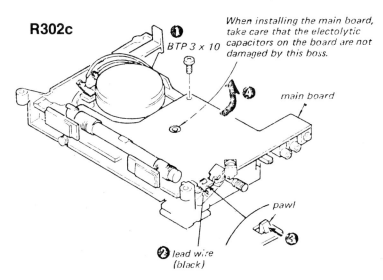

When installing the main board, take care that the electolytic capacitors on the board are not damaged by this boss.

❶ BTP 3 x 10

main board

pawl

❷ lead wire (black)

(R302b,c) DISMANTLING PROCEDURES—MODEL ICF-P2L

VOLUME BOARD REMOVAL

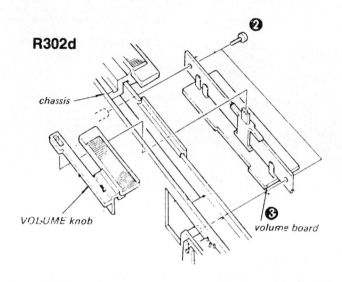

R302d

chassis

VOLUME knob

volume board

(R302d) DISMANTLING PROCEDURES—MODEL ICF-P2L

Drive Cord: (See Fig. R303)

Stringing: Turn the tuning-capacitor shaft fully clockwise, and set the dial drum as illustrated.

Follow the stringing procedure in the numerical order given.

Dial Pointer Installation: Turn the tuning shaft fully counter-clockwise, place the LED and the portion 'A' in a line and apply suitable locking compound to the dial cord as shown.

Alignment

A.M./I.F. 468kHz (IFT1); L.W. 145kHz (L11), 300kHz (CT5), 260kHz (CT7), 170kHz (L13); M.W. 520kHz (L7), 1680kHz (CT6), 1400kHz (CT8), 620kHz (L6); S.W. 18.4MHz (CT1, CT2), 5.8MHz (L5, L4); F.M./I.F. (IFT2, IFT3); F.M./R.F. 108.5MHz (CT3, CT4), 86.5MHz (L3, L2).

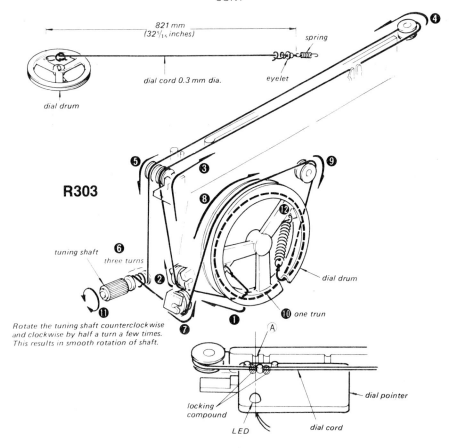

R303

821 mm
(32⁵/₁₆ inches)

dial cord 0.3 mm dia.

dial drum

spring

eyelet

tuning shaft

three turns

dial drum

one trun

Rotate the tuning shaft counterclockwise
and clockwise by half a turn a few times.
This results in smooth rotation of shaft.

locking
compound

dial pointer

LED

dial cord

(R303) DRIVE CORD—MODEL ICF-P2L

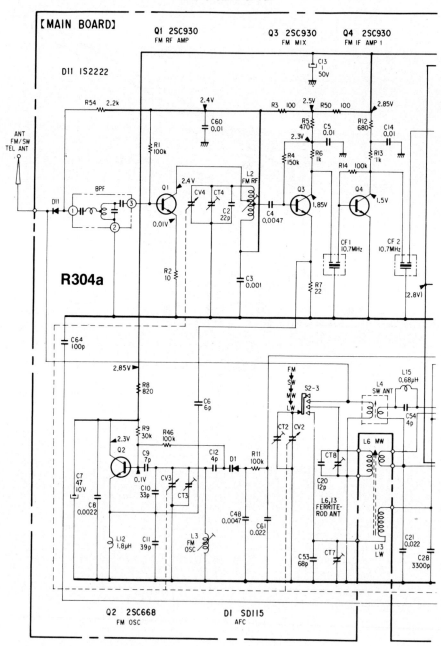

(R304a) CIRCUIT DIAGRAM—MODEL ICF-P2L *(PART)*

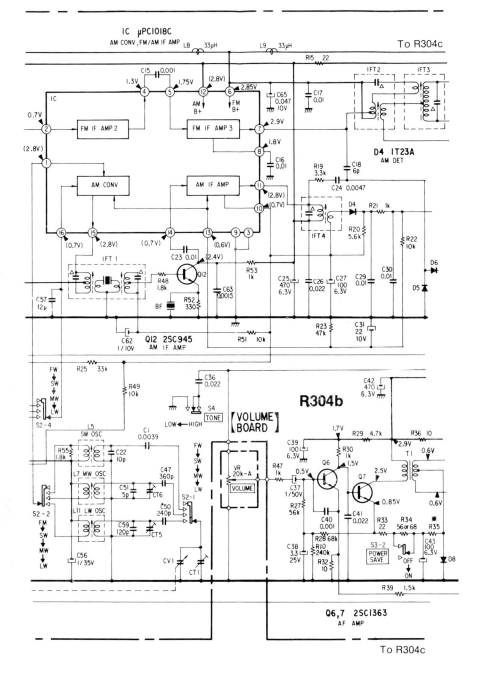

(R304b) CIRCUIT DIAGRAM—MODEL ICF-P2L *(PART)*

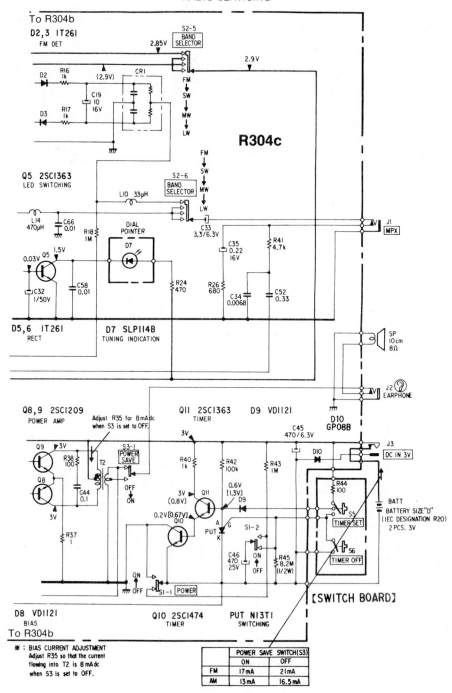

(R304c) CIRCUIT DIAGRAM—MODEL ICF-P2L *(CONTINUED)*

SONY   Model TFM-7720L

General Description: A 3-waveband A.M./F.M. portable radio receiver operating from mains or battery supplies. A socket is provided for the connection of an earphone.

Mains Supply: 240 volts, 50Hz.

Battery: 3 volts (2×1.5 volts).

Wavebands: L.W. 150-255kHz; M.W. 530-1605kHz; F.M. 87.5-108MHz.

Loudspeaker: 8 ohms impedance.

Drive Cord (See Fig. R305): Turn the tuning capacitor fully anti-clockwise and string the drive cord in the order given. Slide the dial pointer to the 'O' position as shown.

Alignment

A.M./I.F. 468kHz (TA-1, TA-2); L.W. 160kHz (L7, CT5), 1400kHz (CT3); M.W. 265kHz (CT6), 520kHz (L6), 1680kHz (CT4); F.M./I.F. 10.7MHz (TF-3, TF-2, TF-1); F.M./R.F. 87.1MHz (L2, L3, L5), 108.5MHz (CT-1, CT-2).

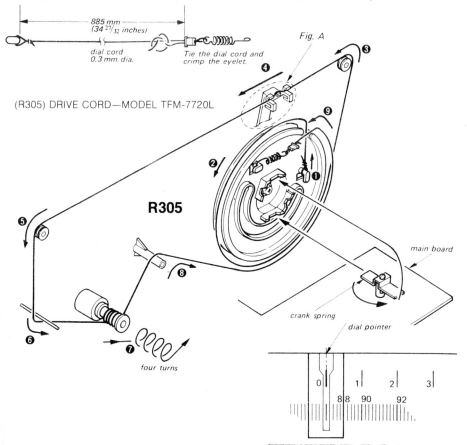

(R305) DRIVE CORD—MODEL TFM-7720L

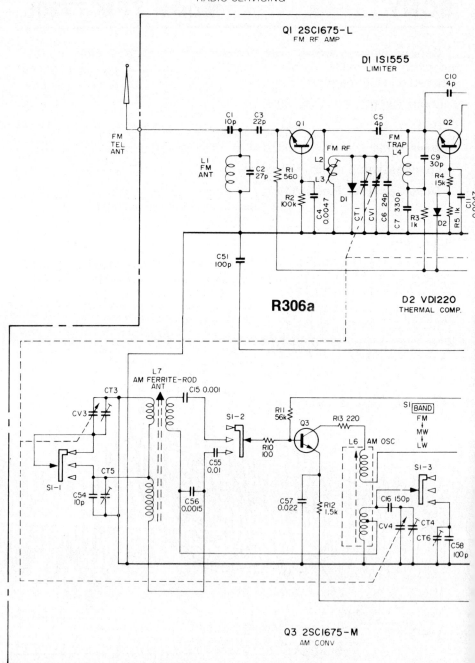

(R306a) CIRCUIT DIAGRAM—MODEL TFM-7720L *(PART)*

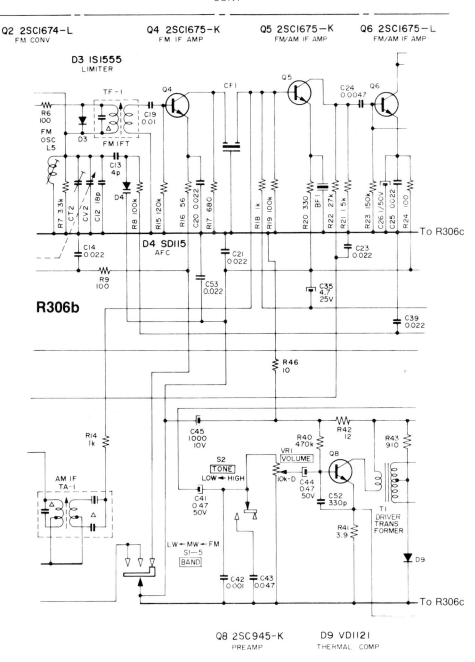

(R306b) CIRCUIT DIAGRAM—MODEL TFM-7720L *(PART)*

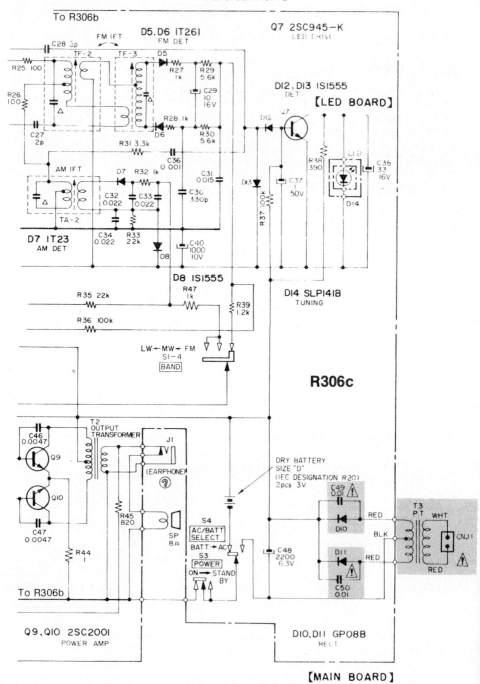

R306c

(R306b) CIRCUIT DIAGRAM—MODEL TFM-7720L *(CONTINUED)*

SONY   Model TR-4150L

General Description: A 2-waveband pocket portable radio receiver operating from battery supplies. A socket is provided for the connection of an earphone.

Battery: 3 volts (2×1.5 volts).

Wavebands: L.W. 150-255kHz; M.W. 530-1605kHz.

Loudspeaker: 8 ohms impedance.

Service Note: When re-installing the printed circuit board, set the band selector switch to Long Wave to avoid damaging the knob. (See Fig. R307.)

Alignment

I.F. 468kHz (IFT1,2,3); M.W. 1400kHz (CT1-1), 620kHz (L1), 1680kHz (CT1-2), 520kHz (L3); L.W. 260kHz (CT4).

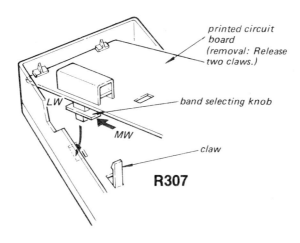

(R307) P.C.B. INSTALLATION—MODEL TR-4150L

687

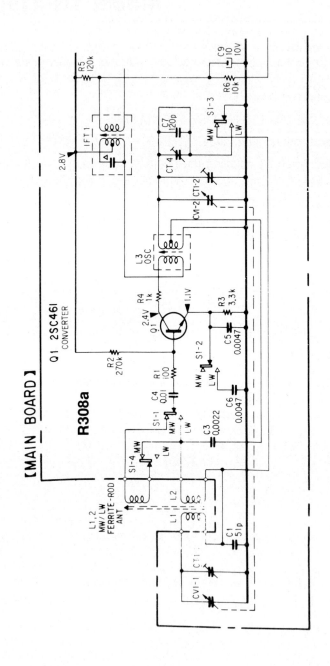

(R308a) CIRCUIT DIAGRAM—MODEL TR-4150L (*PART*)

SONY

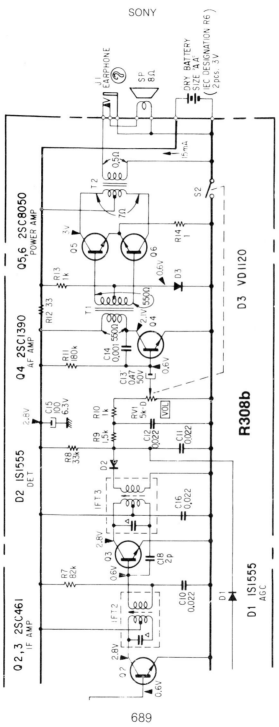

(R308b) CIRCUIT DIAGRAM—MODEL TR-4150L (CONTINUED)

689

ULTRA Model 6192

General Description: A 2-waveband A.M./F.M. portable radio receiver operating from mains or battery supplies. A socket is provided for the connection of an earphone.

Mains Supply: 240 volts, 50Hz.

Battery: 6 volts (4×SP7).

Wavebands: M.W. 520-1620kHz; F.M. 88-104MHz.

Loudspeaker: 8 ohms impedance.

Alignment

Tuning indication can be obtained by connecting a 20,000Ω/V meter, set to the 10V A.C. range, across the loudspeaker terminals.

Throughout alignment the signal input to the receiver should be adjusted, as necessary, so that the meter reading does not exceed 0.63V (50mW).

A.M. I.F. Circuits: Set the Tuning gang fully anti-clockwise (minimum frequency position on tuning scale), the Volume control to maximum and the Waveband switch to M.W. Inject 470kHz, 400Hz (30% modulated) signals via a loop loosely coupled to the ferrite rod aerial.

Adjust L13, L10 and L9 for maximum meter reading.

Repeat adjustments until no further improvement results.

A.M. R.F. Circuits: Inject signals via a loop loosely coupled to the ferrite rod aerial.

Range	Inject	Set cursor to	Adjust for max.
	510kHz	Fully left position (Minimum frequency)	L7
M.W.	1620kHz	Fully right position (Maximum frequency)	C21
	600kHz	600kHz	L6*
	1400kHz	1400kHz	C18

*Adjust by sliding coil along ferrite rod.

Repeat adjustments until no further improvement results.

F.M. I.F. Circuits: Alignment is best obtained using a wobbulator with V.H.F./F.M. and A.M. facilities and a display unit. Connect wobbulator, terminated with a 75 ohm resistor to TP2 and earth line. Unscrew fully core of L12 and switch to V.H.F./F.M.

Inject 10.7MHz (25kHz deviation) signals and adjust L5, L8 and L11 so as to obtain a good shaped 'V' curve with the 10.7MHz marker at the peak of the curve. Finally adjust L12 to present an 'S' curve with the 10.7MHz marker at the centre of the 'S' curve.

Repeat adjustments until no further improvement results.

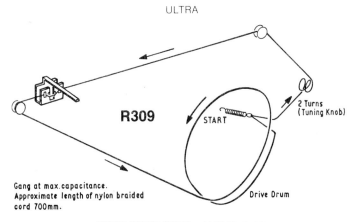

(R309) DRIVE CORD—MODEL 6192

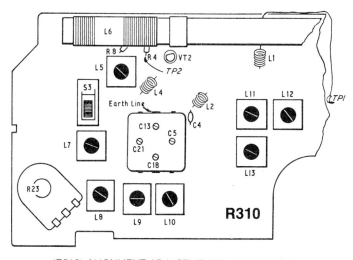

(R310) ALIGNMENT ADJUSTMENTS—MODEL 6192

F.M. R.F. Circuits: With receiver switched to V.H.F./F.M., Volume control at maximum and meter connected to loudspeaker terminals, connect a standard V.H.F. signal generator terminated 75 ohms to TP1 and earth line.

Range	Inject	Cursor position	Adjust for max.
V.H.F./F.M.	87.5MHz	Fully left	L4*
	104.6MHz	Fully right	C1
	88MHz	88MHz	L2*
	104MHz	104MHz	C5

*Adjust by slightly opening or closing coil turns.

Repeat adjustments until no further improvement results.

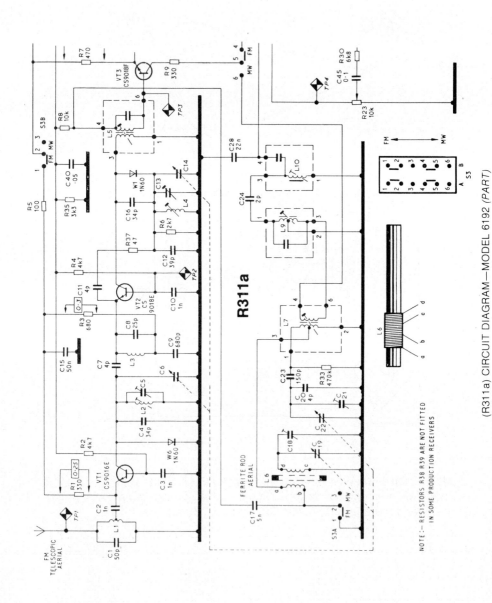

(R311a) CIRCUIT DIAGRAM—MODEL 6192 (PART)

NOTE:— RESISTORS R38 R39 ARE NOT FITTED IN SOME PRODUCTION RECEIVERS

R311a

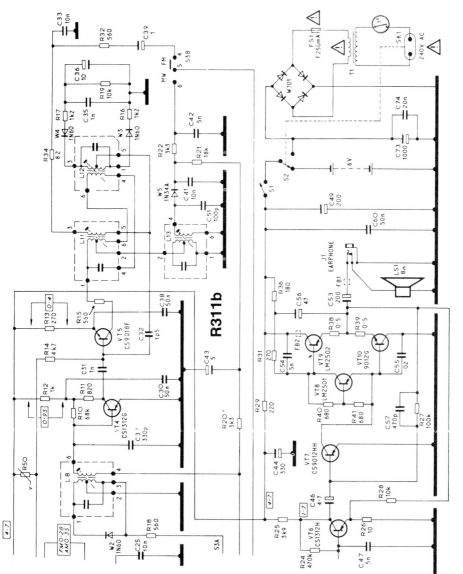

(R311b) CIRCUIT DIAGRAM—MODEL 6192 (CONTINUED)

ULTRA   # Model 6194

General Description: A 4-waveband A.M./F.M. portable radio receiver operating from mains or battery supplies. Automatic changeover from battery to mains occurs when the mains lead is plugged into the socket at the rear of the set. Sockets are provided for the connection of a tape recorder and earphone.

Mains Supply: 240 volts, 50Hz.

Battery: 9 volts (6×SP11).

Wavebands: L.W. 150-260kHz; M.W. 530-1600kHz; S.W. 5.95-6.25MHz; F.M. 88-108MHz.

Loudspeaker: 8 ohms impedance.

Circuit Diagram Notes:

R312 and R331 may be 120kΩ and 470kΩ respectively.

D.C. voltage measurements shown in rectangles were taken relative to the positive chassis line (except where otherwise indicated) under quiescent conditions with a 20,000Ω/voltmeter.

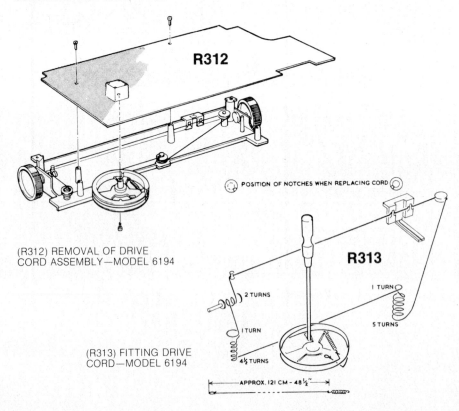

R312

POSITION OF NOTCHES WHEN REPLACING CORD

(R312) REMOVAL OF DRIVE
CORD ASSEMBLY—MODEL 6194

R313

2 TURNS

1 TURN

1 TURN

5 TURNS

(R313) FITTING DRIVE
CORD—MODEL 6194

4½ TURNS

APPROX. 121 CM - 48½"

Alignment

Tuning indication can best be obtained by connecting a 20,000 Ω/V meter, set to the 10V A.C. range, across the loudspeaker terminals.

Throughput alignment the signal input to the receiver should be adjusted as necessary, so that the meter reading does not exceed 0.63V (50mW).

A.M. I.F. Circuits: Set the Tuning capacitor to the minimum frequency end of the Tuning scale (gang fully closed), the Volume control to maximum and depress the Waveband selector switch M.W. Inject 470kHz signals via a loop of wire loosely coiled around the ferrite rod aerial.

Adjust L311, L312 and L313 for maximum meter reading.

Repeat adjustments until no further improvement results.

A.M. R.F. Circuits: Connect test equipment as for I.F. adjustments and proceed as follows:

Range	Inject	Cursor position	Adjust for max.
	510kHz	Fully right (max. capacitance)	L317
M.W.	1640kHz	Fully left (min. capacitance)	C362
	600kHz	600kHz	L314*
	1400kHz	1400kHz	C356
	145kHz	Fully right (max. capacitance)	C366
L.W.	170kHz	170kHz	L315*
	250kHz	250kHz	C360

*Adjust by sliding coil along ferrite rod.

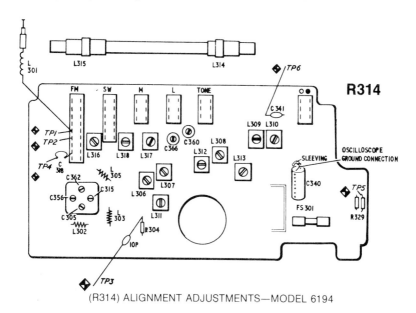

(R314) ALIGNMENT ADJUSTMENTS—MODEL 6194

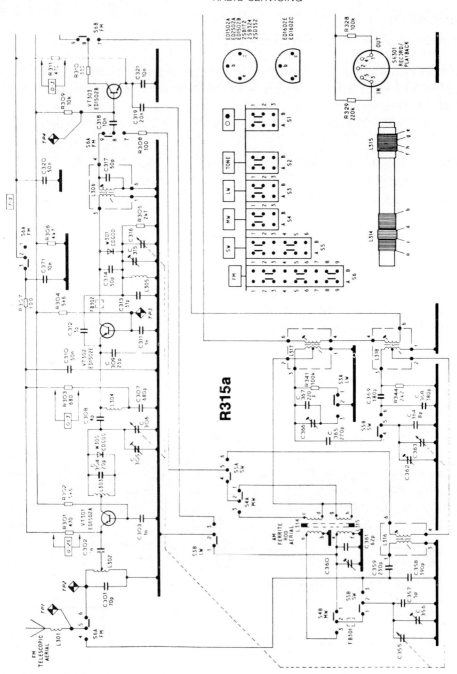

(R315a) CIRCUIT DIAGRAM—MODEL 6194 (PART)

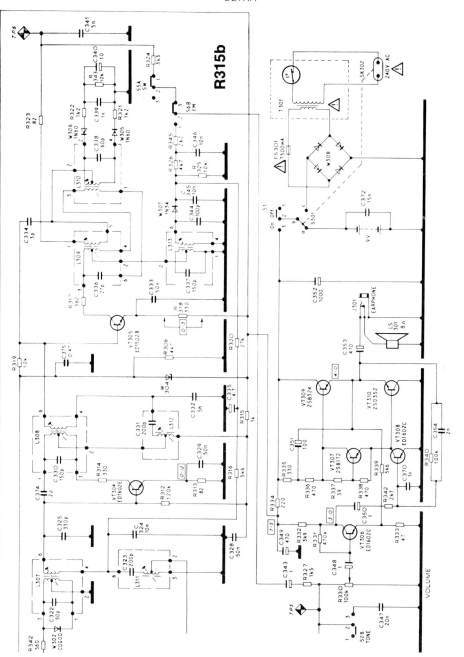

R315b

(R315b) CIRCUIT DIAGRAM—MODEL 6194 *(CONTINUED)*

S.W. R.F. Circuits: Connect Signal generator via a 5pF series capacitor between TP1 and Oscilloscope ground connection and Oscilloscope between TP5 and Oscilloscope ground connection.

Range	Inject	Cursor position	Adjust for max.
S.W.	5.9MHz	Fully right	L318
	6.05MHz	6.65MHz	L316

Repeat adjustments until no further improvement results.

F.M. I.F. Circuits: Alignment is best obtained using a wobbulator terminated with V.H.F./F.M. facilities and a display unit.

Connect the Oscilloscope to TP6, taking care to disconnect C341 (0.005μF capacitor). Connect the wobbulator via a 0.001μF capacitor to TP3. Set the cursor to the extreme left position (min. capacitance), select V.H.F./F.M. on the wobbulator and depress the selector switch F.M. on the radio.

Inject 10.7MHz signals into the circuit and adjust L306, L307, L308 and L309 to obtain a good 'V' curve with the 10.7MHz marker at the peak.

Transfer the Oscilloscope to TP4 and ground via C340 (10μF capacitor).

Adjust L310 to obtain a symmetrical 'S' curve with the 10.7MHz marker at the centre of the 'S' curve.

Repeat the adjustments until no further improvement results.

F.M. R.F. Circuits: With the receiver switched to F.M., the Volume control at maximum and the meter connected across the Loudspeaker terminals, connect a standard F.M. signal generator terminated with 75 ohms, to TP2 and ground connection.

Range	Inject	Cursor position	Adjust for max.
	87.5MHz	Fully right (max. capacitance)	L305*
F.M.	108.5MHz	Fully left (min. capacitance)	C315
	90MHz	90MHz	L303*
	106MHz	106MHz	C305

*Adjust by slightly opening or closing coil turns.

Repeat adjustments until no further improvement results.

VEGA   Model 206

General Description: An A.M. portable radio receiver powered by internal batteries and covering Long, Medium and six bandspread Short wavebands. A socket is provided for the connection of an earphone.

Battery: 9 volts (6×U2).

Quiescent Current: 12/14mA.

Wavebands: Long Wave;   150;   408kHz;
Medium Wave;   525;   1605kHz;
Short Wave 1;   2.0;   5.0MHz;
Short Wave 2;   5.0;   7.5MHz;
Short Wave 3;   9.3;   12.1MHz;
Short Wave 4;   15.1;   15.45MHz;
Short Wave 5;   17.7;   17.9MHz;
Short Wave 6;   21.45; 21.75MHz;

Dismantling

Remove 3 back screws.
Remove Tuning, Volume and Tone control knobs and telescopic Aerial top.
Remove 4 chassis retaining screws located at 4 corners of chassis.
Push telescopic Aerial inside cabinet and stand set up.
Gently remove chassis by holding battery compartment in the right-hand and the case handle in the left-hand. Do not attempt to pull chassis out straight as damage to the Tone control will result. Reverse procedure to assemble taking care to ease the Tone control and other spindle into cabinet first, also check that location of Dial light switch is correct.

Transistor Voltages:

	N423	MN40 or MN41	N423	N423	N422	N422	MN41
	T1	T2	T3	T4	T5	T6	T7
Collector	2.65V	5.3V	1.45V	2.4V	7.0V	5.0V	1.60V
Base	0.55V	3.3V	0.55V	0.75V	1.85V	1.45V	0.30V
Emitter	0.42V	3.1V	0.35V	0.55V	1.65V	1.20V	0.15V

	MN41	MN41	MN41
	T8	T9	T10
Collector	8.8V	9.0V	9.0V
Base	9.0V	0.13V	0.13V
Emitter	1.4V	0.015V	0.015V

Components:

Resistors

R1	6.8K	R13	560	R25	180	R37	560
R2	2.2K	R14	5.1K	R26	8.2K	R38	75
R3	2.7K	R15	10K	R27	15K	R39	820
R4	2.4K	R16	1K	R28	47K	R40	5
R5	75	R17	220	R29	2.7K	R41	220
R6	1.2K	R18	220	R30	1.8K	R42	1K
R7	27	R19	22K	R31	47	R43	2.7K
R8	390	R20	12K	R32	27K	R44	68
R9	8.2K	R21	100K	R33	1.5K	R45	5.1K
R10	6.8K	R22	390	R34	3.9K	R46	10K
R11	2.4K	R23	10K	R35	560	R47	560
R12	270	R24	15K	R36	120		

Capacitors

C1	36	C22	56	C43	68	C64	0.022
C2	360	C23	4-15	C44	180	C65	390
C3	20	C24	2200	C45	0.05	C66	0.01
C4	240	C25	15	C46	0.01	C67	20
C5	18	C26	4-15	C47	0.05	C68	50
C6	20	C27	360	C48	0.05	C69	10
C7	360	C28	5-20	C49	0.05	C70	390
C8	75	C29	8.2	C50	0.05	C71	0.05
C9	240	C30	6.2	C51	1000	C72	20
C10	9.1	C31	9-365	C52	12	C73	500
C11	270	C32	220	C53	1000	C74	0.01
C12	220	C33	5-20	C54	10	C75	0.01
C13	150	C34	43	C55	270	C76	0.05
C14	5-20	C35	82	C56	9.1	C77	390
C15	68	C36	68	C57	1000	C78	20
C16	150	C37	9-365	C58	12	C79	0.01
C17	82	C38	0.01	C59	1000	C80	500
C18	470	C39	0.05	C60	20	C81	3300
C19	5-20	C40	0.05	C61	0.033	C82	4700
C20	62	C41	1000	C62	20		
C21	300	C42	20	C63	0.05		

metric suffixes as applicable.

Alignment Instructions

For tuning the circuits of S.W. ranges an output cord of the standard-signal generator is connected to the Antenna jack A on the terminal block at the power pack. L.W. and M.W. ranges are tuned from the ferrite antenna. The generator output is connected via 80 resistor to the standard frame antenna (380×380mm made of 4mm dia copper wire). The distance from the frame to the middle of the ferrite antenna of the receiver, set perpendicularly to the frame planes, is 1m.

The tuning indicator is in all ranges to the graduated sections of the scale: on the lower tuning frequency—in the right-hand part and to the upper tuning-frequency—in the left-hand part.

The sequence of tuning—first heterodyne and then input, according to this table:

Coils L14, L15, L13 and L12 located on the ferrite rod are tuned in L.W. and M.W. ranges by moving them along the rod axis.

Voltage value of the generator at U out=0.7 shows the receiver sensitivity.

The image channel frequency should be higher than that of the main signal by 930kHz/s and have attenuation in 13m and 16m ranges—not less than 2-fold, in other S.W. ranges—not less than 4-fold, in M.W. not less than 20-fold and in L.W. ranges—not less than 100-fold. In order to check sensitivity in L.W. and M.W. ranges from the external antenna, the standard-signal generator is connected via artificial antenna to the antenna jack A.

Range	Tuning frequency	Tuned elements
S.W. 13m	21.4MHz/s	L1-3, 1-4
	21.8MHz/s	L1-1, 1-2
S.W. 16m	17.6MHz/s	L1-7, 1-8
	18.0MHz/s	L1-5, 1-6
S.W. 19m	15.0MHz/s	L1-11, 1-12
	15.5MHz/s	L1-9, 1-10
S.W. 25m	12.0MHz/s	L3-15, 3-16, C3-17
	9.4MHz/s	L3-13, 3-14
S.W. 41m	7.4MHz/s	L3-19, 3-20, C3-24
	5.1MHz/s	L3-17, 3-18
S.W. 60m	4.75MHz/s	L3-23, 3-24, C3-30
	2.1MHz/s	L3-21, 3-22
M.W.	560kHz/s	L26, 27, L13, 12
	1500kHz/s	C34, C15
L.W.	160kHz/s	L27, 29, L14, 15
	390kHz/s	C16

INSTALLATION OF DRIVE CORD ASSEMBLY

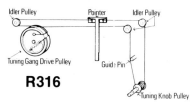

R316

(R316) DRIVE CORD—MODEL 206

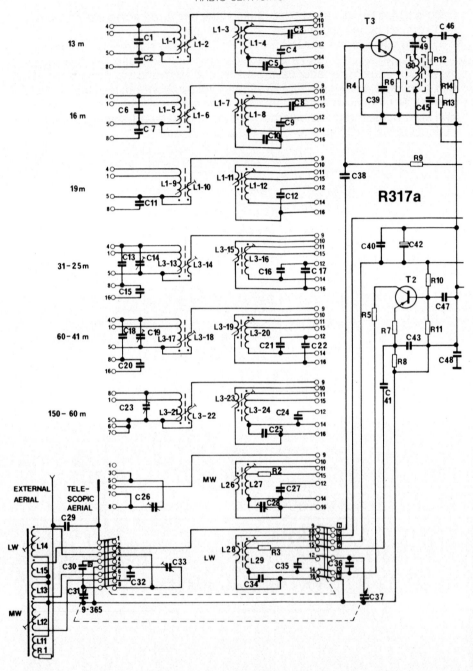

(R317a) CIRCUIT DIAGRAM—MODEL 206 *(PART)*

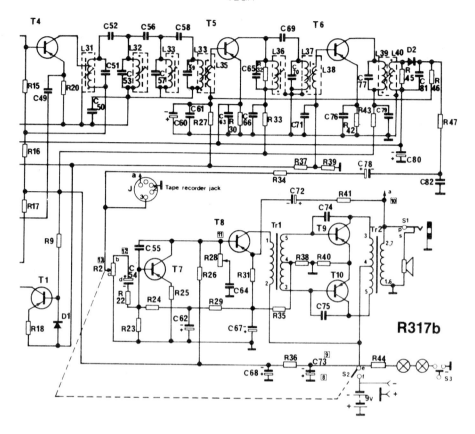

(R317b) CIRCUIT DIAGRAM—MODEL 206 *(CONTINUED)*

VEGA   Model 'Selena'

General Description: A portable multiband A.M./F.M. receiver, the Vega 'Selena' covers the Long and Medium wave broadcast bands, using an internal ferrite aerial, and five Shortwave bands, together with the V.H.F./F.M. broadcast band, using a 9-section telescopic aerial. Coils for each A.M. band are mounted on a rotating turret operated by a band selection control geared to an indicator. A slide switch operated by this control switches from the A.M. turret tuning unit to an independent F.M. tuner on V.H.F. and also provides the necessary I.F. and demodulator switching.

Rotary Volume, Treble and Bass controls, and a meter which combines the functions of signal strength and battery condition indication, are fitted. The 'Selena' can accept an external A.M. aerial, and earth. A.F. output to a tape-recorder, and to an earphone jack are provided.

Modular construction is used, the receiver being made up of five main assemblies: A.M. and F.M. tuning, a combined H.F. and I.F. amplifier, A.F. and audio output, and an internal mains power unit on mains/battery and export models.

Variations: The foregoing describes the basic 'Selena' receiver. Variations occur in facilities and in wavebands fitted, as follows.

Selena Type 1 is a battery-operated only receiver.

Selena Type 2 is a mains- or battery-operated receiver supplied with a separate two-core plug-in mains lead. (This is NOT suitable for the U.K.)

Selena Type 3 is a mains- or battery-operated receiver supplied with a separate three-core plug-in mains lead, with an internal fuse, for use in the U.K. and for export.

In addition, U.K. versions may differ from non-U.K. by incorporating a 75 to 180 metre (1.6 to 4MHz) marine band coil in the SW5 position.

Controls for the Selena therefore vary as follows:

Selena Type 3 has four push-button switches, A.F.C. (for use on F.M.), mains operation, receiver ON/OFF (red), and a Tuning dial and 'S' meter Lamp switch. All switches operate by pressing in. The internal mains power unit assembly U4 is fully wired from the mains input socket and out to the receiver circuits. A 500mA fuse is incorporated.

Selena Type 2 is as for Type 3 except that, because a two-core mains lead is supplied, there is no chassis earth connection. No fuse is fitted.

Selena Type 1 has the mains input leads to the receiver circuits internally disconnected, and the mains input socket blanked off. The mains operations switch is therefore inoperative, and no mains lead is supplied.

Mains Supplies: 127/220 volts, 50Hz.

Battery: 9 volts (6×HP2).

Fuse: 500mA quick blow.

Wavebands (in Turret Sequence):

18MHz version			U.K. marine band version
A.M.	L.W.	150-408kHz	150-408kHz
	M.W.	525-1605kHz	525-1605kHz
	S.W.5	5.97-7.3MHz	1.6-4.1MHz
	S.W.4	9.5-9.77MHz	5.97-7.3MHz
	S.W.3	11.7-12.1MHz	9.5-9.77MHz
	S.W.2	15.1-15.45MHz	11.7-12.1MHz
	S.W.1	17.7-17.9MHz	15.1-15.45MHz
F.M.	V.H.F.	87.5-108MHz	87.5-108MHz

Loudspeaker: 8 ohms impedance.

Dismantling

1. Disconnect mains lead (if fitted) and remove batteries.

2. Remove 4 screws from recesses in back cover panel. Remove waveband control knob.

3. Remove back cover complete with wood surround cabinet, leaving chassis attached to front panel.

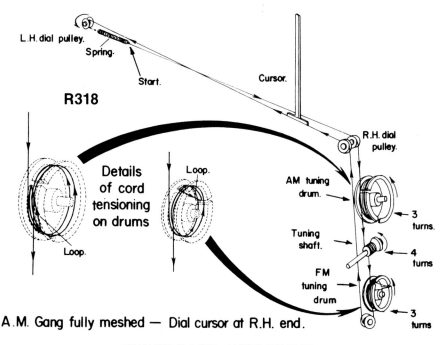

(R318) DRIVE CORD—MODEL 'SELENA'

4. To remove chassis from front panel:

(a). Remove Volume, Treble and Bass control knobs.

(b). Remove 4 hexagon distance pillars from chassis corners (these enter holes in chassis). *Note* earth lead from loudspeaker frame held by lower r.h. pillar.

(c). Ease out chassis to extent of leads. For complete removal, unsolder leads from telescopic aerial and loudspeaker.

5. Access to Modules:

(a). H.F./I.F. board: remove 3 screws.

(b). A.F./O.P. board: remove complete sub-chassis.

(c). V.H.F. tuner: remove sealed screw from bottom, ease off cover.

(d). Turret coil strips: prise open retaining springs at ends; ease strip out carefully.

(e). Mains power unit: remove H.F./I.F. board first, then remove complete unit less mains transformer.

Re-Assembly Note. Before tightening four distance pillars, check that dial cursor moves freely.

Component List

V.H.F. Tuner U1

Resistors

R301	1.5k ohms		R307	6.2k ohms
R302	4.3k ohms		R308	120 ohms
R303	3.9k ohms		R309	5.1k ohms
R304	120 ohms		R310	56k ohms
R305	3k ohms		R311	2.7k ohms
R306	15k ohms			

Capacitors

							Transistors	
C301	6.2uF	C308	6.2pF	C315	0.01uF		Tr301	TT313A
C302	30uF	C309	10pF	C316	56pF		Tr302	TT313A
C303	0.01uF	C310	510pF	C317	4.3pF			
C304	10uF	C311	0.047uF	C318	36pF		**Diodes**	
C305	0.01uF	C312	0.01uF	C319	6.2pF		D301	D20
C306	†	C313	4.3pF	C320	0.01uF		D302	D902
C307	2.2 to 16pF	C314	68pF	†not fitted			D303	D21

A.M. Turret Coil Strips (U2):

16m		**19m**		**25m**		**31m**	
C4	150pF	C4	130pF	C14	300pF	C14	270pF
C5	30pF	C5	43pF	C15	82pF	C15	82pF
C6	62pF	C6	62pF	C16	300pF	C16	270pF
C7	150pF	C7	150pF	C17	82pF	C17	82pF
C8	30pF	C8	43pF	C18	82pF	C18	82pF
C9	56pF	C9	56pF	C19	300pF	C19	300pF
C10	30pF	C10	43pF	C20	110pF	C20	110pF
C11	150pF	C11	150pF				
C12	43pF	C12	43pF				
C13	150pF	C13	100pF				

41 to 50m		50 to 75m		75 to 180m	
C28	68pF	C37	300pF	C47	4-15pF
C29	150pF	C38	47pF	C48	15pF
C30	4-15pF	C39	4-15pF	C49	36pF
C31	100pF	C40	300pF	C50	8-30pF
C32	160pF	C41	68pF	C51	1800pF
C33	8-30pF	C42	8-30pF	C52	10pF
C34	160pF	C43	270pF	C53	6-25pF
C35	110pF	C44	8.2pF		
C36	150pF	C45	62pF		

M.W.		L.W.	
C54	4-15pF	C59	4-15pF
C55	4-15pF	C60	8-30pF
C56	470pF	C61	220pF
C57	8-30pF	C63	82pF
R1	180 ohms	R3	150k ohms
R2	47 ohms	R4	180 ohms
		R5	100 ohms

H.F./I.F. Unit (U3):

Resistors

R11	82 ohms	R28	100 ohms	R45	180 ohms
R12	180 ohms	R29	560 ohms	R46	620 ohms
R14	330 ohms	R30	5.6k ohms	R47	3k ohms††
R15	1.2k ohms	R31	3.3k ohms	R48	100 ohms
R16	18k ohms	R32	1k ohms	R49	6.8k ohms
R17	470 ohms	R33	2k ohms	R50	5.6k ohms
R18	180k ohms	R34	2.4k ohms	R51	6.8k ohms
R19	1.2k ohms	R35	12k ohms	R52	4.7k ohms
R20	27k ohms	R36	4.7k ohms	R53	6.8k ohms
R21	56k ohms	R37	180 ohms	R54	5.6k ohms
R22	390 ohms	R38	680 ohms	R55	820 ohms
R23	270 ohms	R39	3.3k ohms	R56	6.8k ohms
R25	270 ohms	R41	220k ohms*	R57	150k ohms
R26	330 ohms	R42	1k ohms	*variable	
		R43	8.2k ohms	††in series with meter	

Capacitors

C68	0.01uF	C81	36pF	C95	0.01uF	C109	47pF
C69	36pF	C84	5.6pF	C96	0.033uF	C110	36pF
C70	36pF	C85	510pF	C97	10uF	C111	62pF
C71	36pF	C86	0.033uF	C98	22pF	C112	30pF
C72	0.033uF	C87	4.7pF	C99	36pF	C113	0.033uF
C73	0.033uF	C88	510pF	C100	36pF	C114	1000pF
C75	680pF	C89	510pF	C103	0.033uF	C115	3300pF
C76	3300pF	C90	5.6pF	C104	680pF	C116	270pF
C77	0.033uF	C91	0.015uF	C105	6800pF	C117	270pF
C78	0.033uF	C92	0.015uF	C106	50pF	C118	10uF
C79	0.015uF	C93	0.033uF	C107	0.033uF	C119	0.015uF
C80	36pF	C94	510pF	C108	2200pF		

Transistors		Diodes	
Tr1	TT322A	D6 to D9	D9B
Tr2	TT322B	D11	7FE-2a-K
Tr3	TT322A	D12	D103
Tr4	TT322A	D13	D9B
Tr5	TT322B	D14	D9B
Tr6	MN35	D15	D20
Tr7	MN39	D16	D20

Mains Power Supply Unit U4:

Resistors		Capacitors		Transistors		Diodes	
R6	510	C66	500uF	Tr8	N213A	D1 to D4	D226N
R7	3k	C140	0.01uF	Tr9	MN39	D5	D814A
R8	*						
R9	2.7k						

*variable

A.F./Output Unit (U5):

(the second column of co-ordinates refers to the later version p.c. board).

Resistors

R60	10k ohms	R70	6.8k ohms	R80	39 ohms
R61	33k ohms	R71	10k ohms*	R81	330 ohms††
R62	12k ohms	R72	3.9k ohms	R82	1k ohms*
R63	12k ohms	R73	3k ohms	R83	2.4k ohms
R64	430 ohms	R74	3.9k ohms	R84	47 ohms
R65	2.4k ohms	R75	5.6k ohms	R85	47 ohms
R66	620 ohms	R76	24k ohms	R86	1.5k ohms
R67	12k ohms	R77	33k ohms	R87	27 ohms
R68	3.3k ohms	R78	15k ohms*	*variable	
R69	10k ohms*	R79	3.9k ohms	††N.T.C. resistor	

Capacitors

				Transistors	
C123	0.1uF	C131	0.015uF	Tr10	MN40
C124	10uF	C132	0.022uF	Tr11	MN40
C125	20uF	C133	5uF	Tr12	MN40
C126	6800pF	C134	10uF	Tr13	KT315G
C127	20uF	C135	220pF	Tr14	MN40
C128	10uF	C136	50uF	Tr15	MN37
C129	0.022uF	C137	500uF	Tr16	N213G
C130	0.1uF	C138	500uF	Tr17	N213G

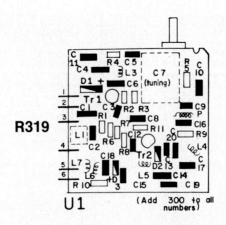

R319

(R319) COMPONENT LAYOUT (TUNER PANEL)—MODEL 'SELENA'

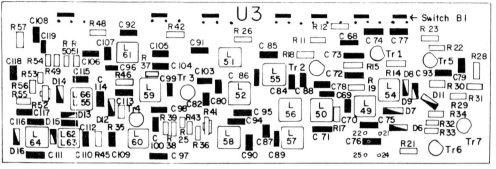

R320

(R320) COMPONENT LAYOUT (MAIN PANEL)—MODEL 'SELENA'

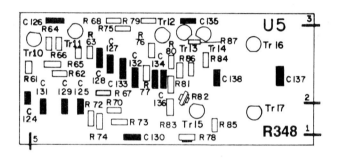

(R348) COMPONENT LAYOUT (A.F. STAGE)—MODEL 'SELENA'

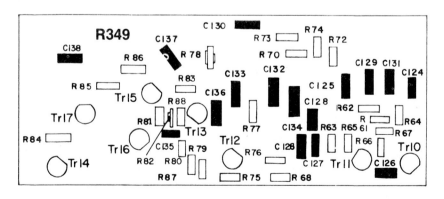

(R349) COMPONENT LAYOUT (A.F. STAGE–LATER VERSION)—MODEL 'SELENA'

Alignment

A.M. I.F. Stages:

1. Connect A.M. Signal Generator, tuned to 465kHz, level 2 to 3mV, via a 0.01uF capacitor to Tr4 base. Connect output meter across Loudspeaker terminals. Set Waveband selector to intermediate position between two A.M. bands, or Tune to no-signal point.

2. Adjust A.M. I.F.T.s L66, L65 for maximum.

3. Transfer Generator input to Tr3 base; adjust L61 for maximum.

4. Transfer Generator output to Tr2 base; adjust L58, L57, L56 and L55 (in that order) for maximum.

5. Transfer Generator input to input point 21 on U3 board: adjust L54, L53 for maximum.

R.F. Stages: Inject signals, level not more than 10mV, via 82 ohm resistor to inductive loop placed near ferrite Aerial or to telescopic Aerial input as appropriate. Adjustments given refer to coils and trimmers on turret coil strips, or to ferrite aerial coils.

L.W. (Select L.W.):

6. Tune Generator and Receiver to 150kHz (2000m); adjust L47 for maximum.

7. Re-tune Generator and Receiver to 408kHz (735m); re-adjust L47 for maximum.

8. Repeat steps 6 and 7 for optimum result.

9. Reduce signal input level to 600uV/m. Tune Signal Generator and receiver to 160kHz. Adjust L1/L2 (by sliding coils along ferrite rod) for maximum.

10. Re-tune Generator and Receiver to 390kHz; adjust Trimmer C59, C60 for maximum.

11. Repeat steps 9 and 10 for optimum result.

M.W. (Select M.W.):

12. Tune Generator and Receiver to 525kHz; adjust L43 for maximum.

13. Re-tune Generator and Receiver to 1605kHz; adjust trimmer C57 for maximum.

14. Repeat steps 12 and 13 for optimum result.

15. Reduce signal level to 300uV/m; tune Generator and Receiver to 560kHz, adjust L43, L41, and then L3, L4 (on ferrite rod) for maximum.

16. Re-tune Receiver and Generator to 1500kHz; adjust trimmers C55, C54 for maximum.

17. Repeat steps 15 and 16 for optimum result.

S.W.5 (75 to 180m Marine Band):

18. Tune Receiver to low frequency end of dial. Inject 1.5MHz signal (level not greater than 4mV) to telescopic Aerial input. Adjust L40, L39 for maximum.

19. Re-tune Receiver to high frequency end of dial, Generator to 4MHz. Adjust Trimmer C53 for maximum.

20. Repeat steps 18 and 19 for optimum result.

21. Tune Generator and Receiver to 2MHz; reduce input level to 100uV and adjust L38, L37, L36 and L35 for maximum.

22. Re-tune Generator and Receiver to 3.6MHz; adjust Trimmers C50 and C47 for maximum.

23. Repeat steps 21 and 22 for optimum result.

S.W.5 or S.W.4 (41 to 50m Band):

24. Tune Receiver to low frequency end of dial, Generator to 6.0MHz, level not more than 4mV. Adjust L28, L27 for maximum.

25. Re-tune Receiver to high frequency end of dial, Generator to 7MHz; adjust Trimmer C63 for maximum.

26. Repeat steps 24, 25 for optimum result.

27. Tune Receiver and Generator to 5.8MHz; adjust L26, L25, L24 and L23, then Trimmers C33, C30 for maximum.

S.W.4 or S.W.3 (30.7 to 31.6m):

28. Tune Receiver to 9.7MHz; inject 9.7MHz signal from Generator (level 50uV), adjust L14, L13, L12 and L11 for maximum.

S.W.3 or S.W.2 (24.8 to 25.6m):

29. Tune Receiver to 11.7MHz; inject 11.7MHz signal (level 50uV). Adjust L14, L13, L12 and L11 for maximum.

S.W.2 or S.W.1 (19.4 to 19.84m):

30. Tune Receiver to 15.4MHz; inject 15.4MHz signal, level 50uV. Adjust L8, L7, L6 and L5 for maximum.

S.W.1 (16.75 to 16.95m):

31. Tune Receiver to 17.8MHz; inject 17.8MHz signal, level 50uV. Adjust L8, L7, L6 and L5 for maximum.

F.M. (Preliminaries):

1. Select V.H.F.
2. Depress A.F.C. switch A.
3. Adjust pre-set R41 to give 0.7V on Tr3 emitter.

I.F. Stages:

1. Inject 10.7MHz signal from F.M. Generator, deviated ±15kHz, level not greater than 20mV, via a 0.01uF capacitor to Tr4 base. Connect output meter across Earphone jack. Adjust L3, L2 for 0.63V meter reading.

2. Remove modulation from signal. Connect D.C. voltmeter across C116 in H.F./I.F. unit U3. Adjust L64 for zero meter reading.

3. Apply 10.7MHz signal with 30 per cent A.M. content. Adjust pre-set R52 for output meter reading less than 150mV.

4. Transfer Signal input, with deviation restored, to Tr3 base; reduce level to 2mV. Adjust L60, L59 for 0.63V output meter reading.

5. Transfer Signal input to Tr2 base, reduce level to 0.2mV. Adjust L52, L51 for 0.63V output meter reading.

6. Transfer Signal input to Tr1 base, reduce level to 0.05mV. Adjust L50, L49 for 0.63V output meter reading.

R.F. Stages (Inject Signals to Telescopic Aerial Input): Increase deviation to ±22.5kHz. Coil, trimmer and resistor numbers refer to those in F.M tuner.

7. Tune Generator and Receiver to 88MHz; inject 0.05mV level signal and adjust L304 for 0.63V output meter reading.

8. Re-tune Generator and Receiver to 108MHz and adjust L304 for 0.63V meter reading.

9. Repeat steps 7 and 8 for optimum result.

10. Tune Generator and Receiver to 90MHz, reduce signal level to 0.012mV. Adjust L303, L302 and L301 for 0.63V output meter reading.

11. Re-tune Generator and Receiver to 100MHz. Adjust trimmer C304 for 0.63V output meter reading.

12. Repeat steps 10 and 11 for optimum result.

13. Tune Receiver to 90MHz. Inject 90MHz signal with 30 per cent A.M. content, modulated 1000Hz, de-tuned ±75kHz, level 12uV. Adjust pre-set R302 for 0.63V output meter reading.

14. A.F.C. check. Tune Receiver to 90MHz. Inject unmodulated 90MHz signal, level 36uV, and adjust L64 in H.F./I.F. unit U3 for 0.63V output meter reading.

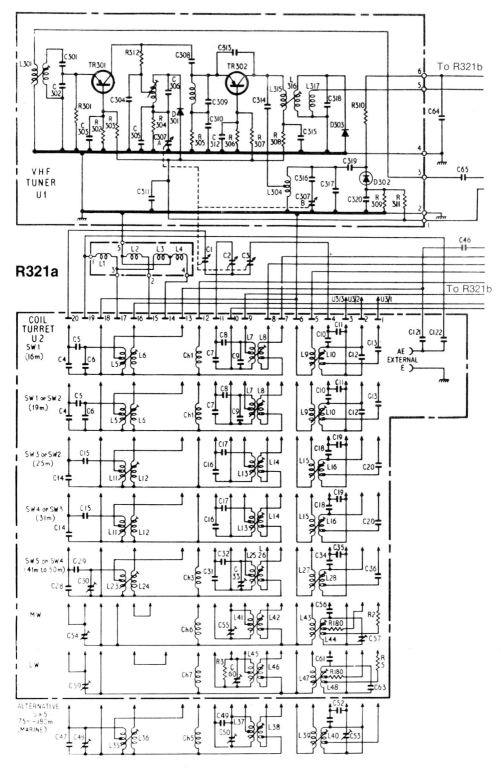

(R321a) CIRCUIT DIAGRAM—MODEL 'SELENA' (PART)

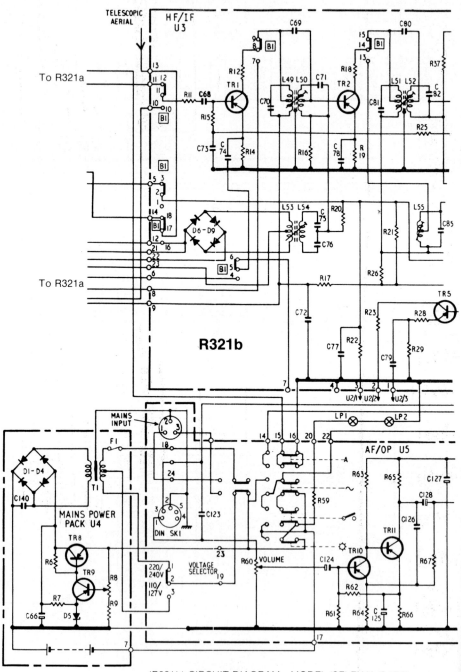

(R321b) CIRCUIT DIAGRAM—MODEL 'SELENA' *(PART)*

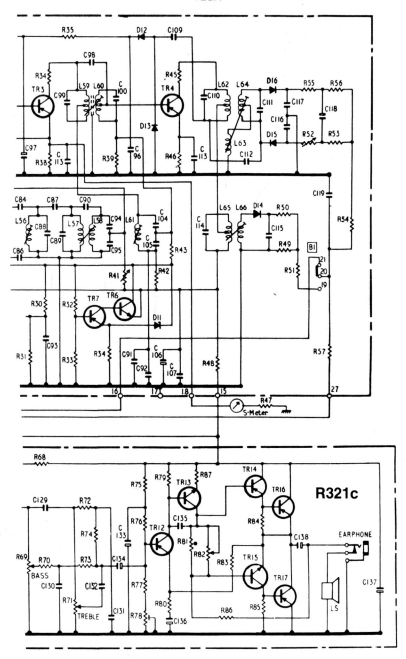

(R321c) CIRCUIT DIAGRAM—MODEL 'SELENA' *(CONTINUED)*

WALTHAM   Model W144

General Description: A portable A.M./F.M. radio receiver operating from mains or battery supplies. A socket is provided for the connection of an earphone.

Mains Supplies: 240 volts, 50Hz.

Batteries: 6 volts (4×1.5 volts).

Wavebands: L.W. 150-260kHz; M.W. 540-1600kHz; Aircraft 118-145MHz; F.M. 88-108MHz.

Loudspeaker: 8 ohms impedance.

Alignment: A.M./I.F. 465kHz (T11, T4, T7); M.W. 600kHz (T10, L9), 1600kHz (CMO, CMA); L.W. 165kHz (L10), 260kHz (CLO, CLA); F.M./I.F. 10.7MHz (T1,2,3,5,6); 88MHz (L4, L2), 108MHz (CAO, CT4).

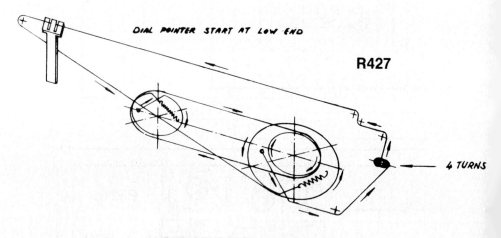

(R427) DRIVE CORD—MODEL W144

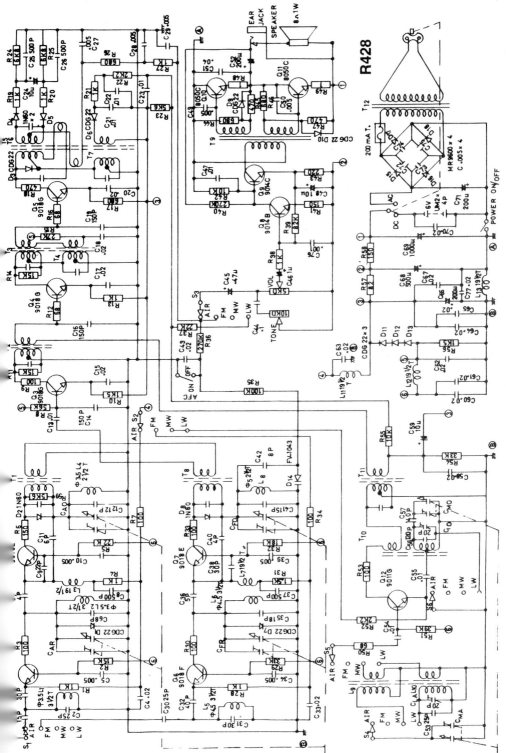

R428

(R428) CIRCUIT DIAGRAM—MODEL W144

WALTHAM   Model W146

General Description: A mains operated digital clock radio covering A.M. and F.M. wavebands. Pre-set alarm and switching facilities are incorporated.

Mains Supplies: 240 volts, 50Hz.

Wavebands: L.W. 148-255kHz; M.W. 535-1620kHz; F.M. 87.5-108MHz.

Alignment: A.M./I.F. 468kHz (T110, T104, T107); F.M./I.F. 10.7MHz (T101-6); M.W. 600kHz (T108, L105), 1600kHz (TC104, TC103); L.W. 150kHz (T109, L106), 255kHz (T106, TC105); F.M. 87.5MHz (L104, L102), 98MHz (L101), 108MHz (TC102, TC101).

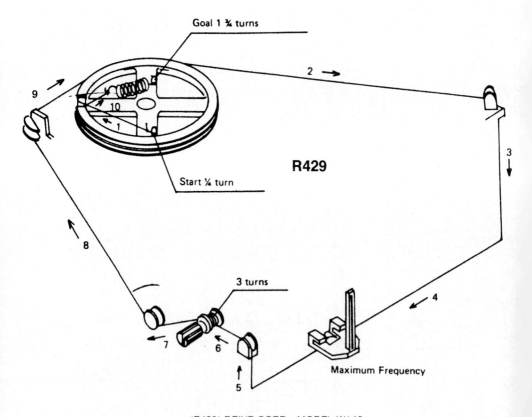

(R429) DRIVE CORD—MODEL W146

718

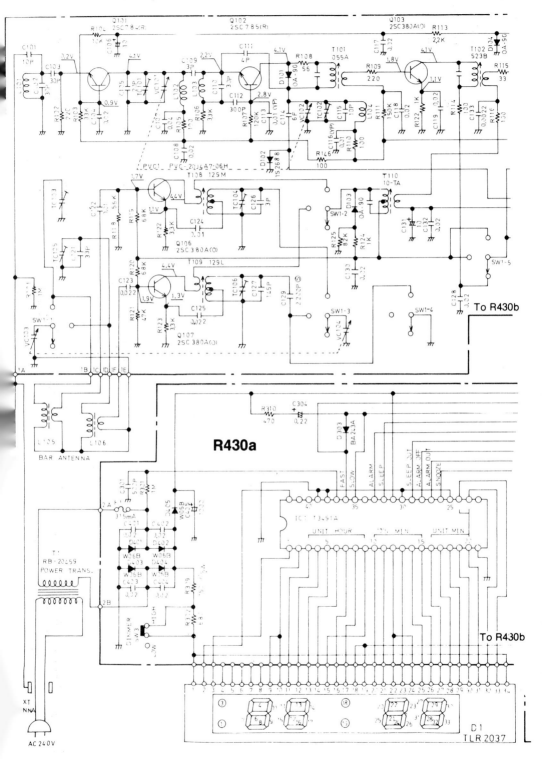

(R430a) CIRCUIT DIAGRAM—MODEL W146 *(PART)*

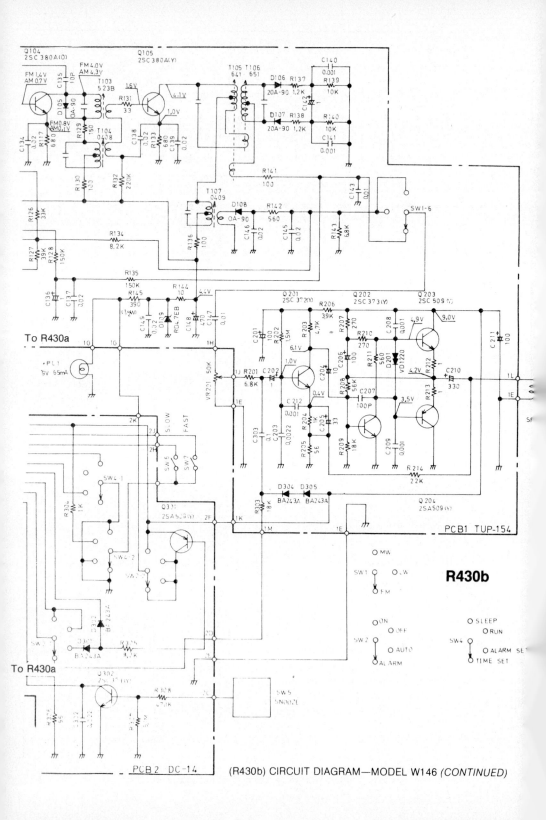

(R430b) CIRCUIT DIAGRAM—MODEL W146 *(CONTINUED)*

WALTHAM   Model W152

General Description: A mains or battery operated A.M./F.M. radio receiver fitted with sockets for auxiliary input/output and earphone.

Mains Supplies: 240 volts, 50Hz.

Batteries: 6 volts (4×SP11).

Wavebands: L.W. 150-350kHz; M.W. 540-1600kHz; S.W. 6-18MHz; F.M. 88-108MHz.

Loudspeaker: 8 ohms impedance.

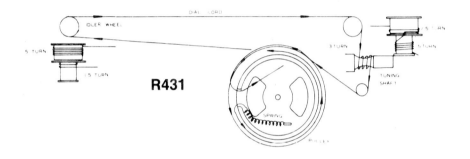

(R431) DRIVE CORD—MODEL W152

Alignment

Preparation: Use a generator which is capable of providing modulated signals from 140kHz to 18MHz (A.M. Mod.) and from 10MHz to 115MHz (F.M. Mod. and Un-mod.) modulated at 30%.

Connect V.T.V.M. across the speaker voice coil. Set the V.T.V.M. on a low A.C. range.

Follow the alignment procedure step by step.

Keep the injected signal low so that A.G.C. action does not produce misalignment.

88mmf capacitor and 330 ohm resistor used in some steps of the alignment are to be used to simulate the capacitance of the rod antenna when it is extended. If they are not used, the high band antenna trimmers will tune very broadly. A definite peak will be obtained when this capacitor and resistor are used.

The Volume control should be at maximum.

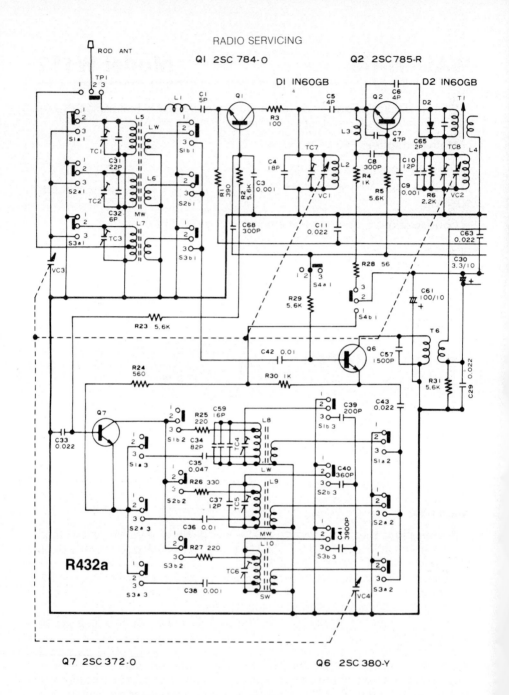

(R432a) CIRCUIT DIAGRAM—MODEL W152 *(PART)*

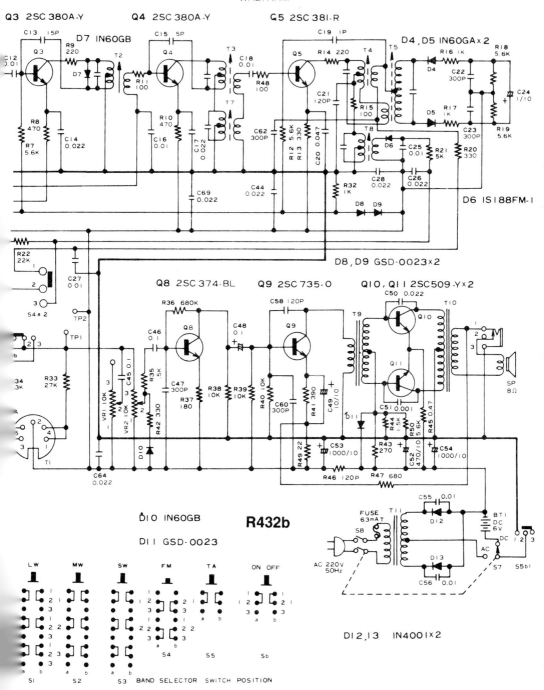

(R432b) CIRCUIT DIAGRAM—MODEL W152 *(CONTINUED)*

F.M. I.F. Alignment:

Signal generator coupling	Signal generator frequency	Radio dial setting	Connect V.T.V.M.	Adjust	Remark
R4 resistor lead through 100mmf (mod.)	10.7MHz	Tuning gang at maximum	A.C. probe across speaker	T1, T2, T3 (I.F. trans.) T4 (ratio det. coil)	Adjust for maximum output
R4 resistor lead through 100mmf (unmod.)	10.7MHz	Tuning gang at minimum	D.C. probe to test point 2 (TP2)	T5 (ratio det. coil)	Adjust for zero reading. A positive and negative reading will be obtained on either side of the correct setting

F.M. Tuner Alignment:

Band switch setting	Signal generator coupling	Signal generator frequency	Radio Radio dial setting	Adjust for maximum
F.M.	Rod ant. through 100mmf	87.25MHz	Tuning gang at max.	L4 (Osc. coil)
		109MHz	Tuning gang at min.	TC8 (Osc. trimmer)
F.M.	Rod ant. through 100mmf	90MHz	Tune for signal	L2 (R.F. coil)
		106MHz		TC7 (R.F. trimmer)

A.M. Alignment:

Band switch setting	Signal generator coupling	Signal generator frequency	Radio dial setting	Adjust for maximum
L.W., M.W., S.W.	Loop	465kHz	Tuning gang at max.	T6, T7, T8 (I.F. transformer)
L.W.	Loop	140kHz	Tuning gang at max.	L8 (Osc. coil)
		360kHz	Tuning gang at min.	TC4 (Osc. trimmer)
L.W.	Loop	160kHz	Tune for signal	L5 (Ant. coil)
		330kHz		TC1 (Ant. trimmer)
M.W.	Loop	520kHz	Tuning gang at max.	L9 (Osc. coil)
		1650kHz	Tuning gang at min.	TC5 (Osc. trimmer)
		600kHz	Tune for signal	L6 (Ant. coil)
		1400kHz		TC2 (Ant. trimmer)
S.W.	Rod ant. through 330 ohm and 8PF	5.7MHz	Tuning gang at max.	L10 (Osc. coil)
		18.5MHz	Tuning gang at min.	TC6 (Osc. trimmer)
S.W.	Rod ant.	6.5MHz	Tune for signal	L7 (Ant. coil)
		16MHz		TC3 (Ant. trimmer)

WALTHAM   Model W168

General Description: A 3-waveband A.M./F.M. radio receiver with electronic clock operating from A.C. mains supplies. A.M. and A.F. functions are contained in a single integrated circuit. The clock section includes alarm facilities.

Mains Supplies: 220-240 volts, 50Hz.

Wavebands: L.W. 145-265kHz; M.W. 510-1640kHz; F.M. 87.2-108.5MHz.

Loudspeaker: 8 ohms impedance.

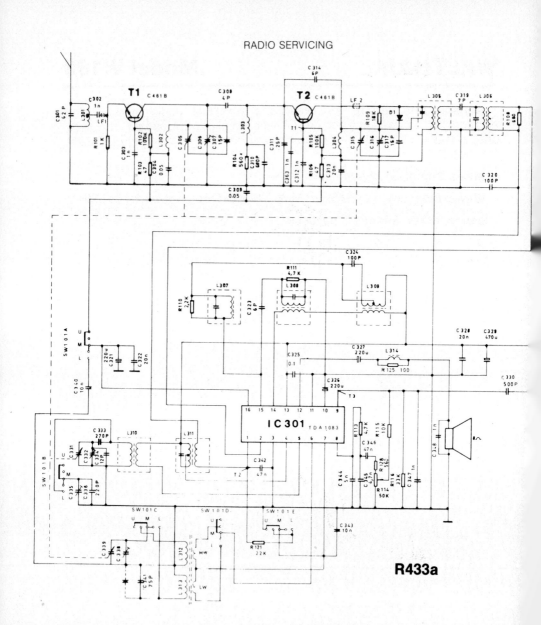

(R433a) CIRCUIT DIAGRAM—MODEL W168 (PART)

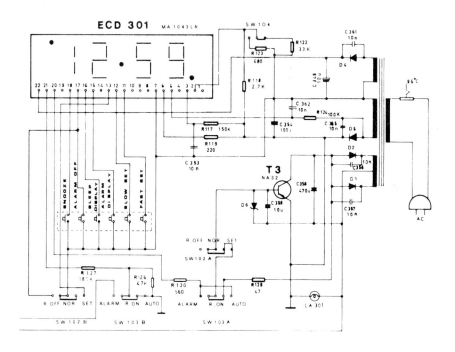

R433b

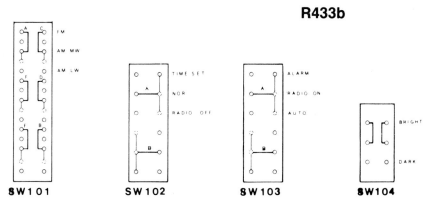

(R433b) CIRCUIT DIAGRAM—MODEL W168 *(CONTINUED)*

WALTHAM   Model W169

General Description: A 3-waveband A.M./F.M. stereo radio with electronic digital clock operating from mains supplies. A socket is provided for the connection of stereo headphones.

Mains Supply: 220-240 volts, 50Hz.

Wavebands: L.W. 150-300kHz; M.W. 540-1600kHz; F.M. 87.5-108MHz.

Loudspeaker: 8 ohms impedance.

Alignment

Medium Wave:

Step	Signal source connected to	Set signal generator to	Set radio dial to	Signal o/p connect to	Adjust	Adjust for
1		Set function switch to M.W. position				
2	R.F. generator standard loop antenna	I.F. frequency	Gang open	A.C. voltmeter across speaker voice coil	T6, T11, T12	Max.
3		Repeat step 2 as necessary to obtain max. sensitivity				
4		525kHz	Gang closed	A.C. voltmeter across speaker voice coil	Osc. coil T7	Max.
5		1625kHz	Gang open		Osc. trimmer C20	Max.
6		Repeat steps 4 and 5 to obtain correct frequency coverage				
7		600kHz	600kHz rock gang	A.C. voltmeter across speaker voice coil	Ferrite bar antenna coil T9	Max.
8			1400kHz rock gang		Antenna trimmer C28	
9		Repeat steps 7 and 8 to obtain best tracking				

Long Wave:

Step	Signal source connected to	Set signal generator to	Set radio dial to	Signal o/p connect to	Adjust	Adjust for
1		Set function switch to L.W. position				
2	R.F. generator with standard radiating loop					
3						
4		145kHz	Gang closed	A.C. voltmeter across speaker voice coil	Osc. coil T8	Max.
5		310kHz	Gang open		Osc. trimmer CT2	Max.
6		Repeat steps 4 and 5 to obtain correct frequency coverage				
7		165kHz	165kHz rock gang	A.C. voltmeter across speaker voice coil	Ferrite bar antenna coil T10	Max.
8		280kHz	280kHz rock gang		Antenna trimmer CT1	Max.
9		Repeat steps 7 and 8 to obtain best tracking				

F.M.:

Step	Signal source connected to	Set signal generator to	Set radio dial to	Signal o/p connect to	Adjust	Adjust for
1	Set function switch to F.M. position					
2	Emitter of Q2 and ground	I.F. frequency 10.7MHz	Gang open	Oscilloscope	T1, T2, T3, T4, T5	Max. and balanced curve
3	F.M. sweep generator through two 0.4μf capacitors	Repeat step 2 to obtain max. amplitude and balanced curve				
4		87MHz	Gang closed	A.C. voltmeter across speaker voice coil	Osc. coil L4	Max.
5		109MHz	Gang open		Osc. trimmer FC2	Max.
6	Marker generator F.M. antenna and ground	Repeat step 4 and 5 to obtain correct frequency coverage				
7		90MHz	90MHz rock gang	A.C. voltmeter across speaker voice coil	F.M. antenna coil L2	Max.
8		106MHz	106MHz rock gang		F.M. antenna trimmer FC1	Max.
9	Repeat steps 7 and 8 to obtain best tracking					

729

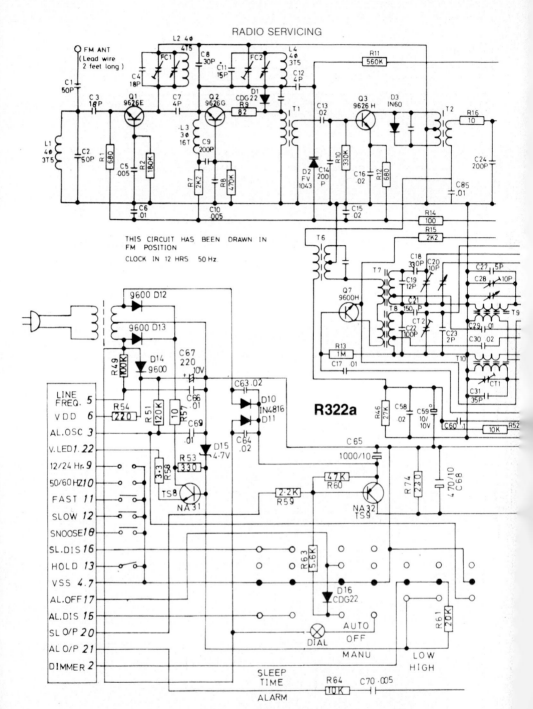

(R322a) CIRCUIT DIAGRAM—MODEL W169 *(PART)*

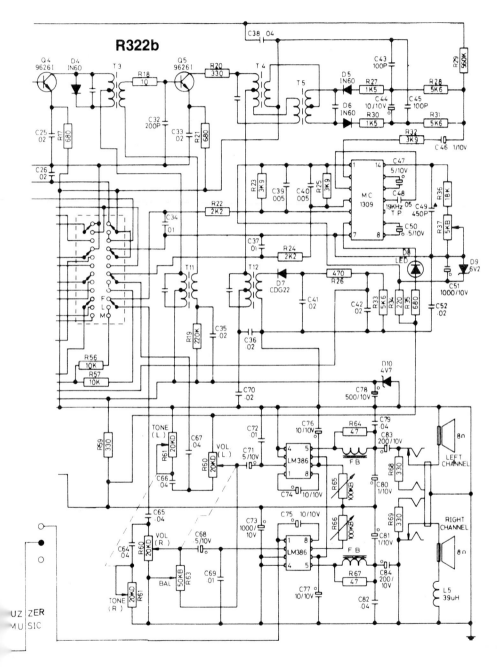

(R322b) CIRCUIT DIAGRAM—MODEL W169 *(CONTINUED)*

WALTHAM   Models W170, W174

General Description: A 3-waveband A.M./F.M. electronic clock radio receiver with 2-track cassette tape-recorder operating from mains supplies. Integrated circuits are used in the clock and A.F. power stages and a microphone is built into the case. Sockets are provided for the connection of auxiliary inputs, remote control and headphones.

Mains Supplies: 220-240 volts, 50Hz.

Wavebands: L.W. 150-300kHz; M.W. 540-1600kHz; F.M. 87.5-108MHz.

Loudspeaker: 8 ohms impedance.

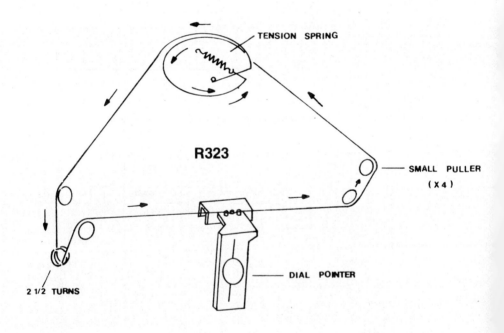

(R323) DRIVE CORD—MODELS W170, W174

Alignment

Medium Wave:

Step	Signal source connected to	Set signal generator to	Set radio dial to	Signal o/p connect to	Adjust	Adjust for
1		Set function switch to M.W. position				
2		I.F. frequency	Gang open	Oscilloscope	T3, T5, T7	Max.
3	R.F. generator standard radiating loop antenna	Repeat step 2 as necessary to obtain max. sensitivity				
4		525kHz	Gang closed	A.C. voltmeter across speaker voice coil	Osc. I.F.T. T9	Max.
5		1625kHz	Gang open		Osc. trimmer CT2	Max.
6		Repeat steps 4 and 5 to obtain correct frequency coverage				
7		600kHz	600kHz lock gang	A.C. voltmeter across speaker voice coil	Ferrite bar M.W. coil L8	Max.
8		1400kHz	1400kHz lock gang		Antenna trimmer CT1	Max.
9		Repeat steps 7 and 8 to obtain best tracking				

Long Wave:

Step	Signal source connected to	Set signal generator to	Set radio dial to	Signal o/p connect to	Adjust	Adjust for
1		Set function switch to L.W. position				
2						
3	R.F. generator with standard radiating loop antenna					
4		145kHz	Gang closed	A.C. voltmeter across speaker voice coil	Osc. I.F.T. T10	Max.
5		310kHz	Gang open		Osc. trimmer C85	
6		Repeat steps 4 and 5 to obtain correct frequency coverage				
7		180kHz	180kHz lock gang	A.C. voltmeter across speaker voice coil	Ferrite bar L.W. coil L9	Max.
8		280kHz	280kHz lock gang		Antenna trimmer C79	Max.
9		Repeat steps 7 and 8 to obtain best tracking				

F.M.:

Step	Signal source connected to	Set signal generator to	Set radio dial to	Signal o/p connect to	Adjust	Adjust for
1	Set function switch to F.M. position					
2	Emitter of Q2 and ground F.M. sweep generator through two 0.4μf capacitors	I.F. frequency 10.7MHz	Gang open	Oscilloscope	T1, T2, T4, T6, T8	Max. and balanced curve
3	Repeat step 2 to obtain max. amplitude and balanced curve					
4	Marker generator F.M. antenna and ground terminals	87MHz	Gang closed	A.C. voltmeter across speaker voice coil	Osc. coil L4	Max.
5		109MHz	Gang open		Osc. trimmer FC2	Max.
6	Repeat steps 4 and 5 to obtain correct frequency coverage					
7		90MHz	90MHz lock gang	A.C. voltmeter across speaker voice coil	F.M. antenna coil L2	Max.
8		106MHz	106MHz lock gang		F.M. antenna trimmer FC1	Max.
9	Repeat steps 7 and 8 to obtain best tracking					

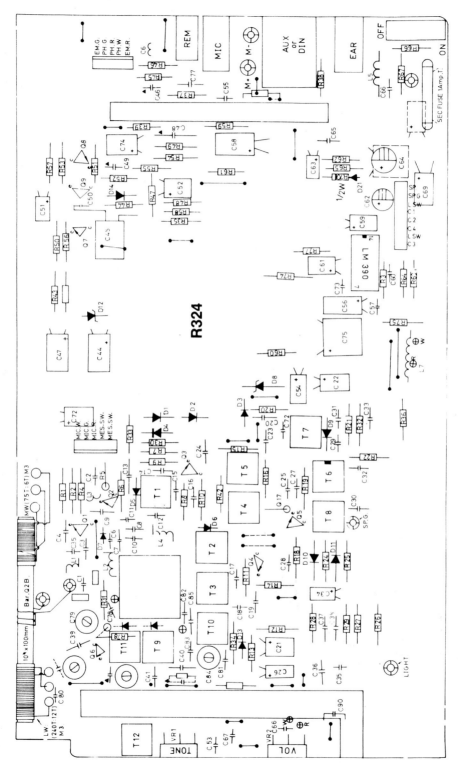

(R324) COMPONENT LAYOUT—MODELS W170, W174

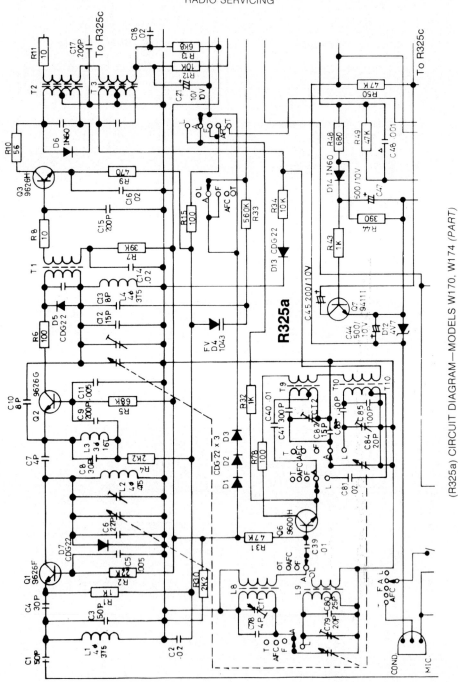

(R325a) CIRCUIT DIAGRAM—MODELS W170, W174 (PART)

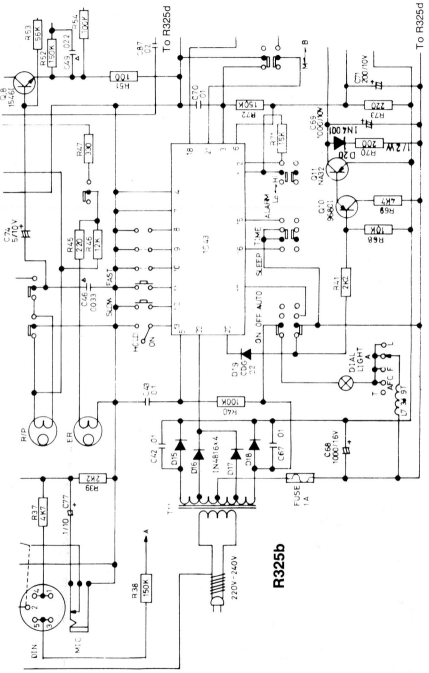

(R325b) CIRCUIT DIAGRAM—MODELS W170, W174 (PART)

R325b

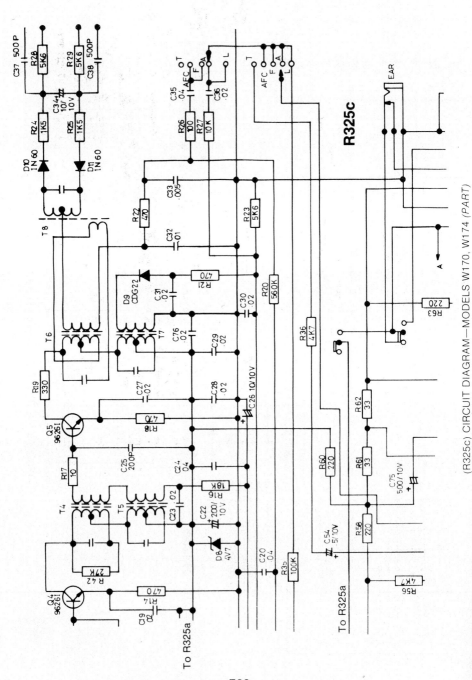

R325c

(R325c) CIRCUIT DIAGRAM—MODELS W170. W174 (PART)

738

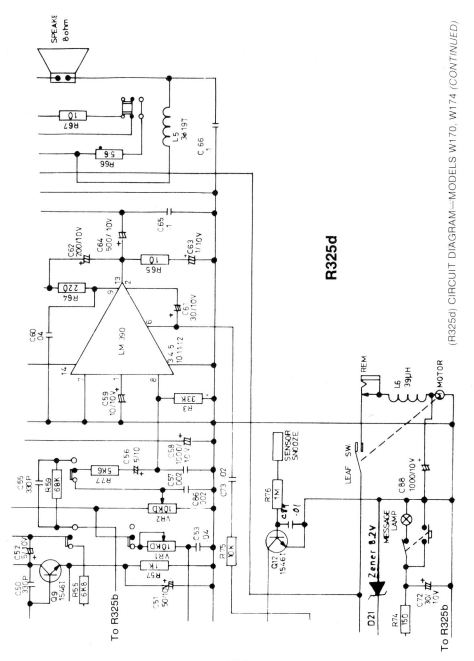

R325d

(R325d) CIRCUIT DIAGRAM—MODELS W170, W174 (CONTINUED)

CROSS REFERENCES

The models listed here will be found to be generally similar to the models referred to in this and earlier volumes of *Radio and Television Servicing*.

Make	Model Number	Refer to	Volume
Alba	70, 71, 75, 91, 95 Series, TC2514, TC2614	Decca 70 Series	1978-79
Bush	Chassis T24E, BC7200	Toshiba C-2090	This volume
Dynatron	CTV60, 61, 62, 63, 64	Philips G11	1978-79
Ferguson	3550, 3552	T.C.E. 1715	This volume
Murphy	MC7240	Toshiba C-2090	This volume
National	TC381, TC481	National PIX-M6A	1978-79
Philips	12B710, 12B912	Philips TX	1978-79
	G22C661/662/663/665/ 666/700/701-6/G26C671/ 674/675/676/678/720/722/ 724/726/728/730/731	Philips G11 Chassis	1978-79
Plustron	TV1200	Plustron TV12	1979-80
Pye	CT454/468/482/494	Philips G11	1978-79
	T182, T185	Philips E2	This volume
	51KT7326, 66K1826	Philips K12	This volume
	193-6	Philips TX	1978-79
	3150, 7225, 7227, 7228, 7323, 7324	Philips KT3	This volume
Roberts Video	RCT223	Philips G11	1978-79
Waltham	W153	Waltham W136	1978-79

SUPPLEMENTARY SERVICING INFORMATION

The following pages contain abstracts from service bulletins issued by the major manufacturers and distributors during the past 12 months. This information, which is of a random nature, lists modifications, setting-up procedures and unusual fault symptoms on circuit designs already published.

The information given here is arranged in manufacturer order (see also 'Supplementary Servicing' and 'Recent Developments' in the 1971-72 volume onwards).

As in some previous volumes, space has been found to include an extended treatment of recent Remote Control systems. A full description of the latest Decca and Thorn systems concludes this section.

1980-81 Supplement

I.T.T. Consumer Product Services
Colour Television: CVC20-CVC45 Chassis.

Philips Service (formerly CES Ltd.) (Philips, Pye, Dynatron)
Colour Television: 'G11', KT3
Monochrome Television: TX, T182, T185
Audio Equipment: 'No data' items.

Rank Radio International (Bush, Murphy)
Colour Television: 20AX, 20AX Chassis, T22, T24, Chassis
Audio Equipment: BS3049, BS3054, BS3082/4

Remote Control Systems
Decca: RC10, RC11, RC12
Thorn: U706, U708

I.T.T. CONSUMER PRODUCT SERVICES

Colour Television

Module Interchangeability

Since the first generation of solid state chassis in 1976 a number of improvements to individual modules have been made, resulting in more than one module performing the same function. In most cases where this occurs the modules are completely interchangeable, later versions giving an improved performance in some particular area. For example, it was found that some T.V. games gave an inferior sync. output. Unacceptable performance resulted when these games units were used with receivers employing original frame and horizontal modules. The later frame and horizontal modules have been modified to cope with all T.V. games. However, if T.V. games are not used by the customer, the original modules are perfectly adequate for normal off-air reception.

The colour decoder presents a further example. It was found necessary to modify the original decoder to match the sharper response curve of the new SWAF I.F. units. In this instance, the CMD 33 decoder designed for SWAF I.F. units, causes slightly impaired definition when used with a discrete I.F. However, the picture quality remains acceptable enough to warrant the use of a CMD 33 decoder with a standard discrete I.F. as a servicing 'stop gap' if the correct unit is not available.

Although most changes are quite small it will be appreciated that new number codes are necessary for updated modules. All chassis now bear clearly marked labels indicating which set of modules give the optimum performance. To assist ease of selection the following 'Chassis-Module' relationship chart, giving appropriate alternatives, is included for servicing purposes. All solid state modular chassis since the advent of the CVC 20 are covered.

NOTES
CMU 10, 11/1 Directly interchangeable.
CMU 30 used with SWAF I.F. CMK 30/1. NOT interchangeable.

CMK 10 & 10/2 interchangeable.
CMK 10/2 gives improved performance.
CMK 30/1 SWAF. I.F. used with CMU 30. NOT interchangeable.

CMD 10 & 30 interchangeable, CMD 30 gives improved performance.
CMD 33 interchangeable with CMD 10 & 30 (impaired definition).
CMD 32 is for Teletext ONLY and is not interchangeable.

CMA 10 & 30 NOT interchangeable.
CMA 30 and 30/1 are interchangeable.

Some chassis are fitted with CMS 30. This must NOT be used with CMF 26 & 31 field time based modules. CMS 32 is a direct replacement for the CMS 30 and can be used in conjunction with CMF 25, 26, 30 & 31 modules.

Some chassis are fitted with CMF 25 in place of CMF 26.
CMF 25 or 26 can be used with CMS 32.
CMF 26 is NOT suitable with CMS 30.
Some chassis are fitted with CMF 30 in place of CMF 31.
CMF 30 or 31 can be used with CMS 32.
CMF 31 is NOT suitable with CMS 30.

CMH 10, 25 & 31 NOT interchangeable.

CMP 10 & 30 NOT interchangeable.
CMP 10 for HT III rail 125V.
CMP 30 for HT III rail 160V.

CMB 10, 25 and 30 NOT interchangeable.

The only CVC 40 series module interchangeable with previous series modules is the CMK 30/1.
CMB 40, 45 NOT interchangeable.
CMU 40, 45 NOT interchangeable.
CMA 40, 41 directly interchangeable.

CHASSIS-MODULE CHART

UNIT	CODE	20	20/2	20/3	20/4	25	25/3	30	30/1	30/2	30/3	32	32/1	32/3	40	40/1	45/1
CHASSIS (MOTHER BOARD)	CVC	20	20/2	20/3	20/4	25	25/3	30	30/1	30/2	30/3	32	32/1	32/3	40	40/1	45/1
TUNER BOARD	CMU	10/11/11/1	10/11/11/1	10/11	10/11/11/1	10/11/11/1	30	10/11/11/1	30	30	30	10/11/11/1	30	30	40	45	40
IF BOARD	CMK	10	10/2	10/2	10/2	10/2	30/1	10/2	30/1	30/1	30/1	10/2	30/1	30/1	30/1	30/1	30/1
DECODER BOARD	CMD	10	10	30	30	30	33	30	33	32	33	30	33	33	40	40	40
AUDIO BOARD	CMA	10	10	10	10	30	30/30/1	30	30/30/1	30/30/1	30/30/1	30	30/30/1	30/30/1	41/40	41/40	41/40
S.M.P.S.	CMP	10	10	10	10	30	30	30	30	30	30	30	30	30	40	40	40
HOR. OSC.	CMS	10	10	11	11	30/32	30/32	30/32	30/32	30/32	30/32	30/32	30/32	30/32	40	40	40
FRAME UNIT	CMF	–	–	–	–	25/26	25/26	30/31	30/31	30/31	30/31	30/31	30/31	30/31	40	40	40
E/W MOD.	CMH	10	10	10	10	25	25	31	31	31	31	31	31	31	–	–	–
CRT BASE	CMB	10	10	10	10	25	25	30	30	30	30	30	30	30	40	45	45
TOL. CORRECTION	CMZ	–	–	–	–	–	–	30	30	30	30	31	31	31	–	–	–
HOR. SUB-BOARD	CMN	–	–	–	–	–	–	–	–	–	–	–	–	–	40	40	40
S.M.P.S. SUB-BOARD	CMN	–	–	–	–	–	–	–	–	–	–	–	–	–	45	45	45
C.R.T.		20" PIL 90°				22" PIL 110°		26" 20 AX 110°				22" 20 AX 110°			16" PIL 90°	22" PIL 90°	20" PIL 90°

I.T.T. CHASSIS-MODULE CHART

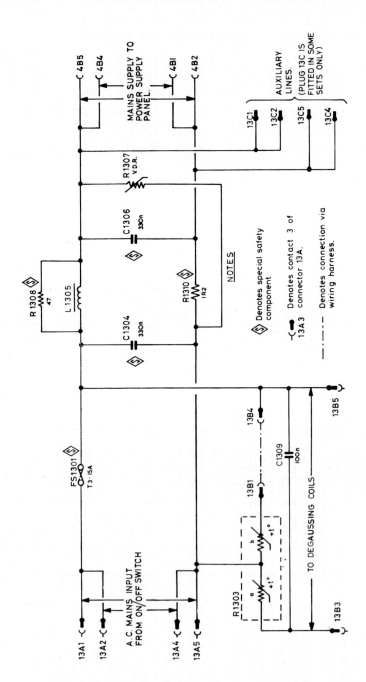

(FIG. 1) MAINS INPUT CIRCUIT—G11' CHASSIS

PHILIPS SERVICE (formerly C.E.S. Ltd.) (Philips, Pye, Dynatron)

Colour Television
Philips/Pye/Dynatron 'G11' chassis

Mains Input Panel: A production change to improve reliability by reducing switch-on current surge has now been introduced, deleting fuse FS1302, and adding a IR2 wirewound safety resistor R1310—see Fig. 2. In addition, C1304 and C1306 have been replaced with types having a smaller dimension. The code number for the panel remains unchanged.

Philips/Pye 'G11' chassis—700 series

Failure of 12 volt Regulator on Viewdata/Teletext I.F. Panel: Some cases of failure of the 12 volt regulator I.C.5073 (type LM340T-12) on the I.F. panel have been reported. The effect is a reducing LT2 supply line voltage which occurs whilst the receiver is warming-up, settling at 8-8,5 volts after approximately 20 minutes.

The symptoms are as follows: On Viewdata receivers the fault may first manifest itself by corrupting the auto-dial telephone number. On both Viewdata and Teletext receivers as the voltage drops the black level will drift upwards and flyback lines may become evident, and as it drops still further the text display may become corrupted or lost completely.

Striations when in Text Mode: On certain Teletext/Viewdata power supply panels (156 volt), a 1μF 63 volt electrolytic capacitor has been added in parallel with D4090, in order to prevent striations occurring when in text mode.

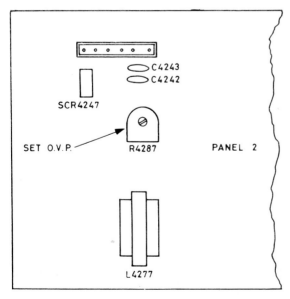

(FIG. 2) POWER SUPPLY PANEL SECTION—'G11' CHASSIS

Failure of Fuse FS4213: To prevent fuse FS4213 blowing on power supply panel 1 which is fitted to later-version Viewdata receivers, the following production changes have been made on power supply panel 2 (5-12 volt unit):

Thyristor SCR4247 changed type from S2060A to BT151/500R.

R4248 changed in value from 1kΩ to 100Ω.

C4249 changed in value from 4μ7 to 100nF foil.

R4286 changed in value from 22Ω to 180Ω.

A diode type IN4148 is added in place of link 'J' between R4267 and R4268—cathode end to R4268 (4k7).

Fuse FS4213—1.6A.

Note: The over-voltage protection preset potentiometer R4287 (see Fig. 2) should be set to 0.4 volt on the slider using a 20kΩ/volt meter.

Philips/Pye KT3 chassis

Field Jump on Programme Change: A further production change has now been introduced on the sync. panel to reduce the effect of momentary loss of sync. on programme change, which is seen as a single jump in field sync.

A new version of the integrated circuit is used which halves the time taken for synchronisation to be restored after a break in syncs. due either to a channel change at the receiver, or a programme change in transmission.

The circuit changes are as follows:

Position	Original	Change
IC8367	TD2571Q	TDA2571AQ
C8368	22μF	10μF
R8368	100kΩ	47kΩ reconnected to pin 18 (LT)
R8375	—	470Ω added in series with C8374
C8375	—	2μ2F added in series with R8374
R8374	1kΩ	1k5
C8389	—	100nF added in parallel with D8388

Note: Luminance/chrominance panel change.
In addition, C3219 on the luminance/chrominance panel is changed in value from 4μ7F to 1μF to reduce colour flash.

C.R.T. discharging: Some receivers have been produced in the factory with the C.R.T. 'discharging spade' omitted. On these receivers, the E.H.T. connection on the C.R.T. must be discharged to the acquadag earthing braid **ONLY** via a clip lead and screwdriver. Any attempt to discharge the C.R.T. to another earth point may result in damage to the semi-conductors.

Replacement of Sound Module U5420: When a replacement sound module is fitted, the volume pre-set control (R5166) should be adjusted as follows:

With the receiver tuned to a normal transmission and the customer volume control set to minimum, adjust R5166 such that the sound in the loudspeaker is barely audible.

Colour Flashes when Signal Interruption Occurs: On all receivers using this chassis, the Automatic Colour Control (A.C.C.) line is used to provide correct ident of the PAL switch, and to work the colour killer. Typically the A.C.C. line is held at 1.0 volts on a normal colour signal, rising through weaker colour signals to become approximately 4 volts for monochrome. Incorrect ident. would produce 7 volts on the line if allowed, but since the colour killer trips when the voltage rises above 2 volts, this situation never occurs.

These conditions rely on the transmitted burst to maintain control. Burst is not transmitted during the field sync. period, so the time constant of the A.C.C. line is arranged to 'span this gap' and retain control, which it will so long as the eight field 'meander gate' sequence is correct at the transmitter end.

A programme interruption or change will cause the receiver to lose ident., the colour killer will operate and the A.C.C. line will rise to give maximum colour gain. This means that at the instant the set re-identifies itself, there is maximum colour gain, until the time constant on the A.C.C. line used to 'bridge the gap' charges-up again—hence the '"colour flash" effect'.

Programmes transmitted by the I.B.A. produce the worst effect since the interruption is made at a commercial break, when the video signal is taken down to Black Level, and therefore accentuating the problem which, incidentally, is usually in the (B-Y) phase due to (R-Y) cancelling out over two fields. B.B.C. broadcasts are generally blocked to the preceding programme, and B.B.C.1 and B.B.C.2 are similarly related. Colour flashes on B.B.C. usually occur just before a programme change, at the instant of locking or re-routing.

Monochrome Television

Philips/Pye TX chassis

Distortion at Low Volume: To reduce distortion at low volume settings, the following production changes have recently been introduced.

Component No.	Original Value	New Value
R312	2k7	3k3
R311	33R	56R
R315	180k	120k
R300	27k	18k

C.R.T. Replacement: Three types of cathode ray tube have been fitted during production as follows:

C.R.T. type	Value of R576
12VBJP4 (Orion)	820k or 470k
12VBJP4 (Philips)	820k
12VCUP4	470k

Note: To ensure a sufficient range of the Brightness control exists, the value of R576 should be 820k in versions where C.R.T. type 12VBJP4 (either version) is fitted, and where a 12VCUP4 is fitted the value of R576 should be 470k.

Pye T182 and T185

Production change to Line Output Transformer: Certain receivers have been fitted with a Line Output Transformer which incorporates an E.H.T. rectifier (code number for complete assembly 140 10165).

In these receivers, the E.H.T. rectifier, its holder and the E.H.T. lead are deleted, and engineers should replace the L.O.P.T. with the appropriate type as necessary.

Audio Equipment

The following list of Philips and Pye products consists of certain 'low-price' domestic items which for economic reasons no specific spare parts nor service documentation are available from Philips Service.

Faulty units should be returned to Philips Service, where an EXCHANGE system is operated at a fixed price.

Make	Type number		Make	Type number	
Philips	90AL070	90RL110	Pye	PT020	1047
	90AL071	90RL113		PT321	1071
	90AL072	90RL114		PT1050	1072
	90AL078	90RL120		PT1120	1172
	90AL162	90RL136		PT1260	1230
	90AL172	90RL152		PT1392	1260
	90AL260	90RL194		PT1400	1280
	90AL262	90RL210		PT1406	1372
	90AL280	90RL221		PT1408	2260
	90AL282	90RL230		PT1409	2271
	90AL360	90AS080W		PT1415	2272
	90AL365	90AS092		SX1082	2273
	90AL380	90AS100		SX7182	2275
	90RL011	90AS180			2300
	90RL020	90AS300			2450
	90RL047	90RN454			4280
	90RL050/15R	N2233			
	90RL051	22AC460			
	90RL052/15R	22AC860			
	90RL053	22AC880			
	90RL076	22AC890			
	90RL077	22RN342			

RANK RADIO INTERNATIONAL (Bush/Murphy)

Colour Television

20AX/30AX Chassis

T130/T160 Signal Panel: There has been a change to the copper layout to allow use of the Plessey TDA2560 I.C.

The copper change isolated the earthy end of R92 from the link that connects 2Z6-2 to earth.

The change to the copper print will allow the panel to be compatible for either Mullard or Plessey I.C.s and the change has been introduced on panels issue 13 and later.

Burst Gate Timing Alteration: The burst gate timing sand castle pulse has been altered to take care of varying transmission waveforms (position of burst) by changing the Capacitor 2C59 (330pf) to 470pf.

T156 Timebase Panel

Prevention of Random Tripping of Protection Circuit: A Capacitor, 2.2 nanofarad, has been added to the circuit between the Collector of TR1 and Emitter of TR2. Production are fitting this capacitor into the existing collector and emitter holes.

T130/T160/T152

Addition of Ferrite Bead: To avoid possible parasitic oscillation of the pre-amplifier at about 500MHz, a ferrite bead has been added to the BASE lead of VT2 on T130/T160 and TR2 on T152.

The oscillation is due to circuit tolerances, and can be recognised as a beat pattern when tuned to a particular channel. The pattern will usually change or disappear with hand capacity around the Surface Wave Filter.

T125A, T136A, Z906 and derivatives

It has been found that with some TBA950 S.I.C.s, the line hold will not break at both ends of its travel and therefore the 'pull-in' could be affected.

To correct this the 11 KΩ fitted in the bottom end of the hold circuit may be changed in value to 10 KΩ.

On the T125A panel the resistor is 14R3, on the T136A 4R59 and on the Z906 it is 4R95.

T22 Chassis

T130 Signal Panel: Capacitor C84 (0.22MFD) which was a tantalum type has now been changed to a polymylor type.

The capacitor has been changed to improve the impedance at burst frequency. Tantalum capacitors exhibiting high impedance at burst frequency may cause lack of colour or colour drop out, as C84 is in the A.C.C. circuit.

T24 Chassis Series

T44 Chassis: To facilitate pre-set adjustments in production, the resistor R221 (100K) is changed in value to 82K.

Use of Alternative Mullard CRT A51-570X: Production will be using the above C.R.T. as an alternative in the T24 Chassis. When the Mullard tube is fitted it is necessary to fit a 5R6 resistor on the C.R.T. base panel in parallel with R920. The resistor should be 'stood off' the panel using 5mm sleeving and a self adhesive label is to be attached to an appropriate lead associated with the C.R.T. panel indicating the change.

The additional resistor is necessary to compensate for the differences in heater current between Mullard and Toshiba C.R.T.s.

The receivers incorporating Mullard C.R.T.s will be given the suffix 'B' instead of 'A', e.g. BC7200AT will become BC7200BT when the Mullard C.R.T. is fitted.

Audio Equipment
BW5503/BW5509

There have been some complaints that the 1 Hz flashing colon has caused interference on sound on the above receivers.

In both cases the trouble can be cleared by the following:

BW5503A: Replace C45 (0.02 MFD) with a 500pF capacitor.

BW5509/B: Replace C54 (0.01 MFD) with a 500pF capacitor.

BS3049, BS3082/4, BS3054

Fuse Rating: Fuse 7FS1 (originally 250mA) has been uprated to 315mA. The fuse label has also been changed.

The reason for the change is that on some receivers the original fuse was found to blow when operating at maximum power.

DECCA INFRA-RED REMOTE CONTROL

Systems RC10, RC11 and RC12

The Decca Infra-Red Remote Control Systems RC10, RC11 and RC12 are designed to interface with the Decca 8 position electronic touch-tune system and 70 Series, 90 Series and 110 Series chassis. The main control element in these systems is a 4-bit microprocessor and an infra-red system using an 8-bit serial code is employed to provide full remote control. A hand held transmitter controls the following receiver functions:

(a) Direct selection of 8 channels.

(b) Remote control of Volume, Brightness and Colour.

(c) Normalising facility for re-setting brightness and colour to the levels set by receiver front controls.

(d) Mute facility for reducing sound to a low level.

(e) Remote switch-off of receiver using a delatching mains switch.

These features are incorporated in the Remote Control System RC10.

In addition, System RC11 provides full control of broadcast Teletext by direct connection to the DATA bus interface for those receivers equipped with a teletext facility.

System RC12 provides full control of broadcast Teletext and also includes Viewdate control by direct connection to the DATA bus interface for receivers equipped with both Teletext and Viewdata facilities.

Automatic sound muting and channel change inhibit is included in these two systems when the text facility is being used.

Modular 'plug-in' construction and compatibility with customer local rotary controls enables easy conversion from non-remote to remote operation; this maintains the full range of controls, both locally and remotely.

Basic System

The basic system is divided into three main blocks. These are the hand held, infra-red remote control transmitter unit, the infra-red remote control receiver/amplifier and the remote control processor panel.

The Transmitter: The major circuit element in the transmitter is the SN76841 N24 integrated circuit which generates an 8-bit transmitted code. The shortest possible transmission consists of the 8-bit code repeated four times with an intercode gap of 8 zeros.

Each logical '1' transmission consists of a 1.56mS burst of 41kHz carrier frequency, followed by a 1.56mS gap. This gap results in a return to zero (RZ) code, which in turn reduces the transmitter current drain.

The resulting signal is fed to a transistor output stage which drives the infra-red emitting diodes.

Depressing any particular button on the hand held remote control transmitter generates a modulated infra-red signal, which has a unique code.

The particular serial code generated is determined on the transmitter keyboard matrix by means of single pole press button switches, which connect any one of the four strobe line outputs on the I.C. with any one of the eight keyboard I.C. inputs.

Each uniquely coded infra-red transmission controls a specific function on the receiver.

Remote Control Receiver/Amplifier: This section is housed in the receiver control unit assembly and is powered from the main receiver chassis.

Interface connections are shown in Fig. 3. The remote receiver/amplifier receives the coded infra-red signals from the transmitter by means of an infra-red diode housed in this assembly. The output from this diode is then passed through a 41kHz filter and high gain amplifier.

The signal is demodulated by a phase-locked loop and the resulting serial data output is routed via SRCD5 to PRCD5 on the Remote Control Processor Panel.

An enable/disable control signal gates the output of the demodulator into the main control input bus. The enable signal reaches the receiver via PRCD1 on the processor panel.

The Remote Control Processor Panel: This panel is housed in the receiver channel selector unit and is powered from the main receiver chassis. Interface and power connections are shown in Fig. 3.

This section contains the microprocessor element, digital-analogue converters and peripheral components.

There are three main sections in both the hardware and software on this panel, as follows:

(i) Channel change drive.

(ii) Analogue control.

(iii) Teletext, Teletext/Viewdate control (employed only on Systems RC11 and RC12 respectively).

(i) Channel Change Drive: Connection is made between the microprocessor and the touch-tune circuit via four interface lines.

Three of these provide a binary coded representation of the selected

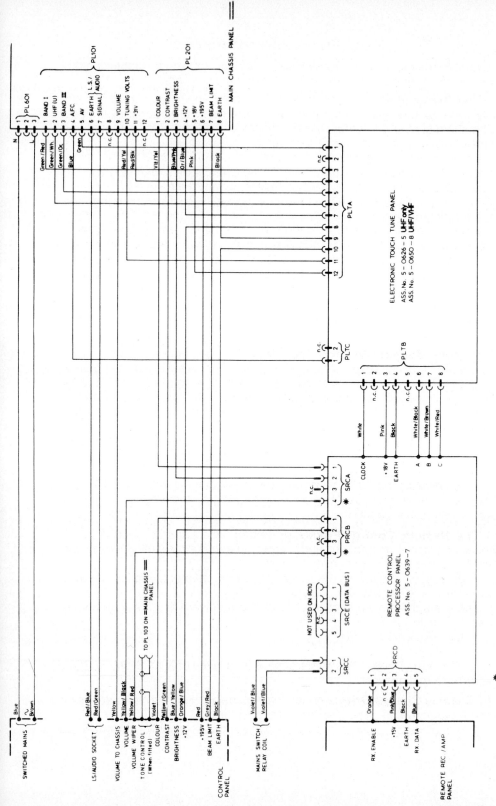

(FIG. 3) SYSTEMS INTERCONNECTION—MODELS RC10/11/12

n.c. DENOTES NO CONNECTION OR BLANKING PIN FITTED

NOTE: PLUG & SOCKET CONNECTIONS TO PRCB & SRCA ARE
LINKED WHEN R/C PROCESSOR PANEL IS NOT USED

channel, connection being made via points A, B and C on the Processor Panel to PLTB6, 7 and 8 respectively on the Touch-Tune Panel.

The fourth provides a channel step command via the 'clock' connection to PLTB1 on the Touch-Tune Panel. When a remote channel change command is signalled, the processor sends sequential stepping pulses until the correct channel code occurs.

(ii) Analogue Control: Connections for this section are taken from PRCB and SRCA on the Processor Panel and interface with the main Receiver Chassis and Control Panel as shown in Fig. 3. Plus and socket connections to PRCB and SRCA, incorporated in the wiring harness, are linked together when remote control is not fitted.

In this system, analogue control is achieved by using a novel technique for relating the receiver local control setting to the remote setting.

In operation the positions of the receiver Volume, Brightness and Colour controls are digitised by an analogue to digital converter, producing a 6-bit word in the range 0 to 63 (value X) for each control.

The remote control + and − switches operate an up/down counter which takes the range from −63 to +63 (value Y).

An arithmetic add is then performed to find the required output as follows:

output=input from local receiver controls + remote offset
Z =value X + value Y.

Since the output can only take values 0 to 63, Z must be modified if it reaches a value less than 0 or greater than 63.

In this event, value Y is modified to bring Z within the permissible range. Thus the logic is arranged so that:

If $X + Y < 0$, Y is modified to Y*, where $X + Y^* = 0$

and similarly,

If $X + Y > 63$, Y is modified to Y*, where $X + Y^* = 63$

The new output Z is then fed through a digital to analogue converter and multiplexer before being routed back to the main receiver. Stepping rate from the remote control is approx. 10 steps/second.

(iii) Teletext/Viewdata Control: Communication between the processor and the Teletext/Viewdata modules is accomplished via a four line serial bus (DATA BUS). This is routed to the Processor Panel socket connections SRCE1 to 5 as follows:

Data out line (SRCE2).
Clock line (SRCE1).
Receive/Execute line (SRCE3).
Data in line (SRCE5).

Data is transferred along the bus from the processor in a serial 10-bit word as shown in Fig. 18 Databus Waveforms.

Command allocations are shown in Table 4 Databus Codes.

Three modes of operation are possible: Picture, Teletext and Viewdata.

The states on entry to a mode are:

(1) Picture: Channel change enabled and sound on.

(2) Teletext: Channel change enabled and sound muted.

(3) Viewdata: Channel change disabled and sound muted.

On switch-on the Picture state is entered.

Mode-changing Commands (See Figs. 15, 16 & 17)

Key	Operation
PICTURE	Teletext to Picture
TEXT	Picture to Teletext
MIX	Picture to Teletext
VIEWDATA	(1) Picture to Viewdata
	or (2) Teletext to Viewdata*
HOLD	Viewdata to Teletext
CLEAR	Viewdata to Picture

* Produces 'PICTURE' code then 'VIEWDATA' code

Transmitter

General Description: The infra-red Remote control transmitter unit comprises two printed circuit panels which are linked by means of a 14-way plug-in flexible ribbon connector.

One panel contains the transmitter circuitry which includes the infra-red emitting diodes D1, D2 (Fig. 4). The second panel contains the press button switch contacts and p.c. keyboard matrix as shown in Fig. 5. Both panels are housed in a case fitted with press buttons to operate the switch contacts. A light emitting diode D3 is located adjacent to the keyboard on the case, which acts as a 'Function Indicator' to provide a visual indication of transmitter operation. When any button is pressed, the LED will be illuminated with a rapidly pulsing light to show normal functioning of the transmitter.

Press Buttons—'Keyboard Matrix': The number of press buttons and their configuration varies on each of the three remote control systems listed. These are shown in Fig. 5 and Table 1. Table 1 shows button symbol markings, designated function and numerical reference of keyboard switches in relation to the circuit diagram of Fig. 5. This table in addition, lists hexadecimal codes and coding reference of keyboard and strobe lines.

Power Source: The unit is powered by a 9 volt replaceable battery type PP3 or equivalent.

Access to this is gained by the removal of the detachable cover on the underside of the unit.

Note: No On/Off switch is fitted on this unit. Care should be taken NOT to leave the unit laying face downwards as this may permit accidental operation of the press buttons, which over an extended period will drain the battery.

The unit should normally function for several months on the same battery. *A discharged battery should not be left in the unit for long periods, as leakage from it may cause damage to the electronic circuitry.*

Access for Servicing: Access is gained by the removal of a single securing screw which is located in the battery compartment.

Removal of this screw will permit the two halves of the moulded case to be

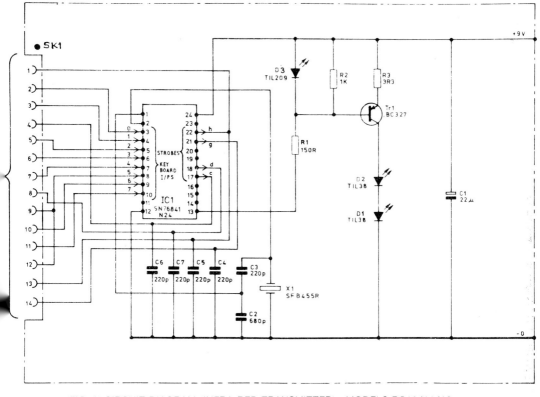

(FIG. 4) CIRCUIT DIAGRAM (INFRA-RED TRANSMITTER)—MODELS RC10/11/12

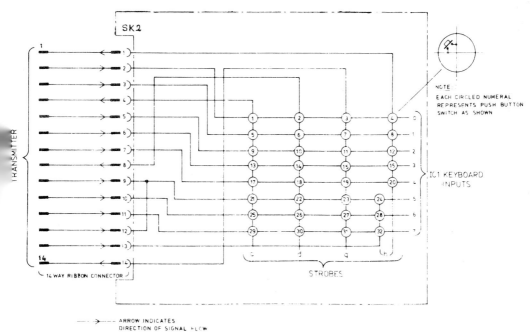

(FIG. 5) CIRCUIT DIAGRAM (KEYBOARD MATRIX)—MODELS RC10/11/12

BUTTON SYMBOL	COMMAND/ FUNCTION	CCT DIAG SWITCH REF NO.	IC1 CODING REF		HEXADECIMAL CODE (INCL. START BIT)	*USED ON MODEL RC10	*USED ON MODEL RC11	*USED ON MODEL RC12
			Keyboard	Strobe				
1	Numeral 1	2	0	d	07	*	*	*
2	Numeral 2	18	4	d	47	*	*	*
3	Numeral 3	10	2	d	27	*	*	*
4	Numeral 4	26	6	d	67	*	*	*
5	Numeral 5	6	1	d	17	*	*	*
6	Numeral 6	22	5	d	57	*	*	*
7	Numeral 7	14	3	d	37	*	*	*
8	Numeral 8	30	7	d	77	*	*	*
9	Numeral 9	4	0	h	0F		*	*
0	Numeral 0	1	0	c	05		*	*
Page *	Page/*	17	4	c	45		*	*
Time #	Time/#	21	5	c	55		*	*
Memory	Memory	5	1	c	15		*	*
Expand	Expand	31	7	g	7D		*	*
☀ +	Brightness +	3	0	g	0D	*	*	*

Table 1. Keyboard and Matrix Table (Functions and Codes)—Model RC10/11/12

	Function							
☼ -	Brightness -	11	2	g	2D	*	*	*
● +	Colour +	7	1	g	1D	*	*	*
● -	Colour -	13	3	c	35	*	*	*
◁ +	Volume +	9	2	c	25	*	*	*
◁ -	Volume -	29	7	c	75	*	*	*
N	Normalise	25	6	c	65	*	*	*
Mute	Mute	27	6	g	6D	*	*	*
OFF	Mains off	23	5	g	5D	*		*
Viewdata	Viewdata	24	5	h	5F			
Reveal	Reveal	28	6	h	7F	*	*	*
Text / Index	Text/Index	32	7	h	7F		*	
Hold	Hold/Clear 1	12	2	h	2F		*	*
Update Tape	Update/Tape	15	3	g	3D		*	
Mix	Mix	16	3	h	3F	*	*	*
Picture Clear	Picture/Clear 2	20	4	h	4F	*	*	*
Not used	Spare A	8	1	h	1F			
Not used	Spare B	19	4	g	4D			

These switch intersection positions are not used in the series listed above.

separated. This should be done carefully, by sliding back towards the rear of the unit the lower half of the moulding incorporating the battery compartment. The transmitter p.c.b. is retained by four moulded spigots and keyways in the p.c.b., together with a sponge rubber retaining pad.

Note: If for any reason the Keyboard p.c.b. or press buttons are removed, it is essential for correct operation that the two operating spigots moulded on the underside of each press button are located correctly before assembly to engage with the sprung contacts on the p.c.b.

Infra-Red Transmitter Circuit Description: In the standby condition the keyboard input lines are 'low' and the strobe lines are 'high'. When a key is pressed connecting a strobe line to an output line, the strobe lines go low, and the 450kHz on-chip oscillator starts up. The strobe lines are then pulsed high one at a time, so that the chip can detect which strobe line is connected to which input line.

An 8-bit serial code is produced at pin 13 of the I.C. Each logic 1 data bit consists of a 1.56mS burst of 40.9kHz carrier followed by a 1.56mS gap. Pin 13 is an open-collector output whose D.C. load is provided by R1 and D3. D3 indicates when a transmission is taking place and provides a constant drive voltage for Tr1, which consequently drives the infra-red emitting diodes with a constant current for all battery voltages in excess of about 4.5V.

The 8-bit code is transmitted at least four times (depending on how long the key is depressed), each transmission being separated by a gap equal in duration to eight bit periods.

The bits are sent in the following order:
Start bit (always 1—least significant bit of strobe line code)
Strobe line code, bit 2

Table 2. Strobe and Input Codes (Hexadecimal)

Decimal	Binary	Hexadecimal
0	0	0
1	1	1
2	10	2
3	11	3
4	100	4
5	101	5
6	110	6
7	111	7
8	1000	8
9	1001	9
10	1010	A
11	1011	B
12	1100	C
13	1101	D
14	1110	E
15	1111	F
16	10000	10
17	10001	11
18	10010	12
MSB	LSB	

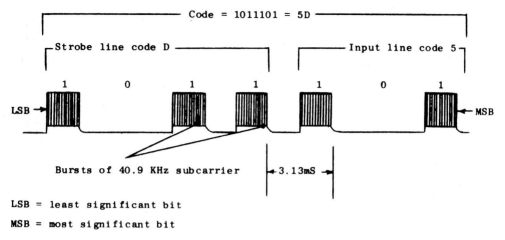

(FIG. 6) EXAMPLE OF TRANSMITTED SIGNAL—MODELS RC10/11/12

Strobe line code, bit 3
Strobe line code, bit 4 (most significant bit)
Input line code, bit 1 (least significant bit)
Input line code, bit 2
Input line code, bit 3 (most significant bit)
Spare or 'expansion' bit (always zero).

Coding Reference: In Table 2 the strobe and input codes are given in hexadecimal code. This is a concise way of expressing numbers in a system based on 16 (four bits of binary can represent numbers 0 to 15; see Table 2).

An example of the transmitted code is shown in Fig. 6.

Transmitter Fault Finding: It will usually be found convenient to disconnect the keyboard from the main transmitter board. A strobe and an input may then be shorted together at SK1 to establish whether the fault is on the keyboard or the transmitter board.

When a strobe line is connected to an input line, a clock waveform should appear across the ceramic resonator X1. This should be about 2V p-p and 450kHz in frequency. Absence of this waveform can be caused by a faulty I.C., a faulty resonator, C2 or C3. The D.C. voltage across the resonator should be about 1V when measured with a 20KΩ/V meter on the 10V range when a strobe line is connected to an input.

The voltage across the infra-red emitting diodes does not fall to zero at any time during a burst of subcarrier, because of stored charge.

Excessive quiescent current may be caused by C4, C5, C6 or C7 being open-circuit. This can result in very short battery life.

Since in operation there are no steady voltages on this unit (except battery supply voltage) only voltage waveforms can be observed. (See Fig. 7.)

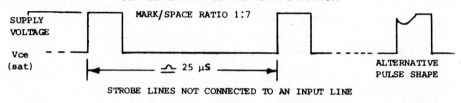

STROBE LINES NOT CONNECTED TO AN INPUT LINE

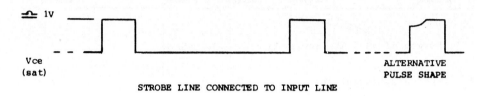

STROBE LINE CONNECTED TO INPUT LINE

(FIG. 7) EXAMPLES OF STROBE LINE WAVEFORMS (TRANSMITTER OPERATING)—
MODELS RC10/11/12

Remote Control Receiver

General Description: The Remote Control Receiver is contained on a single printed circuit panel mounted in the Control Unit Assembly.

This section receives the coded infra-red signals generated by the hand held 'Transmitter Unit'. Signals are detected by the infra-red receiving diode D25, which is mounted within the aperture of the receiving lens on the receiver control panel.

Power and signal connections for this panel are taken via flexible leads and socket connection SRCD, to PRCD on the Remote Control Processor Panel.

Circuit Description (Fig. 8)

The infra-red signals are detected by photodiode D25. This operates under reverse bias, its supply coming from pin 10 of IC25. The current through the diode has a D.C. component (mainly due to ambient lighting) and an A.C. component (noise and wanted signal).

The input amplifier in the SN76832 derives its bias from pin 3. To prevent the D.C. component of the diode current from affecting the bias of the amplifier, this D.C. component is shunted by L25 to the bias supply, which has a sufficiently low impedance to keep the bias voltage constant when the diode current changes.

L25, the input capacitance of the amplifier, the diode capacitance and C25 form a tuned circuit resonant at about 40kHz. This selects the wanted A.C. component of the diode current, which is fed to the input of the first amplifier on pin 11 of the I.C.

The output of the first amplifier appears on pin 12, and is fed via C26 to one input of the second amplifier. Frequencies higher than the wanted signal, such as noise, are shunted to earth by C37.

760

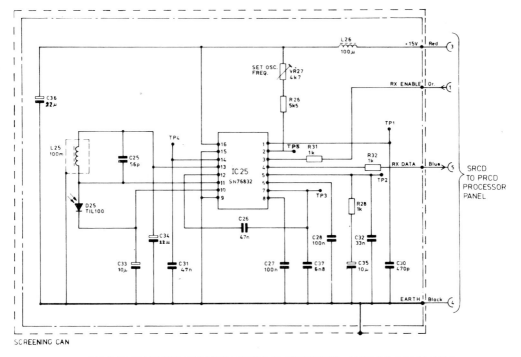

(FIG. 8) CIRCUIT DIAGRAM (REMOTE CONTROL RECEIVER)—MODELS RC10/11/12

C27 and C28 decouple the bias supplies to the inputs of the second amplifier. The output of the second amplifier is connected inside the I.C. to the reference input of a phase-locked loop. The voltage-controlled oscillator in this loop has its free-running frequency governed by R26, VR27 and C30. The loop filter consists of C32, C35 and R28. An extra phase detector is used to detect the 'locked' condition. The output from this detector is filtered by C31 and passes via a Schmitt trigger to the output amplifier.

The output amplifier is switched on and off by an 'enable' signal from the microprocessor. The maximum permissible current into the enable input of the SN76832 is 1mA, corresponding to about 1.5V on the input. The current needed to guarantee that the chip is enabled is about 200µA, so to permanently enable the device for fault-finding a resistor of about 47KΩ must be wired between the enable pin and the +15V supply. The output will be permanently low in absence of an enable signal, although the output is open collector.

In normal operation, the loop will lock during each burst of modulated infra-red from the transmitter. A serial pulse code will appear at the output, and this is fed to the remote control processor panel.

Alignment: If for any reason the I.C. is changed, VR27 must be adjusted so

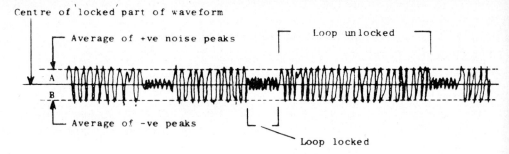

Centre of locked part of waveform

Average of +ve noise peaks

Loop unlocked

A

B

Average of -ve peaks

Loop locked

(FIG. 9) EXAMPLE OF CORRECTLY ALIGNED WAVEFORM (PIN 2 OF IC25)—
MODELS RC10/11/12

that the free-running frequency of the V.C.O. is 40.9kHz. This is most easily done by examining the waveform on pin 2 of the I.C. while most easily done by examining the waveform on pin 2 of the I.C. while a signal is being received from the transmitter. An oscilloscope probe may be clipped onto R26 (with the board in its screening can). When the adjustment of VR27 is correct, a waveform similar to that shown in Fig. 7 should be obtained. The oscilloscope should be adjusted to about 5mV/cm if a x10 probe is used, and to about 2ms/cm.

To check that the receiver does not lock onto the third harmonic of the line oscillator, connect an infra-red emitting diode to a signal generator via a 680Ω resistor. Set the signal generator to 45.9kHz and 4V p-p sine wave. Place the receiver so that the photodiode faces the I.R.E.D. and is about 15cm from it.

Check that the output of the receiver remains low. If necessary, adjust VR27 slightly anti-clockwise.

Note that drifting alignment may be caused by a faulty supply decoupling capacitor (C36).

Remote Control Receiver—Fault Finding

When operating correctly, typical voltages as shown in the accompanying Table 3 should be obtained on the connecting pins of IC25 in the infra-red Remote Control Receiver.

Table 3. IC25 Voltages

IC25 Pin No.	Typical Voltage
*1	5D.C. +3Vp-p triangular wave
2	13
3	0 to 1.5
4	0 to 15
5	13
6	3
7	3
8	3
9	Earth
10	7
11	0.7
12	3
13	0.7
14	2.5 quiescent
15	Earth
16	15 (supply)

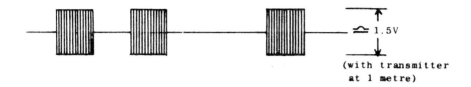

(with transmitter
at 1 metre)

(FIG. 10) TYPICAL RECEIVED WAVEFORM (IC25—PINS 12 AND 7)

N.B. The waveform on pin 1 is the V.C.O. Waveform. The V.C.O. frequency is divided by 2 in the I.C., so it is initially 81.8kHz not 40.9kHz. The period is consequently about 12μS.

With the infra-red Transmitter operating at a distance of 1 metre from the infra-red receiving diode in the Remote Receiver, a waveform similar to that shown in Fig. 10 should be obtained on pins 12 and 7 (output of first amplifier) on IC25.

Remote Control Processor Panel

General Description: The circuit diagram for the Remote Control Processor Panel is shown in Fig. 11.

All circuitry for this panel is contained on a single printed circuit board housed in the Channel Selector Unit, which also contains the Electronic Touch-Tune Panel, shown in block form in the System Interconnection Diagram, Fig. 3.

Power, signal and interface connections between the Processor Panel and other parts of the system are made by colour-coded flexible leads and plug and socket connections.

Reference should be made to Fig. 3 for lead colour coding and inter-connection details.

Telextext and Teletext/Viewdata Facilities: The remote Control Processor Panel employed with Remote Control Systems RC11 and RC12 incorporate some components additional to those incorporated on the Processor Panel employed with Remote Control System RC10.

These additional components provide for the remote operation of receivers equipped with Teletext and Teletext/Viewdata facility on Systems RC11 and RC12 respectively.

These additional components are shown in the circuit diagram of the Remote Control Processor Panel. Fig. 11, and are shown marked with distinguishing symbol thus *.

A table listing the 'DATABUS CODES' employed with Teletext and Viewdata is given in Table 4.

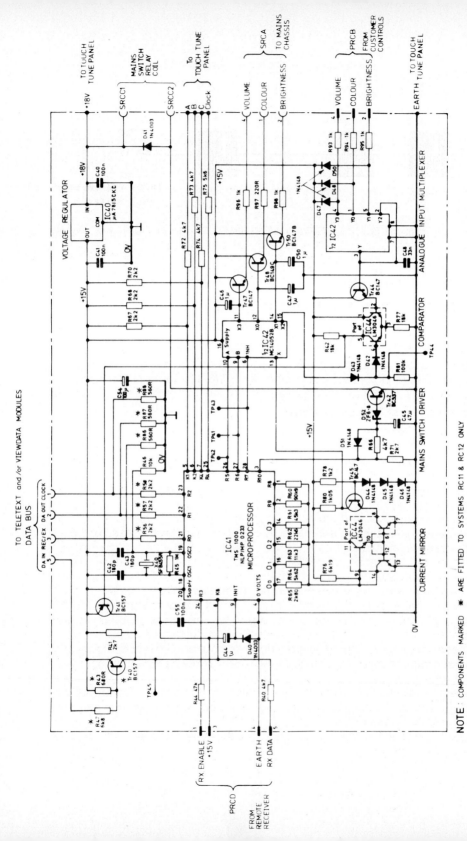

(FIG. 11) CIRCUIT DIAGRAM (REMOTE CONTROL PROCESSOR PANEL)—MODELS RC10/11/12

NOTE : COMPONENTS MARKED ✱ ARE FITTED TO SYSTEMS RC11 & RC12 ONLY

Table 4. Databus Codes—Models RC10/11/12

Command	Data (Hexadecimal)	Function (TXC126)	
0	380	Picture/Clear 2	
1	381	Star*	
2	382	Picture	
3	383	Picture	
4	384	P1	
5	385	Time	
6	386	Hash	
7	387	P2	
8	388	Viewdata	
9	389	Index	
10	38A	Clear 1	
11	38B	Tape	
12	38C	P3	
13	38D	P4	
14	38E	Update	
15	38F	Expand	
16	390	1	
17	391	2	
18	392	3	
19	393	4	
20	394	5	
21	395	6	
22	396	7	
23	397	8	
24	398	9	
25	399	0	
26	39A	Hold	
27	39B	Reveal	
28	39C	Spare A	not used
29	39D	Spare B	
30	39E	Mix	
31	39F	Text	

Remote Control Processor Panel Circuit Description: The microprocessor receives commands from the infra-red receiver in the form of a serial pulse code from PRCD pin 5. This is attenuated, to suit the microprocessor logic levels, by R40 and R41.

The microprocessor has an 'on-chip' clock whose frequency is governed by ceramic resonator X40 connected to pins 18 and 19.

C44 generates a reset pulse to pin 9 of the microprocessor when the receiver is switched on. This sets the internal registers of the microprocessor to their correct states for the device to start executing the stored programme.

Channel Change Operation: The microprocessor is connected by four lines to the SN76705AN touch-tune I.C. on the electronic touch-tune panel. Three of the lines (A, B and C) are the three least significant bits of the button number stored in the touch-tune I.C. (000 for bit 1, 111 for bit 8). The fourth (clock) is a sequential channel change command from the microprocessor. When the microprocessor receives a channel change command from the infra-red receiver, clock pulses are sent to the touch-tune I.C. until the correct code appears on lines A, B and C.

The touch-tune I.C. is intended for systems having up to 16 channel selection buttons, but in this system only eight are employed. To prevent the touch-tune I.C. from ending up with its counter in one of the eight redundant states, the touch-tune panel circuitry is arranged to clock the counter from state 1000 to 1111 and back to 0000. Suppose it is wished to count down from button 6 to button 4. When the command is received, the microprocessor will start sending clock pulses to the touch-tune I.C. When the microprocessor detects code 111 (representing button 8) it sends the clock pulse to put the touch-tune I.C. into its self-clocking mode, and then waits about 2mS to give the touch-tune I.C. time to revert to state 000 (button 1). It then sends the further clock pulses which are required to select the desired button.

Analogue to Digital Conversion (A to D conversion): It was stated previously that the analogue control settings are 'digitised' or converted into digital form. This is done by the successive approximation method (see Fig. 12). In this method a digital-to-analogue converter is fed with various binary numbers and its output is compared, at each step, with the analogue input. If the analogue input is found to be greater than the value represented by the binary number, the binary number is reduced and another comparison made, and vice-versa.

In the system used for RC10, 11 and 12 Remote Control, the control logic is in the microprocessor. The D to A converter consists of the current mirror and the ladder network R60 to R65. By using 64 levels to provide Brightness, Colour and Volume control, the controls operate sufficiently smoothly for the user not to notice the jumps from one level to the next.

Since there is only one D to A converter, it is multiplexed between taking part in the A to D conversions for Brightness, Volume and Colour input and then performing the D to A conversion for each control output. The microprocessor adds the Remote Control offset to the control word for each input before the D

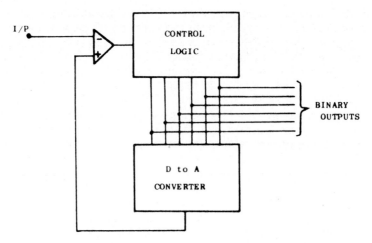

(FIG. 12) BLOCK DIAGRAM (ANALOGUE TO DIGITAL CONVERTER)

to A conversions take place. The analogue outputs are fed to the main chassis via emitter followers Tr47, T448 and Tr50.

The multiplexing of the D to A converter between the analogue outputs and the comparator is done by 'transmission gates' or ' analogue gates' in IC42. This I.C. also switches the comparator between the three analogue inputs. The I.C. acts as a two-pole four-way switch, the switch position being governed by the logic states of the A to B inputs, pins 10 and 9, as shown in Table 5.

The sequence of operations performed by the circuit is as follows: Normally the A address line to IC42 is low and the B line is high. To select the input from the Brightness Control, A is pulsed high, B is pulsed low and the inhibit line to IC42 is pulsed low during the A and B pulses. Input Y1 of the multiplexer is selected, and the local Brightness Control voltage is switched onto C48. This is done three times during periods when the infra-red receiver is inhibited, as shown in Fig. 11. There follows a period during which some of the outputs of the microprocessor may be used to drive a seven-segment display.

Note: The clock waveform on pin 18 of the microprocessor is a sine wave of 5Vp-p at 450kHz.

At the end of this period the A to D conversion of the Brightness Control voltage is performed. C48 is still charged to about the same voltage as that on the Brightness Control slider. The microprocessor produces the trial binary numbers on outputs 0_0, 0_1, 0_2, 0_3, R9 and R8. This gives rise to corresponding analogue voltages on the collector of Tr45 in the current mirror. For explanation of the current mirror, see below. The collector of Tr45 is connected via IC42 to one input of the comparator, and C48 is connected to the other input. The comparator output is inverted by Tr41 and fed to the K8

Table 5. Truth Table for IC42—Models RC10/11/12

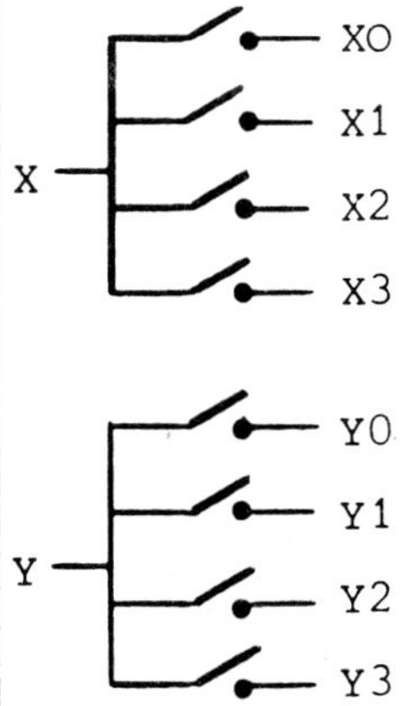

	Inputs (+ve logic)			'On switches'	
	INH	B	A		
	0	0	0	Y0	X0
	0	0	1	Y1	X1
	0	1	0	Y2	X2
	0	1	1	Y3	X3
	1	X	X	NONE	

X = irrelevant

(Switch diagram at left: X — X0, X1, X2, X3; Y — Y0, Y1, Y2, Y3)

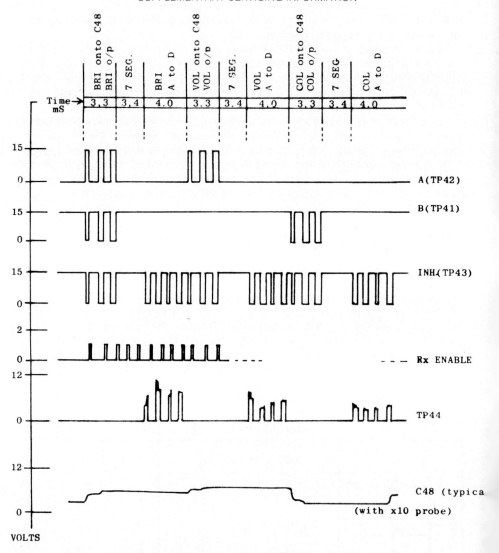

(FIG. 13) TYPICAL WAVEFORMS (PROCESSOR PANEL)—MODELS RC10/11/12

input of the microprocessor. Two steps of the approximation are performed, and the infra-red receiver momentarily enabled. This process is repeated. One step of the approximation is performed and the receiver momentarily enabled. This is also repeated. This gives rise to a waveform on TP44 similar to that shown in Fig. 13. (The height of the pulses will vary with the local control

768

setting.) The A to D conversion is now completed and the binary number corresponding with the Brightness Control setting is added to the Remote Control setting and stored in the microprocessor. Next time the local Brightness Control voltage is sampled and stored on C48, the Brightness Control number stored in the microprocessor will be fed to the D to A converter and the voltage produced fed via IC42 to be stored on C50 and passed via Tr50 to the main chassis.

Next, the Volume Slider voltage is read on to C48 and the previously processed Volume Control voltage fed to the main chassis. After another period set aside for 7-segment driving, the Volume Control voltage on C48 is digitised, processed and stored. The Colour Slider voltage is then sampled and the previously processed Colour Control voltage is fed to the main chassis. After another period for 7-segment driving, the Colour Control voltage is digitised, processed and stored. Next the Brightness Control voltage from the Slider is read onto C48 and the Brightness Control voltage from the current mirror read onto C50, and thus the cycle continues.

The whole process is repeated sufficiently frequently for C46, C47 and C50 to stay charged and provide smoothed analogue control voltages (though there may be about 100mV p-p of ripple on C47).

D47, D48 and D50 protects the inputs of IC42 from any voltage spikes occurring at PRCB by preventing the input voltages from exceeding the supply voltage.

D42 cancels the offset in the comparator caused by the base-emitter voltage of Tr44. D43 introduces a deliberate offset to compensate for the voltage error caused by emitter followers Tr47, Tr48 and Tr50.

Remote Switch-off Facility: When the 'off' button on the hand unit is pressed, pin 3 of the microprocessor goes high. C45 charges through R66. After about half a second the voltage across C45 is sufficient to cause D52 to conduct, turning on Tr42. This energises the relay coil on the mains switch, so that the switch is unlatched and the whole receiver is switched off.

C45 is then discharged through D51 and R71, so that the receiver may be switched back on almost immediately if required.

D41 prevents the relay coil from generating any voltage spikes which might damage Tr42.

Current Mirror: Fig. 14 shows the principle of operation of the D to A converter. The '2' input of the converter is connected to half the resistance 'seen' by the '1' input. Consequently a change in the logic level at the '2' input will cause a change in current twice as large as the change which would result from a change in logic level at the '1' input. Likewise the '4' input can cause twice the change in current caused by the '2' input etc.

The current is therefore proportional to the numerical value of the binary input. However, the analogue controls on the main chassis operate from a varying voltage, so a current mirror is used to obtain this from the varying current. The current mirror is a device which takes a varying input current at a low and fairly constant voltage and produces an output current almost the same as the input current, but which is not affected by variations in output load

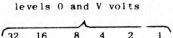

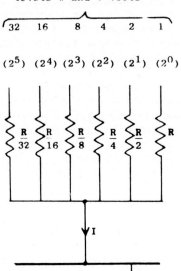

(FIG. 14) PRINCIPLE OF OPERATION OF
D TO A CONVERTER

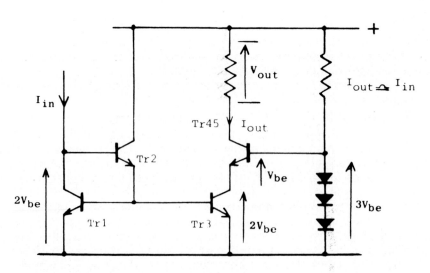

(FIG. 15) CURRENT MIRROR (PROCESSOR PANEL)—MODELS RC10/11/12

or output voltage. The output current may thus be fed through a fixed resistance to produce a voltage proportional to the output current and hence proportional to the input current.

The circuit of the current mirror used on the processor panel is shown in Fig. 15.

Tr2 provides the bias current for Tr1 and Tr3, so that almost all of I_{in} flows in the collector of Tr1. Tr45 is biased so that it keeps the collector voltage of Tr3 the same as that of Tr1.

Tr1, Tr2 and Tr3 are in an I.C. package, so that they are closely matched. Since the base voltage of Tr1 and Tr3 are the same, these transistors have the same collector current, so I_{in} is approximately the same as I_{out}.

Teletext and Viewdata Operation: In the following explanation the word 'teletext' is used to refer only to broadcast systems such as CEEFAX and ORACLE.

When the Remote Control Processor receives a command relevant to Teletext or Viewdata operation, the microprocessor generates another code which can be 'understood' by the Teletext and Viewdata modules. This code will be referred to as the databus code.

MODES OF OPERATION

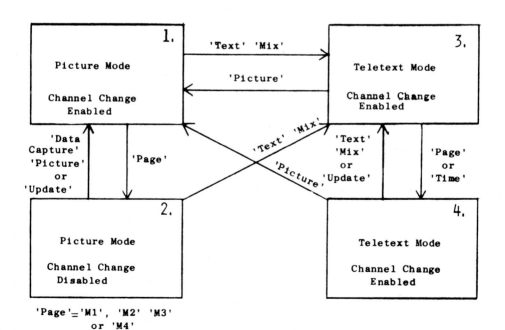

'Page'$=$'M1', 'M2' 'M3'
or 'M4'

(FIG. 16) CHANNEL CHANGE 'ENABLE' STATE DIAGRAM

771

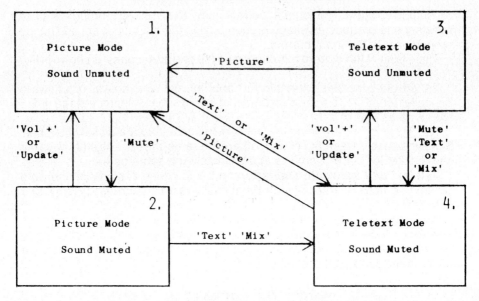

SOUND MUTE STATE DIAGRAM

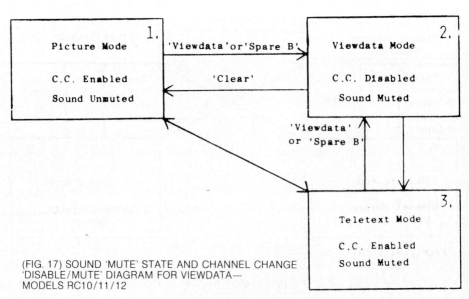

(FIG. 17) SOUND 'MUTE' STATE AND CHANNEL CHANGE
'DISABLE/MUTE' DIAGRAM FOR VIEWDATA—
MODELS RC10/11/12

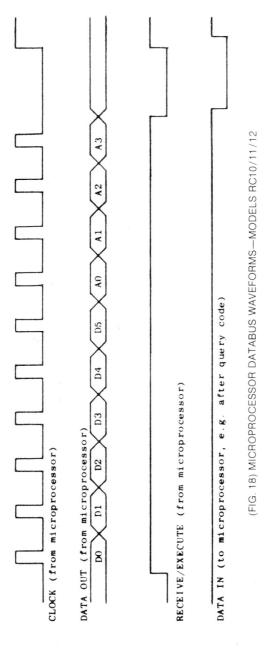

(FIG. 18) MICROPROCESSOR DATABUS WAVEFORMS—MODELS RC10/11/12

When the microprocessor is ready to send the databus code, it first takes the RECEIVE/EXECUTE line high to indicate to the Teletext and Viewdata modules that information is about to be sent. The databus code is then sent serially on the DATA OUT line as 6 data bits and 4 address bits (least significant bit first). Each bit is accompanied by a pulse on the CLOCK bus line to indicate when the data is valid. The mode of operation is shown in Fig. 18.

Picture Mode: The Teletext module may be requested to find and store a page while the receiver is in picture mode. This may be accomplished by keying 'MEMORY' and a numeral in the range 1 to 4, or 'PAGE', followed by the three-digit page number. (The page number duplicates the function of the last MEMORY-digit combination. On switch-on, memory 1 is assumed.)

The channel change is disabled until the page has been captured. When the next channel change command occurs, the microprocessor sends the status enquiry code 3BE (hexadecimal) to the teletext module. Then the RECEIVE/EXECUTE line goes low and the teletext module will put a low logic level on the DATA IN line if the page has not been captured. The microprocessor then disregards the channel change command.

If the page cannot be found for any reason, channel change may be enabled by keying 'PICTURE'. When channel change is enabled, the numeral keys produce no databus codes.

Teletext Mode: In teletext mode when channel change is disabled (see Fig. 17) keying a digit in the range of 1 to 8 causes the microprocessor to send the status enquiry code on the databus in order to determine the Teletex status. If the status is 'low' another digit is required and the relevant databus code is transmitted. If the status is 'high' the digit is ignored.

Digits 9 and 0 always result in the relevant databus code being transmitted.

Viewdata Mode: Channel change is permanently disabled, so numeral keys always produce databus codes.

'Modes of Operation' are shown in Figs. 16 and 17 and show the manner in which various commands affect muting and channel changing.

Fault Finding

Fault Finding Charts, Figs. 19, 20 and 21, are provided to assist in cases where a single fault exists.

In other cases where there may be a combination of faults, other means of diagnosis may need to be employed. As an aid to diagnosis, in many cases it will be found useful to check the waveforms shown in Fig. 13.

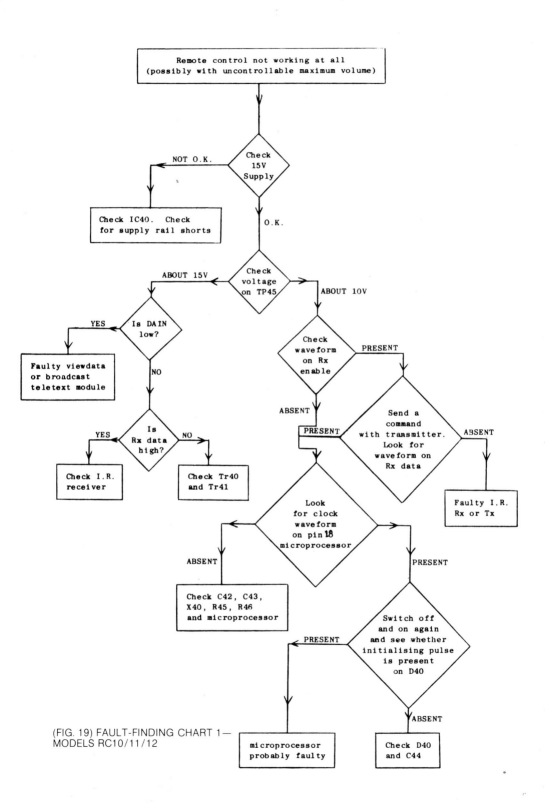

(FIG. 19) FAULT-FINDING CHART 1—
MODELS RC10/11/12

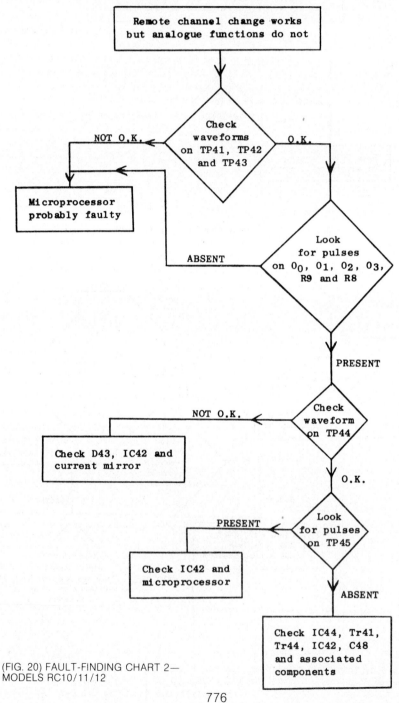

(FIG. 20) FAULT-FINDING CHART 2—
MODELS RC10/11/12

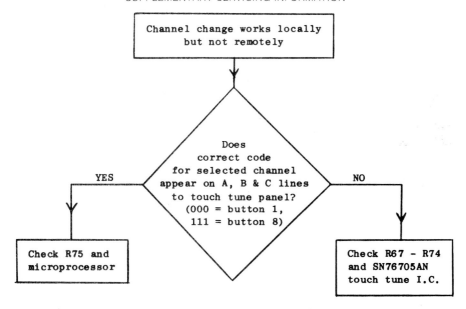

(FIG. 21) FAULT-FINDING CHART 3—MODELS RC10/11/12

THORN CONSUMER ELECTRONICS

Ultrasonic Remote Control Systems U706, U708

U708 Transmitter (see Fig. 22a)

The transmitter is crystal controlled and therefore requires no adjustment. A light-emitting diode gives an indication of battery condition. Twenty-four command frequencies are required to operate the Remote Control Receiver. These are obtained by earthing one of the control inputs—A B C D E simultaneously with one of the control inputs—F G H K L (all inputs are normally at supply potential) via contact 'fingers' on the Transmitter switching panel (Fig. 22b).

Operating error protection recognises the operation of more than one pair of the above inputs as invalid and keeps the oscillator inactive and the internal frequency-divider in a set position.

The oscillator frequency of 4.4336MHz is divided by 2. When one from each group of control inputs A-E and F-L are energised simultaneously an encoded 5-bit word is fed to the adjustable frequency-divider.

The adjustable frequency-divider, working on the blanking principle, blanks out 1-30 pulses from each 128 2.2168MHz pulses. This frequency is further divided by a fixed frequency-divider of 50 resulting in an output at Pin 15 in the range of 34kHz-44kHz. A non-uniform wavetrain occurs due to the blanking process which can result in an audible signal during operation.

As Pin 15 of IC1 must not have a D.C. voltage greater than –0.3V relative to earth, a buffer stage VT1 is used to drive the transducer. T1, an auto-step-up transformer, develops a peak to peak voltage of 340V at the highest frequency and 380V at the lowest frequency. A 20kΩ/V meter, e.g. AVO 72, reads 125V across the transducer. The transducer is of the capacitive type and therefore requires a polarising voltage. This is obtained by W1 conducting on positive peaks and charging the reservoir capacitor C2, C1 acting as a D.C. blocker.

W3 protects the I.C. against incorrect battery connection. There is no requirement for an On/Off switch due to the passive current consumption

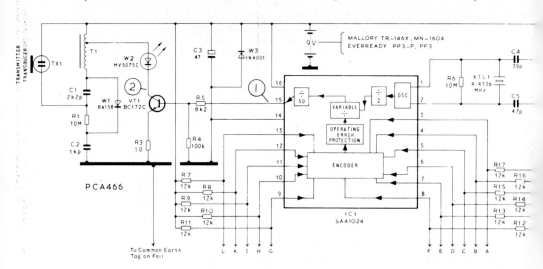

(FIG. 22a) CIRCUIT DIAGRAM (REMOTE CONTROL TRANSMITTER)—U708 *(PART)*

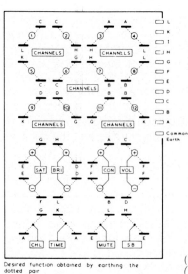

Desired function obtained by earthing the dotted pair

(FIG. 22b) TRANSMITTER SWITCHING PANEL—U708 *(CONTINUED)*

being less than 10μA. In the operating mode, current consumption is approximately 35mA-45mA.

The controls of the Television Receiver must always be adjusted for normal viewing before using the Remote Control Transmitter.

Control Frequencies

Command	Control Inputs Earthed	Approx. Frequency Output (kHz)	Command	Control Inputs Earthed	Approx. Frequency Output (kHz)
1 Standby	H and E	33.95	13 Channel 12	B and K	39.83
2 Sound Mute	L and E	34.29	14 Channel 11	B and G	39.49
3 Colour +	G and E	34.64	15 Channel 10	D and G	40.87
4 Colour –	F and E	35.33	16 Channel 9	D and K	41.22
5 Contrast +	A and F	36.02	17 Channel 8	L and B	42.60
6 Contrast –	B and F	36.72	18 Channel 7	H and B	42.26
7 Volume +	C and F	37.41	19 Channel 6	G and C	40.18
8 Volume –	D and F	38.10	20 Channel 5	K and C	40.53
9 Call Channel	G and A	38.79	21 Channel 4	A and L	41.91
10 Call Channel			22 Channel 3	A and H	41.56
and Time	K and A	39.14	23 Channel 2	C and H	42.95
11 Brightness +	H and D	43.64	24 Channel 1	C and L	43.30
12 Brightness –	L and D	43.99			

Note: The SAA1024 Divider/Encoder incorporates facilities for 30 command frequencies but only 24 are used.

U708 Transmitter Servicing (see Waveforms Fig. 25)

The L.E.D. is a guide to correct operation up to, but not including, the transducer, T1, and polarising voltage circuit. The polarising voltage should read approximately 160V at the junction of R1/C2, if this is correct and no output is obtained, the transducer should be suspected. Voltage across transducer transformer should be 125V A.C.

Transmitter Voltage Measurements: Battery Voltage at 8V (AVO Model 8)

VT1	Passive	Active	IC1 Pin No.	Passive	Active
C	6.4	5.6	3-13	7.4	Any two at 0 depending
B	0	0.75			upon command
E	0	0.3	15	0	3.3

Symptom	Procedure
REDUCED RANGE Assuming normal range of up to 5 metres	Check: Battery voltage on-load which should be at least 5.6V. At distances of 5 metres-7 metres it should be at least 7V. Peak-to-peak voltage across transducer TX1 on . . . STANDBY: 380V p-p 34kHz BRIGHTNESS: 340V p-p 44kHz.
INCORRECT OPERATION	Check: Battery voltage. If on-load voltage is less than 5.6V insert a new battery.

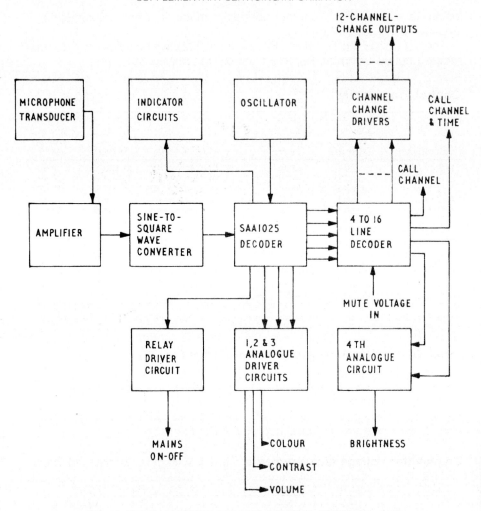

(FIG. 23) BLOCK DIAGRAM (REMOTE CONTROL RECEIVER)—U708

Symptom	Procedure
NO OPERATION	Check: Output Waveform (1) on IC1 Pin 15. Output Waveform (2) on VT1 collector. Check for open-circuit earth terminal from switch-plate; XTL1; W1 short-circuit.
ON-LOAD BATTERY VOLTAGE READS NEAR ZERO With good battery	Check: IC1 as given in Voltage Table; W3 short-circuit.
IF ANY ONE OR GROUP OF COMMANDS IS OPERATIVE	Check: Switch-plate contacts; open-circuit print between pads and terminals.
L.E.D. ILLUMINATED CONTINUOUSLY	Button jammed.

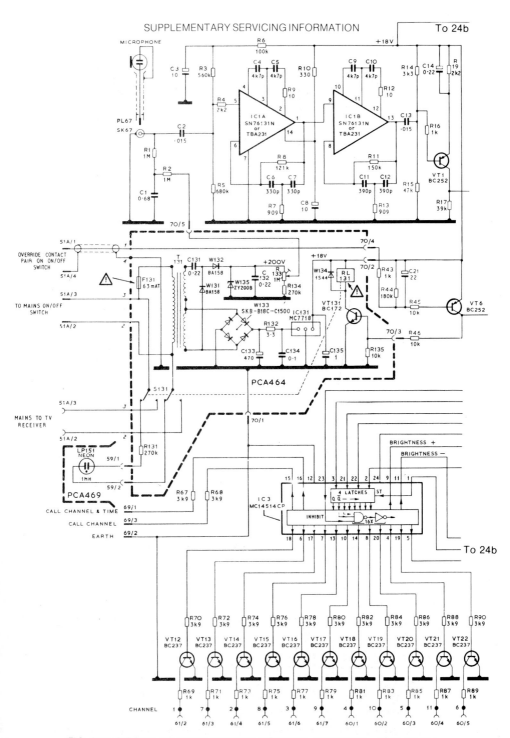

(FIG. 24a) CIRCUIT DIAGRAM (REMOTE CONTROL RECEIVER)—U708 *(PART)*

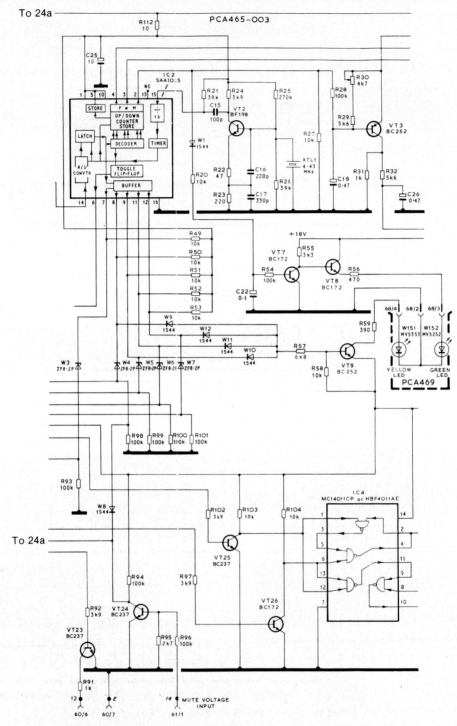

(FIG. 24b) CIRCUIT DIAGRAM (REMOTE CONTROL RECEIVER)—U708 *(PART)*

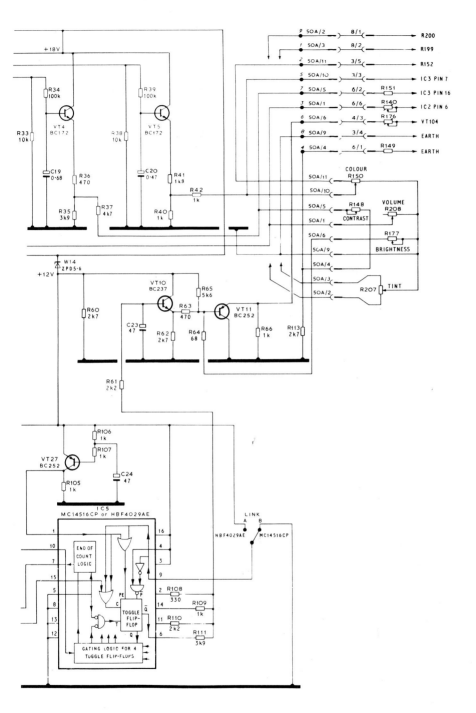

(FIG. 24c) CIRCUIT DIAGRAM (REMOTE CONTROL RECEIVER)—U708 *(CONTINUED)*

U708 Receiver Command Code

Command Received	Frequency kHz	Code (Positive Logic) IC2 PIN No.				
		E 8	D 9	C 11	B 12	A 7
1 Standby	33.95	1	1	1	0	1
2 Sound Mute	34.29	1	1	1	0	0
3 Colour +	34.64	*1	1	0	1	1
4 Colour –	35.33	1	1	0	0	1
5 Contrast +	36.02	1	0	1	1	1
6 Contrast –	36.72	1	0	1	0	1
7 Volume +	37.41	1	0	0	1	1
8 Volume –	38.10	1	0	0	0	1
9 Call Channel	38.79	0	1	1	1	1
10 Call Channel and Time	39.14	0	1	1	1	0
11 Brightness +	43.64	0	0	0	0	1
12 Brightness –	43.99	0	0	0	0	0
13 Channel 12	39.83	0	1	1	0	0
14 Channel 11	39.49	0	1	1	0	1
15 Channel 10	40.87	0	1	0	0	1
16 Channel 9	41.22	0	1	0	0	0
17 Channel 8	42.60	0	0	1	0	0
18 Channel 7	42.26	0	0	1	0	1
19 Channel 6	40.18	0	1	0	1	1
20 Channel 5	40.53	0	1	0	1	0
21 Channel 4	41.91	0	0	1	1	0
22 Channel 3	41.56	0	0	1	1	1
23 Channel 2	42.95	0	0	0	1	1
24 Channel 1	43.30	0	0	0	1	0

* Testing outputs. Transmit Brightness—when all pins of IC2 are being switched.

Logic 1 represents maximum D.C. voltage,   1V below supply rail.
Logic 0 represents minimum D.C. voltage,   9V below supply rail.

24-Channel Remote Control Receiver (Figs. 23, 24)

The receiver is a self-contained unit including its own power supply. The output requirements from the ultrasonic remote receiver to control T.V. receiver from the 24 command signals are:

(i) Four separate variable D.C. voltages to control Colour, Contrast, Volume and Brightness.

(ii) An independent control for Sound Mute.

(iii) A D.C. voltage switching from 0V to +17V to operate the Standby and On-from-Standby function.

(iv) Twelve independent pulsed outputs to select the Channel required.

(v) Two independent pulsed outputs to select Channel or Channel-and-Time on screen display.

When the T.V. mains switch is operated the remote receiver power supply is energised, supplying +18V (70/2), +12V (70/2 via zener W14) to the remote receiver. 200V is also supplied (via 70/5) and is fed to the microphone which requires a maximum D.C. polarising voltage of 200V. This voltage may be lowered by a preset on the power supply to give reduced sensitivity.

IC2 (SAA1025): At switch-on IC2 outputs are:

(i) Pins 2, 3 and 4: 9kHz square wave which gives D.C. voltages of 6V at Pin 2, 10V at Pin 3 and 9V at Pin 4 (see Ultrasonic Control). These voltages are used to set the standardised conditions of Volume, Contrast and Colour via their respective output transistors VT3, VT4 and VT5.

(ii) Pin 6 initially at 0V, but on operating the On/Off switch the override contacts momentarily earth the base of VT6. VT6 conducts, switching on VT131 which operates the relay and switches mains to the T.V. receiver. The output from VT6 collector also takes Pin 6 positive which resets the toggle flip-flop in IC2, and Pin 6 then supplies +17V to hold VT131 on. VT6 switches off as the capacitor across its base/emitter diode.

(iii) Pins 7, 9, 11, 12, 8: all at +16V.

The Remote Control Receiver will always return to these conditions when the T.V. receiver is switched off and on again.

Ultrasonic Control: The microphone picks up any one of the 24 command signals between 34kHz and 44kHz. The signal is amplified by IC1 which contains two operational amplifiers with a bandpass response of 30kHz-46kHz.

VT1 amplifies and limits the sine wave input producing a square wave of approximately 17Vp-p at Pin 14 IC2. Correct operation of these stages is indicated by measuring the A.C. voltage on Pin 14.

IC2 accurately counts the input frequency over a fixed time period, the accuracy of counting being dependent upon the input at Pin 15 from the crystal oscillator VT2. Depending upon the frequency transmitted, IC2 produces a coded 5-bit pulse output signal on Pins 7, 9, 11, 12 and 8. Seven of the 24 instructions are processed further in the decoder of which six control the pulse-width modulator circuit. This produces variable mark-space ratio outputs at Pins 2, 3 and 4 to provide Volume ±, Contrast ±, Colour ± controlling voltages. The seventh, in producing 0V D.C. at Pin 2, is used for sound mute.

In the standardised condition the mark-space ratios at Pins 2, 3 and 4 are different producing the voltages given in paragraph (i) under IC2 (SAA1025).

Colour Control: The square-wave output at Pin 4 of IC2 is fed to the base of emitter follower VT5 via an integrating network consisting of R39 and C20. The two resistors in the emitter of VT5 divide the emitter voltage so that the required voltage swing appears at the output. R42 limits the maximum current which may be taken through the slider of the Colour Control.

The output voltage swing of 5V (minimum mark-space ratio: minimum

U708 Transmitter

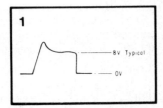
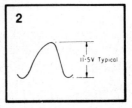

U708 Receiver

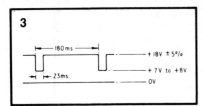
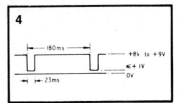

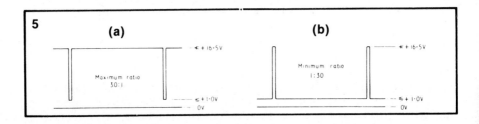

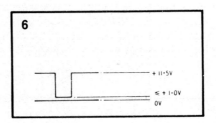

(FIG. 25) CIRCUIT WAVEFORMS—U708

saturation) to 9.5V (maximum mark-space ratio: maximum saturation) is obtained when the Colour Control is set to the centre of its travel.

Contrast Control: The square-wave output at Pin 3 of IC2 drives a circuit similar to that for Colour but with different value resistors in the emitter follower output stage to give the required voltage swing of 4.3V to 8.1V when the control is set at mid position.

Volume Control: The operation of the circuit is similar to the Colour and Contrast Control ciruits but a PNP transistor is used instead of NPN.

With the Remote Control not connected, set receiver Volume Control midway and adjust R140 (I.F. Decoder Module) for 1V D.C. on slider of Volume Control.

Connect Remote Control and adjust R30 on remote control until voltage on slider of receiver Volume Control is 1.6V.

Sound Mute: When the Sound Mute command is transmitted, Pin 2 of IC2 falls to 0V, VT3 turns off thus muting the sound and the green L.E.D. illuminates. When the Sound Mute command is repeated the square wave output at Pin 2 returns to its previous mark-space ratio so that volume returns to the pre-muted level.

IC3 4-Line to 16-Line Latch Decoder: The 5-bit pulsed outputs at Pins 7, 9, 11, 12 and 8 of IC2 are passed to IC3 via 8.2V zener diodes W3-W7 to keep the input voltage at or below the 12V supply of IC3. Two of the outputs of IC3 (Pins 9 and 11) are used to operate the Brightness Control circuit, the other 14 outputs are used for Channel Change and to call Channel or Channel-and-Time display on the screen.

Pin 8 of IC2 is connected to the inhibit input of IC3, and IC3 will only operate when the inhibit input falls to 0V, this only occurs during Channel Change, Brightness ±. Call Channel and Call Channel-and-Time commands.

Channel Change: For Channel Change a positive output from IC3 of at least 60ms duration is required, but as the pulse output of IC3 consists of 23ms pulses every 180ms, pulse stretching is necessary.

Pulse stretching is achieved by using the sound mute pulse which is given out from the channel change I.C. and lasts for approximately 400ms. This positive pulse turns on VT24 pulling down the voltage to the strobe input of IC3. If the inhibit line (normally held down for 23ms) was to go high, IC3 would cease to give an output. W8 is therefore included so that whilst VT24 is on the inhibit line is also held down.

Positive-going pulses of approximately 400ms appear at the channel change outputs of IC3 switching on the required output transistor. This in turn reduces the input voltage to the appropriate channel change I.C. input pin, latching it to the required channel.

Switching the Receiver to Standby: The red button (Standby command) must be held down until the red neon illuminates to show that the receiver is in the standby mode. The toggle flip-flop in IC2 is switched so that the output at Pin 6 changes from 17V to 0V, VT131 turns off and the receiver goes to standby.

Switching on the Receiver from Standby: The T.V. may be switched on from Standby by operating any one of the remote Channel Change commands until the red neon is extinguished. When the button is held down longer a channel other than 1 will be directly selected, the L.E.D. indicating the channel number corresponding to the button. If a Channel Change control button is not pressed until the corresponding number is displayed, the T.V. receiver selects Channel 1.

The toggle flip-flop for the above operation is reset within IC2, Pin 6 goes to +17V, VT131 is then held in a conducting state operating the relay and power is switched to the T.V. receiver.

Brightness Control: The requirement of the Brightness Control is similar to that for Volume, Colour, etc. IC2 has only three variable D.C. outputs, therefore a 16-Step Binary Up/Down Counter, IC5, is used to generate a variable D.C. output to control brightness. The binary coded outputs of Pins 2, 14, 11, 6 of IC5 are added together by the resistor network R108 to R111 and passed via integrator R61/C23 to emitter-follower VT10 and VT11 to give the controlling voltage swing of 3V to 9.7V.

Maximum D.C. output is obtained when IC5 Pins 2, 14, 11 and 6 are all at 9.7V, resulting in minimum brightness. Minimum D.C. output is obtained when the pins are at 0V, resulting in maximum brightness.

At switch-on the output voltage sits at approximately half of the output voltage maximum/minimum limits (standardised condition). This is achieved by the reset circuit VT27 and Pin 1 of IC5. When Pin 1 is driven to rail supply the voltage conditions on Pins 3, 4, 12 and 13 are transferred to the output Pins 2, 14, 11 and 6 so that Pins 2 and 6 are 9.7V and Pins 14 and 11 are 0V.

At switch-on VT27 conducts taking Pin 1 to the rail supply. As the capacitor in the base charges, VT27 turns off, and Pin 1 drops to 0V.

IC5 Counter Instructions: The I.C. requires three instructions:
(i) Direction fo count (up or down) input to Pin 10.
(ii) Clock pulse input to Pin 15.
(iii) Clock pulse inhibit output from Pin 7 when maximum count (minimum brightness) or minimum count (maximum brightness) is reached.

Direction of Count: The counter counts up when Pin 10 is 11.5V and counts down when Pin 10 is at 0V. This instruction is obtained from the two NAND gates connected to operate as a bistable driven by VT25/26.

With no Brightness command VT25/26 bases are at 0V. When Brightness— is transmitted VT26 is pulsed by the output of IC3 switching the bistable to give 11.5V (count up command) at Pin 10 IC5. The output will stay in this state until a different instruction is given. If Brightness + instruction is transmitted, IC3 pulses VT25, the output of which reverses the state of the bistable to give 0V, instructing IC5 to count down.

Clock Pulse Input to Pin 15 IC5: When a Brightness command is transmitted, IC3 gives out at Pin 9 or Pin 11 a 23ms pulse every 180ms. These pulses are passed via VT25 or VT26 to Pins 12 or 13 of IC4 and via the two NAND gates to the clock pulse input at Pin 15 IC5.

Clock Pulse Inhibit: When the counter IC5 reaches maximum count (all output pins at 11.5V) or minimum count (all output pins at 0V), the end of count circuit switches the voltage on Pin 7 of IC5 from 11.5V to 0V. This inhibits a NAND gate in IC4 resulting in non clock pulse output at Pin 10.

If the clock pulses were not inhibited at the minimum/maximum counts, the counter would re-cycle causing the brightness to vary continuously.

Visual Indicators: The following indicators are used:
(i) Red neon to indicate the Standby condition.
(ii) Yellow L.E.D. to indicate signal reception from the Remote transmitter.
(iii) Green L.E.D. to indicate the sound mute condition.

A double-pole change-over relay is used with the mains fed to the pole contacts and the neon connected to the contacts of the unenergised condition of the relay. Hence, the neon only illuminates whilst the T.V. receiver is off.

The yellow L.E.D. is driven from VT9, the base of which is lowered relative to emitter whenever one, or more, of all four of the outputs of IC2 (Pins 8, 9, 11 and 12) are available. The L.E.D. will flash in sympathy with the outputs as they consist of 23ms wide pulses with a pulse repetition rate of 180ms.

The green L.E.D. is driven by VT8 which in turn is driven by VT7. As long as a pulse output is present at Pin 2 of IC2, VT7 is conducting and its collector voltage is virtually 0V. Hence VT8, the base of which is driven from VT7 collector, is off. When Pin 2 goes to 0V (indicative of a mute command) VT7 is cut-off, its collector voltage rises to rail supply, and VT8 is driven into conduction thus causing the L.E.D. to illuminate.

Power Supply: Mains potential is always present at isolation transformer T131 with the T.V. receiver on or in the standby mode. T131 feeds the bridge rectifier W133 which supplies 25V to IC131 18V regulator. The 18V supplies the relay driver, VT131, and the remote control receiver via Plug 70/2.

At switch-on the override contacts momentarily ground the base of VT6 via R43, turning VT6 hard on and charging C21. VT6 collector drives VT131 on, operating the relay and switching on the television receiver. The positive output at VT6 collector also drives Pin 6 of IC2 positive, resetting the toggle flip-flop output from 0V to +17V.

R45/C21 in VT6 base is to keep VT6 conducting for a period after the override contacts have open-circuited, keeping the relay RL131 in until the toggle flip-flop output changes from 0V to 17V.

200V Supply for Microphone: Voltage doubler C131, W131, W132 and C132 produces approximately +240V which is stabilized by zener diode W135 to 200V. R133 adjusts the voltage supplied to the microphone and is normally set for maximum voltage. Reducing the voltage will result in decreased sensitivity of the remote receiver.

U706 (Mk 2) Clock and Channel Display Unit (Figs. 26, 27)

The Clock and Channel Display Unit U706 is used in conjunction with the 12-channel ultrasonic remote control unit U708, to enable the selected channel number and the time to be displayed when required on the 9500-9600 series receiver C.R.T.

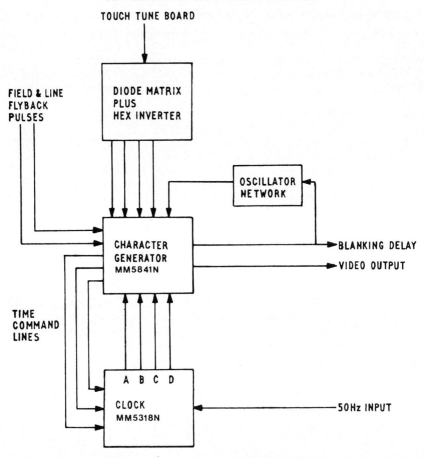

(FIG. 26) BLOCK DIAGRAM (CLOCK AND CHANNEL UNIT)—U706

The U708 remote control unit is operated with a conventional L.E.D. channel number display.

The basic elements of the clock and channel unit are shown in the simplified block-schematic diagram.

Display Functions: The U706 provides facilities to display the selected channel number, with or without time, as yellow figures on a black background (referred to as the black box in this description). The black box is factory set to be positioned in the top right hand area of the C.R.T.

When changing channel, by touch-pads or remote control, the selected channel number will be displayed for a period of approximately 2 seconds. It is possible to recall the selected channel number by remote control, the number will remain displayed for the period that the remote control button is depressed,

790

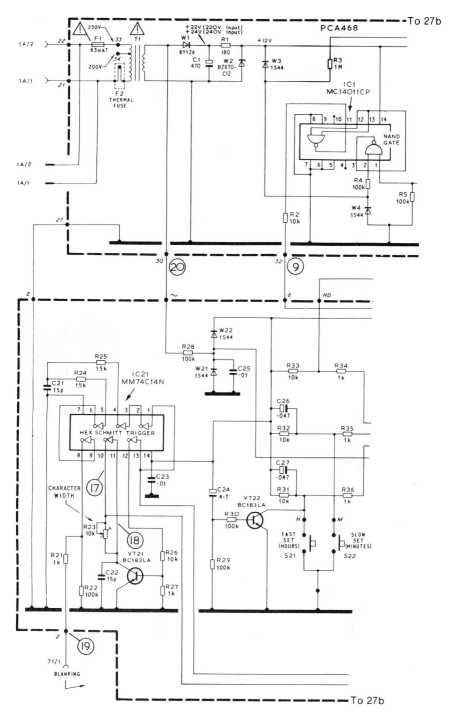

(FIG. 27a) CIRCUIT DIAGRAM (CLOCK AND CHANNEL UNIT)—U706

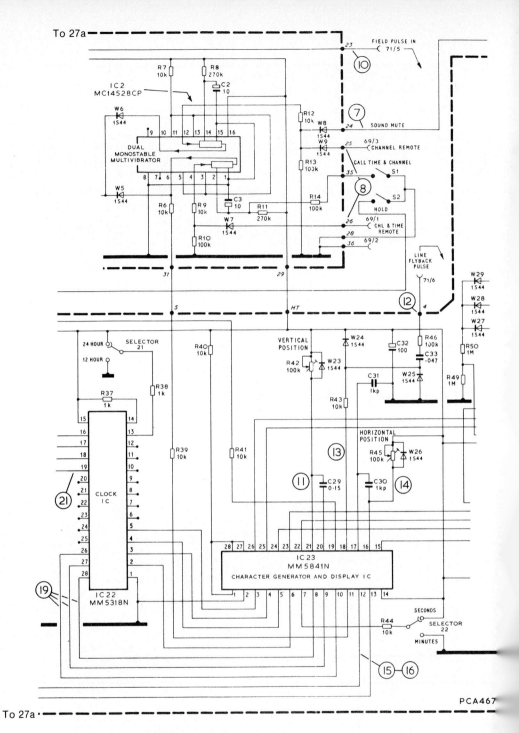

CLOCK & CHANNEL CIRCUIT

(FIG. 27b) CIRCUIT DIAGRAM (CLOCK AND CHANNEL UNIT)—U706

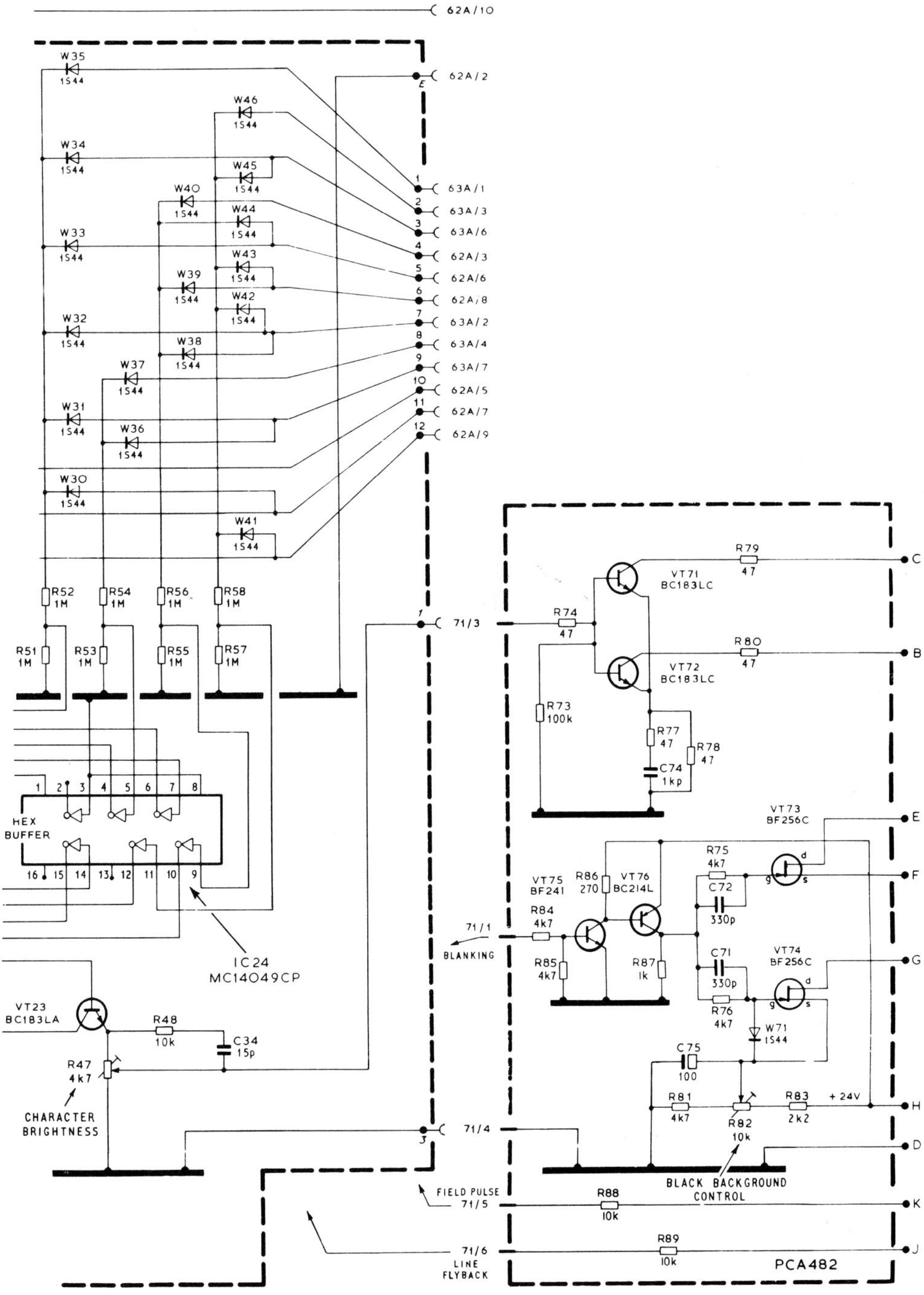

INTERFACE CIRCUIT

(FIG. 27c) CIRCUIT DIAGRAM (CLOCK, CHANNEL AND INTERFACE)—U706 and for a few seconds after the button is released. The time in hours, minutes and seconds, together with the channel number, can be displayed either via the remote control unit or by a manual switch on the receiver. When calling time and channel by remote control the display will remain for the period that the button is depressed and will disappear a few seconds after the button is released. A hold (stop/start clock) facility is available on the unit to enable the time to be set.

U706 Printed Circuit Boards: U706 consists of three P.C. boards, PCA467 and PCA468 to generate the time and channel information, the third is used to interface with the receiver and can be changed to accommodate other models. In the case of the 9500-9600 series receiver the correct interface board is PCA482.

Power Supply and Switching Circuit PCA468: P.C. board PCA468 carries the power supply for the clock and channel unit and also the switching circuit for the field flyback pulse which is used to initiate the display circuitry.

Power Supply: Mains is fed, via a double-wound mains transformer, to a simple half-wave rectifier stabilized by zener diode W2 to provide +12V D.C. for the channel and time boards. A low voltage 50Hz signal is taken from the anode of the rectifier diode W1, and fed to Pin 19 of IC22, the clock I.C. Because IC22 relies on the mains frequency for counting, the unit is permanently connected to the mains supply side of the T.V. receiver on-off switch.

The mains transformer primary has a low voltage tapping (Tag 34) which should only be used in areas where mains supplies are permanently below 200V.

As the complete unit only draws typically 20mA from the mains, extra protection is provided for faults which will not blow the time-lag fuse F1. This takes the form of a thermal link F2 wired in the primary of the transformer and fitting into a slot in the transformer moulding. The transformer, normally warm during operation, rises in temperature on overload causing the link to open.

Switching Circuit: IC1 and IC2 provide the switching circuit for the negative-going field pulse which is fed in from the interface board PCA482 via PL/SK 71/5 and Tag 23. R3/R4/W3/W4 provide simple clipping to protect IC1 which is a 2-input NAND gate package.

One section is used as a gate to allow the field pulse to pass when the correct command is received. The pulse appears on Pin 2, but Pin 3 stays at rail potential until Pin 1 is pulled up towards rail potential by either W5 or W6. When Pin 1 is high, an inverted field pulse appears at output Pin 3 and passes to the second NAND gate which is used as an inverter so that a negative pulse appears at output Pin 11. This passes via R2 and Tag 32 to Tag 6 of PCA467 and on via R41 to Pin 19 of IC23, the character generator, to initiate the display. R2 and R41 provide flashover protection.

IC2 is a dual, retriggerable, resettable monostable multivibrator. The command pulses from the remote control and the sound mute pulse pass through the diodes W7, W8 or W9 to raise the potential on Pins 4 or 12 up

794

towards rail supply. The I.C. responds to the positive edges of these pulses and produces a positive output voltage on either Pin 6 or Pin 10 for a two- to three-second period after receiving each pulse. The time constants for the two halves of the I.C. are set by the components R8/C2 and R11/C3.

At channel-change (by touch-pad or remote), the single 300ms to 600ms sound mute pulse generated by the channel-change I.C.s in the T.V. receiver pulls up Pin 12 via W8, Pin 10 rises for the two- to three-second period which causes Pin 1 of IC1 to be pulled up via W6 so allowing the field pulse to pass to IC23 as described earlier.

When the remote control is operated to Call Channel or Call Channel and Time, a series of 23ms pulses passes through either W9 or W7 triggering the appropriate input (Pin 12 or Pin 4) so that one of the outputs (Pin 10 or Pin 6) rises and pulls up Pin 1 of IC1. Because a stream of pulses is generated in the remote receiver the display will remain on the screen while the remote control transmitter button is pressed and for a few seconds after it is released. When the Call Channel and Time command is received, Pin 11 of IC23 is pulled towards rail supply via R6 and R39 so that time and channel information are displayed. When only the channel information is required Pin 11 of IC23 is kept at chassis potential.

To simplify setting-up, toggle switches S1 and S2 are provided; S1 to permanently display the channel and time information and S2 to stop the clock counting. Setting-up the time is achieved by throwing the switches to give a permanent on-screen static display and using the fast and slow set push-button switches S21 and S22 to set the required time in hours and minutes. Setting the seconds to display correctly can be achieved by using the Hold switch S2. If the display is set-up before a transmitted time check, then at the required instant the Hold switch can be set to normal and the clock will then start to count.

Example: To set clock to 12.00h precisely.

Set switches to DISPLAY and HOLD.

Press FAST push-button and release when 11h is displayed, then operate SLOW push-button until approximately 11.58. Switch from HOLD to NORMAL. The clock will now advance at 1 second intervals so watch the display carefully and switch to HOLD when 12.00.00 appears.

Return Hold switch to NORMAL operation at 12.00h time check. Then return Display switch to NORMAL operation.

The Character Generator and Display Circuit: This is the heart of the Clock and Channel Unit; by taking line and field flyback pulses IC23 produces the voltages required to blank out an area of the screen and insert channel and time characters. The negative line pulse passes through R46 and C33 and is clipped by W24 and W25 before passing through R43 to Pin 18 to trigger a monostable circuit within the IC. The circuit is used with preset R45 and its timing capacitor C30 to adjust the horizontal position of the display. The negative field pulse is fed from the NAND gate circuit IC1 on PCA468, via R2 and R41 and into Pin 19 to trigger a second monostable circuit, which is used with preset R42 and timing capacitor C29 to set the vertical position of the display. The values of R42 and R45 allow almost any position to be chosen, but are factory adjusted to place the display near the top right hand side of the screen. Diodes W23 and W26 together with capacitor C31 reduce spurious outputs affecting the top line of the display.

The presence of the field pulse initiates the operation of IC23 whose circuitry interrogates both the channel number information and IC22, the clock IC, to produce the required display. A positive pulse appears on Pin 12 of IC23 on each of the display lines (see Waveform 16 on Fig. 30) and is used as the blanking pulse for the T.V. receiver Signals Module. It is fed to Pins 1 and 13 of IC21 which is a Hex Schmitt Trigger. The four sections of IC21 between Pins 1 and 8, together with R24, R25 and C21, provide a short delay for the blanking signal to ensure that on the tube face the black box is positioned symmetrically around the characters.

The pulse from Pin 12 of IC23 also starts the Schmitt trigger oscillator between Pins 10 and 11 of IC21. This simple positive feedback oscillator provides timing pulses for the character generator IC23. Outside the blanking period VT21 is switched on and the oscillator is stopped. When the blanking pulse starts, Pin 13 of IC21 rises so Pin 12 falls and VT21 is switched off allowing the oscillator to start. When VT21 switches off, Pin 11 of IC21 rises; causing Pin 10, the output of this Schmitt trigger stage, to fall. This, in turn, pulls Pin 11 back down towards chassis so reversing the output. The frequency is set by the preset R23 (Character Width) and the capacitor C22. IC23 is designed to operate with a frequency between 4MHz and 5MHz giving an approximate 6-inch display on a 26-inch TV screen. The pulses are fed into Pin 13 of IC23 which counts them and provides the orders for the clock I.C. as well as providing the drive information for the video output stages. This appears on Pin 15 and drives the emitter follower VT23. The preset R47 (Character Brightness) is used as an amplitude control to adjust the intensity of the characters and R48 and C34 provide transient compensation.

The option to remove seconds from the display is provided by taking Pin 7 of IC23 down to earth using Selector 22, a simple tag lead connector. This alters the count functions so that the Schmitt trigger oscillator provides 48 pulses when only hours and minutes are required instead of 64 when the seconds are added.

The Diode Matrix and Hex Inverter Circuitry: Only one of the output pins of the touch tune circuitry is switched up to the +35V stabilized supply at any one time, the remaining 11 being at zero volts. The character generator IC23 is an NMOS device requiring the channel number information to be presented in digital form for both the tens and units digits with zero volts as the on state, i.e. negative logic. The diode matrix takes the single voltage from the touch tune circuit and switches it to the correct combination of inputs to Pins 5, 7, 9, 11 and 14 of the hex inverter IC24 as shown below. The five line B.C.D. (Binary Coded Decimal) code representing the channel information is inverted within IC24 and then fed to Pins 22 to 26 inclusive on IC23.

IC24 Voltages:

Channel No.	Input resistors at +35V	Output pins of IC24 at 0V
1	R52	15
2	R58	12
3	R52, R58	12,15
4	R56	10
5	R52, R56	10,15
6	R56, R58	10,12
7	R52, R56, R58	10,12, 15
8	R54	4
9	R52, R54	4, 15
10	R50	6
11	R50, R52	6, 15
12	R50, R58	6, 12

The Clock Circuit: IC22 and its associated components provide the time information for the display. The clock takes the nominal 50Hz mains frequency as its reference. This means that the long term accuracy will be excellent but the seconds indicated will not necessarily correspond exactly to transmitted time signals. Because of the dependence on the mains, the clock unit is not switched off by the T.V. receiver on-off switch and is permanently counting as long as the receiver is plugged into an uninterrupted mains supply.

The 50Hz signal is taken from the anode of W1, passed through filter network R28/C25 and into Pin 19 of IC22 to operate a divider which produces a series of 1s pulses. These are fed to counters within IC22 to produce seconds, minutes and hours information. W21 and W22 prevent excessive voltage reaching the I.C.

Push-buttons S21 and S22 are time set-up switches, which pull down Pins 18 and 17 of IC22 to provide fast and slow functions by altering the counting within the I.C. S21 gives a 60-minute change every second and S22 gives a 60-second change every second. Pins 18 and 17 are normally held up to rail supply by R31 and R32. R35 and R36 provide flashover protection. The two tantalum capacitors C26 and C27 eliminate pickup effects which could give spurious time changes, caused by the large pulses which are present, especially when the T.V. receiver is switched on and off.

Transistor VT22 and associated circuitry are added to avoid the time display coming up as a series of blanks during installation. C24 is not charged when power is first applied so for a few seconds VT22 will be held switched on. This pulls Pin 18 of IC22 down to chassis causing the fast function to operate for a few seconds and prevent a blank time display when the picture appears. When C24 has charged, VT22 switches off and plays no further part in the operation of the clock.

A Hold (stop/start clock) switch, S2, pulls Pin 16 down to chassis and stops the clock counting by inhibiting the divider, a useful feature during the set-up procedure. Selector S21 can be set to take Pin 13 of IC22 either to rail supply or chassis to give a choice of 12- or 24-hour clock display.

Under normal operation the clock I.C. counts continuously. It provides the output information in digital form on the four output Pins 2, 3, 4 and 5. These provide the D, C, B and A information respectively. This is switched from hour tens, hour units, colon, minute tens, minute units, colon, second tens to second units as required by character generator IC23 during the period of the display. Zero volts on these pins indicates the active on state. Each of the six counters within IC22 gives a 4-line binary output and as only four lines are available between IC22 and IC23, the output from each counter must be sampled in sequence. This sequential sampling is achieved by the 'select digit logic' switch in IC22 which is controlled by a code sent on three lines from IC23 to Pins 26, 27 and 28 of IC22. These three lines are coded as shown in the table below.

| | IC22 Pin No. | | |
Output	26	27	28
Hour tens	HT	HT	HT
Hour units	0	HT	HT
Zero	0	0	HT
Minute tens	HT	0	HT
Minute units	HT	0	0
Zero	0	0	0
Second tens	0	HT	0
Second units	HT	HT	0

Waveform 19 on page 13 shows the switching waveforms relative to the black box blanking pulse. The eight separate commands correspond to the eight equal time periods into which the character generator divides the blanking pulse. However, to allow for transit time effects, the clock is ordered to yield the information for the particular unit of time one period before it is to be displayed on the screen. So outside the black box period all three pins are at supply rail potential and the output of the clock gives the hour tens information. The clock gives out zeros during the two blank periods.

The Interface Circuit (Fig. 27c and Fig. 28): The small interface board, PCA482, is mounted on the chassis framework adjacent to the I.F. Decoder Module to keep signal leads short to avoid feedback and other undesirable effects. The interface circuitry is capable of:

(i) Blanking luma and chroma information whilst altering the D.C. level of the C.R.T. cathodes to produce the black box on the screen.

(ii) Producing yellow figures within the black box to convey the channel and time information.

With reference to the Interface diagram (Fig. 28), the blanking pulse is fed via VT75/VT76 amplifiers into the gate circuits of two F.E.T.s, VT73 and VT74, switching them on. VT73 becomes short-circuited across L115 at the start of the chroma delay line and so blanks out the chroma. VT74 has the source connected to an adjustable D.C. potential and the drain connected to the luma signal at the output of IC3. Therefore, when VT74 is switched on, the luma signal is shorted down to the capacitor C75, lowering the D.C. on Pin 3 of IC4, and thus raising the C.R.T. cathode voltages to black level. The preset R82

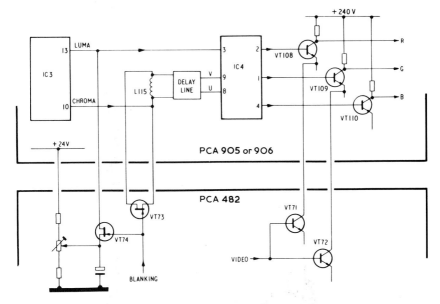

(FIG. 28) INTERFACE DIAGRAM—U706

enables setting the blackness of the black box to allow for variations between signal boards.

To produce yellow figures and colons within the black box the red and green output stages must be switched on at the appropriate time. This is achieved by taking the character drive voltage from the slider of preset R47, which acts as a brightness-contrast setting adjustment, and using the signal to switch on two simple transistor stages VT71 and VT72.

Their collectors are taken to the emitters of the red and green video output stages on the I.F. Decoder Module. When VT71 and VT72 are effectively reduced, so increasing the current in the two output stages.

This combination of the red and green output stages gives yellow characters on the screen. The emitter components act as transient compensation to give a crisp response, and resistors R79 and R80 provide flashover protection. Additional connections between the T.V. receiver and PCA482 provide +24V, earth and the line and field pulses. The waveforms (Fig. 29) show the pulse voltages; the video drive pulse changes with time information.

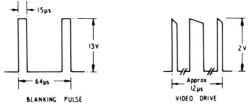

(FIG. 29) INTERFACE WAVEFORMS—U706

Servicing Notes and Fault-Finding Guides

Important. Please Note Before Servicing:

Live Chassis: One side of the mains supply is connected to the T.V. receiver chassis via a bridge rectifier. This results in the chassis being at half-mains voltage whenever the receiver is switched on, and this also applies to the U708 and U706 when fitted. An additional servicing hazard concerns the U706 clock facility which necessitates this unit being connected to the mains side of the T.V. on-off switch so that it remains live even when the T.V. is switched off. It is important, therefore, that whenever possible an isolated supply should be used for any fault investigations. The isolating transformer should have a minimum rating of 500VA.

Double-sided Printed Boards: Where double-sided printed boards with through-plated holes are employed, any component replacement must be undertaken with especial care. Correct diagnosis of faults is therefore very important, fault-finding by a process of elimination could result in a damaged print. A low-wattage small-bit soldering iron should always be used when changing components. All measurements can be taken from the top of the board using the I.C. pins. By this method a fault can be isolated to a few components.

The use of a not less than 20k Ω/V meter for fault-finding is suggested if it is found difficult to lock a C.R.O. to the pulses generated for the U708 due to their repetition rate being approximately 5Hz. Whenever possible, voltage indication of the presence of pulses is also given for the U706 but as these are mainly at line and field frequencies, the preferred method is to use a C.R.O.

MOS Integrated Circuits: The integrated circuits used in the remote control receiver and clock-and-channel display unit must be handled with care to avoid damage resulting from static charges. Never loosen, remove, or insert a device whilst the rail supply is applied. Touch an earthed object before handling a replacement I.C. Avoid touching contact pins—handle by the casing only.

Replacement I.C.s are placed in conductive foam. Do not remove the foam until you are ready to fit the I.C. into the printed-circuit panel.

U708 Receiver Servicing

The mains input to the television receiver is connected via relay switch contacts on the Remote Control Power Supply Board.

Whenever there is doubt whether mains failure is due to the relay drive circuit, the plug/socket connecting the mains input via the relay contacts can be unplugged and the mains connected directly to the television receiver from the On/Off switch.

The relay and relay driver VT131 can be checked by connecting a 10kΩ 0.5W resistor between SK70/2 and SK70/3. If the receiver will only come on in the standby mode the override contacts (mounted on rear of On/Off switch) can be checked by momentarily short-circuiting them with a screwdriver.

Note: The plastic spigot which operates the override switch must be engaged in its locating hole.

U708 receivers have a 'keyhole' pierced in the housing to enable the unit to be parked outside the cabinet for servicing.

Receiver Voltage Measurements

I.C.s: Typical AVOmeter readings, 25V range. Standardised condition for all analogues. Any channel selected. Quiescent conditions, 18V supply 17.7V; 12V supply 12.0V.

Pin	IC1	IC2	IC3	IC4	IC5
1	9.2	17.7	10.0*	11.8*	0
2	14.8	6.0	8.3*	0*	8.5*
3	12.5	10.6	8.4*	12.0*	12.0
4	12.5	9.5	0*	0*	12.0
5	5.5	17.7	0*	12.0*	0
6	8.2	17.5	0*	11.8*	11.0*
7	0	16.5*	0*	0	11.8*
8	9.2	16.5*	0*	11.8*	0
9	9.2	16.5*	0*	0*	12.0†
10	12.5	17.7	0*	12.0*	0*
11	12.5	16.5*	0*	0*	0*
12	14.8	16.5*	0	11.8*	0
13	9.4	—	0*	11.8*	0
14	15.7	9.9	0*	12.0	0*
15	—	16.3	0*	—	12.0*
16	—	0	0*	—	12.0
17	—	—	0*	—	—
18	—	—	0*	—	—
19	—	—	0*	—	—
20	—	—	0*	—	—
21	—	—	8.4*	—	—
22	—	—	8.4*	—	—
23	—	—	8.3*	—	—
24	—	—	12.0	—	—

* **When a signal is present:**
IC2 voltage drops to 7V. A 20k Ω/V meter (e.g. AVOmeter Model 8) will indicate an oscillatory reading between 14V and 16V.
IV3, IC4, IC5
(a) Normal high voltage drops to zero. A 20kΩ/V meter will indicate an oscillatory reading between 10V and 12V.
(b) Nominal low voltage increases to rail supply. A 20kΩ/V meter will indicate an oscillatory reading between 1V and 1.5V.
(c) Pins 2, 3, 21, 22 and 23 of IC3 will indicate an oscillatory reading between 7V and 8V when checked with a 20kΩ/V meter.
† +12V for **SGS-ATES HBF4029AE** 0V for **Motorola MC14516CP.**

Transistors

VT	E	B	C	VT	E	B	C
1	17.0	16.3	9.9	10	5.0	5.7	12.0
2	—	1.3	8.8	11	5.0	5.7	12.0
3	17.6	17.0	2.2	12			
4	8.6	—	17.7	to	0	0	33.0
5	7.5	—	17.6	23			
6	17.7	17.0	17.5	24	0	0	10.0
7	0	0.7	0	26	0	0	11.8
8	0	0	17.7	26	0	0	11.8
9	12.0	11.7	0	27	12.0	12.0	0

Fault Finding Guide

Symptom	Procedure
T.V. WILL NOT SWITCH ON BY ON-OFF SWITCH OR REMOTE TRANSMITTER (a) No neon or L.E.D.s illuminated.	Check: F1, 2.5A mains input fuse (T.V. receiver). F131 63mA fuse (Remote Receiver Power Board). PL/SK3B; On-Off switch. T131 (Remote Receiver Power Board).
(b) Standby neon permanently illuminated.	Check: +18V at PL70 Pin 2; PL/SK70. Bridge rectifier W133, IC131 (Remote Receiver Power Board).
2. SWITCHES ON FOR FIVE SECONDS APPROXIMATELY With or without Yellow and Green L.E.D.s illuminated.	Check: VT2 D.C. conditions as given in Voltage Table. If correct, check: XTL1 crystal for dry-joint. Poor contact between VT2 collector and IC2 Pin 15. C16 or C17 open-circuit. If incorrect, check: C16 and/or C17 short-circuit. Check that voltage does not remain at 17V on IC2 Pin 6.
3. VOLUME, CONTRAST, COLOUR, SOUND MUTE & STANDBY ONLY FUNCTIONING With or without Yellow L.E.D. illuminated.	Check: +12V supply rail; W4 open-circuit; R50 open-circuit; R98 open-circuit. Check for pulse Waveform 3 on IC2, Pin 8. An AVOmeter, 25V or 30V range, connected between Pin 8 and earth will indicate voltage swing 12V-17V approx.
4. EVERY ALTERNATE FUNCTION MISSING ON CHANNEL-CHANGE, BRIGHTNESS AND CLOCK & CHANNEL NUMBER COMMANDS e.g. Channel 1, Channel 2 selected by Channel 1; Brightness +, Brightness— selected by Brightness —	Check for pulse Waveform 3 on IC2, Pin 7. An AVOmeter, 25V or 30V range, connected between Pin 7 and earth will indicate voltage swing 12V-17V approx. Check: W3 for open-circuit; R49 open-circuit. Check for pulse Waveform 4 on IC3, Pins 2, 3, 21, 22, 23. An AVOmeter, 25V or 30V range, connected between appropriate pin and earth will indicate voltage swing of approximately 1V (i.e. within 7V-9V). Check: R93 open-circuit.
5. CHANNEL-CHANGE, BRIGHTNESS, AND CLOCK & CHANNEL COMMANDS CORRECT All other functions correct.	Operate Standby Command If Yellow L.E.D. does not flash, then there is no output from IC2 Pin 12. Operate Colour + If Yellow L.E.D. does not flash, then there is no output from IC2 Pin 11. Operate Contrast + If Yellow L.E.D. does not flash, then there is no output from IC2 Pin 9.
6. REDUCED SENSITIVITY	Check: +200V (-7.5% +5%) at SK67. If incorrect, check: Relevant section of Power Board. If correct, check: IC1, VT1 as given in Voltage Tables.

Sympton	Procedure
7. NO CONTROL OF VOLUME, CONTRAST OR COLOUR	Check: VT3, VT4, VT5 as given in Voltage Table. If correct, check: SK/PL5C. Check for output Waveforms 5a/5b on IC2 Pins 2, 3 and 4. An AVOmeter, 25V or 30V range, connected between appropriate pin and earth will indicate voltages of: Pin 2, 6V; Pin 3, 10V; Pin 4, 9V.
8. NO CONTROL OF BRIGHTNESS	Check: IC4, IC5 as given in Voltage Table; VT27; VT25; VT26; IC3 Pins 9 and 11. Voltage swing on AVOmeter between 1V and 1.5V.
9. BRIGHTNESS CYCLES CONTINUOUSLY	Check for Waveform 6* on IC5 Pin 7. An AVOmeter, 25V or 30V range, connected between Pin 7 and earth should indicate +12V (±5%) and then 0V for correct operation. A periodic low reading indicates that IC4 is faulty. * This pulse appears only at maximum (15) and minimum (0) counts and is used to inhibit the clock pulse to IC5 Pin 15 so that the counter does not reset automatically.
10. FAILURE TO INITIATE CHANNEL CHANGE Brightness functions correctly.	Check: VT24* as given in Voltage Table. PL/SK60 and PL/SK61 connections. * VT24 only operates when the sound-mute voltage of the channel change IC is present. The collector stays at 10V and exhibits a drop to 0V for as long as the sound-mute voltage exists, typically 300ms. An AVOmeter will indicate whether VT24 is operating or not.
11. RECEIVER SWITCHED ON PERMANENTLY With or without Yellow and Green L.E.D.s illuminated.	Check: IC2 and VT6 as given in Voltage Table. PL3B contacts 1 and 4 short-circuit; Override contacts short-circuit on On-Off switch; VT2 D.C. conditions as given in Voltage Table.
12. YELLOW LED PERMANENTLY ILLUMINATED	Check: VT24 collector short-circuit to earth. IC3 Pins 2, 3, 21, 22 or 23 short-circuited to earth.

U706 Clock and Channel Servicing

Fault diagnosis can be simplified if the effect can be displayed on the screen and from careful observation it should be possible to identify the problem as falling within one of the following basic categories.

Type A: No Channel or Time & Channel Display or no Black Box—T.V. and Remote Control normal.

Type B: No T.V. Picture but Audio normal, Display may or may not appear on command.

Type C: Time Fault.

Type D: Channel Faults.

Type E: Black Box Faults.

Type F: Display Present but Faulty.

U706 Clock and Channel Unit

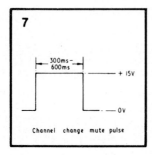

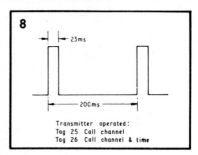

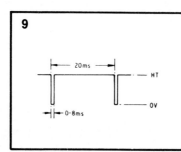

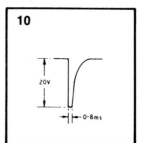

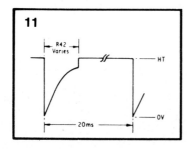

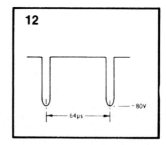

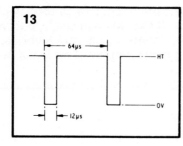

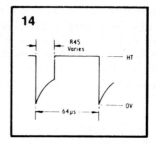

(FIG. 30a) CIRCUIT WAVEFORMS—U706 *(PART)*

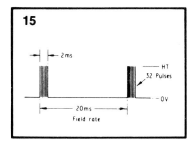

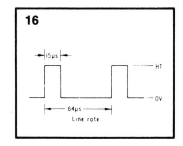

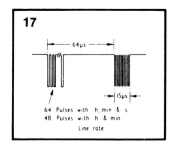

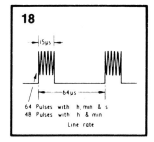

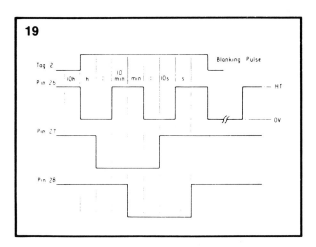

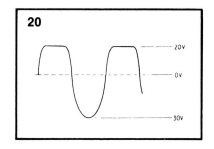

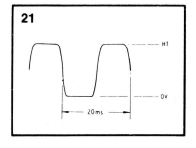

(FIG. 30b) CIRCUIT WAVEFORMS—U706 *(CONTINUED)*

Having decided on the type of fault, before referring to the relevant section, it should be noted that S1 may be closed to give a permanent on-screen display and that S2 should interrupt the normal counting sequence. If the mains supply to the T.V. is interrupted, however briefly, when restored, the clock will show random time. Should the mains interruption occur whilst the T.V. is switched on, the set will switch to Standby and the cause made obvious; but if the T.V. was off and the interruption of the supply passed unnoticed, then a false assumption of a Time Fault condition could be made.

With any type of fault, first check plugs and sockets 62, 63, 69, 71 and 58.

Type A. No Channel or Time and Channel Display or No Black Box: If closing S1 gives the correct display but the remote control transmitter is inoperative despite the yellow light flashing, then suspect IC2 circuitry and PL69. Check for pulses on Pins 24 (on channel change), 25 and 26, see Waveforms 7 and 8. The presence of these pulses can be checked with an AVOmeter; Pin 24, 15V; Pins 25 and 26, 1.5V.

If these pulses are present check Pins 4 and 12 of IC2. If they are present there suspect IC2 or the socket. If either display is present even with S1 open, suspect IC2 or the appropriate R.C. network. (R8/C2 for permanent channel display and R11/C3 for permanent time-and-channel display.)

If closing S1 has no effect and the display is missing keep S1 closed and check for supply voltage across W2; if absent, bearing in mind mains voltage check F1 and F2, then R1/C1 (PC468).

The Thermal fuse F2 is **NOT** repairable. If it has gone open-circuit it must be replaced with a new fuse, Part No. 00E6-040-001.

If the supply is normal, ensure that with S1 closed Tag 31 has risen to the rail voltage.

If Tag 31 is correct, check that Pin 1 of IC1 also rises when S1 is closed. If not, suspect IC2 or socket. If these are normal, check for field flyback pulse on Tag 32, see Waveform 9 (indicated by 0V-12V swing on AVOmeter as S1 closes). If absent, check Tag 23, see Waveform 10, and IC1 circuit as necessary.

If Tag 32 is normal, check for same field pulse on Pin 19 of IC23. Also check for monostable Waveform 11 on Pin 21 of IC23 (indicated by 1V drop when S1 is closed). If normal, check for line flyback pulses on Tag 4, see Waveform 12; then Pin 18 IC23, see Waveform 13. If necessary, check that line monostable Waveform 14 is present on Pin 16 IC23.

If these are normal, black box blanking pulses should appear as shown in Waveforms 15 or 16 on Pin 12 IC23 (AVOmeter indication: 0V to 0.5V D.C. approx. when S1 is closed). If pulses are absent on Pins 12 or 16, IC23 or its socket should be suspected of being faulty.

If a pulse is present on Pin 12 but there is no black box display, check IC21 for Waveform 17 on Pin 10 and Waveform 18 on Pin 11 (using an AVOmeter, Pin 10 drops 0.25V and Pin 11 rises 0V or 0.5V when S1 is closed). If oscillations are absent, suspect IC21 or socket, or VT21 circuit. If present, confirm same signal is on Pin 13 of IC23.

If normal, check for presence of character information on Pin 15 of IC23. If absent, suspect IC23 or socket. If pulses are present on Pins 12 and 15 of IC23 they should appear on Tags 1 and 2 (Tag 2 rises 0V to 0.5V D.C. on AVOmeter). If not, IC21 or VT23 circuits could be faulty. If Tags 1 and 2 are correct, then the fault should be on Interface Board PCA482.

Type B. No T.V. Picture But Audio Normal, Display May or May Not Appear on Command: Clock faults could blank out the normal T.V. picture, i.e. Brightness and Contrast effectively turned down. The display may or may not appear on command, or when S1 is closed. Should the fault remain after disconnecting PL71 then PCA482 should be investigated. VT73, VT74, VT75 or VT76 faults will cause loss of T.V. picture. If the fault is removed when PL71 is disconnected then the Main Assembly PCA467 is faulty.

Reconnect PL71 so that fault reappears and the field and line flyback pulses can pass to the clock unit to produce the display.

If the characters are present then IC21/VT21 oscillator must be working. This means that the blanking pulse can be present on Pins 1 and 13 of IC21 so the fault must occur beyond this point. Check IC21 and Tag 2 as in Type A procedure.

If the characters are absent, check IC23 as in Type A procedure.

Type C. Time Faults: There are three basic types of Time Fault:
(i) No Time characters—just colon dots.
(ii) Changing Time characters but sequence wrong.
(iii) Random Time Changes or other Clock faults.

(i) No Time Characters—Just Colon Dots: Suspect IC23 after checking for pulses at Pins 8, 9, 10. Or suspect IC22 after checking for pulses on Pins 2, 3, 4, 5.

(ii) Changing Time Characters but Sequence Wrong: This type of fault requires an understanding of the B.C.D. (Binary Coded Decimal) code and the exact pin functions of IC22 and IC23.

The clock I.C. supplies all the time-information to IC23 on the four Pins 2, 3, 4, 5 on a time-sharing basis. The commands from IC23 which control these clock outputs are applied to Pins 26, 27, 28 of IC22 (when S1 is closed an AVOmeter will indicate a voltage drop between 0.25V and 0.5V).

The interconnections between these I.C.s are shown in Fig. 31.

The three command pulses are as shown in Waveform 19. The relative times of these are critical so the blanking pulse is shown as a reference.

Combining the three input signals within the clock I.C. provides eight separate commands, the relevant time information appearing on the output pins (six times and two blanks). The time outputs are also negative-going and B.C.D. coded. They change not only with time but also across the display as described. These will not respond to an AVOmeter check.

As can be seen in the Time and Command diagram, with such a large number of interconnections many fault conditions could arise if one or more of these pins should develop a fault or become loose in its I.C. socket.

With such a fault, the facility of seeing the screen display and the use of the

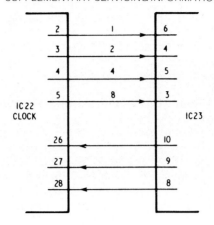

(FIG. 31) CLOCK INTERCONNECTIONS—U706

Hold, Fast and Slow Set switches should help in diagnosing what is wrong. An oscilloscope will show whether the necessary pulses are on the 14 pins to enable the reason for the fault to be established.

(iii) Random Time Changes or Other Obvious Clock Faults: IC22 counts the 50Hz mains pulses and derives the time from this so any random changes could be associated with IC22, its socket, or the peripheral circuit. Check Tag 30 with an Oscilloscope for the 50Hz signal shown in Waveform 20.

If Waveform 21 is absent on Pin 19, check W1/W22. An incorrect count will occur if the IC21/VT21 oscillator is too low in frequency, i.e. display too wide (6in on 26in receiver). If R23 requires adjustment or has become faulty, obvious errors such as '70-second minutes' could arise.

Faults associated with either S21, S22 or VT22 would give a rapid count; and S2 faults would stop the clock. Pin 13 of IC22 gives a 12h or 24h option. Pin 7 of IC23 gives hours-minutes or hours-minutes-seconds display depending upon the selectors 21 and 22. Faults to these selectors could cause intermittent faults but these should be comparatively straightforward to correct after observation.

Type D. Channel Faults: Either the call-channel command will not operate; or the displayed channel number will be wrong, i.e. different to the L.E.D. or touch-pad channel number. If the display fails to respond to the appropriate remote command or fails to appear at channel-change, check for the presence of the correct pulses on Tags 24 and 25. If these are present and S1 gives a correct time-and-channel display, suspect IC2 or the R8/C2 network. A short-circuit across R8 or an open-circuit C2 could cause this type of fault.

If the channel display is present but different to the L.E.D. display, before suspecting the clock unit establish whether the fault shows up on more than one channel, in which case the clock unit would be the most likely source of

808

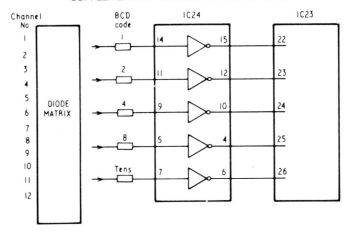

(FIG. 32) B.C.D. INTERCONNECTIONS—U706

the problem. If just one channel is incorrect, check whether adjusting the drawer control on that channel alters the situation. If it does, the touch-tune board or drawer unit could be faulty.

If it is a clock unit fault, comparison with the L.E.D. display and noting the exact differences could help in an assessment of the fault since both circuits operate with a similar B.C.D. (Binary Coded Decimal) system.

Having selected a channel with a faulty display, check for the presence of the +35V supply at the appropriate tag on PCA467. If this is absent, Channel 0 should be displayed on the screen and the fault will lie in the interconnections between the clock unit and the touch-tune board. If present, by reference to Table and B.C.D. Interconnections diagram (Fig. 32), it should be possible to proceed through the diode matrix and IC24 to establish where a fault has occurred.

The table shows which channels the 35V supply is matrixed on to the resistors R50/R52/R54/R56/R58.

If these are correct on the appropriate channel, proceed to the inputs and outputs of IC24. Short-circuits I.C. or socket faults could be the cause.

Channel	R50	R52	R54	R56	R58
1	L	H	L	L	L
2	L	L	L	L	H
3	L	H	L	L	H
4	L	L	L	H	L
5	L	H	L	H	L
6	L	L	L	H	H
7	L	H	L	H	H
8	L	L	H	L	L
9	L	H	H	L	L
10	H	L	L	L	L
11	H	H	L	L	L
12	H	L	L	L	H

L=Low (0V)   H=High (35V)

The interconnection diagram shows the B.C.D. arrangement. The 0 to 9 display is standard binary with the tens separate. So, for example on Channel 7, W32/W38/W42 should be biased on to provide +35V on R52/R56/R58. This activates the 1, 4 and 2 B.C.D. lines at the inputs of IC24 because 7 in the B.C.D. code is 1+2+4. Therefore, if the 2 input is faulty the display would show as 5, and one would expect the fault to be associated with this 2 line. As can be seen, similar errors can occur on other channels:

Channel	BCD Code
1	1
2	2
3	1+2
4	4
5	1+4
6	2+4
7	1+2+4
8	8
9	1+8
10	10
11	1+10
12	2+10

These positive inputs to IC24 are inverted at the output pins because IC23 is an NMOS device and requires this reversal.

Usually in digital applications, the 1, 2, 4 and 8 code lines are referred to as the A, B, C and D lines respectively. This should not be confused with the B.C.D. of binary coded decimal.

Type E. Black Box Faults: If the character display is correct, IC21/VT21 oscillator must be functioning to provide IC23 with the correct pulses. The black box output must therefore be present on Pin 12 of IC23. This means that 'Black Box only' faults can only be due to conditions beyond Pin 1 of IC21. Check for these pulses, see Waveforms 15 and 16, on Pins 1, 4 and 8 of IC21.

If these pulses are correct, check that they reach Tag 2 and SK71/1. The pulse turns on the two transistors and two F.E.T.s on the Interface Board to blank the luma (VT74) and chroma (VT73) stages. The preset R82 will be set to between 10V and 12V on the slider to clamp the luma signal to give a 'black' blanked-out area. If the signal is present on SK71/1, checking these four stages will expose the fault. A supply line fault, e.g. 24V missing, should be checked for on Tag H.

Type F. Display Present But Faulty: The five U706 presets can cause problems if out of adjustment or faulty when S1 and S2 are operated.

If R23 is incorrect, the display will be too narrow or too wide. If too wide, much more than the nominal 6in-7in (26in C.R.T.), time errors can occur.

If R42 is incorrect, the display will be in the wrong vertical position and could move off the screen altogether.

If R43 is incorrect, the display will be in the wrong horizontal position and could move off the screen, or give a display which only appears on alternate or every third line.

If R47 or R82 is incorrect, the characters could be too bright or too dark. These two presets are interdependent where the characters are concerned.

R82 should always be set to give a blanked area which is just black under normal picture conditions and . . .

R47 may then be set to give characters which are bright but do not cause flaring.

Note: If R82 is out of adjustment, in addition to bright characters, the blanked area could be bright rather than dark.

INDEX